PHILIP'S

STREET

Co Antrim
Co Londonderry

Antrim, Ballymena, Belfast, Coleraine, Lisburn, Londonderry, Newtownabbey

First published 2006 by

Philip's, a division of
Octopus Publishing Group Ltd
2-4 Heron Quays, London E14 4JP

First edition 2006
First impression 2006
LDYAA

ISBN-10   0-540-08931-1 (spiral)
ISBN-13   978-0-540-08931-4 (spiral)

© Philip's 2006

ORDNANCE SURVEY®
OF NORTHERN IRELAND

is a registered Trade Mark of Ordnance Survey
of Northern Ireland

Reproduced from Ordnance Survey of Northern
Ireland digital data with the permission of the
Controller of Her Majesty's Stationery Office.
© Crown copyright and database rights 2006.
Licence number LA125.

Includes Ordnance Survey of Ireland data
reproduced by permission of OSi. Unauthorised
reproduction infringes Ordnance Survey Ireland
and Government of Ireland Copyright.
© Ordnance Survey Ireland 2005

Printed and bound in Spain
by Cayfosa-Quebecor

Contents

II   **Key to map pages**

IV   **Route planning**

VI   **Administrative and Postcode boundaries**

VII   **Key to map symbols**

2   **Street maps** at 1¾ inches to 1 mile

122   **Street maps** at 3½ inches to 1 mile

188   **Street map of Belfast city centre** at 7 inches to 1 mile

190   **Index** of towns, villages, townlands, streets, hospitals, industrial estates, railway stations, schools, shopping centres, universities and places of interest

Digital Data

The exceptionally high-quality mapping found in this atlas is available as digital data in TIFF format, which is easily convertible to other bitmapped (raster) image formats.

The index is also available in digital form as a standard database table. It contains all the details found in the printed index together with the Irish Grid reference for the map square in which each entry is named.

For further information and to discuss your requirements, please contact Philip's on 020 7644 6932 or james.mann@philips-maps.co.uk

Key to map pages

26 Map pages at 7 inches to 1 mile

185 Map pages at 3½ inches to 1 mile

42 Map pages at 1¾ inches to 1 mile

Scale

0 5 10 15 20 km

0 5 10 miles

R238

R240

R247

R238

4 5

173 A2

Portstewart/ *Port Stíobhaird*

Portrush/ *Port Rois*

72

11

12 Downhill

13 Castlerock

14

15

Coleraine/ *Cúil Raithin*

Ballybogy

174

Ballyscullion

A2

Castleroe

22

23

24

25 Macosquin

26

27

A37

B201

A26

Artikelly

Ballylintagh

B186

Muff

35

Culmore

City of Derry Airport

Greysteel

Ballykelly

180

Limavady/ *Léim An Mhadaidh*

B66

Ringsend

Aghadowey

42

43

Bridge End

34

176 177

Strathfoyle

36

37

A2

38

39

Drumsurn

40

41 Ballyrogan

A29

Moneydig

Eglinton

B118

Londonderry/*Doire*

Kildrum

178 179

Lettershendoney

Bonnanaboigh

B69

B64

Brockaghboy

B64

Garvagh

A54

Kilrea

50

51

52

53

54

55

56

57

Bovedy

B64

New Buildings

A6

Ballymoney

Dungiven

A29

58

59

B48

N13

Claudy

Craigdarragh

B74

Feeny

B74

Cashel

A6

Swatragh

B75

75

67

68

Liscloon

B49

69

70

71

72

73

74

Upperlands

A42

Dunnamanagh

Park

B44

Maghera

N14

R265

A5

R236

B40

B42

Knockcloghrim

A6

R264

B48

Moneyneany

Tobermore

90

B42

85

86

87

88

89

B40

Desertmartin

Strabane

B83

Draperstown

B165

B72

Cranagh

B47

Mount Hamilton or Sperrin

The Six Towns

Mooreside Cottages

183

Magherafelt / *Machaire Fiolta*

N15

B165

101

102

103

104

B235

B164

B46

B162

A29

A31

B84

B46

Churchtown

Moneymore

112

185

113

114

B50

B48

Co Tyrone and Co Fermanagh STREET ATLAS

A505

Cookstown/ *An Chorr Chríochach*

Coagh

B50

B160

B160

B46

B4

A29

B160

B161

B50

B158

B46

B4

B43

B84

A32

Omagh

B122

B83

B46

Coalisland

A45

B4

B4

B80

B122

B168

A5

B83

Dungannon

A29

B199

B123

B46

A4

B35

A29

A4

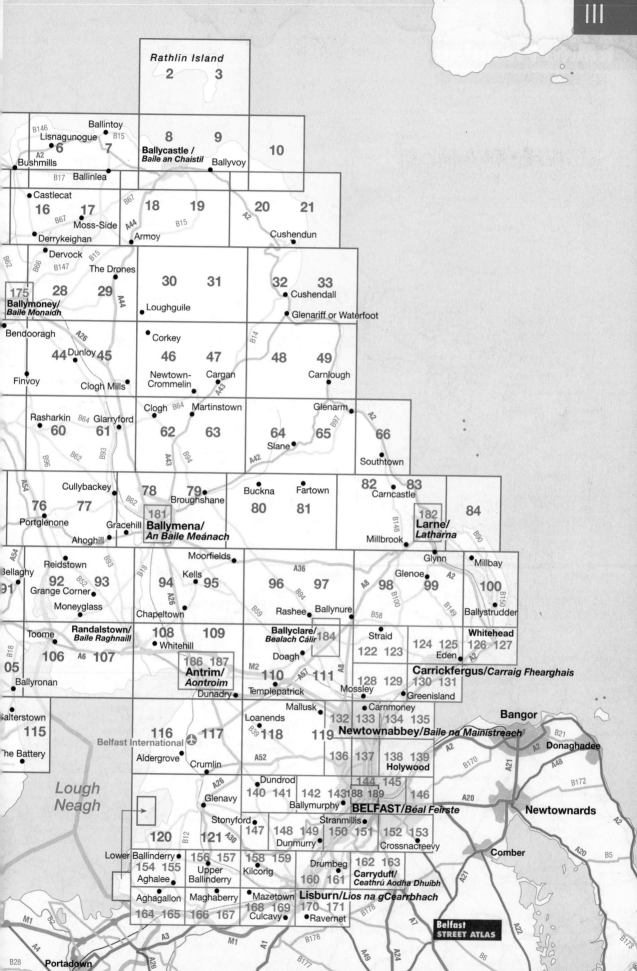

Rathlin Island
2 3

B146 Ballintoy
Lisnagunogue 7 B15
6 7
Bushmills A2
B17 Ballinlea
8 9 10
Ballycastle /
Baile an Chaistil Ballyvoy

Castlecat
16 17 18 19 20 21
Moss-Side A44 B15 A2 Cushendun
B67 B67 Armoy
Derrykeighan

Dervock
The Drones 30 31 32 33
175 28 29 A44 Cushendall
Ballymoney/ Loughguile Glenariff or Waterfoot
Baile Monaidh

Bendooragh A26 Corkey
44 Dunloy 45 46 47 48 49
Finvoy Newtown- Cargan Carnlough
Clogh Mills Crommelin A43

Clogh B64 Martinstown Glenarm
Rasharkin B64 Glarryford 62 63 64 65 66
60 61 A43 B94 Slane A2
B96 B62 B93 A42 Southtown

A54 Cullybackey 78 79 Buckna Fartown 82 83
76 77 B62 Broughshane 80 81 Carncastle
Portglenone 181 Gracehill 182 84
Ahoghill Ballymena/ Millbrook Larne/ B90
An Baile Meánach Latharna

A54 Moorfields Glynn Millbay
Bellaghy Reidstown B93 A36 Glenoe A2
92 93 94 Kells 95 96 97 98 99 100
91 Grange Corner B52 A8 B100 Ballystrudder
Moneyglass A26 B94 B58 B149
Chapeltown Rashee Ballynure B150

Toome Randalstown/ 108 109 Ballyclare/ 184 Straid 124 125 Whitehead
Baile Raghnaill Whitehill Bealach Cáir 122 123 Eden 126 127
106 A6 107 Doagh 128 129 Carrickfergus/Carraig Fhearghais
105 186 187 M2 110 111 Mossley 130 131
Ballyronan Antrim/ Templepatrick A67 A8 Greenisland
Aontroim
Dunadry Mallusk 132 133 134 135
Salterstown Loanends Carnmoney
115 116 117 B39 118 119 Newtownabbey/Baile na Mainistreach
The Battery Belfast International 136 137 138 139
Aldergrove Crumlin A52 Holywood
Dundrod 144 145
120 140 141 142 143 188 189 146
Glenavy Ballymurphy BELFAST/Béal Feirste
121 Stonyford 147 148 149 150 151 152 153
B12 A30 Dunmurry Crossnacreevy
Lower Ballinderry 156 157 158 159 Drumbeg 162 163
154 155 Upper Kilcorig 160 161 Carryduff/
Aghalee Ballinderry Ceathrú Aodha Dhuibh
Aghagallon Maghaberry Mazetown Lisburn/Lios na gCearrbhach
164 165 166 167 168 169 170 171
Culcavy Ravernet

Lough Neagh

Bangor
B21
Donaghadee
A2 B170 A21 A48
A2 B172
Newtownards
A2
A20
Comber
A21 A20 B5
A7
Belfast A22
STREET ATLAS B173

M1 B2 M1 A1 B178 A49 A24 B6
A4
Portadown A26 B177
B28

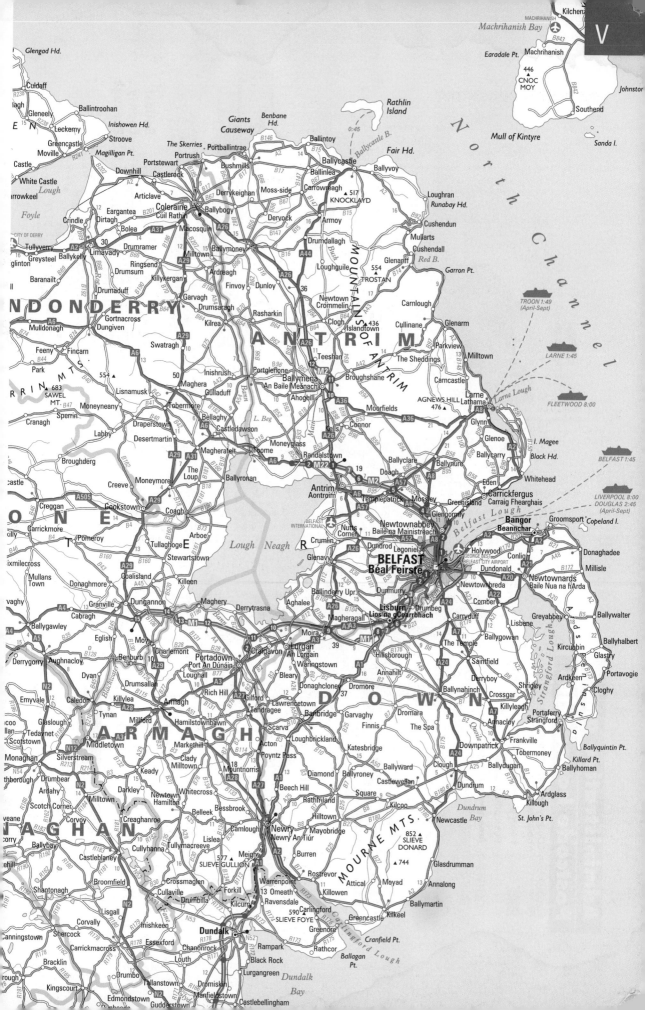

VI

Administrative and Postcode boundaries

- County and county borough boundaries
- Local government district boundaries
- Postcode boundaries
- Area covered by this atlas

Scale

0 5 10 15 20 km
0 5 10 miles

Motorway with junction number (10)	
Primary route – dual/single carriageway	
A road – dual/single carriageway	
B road – dual/single carriageway	
Minor road – dual/single carriageway	
Other minor road – dual/single carriageway	
Road under construction	
Tunnel, covered road	
Track, private road or narrow road in urban area	
Gate or obstruction to traffic (restrictions may not apply at all times or to all vehicles)	
Path, or track	
Pedestrianised area	
Postcode boundaries (BT23)	
International boundary	
County and county borough boundaries	
Railway, tunnel, railway under construction	
Miniature railway	
Railway station (Lisburn)	
Private railway station	
Bus, coach station	

◆	Ambulance station
◆	Coastguard station
◆	Fire station
◆	Police station
✚	Accident and Emergency entrance to hospital
H	Hospital
+	Place of worship
i	Information Centre (open all year)
🛒	Shopping Centre
P	Parking
PO	Post Office
Δ	Camping site
⌂	Caravan site
►	Golf course
⋈	Picnic site
(Prim Sch)	Important buildings, schools, colleges, universities and hospitals
	Built up area
	Woods
(River Bann)	Tidal water, water name
	Non-tidal water – lake, river, canal or stream
	Lock, weir, tunnel
Church	Antiquity
87	Adjoining page indicators and overlap bands
246	The colour of the arrow and the band indicates the scale of the adjoining or overlapping page (see scales below)

Acad	Academy	Ct	Law Court	Resr	Reservoir
Cemy	Cemetery	L Ctr	Leisure Centre	Ret Pk	Retail Park
C Ctr	Civic Centre	LC	Level Crossing	Sch	School
CH	Club House	Liby	Library	Sh Ctr	Shopping Centre
Coll	College	Mkt	Market	TH	Town Hall/House
Crem	Crematorium	Meml	Memorial	Trad Est	Trading Estate
CC	Cricket Club	Mon	Monument	Univ	University
Ent	Enterprise	Mus	Museum	W Twr	Water Tower
Ex H	Exhibition Hall	Obsy	Observatory	Wks	Works
Ind Est	Industrial Estate	Pal	Royal Palace	YC	Yacht Club
IRB Sta	Inshore Rescue	PH	Public House	YH	Youth Hostel
	Boat Station	Recn Gd	Recreation		
Inst	Institute		Ground		

Enlarged mapping only

	Railway or bus station building
	Place of interest
	Parkland

■ The representation on this map of a Road, Track or Path is no evidence of the existence of a right of way

■ The small numbers around the edges of the maps identify the 1 kilometre Irish Grid lines

■ The dark grey border on the inside edge of some pages indicates that the mapping does not continue onto the adjacent page

The scale of the maps on the pages numbered in blue is 5.52 cm to 1 km • 3½ inches to 1 mile • 1: 18103	0 ¼ ½ ¾ 1 mile 0 250m 500m 750m 1 kilometre
The scale of the maps on pages numbered in green is 2.76 cm to 1 km • 1¾ inches to 1 mile • 1: 36206	0 ¼ ½ ¾ 1 mile 0 250m 500m 750m 1 kilometre
The scale of the maps on pages numbered in red is 11.04 cm to 1 km • 7 inches to 1 mile • 1: 9051	0 220 yards 440 yards 660 yards ½ mile 0 125m 250m 375m ½ kilometre

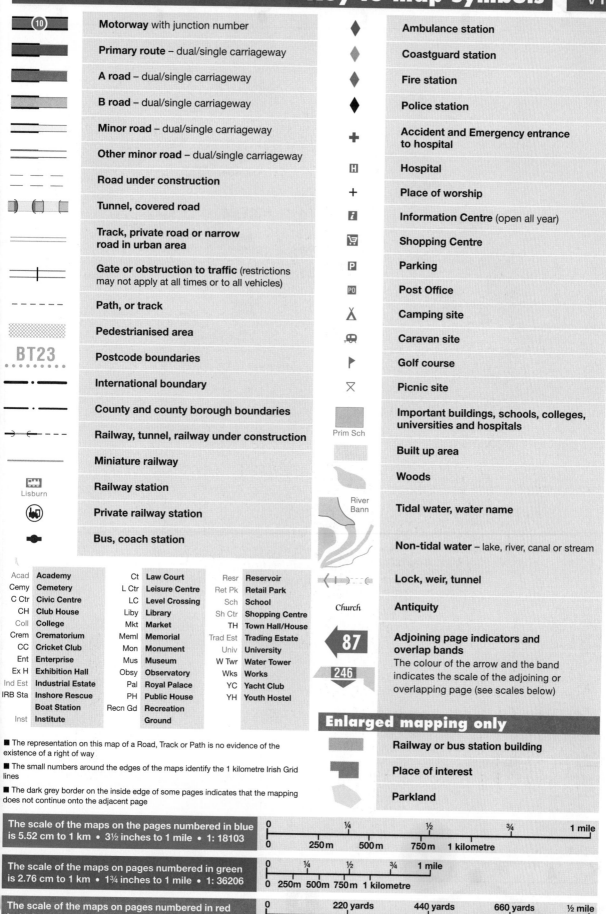

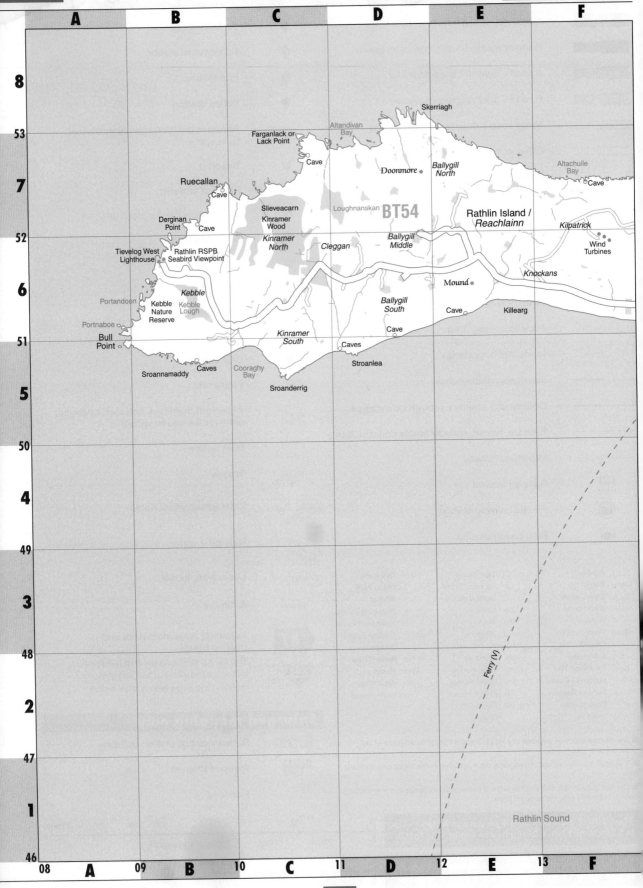

A   B   C   D   E   F

8

53

7

52

6

51

5

50

4

49

3

48

2

47

1

46

Skerriagh

Altandivan Bay

Farganlack or Lack Point

Cave

Doonmore

Ballygill North

Altachuile Bay

Cave

Ruecallan

Cave

Slieveacarn

Kinramer Wood

Loughnanskan

BT54

Rathlin Island / Reachlainn

Kilpatrick

Derginan Point

Cave

Kinramer North

Cleggan

Ballygill Middle

Wind Turbines

Tievelog West Lighthouse

Rathlin RSPB Seabird Viewpoint

Knockans

Portandoon

Kebble

Kebble Lough

Mound

Kebble Nature Reserve

Ballygill South

Cave

Killearg

Portnaboe

Cave

Bull Point

Kinramer South

Caves

Sroannamaddy

Caves

Cooraghy Bay

Stroanlea

Sroanderrig

Ferry (V)

Rathlin Sound

08   A   09   B   10   C   11   D   12   E   13   F

Scale: 1¾ inches to 1 mile

0   ¼   ½   mile
0   250m 500m 750m 1 km

A   B   C   D   E   F

8
53
7
52
6
51
5
50
4
49
3
48
2
47
1
46

Coastguard Lookout
Cantruan
Altacorry Bay
Slieveanaille

East Lighthouse

Ballyconagan
Bruce's Cave
Inannanooan

Ballynagard
Slieveard

Cave
Bruce's Castle
Portcastle

Church Quarter
Mullindress

Portawillan

St Mary's Prim Sch
The Richard Branson Activity Centre
Ballycarry

Standing Stone Glebe
Brackens Cave

Harbour
Mus PO
Ballynoe

Demesne
Carrickagile

Church Bay
Portnaminnan

Mill Bay
BT54

Ruenascarrive

Craigmacagan
Craigmacagan Lough

Caves
Kinkeel
Kinkeel Lough
Arkill Point

Caves
Grave Yard
Arkill Bay

Cloghadoo
Ally Lough

Carravinally
Illancarragh Bay

Oweyadoo
Carravindoon
Doon Point

Ushet Lough
Doon Bay

Maddygalla

Roonivoolin

Park Cove
Ushet Point

South Lighthouse
Rue Point

14   A   15   B   16   C   17   D   18   E   19   F   46

Scale: 1¾ inches to 1 mile

0   ¼   ½   mile
0   250m   500m   750m   1 km

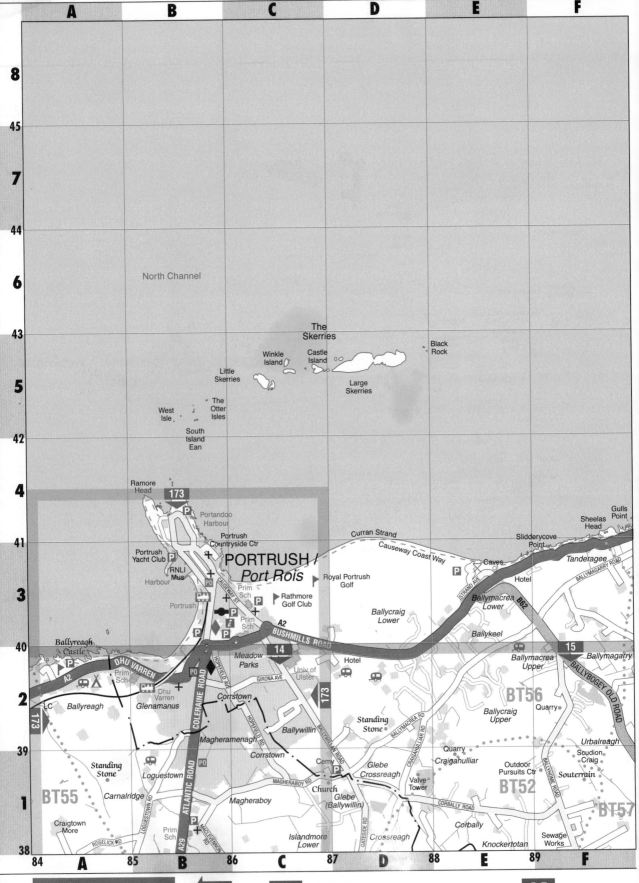

For full street detail of the highlighted area see page 173.

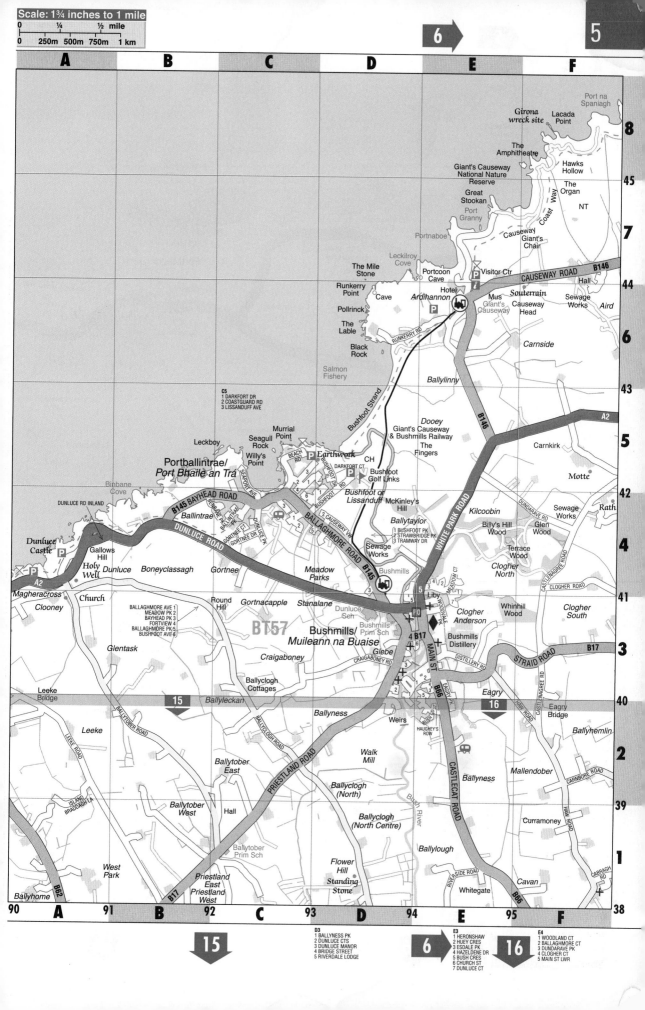

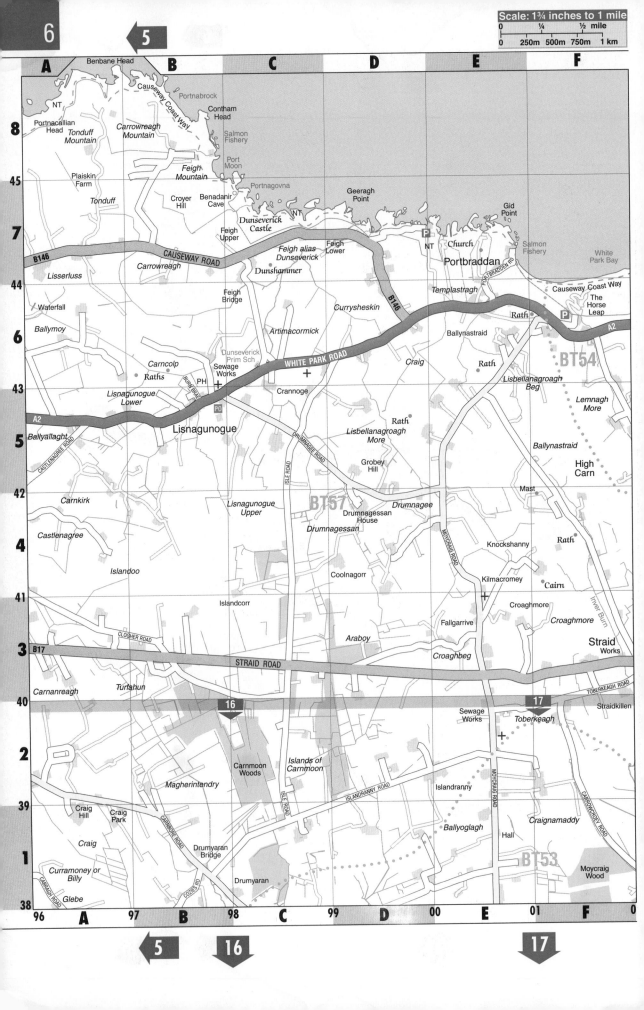

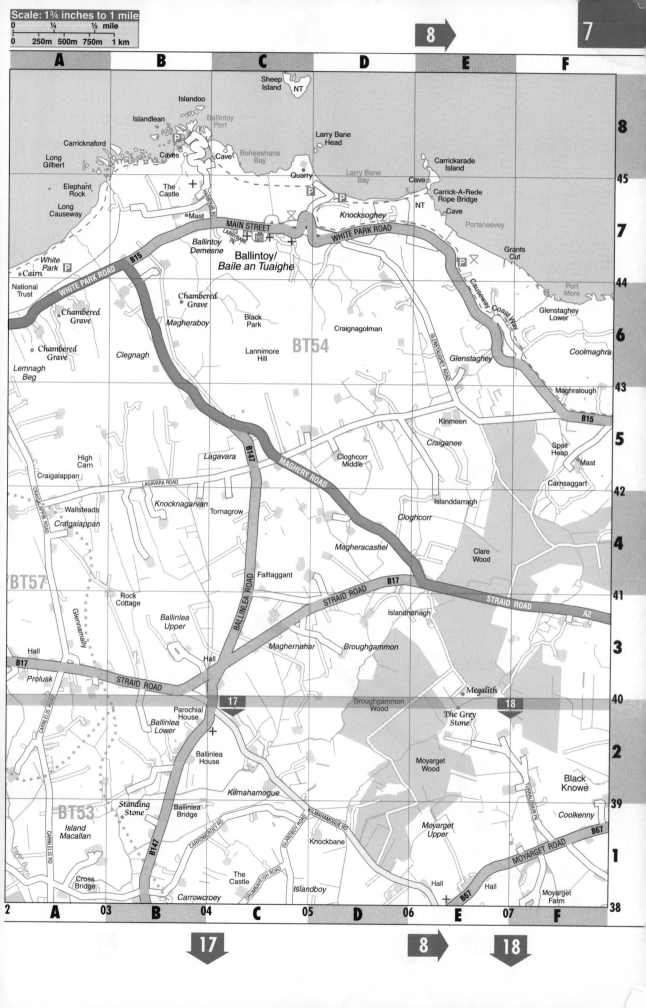

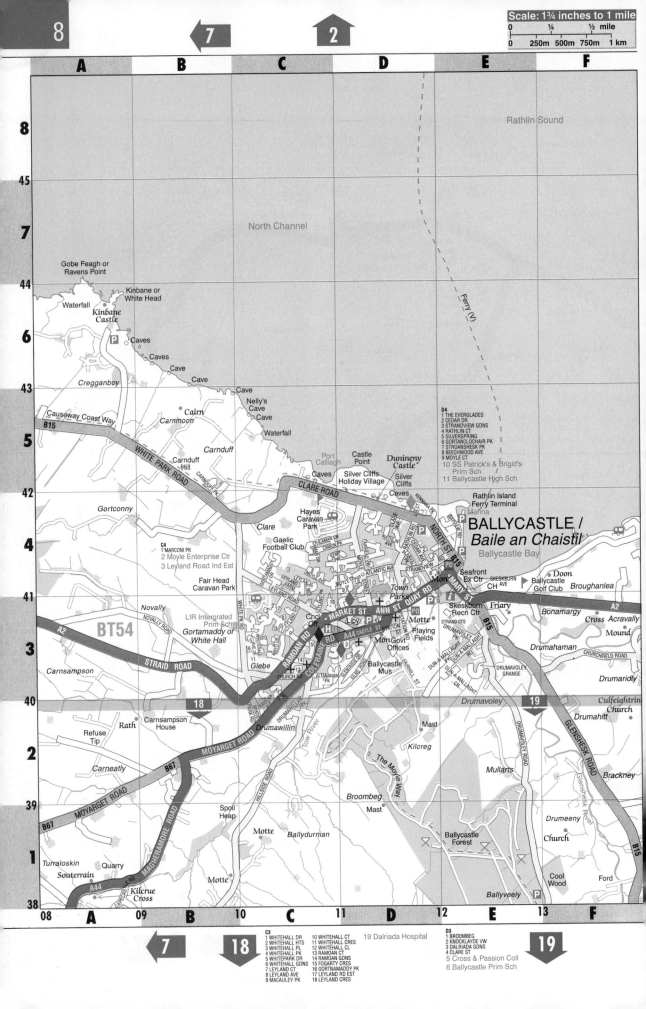

A   B   C   D   E   F

8

45

7

North Channel

Rathlin Sound

44

Gobe Feagh or
Ravens Point

Kinbane or
White Head

Waterfall

Kinbane
Castle

6

P

Caves

Caves

Cave

Cregganboy

Cave

43

Cairn

Carnmoon

Nelly's
Cave

Cave

Cave

Ferry (V)

Causeway Coast Way

Carnduff

Waterfall

Port
Calliagh

Castle
Point

Dunineny
Castle

D4
1 THE EVERGLADES
2 CEDAR DR
3 STRANDVIEW GDNS
4 RATHLIN CT
5 SILVERSPRING
6 GORTANCLOCHAIR PK
7 STROANSHESK PK
8 BEECHWOOD AVE
9 MOYLE CT
10 SS Patrick's & Brigid's
     Prim Sch
11 Ballycastle High Sch

5

B15

WHITE PARK ROAD

Carnduff
Hill

CARNDUFF PK

Caves

Silver Cliffs
Holiday Village

Silver
Cliffs

CLARE ROAD

Caves

42

Gortconny

Clare

Hayes
Caravan
Park

Rathlin Island
Ferry Terminal

Marina

BALLYCASTLE /
Baile an Chaistil

4

Gaelic
Football Club

NORTH ST

B15

Ballycastle Bay

C4
1 MARCONI PK
2 Moyle Enterprise Ctr
3 Leyland Road Ind Est

Fair Head
Caravan Park

Seafront
Ex Ctr

CH

SKESKBURN AVE

Doon
Ballycastle
Golf Club

Broughanlea

41

Novally

NOVALLY ROAD

LIR Intergrated
Prim Sch

Gortamaddy or
White Hall

WHITE PK RD

Town
Park

MARY ST

Skeskburn
Recn Ctr

i

Friary

Bonamargy

A2

Cross Acravally
Mound

BT54

A2

Liby

P

Motte

STRAID ROAD

MARKET ST

ANN ST

QUAY RD

CASTLE ST

Playing
Fields

DRUMAVOLEY RD

B15

3

Carnsampson

Cnch
Off

H

RAMOAN RD

COLERAINE RD

A44

Mon Govt
Offices

Ballycastle
Mus

DUN-A-MALLAGHT RD

DUN-A-MALLAGHT
CR

DRUMAVOLEY
GRANGE

Drumahaman

CHURCHFIELD ROAD

Drumaridly

Glebe

CHURCH RD

Drumavoley

40

18

19

Culfeightrin
Church

Drumahitt

Refuse
Tip

Rath

Carnsampson
House

Drumawillin

MOYARGET ROAD

Tow River

Mast

Kilcreg

The Moyle Way

Mullarts

GLENSHESK ROAD

DRUMAVOLEY ROAD

Brackney

Glenshesk River

2

Carneatly

B67

HILLSIDE ROAD

39

B67

MOYARGET ROAD

Spoil
Heap

Broombeg

Mast

Drumeeny

Church

1

Turraloskin
Souterrain

Quarry

MAGHERAMORE ROAD

CAPECASTLE RD

A44

Kilcrue
Cross

Motte

Ballydurnian

Motte

Ballycastle
Forest

Ballyveely

P

Cool
Wood

Ford

38

08   A   09   B   10   C   11   D   12   E   13   F

C3
1 WHITEHALL DR
2 WHITEHALL HTS
3 WHITEHALL PL
4 WHITEHALL PK
5 WHITEPARK DR
6 WHITEHALL GDNS
7 LEYLAND CT
8 LEYLAND AVE
9 MACAULEY PK
10 WHITEHALL CT
11 WHITEHALL CRES
12 WHITEHALL CL
13 RAMOAN CT
14 RAMOAN GDNS
15 FOGARTY CRES
16 GORTNAMADDY PK
17 LEYLAND RD EST
18 LEYLAND CRES

19 Dalriada Hospital

D3
1 BROOMBEG
2 KNOCKLAYDE VW
3 DALRIADA GDNS
4 CLARE ST
5 Cross & Passion Coll
6 Ballycastle Prim Sch

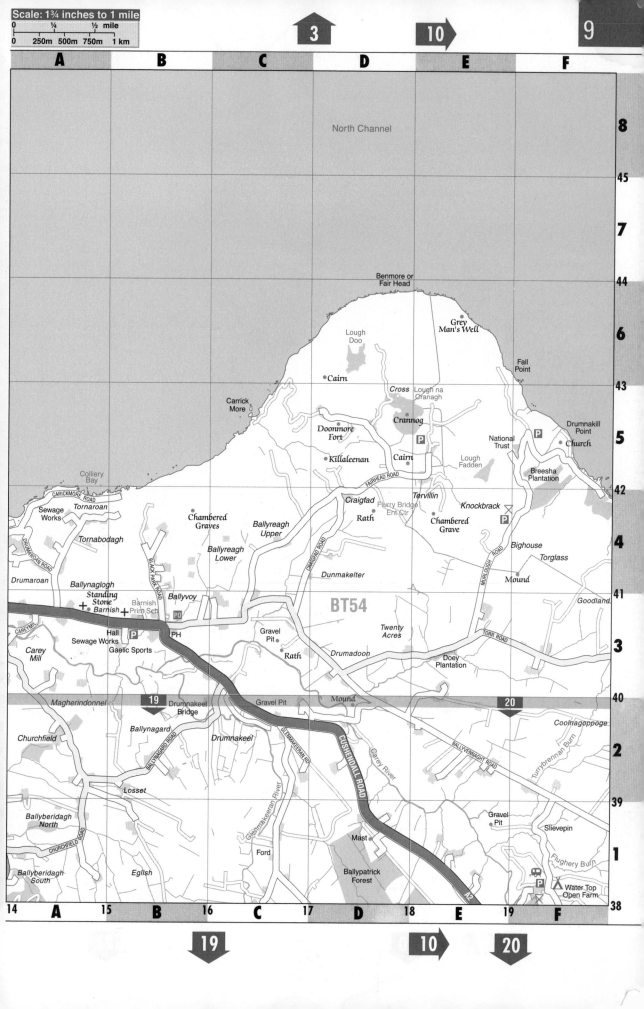

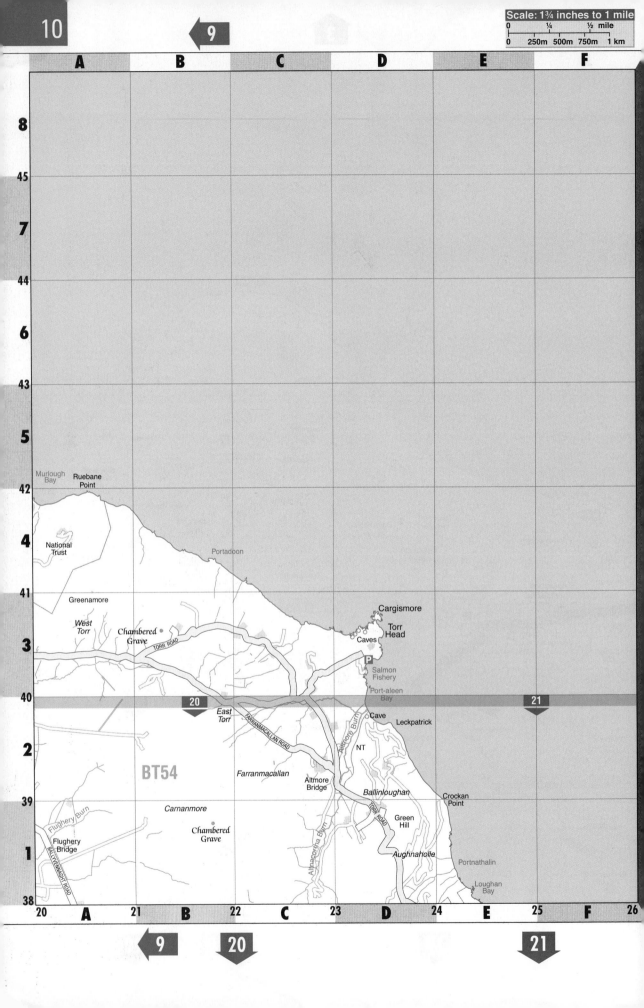

Scale: 1¾ inches to 1 mile

0   ¼   ½   mile
0 250m 500m 750m 1 km

A   B   C   D   E   F

8
45
7
44
6
43
5
42

Murlough
Bay
Ruebane
Point

National
Trust

Portadoon

41

Greenamore

Cargismore

West
Torr

Chambered
Grave

TORR ROAD

Torr
Head

Caves

3

P

Salmon
Fishery

40

Port-aleen
Bay

21

20

East
Torr

Cave

Leckpatrick

FARRANMACALLAN ROAD

Altmore Burn

NT

2

BT54

Farranmacallan

Altmore
Bridge

Ballinloughan

Crockan
Point

39

Carnanmore

Chambered
Grave

Altnagarraha Burn

TORR ROAD

Green
Hill

Flughery Burn

Flughery
Bridge

BALLYVENNAGHT ROAD

Aughnaholle

Portnathalin

1

Loughan
Bay

38
20   A   21   B   22   C   23   D   24   E   25   F   26

A   B   C   D   E   F

8

Ferry (V) to Greencastle (Co Donegal)

Magilligan Point

Magilligan Martello Tower

PH

P

Magilligan Point Nature Reserve

39

POINT RD

Dunes

7

B202

Lower Doaghs

Dunes

38

PH

Lower Middle Doaghs

Benone Beach

6

Magilligan   Strand

37

DANGER ZONE

Nature Reserve

POINT ROAD

Lower Drummans

5

Middle Doaghs Upper

Doaghs Upper

Lough   Foyle

Drummans Middle

36

A

Sandyville

Dunes

Ballymagoland

4

Oughtymore

Upper Drummans

Big Drain

Drumahorgan

Magilligan or Big Drain Bridge

35

Ballymulholland

Sewage Works

St Aidan's Magilligan Prim Sch

3

BT49

North Base Tower

B202

A2

Aughil

SEACOAST ROAD

PH

Clooney

34

Lenamore

Margymonaghan

Field Ctr

LC

Tircreven Road

2

CURRAGH RD

Drumavally

Big Drain Bridge

Tircreven Bridge

33

CARRIAGE COURT

PO

DRUMAVALLEY

Ballyscullion

LC

The Castle

Lower Ballyleighery

Playing Field

LIMESTONE ROAD

LC   Cross

Church Hill   Duncrun

1

DUNCRUN ROAD

LEIGHRY RD

Ballymultimber

Manse

Rath

32

64   A   65   B   66   C   67   D   68   E   69   F   70

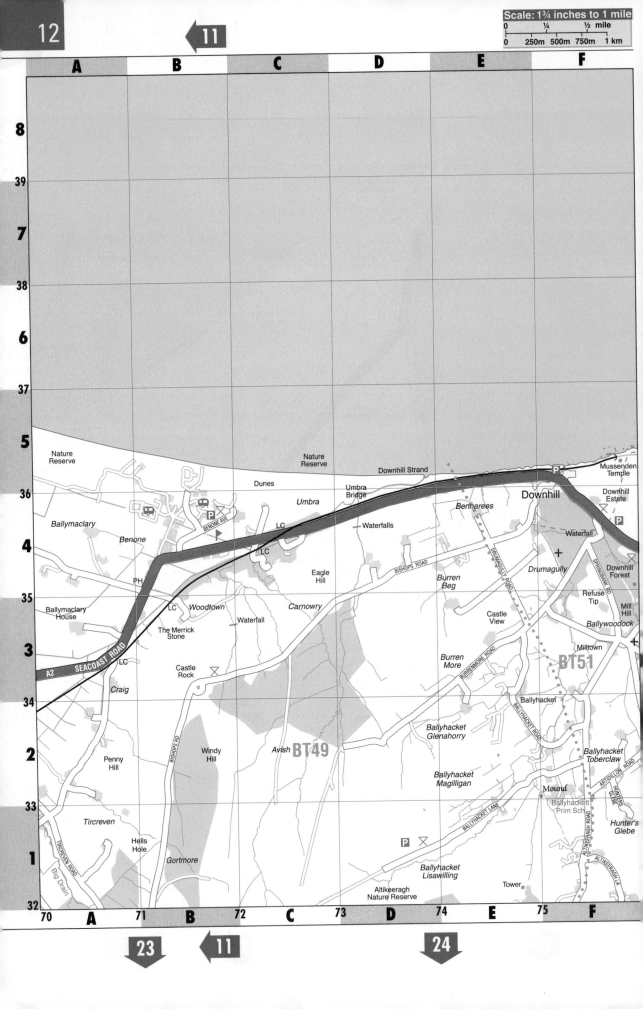

Scale: 1¾ inches to 1 mile

0	¼	½	mile
0	250m 500m 750m	1 km	

14

For full street detail of the highlighted area see page 172.

13

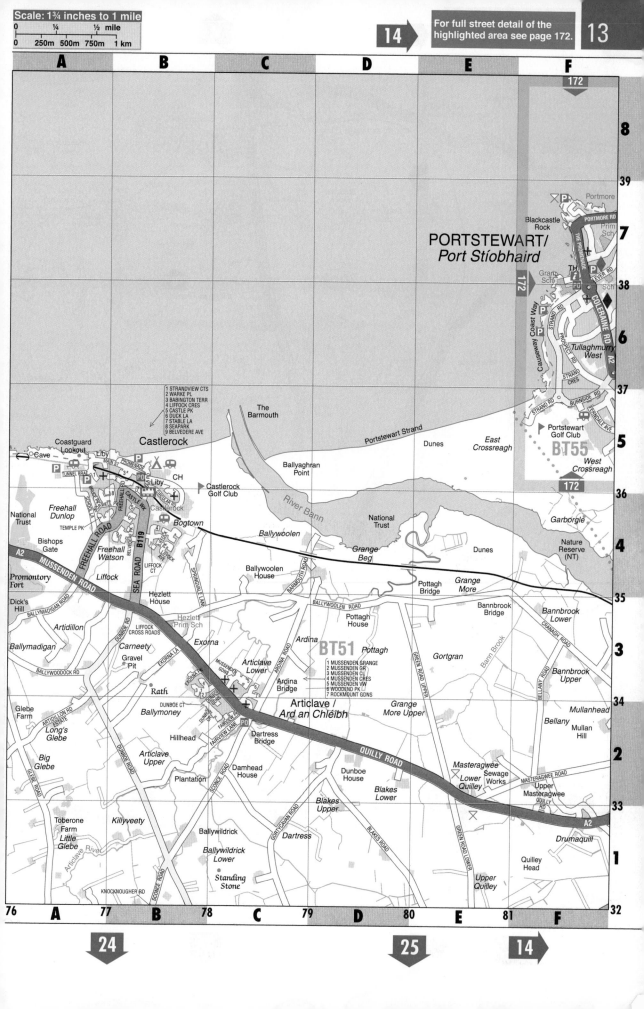

172

PORTSTEWART/
Port Stíobhaird

Blackcastle Rock

Portmore

PORTMORE RD

Prim Sch

THE PROMENADE

FEVER RD

COLERAINE RD

Gram Sch

Tullaghmurry West

Causeway Coast Way

STRAND RD

PROSPECT RD

STRAND CRES

BURNSIDE RD

FERNDALE AVE

Portstewart Golf Club

BT55

West Crossreagh

East Crossreagh

Dunes

172

The Barmouth

1 STRANDVIEW CTS
2 WARKE PL
3 BABINGTON TERR
4 LIFFOCK CRES
5 CASTLE PK
6 DUCK LA
7 STABLE LA
8 SEAPARK
9 BELVEDERE AVE

Castlerock

Portstewart Strand

Coastguard Lookout

Cave

TUNNEL BRAE

Main St

PROMENADE

Liby

Liby

CH

Castlerock Golf Club

Bogtown

Ballyaghran Point

River Bann

Ballywoolen

National Trust

Dunes

Garborgle

Nature Reserve (NT)

National Trust

Freehall Dunlop

TEMPLE PK

Freehall Watson

Liffock

FREEHALL ROAD

SEA ROAD

B119

LIFFOCK CT

SPRINGVALE LANE

Ballywoolen House

Grange Beg

Pottagh Bridge

Grange More

BALLYWOOLEN ROAD

Bannbrook Bridge

Bannbrook Lower

CRANAGH ROAD

BELLANY RD

Bannbrook Upper

National Trust

A2

MUSSENDEN ROAD

Promontory Fort

Dick's Hill

BALLYMADIGAN ROAD

Hezlett House

Hezlett Prim Sch

Liffock Cross Roads

Ardina

Pottagh House

Pottagh

BT51

1 MUSSENDEN GRANGE
2 MUSSENDEN GR
3 MUSSENDEN CL
4 MUSSENDEN CRES
5 MUSSENDEN VW
6 WOODEND PK
7 ROCKMOUNT GDNS

Gortgran

Bann Brook

Mullanhead

Artidillon

Ballymadigan

BALLYWOODOCK RD

Carneety

Gravel Pit

EXORNA LA

Exorna

ARDINA ROAD

BARMOUTH ROAD

Ardina Bridge

Articlave Lower

GREEN ROAD UPPER

Grange More Upper

Bellany

Mullan Hill

Glebe Farm

ARTIDILLON RD ESTATE

Long's Glebe

Big Glebe

DUNBOE ROAD

Rath

DUNBOE CT

Ballymoney

FAIRVIEW LANE

MUSSENDEN GDNS

Articlave / Ard an Chléibh

Dartress Bridge

Damhead House

Masteragwee Lower

Lower Quilley

MASTERAGWEE ROAD

Sewage Works

Upper Masteragwee

Hillhead

Articlave Upper

SCONCE ROAD

Plantation

Dunboe House

Blakes Lower

QUILLY ROAD

Upper Quilly

A2

Drumaquill

GLEBE ROAD

Toberone Farm

Little Glebe

Articlave River

Killyveety

Ballywildrick

GORTYCAVAN ROAD

Dartress

Ballywildrick Lower

BLAKES ROAD

Blakes Upper

GREEN ROAD LOWER

Upper Quilley

Quilley Head

KNOCKNOUGHER RD

Standing Stone

8
39
7
38
6
37
5
36
4
35
3
34
2
33
1

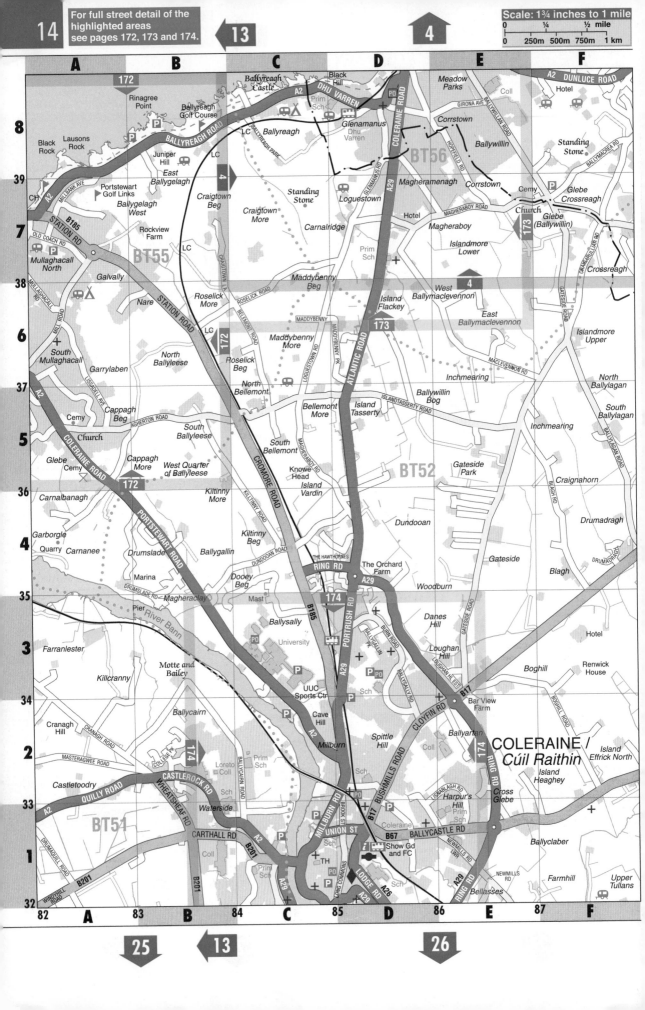

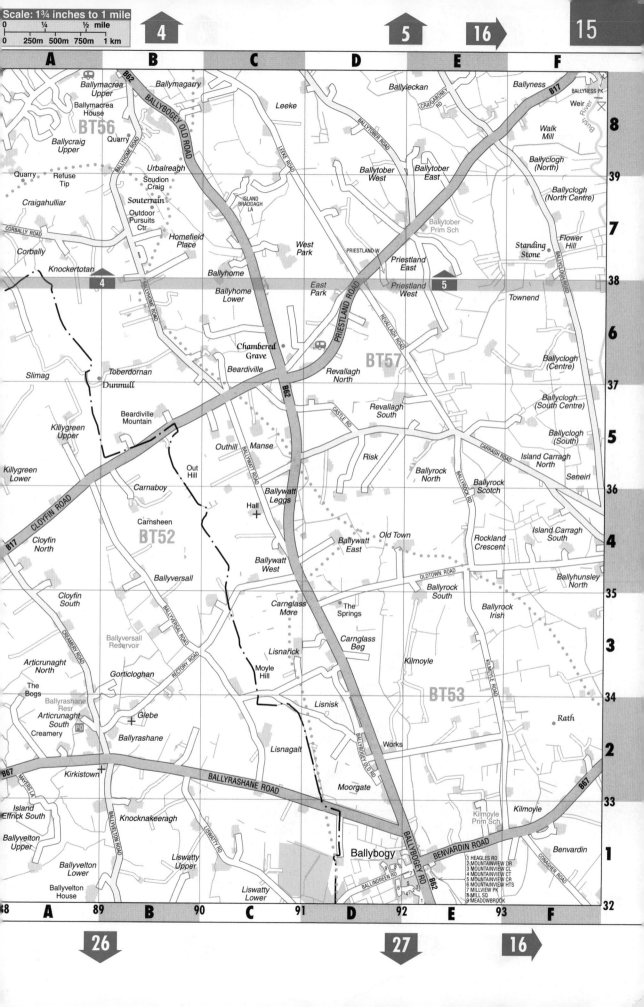

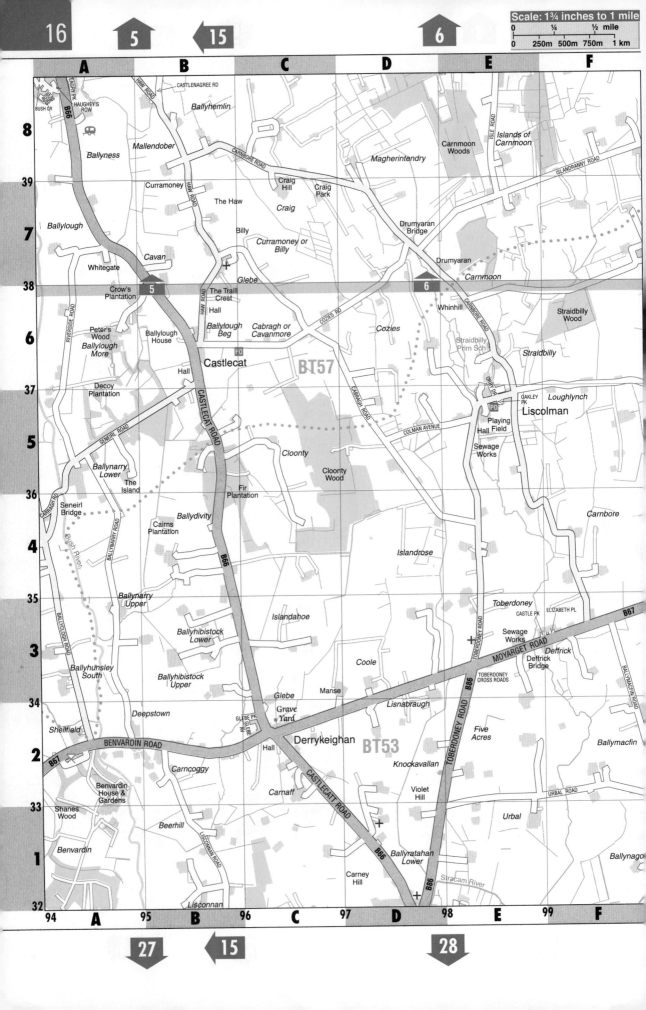

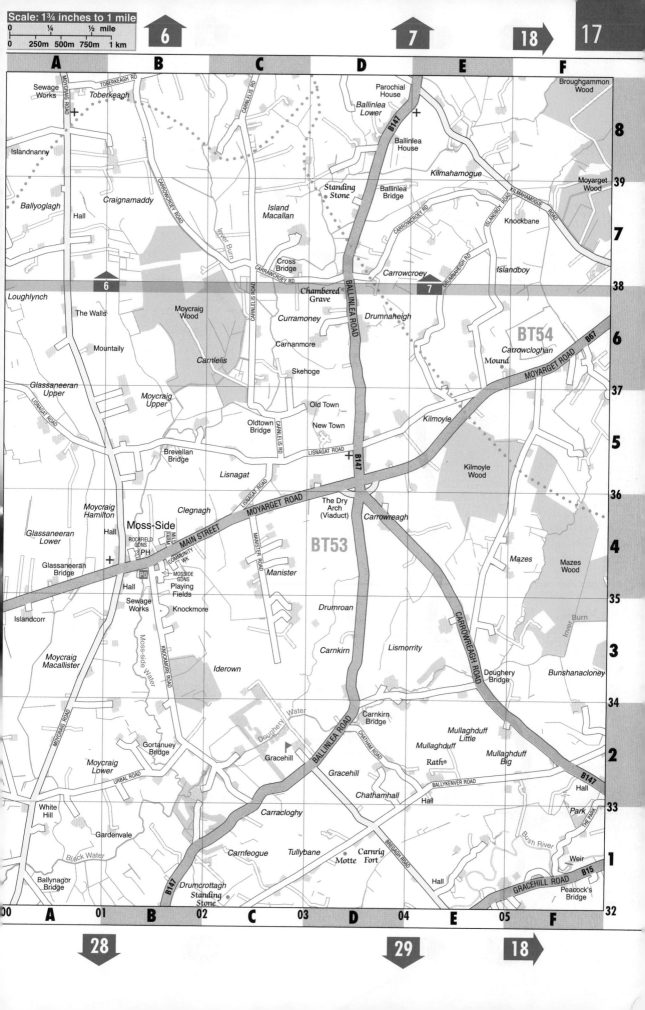

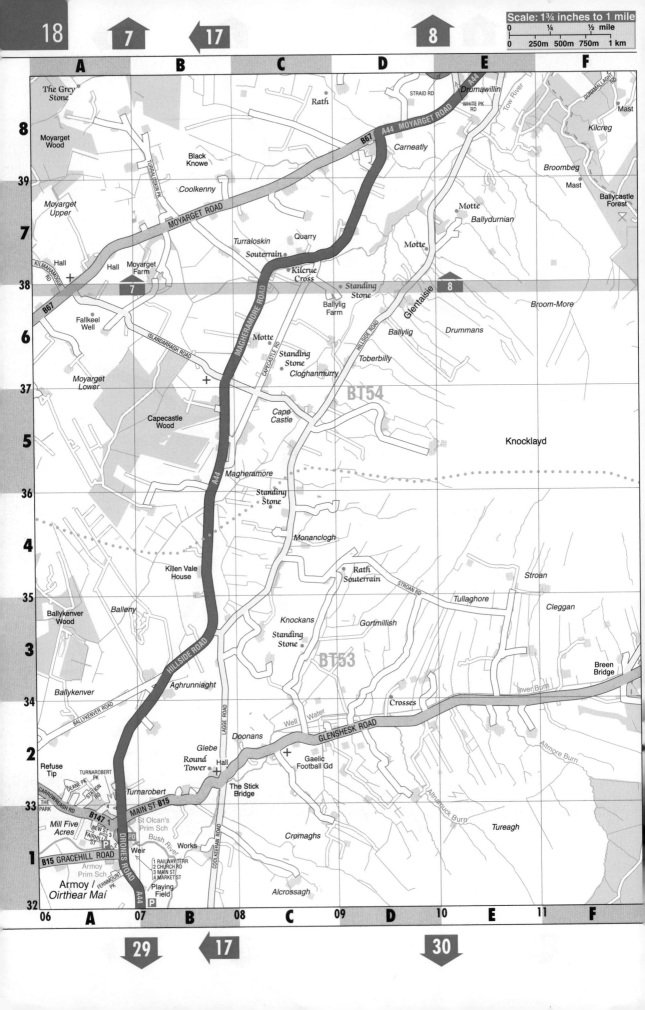

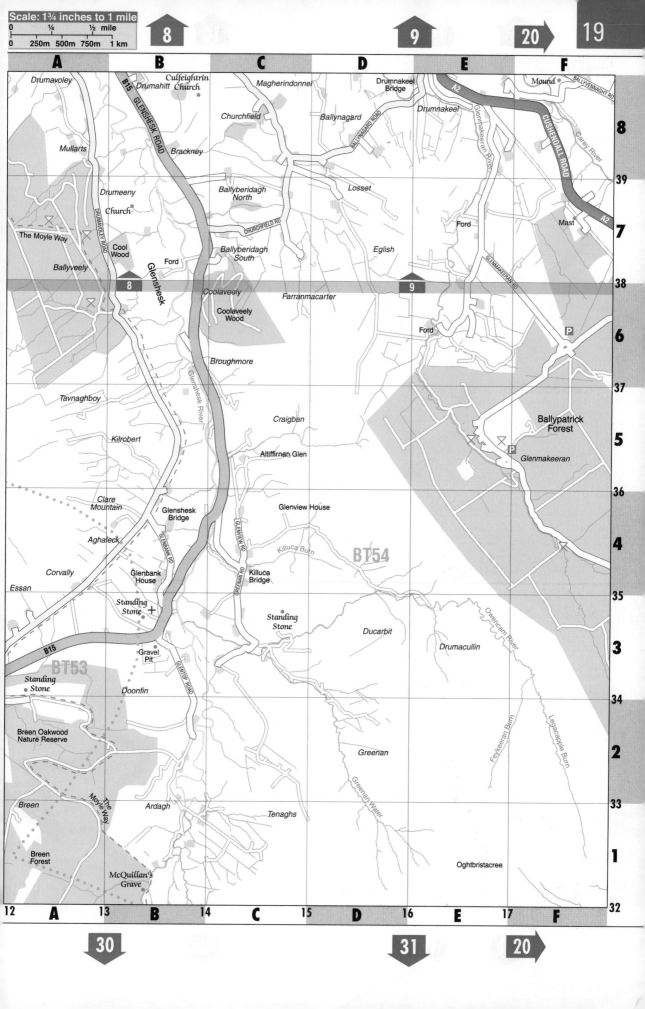

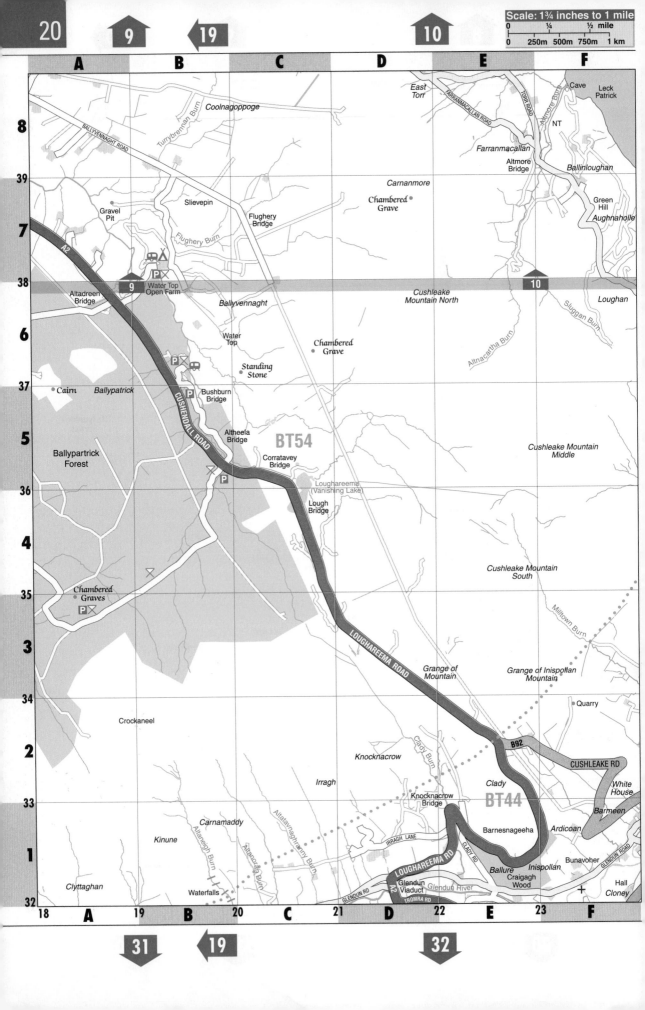

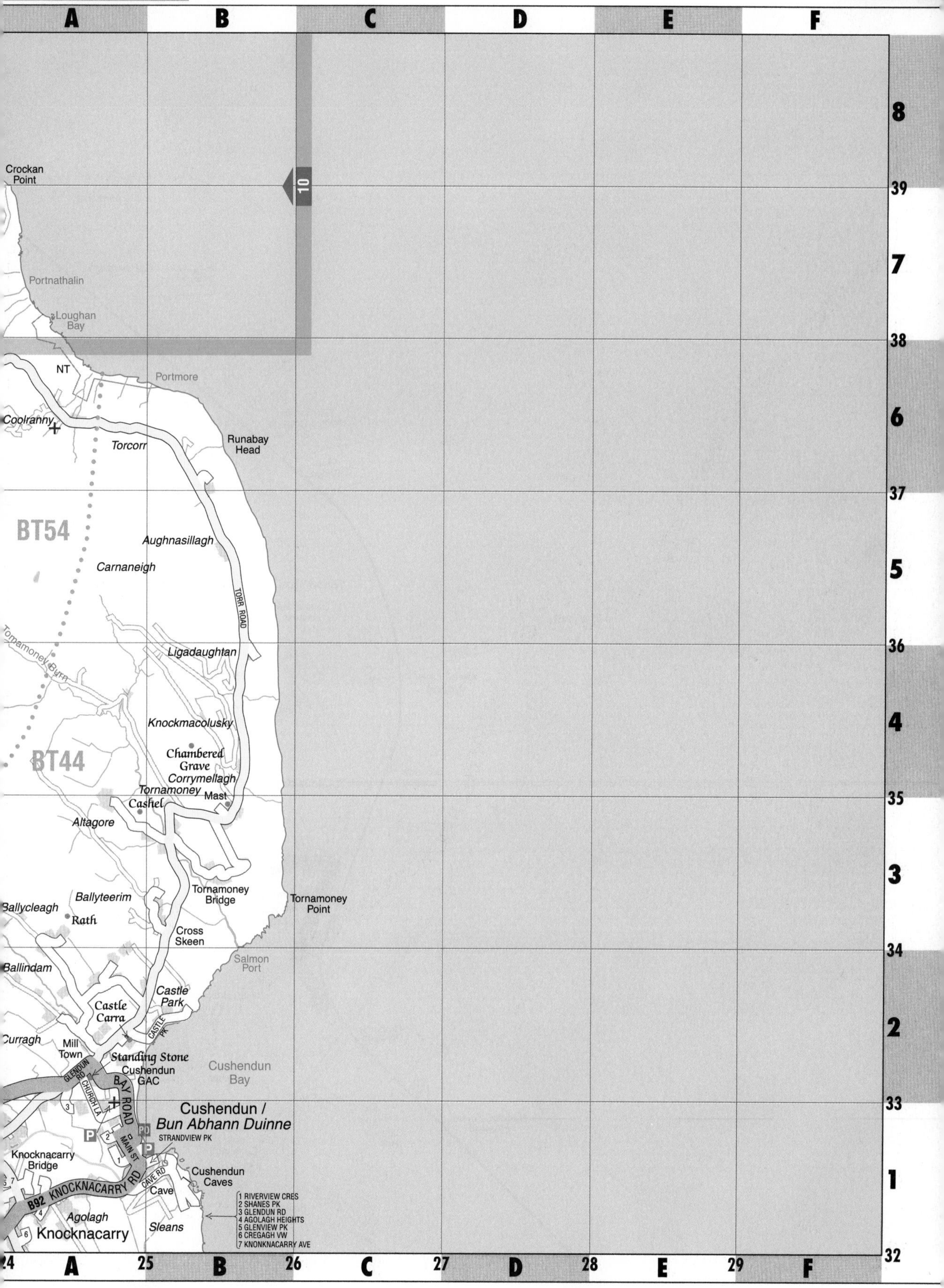

A   B   C   D   E   F

8

Crockan
Point

10

39

7

Portnathalin

Loughan
Bay

38

NT

Portmore

6

Coolranny

Torcorr

Runabay
Head

37

BT54

Aughnasillagh

Carnaneigh

TORR ROAD

5

Tornamoney Burn

Ligadaughtan

36

Knockmacolusky

4

BT44

Chambered
Grave
Corrymellagh
Tornamoney
Cashel   Mast

35

Altagore

Tornamoney
Bridge   Tornamoney
Point

3

Ballyteerim

Ballycleagh Rath

Cross
Skeen

34

Salmon
Port

Ballindam

Castle   Castle
Carra   Park

CASTLE PK

2

Curragh   Mill
Town

Standing Stone
Cushendun
GAC

Cushendun
Bay

GLENDUN
CHURCHILLA
BAY ROAD

33

Cushendun /
Bun Abhann Duinne

STRANDVIEW PK

Knocknacarry
Bridge

MAIN ST

Cushendun
Caves

1 RIVERVIEW CRES
2 SHANES PK
3 GLENDUN RD
4 AGOLAGH HEIGHTS
5 GLENVIEW PK
6 CREGAGH VW
7 KNONKNACARRY AVE

1

CAVE RD

B92 KNOCKNACARRY RD

Cave

Agolagh
Knocknacarry   Sleans

6

32

24   A   25   B   26   C   27   D   28   E   29   F   32

32

33

Lough
Foyle

Gliding
Club

Minearny

Base
Tower

Carrowreagh

LC

Balls
Point

Bellarena

Scotchtown
Carrowmuddle

Carrowmuddle

Sheep
Marsh

River Roe

Roe Estuary
Nature Reserve

Roe
Bridge

CARROWCLARE ROAD

Carrowmenagh

Carrowmena
House

SHORE AVE

LC

Myroe Level
(Intake)

Carrowreagh

Crindle

Carrowmena Outdoor
Education Ctr

BT49

Barnacle
Lodge

Carrowclare

LC

LC

CARROWCLARE RD

B510

LOMOND ROAD

Ballymacran
Widgeon
Lodge

Back

Lomond

Burnfoot River

Broighter
House

Broighter

BROIGHTER ROAD

Broharris
Bridge

Broglasco
House

LC

Broglasco

Ballykelly Level
(Intake)

Carse
Hall

Rush
Hall
Cottages

CARSE ROAD

BURNALLY ROAD

Broharris

Rush Hall
Bridge

Cricket
Ground

FARLOW RD

Farlow

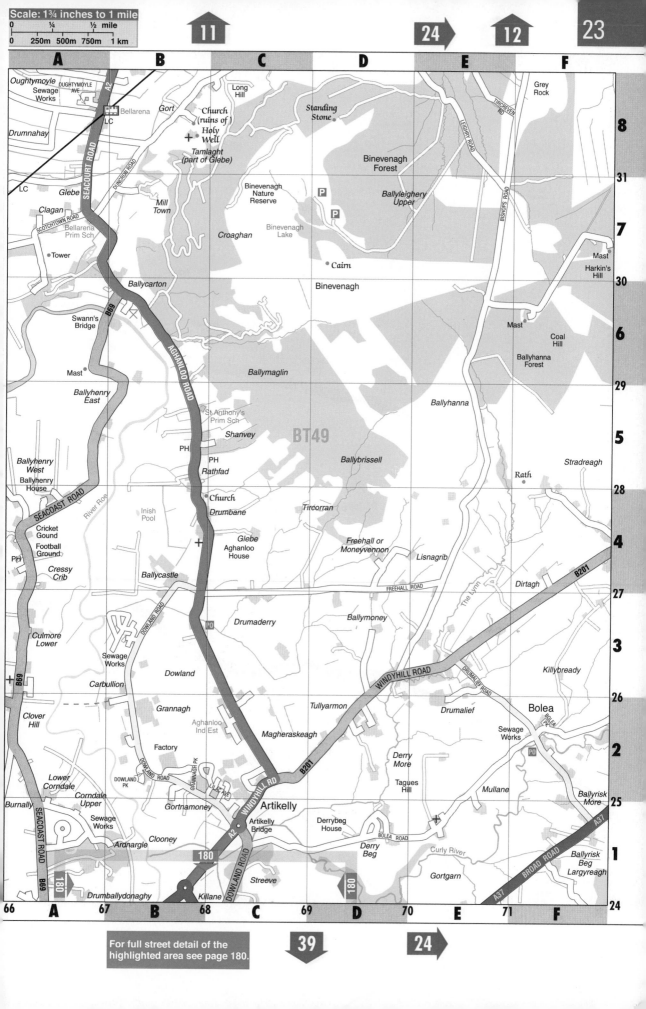

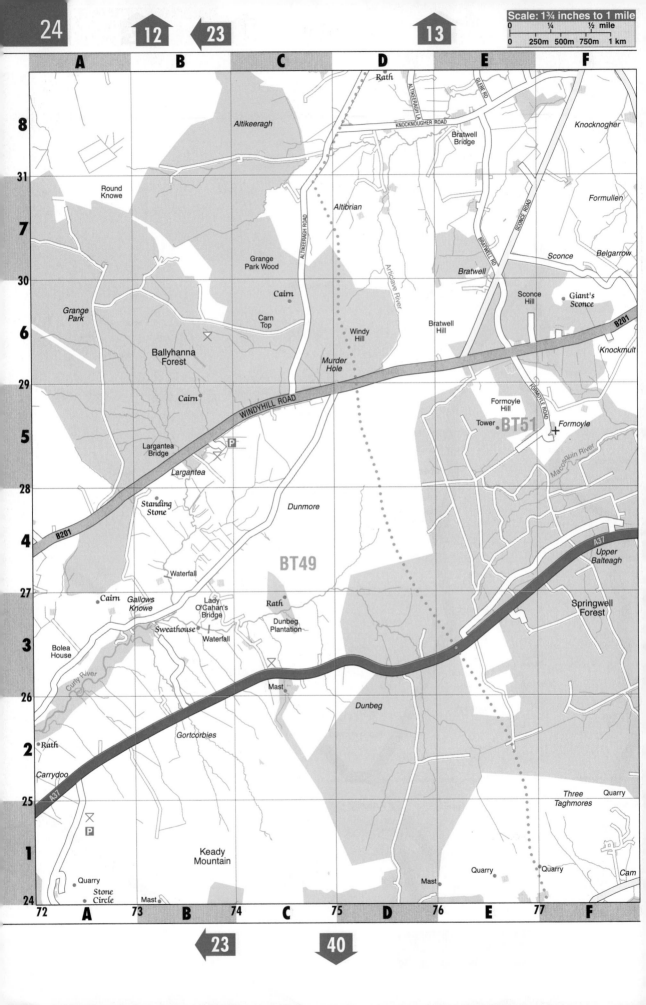

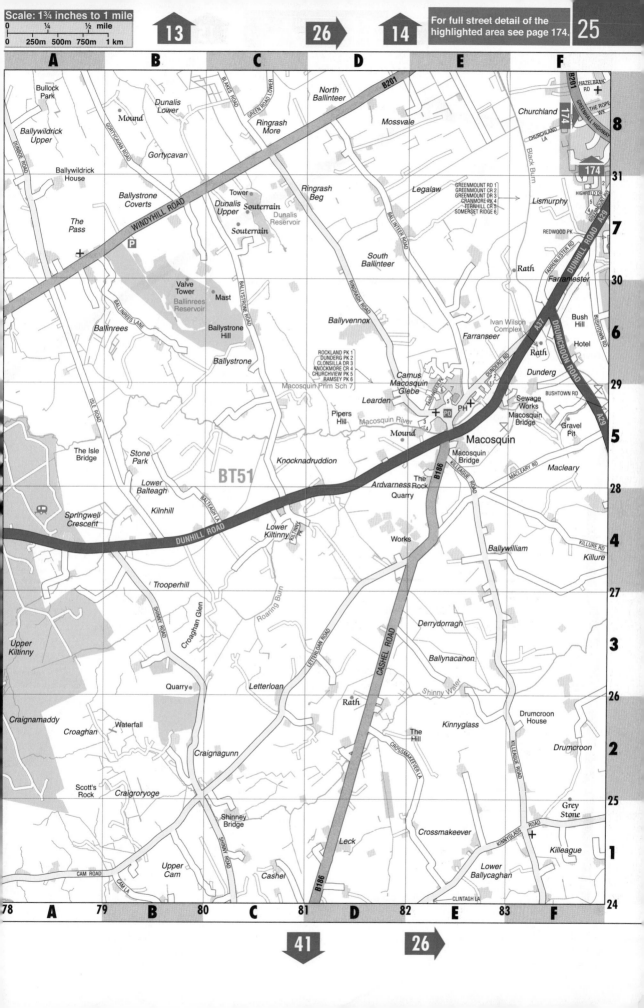

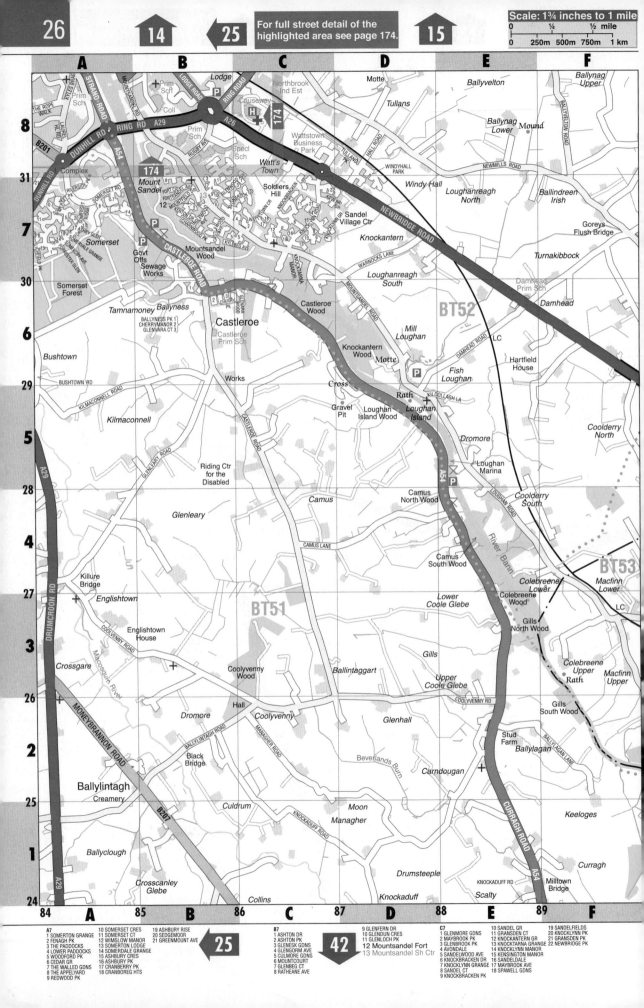

26
14
25
For full street detail of the highlighted area see page 174.
15
Scale: 1¾ inches to 1 mile
0   ¼   ½   mile
0 250m 500m 750m 1 km

25
42
25

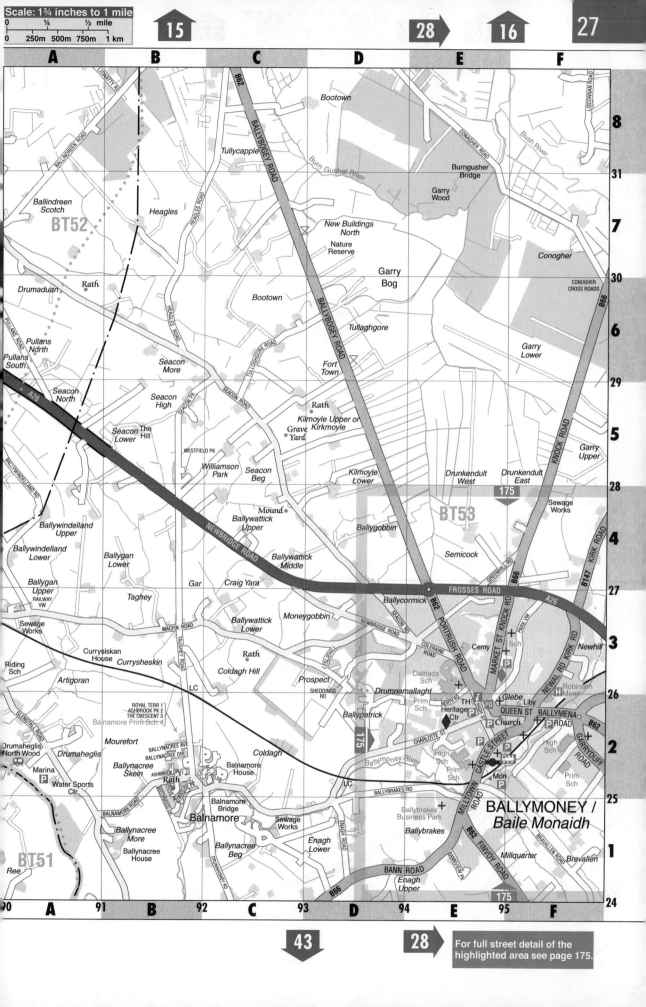

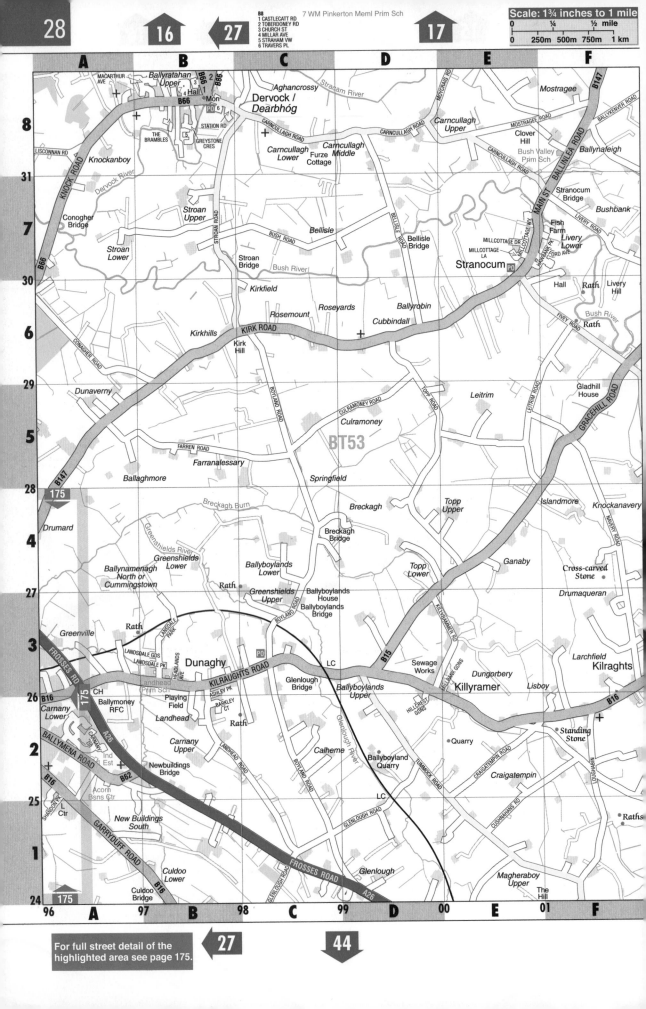

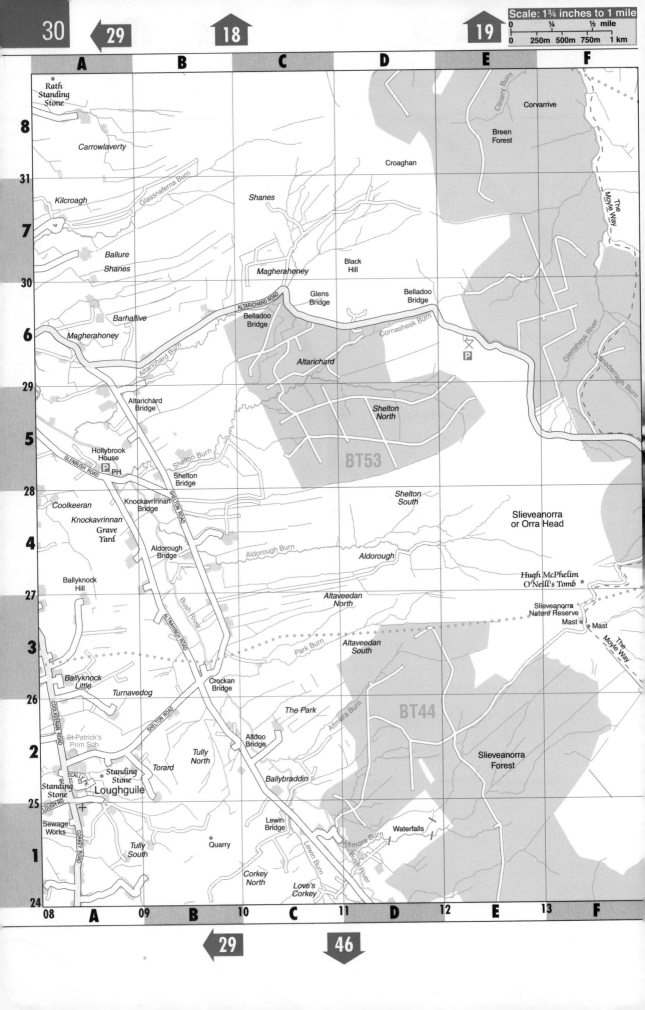

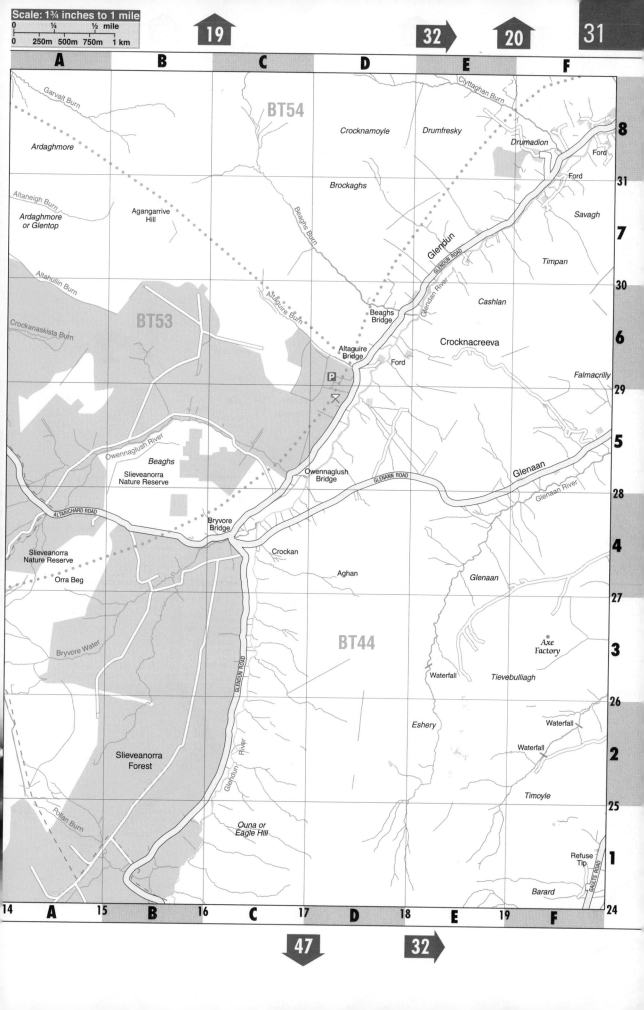

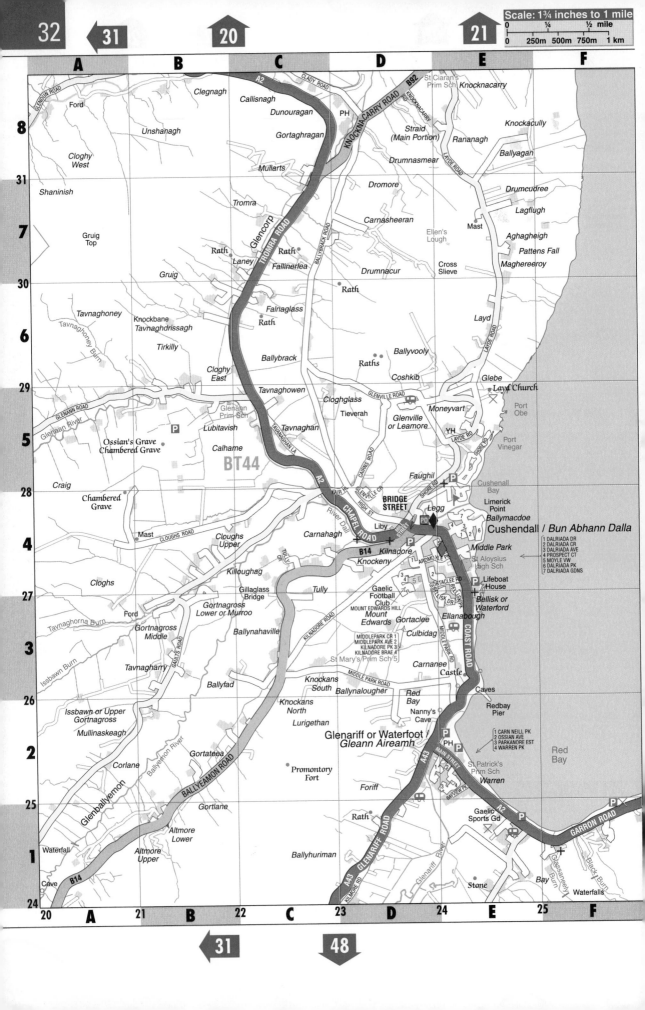

GARRON ROAD

Ardclinis Bridge
Church

Crealargh Burn

Waterfall

Galboly Upper

Fallowvee

Cushenlit Burn

Ardclinis Burn

Ardclinis

BT44

Lough Galboly

Waterfall

Galboly Lower

TOWER RD

A2

Cloghastucan or White Lady

Inscribed Stone

Garron Point

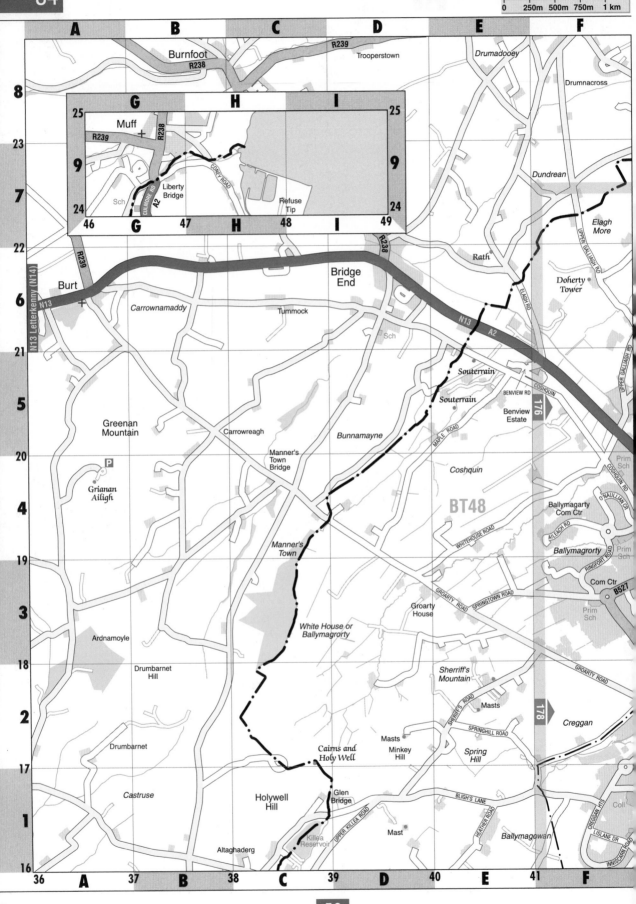

Scale: 1¾ inches to 1 mile

0   ¼   ½   mile
0 250m 500m 750m 1 km

A B C D E F

G H I

8
23
7
22
6
21
5
20
4
19
3
18
2
17
1
16

36 A 37 B 38 C 39 D 40 E 41 F

25 G H I
9
24
46 G 47 H 48 I 49

Burnfoot
R238
R239
Trooperstown
Drumadooey
Drumnacross

Muff
R239
R238
CONEY ROAD
CULMORE RD
A2
Sch
Liberty Bridge
Refuse Tip

Dundrean
Elagh More

Burt
R239
N13 Letterkenny (N14)
N13
Carrownamaddy
Tummock
Bridge End
R238
Rath
Doherty Tower

UPPER GALLIAGH RD

N13 A2
Souterrain
Souterrain
BENVIEW RD
Benview Estate
COSHQUIN
176
ELAGH RD

UPPER GALLIAGH RD

Greenan Mountain
Carrowreagh
Manner's Town Bridge
Bunnamayne
MAPLE ROAD
Coshquin
COSHQUIN RD
Prim Sch

P
Grianan Ailigh
BT48
Ballymagarty Com Ctr
AILEACH RD
O NAULLIAN CR
Ballymagrorty
Prim Sch

Manner's Town
WHITEHOUSE ROAD
RINGFORT ROAD
Com Ctr
B527

Ardnamoyle
White House or Ballymagrorty
Groarty House
GROARTY ROAD
SPRINGTOWN ROAD
GROARTY ROAD
Prim Sch

Drumbarnet Hill
Sherriff's Mountain
SHERRIFF'S ROAD
Masts
178
Creggan

Drumbarnet
Masts
Minkey Hill
SPRINGHILL ROAD
Spring Hill
CREGGAN HTS
Coll

Cairns and Holy Well
Mast
BLIGH'S LANE
HEATHER ROAD
LISLANE DR

Castruse
Holywell Hill
Glen Bridge
UPPER KILLEA ROAD
Mast
Ballymagowan
INNISCARN ROAD

Altaghaderg
Killea Reservoir

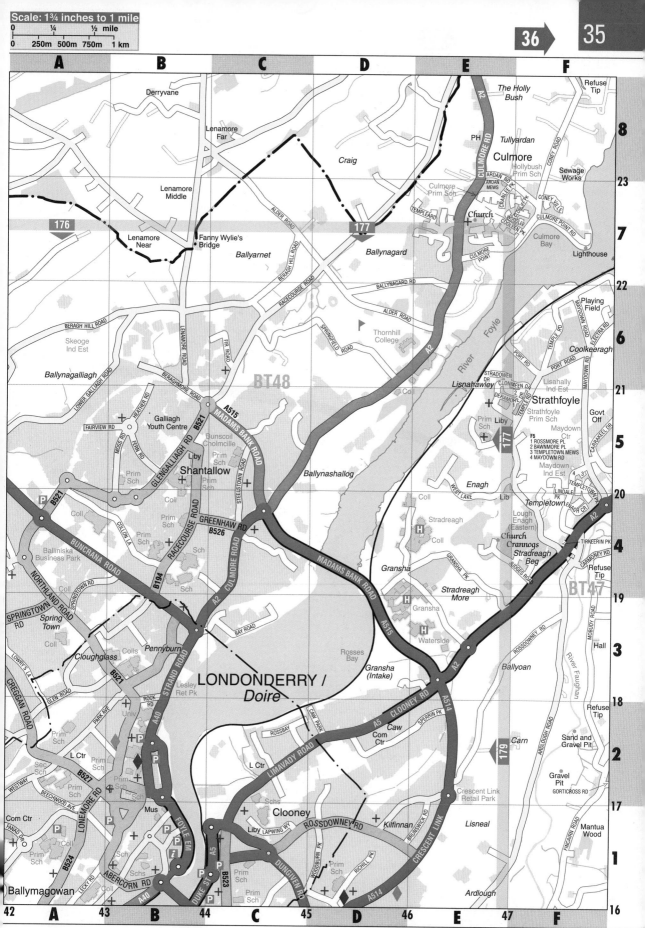

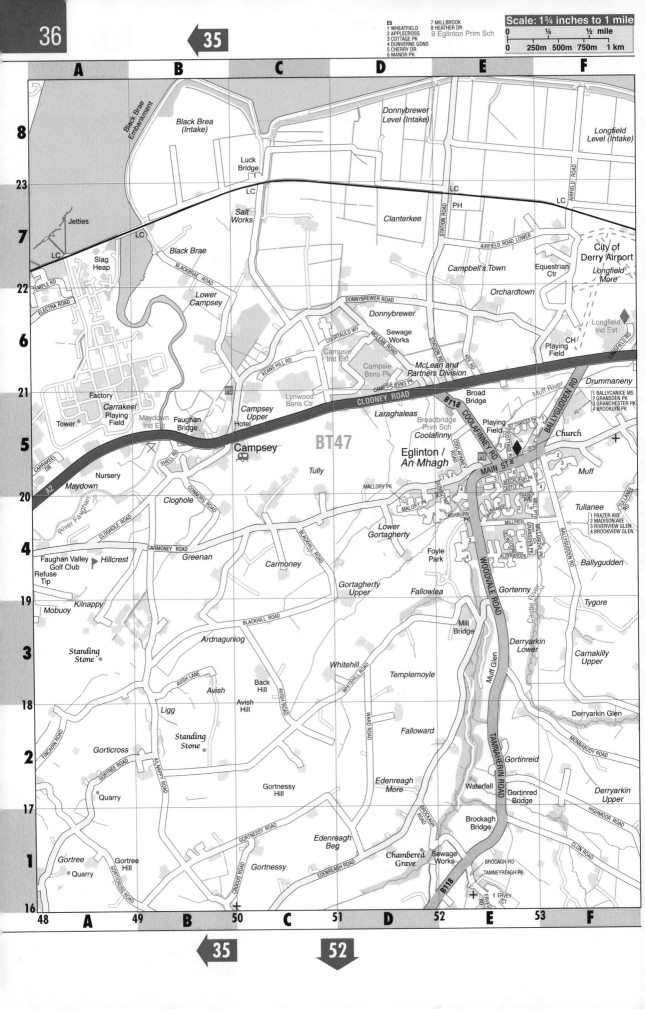

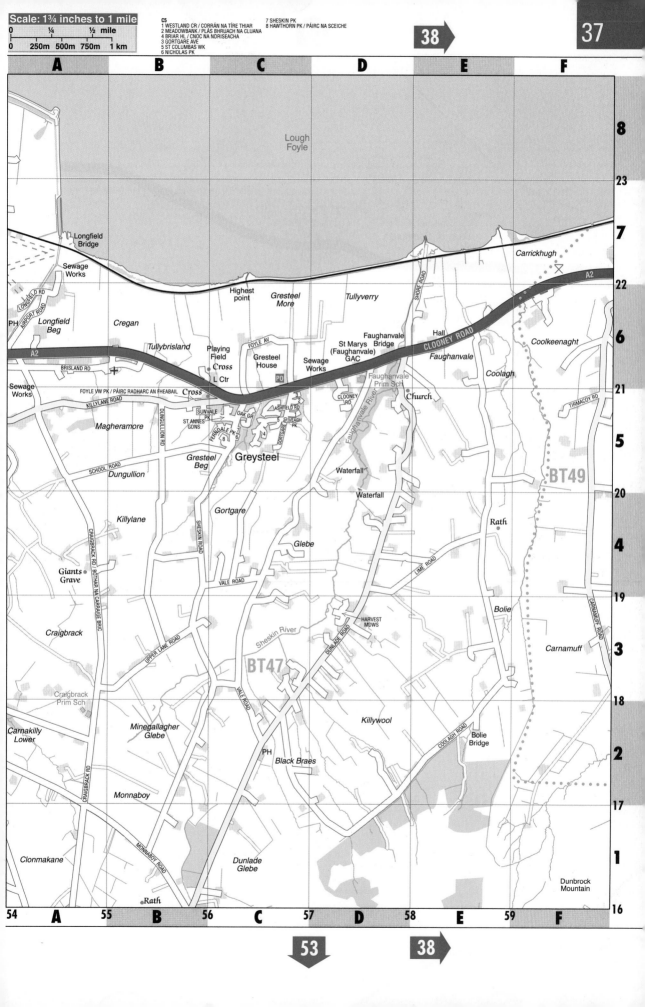

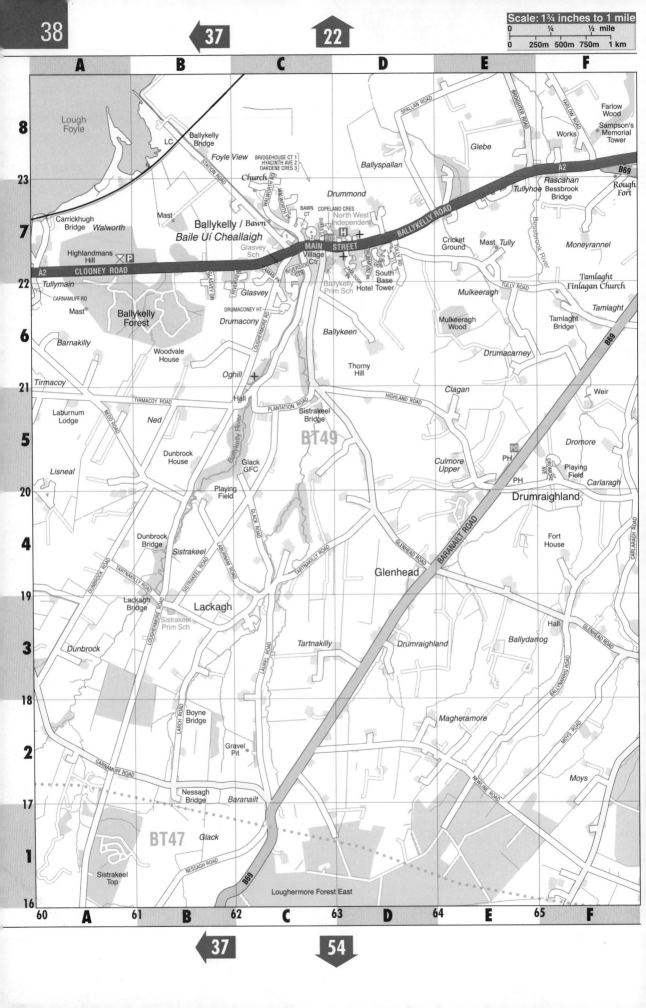

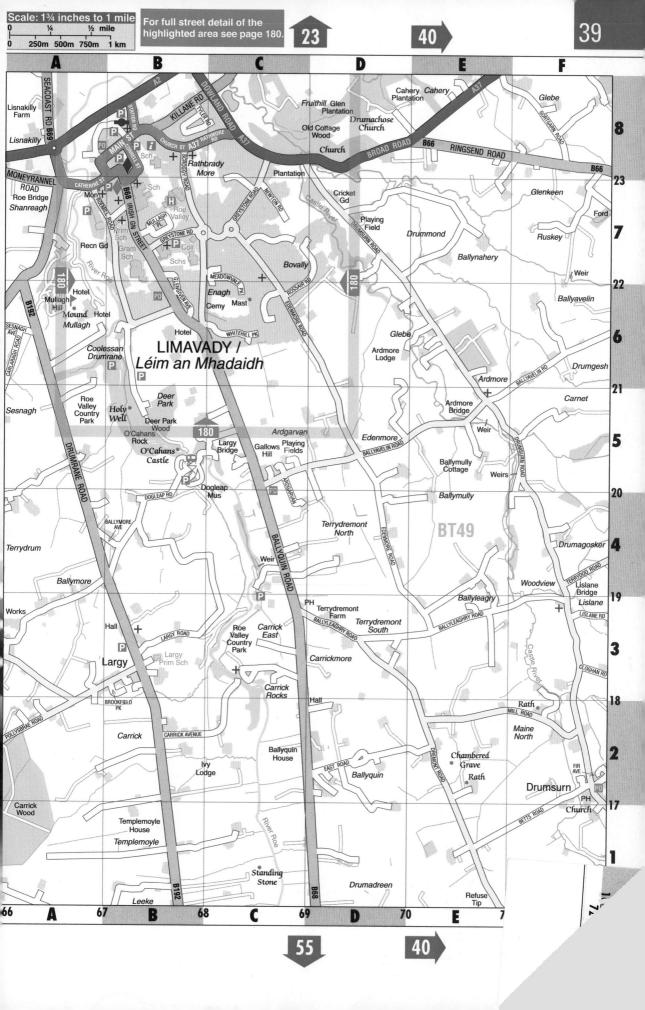

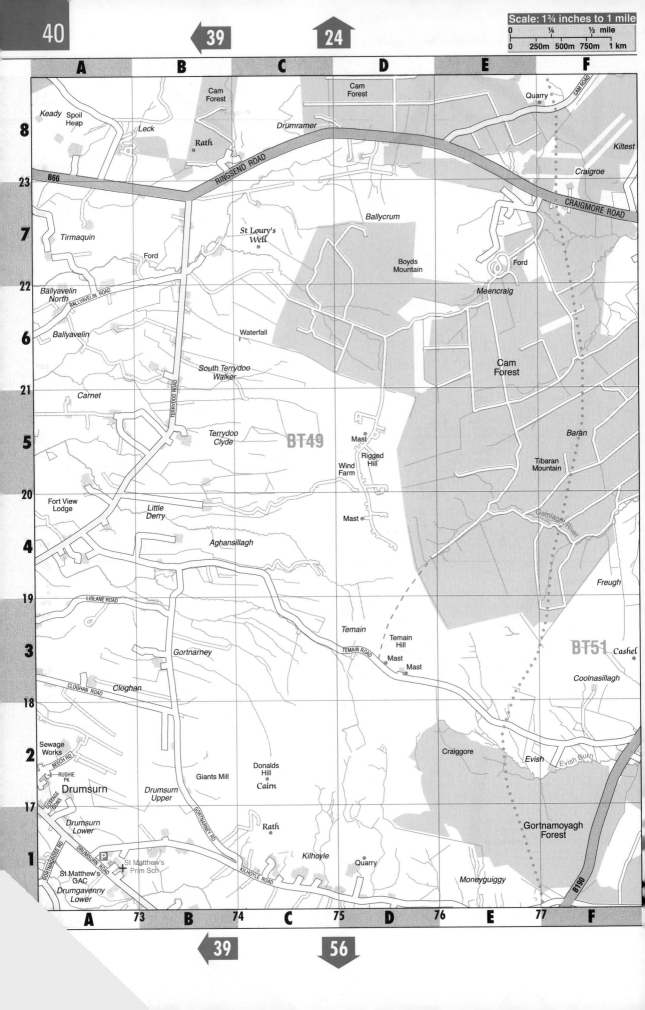

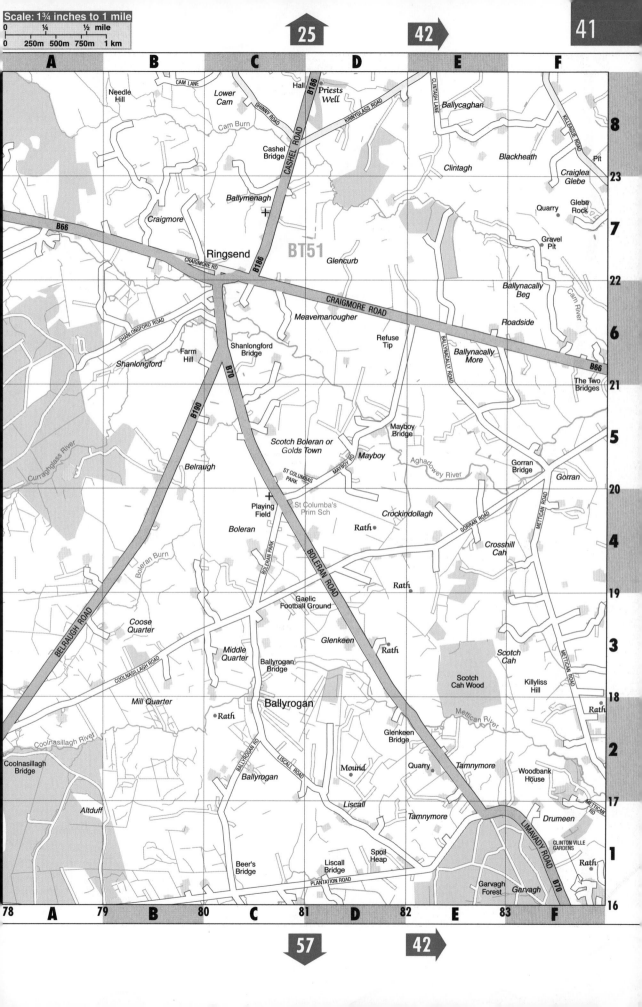

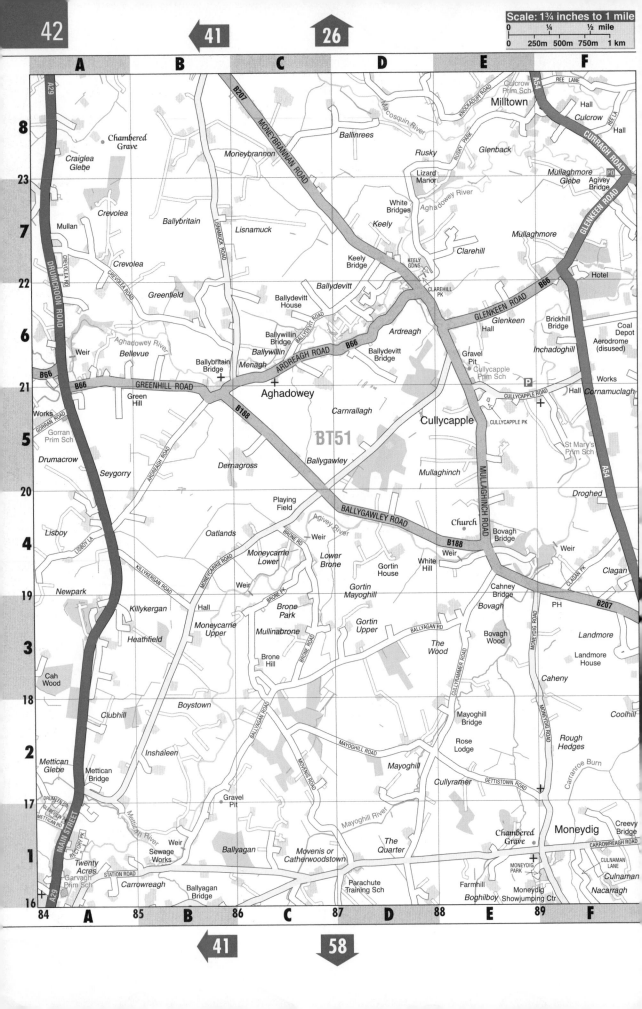

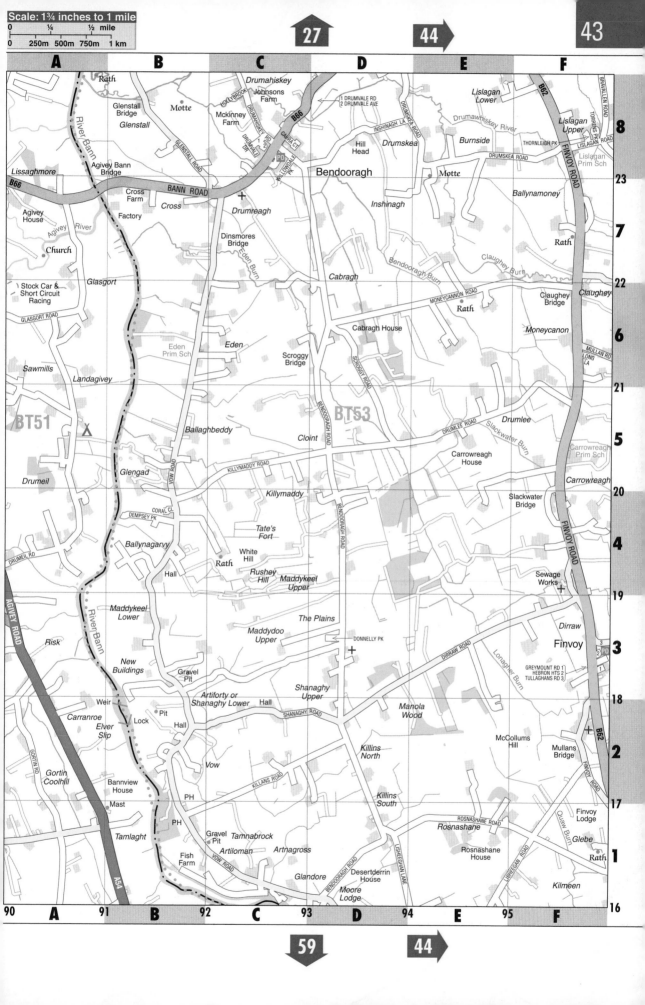

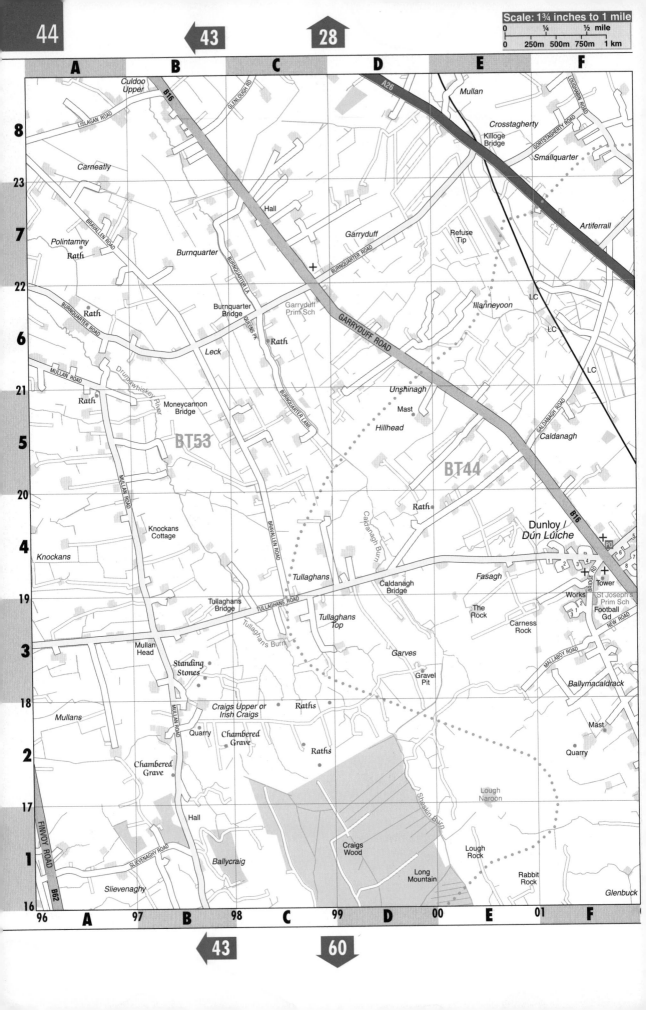

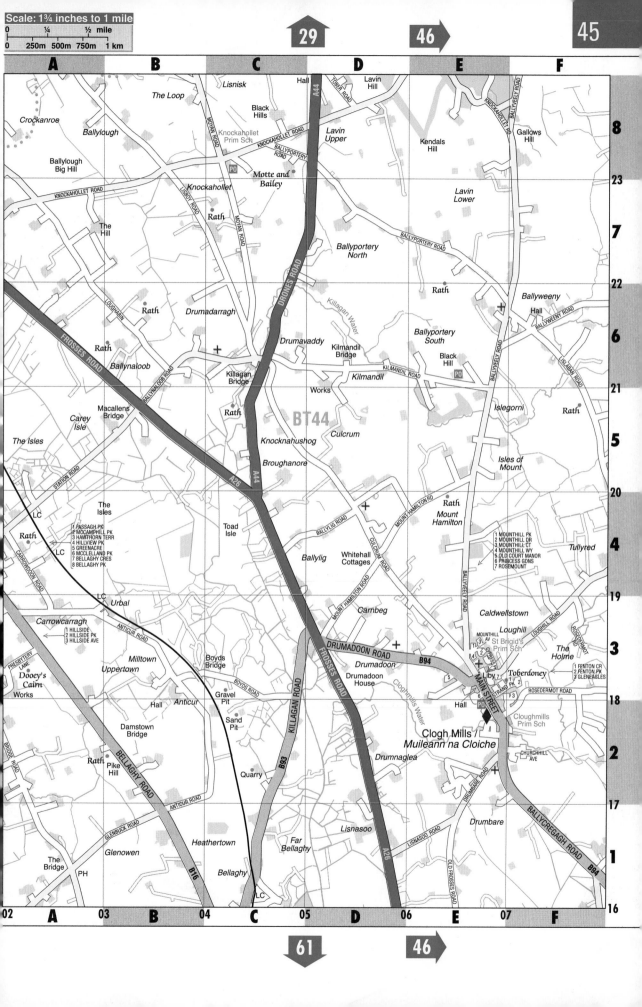

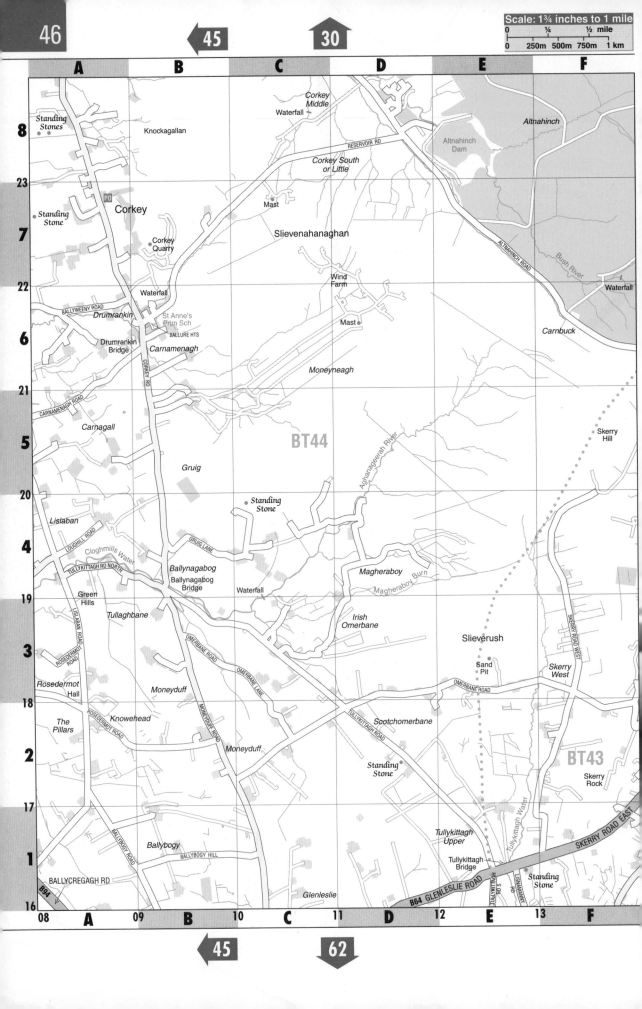

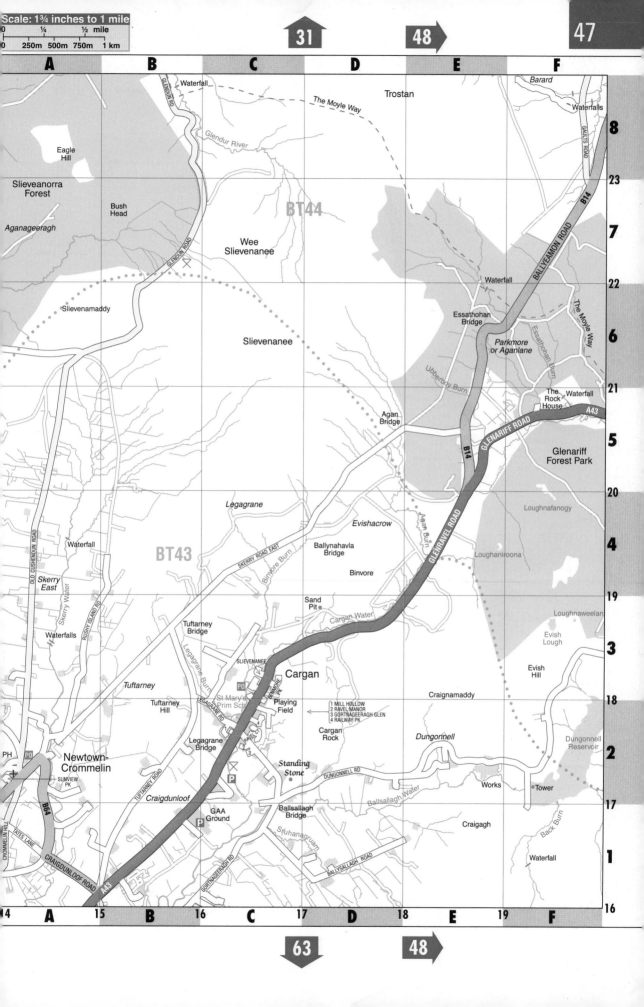

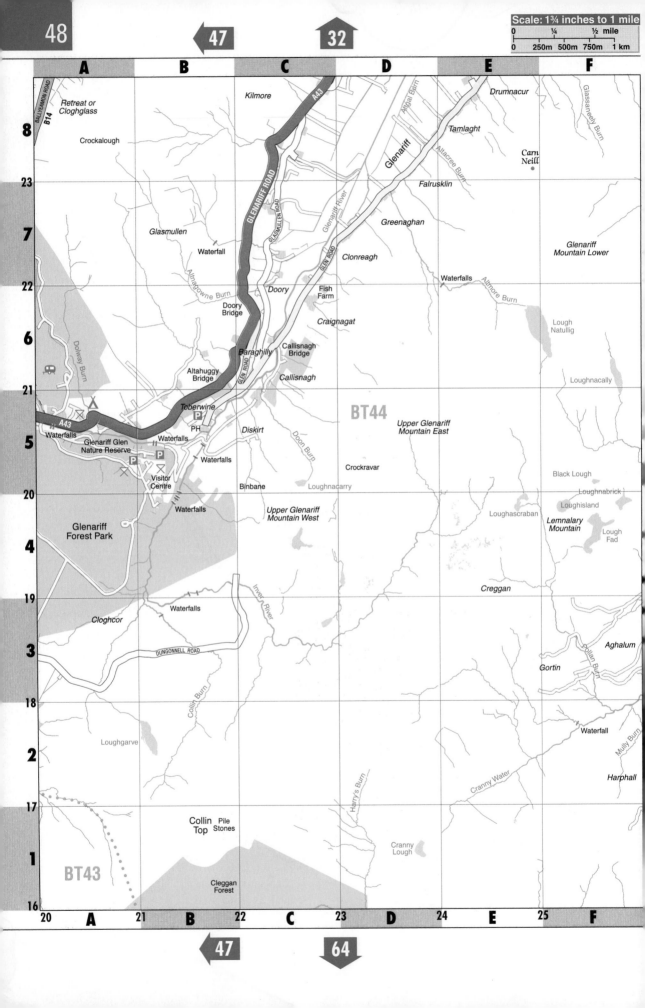

A   B   C   D   E   F

8
23
7
22
6
21
5
20
4
19
3
18
2
17
1
16

Carrivemurphy

Cushenlit Burn

Ardclinis

Ardclinis Burn

Lough
Galboly

Promontory
Fort
St MacNissis
College

Garron
Tower

A2

P

Knockore

Nappan

Drumnasole

Loughan

Mound

Ballyvelligan

Newtown

Craigatinnel

Cross Burn

Broken
Bridge

Burnside

Turnly's
Port

Black Burn

Binabanan

BT44

Drumnacross

Ringfad

GARRON ROAD

TOWER RD

LARGY ROAD

Loughfine

Castle
Hill

Highlandtown

Denny's
Lough

Scaryhill

Big
Trosk

Loughnatrosk

Longtown

Hunters
Point

Little
Trosk

Gortnagory

Lemnalary

A2

Tommy's Port

Bottle
Point

Seal
Rock

GARRON ROAD

GORTNAGORY ROAD

BRANCH RD

C3
1 CRANNIE AVE
2 MOYLE GDNS
3 CAIRNHILL MANOR
4 HERBERT ST
5 HAVELOCK PL
6 CROFT CL
7 CROFT GR
8 GORTIN HL

WATERFALL RD

Gortin
Quarry

Creggan
Quarry

Campbeltown

Carnlough
North

Cranny
Falls

Drumnahoe

Carnlough River

Carnlough South

Carnlough /
Carnlach

CLINTON HILL

CLIFF AVE

HIGH ST

LARGY RD

CROFT AVE

BRIDGE ST

PO

WHITEHILL RD

Carnlough
Prim Sch

MARINE RD

White
Hill

St John's
Prim Sch

Cemy Hall

Mill
Tenement

ATLANTIC AVE

Carnlough
Bay

DRUMOURNE RD

Knock Burn

Knockaneffrin

GARTFORD LA

Bonnytober

Playing
Field

Stony
Hill

1 HILLVIEW PK
2 GLENBROOK
3 STONYHILL

Black
Rock

Straidkilly
Point

Craigfad
Loughs

BAY ROAD

BRECKLAND ST

SHINGLE
COVE

THE CLONEY

Binnagee

Gartford

A42 BALLYMENA ROAD

GARTFORD LA

GALDANAGH RD

BALLYVADOY RD

Straidkilly Road

Straidkilly

A2

Straidkilly
Nature
Reserve

Drumourne

Gortcarney

Drumnacole

Druminagh

P

Scale: 1¾ inches to 1 mile

0   ¼   ½ mile

0   250m 500m 750m 1 km

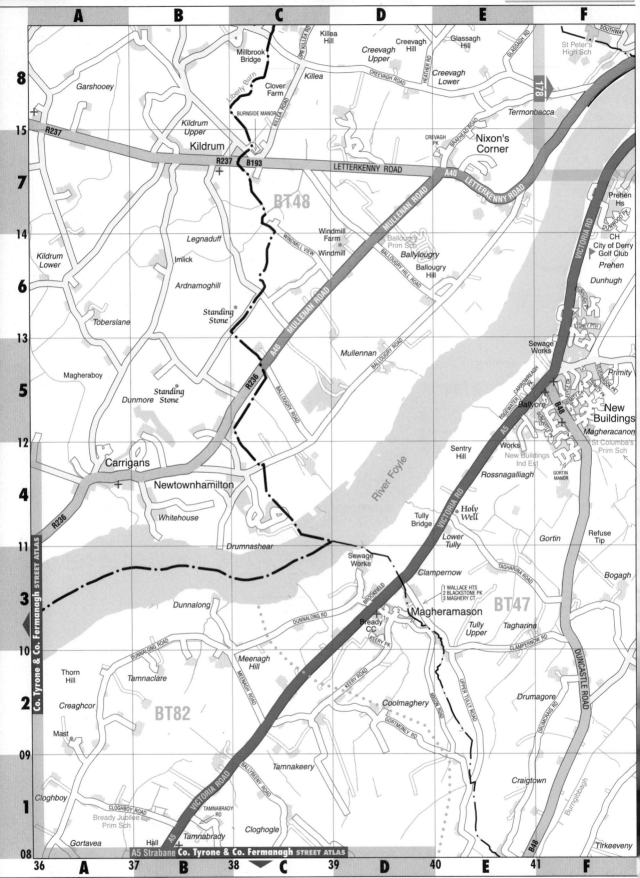

Co. Tyrone & Co. Fermanagh STREET ATLAS

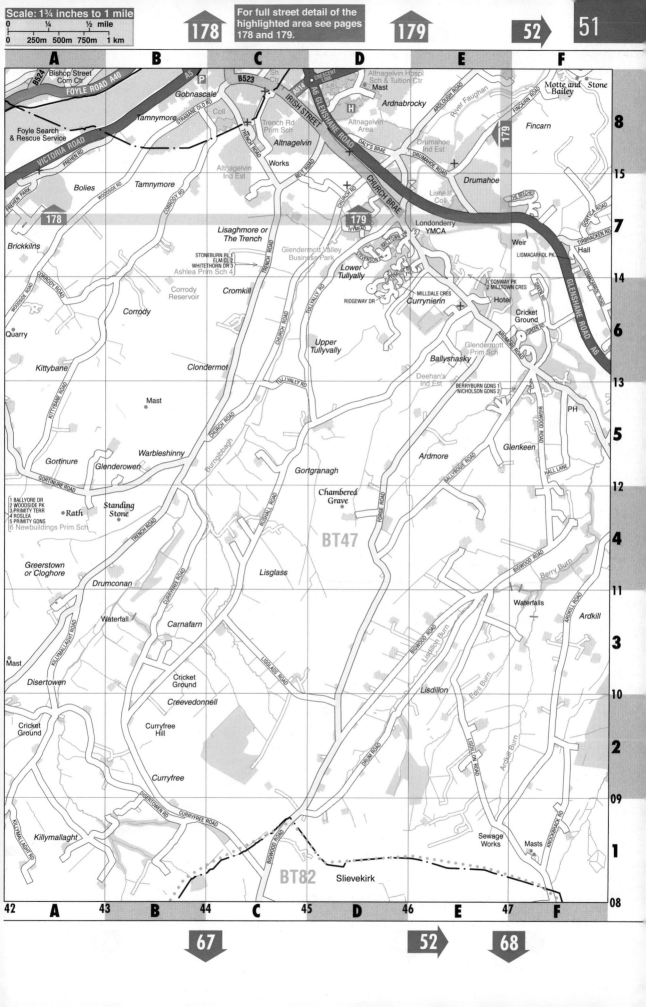

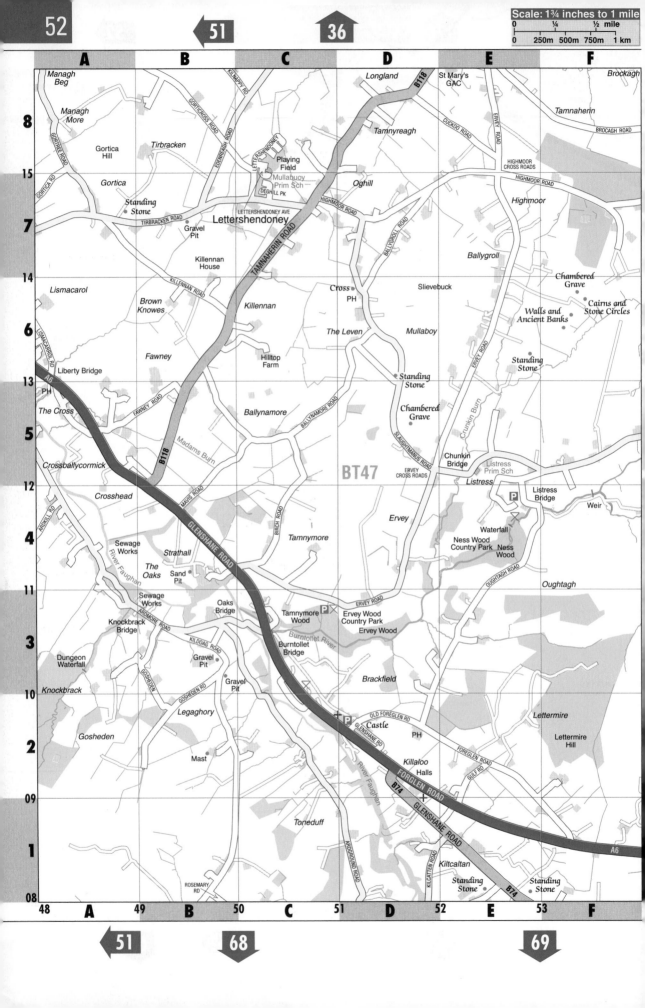

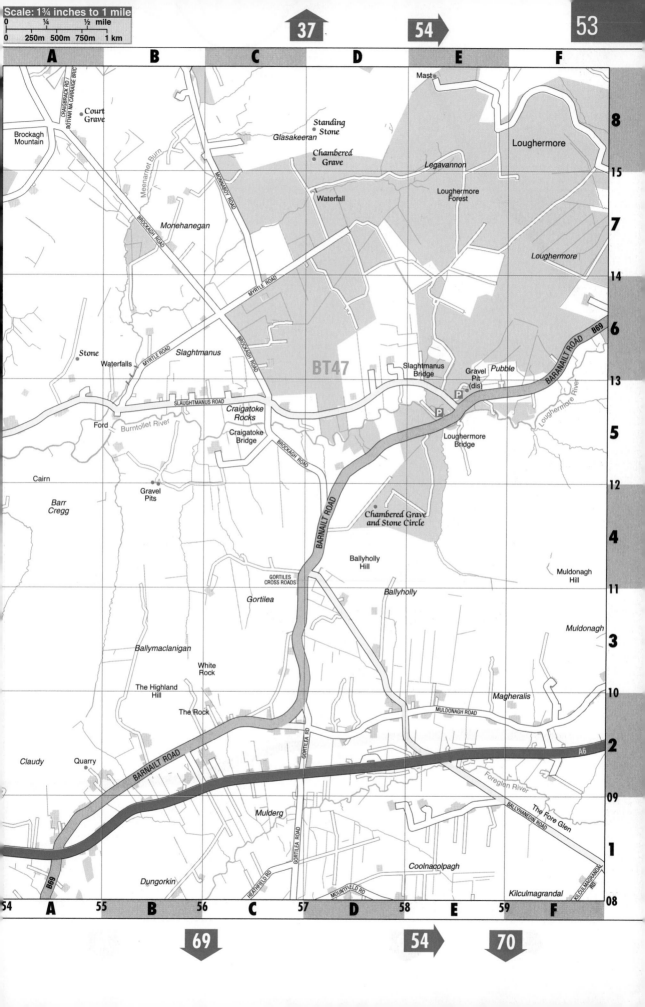

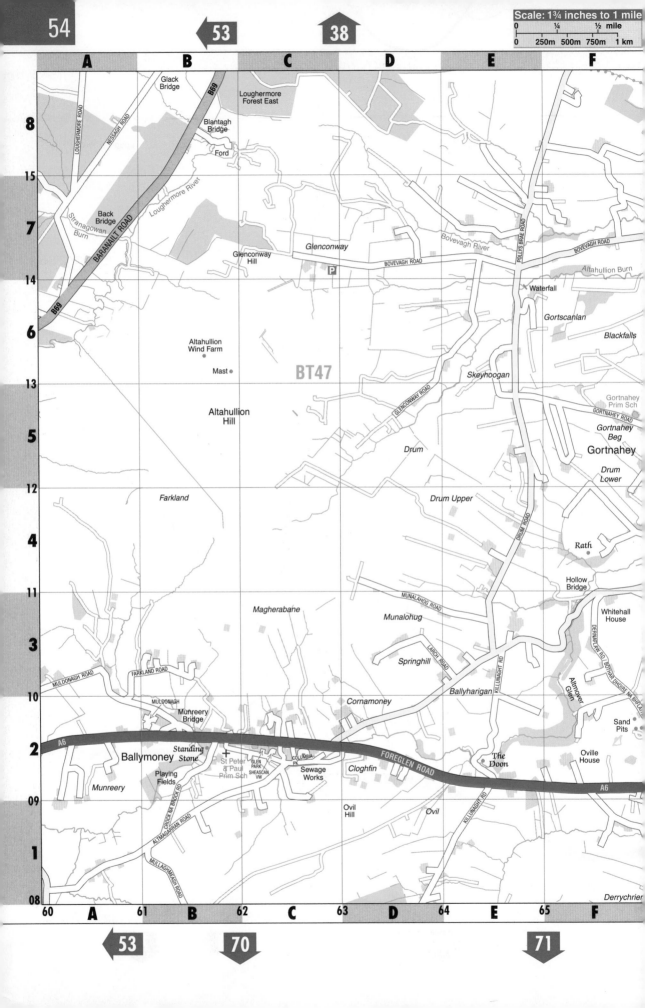

A   B   C   D   E   F

8

15

7

14

6

13

5

12

4

11

3

10

2

09

1

08

Glack Bridge

Loughermore Forest East

Blantagh Bridge

Ford

LOUGHERMORE ROAD

NESSAGH ROAD

B69

Loughermore River

Back Bridge

Stranagowan Burn

BARANAILT ROAD

B69

Glenconway Hill

Glenconway

Bovevagh River

BOVEVAGH ROAD

POLLYS BRAE ROAD

BOVEVAGH ROAD

Altahullion Burn

Waterfall

Gortscanlan

Blackfalls

P

BT47

Altahullion Wind Farm

Mast

Skeyhoogan

GLENCONWAY ROAD

Gortnahey Prim Sch

GORTNAHEY ROAD

Altahullion Hill

Drum

Gortnahey Beg

Gortnahey

Drum Lower

Farkland

Drum Upper

DRUM ROAD

Rath

Hollow Bridge

Magherabane

MUNALAHOG ROAD

Munalohug

Whitehall House

DERNAFLAW RD / BÓTHAR DHOIRE NA BHFEÁL

Springhill

LARCH ROAD

Ballyharigan

KILLUNAGHT RD

Altnover Glen

Sand Pits

MULDONAGH ROAD

FARKLAND ROAD

Muldonagh

Munreery Bridge

Cornamoney

A6

Standing Stone

Ballymoney

St Peter & Paul Prim Sch

GLEN PARK

COLUMBIA PK

SHEASCAN VW

Sewage Works

Cloghfin

FOREGLEN ROAD

The Doon

Oville House

A6

Playing Fields

CNOC NA BROCK RD

Munreery

Ovil Hill

Ovil

KILLUNAGHT RD

ALTMAGARRAN ROAD

MULLAGHMEASH ROAD

Derrychrier

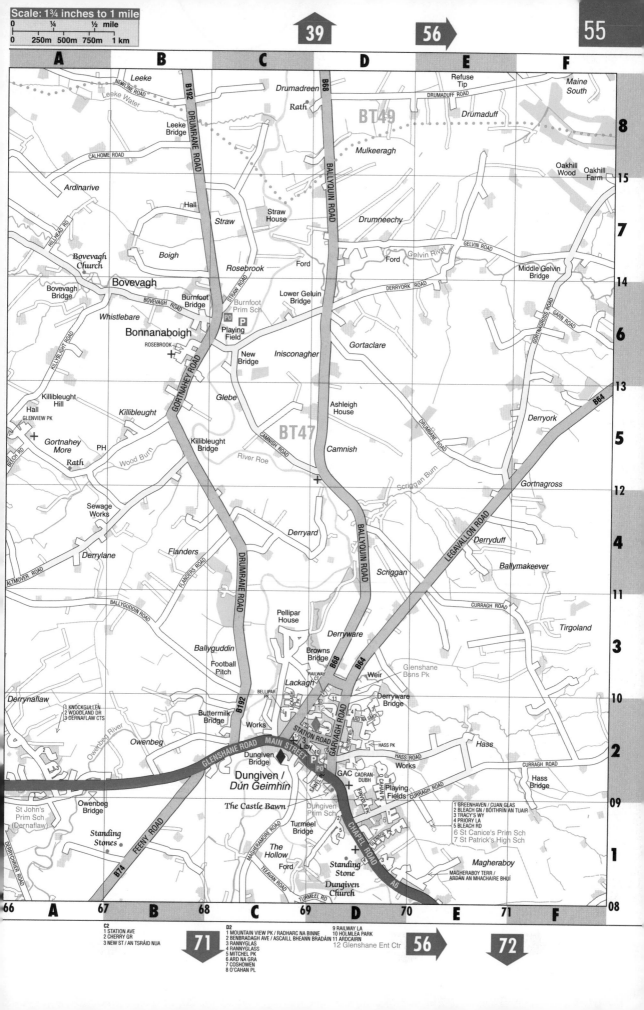

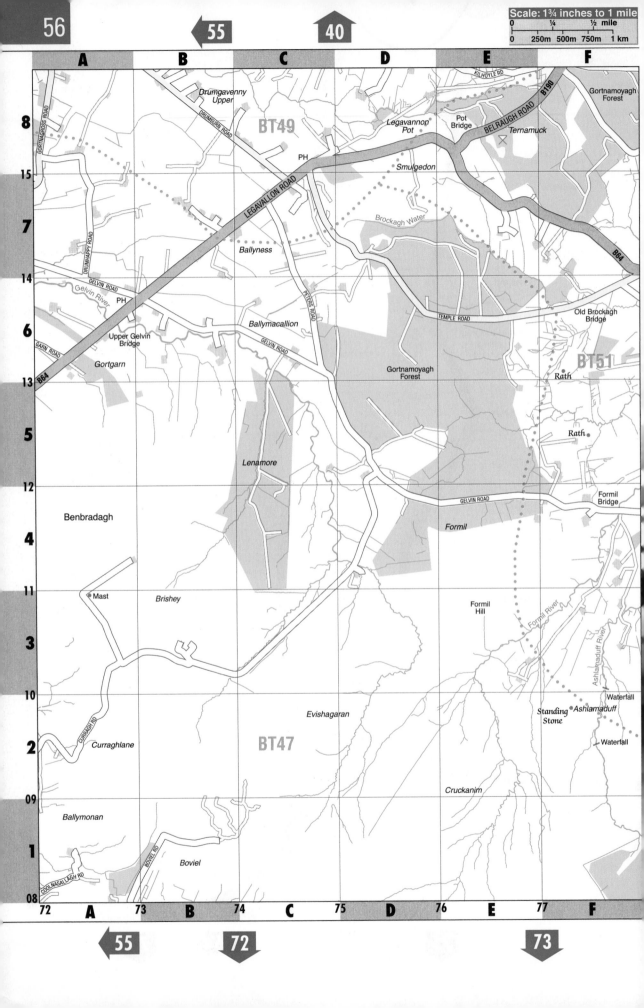

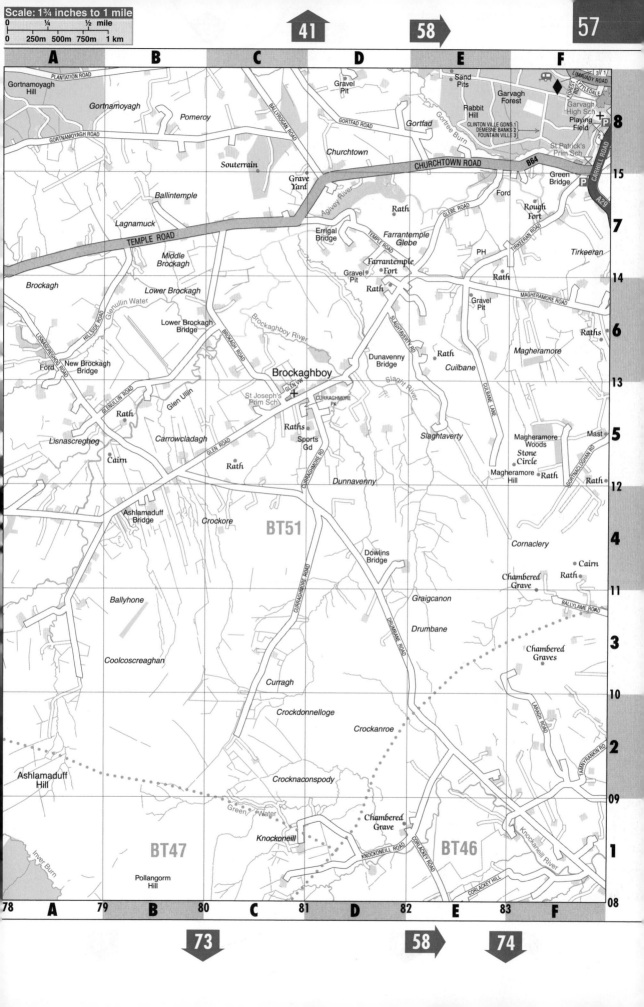

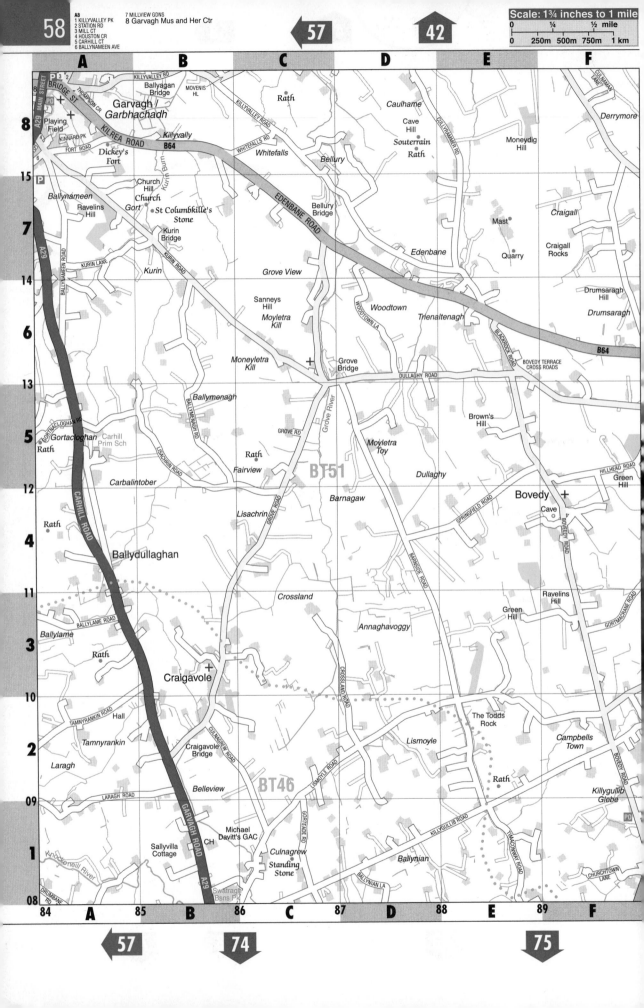

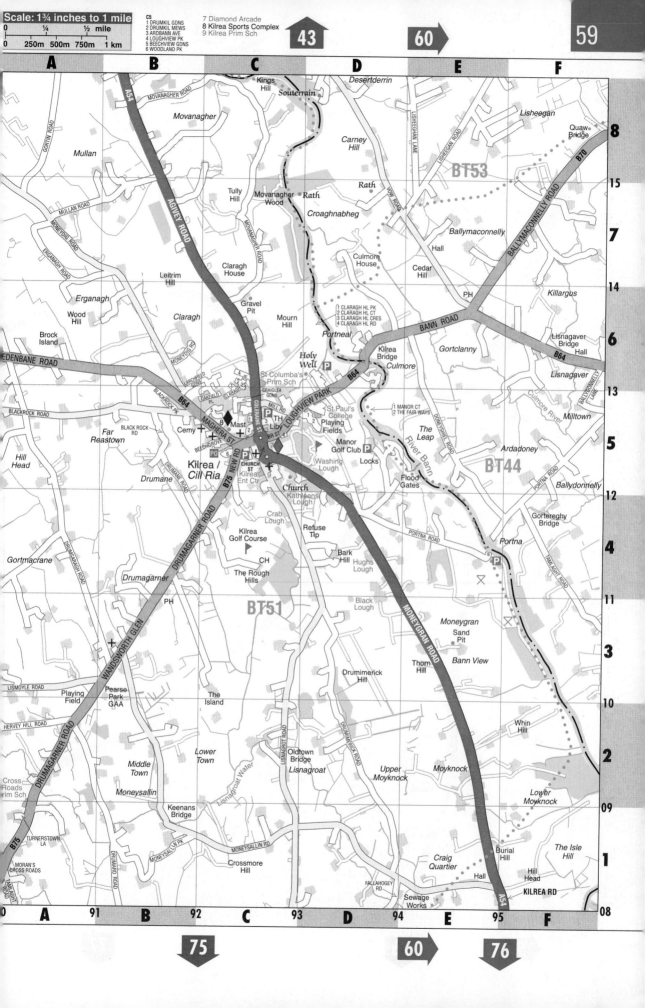

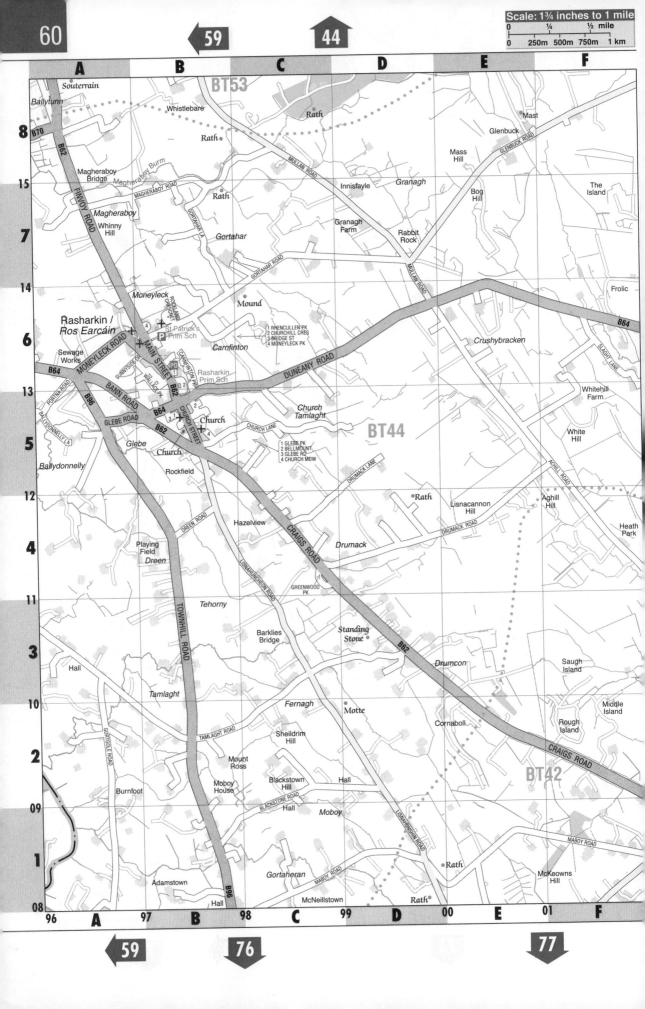

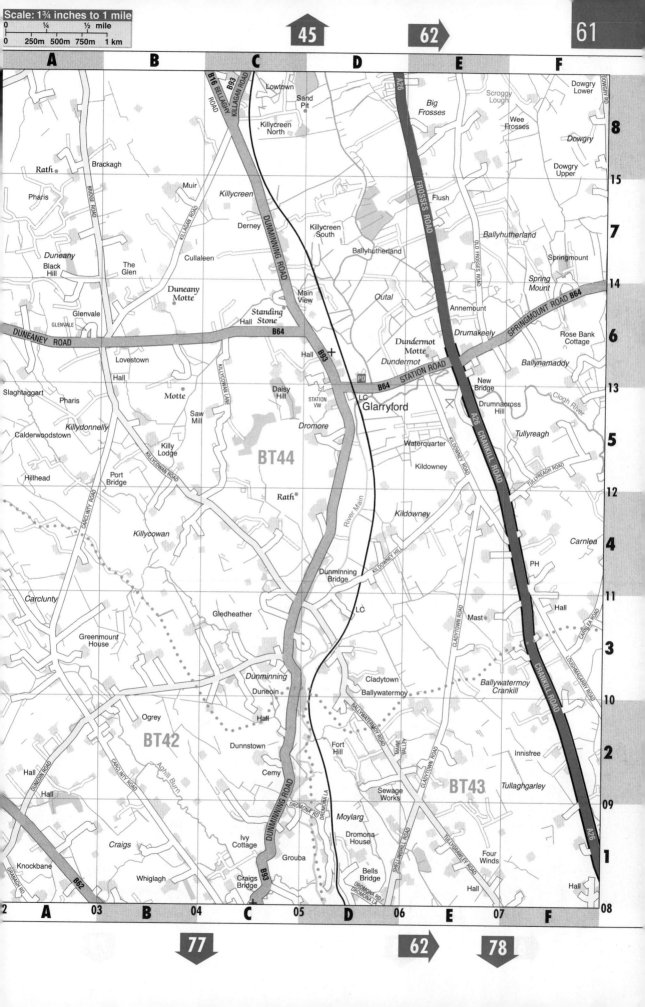

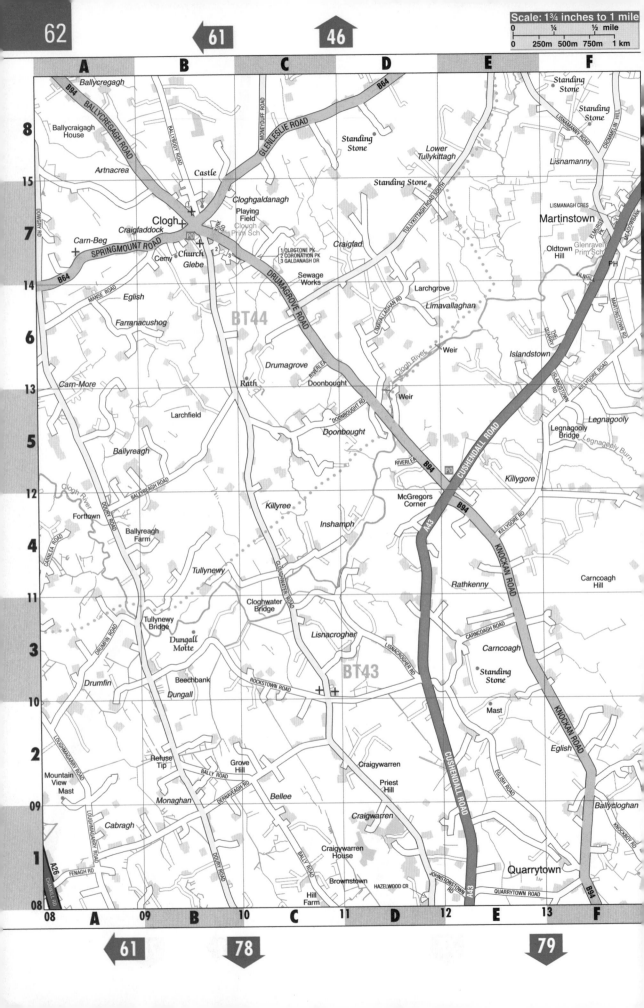

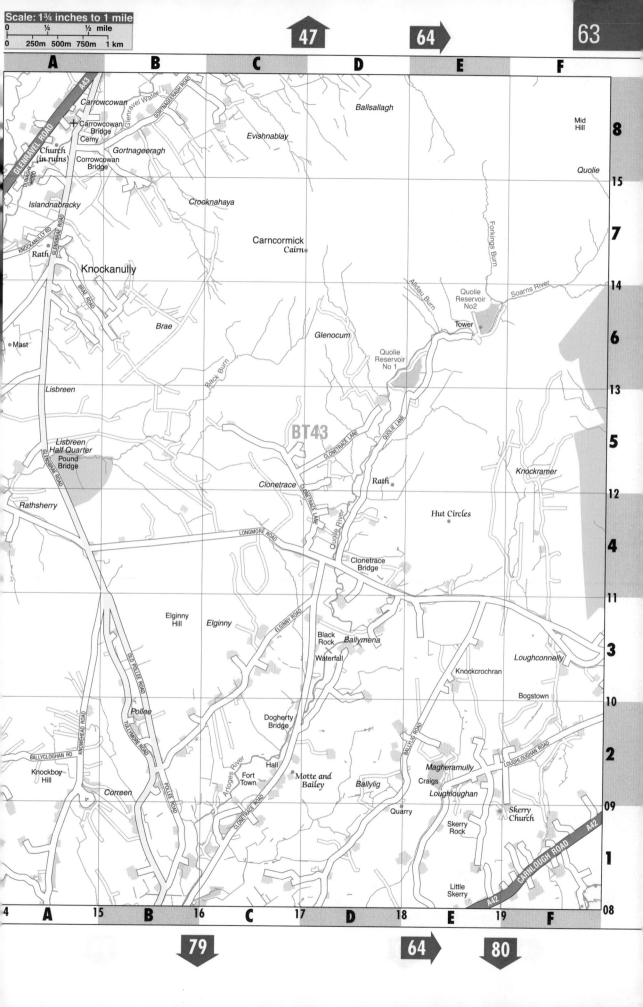

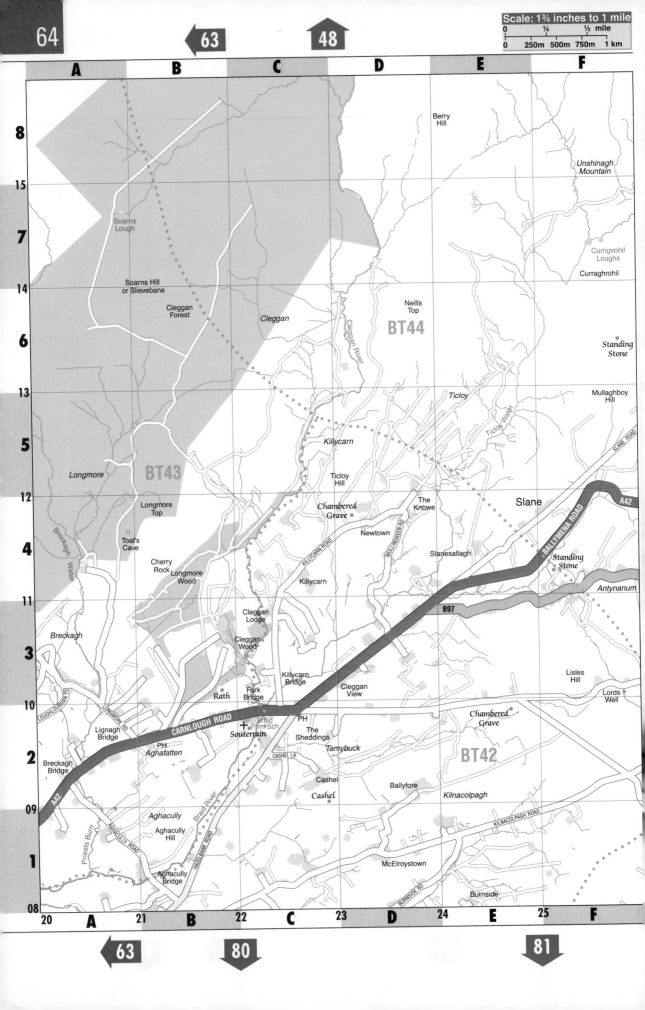

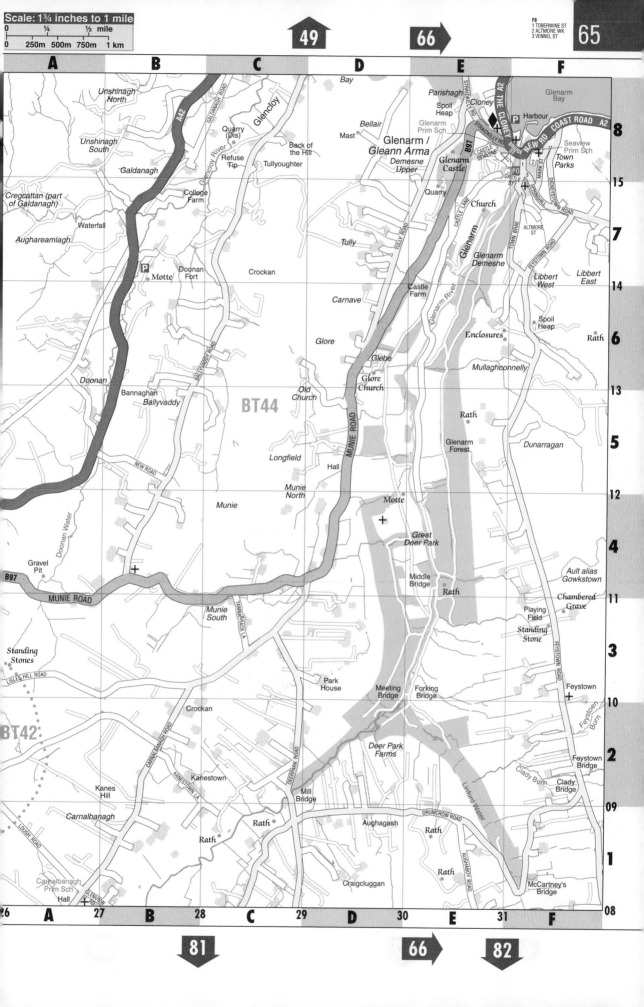

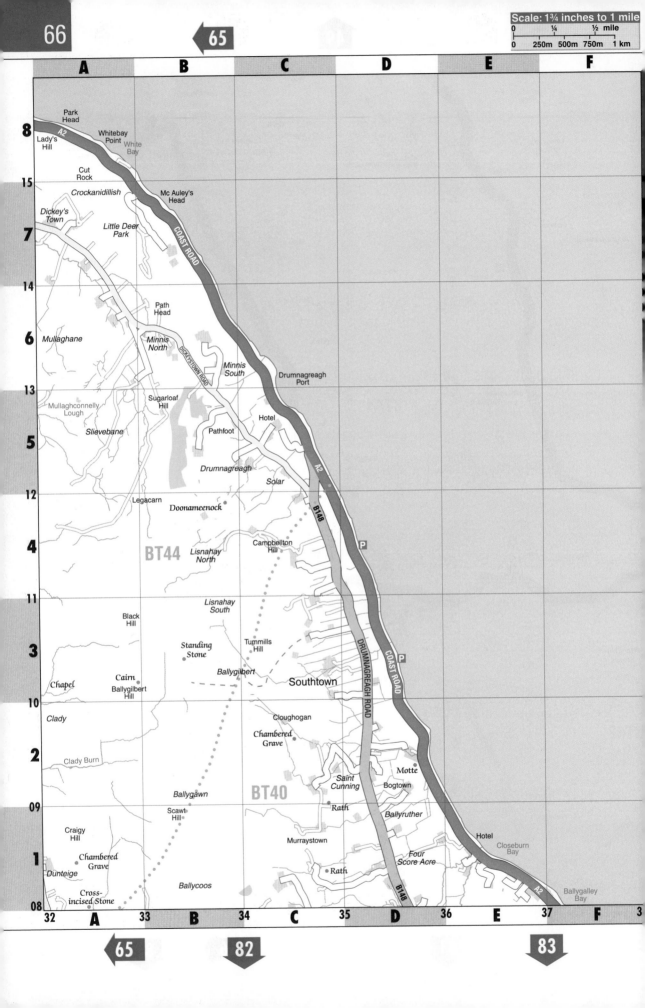

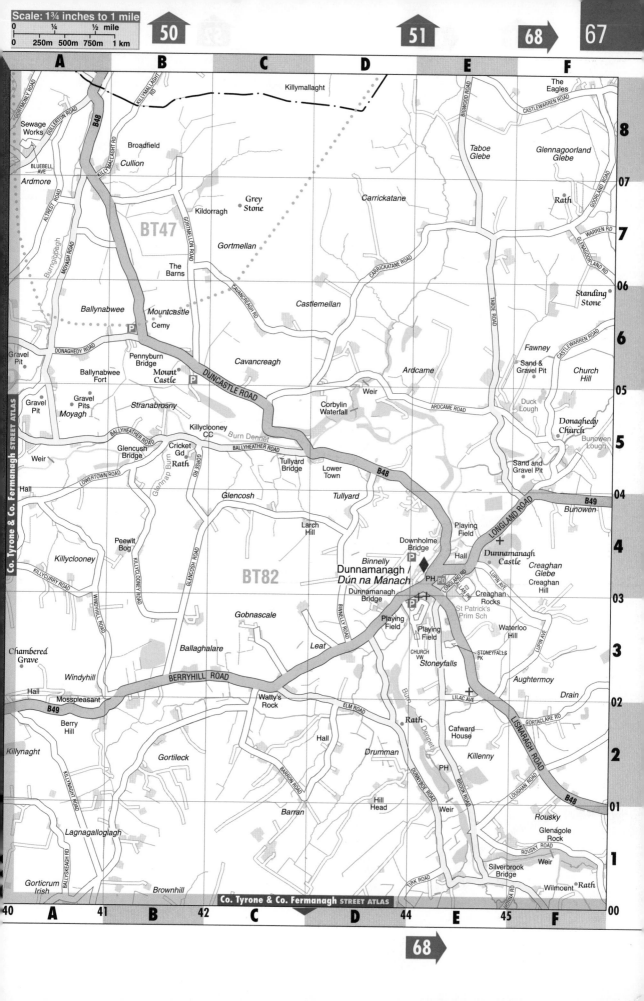

A   B   C   D   E   F

Killymallaght

The
Eagles

Castlewarren Road

Sewage
Works

BLUEBELL
AVE

Ardmore

Broadfield

Cullion

Taboe
Glebe

Glennagoorland
Glebe

8

07

Carrickatane

Rath

Kildorragh

Grey
Stone

GOORLAND RD

BT47

WARREN RD

7

Gortmellan

Standing
Stone

06

The Barns

CAVANCREAGH RD

Castlemellan

GL FAGOORLAND RD

Ballynabwee

Mountcastle

Cemy

Fawney

Church
Hill

6

Gravel
Pit

Donaghedy Road

Cavancreagh

Ardcame

Sand &
Gravel Pit

CASTLEWARREN ROAD

Pennyburn
Bridge

TABOE ROAD

Duck
Lough

05

Ballynabwee
Fort

Mount
Castle

DUNCASTLE ROAD

Weir

ARDCAME ROAD

Donaghedy
Church

Gravel
Pit

Stranabrosny

Corbylin
Waterfall

Sand and
Gravel Pit

Bunowen
Lough

5

Moyagh

Gravel
Pits

BALLYHEATHER ROAD

Burn Dennet

BALLYHEATHER ROAD

04

Weir

Glencush
Bridge

Cricket
Gd
Rath

Killyclooney
CC

Tullyard
Bridge

Lower
Town

B48

Bunowen

LONGLAND ROAD

B49

Hall

LOWERTOWN ROAD

Glencosh

Tullyard

Playing
Field

Dunnamanagh
Castle

Creaghan
Glebe

4

Hall

Peewit
Bog

Larch
Hill

Downholme
Bridge

Hall

Creaghan
Hill

03

Killyclooney

BT82

Binnelly
Dunnamanagh /
Dún na Manach

PH PO

Creaghan
Rocks

St Patrick's
Prim Sch

Waterloo
Hill

LUPIN AVE

Gobnascale

Dunnamanagh
Bridge

Playing
Field

Playing
Field

STONEYFALLS
PK

3

Chambered
Grave

Ballaghalare

Leat

CHURCH
VW
Stoneyfalls

Aughtermoy

02

Windyhill

BERRYHILL ROAD

Watty's
Rock

LILAC AVE

Drain

Hall

Mosspleasant

ELM ROAD

Rath

Cafward
House

Killenny

LISMARAGH ROAD

GORTACLARE RD

B49

Berry
Hill

Gortileck

Hall

Drumman

PH

B48

01

Killynaght

BARRON ROAD

Hill
Head

Weir

Rousky

Glenágole
Rock

2

Lagnagalloglagh

KILLYNAGHT ROAD

Barran

ROUSKY ROAD

Weir

Silverbrook
Bridge

Wilmount

Rath

1

Gorticrum
Irish

BALLYSKEAGH RD

Brownhill

TIRK ROAD

40   A   41   B   42   C   D   44   E   45   F   00

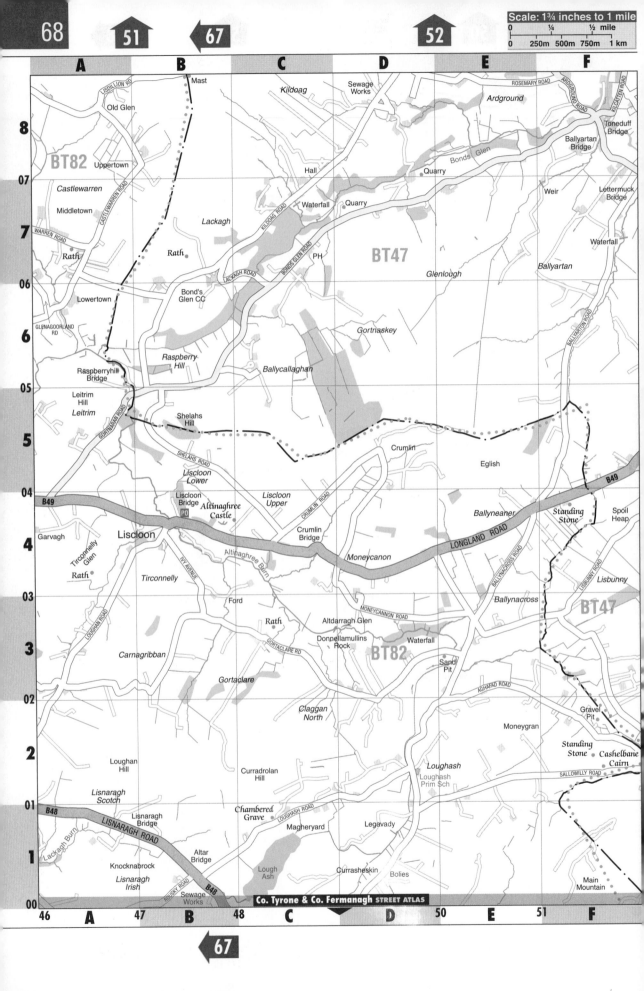

A   B   C   D   E   F

8

07

BT82

7

06

6

05

5

04

B49

4

03

3

02

2

01

B48

1

00

46   A   47   B   48   C   D   50   E   51   F

LISDILLION RD
Mast
Old Glen
Kildoag
Sewage Works
Ardground
ROSEMARY ROAD
ARDGROUND ROAD
KILCATTEN ROAD
Uppertown
Toneduff Bridge
Ballyartan Bridge
Castlewarren
CASTLEWARREN ROAD
Lackagh
Bonds Glen
Weir
Lettermuck Bridge
Middletown
WARREN ROAD
Rath
Rath
KILDOAG ROAD
BONDS GLEN ROAD
Hall
Waterfall
Quarry
Quarry
BT47
Waterfall
Ballyartan
Rath
LACKAGH ROAD
PH
Glenlough
Lowertown
Bond's Glen CC
GLENAGOORLAND RD
Raspberry Hill
Gortnaskey
Raspberryhill Bridge
Ballycallaghan
Leitrim Hill
Leitrim
GORTINWARRAN ROAD
Shelahs Hill
SHELAHS ROAD
Crumlin
Eglish
B49
Liscloon Lower
Liscloon Upper
Liscloon Bridge
PO
Altinaghree Castle
CRUMLIN ROAD
Ballyneaner
Standing Stone
Spoil Heap
B49
Garvagh
Liscloon
Crumlin Bridge
Altinaghree Burn
Moneycanon
LONGLAND ROAD
BALLYVARTON ROAD
Tirconnelly Glen
IVY AVENUE
BALLYNACROSS ROAD
Standing Stone
Ballynacross
LISBUNNY ROAD
BT47
Rath
Tirconnelly
Ford
MONEYCANNON ROAD
Lisbunny
LOUGHAN ROAD
Rath
GORTACLARE RD
Altdarragh Glen
Donnellamullins Rock
Waterfall
BT82
Sand Pit
AGHAFAD ROAD
Carnagribban
Moneygran
Gravel Pit
Gortaclare
Standing Stone
Cashelbane Cairn
SALLOWILLY ROAD
Loughan Hill
Curradrolan Hill
Claggan North
Loughash
Loughash Prim Sch
Lisnaragh Scotch
Chambered Grave
LOUGHASH ROAD
Magheryard
Legavady
B48
LISNARAGH ROAD
Lisnaragh Bridge
Lackagh Burn
Knocknabrock
Altar Bridge
B48
ROUSKY ROAD
Lough Ash
Currasheskin
Bolies
Main Mountain
Lisnaragh Irish
Sewage Works

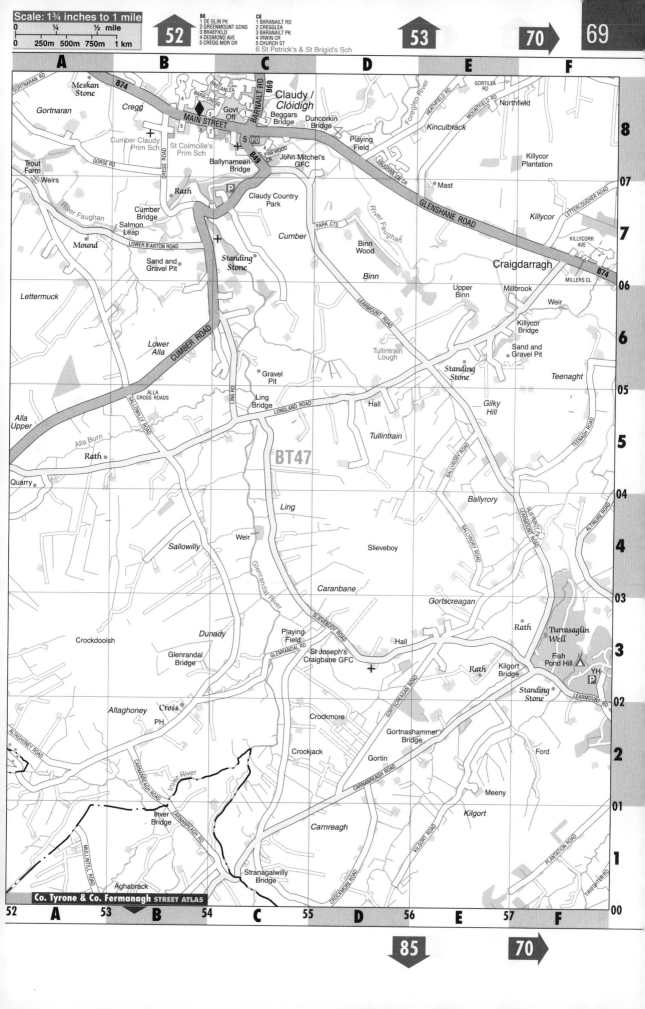

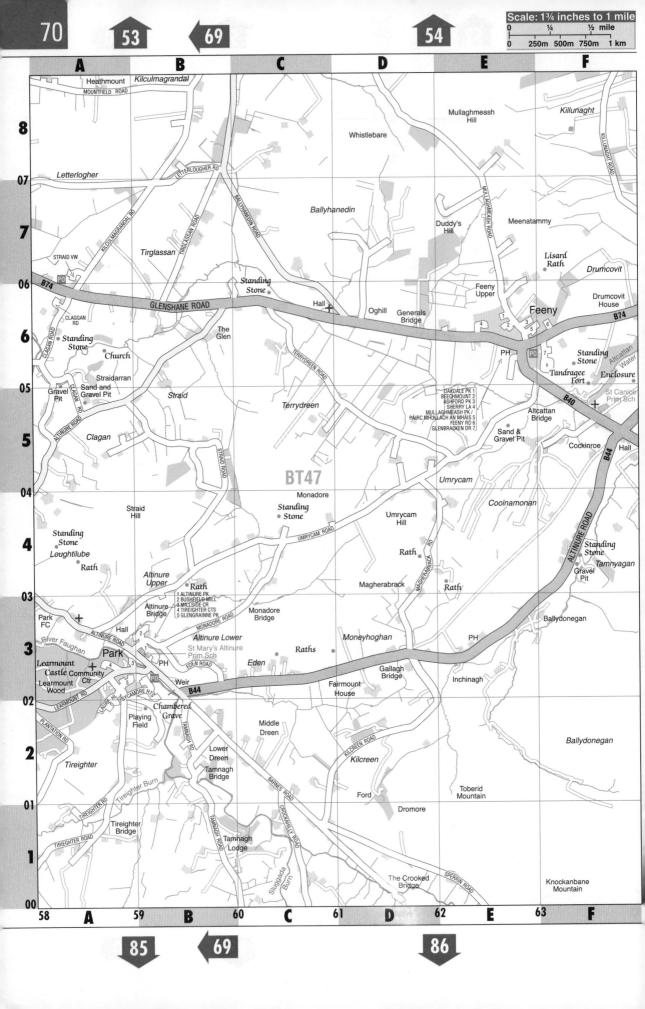

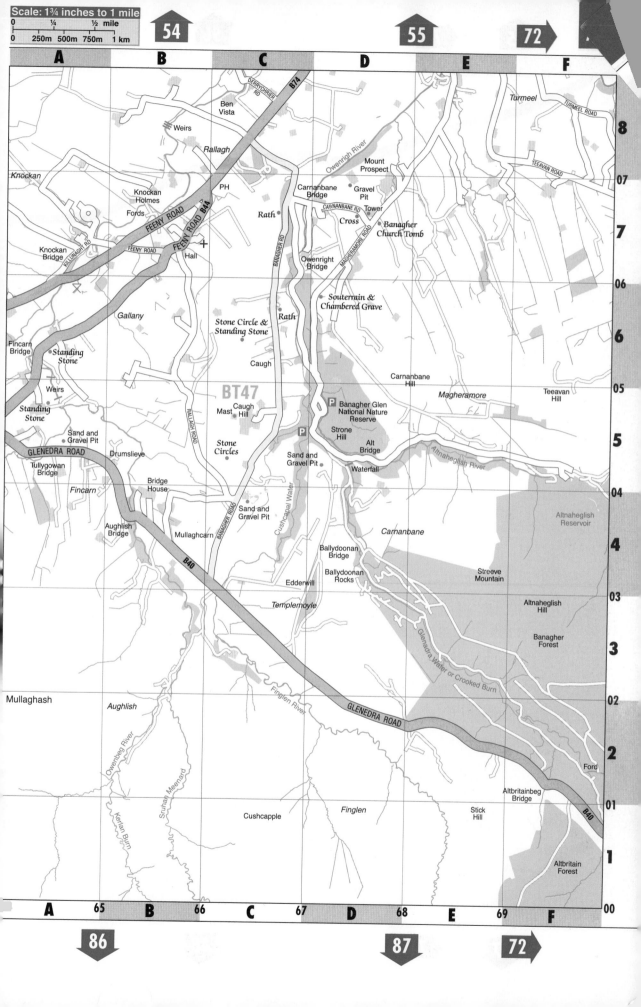

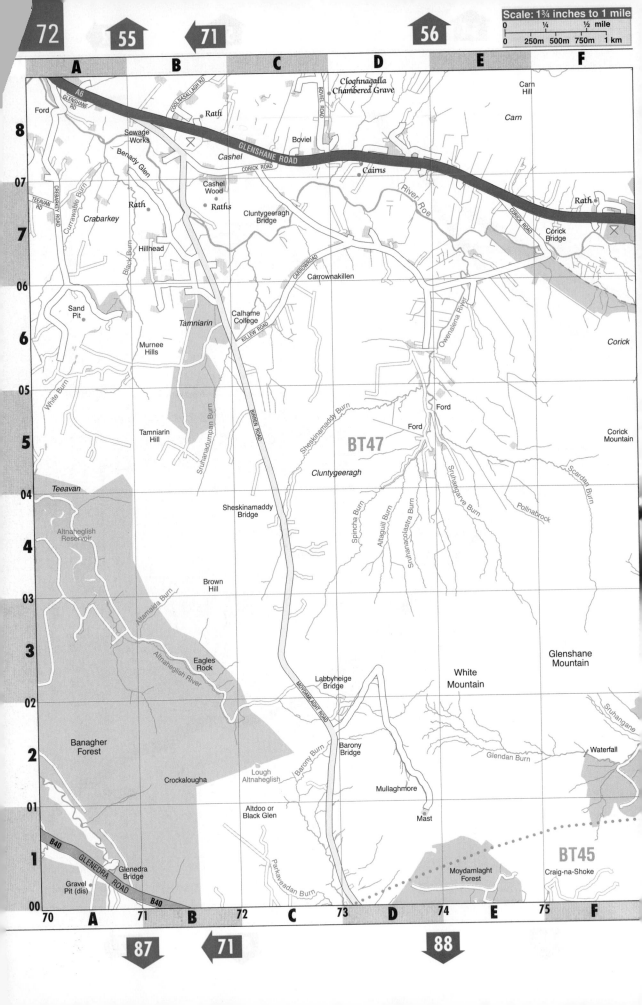

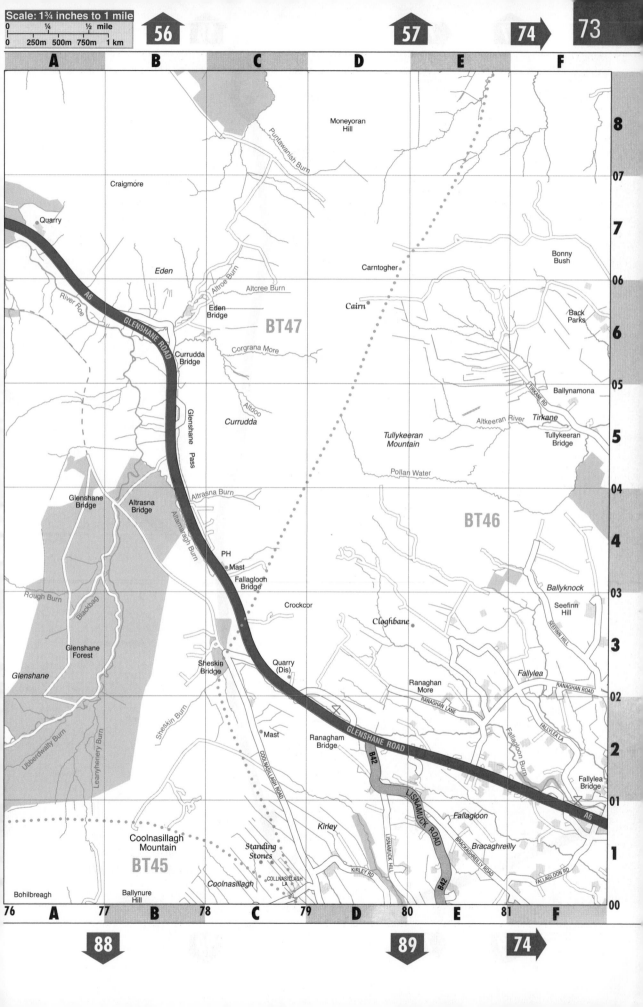

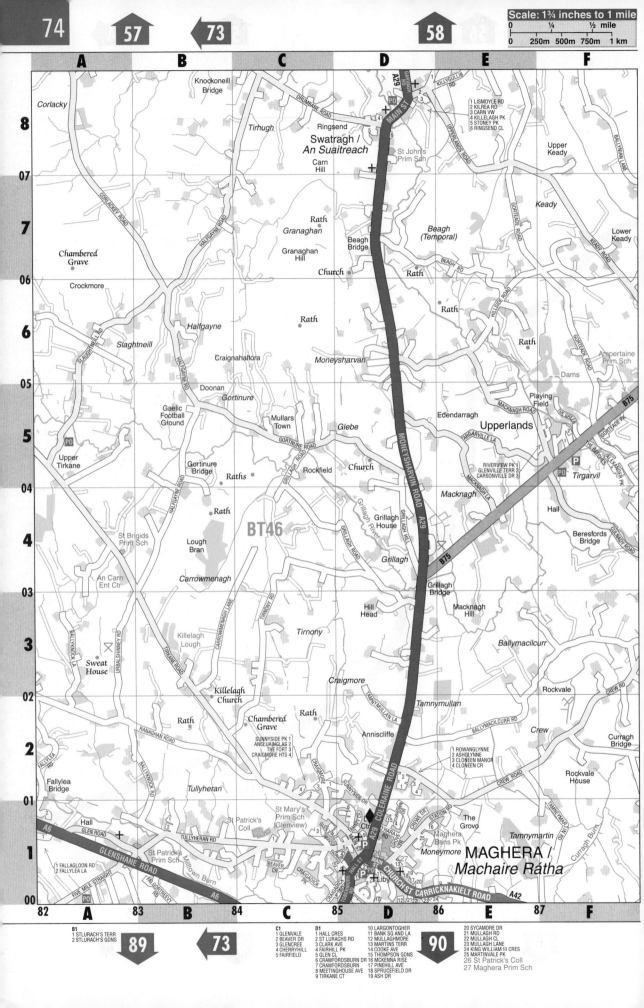

Scale: 1¾ inches to 1 mile

0   ¼   ½ mile
0   250m   500m   750m   1 km

A   B   C   D   E   F

Corlacky

Knockoneill Bridge

1 LISMOYLE RD
2 KILREA RD
3 CARN VW
4 KILLELAGH PK
5 STONEY PK
6 RINGSEND CL

Tirhugh

Ringsend

Swatragh /
An Suaitreach

Carn Hill

St John's Prim Sch

Upper Keady

Chambered Grave

Crockmore

Rath
Granaghan

Granaghan Hill

Beagh Bridge

Beagh (Temporal)

Keady

Lower Keady

Church

Rath

Rath

Halfgayne

Slaghtneill

Craignahaltora

Moneysharvan

Rath

Rath

Ampertaine Prim Sch

Doonan

Gortinure

Mullars Town

Glebe

Edendarragh

Upperlands

Dams

Playing Field

Gaelic Football Ground

Gortinure Bridge

Rockfield

Church

RIVERVIEW PK 1
GLENVILLE TERR 2
CARSONVILLE DR 3

Tirgarvil

Upper Tirkane

Raths

Rath

Macknagh

Hall

BT46

Rath

Lough Bran

Grillagh House

Grillagh

Beresfords Bridge

St Brigids Prim Sch

Carrowmenagh

Grillagh Bridge

Macknagh Hill

An Carn Ent Ctr

Killelagh Lough

Tirnony

Hill Head

Ballymacilcurr

Sweat House

Craigmore

Rockvale

Killelagh Church

Rath

Chambered Grave

Rath

Tamnymullan

Crew

Curragh Bridge

Fallylea Bridge

Tullyheran

SUNNYSIDE PK 1
ANCLUAINGLAS 2
THE FORT 3
CRAIGMORE HTS 4

Anniscliffe

1 ROWANGLYNNE
2 ASHGLYNNE
3 CLONEEN MANOR
4 CLONEEN CR

Rockvale House

Hall

St Mary's Prim Sch (Glenview)

St Patrick's Coll

The Grove

Tamnymartin

Moneymore

MAGHERA /
Machaire Rátha

St Patrick's Prim Sch

Maghera Bsns Pk

1 FALLAGLOON RD
2 FALLYLEA LA

GLENSHANE ROAD

A6

Libry

CHURCH ST   CARRICKNAKIELT ROAD   A42

82   A   83   B   84   C   85   D   86   E   87   F

B1
1 STLURACH'S TERR
2 STLURACH'S GDNS

89   ← 73

C1
1 GLENVALE
2 BEAVER DR
3 CLARK AVE
4 CHERRYHILL
5 FAIRFIELD

D1
1 HALL CRES
2 ST LURACHS RD
3 CLARK AVE
4 FAIRHILL PK
5 GLEN CL
6 CRAWFORDSBURN DR
7 CRAWFORDSBURN
8 MEETINGHOUSE AVE
9 TIRKANE CT

10 LARGONTOGHER
11 BANK SQ AND LA
12 MULLAGHMORE
13 MARTINS TERR
14 COOKE AVE
15 THOMPSON GDNS
16 MCKENNA RISE
17 PINEHILL AVE
18 SPRUCEFIELD DR
19 ASH DR

20 SYCAMORE DR
21 MULLAGH RD
22 MULLAGHMORE
23 MULLAGH LANE
24 KING WILLIAM III CRES
25 MARTINVALE PK
26 St Patrick's Coll
27 Maghera Prim Sch

90

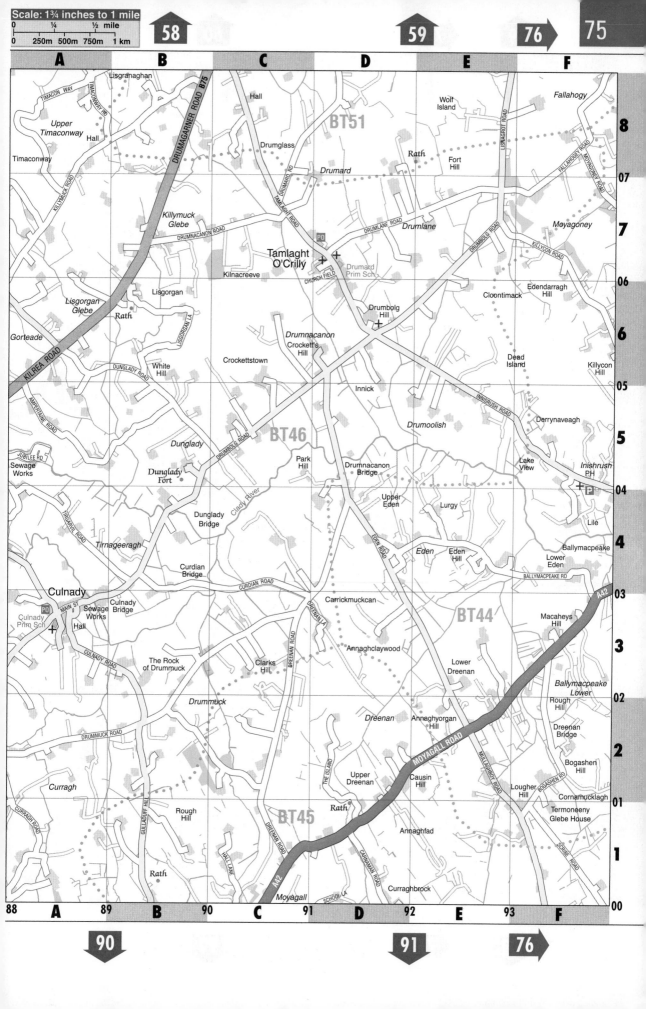

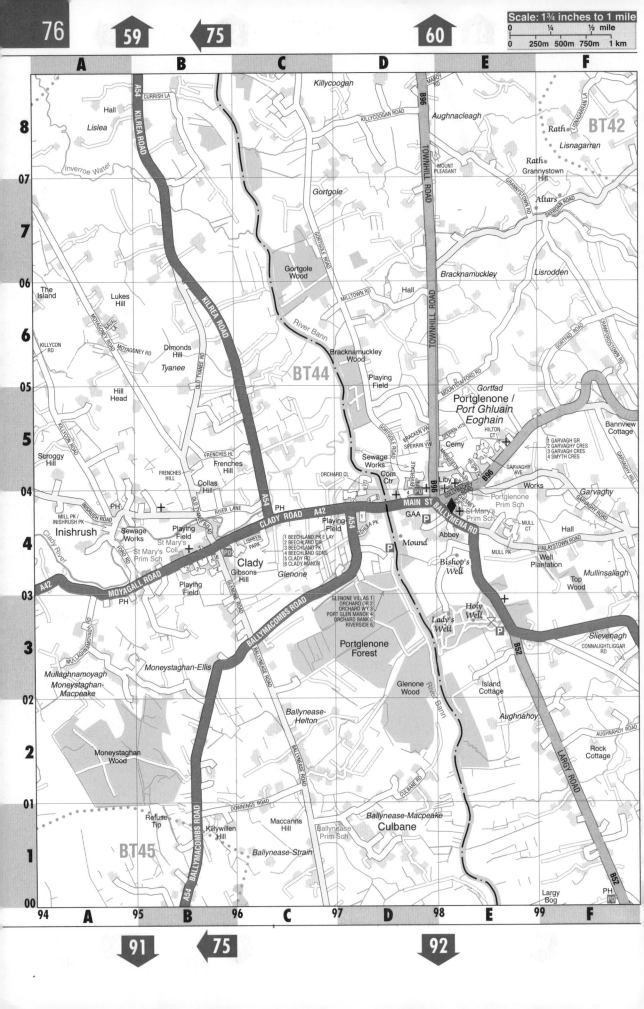

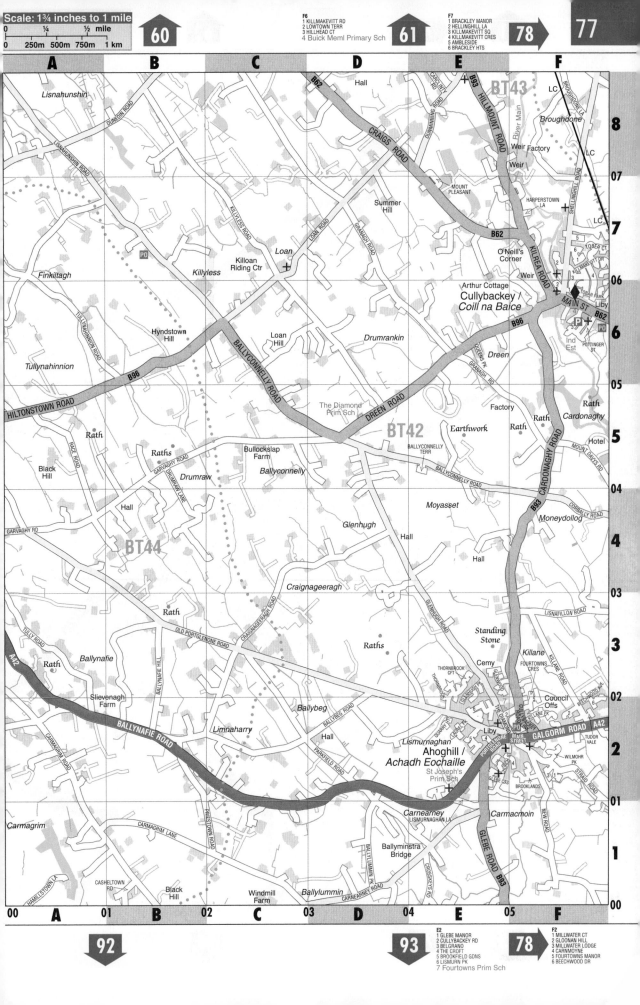

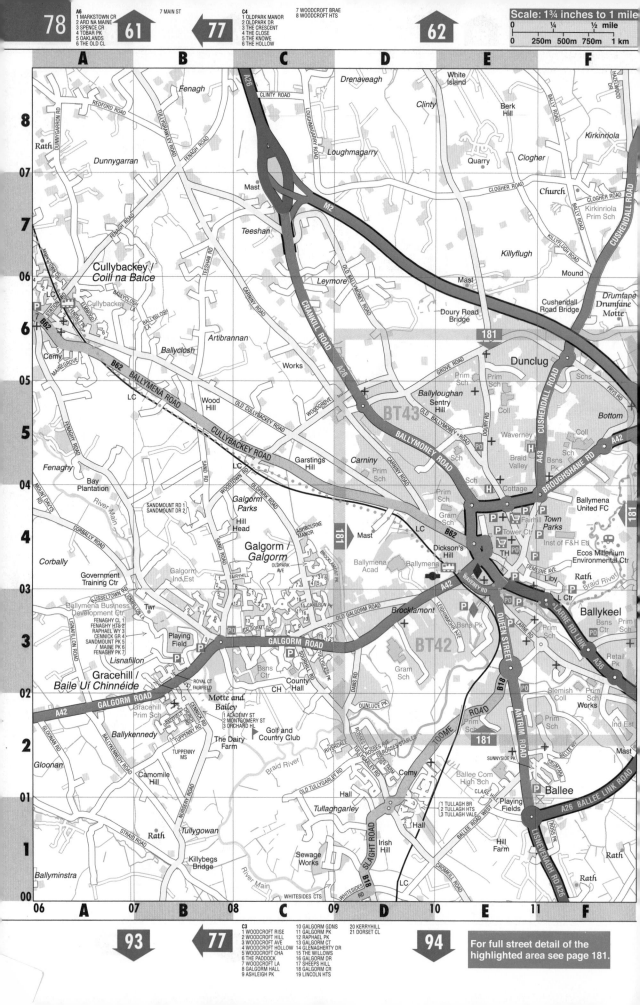

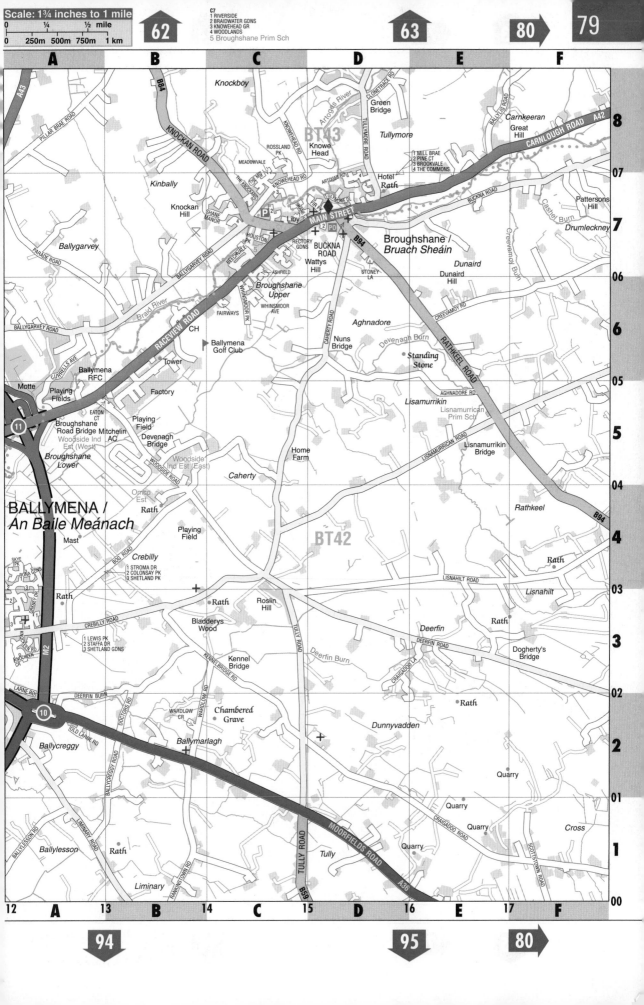

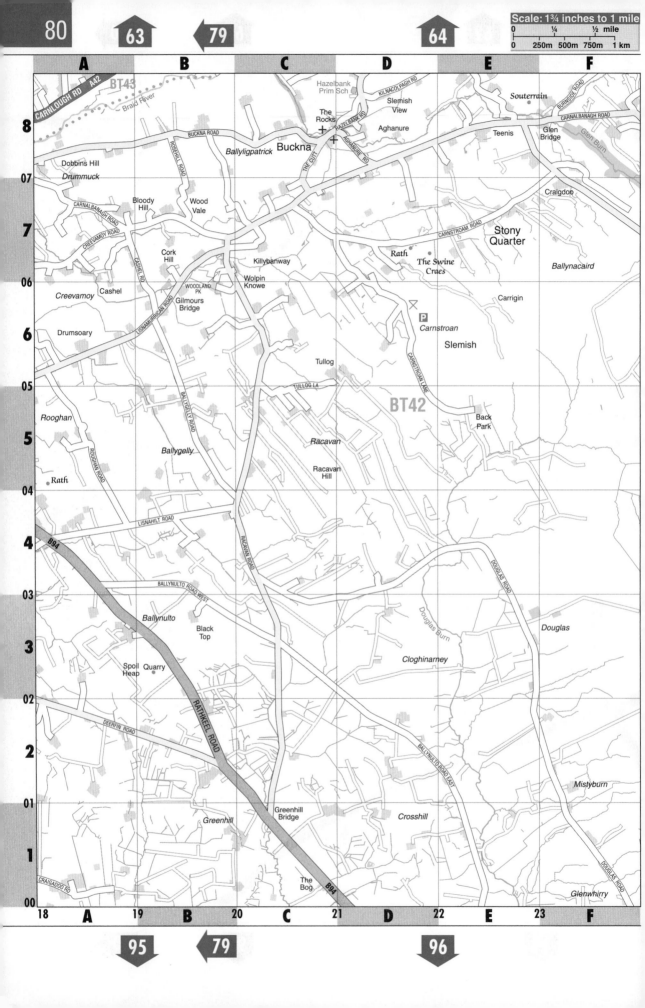

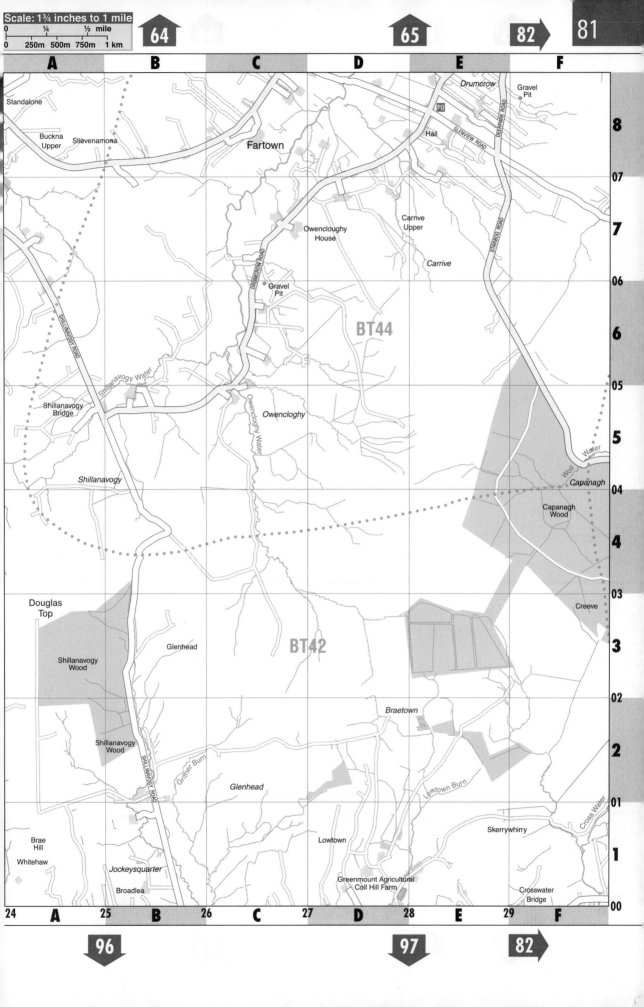

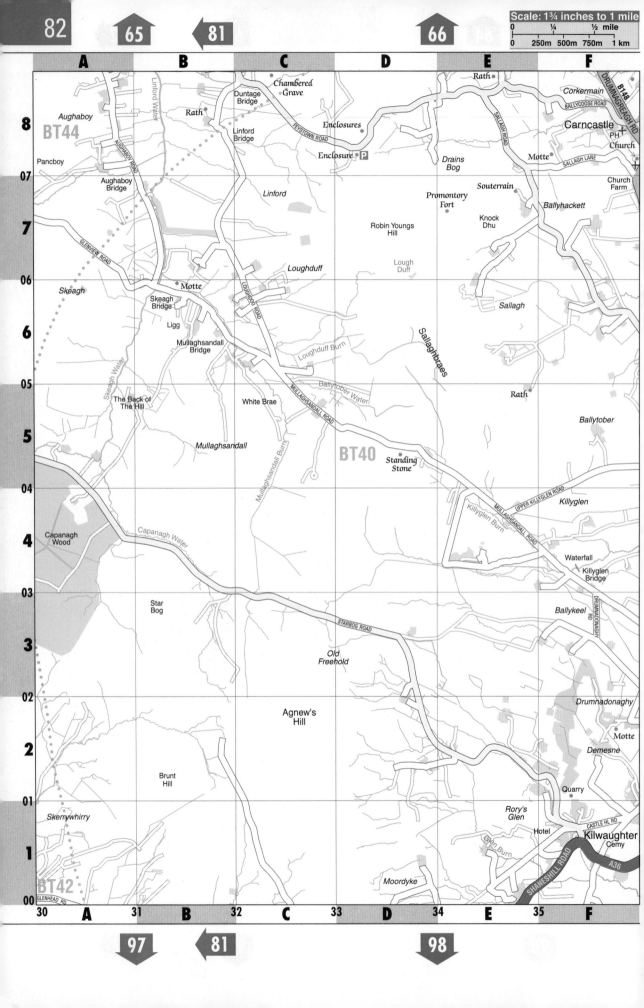

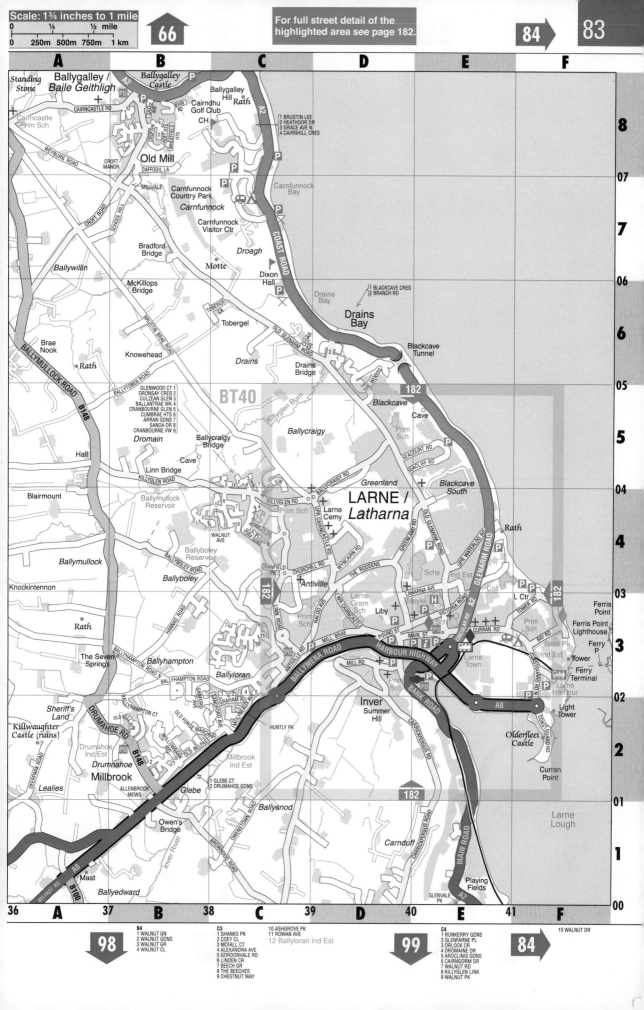

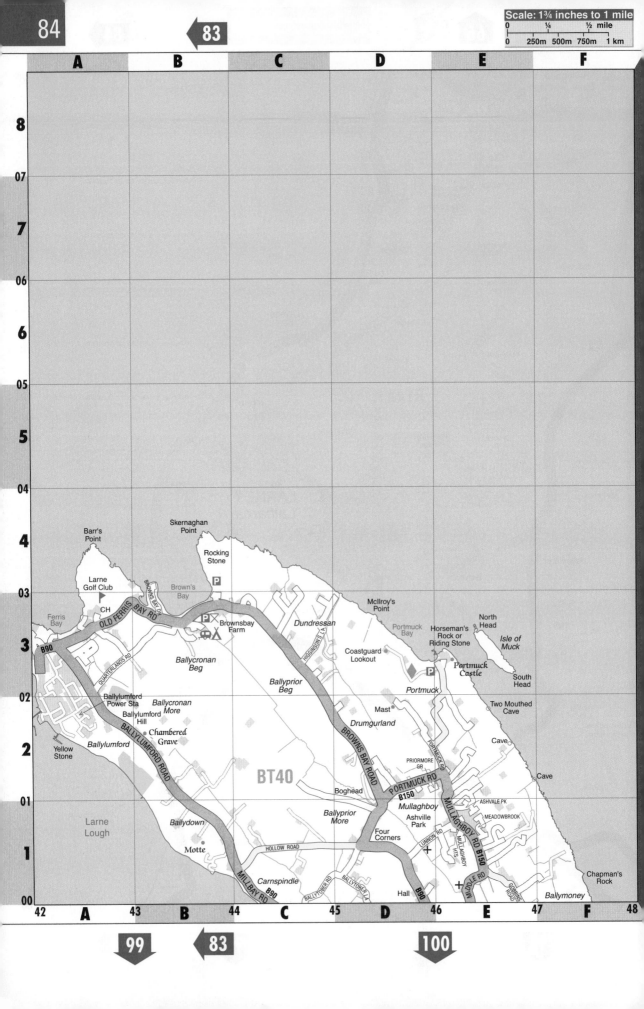

Scale: 1¾ inches to 1 mile

Barr's Point

Skernaghan Point

Larne Golf Club

CH

Ferris Bay

Rocking Stone

Brown's Bay

Old Ferris

Bay Rd

Browns Bay Dr

Brownsbay Farm

Dundressan

McIlroy's Point

North Head

Isle of Muck

South Head

B90

Quarterlands Rd

Ballycronan Beg

Higginson's

Coastguard Lookout

Portmuck Bay

Horseman's Rock or Riding Stone

Portmuck Castle

Ballyprior Beg

Ballylumford Power Sta

Ballylumford Hill

Ballycronan More

Chambered Grave

Portmuck

Two Mouthed Cave

Yellow Stone

Ballylumford

Ballylumford Road

Mast

Drumgurland

Browns Bay Road

Portmuck Rd

Cave

Cave

Larne Lough

Ballydown

Motte

Ballyprior More

Boghead

Priormore Gr

Portmuck Rd

B150

Mullaghboy

Ashville Park

Ashvale Pk

Meadowbrook

Mullaghboy Rd

B150

Chapman's Rock

Hollow Road

Carnspindle

Mill Bay Rd

B90

Ballytober Rd

Ballytober La

Four Corners

Hall

Lunnon Rd

Mullaghboy Hts

Middle Rd

Gibbis Road

Ballymoney

B90

BT40

BT40

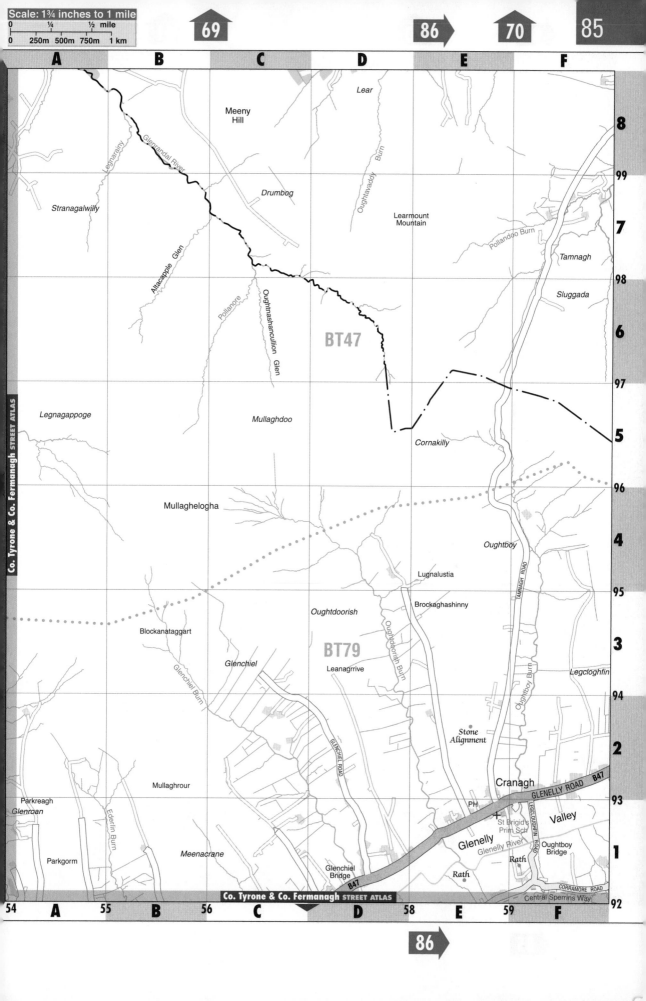

Co. Tyrone & Co. Fermanagh STREET ATLAS

Lear

Meeny Hill

Legnarainy

Glenrandal River

Drumbog

Oughtavaddy Burn

Learmount Mountain

Pollanddo Burn

Tamnagh

Stranagalwilly

Altacapple Glen

Sluggada

Pollanore

Oughtnashancullion Glen

BT47

Legnagappoge

Mullaghdoo

Cornakilly

Mullaghelogha

Oughtboy

Tamnagh Road

Blockanataggart

Oughtdoorish

Lugnalustia

Brockaghashinny

Legcloghfin

BT79

Glenchiel

Leanagrrive

Oughtdoorish Burn

Oughtboy Burn

Glenchiel Burn

Glenchiel Road

Stone Alignment

Cranagh

GLENELLY ROAD

B47

Mullaghrour

PH

St Brigid's Prim Sch

Valley

Parkreagh

Glenroan

Ederlin Burn

Glenelly

Glenelly River

Oughtboy Bridge

Parkgorm

Meenacrane

Glenchiel Bridge

B47

Rath

Rath

Legcloghfin Road

CORRAMORE ROAD

Central Sperrins Way

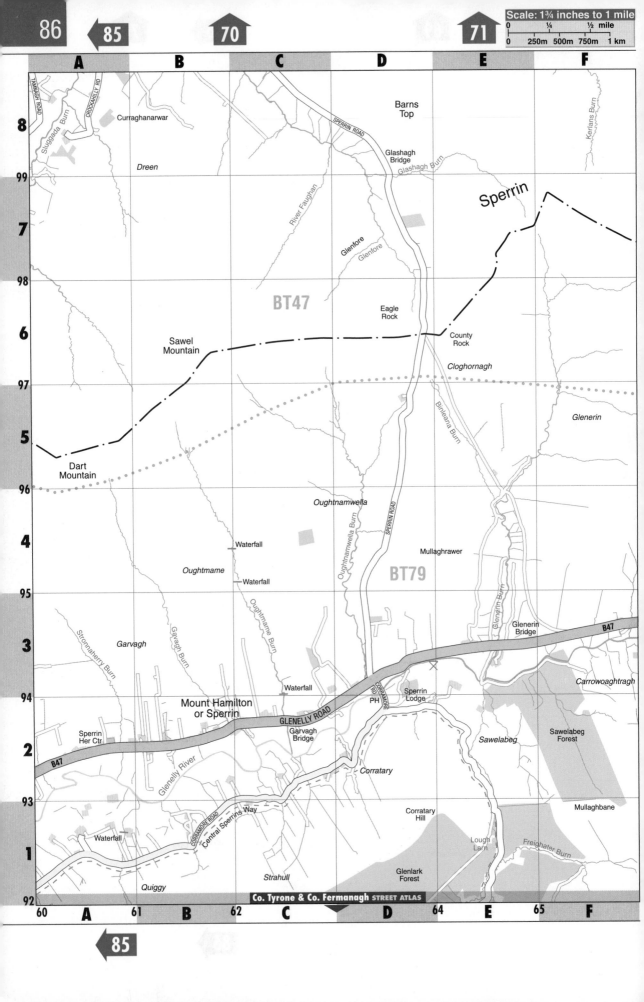

Scale: 1¾ inches to 1 mile
0   ¼   ½ mile
0   250m 500m 750m 1 km

A **B** **C** **D** **E** **F**

8

Curraghanarwar

Dreen

TAMNAGH ROAD
CROCKAHILLY RD
Sluggada Burn

99

Barns
Top

SPERRIN ROAD

Glashagh
Bridge
Glashagh Burn

Kerlans Burn

7

Sperrin

River Faughan

Glenfore
Glenfore

98

BT47

Eagle
Rock

6

Sawel
Mountain

County
Rock

Cloghornagh

Binleana Burn

Glenerin

97

5

Dart
Mountain

96

Oughtnamwella

Oughtnamwella Burn

SPERRIN ROAD

Mullaghrawer

4

Waterfall

Oughtmame

Waterfall

BT79

95

Oughtmame Burn

Garvagh

Gavagh Burn

Glenerin
Bridge

B47

3

Stronnaherry Burn

Carrowoaghtragh

Glenerin Burn

94

Waterfall

Mount Hamilton
or Sperrin

GLENELLY ROAD

Sperrin
Lodge

PH

Sperrin
Her Ctr

Garvagh
Bridge

CORRAMORE ROAD

Sawelabeg

Sawelabeg
Forest

2

B47

Glenelly River

Corratary

Mullaghbane

93

CORRAMORE ROAD
Central Sperrins Way

Corratary
Hill

Lough
Larn

Freighater Burn

1

Waterfall

Glenlark
Forest

Quiggy

Strahull

92

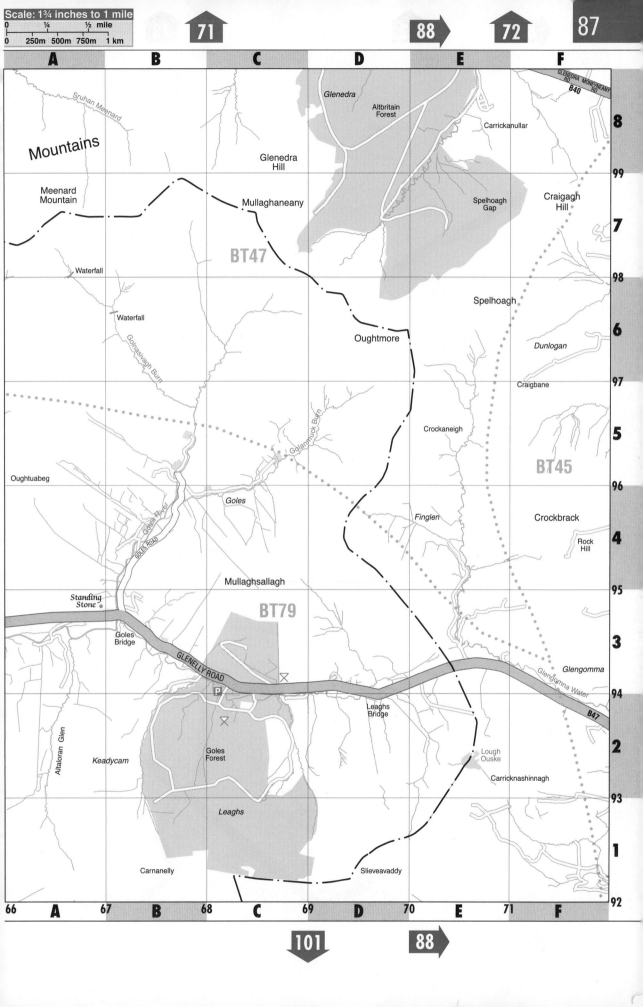

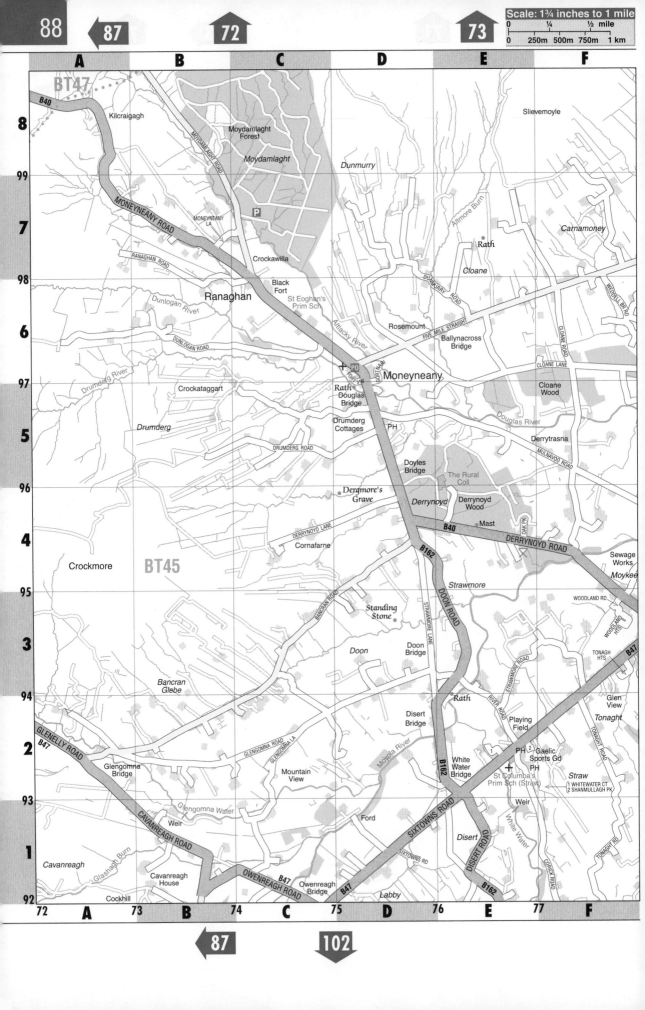

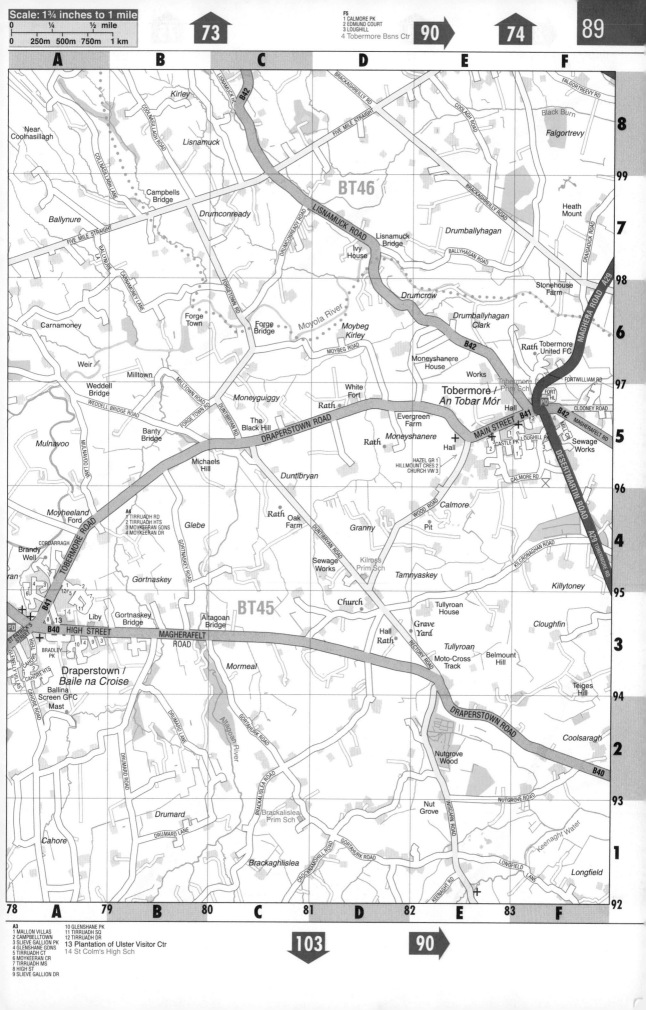

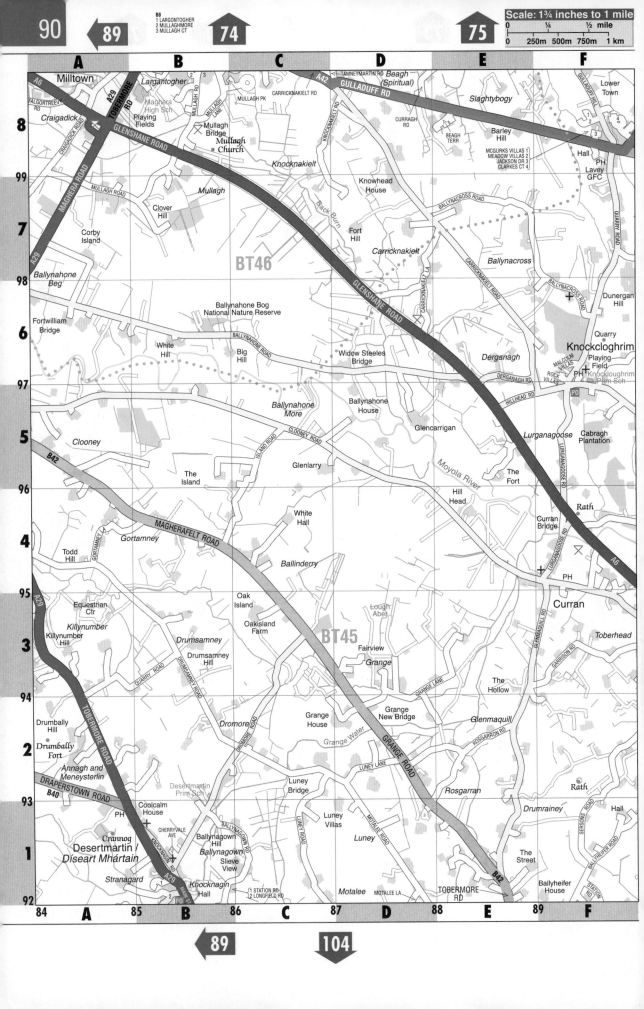

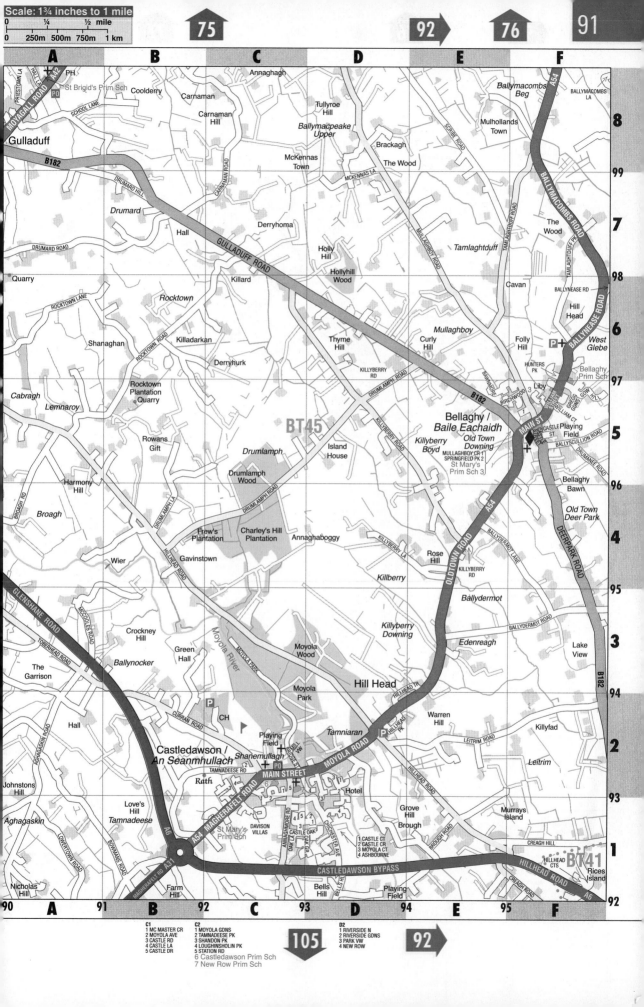

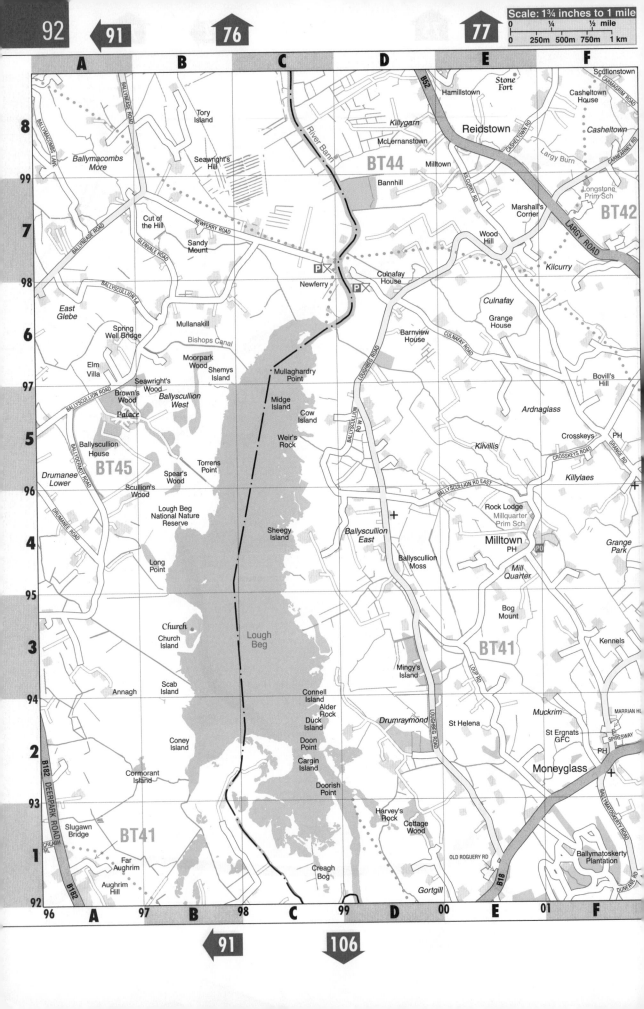

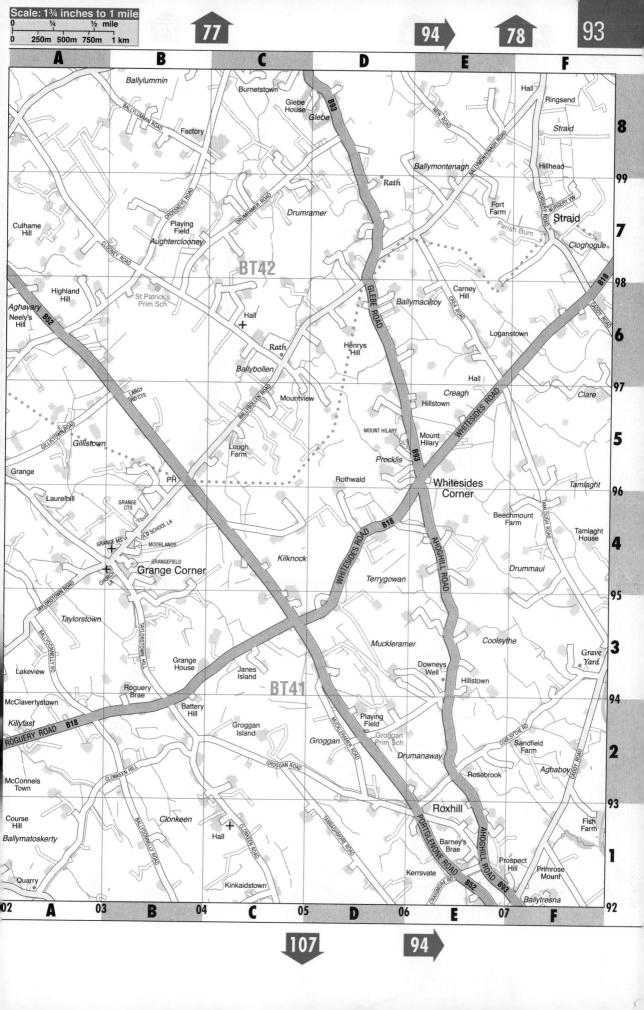

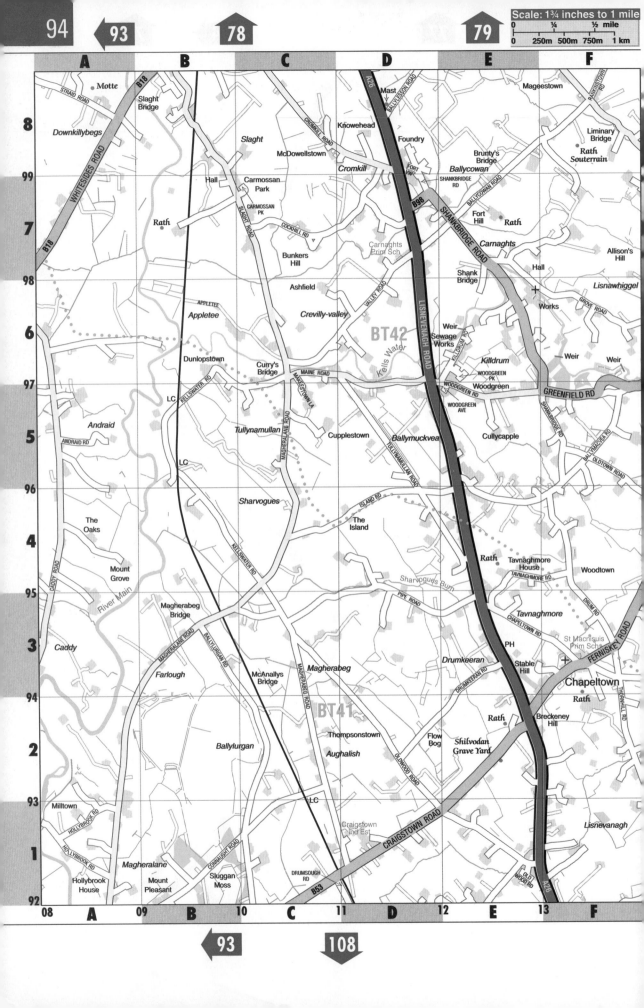

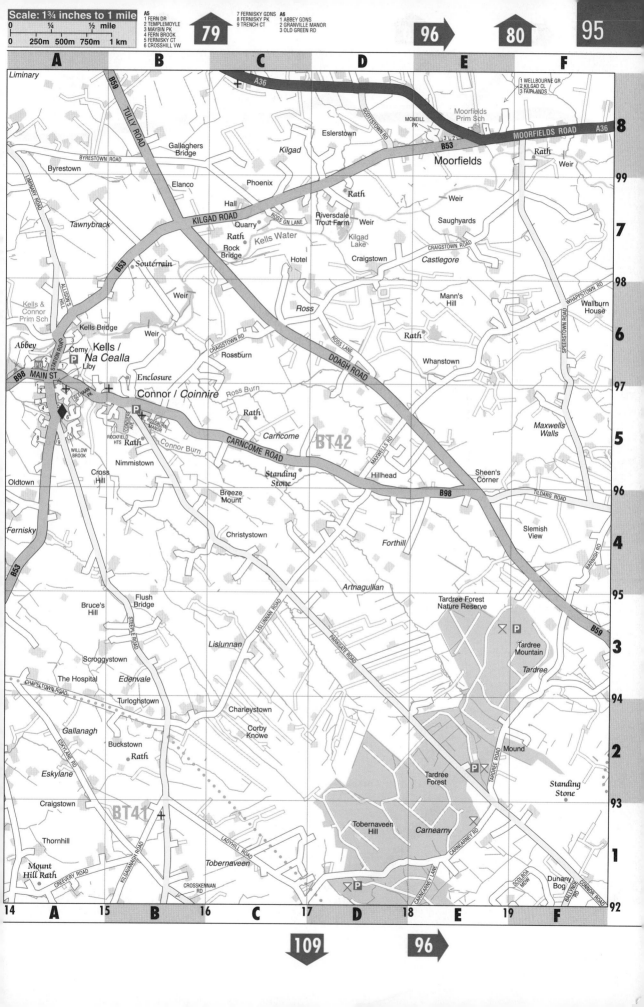

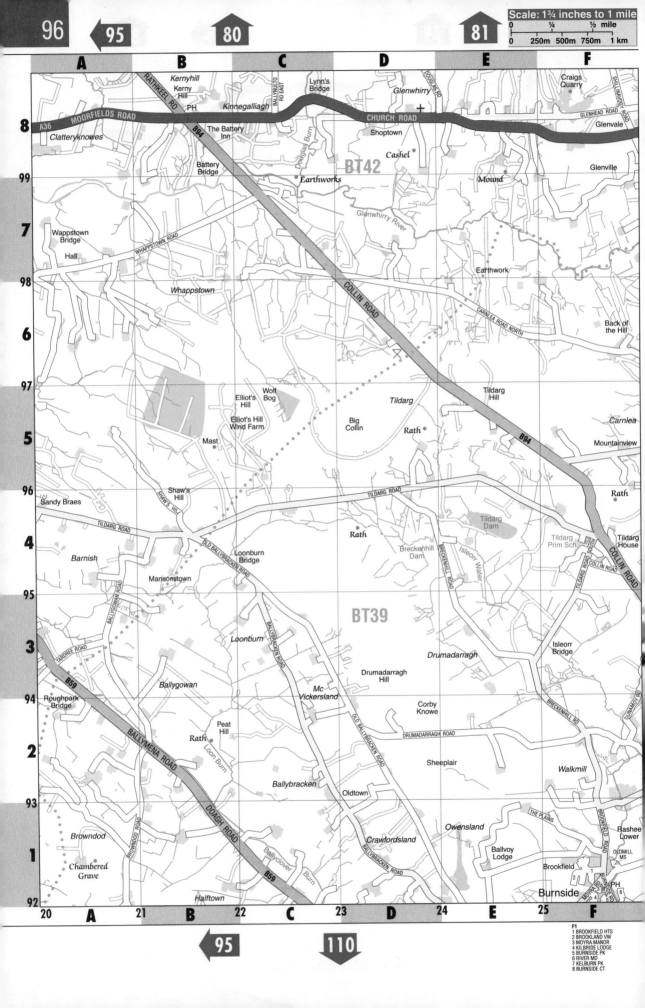

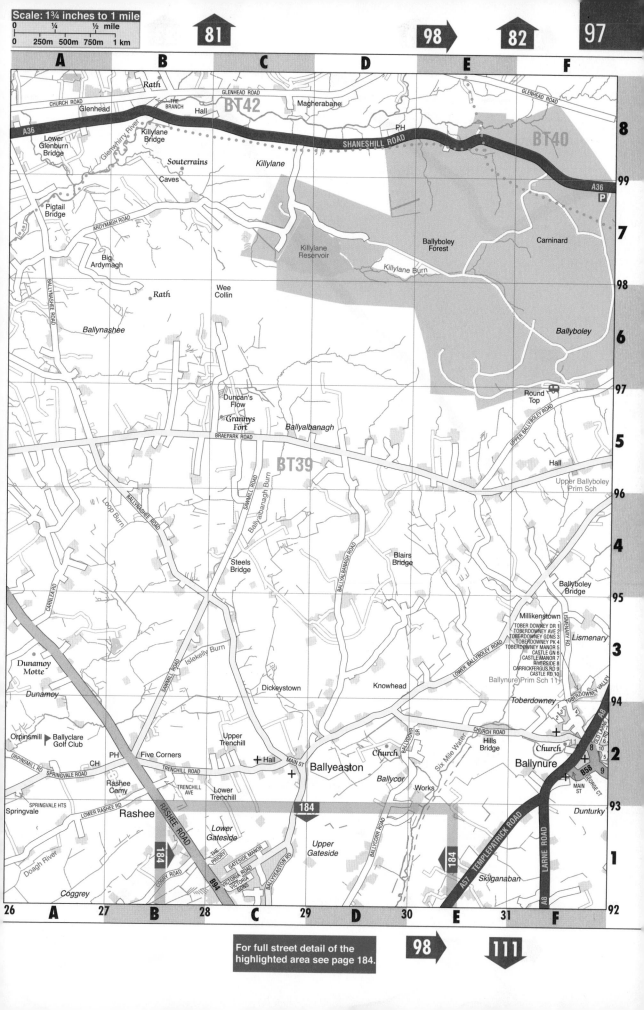

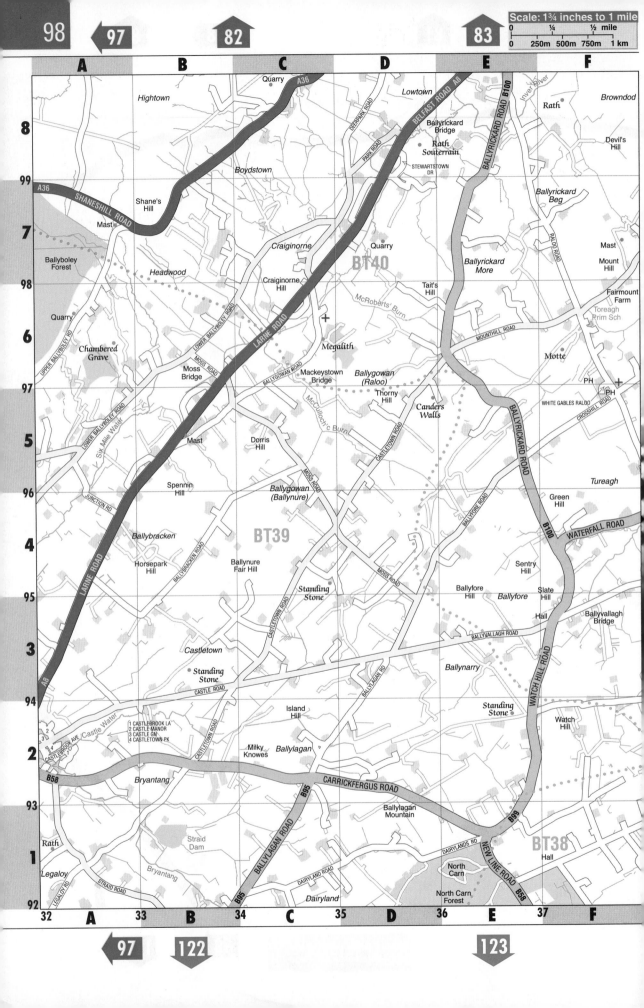

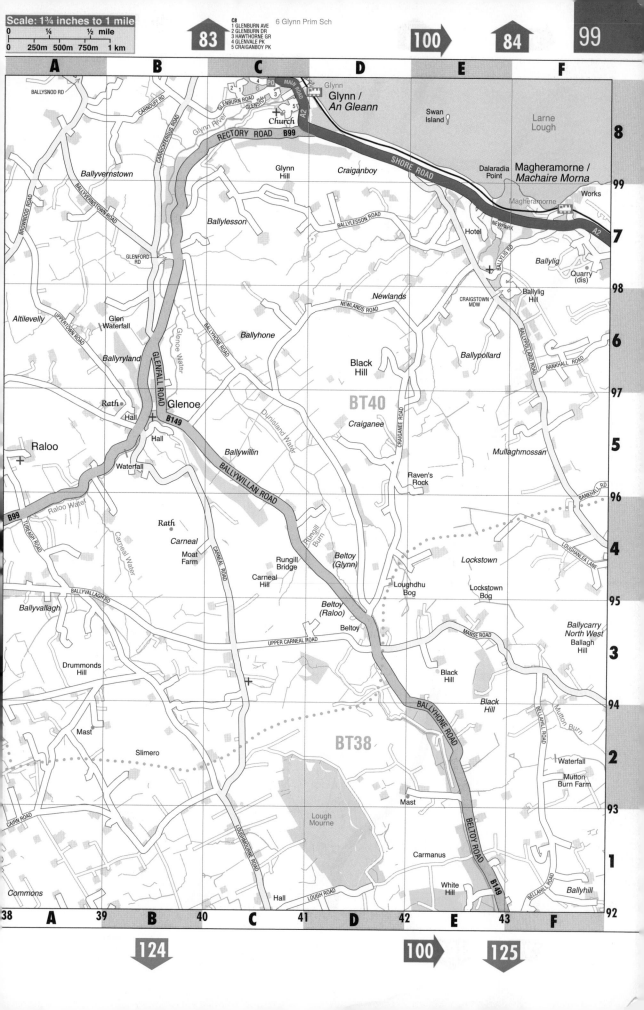

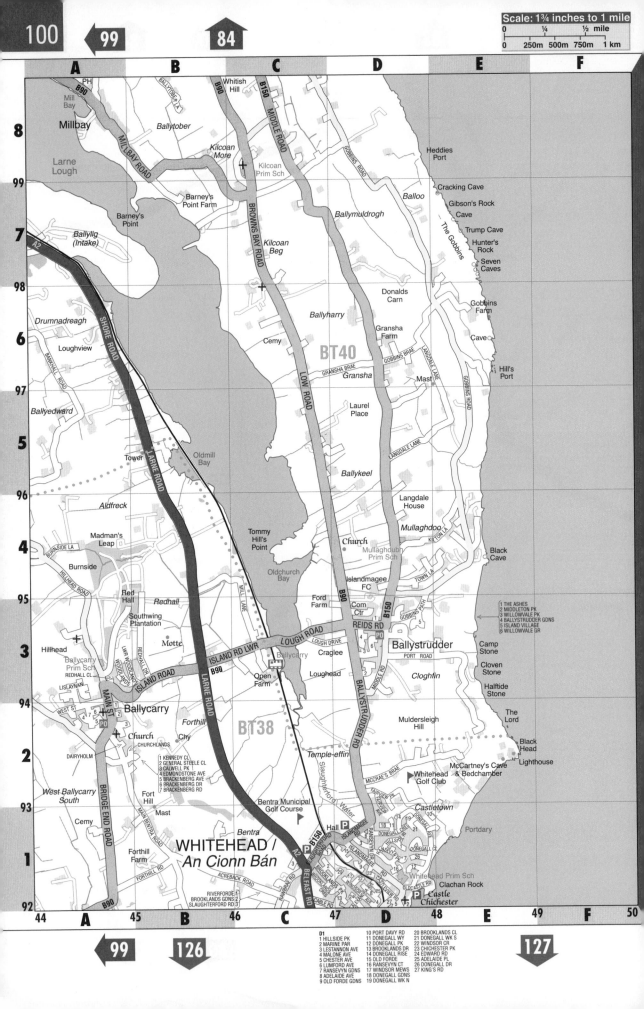

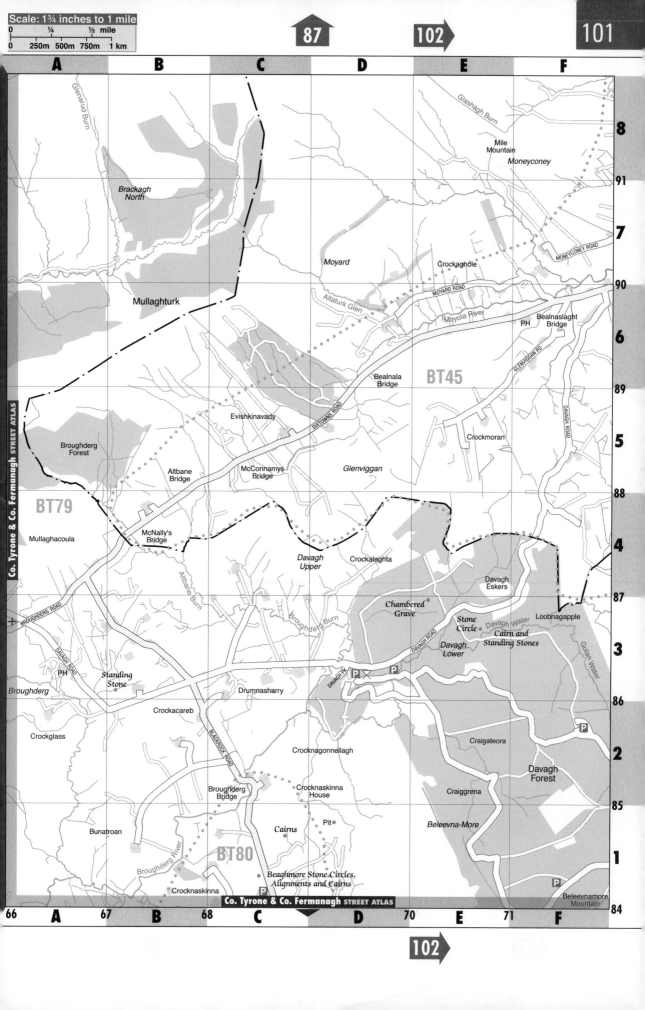

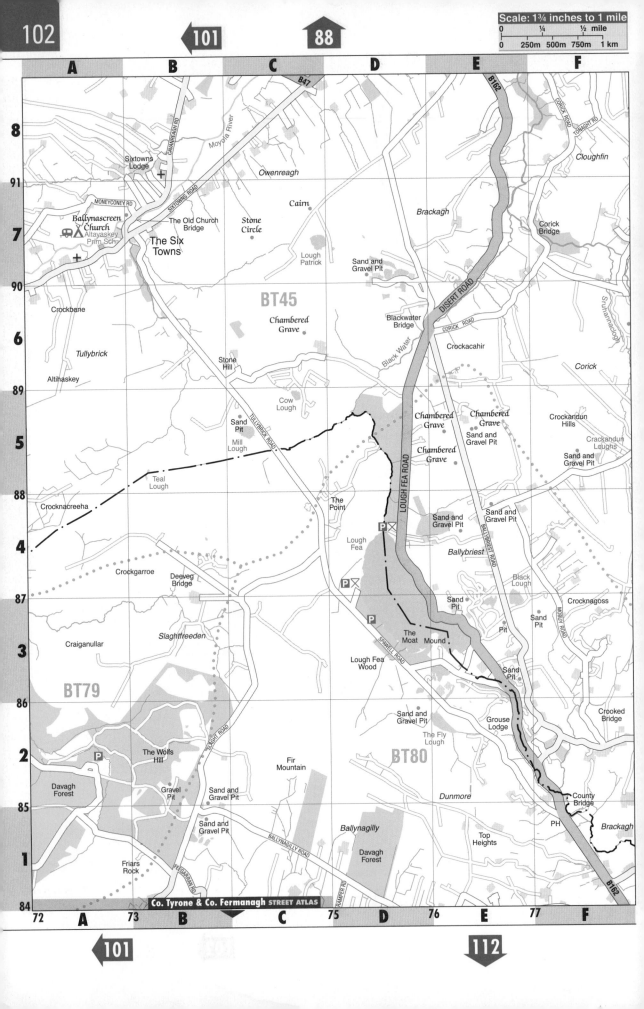

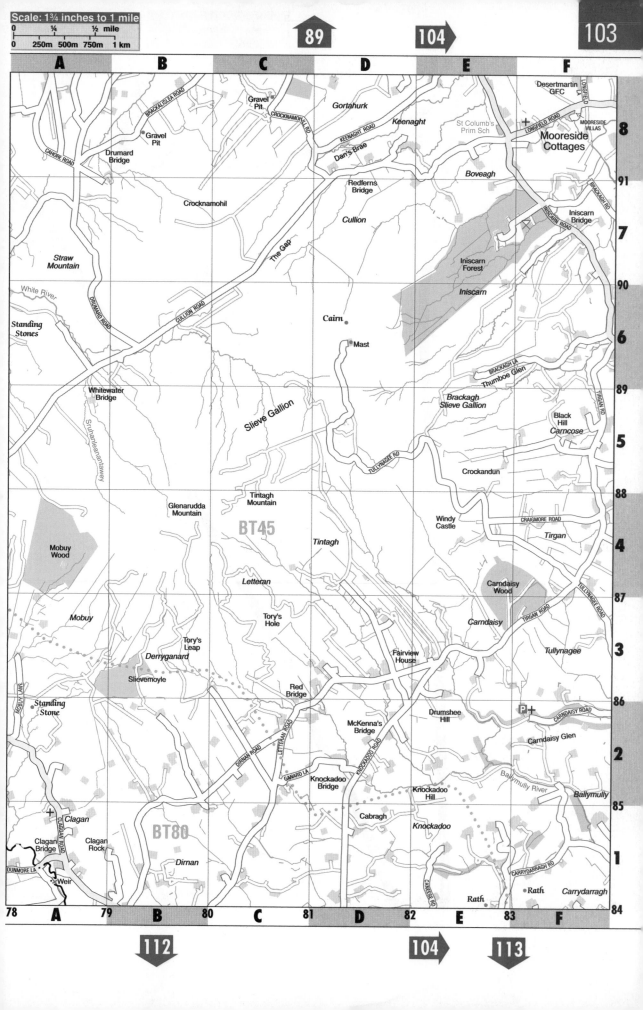

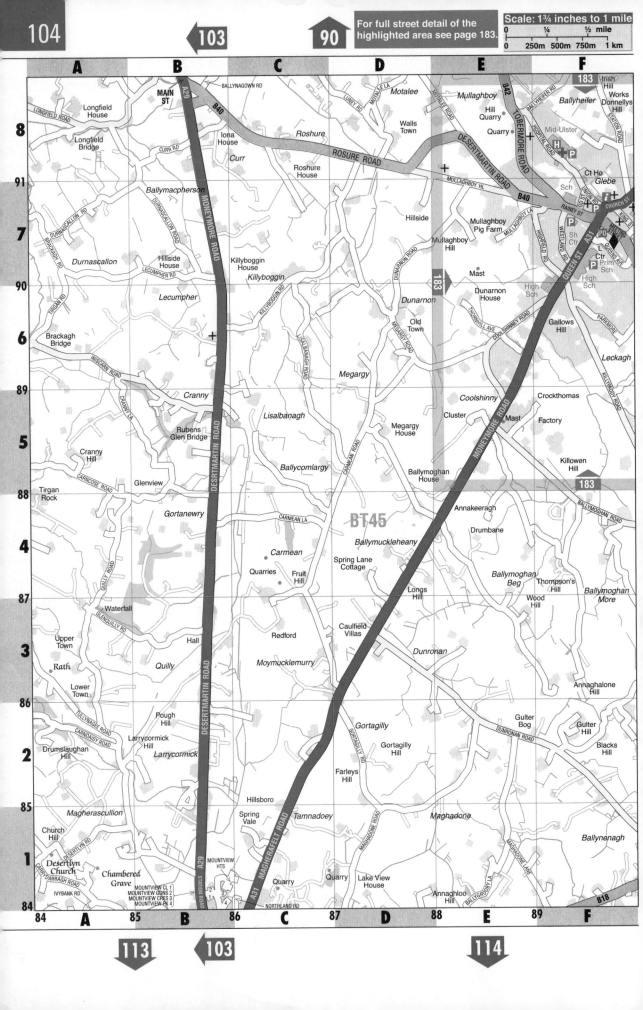

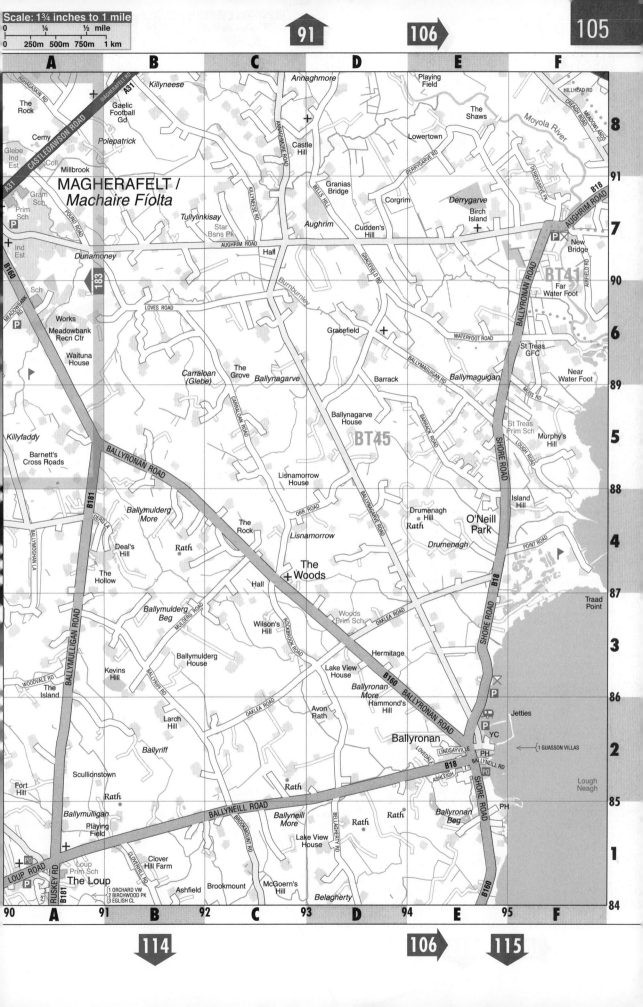

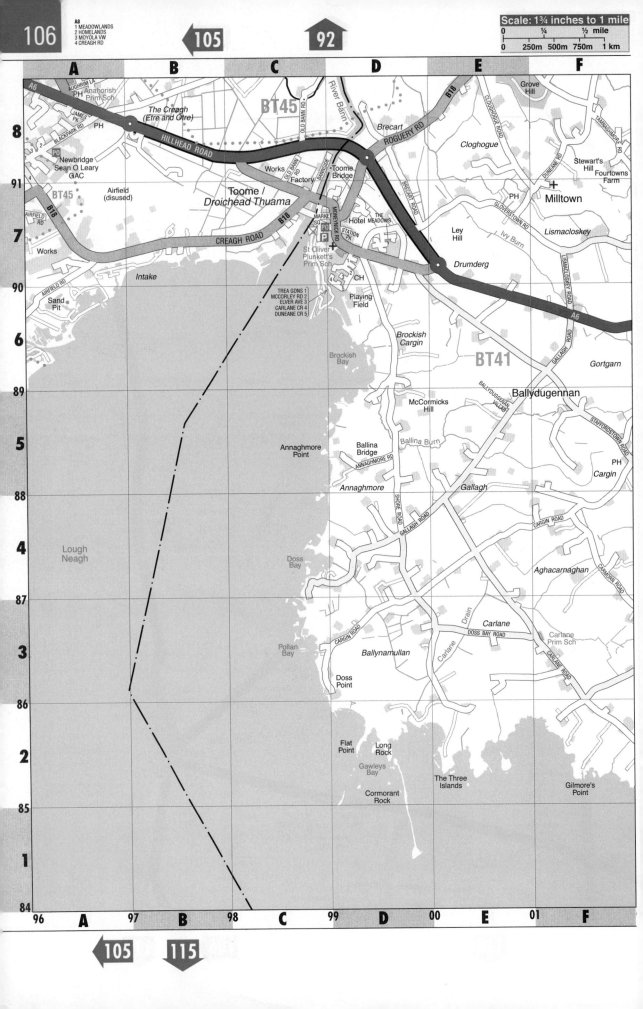

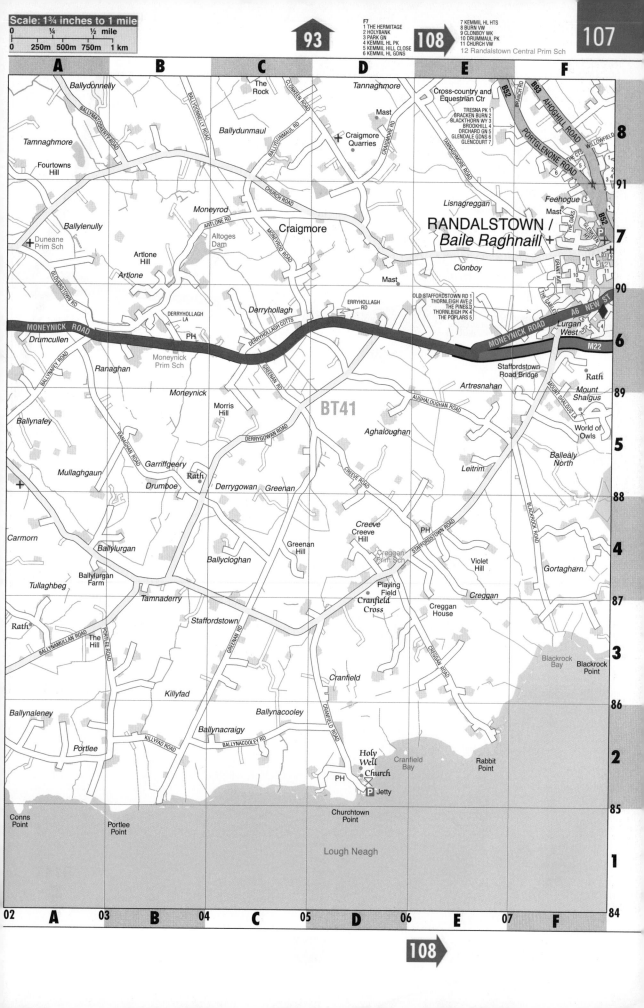

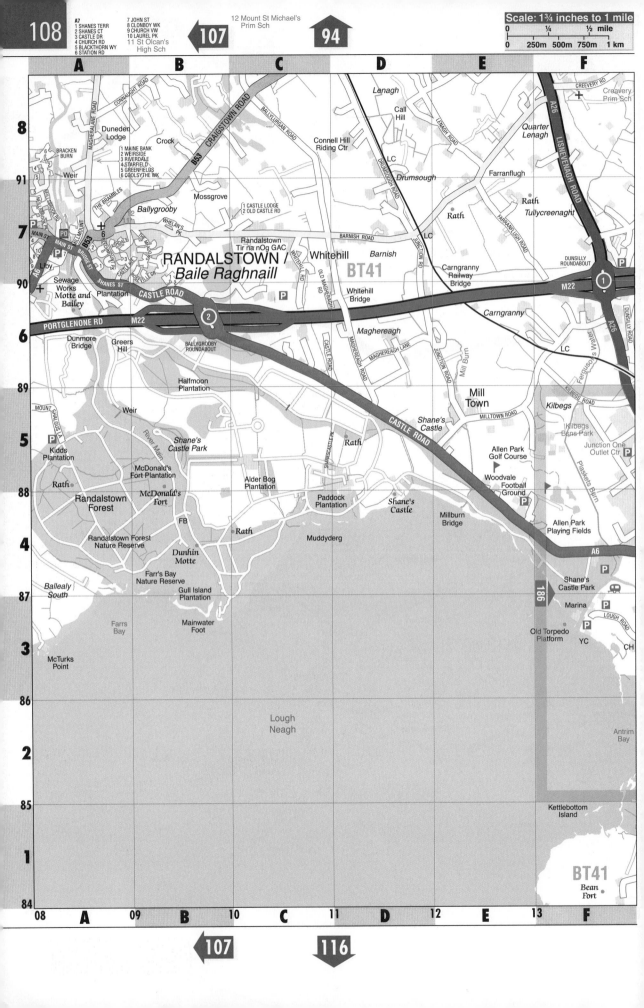

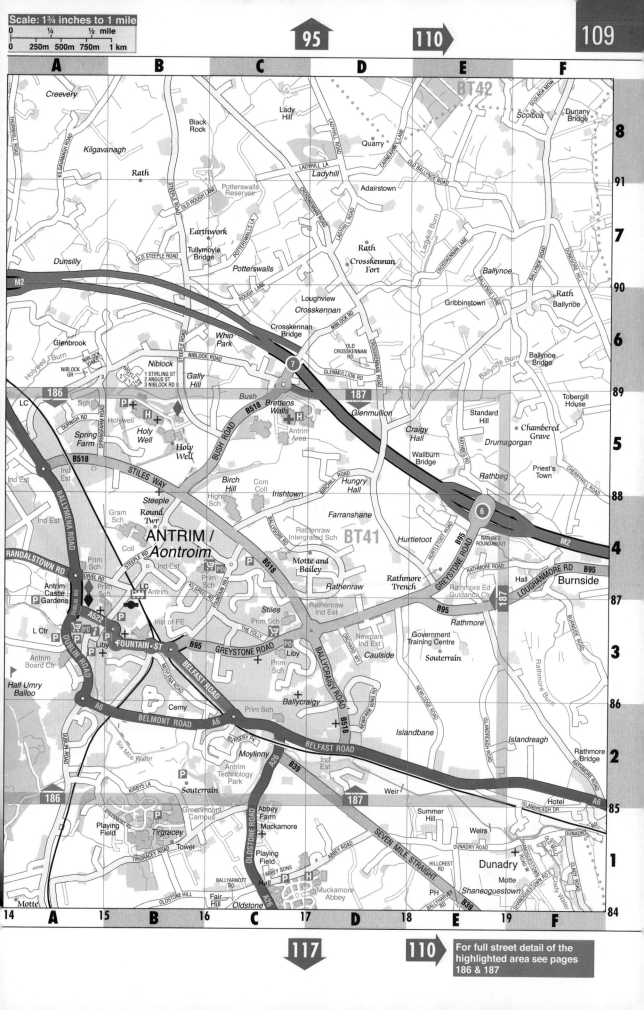

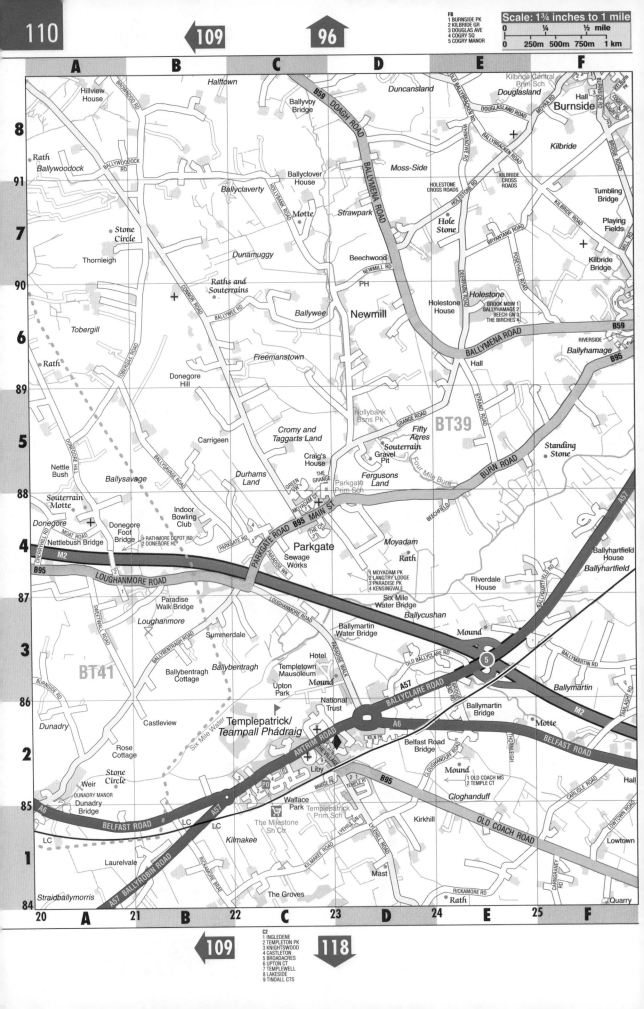

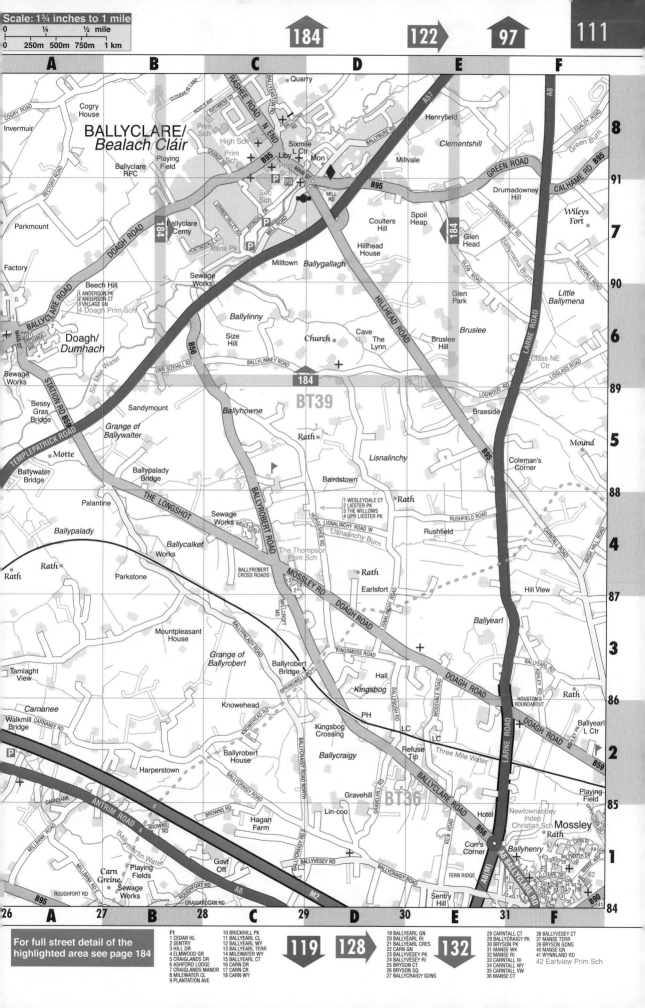

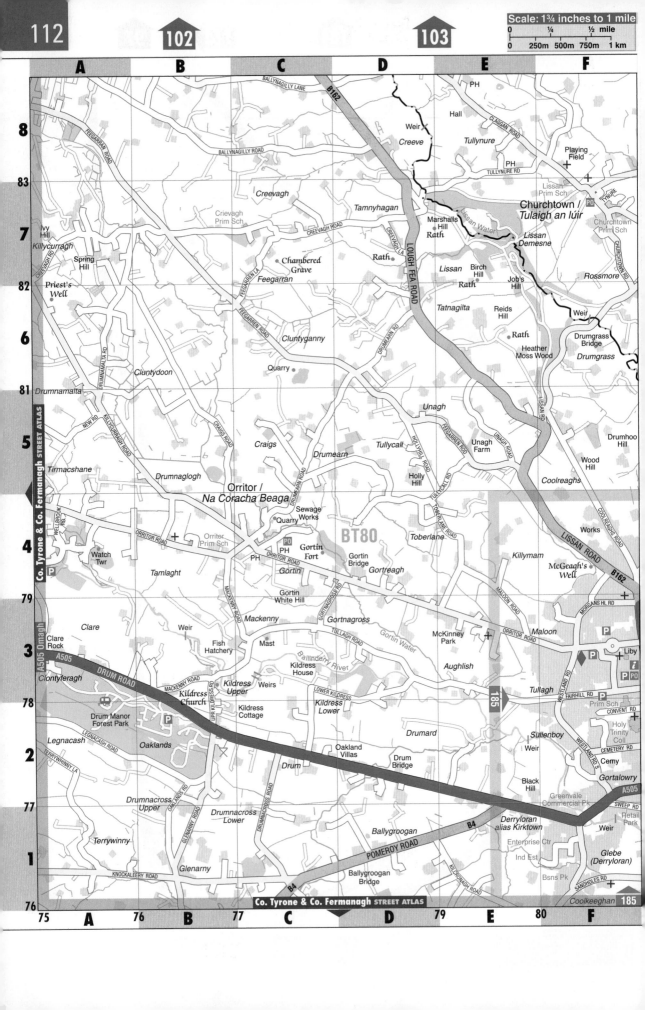

Scale: 1¾ inches to 1 mile

0   ¼   ½   mile
0   250m 500m 750m 1 km

103 ↑

E8
1 MOUNTVIEW CT
2 NORTHLAND RD
3 NORTHLAND GDNS
4 NORTHLAND DR
5 HIGH ST
6 MILL LA

7 OLD MILL CT
8 WOODVALE CRES
9 MARKET ST
10 CONYNGHAM ST
11 Moneymore Prim Sch

114 →   **104** ↑   **113**

A   B   C   D   E   F

Caneese

CARRYDARRAGH RD
CANEESE RD

TURNAFACE ROAD
IVYBANK RD

Carrydarragh RD
The Brewery Bridge

STATION RD
SANFORD ST
SMITH ST
FAIRLEA HTS
FAIRLEA GL
CIRCULAR ST

Turnaface

Drumard Hill
Drumard

Feenan More
Feenan Beg

Liby
ELM PK RD

LOUP RD B18
8

Moneymore / Muine Mór

STONARD ST
BRIDGE ST
MINISTERS W
HAMMOND ST
HALL

Playing Field
The Hill

83

Drummeen Farm
Beech Hill

A29 COOKSTOWN ROAD
SPRINGVALE
Tower Crossnarea

Playing Field
Spring Hill

Twr
Springhill House

SPRINGHILL ROAD B18

Drummeen
Rath

Killybasky

DRUMGRASS ROAD
MUFF ROAD
TAMLAGHTMORE RD

DUNNABRAGGY ROAD
Coltrim
COLTRIM CROSS ROADS

CLONEEN DR 1
MAGHERAFELT RD 2
St Patrick's Prim Sch 3

Grania's Well

7

82

Muff
Dunnabraggy

COLTRIM LANE

DRUMROT ROAD

Ballymully River

6

Derrycrummy
CLAGGAN LA

TULLAGHBOY RD
Rath Glebe
Dunman Bridge

Moneyhaw House
Moneyhaw

81

Ford
Weir

MONEYMORE ROAD
Ballyforlea
BALLYFORLEA RD

Drumrot

BT45

BT80
Claggan
Dunman

Ballyloughan Bridge

CROSSPATRICK ROAD

5

Tamlaghtmore Hall
RIVERSIDE
Factory

Tullyboy

Crosspatrick Bridge

80

185

Glasgows Hill

Ballymenagh House
LISMONEY RD

Sewage Works
Hall
Ringsend

Annahavil House
Annahavil
Forthill

Crosspatrick Bridge

4

Monrush
Ballymenagh

Lismoney
Lismoney House

TULLAGHBOY ROAD
Green Lodge

RED BRIDGE RD
Red Bridge

Drummullan Bridge
DRUMULLAN RD

A29
Lissan Water

Drumgarrell

DRUMGARRET ROAD
Ballyloughan

St Malachy's Prim Sch

79

COOKSTOWN / An Chorr Chríochach

HAWTHORNE MANOR

P   EAST CIRCULAR RD
OLD COAGH RD
COAGH ST
Station Square Retail Park
UNION ST
WILLIAM ST
LOY ST

Tullygare
Cranfield

Drummullan
Little Bridge
LITTLEBRIDGE RD

3

Sports Ctr
B73
MOLESWORTH RD
Loy

COAGH ROAD
Drumcraw

KILLYBEARN ROAD
BALLYLOGHAN ROAD

KILLYBEARN ROAD
B73

Playing Field
PH

78

P
CHAPEL ST
CHURCH ST
Prim Sch
L Ctr
High Sch

185
New Buildings
Standing Stone

CLARE LANE
Terressan
Rath

DERRYGONIGAN ROAD
Killybearn

BALLYGONNY RD EAST
Bullet Green

2

Scotchtown
KILLYMOON RD

Clare
CLOGHOG RD
FOUNTAIN ROAD

Cloghog
Sandy Row

Derrygonigan

Ballinderry River

Ballynahone
MOORVILLE
Ardtrea Bridge

77

P
DUNGANNON ROAD
Coolnahavil
CASTLE ROAD

The Killymoon Golf Club
CH
Chambered Grave

DRAPERSFIELD ROAD
Cookstown United FC
Weir

Big Bridge House
Weir

BT71
Lisnahall
Kingsmill Bridge

B160

1

Weir
Killymoon Castle
Killymoon Demesne

Bellinderry River
New Bridge
LWR GRANGE RD

Rath

TULLYVEAGH ROAD
DUFLESS RD
Tullyveagh
Doorless

Tullyraw
Tullyyeagh

KNOCKNACLOY ROAD
Claggan

BALLYMAGUIRE RD
LISNAHALL ROAD
Hall
Rath
ARDTREA ROAD

76

A29 Dungannon
Drummond Wood   Drummond

81   A   82   B   83   C   84   D   E   86   F

114 →

For full street detail of the highlighted area see page 185.

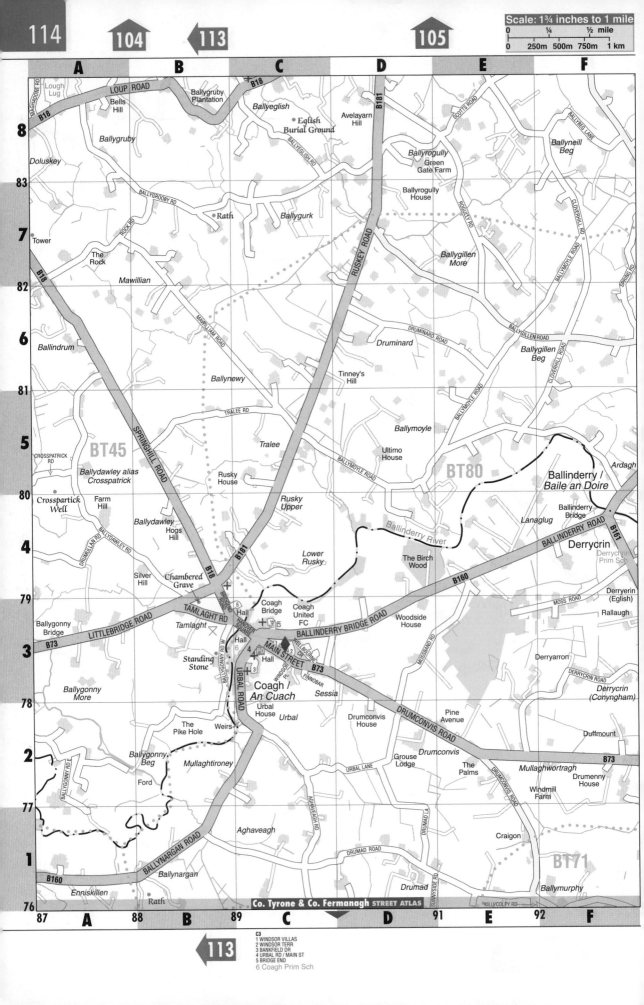

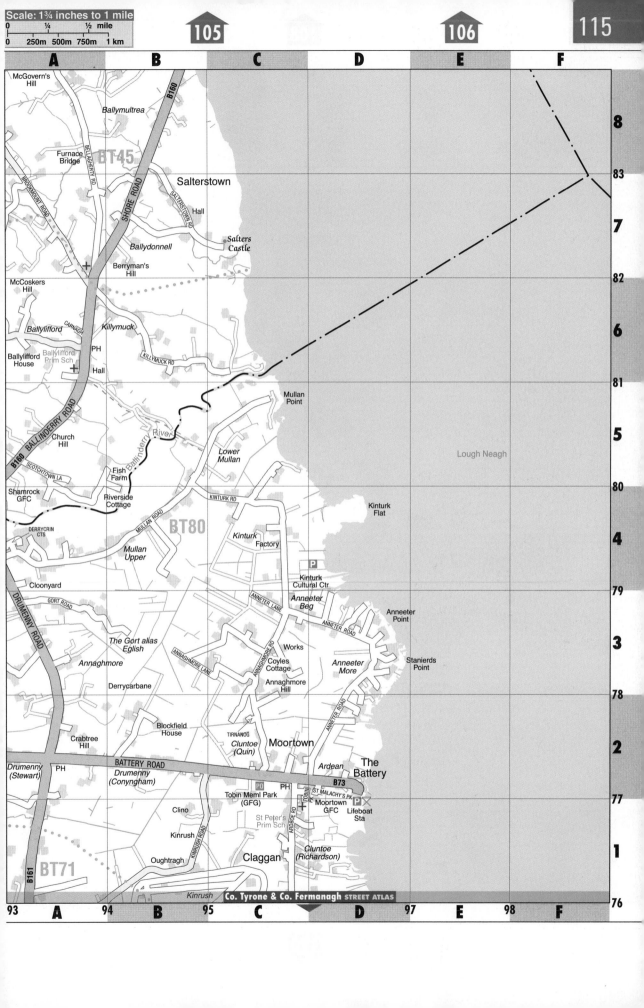
A   B   C   D   E   F

McGovern's
Hill

Ballymultrea

BT45

Furnace
Bridge

BELLAGHERRY RD

SHORE ROAD

SALTERSTOWN RD

B160

Salterstown

Hall

BROOMDRUM ROAD

Ballydonnell

Salters
Castle

Berryman's
Hill

8

83

7

82

McCoskers
Hill

CARNAGH

Ballylifford

Killymuck

KILLYMUCK RD

6

Ballylifford
Prim Sch

PH

Ballylifford
House

Hall

BALLINDERRY ROAD

B160

Church
Hill

SCOTCHTOWN LA

Ballinderry River

Mullan
Point

Lower
Mullan

81

5

Fish
Farm

Riverside
Cottage

KINTURK RD

80

Shamrock
GFC

DERRYCRIN
CTS

MULLAN ROAD

BT80

Mullan
Upper

Kinturk

Factory

Kinturk
Flat

Lough Neagh

4

Cloonyard

GORT ROAD

DRUMENNY ROAD

79

P

Kinturk
Cultural Ctr

ANNETER LANE

Anneeter
Beg

ANNEETER ROAD

Anneeter
Point

The Gort alias
Eglish

ANNAGHMORE LANE

ANNAGHMORE RD

Works

Coyles
Cottage

Anneeter
More

Stanierds
Point

3

Annaghmore

Derrycarbane

Annaghmore
Hill

78

Blockfield
House

TIRNANOG

Cluntoe
(Quin)

Moortown

ANNEETER ROAD

2

Crabtree
Hill

BATTERY ROAD

Drumenny
(Stewart)

PH

Drumenny
(Conyngham)

PO

PH

TOBIN

ST. MALACHY'S PK

Ardean

The
Battery

B73

77

Clino

Tobin Meml Park
(GFG)

St Peter's
Prim Sch

ARDBOE RD

Moortown
GFC

Lifeboat
Sta

Kinrush

KINRUSH ROAD

Oughtragh

Claggan

Cluntoe
(Richardson)

1

B161

BT71

93   A   94   B   95   C   96   D   97   E   98   F   76

	A	B	C	D	E	F

Deer Park

BT41

Dunore Point

Rath

Spoil Heap

Rath

Oldlodge Wood

Rath

Rath

Rath

DUNORE ROAD

Corbally

Rath

Rath

DUNGONNELL ROAD

Corbally House

CORBALLY ROAD

PH

Dungonnell

Lough Neagh

Quay

Ballyginniff Milltown

Mount Cottage

BALLYGINNIFF ROAD

PH

BRITISH ROAD

SEACASH RD

Black Burn

LOUGHVIEW ROAD

Rath

DUNGONNELL ROAD

Ballyginniff

Ballyginniff House

Rath

Clover Hill

Rath

TOWNLAND ROAD

BALLYQUILLAN ROAD

Moores Grove

Ardmore House

Rath

Ballynageeragh

Ballyquillin

Ballyquillin House

Ardmore Point

Grove Cottage

Oakfield House

BT29

Aldergrove

PH

STATION RD

Ardmore

Ballymacilhoyle

Playing Field

DIAMOND ROAD

Moores Quay

The Elms

The Diamond

Firfield

Solitude

Blackstown

ARDMORE ROAD

BLACKSTOWN ROAD

McVeaghstown

Ballynadrentagh

Plantation House

BALLYCLAN ROAD

Ballyclan House

Ballyclan

Ravenhill

Ashfield

Gortnagallon

Rathvale

Gortnagallon Cottages

LARGY ROAD

Cidercourt Bridge

Mast

GORTNAGALLON RD

Factory

Largy Cottages

Crumlin River

Waterfall

CIDERCOURT ROAD

Airfield (private)

Largy House

Largy

Lake View

Ballymacmary

BAY RD

08	A	09	B	10	C	11	D	12	E	13	F

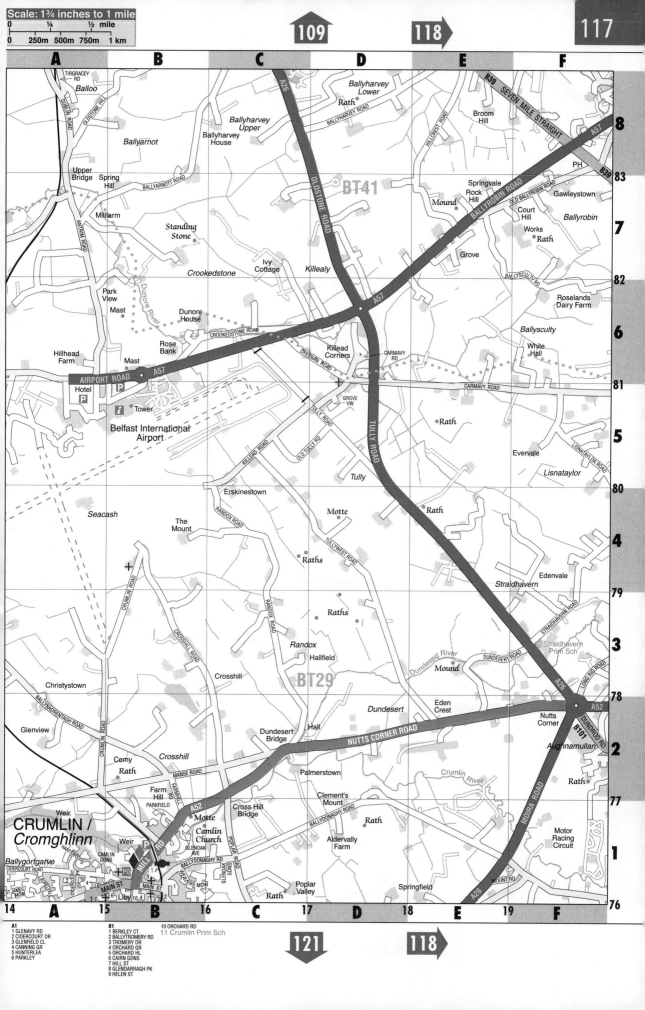

117
110

Scale: 1¾ inches to 1 mile
0   ¼   ½   mile
0   250m   500m   750m   1 km

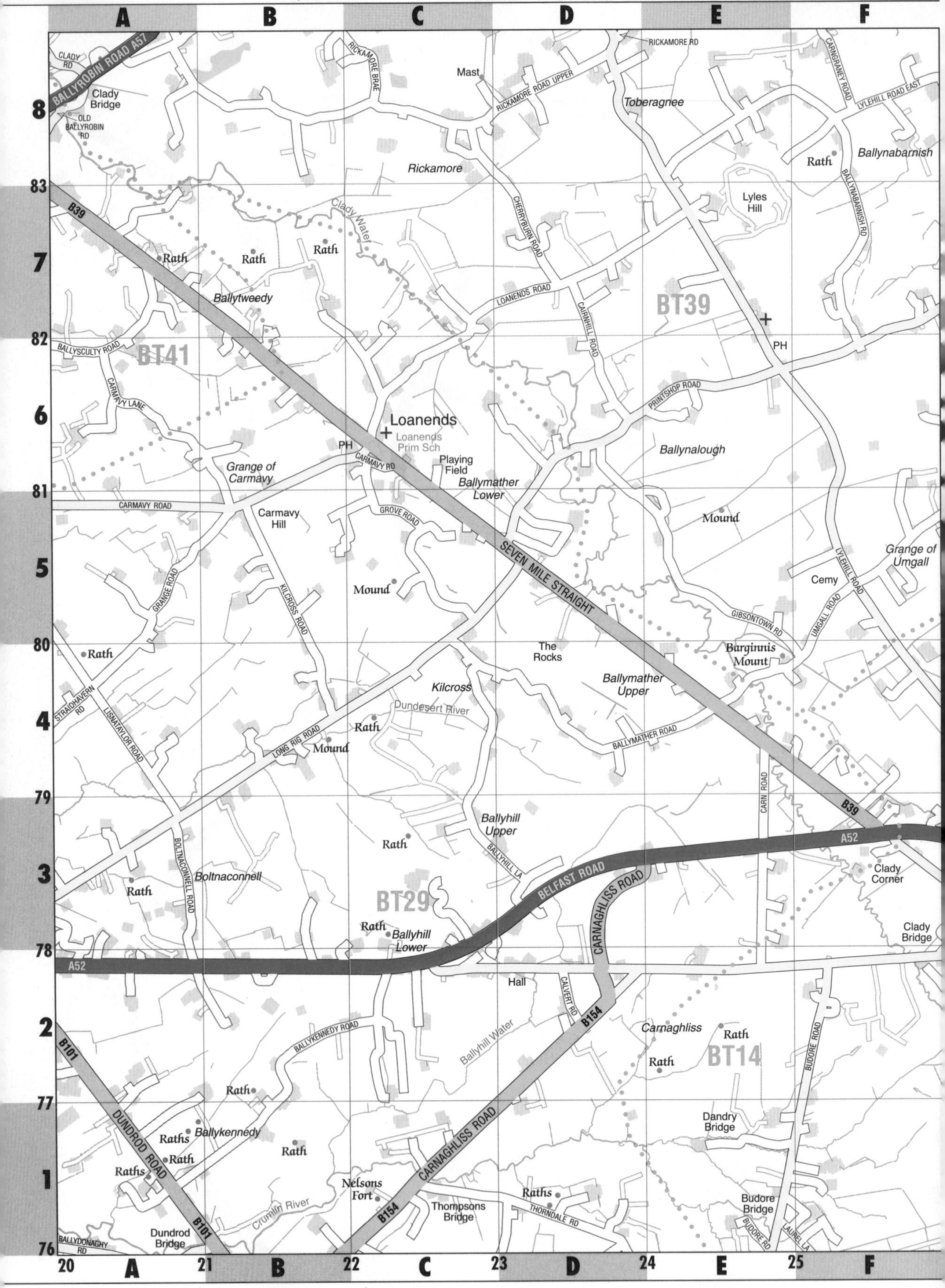

A   B   C   D   E   F

8

CLADY RD
BALLYROBIN ROAD A57
Clady Bridge
OLD BALLYROBIN RD
Mast
RICKAMORE BRAE
RICKAMORE RD
RICKAMORE ROAD UPPER
Toberagnee
Rath
Ballynabarnish

83

B39
Rickamore
Clady Water
CHERRYBURN ROAD
CARNGRANEY ROAD
LYLEHILL ROAD EAST
Lyles Hill
BALLYNABARNISH RD

7

Rath   Rath   Rath
Ballytweedy
LOANENDS ROAD
CARNHILL ROAD
BT39
PH

82

BALLYSCULTY ROAD
BT41
CARMAVY LANE
PRINTSHOP ROAD

6

Grange of Carmavy
PH
CARMAVY RD
Loanends
Loanends Prim Sch
Playing Field
Ballymather Lower
Ballynalough

81

CARMAVY ROAD
Carmavy Hill
GROVE ROAD
SEVEN MILE STRAIGHT
Mound
Grange of Umgall

5

GRANGE ROAD
KILCROSS ROAD
Mound
Cemy
LYLEHILL ROAD
UMGALL ROAD
GIBSONTOWN RD

80

Rath
The Rocks
Ballymather Upper
Barginnis Mount

4

STRAIDHAVERN RD
LISNATRUNK ROAD
Kilcross
Dundesert River
Rath
LONG RIG ROAD
Mound
BALLYMATHER ROAD

79

Ballyhill Upper
CARN ROAD
B39
A52

3

BOLTNACONNELL ROAD
Rath
Boltnaconnell
BT29
Rath
BALLYHILL LA
BELFAST ROAD
CARNAGHLISS ROAD
Clady Corner
Clady Bridge

78

A52
Rath
Ballyhill Lower
Hall
CALVERT RD
B154

2

B101
BALLYKENNEDY ROAD
Ballyhill Water
Carnaghliss
Rath
Rath
BT14
BUDORE ROAD

77

Rath
DUNDROD ROAD
Raths   Ballykennedy
Rath
Rath
Dandry Bridge

1

Raths
CARNAGHLISS ROAD
Nelsons Fort
Raths
Budore Bridge
THORNDALE RD
LAUREL LA
BUDORE RD

76

BALLYDONAGHY RD
B101
Dundrod Bridge
Crumlin River
B154
Thompsons Bridge

20   A   21   B   22   C   23   D   24   E   25   F

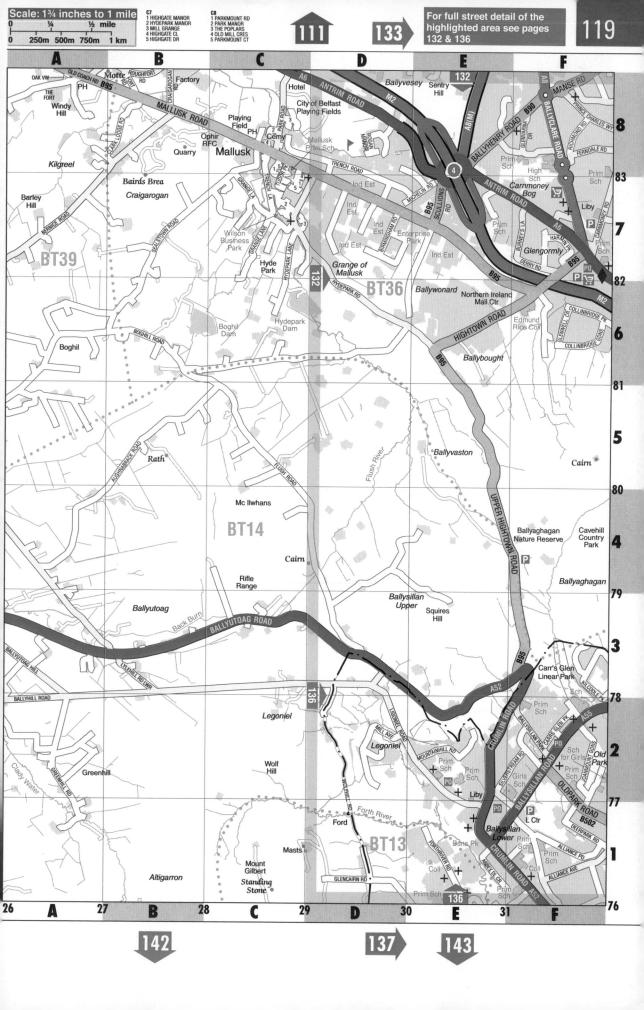

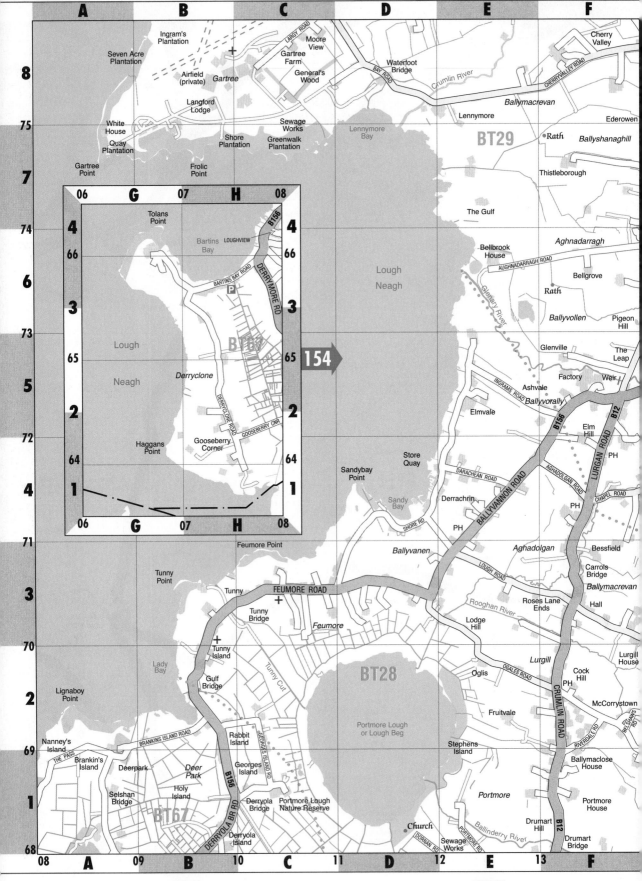

Scale: 1¾ inches to 1 mile

0 ¼ ½ mile
0 250m 500m 750m 1 km

A B C D E F

8

Seven Acre
Plantation

Ingram's
Plantation

Gartree
Farm

Moore
View

Largy Road

General's
Wood

Waterfoot
Bridge

Bay Road

Cherry
Valley

Cherryvalley Road

Crumlin River

Airfield
(private) *Gartree*

Langford
Lodge

Ballymacrevan

Lennymore

Ederowen

75

White
House

Sewage
Works

Lennymore
Bay

BT29

Rath

Ballyshanaghill

Quay
Plantation

Shore
Plantation

Greenwalk
Plantation

Thistleborough

7

Gartree
Point

Frolic
Point

The Gulf

06 **G** 07 **H** 08

Bellbrook
House

Aghnadarragh

74

4 66

Tolans
Point

Bartins
Bay

LOUGHVIEW

B156

4
66

Aughnadarragh Road

Bellgrove

Lough
Neagh

Rath

Ballyvollen

Pigeon
Hill

66

Bartins Bay Road

Derrymore Rd

P

Glenary River

3

3 3

Glenville

The
Leap

73

65 65

Lough

BT67

Derryclone

154

Ashvale

Factory

Weir

Ingrams Road

Ballyvorally

B156

5

2

Neagh

Derryclone Road

Gooseberry Cnr

2 2

Elmvale

Elm
Hill

B12

PH

72

64

Haggans
Point

Gooseberry
Corner

64

Store
Quay

Daraichean Road

Derrachrin

Aghadolgan Road

PH

Lurgan Road

Chapel Road

4

1

Sandybay
Point

Sandy
Bay

Shore Rd

1

PH

Ballyvanmon Road

PH

71

Feumore Point

Ballyvanen

Aghadolgan

Bessfield

Carrols
Bridge

Tunny
Point

Tunny

FEUMORE ROAD

Rooghan River

Lough Road

Roses Lane
Ends

Ballymacrevan

Hall

3

Tunny
Bridge

Feumore

Lodge
Hill

70

Tunny
Island

Lady
Bay

Tunny Cut

BT28

Ogales Road

Lurgill

Oglis

PH

Lurgill
House

Cock
Hill

Crumlin Road

2

Lignaboy
Point

Gulf
Bridge

Portmore Lough
or Lough Beg

Fruitvale

McCorrystown

Belshaws Rd

Nanney's
Island

Brankins Island Road

Rabbit
Island

Georges Island Rd

Stephens
Island

Portmore

Ballymaclose
House

69

THE PASS

Brankin's
Island

Deerpark

*Deer
Park*

B156

Georges
Island

Riverdale Rd

Portmore
House

1

Selshan
Bridge

Holy
Island

Derryola
Bridge

Portmore Lough
Nature Reserve

Church

Ballinderry River

Drumart
Hill

B12

Drumart
Bridge

BT67

Derryola Br Rd

Derryola
Island

Dornan Rd

Portmore Rd

Sewage
Works

68

08 **A** 09 **B** 10 **C** 11 **D** 12 **E** 13 **F**

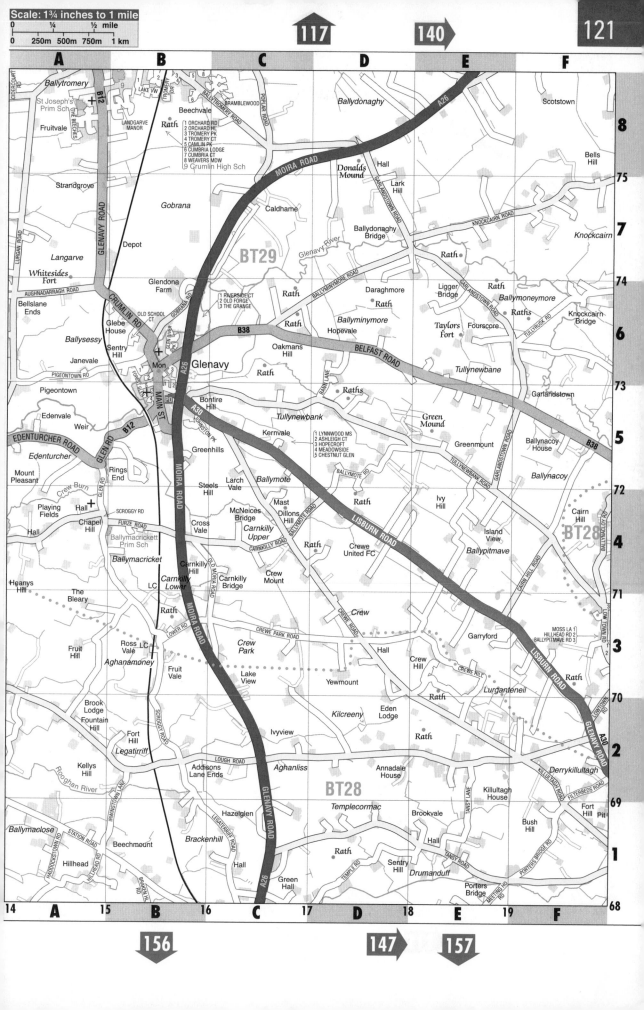

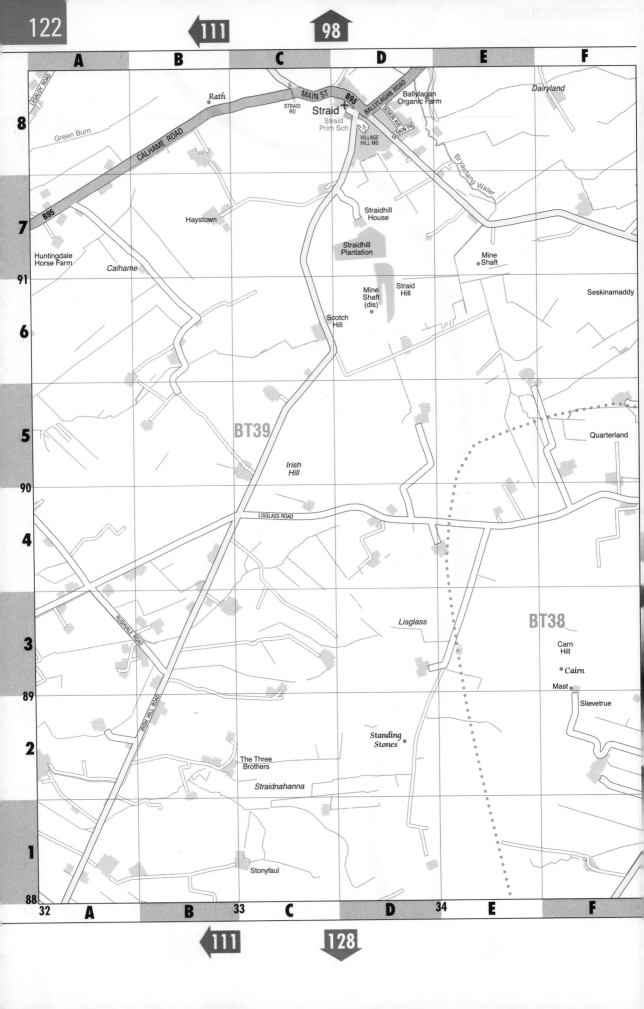

A B C D E F

8
7
91
6
5
90
4
3
89
2
1

North Carn
Forest

BT39

Billy's
Hill

SESKIN ROAD

B58

P

North
Woodburn
Reservoir

NEW LINE ROAD

PAISLEY ROAD

LIBERTY ROAD

COUNCILLORS ROAD

Aldoo

BT38

Waterfall

Mounds

Woodburn River

LISGLASS ROAD

WOODBURN ROAD

Woodburn
Forest

WOODBURN ROAD

B58

South
Woodburn
Reservoirs

KNOCKAGH ROAD

35 A B 36 C D 37 E F 88

A B C D E F

8

Commons

Horse
Park

PAISLEY ROAD

7

91

Burleigh
Hill

6

LIBERTY ROAD

BT38

French
Park

5

90

Motte

Carnrawsy
Well

COPELAND
VIEW TERR

WINDSLOW MS 1
WINDSLOW CT 2
HAMPTON CT 3
CAMPDEN PK 4
RICHMOND PK 5
WINDSLOW CL 6

*Middle
Division*

4 B58 NEW LINE ROAD

Carrickfergus
CC

THORNDENE PK

Woodburn River

NEW LINE ROAD

MEADOWHILL CL

B90

MEADOWHILL CV

WINDSLOW HTS

WINDSLOW
RISE

BERKLEY DR

HESTON
DR

MILEBUSH PARK

MILEBUSH CRES

Bryantang

Refuse
Tip

NEW LINE

HILLVIEW GN

HILLVIEW
GDNS

WINDSLOW RD

WINDSLOW
DR

WINDSLOW
GN

SANDRINGHAM
GN

MILEBUSH
DR

MIDDLE ROAD

B58

HILLVIEW
GR

HILLVIEW
AVE

HILLVIEW

HENLY RD

SANDRINGHAM
HTS

SANDRINGHAM
AVE

3

Waterfall

WOODBURN ROAD

B58

KNOCKAGH
HTS

CARRON
HTS

RATHLIN
HEIGHTS

HENLY HTS

SANDRINGHAM
PLACE

Carrickfergus
Gram Sch

Carrickfergus
Coll

89

B90

SHANE
HTS

DRUMRAMER

TARDREE HTS

LEMISH
HTS

COLLIN
HTS

PROSPECT HTS

HENLY
DR

HENLY
GR

HENLY

SANDRINGHAM

Playing
Fields

Animal
Shelter

Farmhill

PROSPECT ROAD

LEICESTER
CT

PROSPECT
GR

HENLY
GDNS

PROSPECT DR

2 **CARRICKFERGUS /**
Carraig Fhearghais

DRUMHOY
CT

Woodburn
Prim Sch

Weston
Bsns
Pk

RATH VW

PROSPECT AVE

NORTHLAND

THORNFIELD
CT

THORN
SQ

Com
Ctr

WOODBURN ROAD

PROSPECT DOWNS

PROSPECT PK

PROSPECT
DOWNS

OAKWOOD ROAD

THE
BLACKTHORN

THORNFIELD
SQ

EDERNY

DRUMHOY

1

*Dorisland
Reservoir*

UPPER ROAD

B90

PROSPECT
GN

CROSS GN

BLINN

WALK

HOLLIES
THE BIRCHES

WOODBURN AVE

THE
CHERRY
WK

THE
MAPLE

SUNNYLANDS
AVENUE

KIRKLAND

SANDRINGHAME GDNS

CHICHES
SQ

SANDES CT

WOODLAND
AVE

WOODLAWN

BURLEIGH
WK

CARNMARY
WK

WHINFIELD WK

TOWN

BURLEIGH
GR

HAWTHORN

Woodlawn
Prim Sch

HAWTHORN
GR

HAWTHORN
AVE

Sunnylands
Prim Sch

Com
Ctr

88

38 A B 39 C D 40 E F

D2
1 PROSPECT LOANEN
2 LEICESTER CT
3 MOURNEVIEW PK

E1
1 GLENFIELD WK
2 WOODBURN AVE

F1
1 SHAFTESBURY PL
2 SHAFTESBURY CROSS
3 SANDES CT
4 THE LARCHES

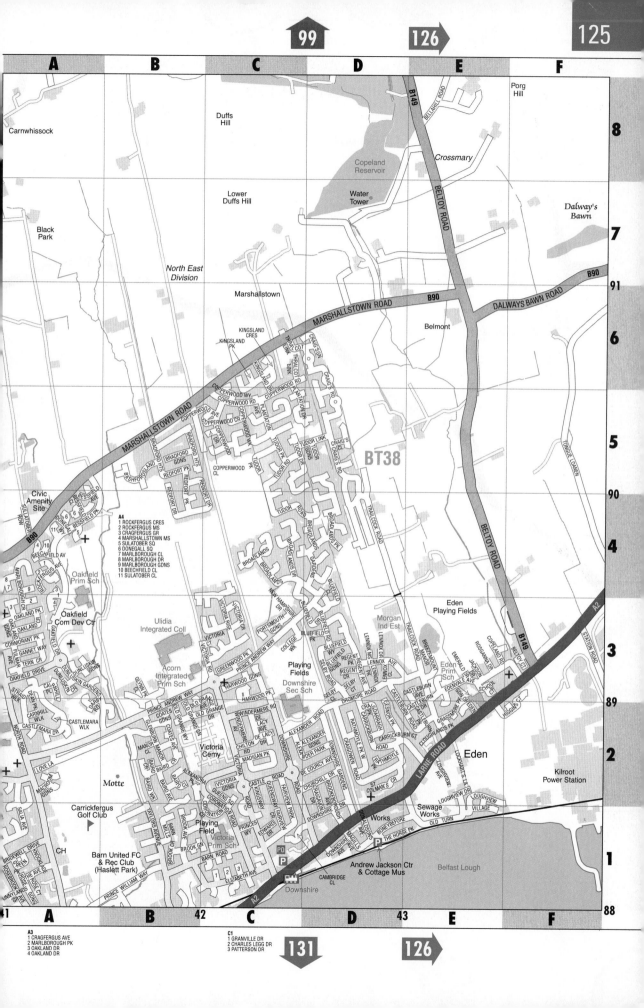

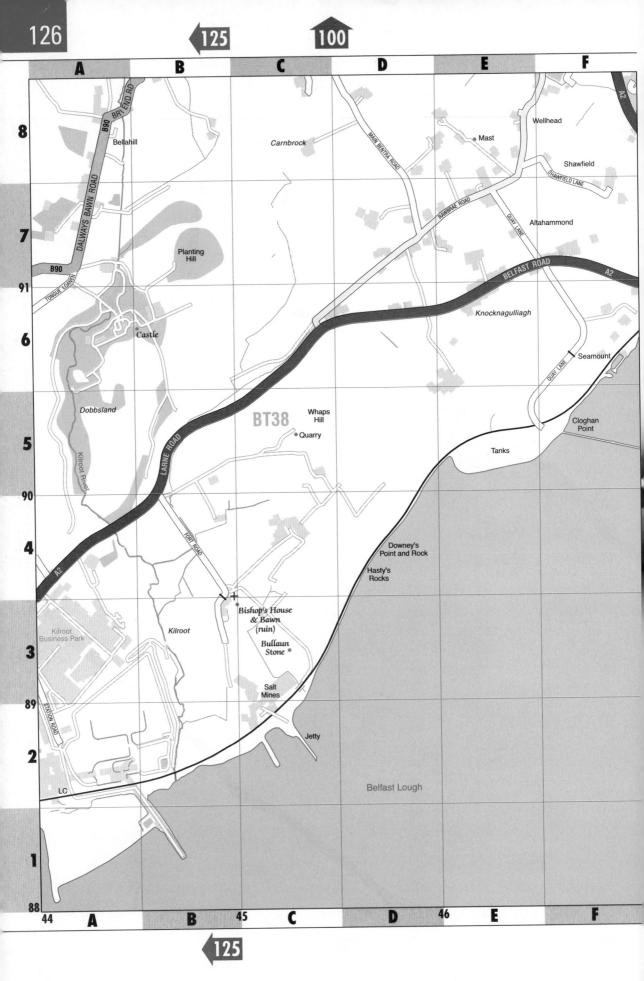

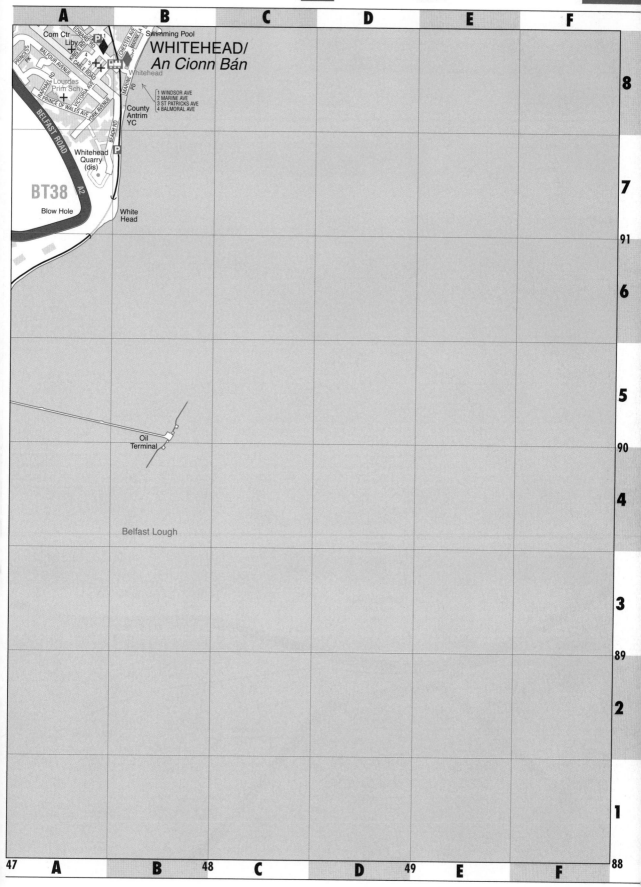

WHITEHEAD/
An Cionn Bán

1 WINDSOR AVE
2 MARINE AVE
3 ST PATRICKS AVE
4 BALMORAL AVE

Com Ctr
Liby
Swimming Pool
Whitehead
County
Antrim
YC

Lourdes
Prim Sch

Whitehead
Quarry
(dis)

BT38
Blow Hole
White
Head

BALFOUR AVENUE
PRINCES PK
RAPHAEL RD
PRINCE OF WALES AVE
VICTORIA AVE
YORK AVENUE
BELFAST ROAD
A2
EDWARD RD
KING'S RD
CABLE ROAD
CHESTER AVE
MARINE LA
MARINE RD
BEACH RD

Oil
Terminal

Belfast Lough

← 111
122

A B C D E F

8
87
7
6
5
86
4
3
85
2
1
84

BT39

BT38

BT36

BT37

Hillmount House

Rea Hill

Halftown

Carntall

Mast

Leiganfield

Mast

Burnfield House

Ballyhowne

Rath

Hall

Cully's Burn

REHILL ROAD

CARNTALL ROAD

SLIEVETRUE ROAD

KNOCKAGH ROAD

CULLYBURN ROAD

Pound Burn

1 OAKLANDS CT
2 OAKLANDS PK
3 BRAMBLE PK
4 SORRELL PK
5 SORRELL AVE
6 SORRELL DR
7 BRAMBLE GRANGE
SORRELL AVE
SORRELL AVE

CHRISTINE GR 1
WOODFORD GR 2
WOODFORD DR 3
WOODFORD MANOR 4
KNOCKVIEW CRES 5
KNOCKVIEW GDNS 6
KNOCKVIEW DR 7
WOODFORD PAR 8

Burnfield House Golf Club

CH

Old Carrick Road

B59
DOAGH ROAD

B90

Mossley West

Mossley

EARLFORD HTS

Mossley Mill Civic Ctr

UPPERTOWN DR

CHERRYMOUNT Recn Gds

Playing Fields

THE GLADE

BRICKHILL

CARNMONEY RD NORTH

PLANTFIELD

MANSE WY

CAMPBELL RD

Playing Field

St MacNissi's Prim Sch

B59

LAKEVIEW AVE

Mossley Prim Sch

RAVENSDALE

CHURCH RD

Knockview Manor

DOAGH RD

Knockview Ave

WOODFORD RD

WOODFORD AVE

CHRISTINE RD

Christine Park

GLENKYLE CRES

Woodford

Ballyduff Prim Sch

Ballyduff Com Ctr

Playing Field

FAIRVIEW PK

FAIRVIEW GDNS

FAIRVIEW DRIVE

RAVELSTON CRES

RAVELSTON WY

FAIRVIEW RD

FAIRVIEW AVE

RAVELSTON PK

RAVELSTON AVE

Ballyduff

DOWNHILL AVE

CORNHILL

BALLYFORE

BALLYFORE WK

FORTHILL DRIVE

BRAESIDE DR

Factory

Three Mile Water

Three Mile Water Conservation Park

Three Mile Water Playing Fields

BRIDGE ROAD

BRAESIDE AVE

Playing Fields

1 Victoria La

BALLYDUFF ROAD

BT37

TWINBURN GDNS

TWINBURN CR

TWINBURN RD

HAWTHORNE ROAD

LISBANE DRIVE

LISSANE AVE

MONKSTOWN ROAD

Monkstown Com Sch

Monkstown

OAKLANDS AVE

OAKLANDS RI

OAKLANDS CL

OAKLANDS SOUTH

OAKLANDS VW

BRAMBLE AVE

BURNIE AVE

BURNET PK

MULBERRY PK

BLACKTHORN WY

BRIAR PK

BRIAR CT

BREEN CT

RAILWAY HALT

LARAL PK

LARAL GDNS

Liby

Monkstown GDNS

JORDANSTOWN ROAD

JENNINGS DRIVE

MEADOWBANK CT

BALLYALTON DR

CASHEL CL

ADARE

CLOYNE GDNS

1 DOWNPATRICK GN

GREYABBEY GDNS

DERWENT DRIVE

FINNER WK

HOLLYBANK

Com Ctr

Playing Field

Hollybank Prim Sch

B90

Beverley Sh Ctr

WAVERLEY DR

WAVERLEY GDNS

BEVERLEY RD

CARNMONEY ROAD

P

32 33 34
A B C D E F

← 111
133

A1
1 WAVERLEY CRES
2 GLENKYLE GR
3 BEECHGROVE DR
4 BEVERLEY CRES

A2
1 LAKEVIEW GR
2 LAKEVIEW PK
3 ROWAN GR
4 BIRCHMOUNT
5 ELDERBURN
6 HOLLYVALE

B1
1 GLENKYLE PK AVE
2 GLENKYLE DR
3 GLENKYLE PAR
4 RAVELSTON GDNS
5 RAVELSTON LINK
6 RAVELSTON GR

F2
1 MULBERRY GRANGE
2 BLACKTHORN GRANGE
3 BLACKTHORN MEWS
4 MULBERRY PK
5 MULBERRY MEWS
6 OAKLANDS MDW
7 BURNET CL
8 OAKLANDS WY

Woodburn Forest

West Division

Fire Tower

Cave

My Lords Mountain

Masseys Mountain

Mound

Cave

Knockagh House

8

Knockagh Road

O'Kane's Bog

7

BT36

87

County Antrim War Memorial

O'Haughan's Cave

6

B90

BT38

Mast

Greenisland Golf Club

WOODGREEN

CH

UPPER ROAD

DOWNVIEW RD

DOWNVIEW PK

DOWNVIEW GDNS

DOWNVIEW CRES

DOWNVIEW ROAD

GORMAN CLOSE

5

Monkstown Church

Knockmhore House

WHITETHORN

THE PADDOCK

BERKELEY DEANE

TINAMARA

UPPER STATION RD

Greenisland Prim Sch

SCHOOL LA

86

Mast

FARM LODGE RD

FARM LODGE CL

FARM LODGE GDNS

Playing Field

FARM LODGE PK

GLENISLAND TERR

LOUGHVIEW TERR

Greenisland

B90

GOLDENVIEW PK

4

HEDGELEA PK

HEDGELEA MANOR

OLD CARRICK ROAD

FARM LODGE CT

FARM LODGE GN

FARM LODGE WK

FARM LODGE

FARM LODGE DR

FARM LODGE WY

KNOCK'S ALLAGH PARK

KNOCKFERGUS

Greenisland Com Ctr

Liby

Greenisland Knockagh Youth Ctr

STATION ROAD

Greenisland / Inis Glas

GLASSILLAN CT

LONGFIELD LA

LONGFIELD CT

JOHNSTONE CL

3

HEDGELEA LA

HEDGELEA GR

HEDGELEA AVE

BERRYFIELDS

BERRY PK

BERRY CR

BERRY LA

BERRY DR

BT37

MEADOWVIEW

MEADOW DALE

1 MOUNT PLEASANT GDNS
2 CLONASLEA CT
3 ROSEMOUNT CT

Jordanstown

KINRATNE AVE

KNOX'S GORT LANE

KINRATNE DR

GLENKEEN AVE

GLENGEEN DR

GLENGEEN DR

KNOCKLEIGH DR

KNOCKLEIGH RD

ISLYNNAGH AVE

ROSSMORE DR

HAINORAN

CARRICKMORE

PO

GDNS

Silverstream Prim Sch

Playing Field

MOYARD GDNS

BATES PK

THE GLADE

SHORELANDS GDNS

SHORE RD

A2

85

B90

ROSEMOUNT PK

MOUNT PLEASANT RD

MOUNT PLEASANT LA

JORDANSTOWN RI

MEADOWBANK LA

MEADOWLANDS

1 DOWNPATRICK GN

NEILL'S LANE

Playing Fields

KNOCKLEIGH RD

KNOCKLEIGH

SHORELANDS

OLD STONE CL

Cloch-na-larty

SHORE ROAD

2

TYNAN DR

ARDS DRIVE

ARDS

HAMPTON CT

HAMPTON CT GDNS

MOUNT PLEASANT PK

ROYAL AVE

GLENKEEN CT

GLENKEEN MANOR

WOODFIELD

WOODFIELD DR

WOODFIELD GLEN

LENAMORE DRIVE

LENAMORE AVE

LENAMORE PARK

Jordanstown Sch

Playing Fields

Playing Fields

SILVERSTREAM ROAD

University of Ulster at Jordanstown

Belfast High Sch

Belfast Lough

1

LYNDA GDNS

SYCAMORE DR

SYCAMORE PK

JORDANSTOWN ROAD

CHURCH AVENUE

LENAMORE CRES

LENAMORE GDNS

CLONAVON

CORNATION DR

VINDA FARM

LYNDA CRES

LC

RAILWAY

CORNATION

Playing Fields

JORDANSTOWN AVE

ROSS PARK

GREEN LINK

ROSS AVENUE

MEADOWBANK LA

LANGLEY

A2

SILVERSTREAM BANKS

SCHOONER CT

84

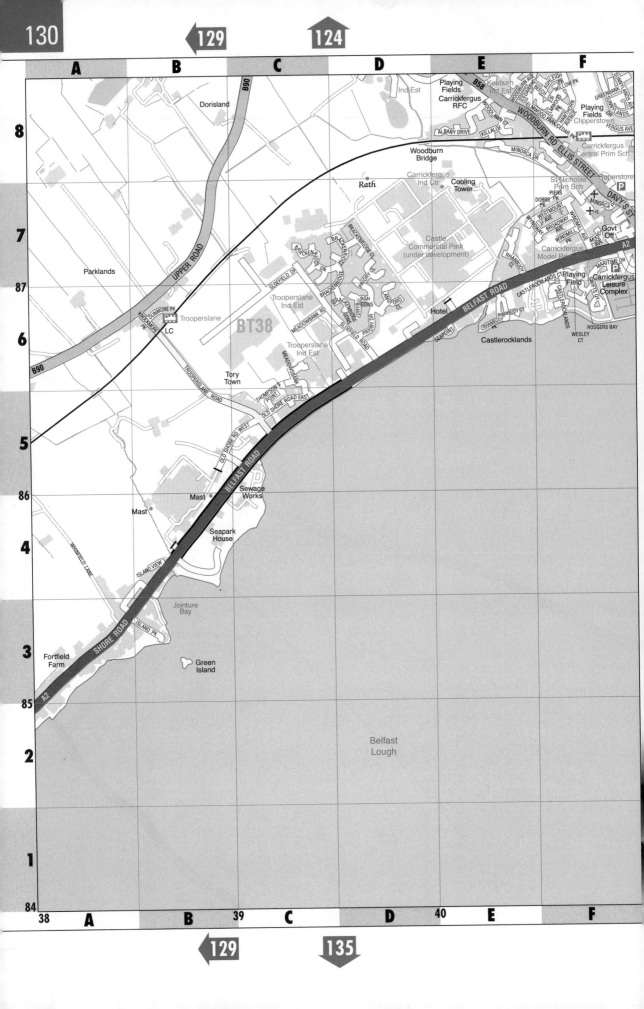

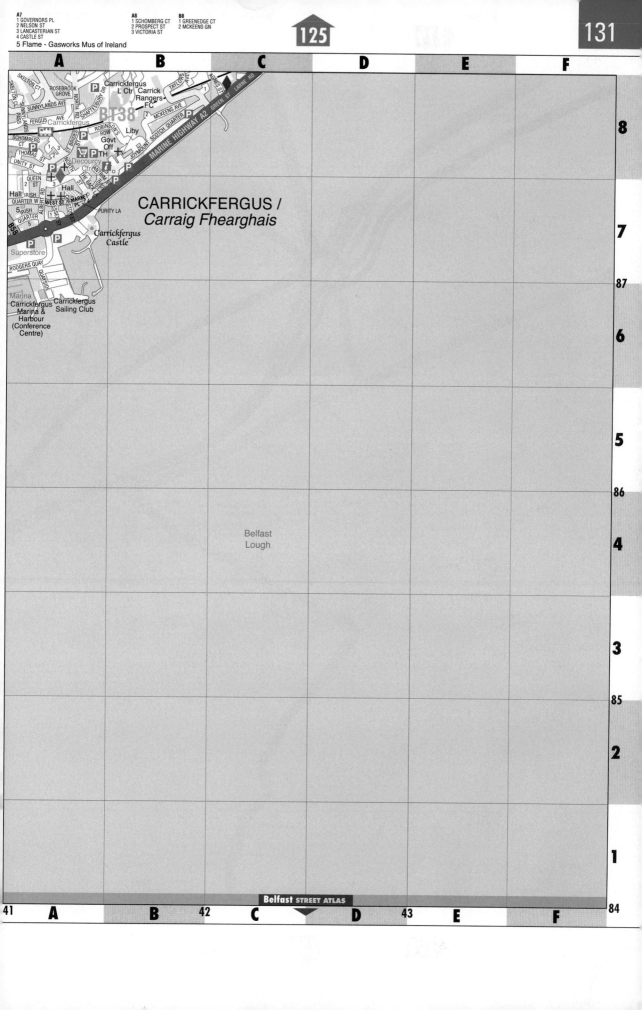

CARRICKFERGUS /
Carraig Fhearghais

Belfast
Lough

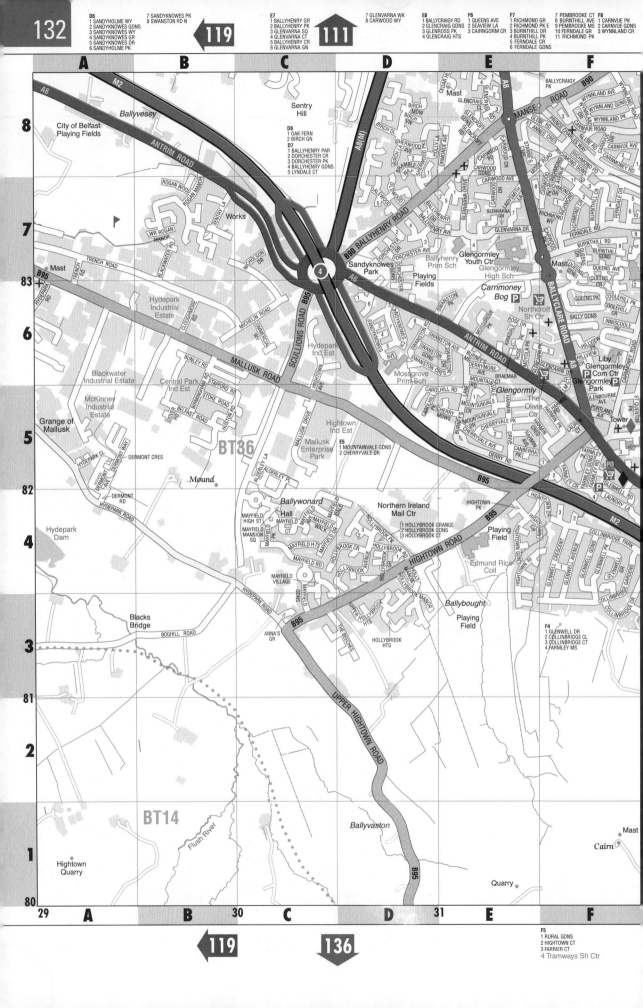

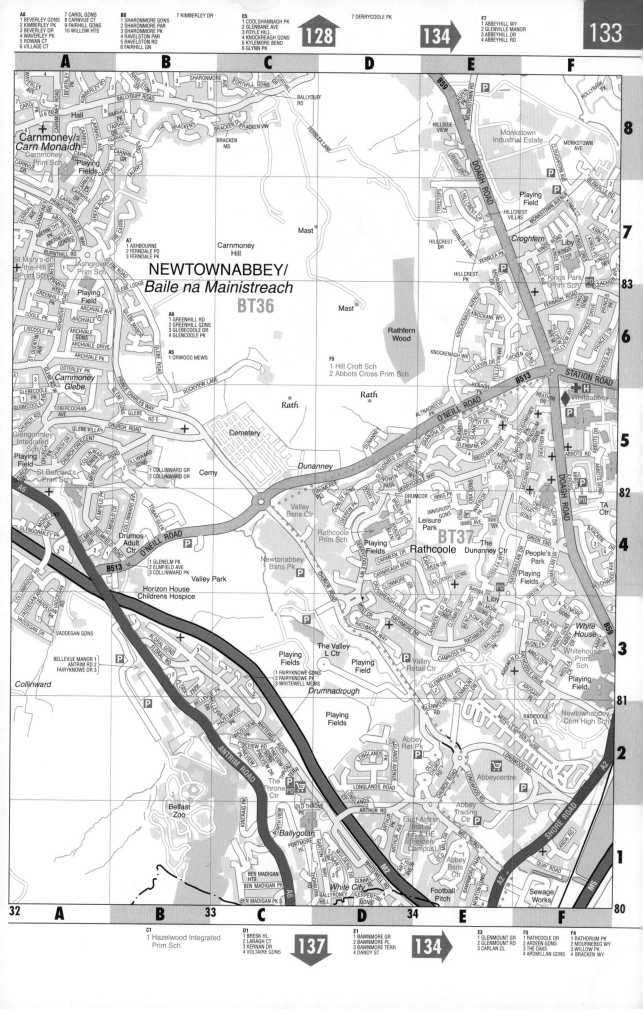

Belfast Lough

North Down Coastal Path

CLANBRASSIL ROAD
CLANBRASSIL TERR
OLD CULTRA RD
TARAWOOD
OLD DUAY RD
FARMHILL ROAD
FARMHILL
OLD CULTRA LA
OLD CULTRA RD
YC CULTRA AVE

BT18
Cultra

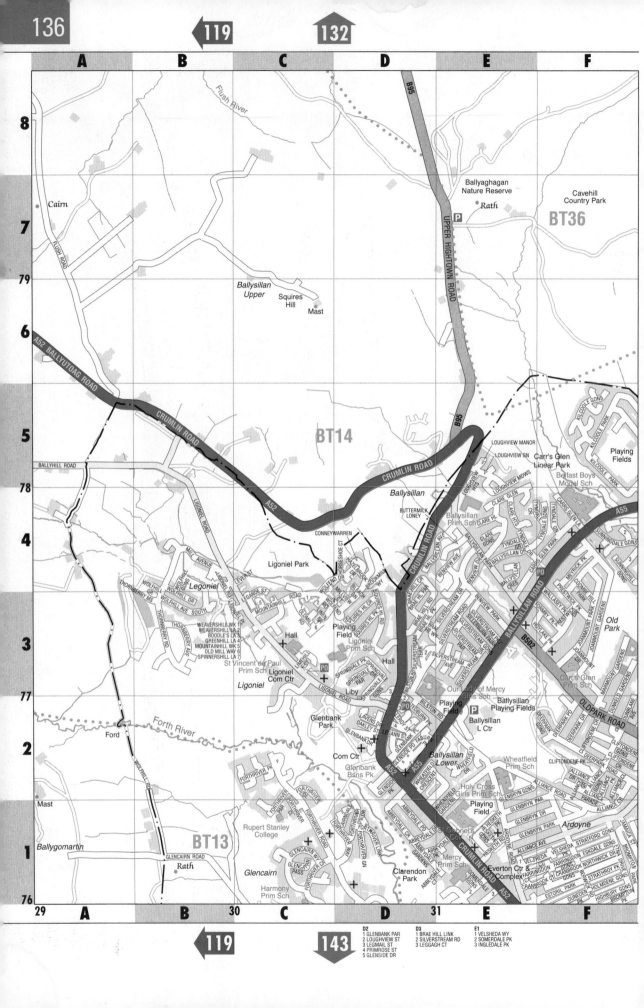

D8
1 SERPENTINE PAR
2 SERPENTINE GDNS

A B C D E F

Cave

St Clement's
Retreat House

SLIEVEGOLAND PK

BT36

Cairn

Volunteers'
Well

St Gerard's
Com Ctr

Ballygolan
Prim Sch

Liby

Belfast
Lough

McArt's
Fort

Cave Hill
Country Park

Green
Castle

Cedar
Lodge Sch

Hazelwood
Integrated
Coll

Graymount

1 GREENCASTLE CL
2 GREENCASTLE PL
3 GRAYMOUNT GR
4 GRAYMOUNT TERR

Our Lady
of Lourdes
Prim Sch

Ben Madigan
Prep Sch

Downview
Lodge

Fortwilliam
Golf Club

Gray's Lane

Loughshore
Education &
Resource Ctr

Belfast Castle
(Cave Hill
Visitor Centre)

Playing
Fields

Grove
United FC

Ballyaghagan

St Mary's
Star of the Sea
Prim Sch

DOWNVIEW
PK

DOWNVIEW AVENUE

BEN EDEN GN

DOWNVIEW MS

1 INNISFAYLE PASS
2 PARKMOUNT PASS
3 PARKMOUNT WY
4 PARKMOUNT LA
5 BEN EDEN PK
6 PARKMOUNT PL

WATERLOO
PK

WATERLOO GDNS

B5
1 MERRYFIELD DR

WATERLOO PK S

WATERLOO PARK

DONEGALL PK AVE

Loughside
Park

INNISFAYLE PARK

STRATHMORE PARK

Low-Wood

PARKMOUNT ROAD

1 SHERINGHURST PK
2 SHERINGHURST CT

Cavehill
Prim Sch

Playing
Field

LISMOYNE PK

STRATHMORE PARK S

Castle Ave

Lowwood
Prim Sch

Loughside
Recn Ctr

A55

Fort William

SLIEVEMOYNE

LANSDOWNE ROAD

Mount
Vernon
Com
House

NORTH CIRCULAR ROAD

OLD CAVEHILL ROAD

BT15

Somerton
Grange

BT3

Cliftonville
Golf Club

B4
1 WOODBURN DR
2 TOKIO GDNS
3 CHICHESTER MS

St Patrick's
Coll

Little
Flower
Girls Sch

E4
1 MOUNT VERNON PASS
2 MOUNT VERNON WLK
3 MOUNT VERNON LA
4 FORTWILLIAM CR

Dargan Road
Landfill Site

Belfast Model
Sch for Girls

CAVEHILL ROAD

1 OLD BALLYSILLAN RD
2 SUNNINGDALE GR
3 SUNNINGHILL PK

Belfast
Inst of FE & HE
Liby

St Therese
of Lisieux Prim Sch

Dominican
Carmel Coll

Fortwilliam
Youth Ctr

DARGAN ROAD

Loughside
Ind Pk

BT14

Castle
High Sch

N.I. Hospice
(Somerton
House)

Seaview
Prim Sch

Duncrue
Industrial
Estate

Quayside
Office Park

Mast

Our Lady's
Girls Prim Sch

Earthwork

Crusaders
FC & AC

DUNCRUE ST

Sewage
Works

Works

Skegoneill

Brantwood
FC

SKEGONEILL AVENUE

Liby

Mast Govt
Offs

M2 Business
Park

RICHMOND SQ 1

Dunmore
Ind Est

C4
1 CHICHESTER CT
2 CHICHESTER CL

Keadyville
Com Ctr

Cliftonville

Cliftonville
FC

LIMESTONE RD

Alexandra
Park

The Grove
Playing Fields

Grove
Prim Sch

Grove
L Ctr

Tower

Cliftonville
Prim Sch

ANTRIM ROAD

Hall

Bowling
Green

Herdman
Channel

OLDPARK ROAD

Sacred Heart
Prim Sch

Playing
Fields

LIMESTONE RD

Currie
Prim Sch

B95

Duncairn
Com Ctr

NORTH QUEEN ST

YORK ROAD

M2

A1
1 OLDPARK SQ
2 TORRENS CT
3 WYNDHAM DR

B1
1 BALLYNURE ST
2 BALLYCLARE ST
3 ARBOUR ST
4 ROSAPENNA PAR
5 SYLVAN ST
6 CHESTNUT GDNS
7 CLIFTONVILLE DR
8 CLIFTONVILLE PAR
9 ELIMGROVE ST

10 BENNETT DR
11 BROOKVALE PAR
12 Bunscoil Bheann
Mhadagain

C1
1 CLIFTONPARK AVE
2 WOODLAND AVE
3 NEWINGTON ST
4 DUNCAIRN GDNS
5 Belfast Royal Acad

C3
1 HOPEFIELD CT
2 KANSAS AVE FLATS
3 SOMERTON DR
4 FORTWILLIAM CT

D1
1 PARKMOUNT CL
2 SEAVIEW CL
3 MERVUE ST
4 MOUNTCOLLYER CL
5 CLANCHATTAN ST

D3
1 QUEEN VICTORIA GDNS
2 SEASCAPE PAR
3 FORTWILLIAM PAR
4 JELLICOE PK

E1
1 SEAVIEW ST
2 CASTLETON AVE
3 ALEXANDRA PARK AVE
4 GROVE PL

E3
1 SEAMOUNT
2 ST VINCENT ST
3 ST AUBYN ST
4 LOUGHVIEW TERR
5 NORTHWOOD CRES
6 SEAVIEW GDNS
7 SEAGROVE PAR
8 SEABANK PAR

144 138

A   B   C   D   E   F

8

7   Belfast
           Lough

79

6   Refuse
        Tip

5   HERON
                                                      AVE
78   Sydenham
        Edgewater Road   Bsns Park
     Edgewater   Harbour   HERON VIEW
     Bsns Pk WEST BANK ROAD   Lagoon
Low-Wood   WEST BANK DL   HERON ROAD
  Intake   Airport Road West
4   DARGAN RD   Belfast Harbour   Mast Belfast Lough
     Round Tower Ind Est   Reserve   Tower
DARGAN CRESCENT

     Commericial Park Liverpool
Fortwilliam Ferry Terminal   Portside
  Ind Est Westbank   Bsns Park   Tower
Council   Dargan Bsns Park   Tower
Offices   Ind Park Heysham   BT3   Tower
Bayview   Quayside Ferry Terminal
Ind Park Office Park   Loughview
     Loughside   Sydenham   Bsns Park
3   Ind Park Graham   Intake
            Ind Park Tower   MOSCOW ROAD

          HERDMAN CHANNEL ROAD
77 Somerton Sewage
    Ind Park Works   Mast
          Light
          Tower   George Best
HERDMAN CHANNEL ROAD   Belfast City
2   Airport   P

     Herdman West Twin   Works
     Channel Island
          MCCAUGHEY ROAD   P   DEPOT ROAD
          Victoria Channel East
STORMONT RD WORKMAN ROAD Twin   Musgrave Channel   SYDENHAM BY-PASS
SINCLAIR RD   EAST TWIN ROAD Island   Airport   Sydenham
1   Tower THOMPSON WHARF RD WOLFF ROAD Mast Works Terminal Playing
                                AIRPORT ROAD   A2   Fields
76   P   BT4
35   A   B   36   C   D   37   E   F

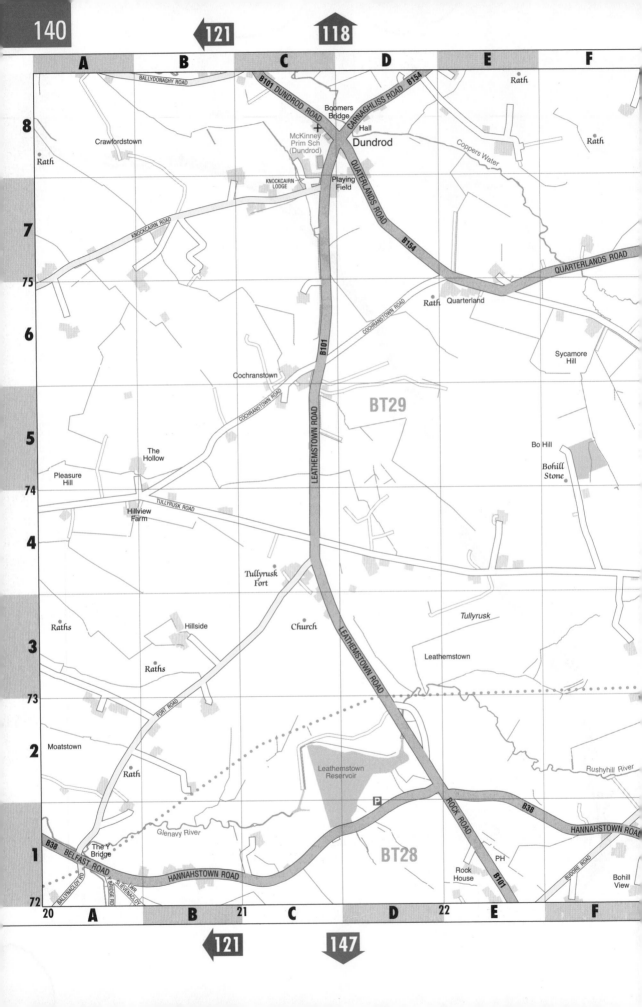

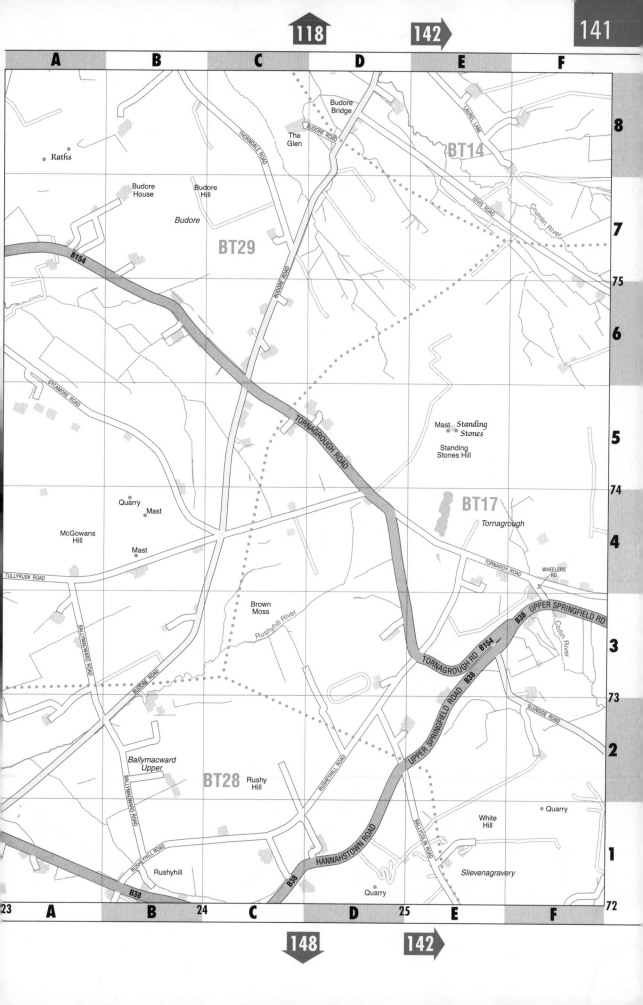

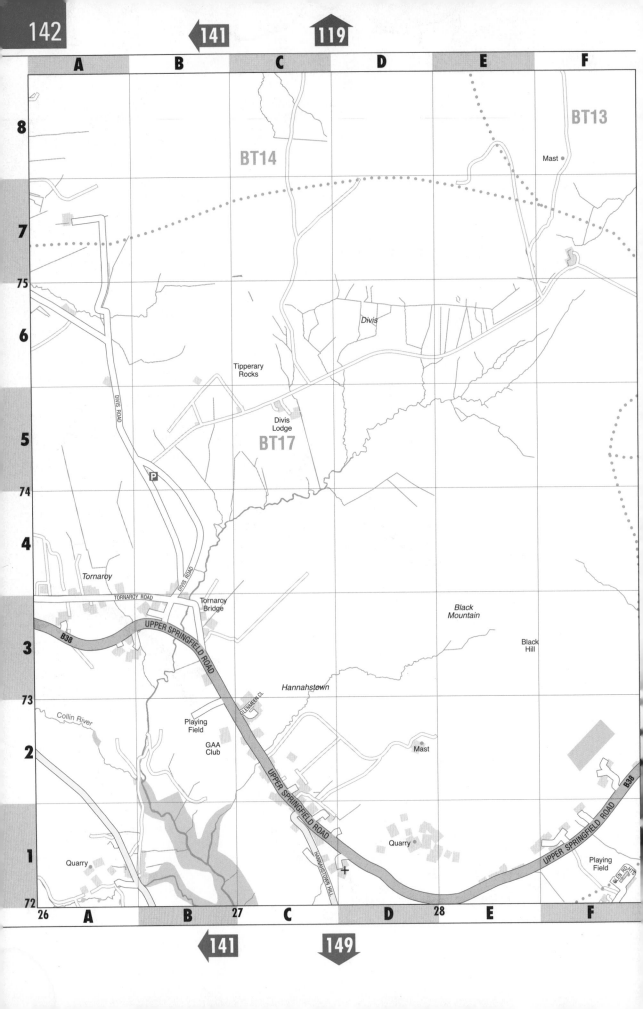

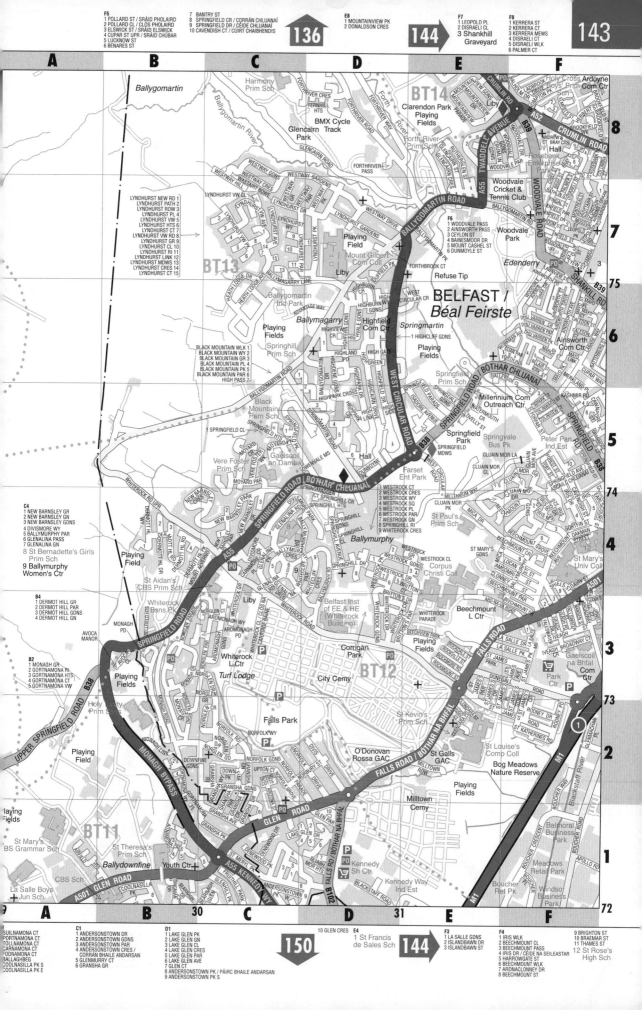

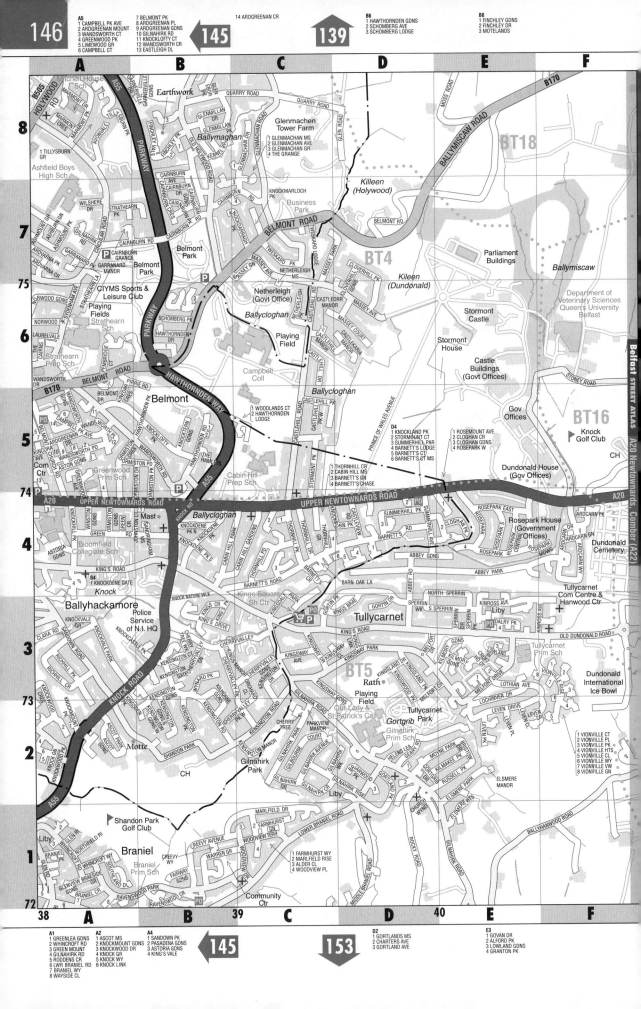

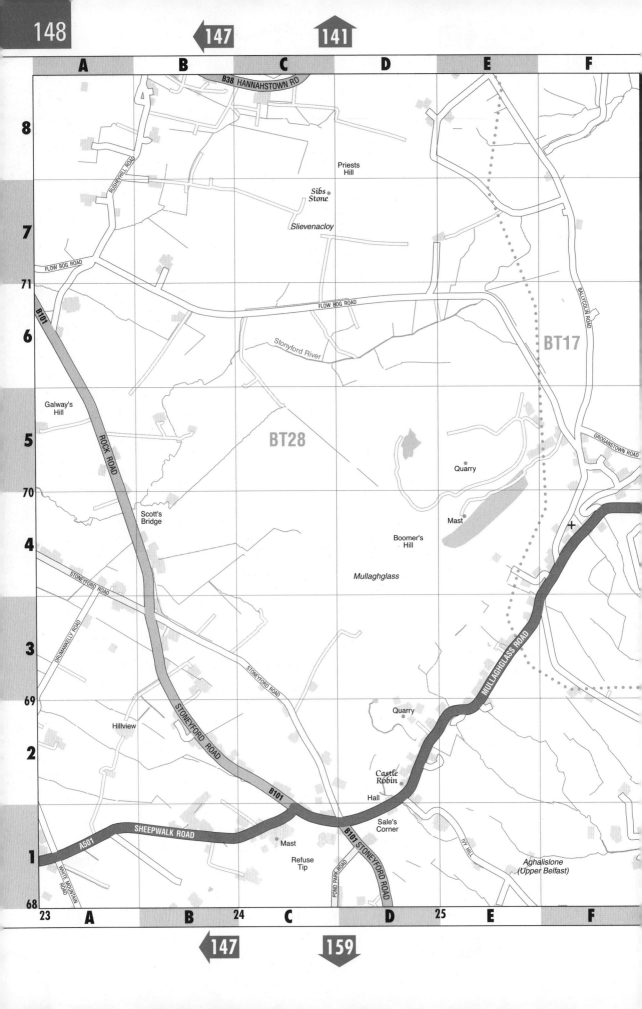

A B C D E F

8

Priests
Hill

Sibs
Stone

Slievenacloy

7

RUSHEY HILL ROAD

FLOW BOG ROAD

71

B101

Flow Bog Road

6

BT17

BALLYCOLIN ROAD

Stonyford River

Galway's
Hill

ROCK ROAD

BT28

5

Quarry

GROGANSTOWN ROAD

70

Scott's
Bridge

Mast

4

STONEYFORD ROAD

Boomer's
Hill

DRUMANKELLY ROAD

Mullaghglass

3

STONEYFORD ROAD

MULLAGHGLASS ROAD

69

Hillview

STONEYFORD ROAD

Quarry

2

Castle
Robin

Hall

B101

Sale's
Corner

SHEEPWALK ROAD

IVY HILL

A501

B101 STONEYFORD ROAD

Mast

Aghalislone
(Upper Belfast)

1

Refuse
Tip

WHITE MOUNTAIN ROAD

POND PARK ROAD

68

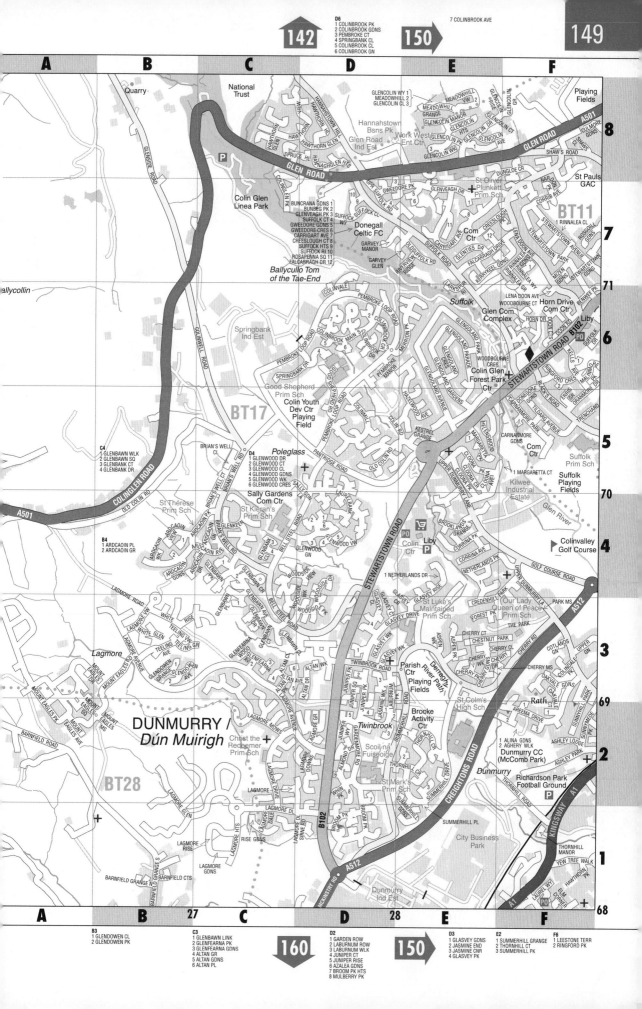

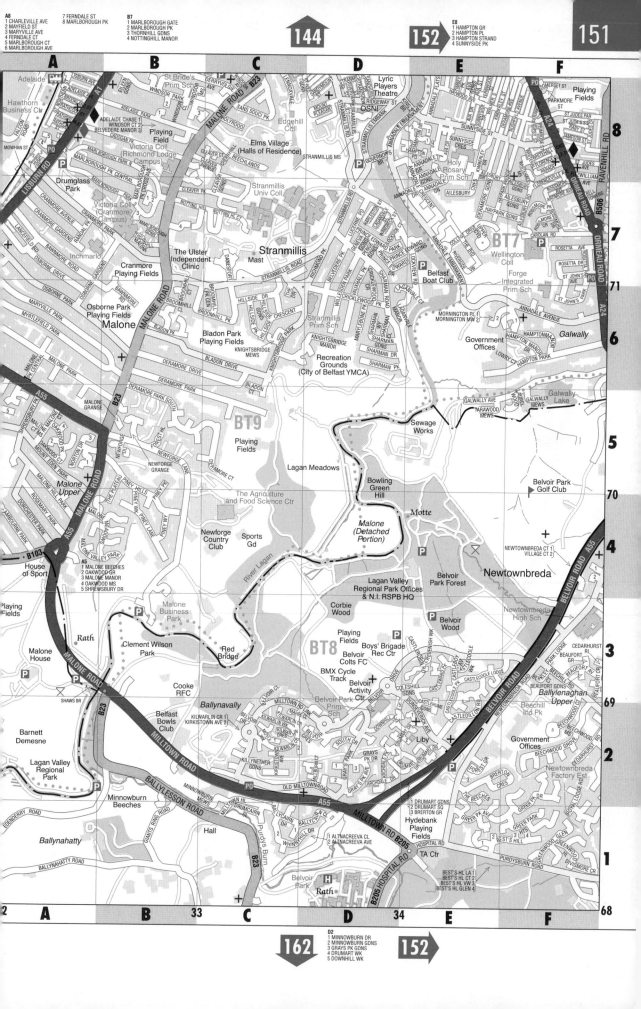

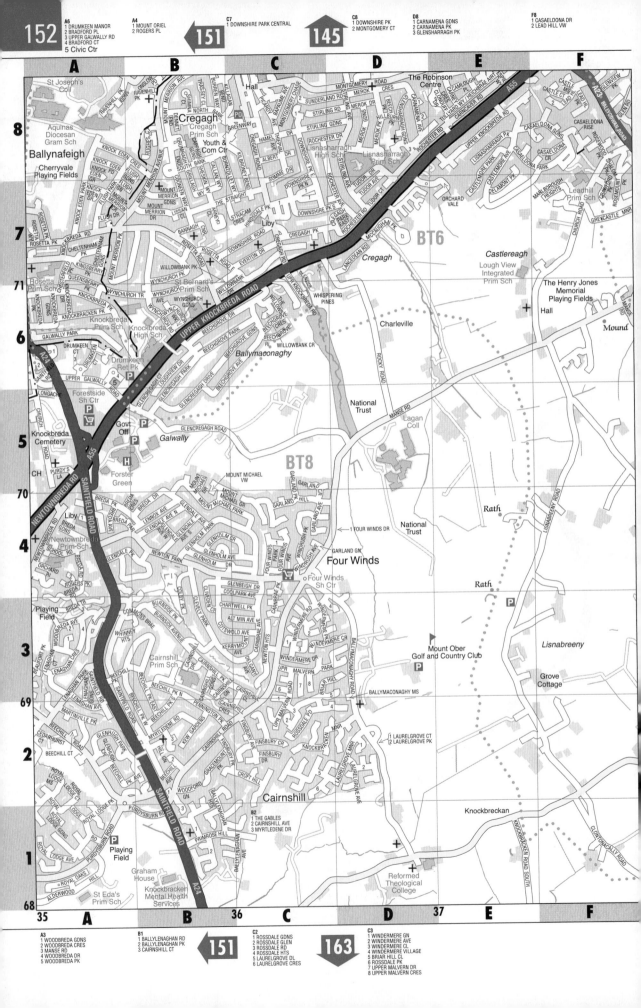

A   B   C   D   E   F

8

7

71

6

5

70

4

3

69

2

1

8   A   B   39   C   D   40   E   F   68

Ballyhanwood

Lower Braniel Road
GLENVIEW DR
CORMORANT PK
WOODCROFT HTS
WOODCROFT RISE
SHANDON HTS
GLENVIEW GDNS
GLENVIEW AVE
CASTLE GRANGE
GLENVIEW CRES
FRIAR'S H
CASTLE

Gilnahirk Rd W

Gilnahirk Road

QUARRY HILL

MIDDLE BRANIEL ROAD

Braniel

Rocky Road

CH

Mast

Gilnahirk

BALLYGOWAN ROAD

BT5

UPPER BRANIEL ROAD

Gilnahirk
Golf Club

MANN'S ROAD

Rath

71

Knockbreda
FC

The
Thorn

BT5

Lisleen Road

EDEN RD

RYAN PK

Slatady

SCHOOL ROAD

MANN'S ROAD

Beechmount

P

Roselawn
Crematorium

A23 BALLYGOWAN ROAD

Roselawn
Cemetery

Thorndale

70

LISLEEN ROAD EAST

Alderside

LISMAGREEN ROAD EAST

School Rd

4

FORD CRES
ILFORD PK
ILFORD AVE
HOUSTON RD
ILFORD DR
ILFORD RD

Crossnacreevy

Lisleen

BT23

3

BT6

LISLEEN ROAD

Lisleen

LISLEEN RD E

69

KNOCKBRACKEN ROAD

GRANSHA ROAD

Maryland
Ind Est

2

MERRYLAND
CROSS ROADS

MONEYREAGH ROAD

Threetown
Bridge

BALLYKEEL ROAD

LISLEEN ROAD SOUTH

1

BT8

A23

A23 Ballygowan

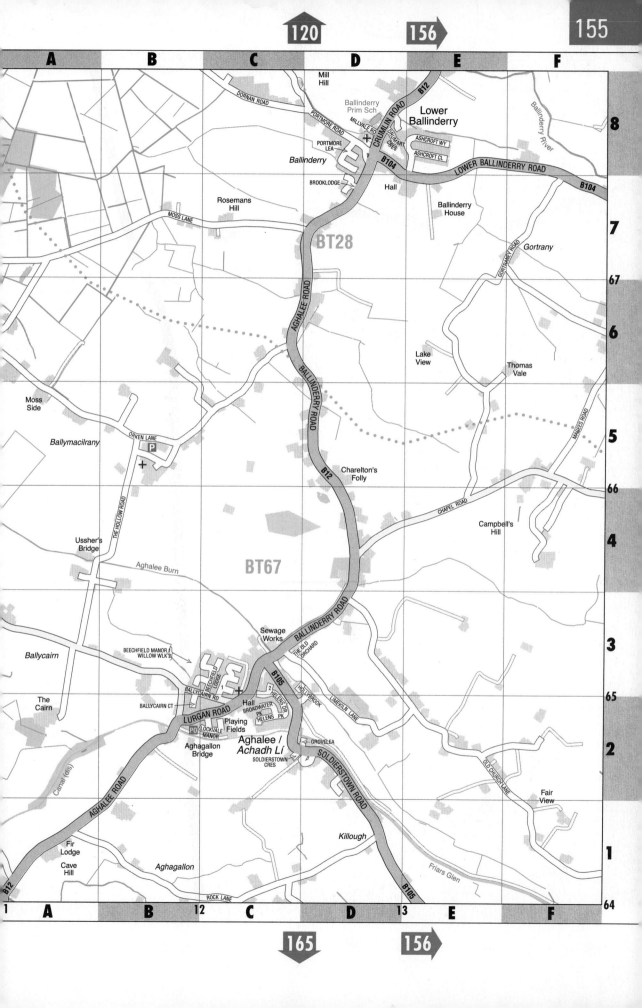

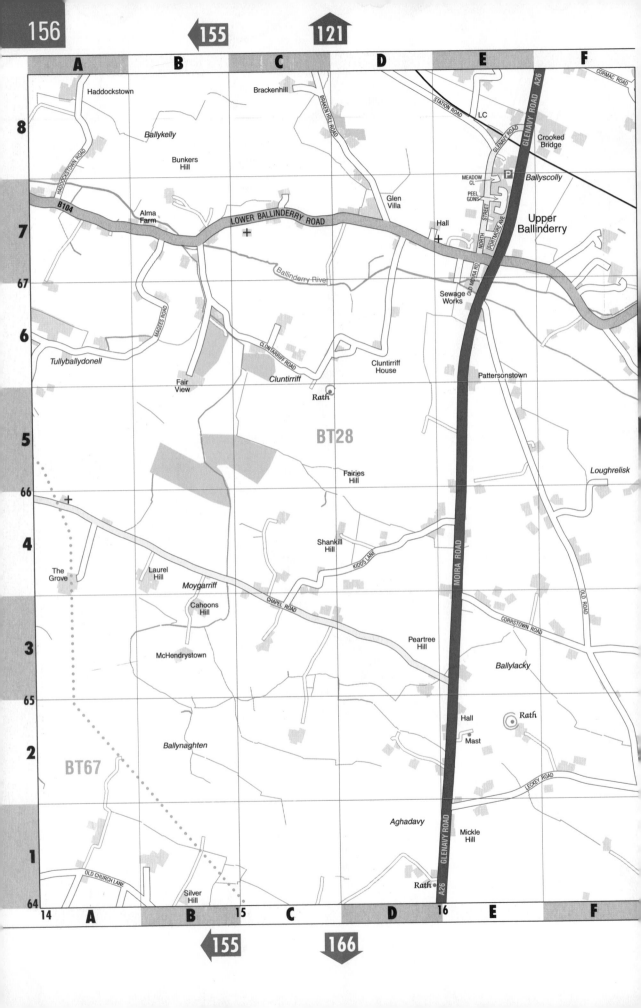

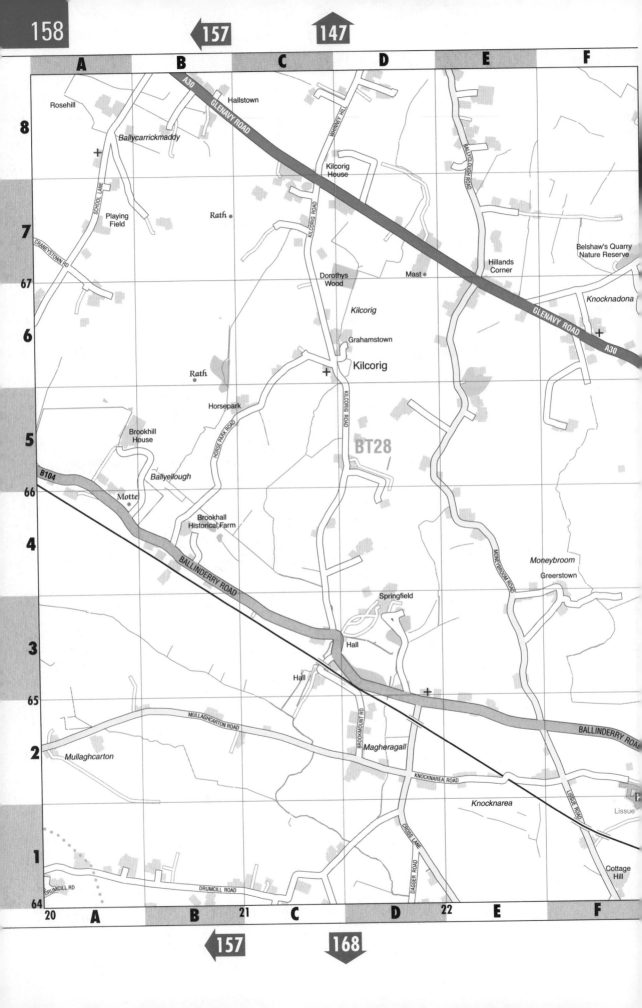

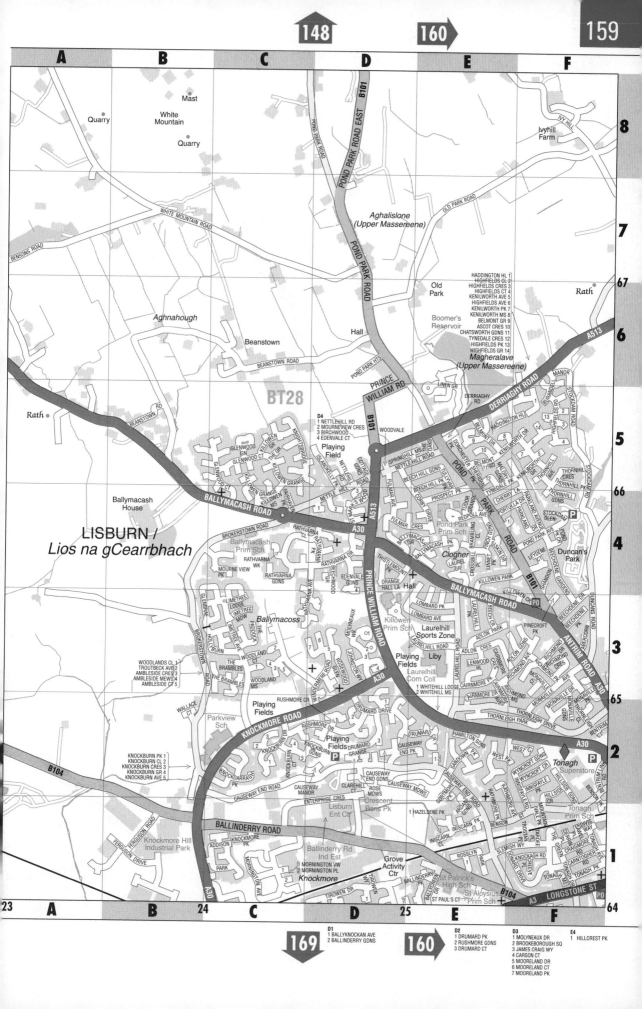

A B C D E F

8
67
7
6
5
66
4
3
65
2
1
64

Quarry
Mast
White Mountain
Quarry

Ivyhill Farm

WHITE MOUNTAIN ROAD

BENSONS ROAD

Aghnahough

Beanstown

Hall

Aghalislone
(Upper Massereene)

Old Park Road

Rath

POND PARK ROAD EAST
B101

POND PARK ROAD

Old Park

Boomer's Reservoir

HADDINGTON HL 1
HIGHFIELDS CL 2
HIGHFIELDS CRES 3
HIGHFIELDS CT 4
KENILWORTH AVE 5
HIGHFIELDS AVE 6
KENILWORTH PK 7
KENILWORTH MS 8
BELMONT GR 9
ASCOT CRES 10
CHATSWORTH GDNS 11
TYNEDALE CRES 12
HIGHFIELDS PK 13
HIGHFIELDS GR 14

Magheralave
(Upper Massereene)

A513

Rath

BEANSTOWN ROAD

Beanstown

BT28

POND PARK HTS

PRINCE WILLIAM RD

B101

Woodvale

DERRIAGHY ROAD

Linen GR

Derriaghy Rd

MANOR
STOCKDAM ROAD

D4
1 NETTLEHILL RD
2 MOURNEVIEW CRES
3 BIRCHWOOD
4 EDENVALE CT

Playing Field

BALLYMACASH ROAD

Rath

Ballymacash House

LISBURN /
Lios na gCearrbhach

BROKERSTOWN ROAD

Ballymacash Prim Sch

RATHVARNA WK

RATHVARNA PK
MOURNE VIEW PK
RATHVARNA GDNS

Ballymacoss

GLENBRAE
LIMETREE LODGE
LIMETREE MDW
THE PADDOCK
HOLLYBURN
WOODLAND CT
THE BRAMBLES
WOODLAND MS
THE BRAMBLES

WOODLANDS CL 1
TROUTBECK AVE 2
AMBLESIDE CRES 3
AMBLESIDE MEWS 4
AMBLESIDE CT 5

WALLACE CT

Parkview Sch

KNOCKMORE ROAD

Playing Fields

RUSHMORE CR

B104

Knockmore Hill Industrial Park

FERGUSON DRIVE

ADDISON
KNOCKMORE PK

KNOCKBURN PK 1
KNOCKBURN CL 2
KNOCKBURN CRES 3
KNOCKBURN GR 4
KNOCKBURN AVE 5

KNOCKDARRAS

CAUSEWAY END ROAD

CAUSEWAY MANOR

ENTERPRISE CRES

Lisburn Ent Ctr

BALLINDERRY ROAD

MORNINGTON AVE

PARK

A30

Ballinderry Rd Ind Est

1 MORNINGTON VW
2 MORNINGTON PL

Knockmore

TIROWEN DR

Grove Activity Ctr

A30

GLENWOOD GN
GLENWOOD CT

KILLOWEN GR
THE DR
GLENWOOD CT

KILLOWEN GRANGE
KILLOWEN MS
FAIRHAVEN
KILLOWEN GRANGE

KNIGHTSBRIDGE

NETTLEHILL ROAD
COTTAGE GDNS

SPRINGHILL MS THE OAKS
NETTLE HILL RD

A513

BECKERS WOOD

NETTLE HILL RD
BEECH HILL GDNS
CORBY DRIVE
PROSPECT PK

SHERIDAN
DORCHESTER
SPRINGHILL

FULMAR AVE

FULMAR CRES

BELMONT DR
BELMONT DR

TILLYARD
TUDOR
REDPOLL AVE

Pond Park Prim Sch

BRAMBLING

FINCH
CROSSBILL
LINNET

KENILWORTH DR

KENILWORTH PK

CHERRY LA
PORTULLA PK
PARKLAND AVE
PARKLAND
PARKLAND

THORNHILL CRES
THORNHILL PK
THORNHILL GDNS

BRANDEL

STOCKDAM GLEN

STOCKDAM ROAD

HIGHFIELDS

POND PARK ROAD

LEYDENE CT

BECCROFT DR

Duncan's Park

P

BALLYMACASH RD
BALLYMACASH PK

Clogher

KILLOWEN PARK

KILLOWEN CR PO

BALLYMACASH ROAD

ANTRIM ROAD

BEECHDENE DR
BECCHDENE
BECCHDENE GDNS

DUNCANS ROAD

RATHVARNA CL
RATHVARNA
RATHVARNA DR
RATHVARNA
BEECHWOOD GR

EDENVALE GDNS

PRINCE WILLIAM ROAD

THISTLEMOUNT
ORANGE HALL LA
LAUREL
Hall

LOMBARD PK
LOMBARD AVE

Killowen Prim Sch

Laurelhill Sports Zone

LAURELHILL ROAD

Playing Fields

Liby

Laurelhill Com Coll

LAUREL
BEECH

LAURELHILL

ADLON PARK
ADLON CRES
ADLON

PINECROFT

CAIRNMORE

LENWOOD GDNS
CAIRNMORE
CAIRNMORE DR
CAIRNMORE GDNS

RICHMOND GDNS
RICHMOND
RICHMOND CRES
RICHMOND CT

MONAVILLE GDNS
MONAVILLE

MONAVILLE AVE
MONAVILLE
THORNLEIGH

A30

BENTRIM

THORNLEIGH PARK
THORNLEIGH DRIVE

1 WHITEHALL LODGE
2 WHITEHALL MS

65

WINDERMERE ROAD

JOHNSTON
MOLYNEAUX WK

ROSEWOOD GLEN

RUSHMORE CR

DRUMARD DRIVE

HAMILTON GDNS

WEST PK
WEST

SANDOWN

WYNCROFT GDNS
WYNCROFT CR
INNISFAYLE
INNISFAYLE CR

HILLSIDE GDNS
HILLSIDE
CR

BENSON

BENTRIM LINK

RATHMORE AVE
RATHMORE PK

Tonagh Superstore

P

Tonagh Prim Sch

KNOCKBURN
KNOCKBURN GDNS

Playing Fields

P

DRUMARD GRANGE

CAUSEWAY END PK

CAUSEWAY END GDNS
CAUSEWAY MDWS

CLAREHILL
ROSE MDWS
CT

Crescent Bsns Pk

1 HAZELDENE PK

RATHMORE AVE
TROSNAGH
RATHMORE VALE PK

INISCARN
INISCARN CR

DORTMORE GDNS
ARDANE GDNS
BENSON

ROSSLYN PARK

SLEMISH WY

KNOCKAGH RD

DIVIS
CONLIG
DRIVE

TONAGH
TONAGH
THE GREEN
CRAIGMORE
CARNTOGHER

LONGSTONE ST

A3
B104

St Patrick's High Sch
St Aloysius' Prim Sch
St Paul's CT

BALLINDERRY

Ballinderry

64

169
D1
1 BALLYKNOCKAN AVE
2 BALLINDERRY GDNS

160
D2
1 DRUMARD PK
2 RUSHMORE GDNS
3 DRUMARD CT

D3
1 MOLYNEAUX DR
2 BROOKEBOROUGH SQ
3 JAMES CRAIG WY
4 CARSON CT
5 MOORELAND DR
6 MOORELAND CT
7 MOORELAND PK

E4
1 HILLCREST PK

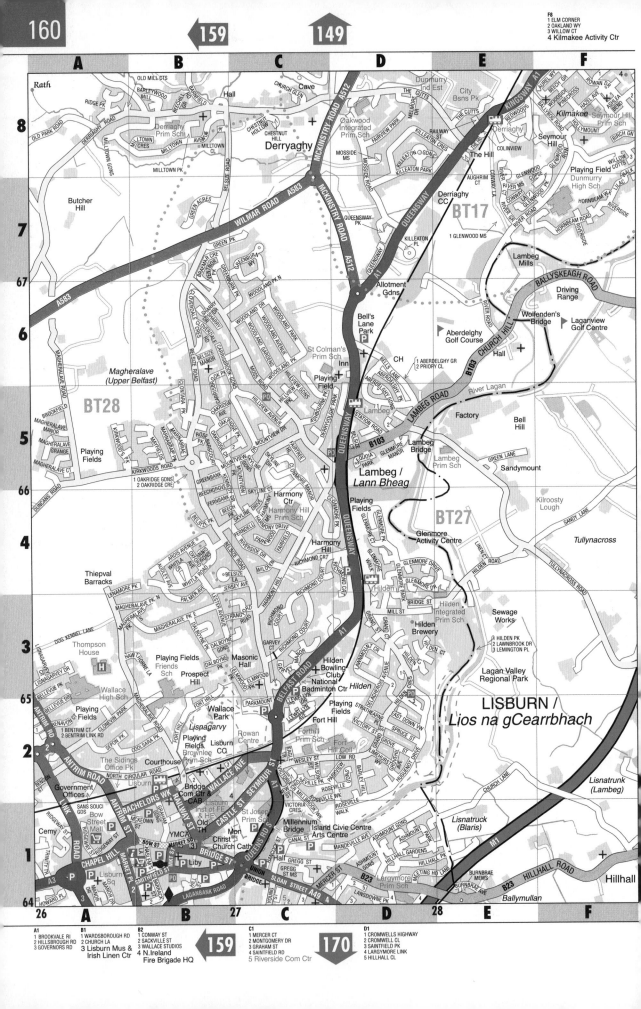

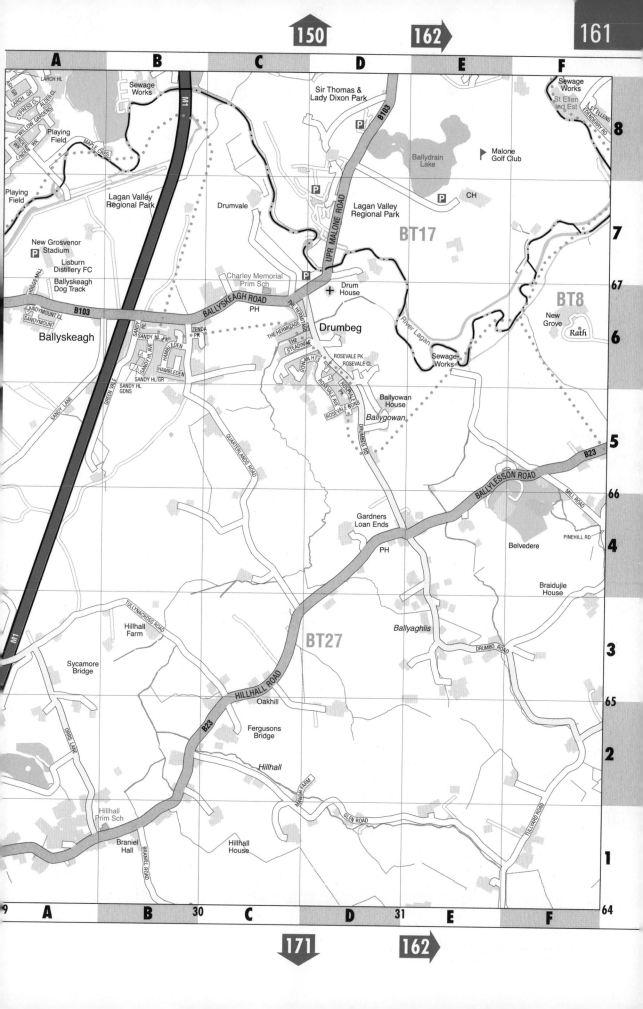

A **B** **C** **D** **E** **F**

Giants Ring
Earthwork and
Chambered Grave

Edenderry

EDENDERRY RD

PINEHILL ROAD

BALLYLESSON ROAD

BALLYNAHATTY RD

B23

Belvoir Park

H

HOSPITAL ROAD

B205

Beechwood

Govt
Offs

Ballydollaghan

Scoot
Hill

Purdysburn

PURDYSBURN HILL

BALLYCOAN ROAD

Purdys Burn

Ballylesson

LAGANVALLEY
HTS

FORT
RD

B205

Ballycowan

Moorcrofts
Milltown

Black
Bridge

B23

Ballycarn

FORT ROAD

BT8

Hall

BALLYLESSON ROAD

Drumbo
Rectory

Rath

BALLYCOAN ROAD

MOORCROFT ROAD

DOWS ROAD

Waterfall

MEALOUGH ROAD

BALLYMAGARRICK ROAD

Round
Tower

PINEWOOD
PK

Drumbo

GLENSIDE AVE

GLENSIDE PK

Sewage
Works

Mast

DRUMBO RD

PINEHILL RD

BACK ROAD

CHESTNUT
LODGE

Leveroge

LEVEROGUE ROAD

Drumbo
Prim Sch

TITTERINGTON
GDNS

Playing
Field

BT27

FRONT ROAD

THE COOPER

Rural
Cottage

8 **7** **67** **6** **5** **66** **4** **3** **65** **2** **1** **64**

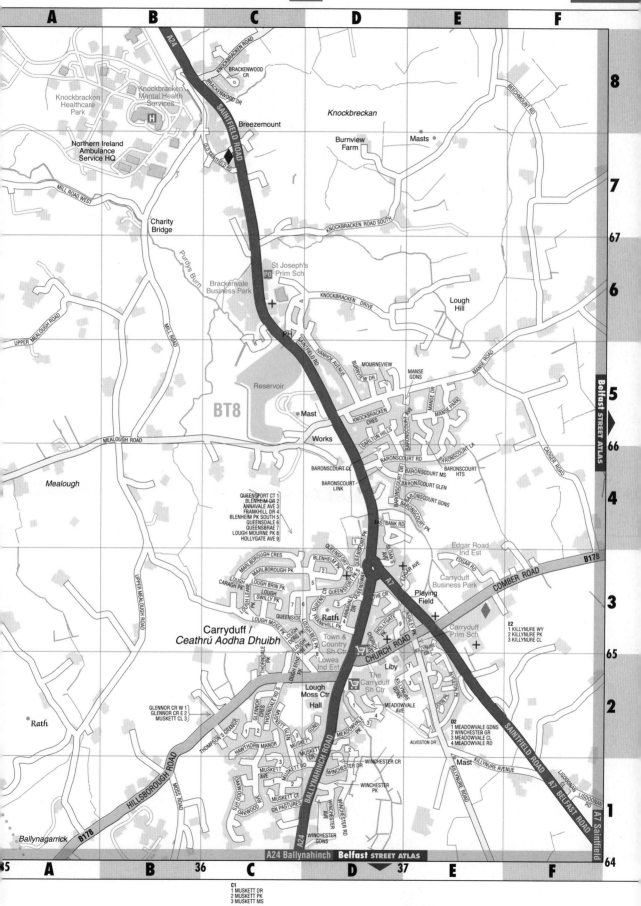

Knockbracken Healthcare Park

Knockbracken Mental Health Services

H

Northern Ireland Ambulance Service HQ

MILL ROAD WEST

Charity Bridge

Purdy's Burn

Brackenvale Business Park

UPPER MEALOUGH ROAD

MILL ROAD

Reservoir

BT8

Mast

Works

Mealough

MEALOUGH ROAD

UPPER MEALOUGH ROAD

Rath

A24

BRACKENWOOD ROAD

BRACKENWOOD CR

BRACKENWOOD DR

Breezemount

OLD SAINTFIELD RD

SAINTFIELD ROAD

Knockbreckan

Burnview Farm

Masts

Lough Hill

KNOCKBRACKEN ROAD SOUTH

St Joseph's Prim Sch

PO

KNOCKBRACKEN DRIVE

SAINTFIELD RD

PH

IVANHOE AVENUE

MOURNEVIEW

BURNVIEW DR

MANSE GDNS

MANSE DR

MANSE ROAD

MANSE PARK

BARONSCOURT AVE

Knockbracken Cres

CARLTON HILLS

BARONSCOURT DR

BARONSCOURT RD

BARONSCOURT LA

BARONSCOURT MS

BARONSCOURT HTS

BARONSCOURT CL

BARONSCOURT GLEN

BARONSCOURT GDNS

BARONSCOURT LINK

BARONSCOURT PK

BEECHMOUNT RD

CADGER ROAD

Belfast STREET ATLAS

QUEENSFORT CT 1
BLENHEIM DR 2
ANNAVALE AVE 3
FRANKHILL DR 4
BLENHEIM PK SOUTH 5
QUEENSDALE 6
QUEENSBRAE 7
LOUGH MOURNE PK 8
HOLLYGATE AVE 9

EASTBANK RD

QUEENSFORT RD

QUEENSFORT PK

BLENHEIM PK

MARLBOROUGH CRES

MARLBOROUGH PK

LOUGH BRIN PK

LOUGH LEANE

LOUGH CARAGH PK

LOUGH SWILLY PK

LOUGH MOSS PK

QUEENSIDE

LOUGH BEG PK

LOUGH ERNE PK

LOUGH DERG PK

QUEENSWAY

QUEENSCR

THE CR

STAN'S AVE

A7

EDGAR AVE

Edgar Road Ind Est

EDGAR RD

Carryduff Business Park

COMBER ROAD

B178

E2
1 KILLYNURE WY
2 KILLYNURE PK
3 KILLYNURE CL

Playing Field

Carryduff Prim Sch

ASHLEY PK

Rath

FRANKHILL PK

Carryduff /
Ceathrú Aodha Dhuibh

Town & Country Sh Ctr

Lowes Ind Est

CHURCH ROAD

Liby

HOLLYGATE

CHURCH AVE

KILLYNURE

KILLYNURE GDNS

KILLYNURE PK

The Carryduff Sh Ctr

MEADOWVALE AVE

ALVESTON PK

THORNDALE PK

GLENNOR CRES

THORNDALE GLEN

THORNDALE RD S

MUSKETT GDNS

MEADOWVALE PK

MEADOWVALE

ALVESTON DR

D2
1 MEADOWVALE GDNS
2 WINCHESTER GR
3 MEADOWVALE CL
4 MEADOWVALE RD

Lough Moss Ctr Hall

GLENNOR CR W 1
GLENNOR CR E 2
MUSKETT CL 3

THOMPSON'S GRANGE

HAWTHORN MANOR

MUSKETT RD S

MUSKETT AVE

MUSKETT CT

OAKWOOD HTS

OAKWOOD AVE

GN PASTURES

HILLSBOROUGH ROAD

MOSS ROAD

B178

Ballynagarrick

BALLYNAHINCH ROAD

A24

WINCHESTER DR

WINCHESTER CR

WINCHESTER PK

WINCHESTER RD

WINCHESTER AVE

WINCHESTER GDNS

Mast

KILLYNURE ROAD

KILLYNURE AVENUE

SAINTFIELD ROAD

A7 BELFAST ROAD

LISDOONAN RD

LISDOONAN CL

A7 Saintfield

C1
1 MUSKETT DR
2 MUSKETT PK
3 MUSKETT MS

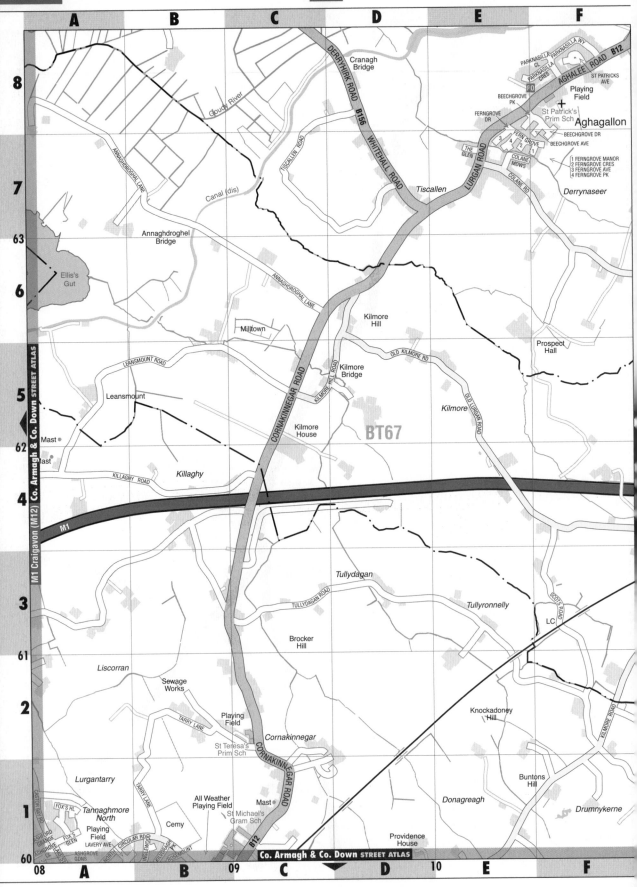

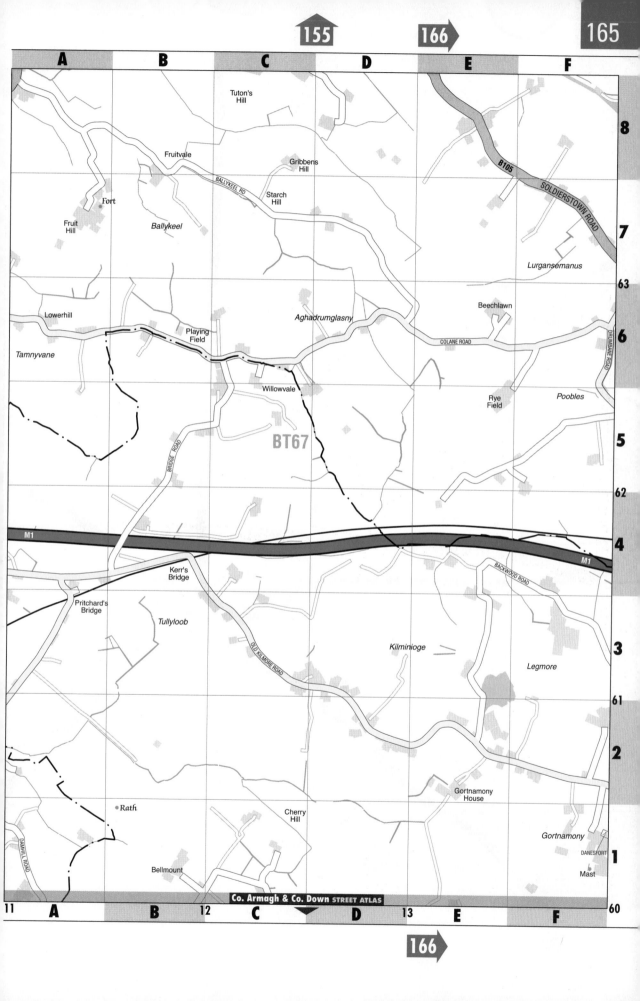

A   B   C   D   E   F

8
7
63
6
5
62
4
61
2
1
60

Tuton's
Hill

Fruitvale

Gribbens
Hill

BALLYKEEL RD

Starch
Hill

Fort

Fruit
Hill

Ballykeel

B105

SOLDIERSTOWN ROAD

Lurgansemanus

Lowerhill

Aghadrumglasny

Beechlawn

Playing
Field

COLANE ROAD

DRUMBANE ROAD

Tamnyvane

Willowvale

Rye
Field

Poobles

BRIDGE ROAD

BT67

M1

M1

Kerr's
Bridge

Pritchard's
Bridge

Tullyloob

OLD KILMORE ROAD

Kilminioge

BACKWOOD ROAD

Legmore

DAMHILL ROAD

Rath

Cherry
Hill

Gortnamony
House

Gortnamony

DANESFORT

Bellmount

Mast

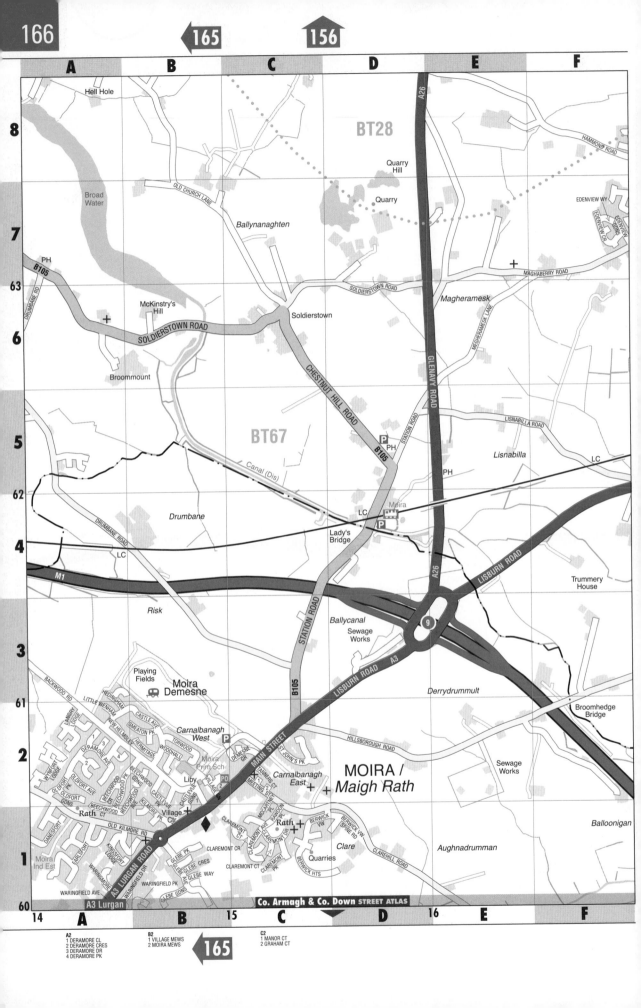

A · B · C · D · E · F

Hell Hole

BT28

Broad Water

Old Church Lane

Ballynanaghten

Quarry Hill

Quarry

EDENVIEW WY

EDENVIEW GDNS

EDENVIEW CR

PH

B105

DRUMBANE RD

McKinstry's Hill

SOLDIERSTOWN ROAD

Soldierstown

SOLDIERSTOWN ROAD

Magheramesk

MAGHABERRY ROAD

MAGHERAMESK LANE

GLENAVY ROAD

Broommount

BT67

CHESTNUT HILL ROAD

B105

STATION ROAD

PH

LISNABILLA ROAD

Lisnabilla

PH

LC

Canal (Dis)

Drumbane

DRUMBANE ROAD

LC

Moira

Lady's Bridge

M1

LC

LISBURN ROAD

Trummery House

Risk

STATION ROAD

Ballycanal

Sewage Works

9

A26

A3

LISBURN ROAD

Derrydrummult

Broomhedge Bridge

Playing Fields

Moira Demesne

BACKWOOD RD

LITTLE WENHAM

HEDINGHAM

LANGRY LODGE

DERAMORE AVE

WYNFORD LODGE

OLDFORT

OLDFORT AVE

CASTLE AVE

NEW HELMSLEY

SMEATON PK

HERMITAGE

TORWOOD

WOODHALL

Carnalbanagh West

B105

Moira Prim Sch

DEMESNE GR

TANNERS CT

ST JOHN'S PK

Carnalbanagh East

MAIN STREET

HILLSBOROUGH ROAD

Sewage Works

MOIRA / Maigh Rath

BEECHWOOD

BEECHWOOD PK

BEECHWOOD GDNS

BEECHWOOD

CASTEVE

KILMORE PK

Liby

Village Ctr

PO

MEETING ST

CASTLEVUE

CASTLEVUE PK

MCCATSON

BANDON CT

MCCATSON PK

Rath CT

OLD KILMORE RD

Rath

BERWICK VW

BERWICK VW

BERWICK SPINE RD

Clare

Balloonigan

DANESFORT

EARLSFORT

KINGSFORT LODGE

WARINGMORE

A3 LURGAN ROAD

Moira Ind Est

WARINGFIELD AVE

WARINGFIELD PK

WARINGFIELD DR

GLEBE GDNS

GLEBE PK

GLEBE AVE

GLEBE CRES

GLEBE WAY

CLAREMONT CR

CLAREMONT CT

CLAREMONT AVE

CLAREMONT TCE

CLAREMONT PK

Quarries

BERWICK HTS

CLAREHILL ROAD

Aughnadrumman

A3 Lurgan

Co. Armagh & Co. Down STREET ATLAS

14 · A · 15 · B · C · 16 · D · E · F

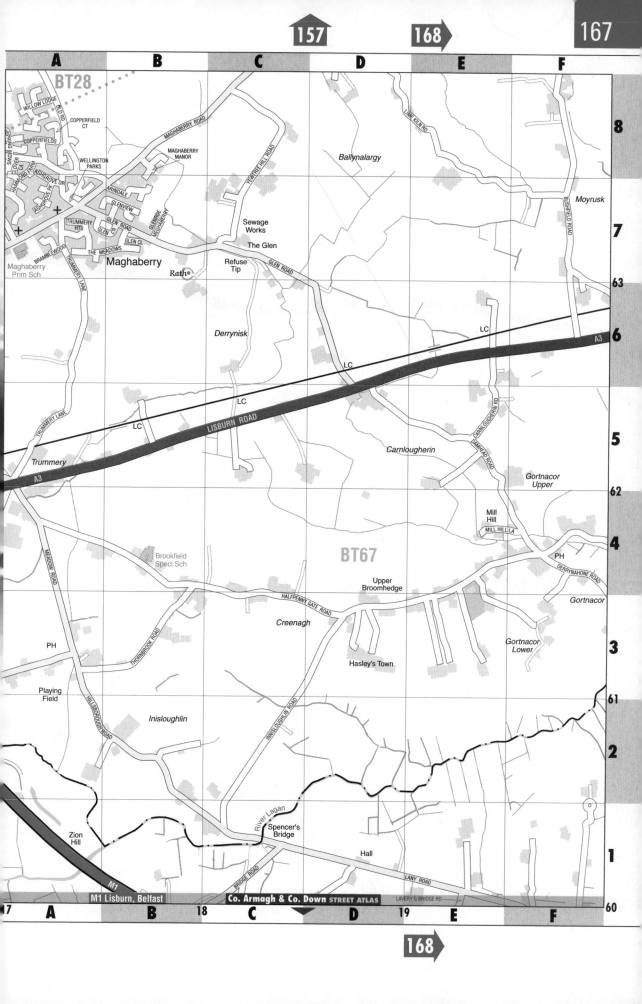

BT28

A B C D E F

8
7
63
6
5
62
4
3
61
2
1
60

Willow Lodge
Old Rd
Copperfield
CT
Copperfields
Wellington Parks
Maghaberry Road
Maghaberry Manor

Yewtree Hill Road

Lime Kiln Rd

Moyrusk

Ballynalargy

Bushfield Road

Smithswondeni
Clover
Arindale
Ashgrove Dr
Ashgrove Pk
Hammond Farm
Glenview
Glen Road
Glen Cr
Glenmore Meghaberry
Glen Cl
Trummery HTS
The Meadows

Sewage Works

The Glen

Maghaberry
Bramblewood
Maghaberry Prim Sch

Rath

Refuse Tip

Glen Road

Derrynisk

LC

A3

6

LC

Trummery Lane

LC

Lisburn Road

LC

Carnlougherin Rd

LC

Carnlougherin

Damhead Road

Gortnacor Upper

Trummery

A3

Mill Hill

5

Mill Hill La

Meadow Road

Brookfield Specl Sch

BT67

PH

Derrynahone Road

4

Gortnacor

Upper Broomhedge

Halfpenny Gate Road

Thornbrook Road

PH

Creenagh

Gortnacor Lower

Hasley's Town

Playing Field

Hillsborough Road

Inisloughlin

Innisloughlin Road

61

River Lagan

Spencer's Bridge

Zion Hill

Hall

Lany Road

M1

Bridge Road

17 A B 18 C D 19 E F 60

8

7

63

6

5

62

4

3

61

2

1

60

A B C D E F

Drumsill

BT28

Moyrusk

Rath

LC

A3

LC LC

LC

Bushfield Rd OLD FORGE
MS

LISBURN ROAD MOIRA ROAD Lurganure

A3

Church Lane Hall Lurganure Road Mazetown

BT67 THE
FIRST
DOWN
ROYAL

Broughmore CAMPBELL
CT

River Lagan LAGANVALE

Sand
Pit

The
Bog

Maze Race Course BOG ROAD

GRAVELHILL ROAD

BT27

Halfpenny Gate Rd Maze

Dungarton Road KINGSCHASE

PH

Lagan
View Thorn Maze
Hill Prim Sch

Robbery Road KESH ROAD

Ashfield Hall

The
Deerfinhone Rd Long Kesh

The
New
Bridge

Cockhill Road Cock
Hill

St James Road

Rosmead Kesh
Bridge

WALNUT HL

BT26

Aghnatrisk Annacloy

M1 Aghnatrisk Road

AGHNATRISK ROAD Priest
Hill

TRENCH ROAD

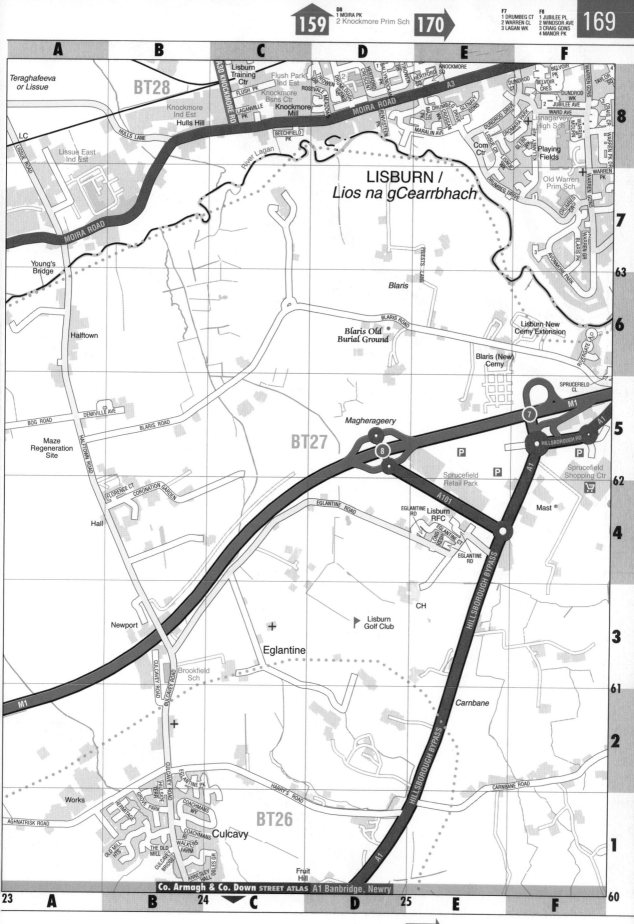

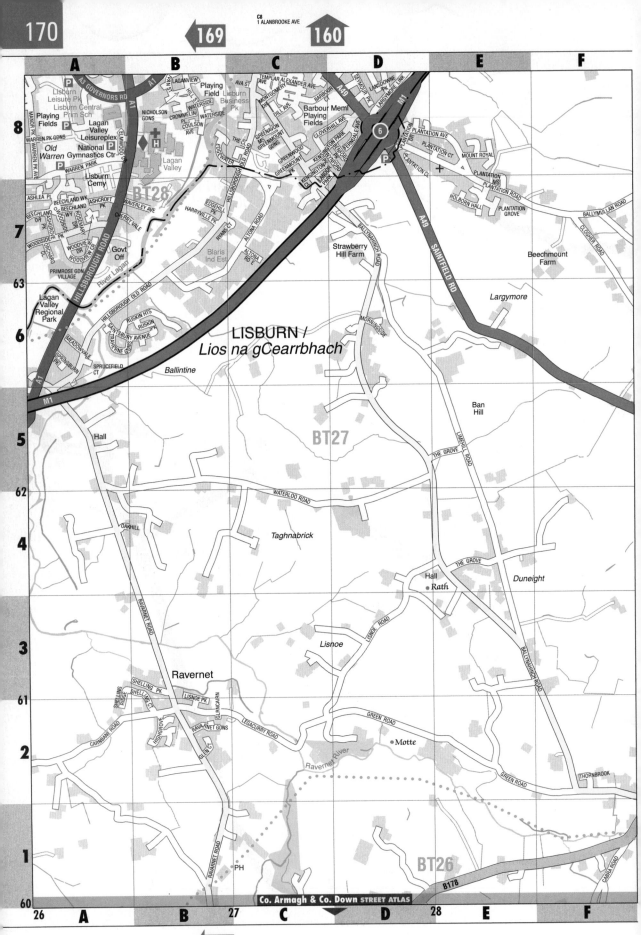

A **B** **C** **D** **E** **F**

8

7

63

6

5

62

4

3

61

2

1

60

LISBURN /
Lios na gCearrbhach

BT28

BT27

BT26

Ravernet

Taghnabrick

Lisnoe

Ballintine

Largymore

Beechmount
Farm

Strawberry
Hill Farm

Ban
Hill

Duneight

Hall
Rath

Motte

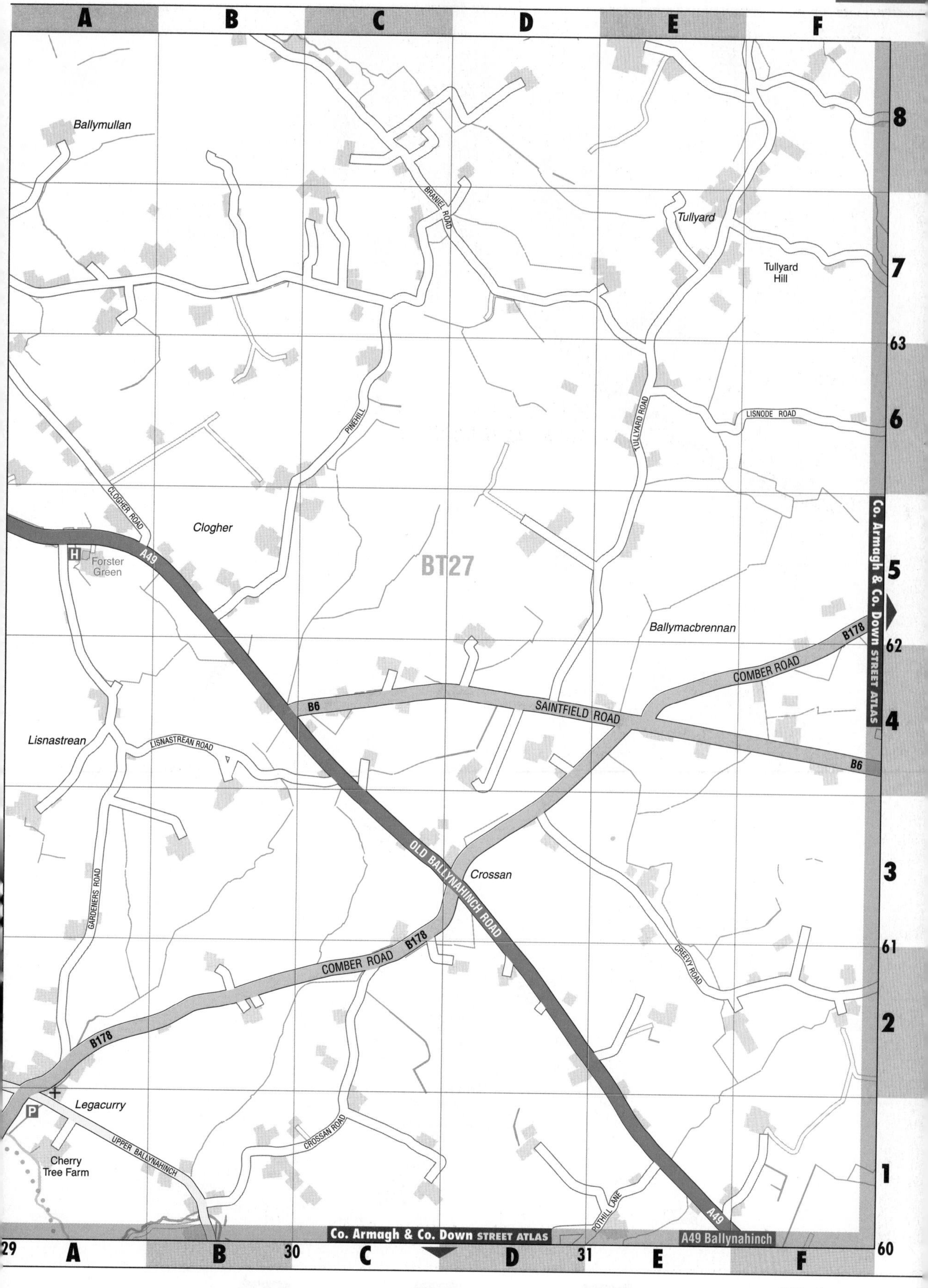

A   B   C   D   E   F

8

Ballymullan

Tullyard

7

63

BRANIEL ROAD

6

Tullyard Hill

LISNODE ROAD

PINEHILL

TULLYARD ROAD

CLOGHER ROAD

Clogher

A49

H Forster Green

BT27

5

62

Ballymacbrennan

B178

COMBER ROAD

B6

SAINTFIELD ROAD

4

LISNASTREAN ROAD

Lisnastrean

B6

OLD BALLYNAHINCH ROAD

Crossan

3

GARDENERS ROAD

61

COMBER ROAD

B178

CREETY ROAD

2

B178

CROSSAN ROAD

Legacurry

P

POTHILL LANE

A49

1

Cherry Tree Farm

UPPER BALLYNAHINCH

A49 Ballynahinch

29   A   B   30   C   D   31   E   F   60

Co. Armagh & Co. Down STREET ATLAS

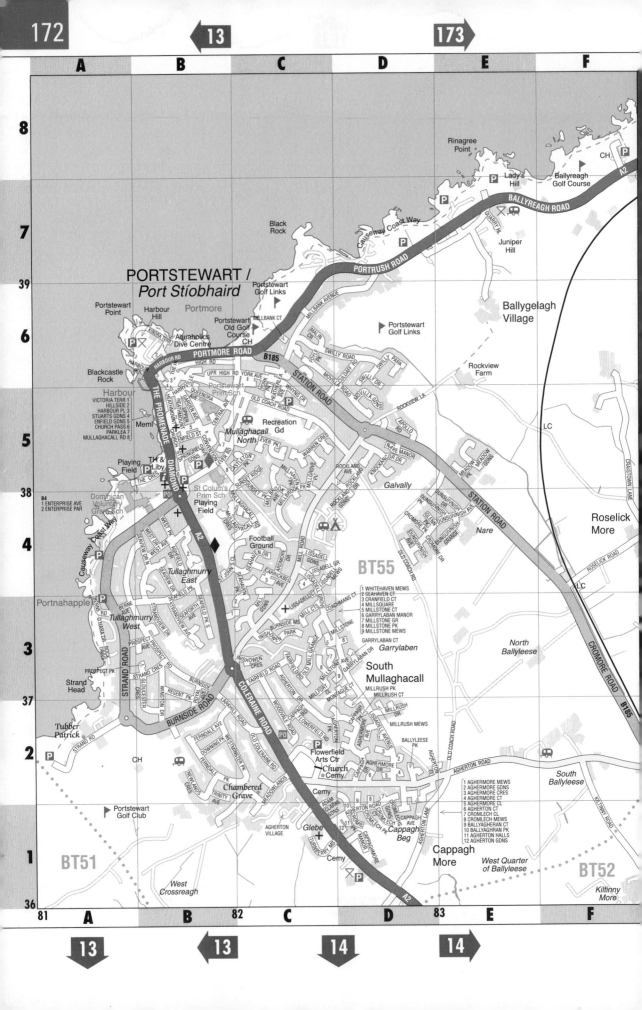

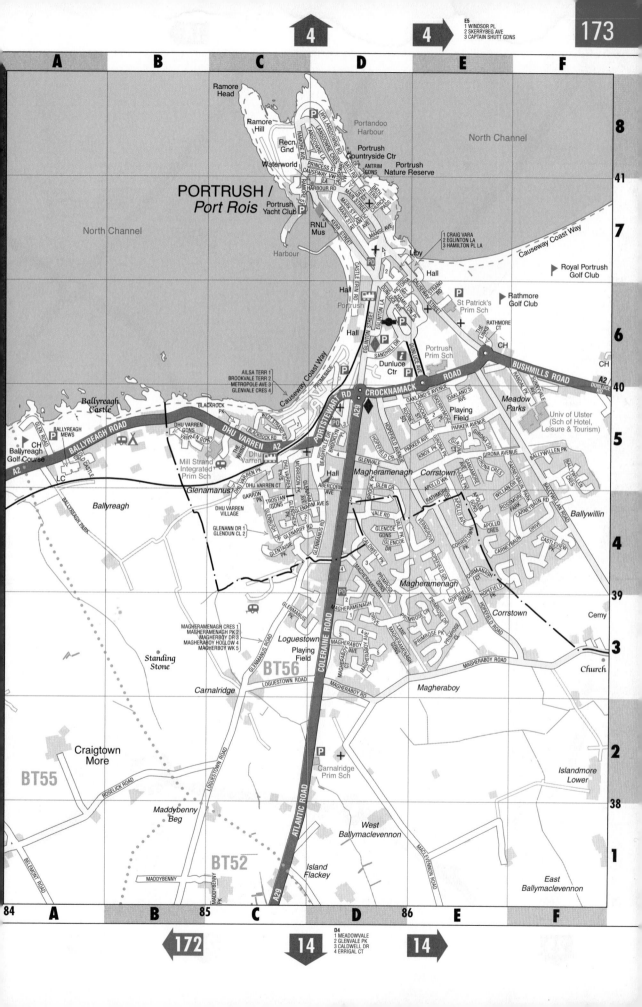

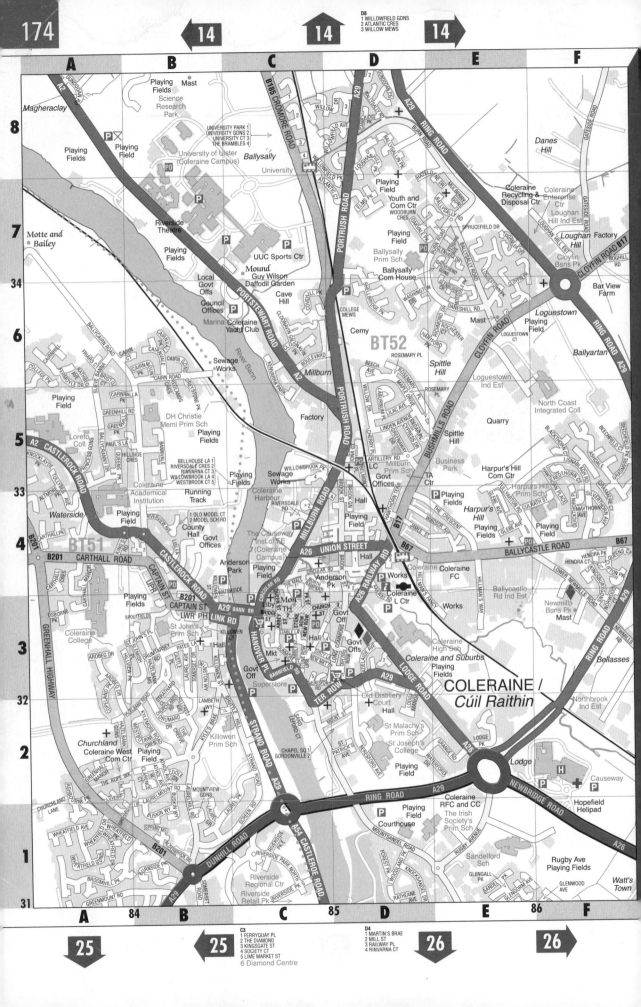

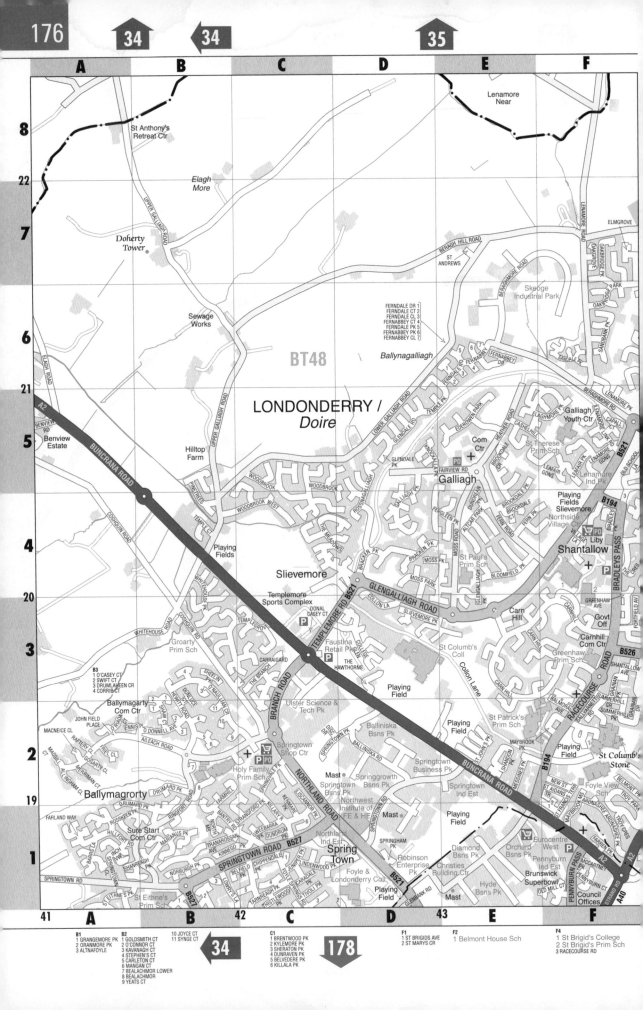

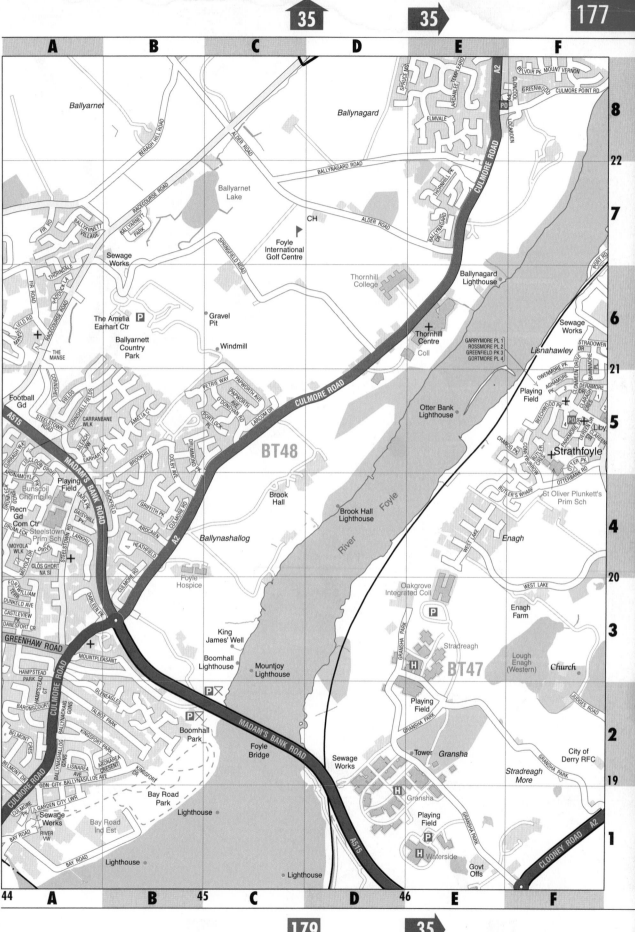

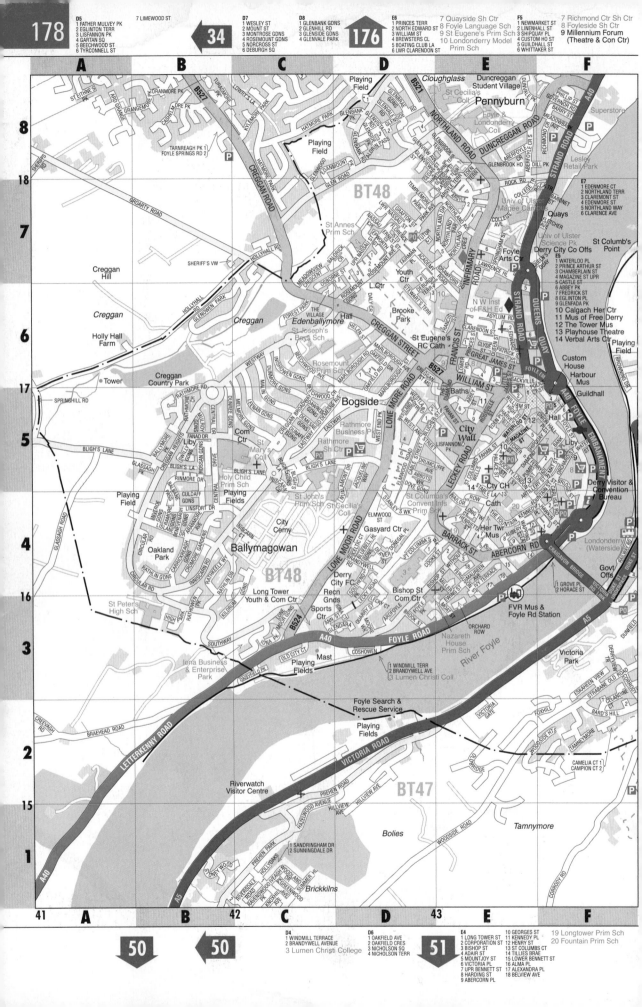

178

D5
1 FATHER MULVEY PK
2 EGLINTON TERR
3 LISFANNON PK
4 GARTAN SQ
5 BEECHWOOD ST
6 TYRCONNELL ST

7 LIMEWOOD ST

34

D7
1 WESLEY ST
2 MOUNT ST
3 MONTROSE GDNS
4 ROSEMOUNT GDNS
5 NORCROSS ST
6 DEBURGH SQ

D8
1 GLENBANK GDNS
2 GLENHILL RD
3 GLENSIDE GDNS
4 GLENVALE PARK

176

E6
1 PRINCES TERR
2 NORTH EDWARD ST
3 WILLIAM ST
4 BREWSTERS CL
5 BOATING CLUB LA
6 LWR CLARENDON ST

7 Quayside Sh Ctr
8 Foyle Language Sch
9 St Eugene's Prim Sch
10 Londonderry Model
   Prim Sch

F5
1 NEWMARKET ST
2 LINENHALL ST
3 SHIPQUAY ST
4 CUSTOM HO ST
5 GUILDHALL ST
6 WHITTAKER ST

7 Richmond Ctr Sh Ctr
8 Foyleside Sh Ctr
9 Millennium Forum
   (Theatre & Con Ctr)

50

50

D4
1 WINDMILL TERRACE
2 BRANDYWELL AVENUE
3 Lumen Christi College

D6
1 OAKFIELD AVE
2 OAKFIELD CRES
3 NICHOLSON SQ
4 NICHOLSON TERR

51

E4
1 LONG TOWER ST
2 CORPORATION ST
3 BISHOP ST
4 ADAIR ST
5 MOUNTJOY ST
6 VICTORIA PL
7 UPR BENNETT ST
8 HARDING ST
9 ABERCORN PL

10 GEORGES ST
11 KENNEDY PL
12 HENRY ST
13 ST COLUMBS CT
14 TILLIES BRAE
15 LOWER BENNETT ST
16 ALMA PL
17 ALEXANDRA PL
18 BELVIEW AVE

19 Longtower Prim Sch
20 Fountain Prim Sch

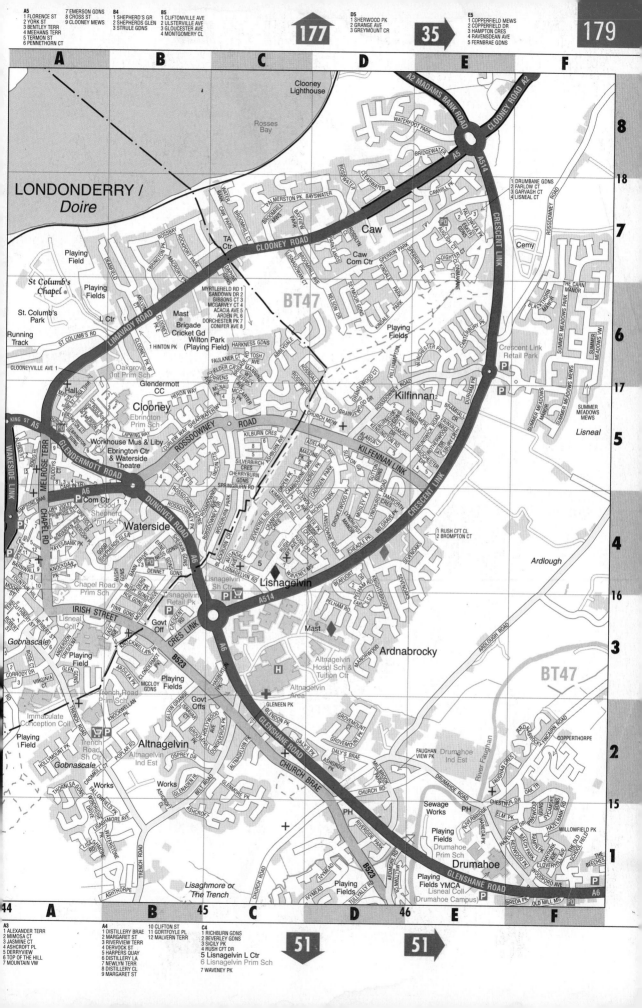

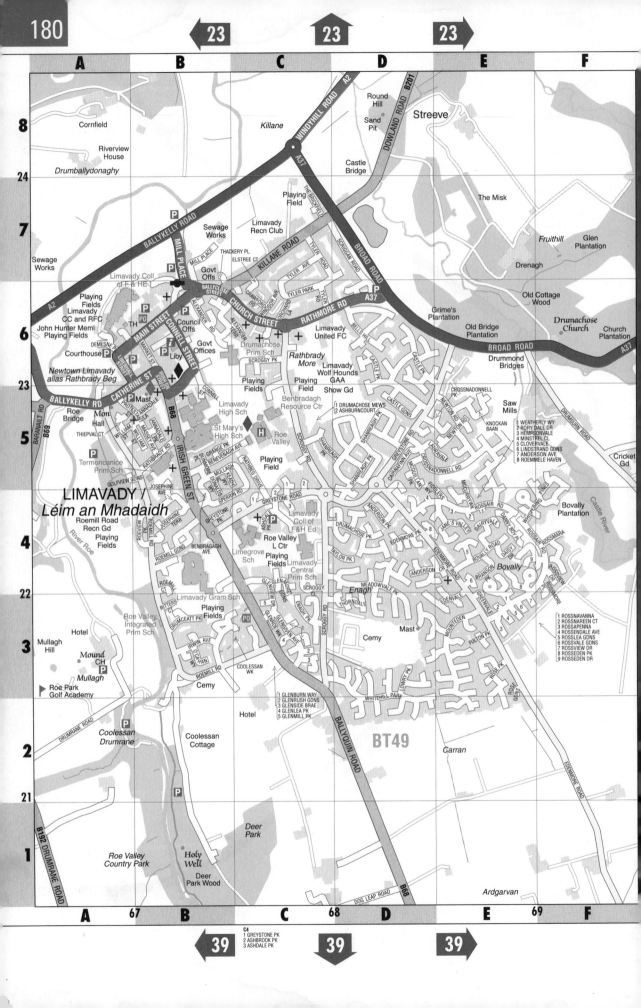

A   B   C   D   E   F

8
24
7
6
23
5
4
22
3
2
21
1

LIMAVADY /
Léim an Mhadaidh

BT49

Cornfield
Riverview
House
Drumballydonaghy

Killane
Round
Hill
Sand
Pit
Streeve

Castle
Bridge
The Misk

Playing
Field

Sewage
Works
Limavady
Recn Club
Fruithill
*Glen
Plantation*

Thackery Pl
Elstree Ct
Drenagh
Old Cottage
Wood

Mill Place
Govt Offs
Grime's
Plantation
*Drumachose
Church*
Church
Plantation

Sewage
Works
Limavady Coll
of F & HE
Council
Offs
Govt
Offices
Limavady
United FC
Old Bridge
Plantation
Drummond
Bridges

Playing
Fields
Limavady
CC and RFC
*Rathbrady
More*
Limavady
Wolf Hounds
GAA

John Hunter Meml
Playing Fields
Drumachose
Prim Sch
Scroggy Pk
Playing
Field
Show Gd
Crossnadonnell
Pk

Courthouse
Liby
Playing
Fields
Benbradagh
Resource Ctr
1 DRUMACHOSE MEWS
2 ASHBURNCOURT
Saw
Mills

*Newtown Limavady
alias Rathbrady Beg*
Mast
Limavady
High Sch
Bells Hill
Knockan
Baan
1 WEATHERLY WY
2 RORY DALL DR
3 HEMPSONVALE
4 MINSTREL CL
5 CLOVERVALE
6 LINDSTRAND GDNS
7 ANDERSON AVE
8 ROEMMELE HAVEN

Roe
Bridge
Mon
Hall
St Mary's
High Sch
Roe
Valley
Cricket
Gd

Thiepval Ct
Playing
Field
Bovally
Plantation

Termoncanice
Prim Sch
Limavady
Coll of
F&H Ed
1 ROSSNAVANNA
2 ROSSNAREEN CT
3 ROSSAPENNA
4 ROSSENDALE AVE
5 ROSSLEA GDNS
6 ROSSVALE GDNS
7 ROSSVIEW DR
8 ROSSEDEN PK
9 ROSSEDEN DR

Roemill Road
Recn Gd
Playing
Fields
Roe Valley
L Ctr
Limegrove
Sch
Playing
Fields
Limavady
Central
Prim Sch
Bovally

River Roe
Enagh
Anderson

Hotel
*Mullagh
Hill*
Limavady Gram Sch
Playing
Fields
Enagh
Cemy
Mast

Mullagh
Mound
CH
Roe Valley
Integrated
Prim Sch
Hotel

Roe Park
Golf Academy
Cemy
1 GLENBURN WAY
2 GLENRUSH GDNS
3 GLENSIDE BRAE
4 GLENLEA PK
5 GLENMILL PK

*Coolessan
Drumrane*
Coolessan
Cottage
Carran

*Roe Valley
Country Park*
Holy
Well
*Deer
Park*

*Deer
Park Wood*
Dog Leap Road
Ardgarvan

A   B   C   D   E   F
67   68   69

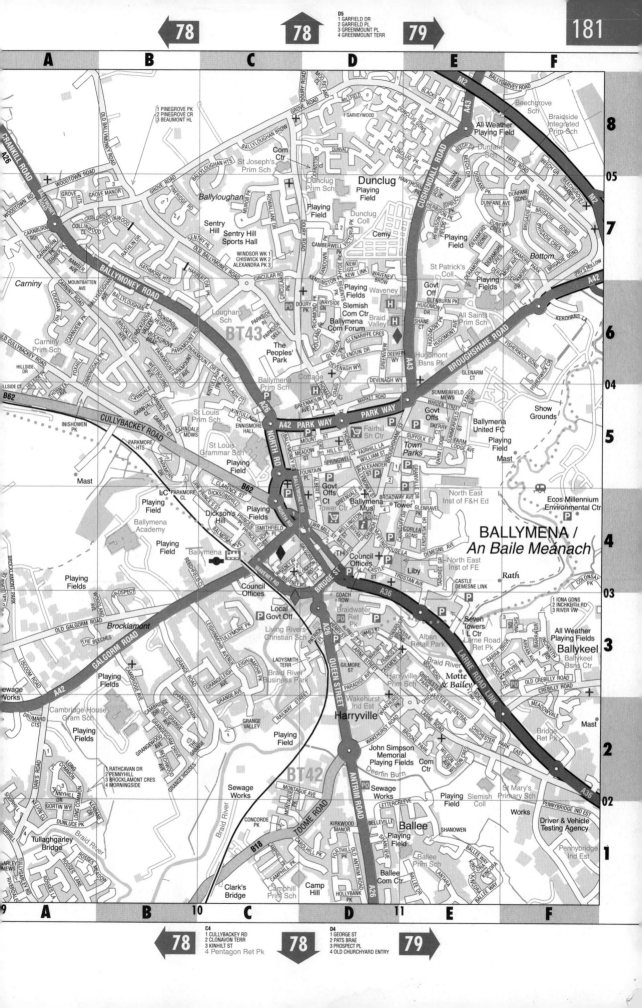

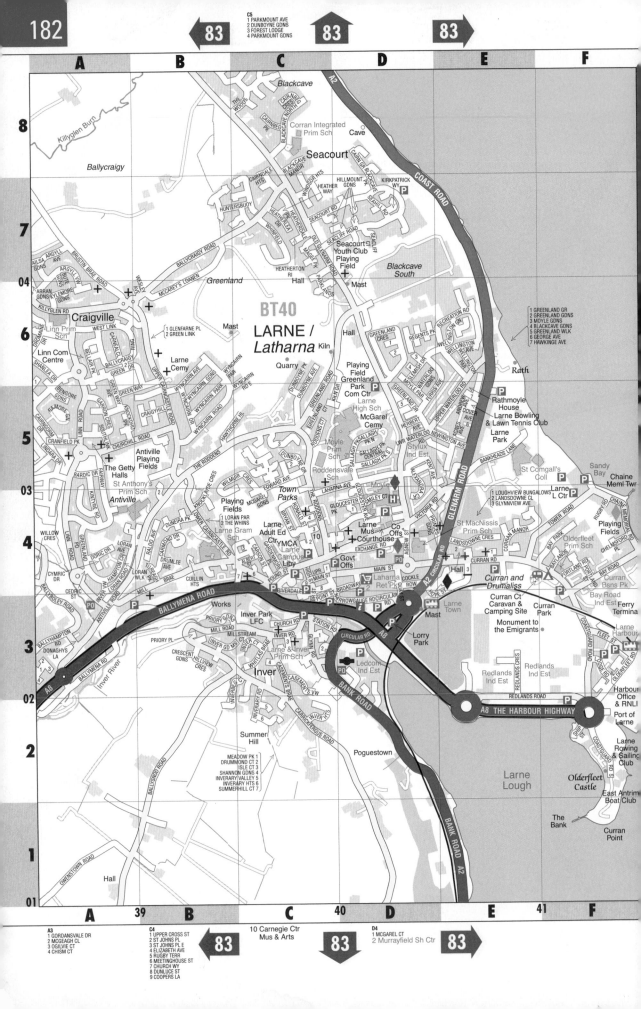

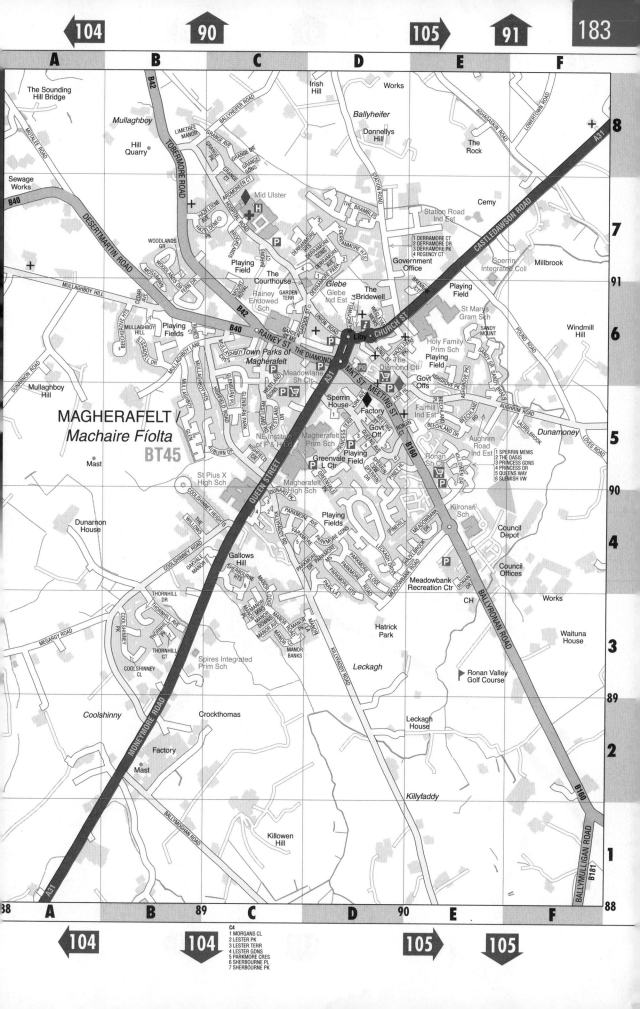

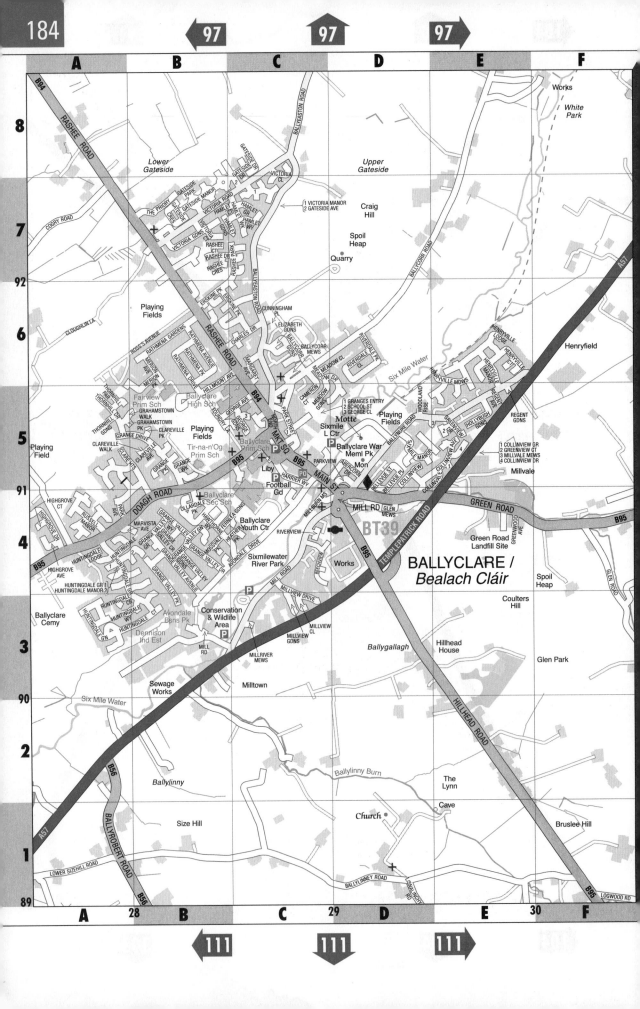

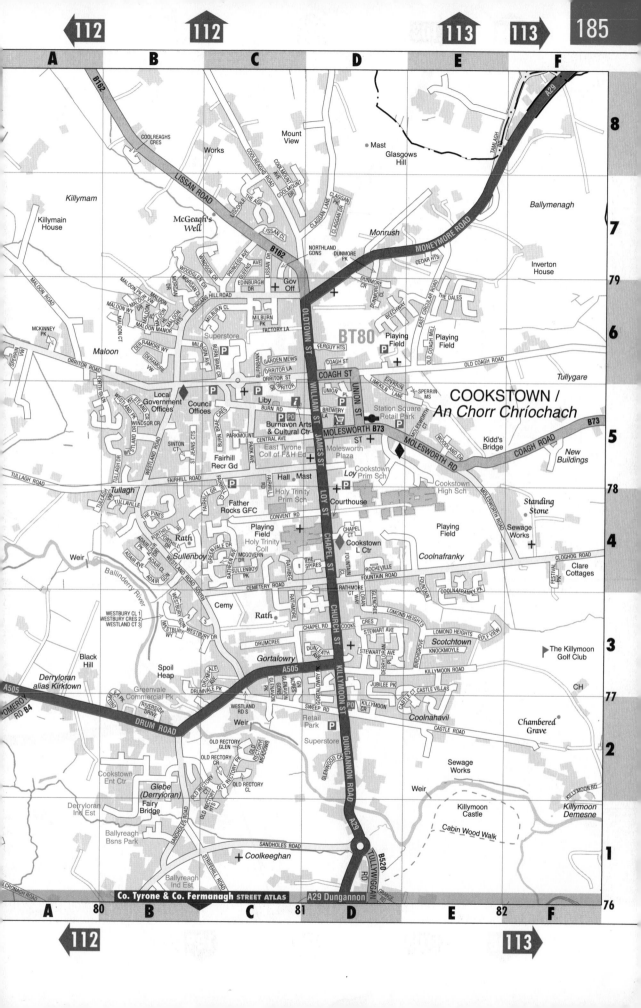

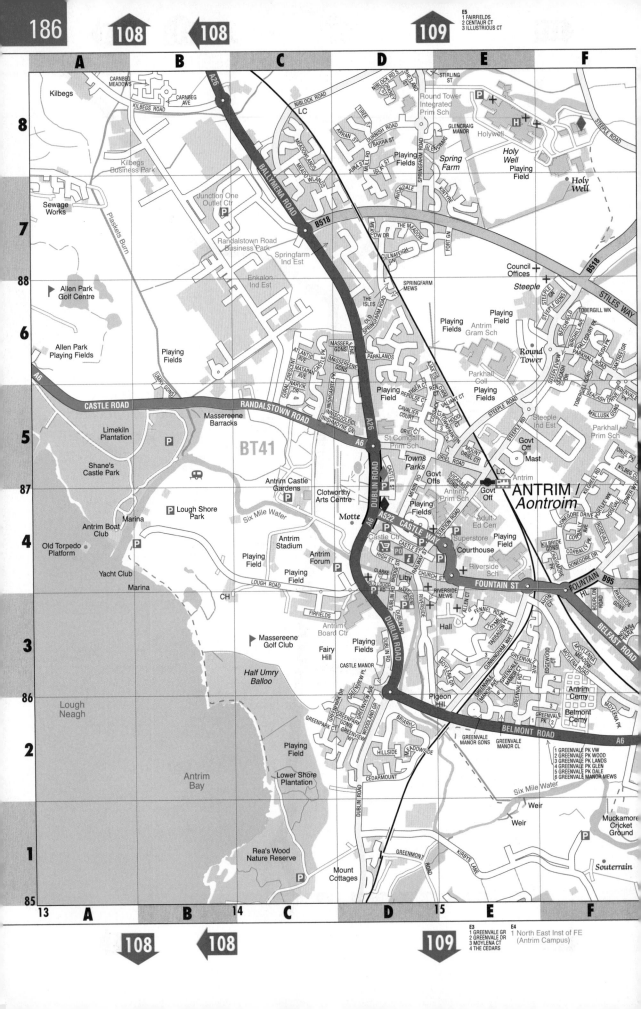

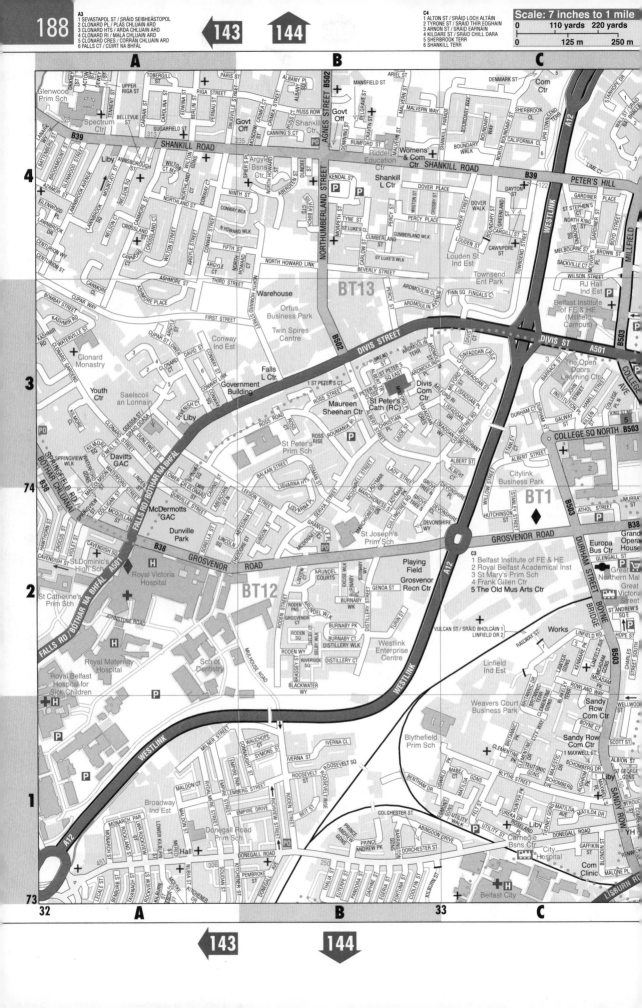

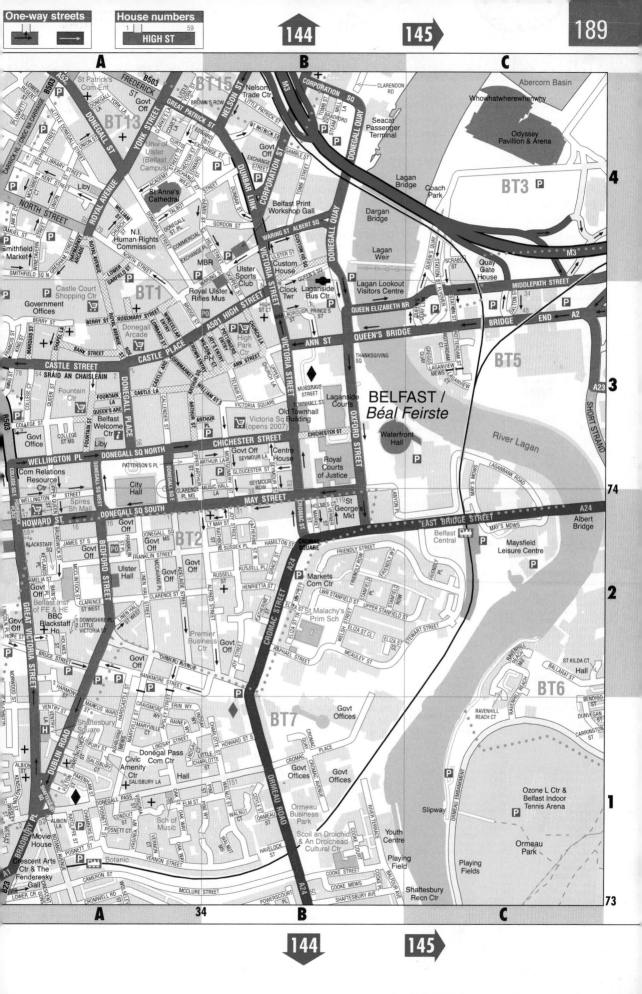

Index

Place name May be abbreviated on the map

→ **Church La 2** Lisburn BT28..........**26** B1

Location number Present when a number indicates the place's position in a crowded area of mapping

Locality, town or village Shown when more than one place has the same name

Postcode district District for the indexed place

Page and grid square Page number and grid reference for the standard mapping

Cities, towns and villages are listed in CAPITAL LETTERS   Public and commercial buildings are highlighted in magenta
Places of interest are highlighted in blue with a star★   Townlands are indicated by ❶ in the index and *italic* type on the maps

Abbreviations used in the index

Acad	Academy	Comm	Common	Gd	Ground	L	Leisure	Prom	Promenade
App	Approach	Cott	Cottage	Gdn	Garden	La	Lane	Rd	Road
Arc	Arcade	Cres	Crescent	Gn	Green	Liby	Library	Recn	Recreation
Ave	Avenue	Cswy	Causeway	Gr	Grove	Mdw	Meadow	Ret	Retail
Bglw	Bungalow	Ct	Court	H	Hall	Meml	Memorial	Sh	Shopping
Bldg	Building	Ctr	Centre	Ho	House	Mkt	Market	Sq	Square
Bsns, Bus	Business	Ctry	Country	Hospl	Hospital	Mus	Museum	St	Street
Bvd	Boulevard	Cty	County	HQ	Headquarters	Orch	Orchard	Sta	Station
Cath	Cathedral	Dr	Drive	Hts	Heights	Pal	Palace	Terr	Terrace
Cir	Circus	Dro	Drove	Ind	Industrial	Par	Parade	TH	Town Hall
Cl	Close	Ed	Education	Inst	Institute	Pas	Passage	Univ	University
Cnr	Corner	Emb	Embankment	Int	International	Pk	Park	Wk, Wlk	Walk
Coll	College	Est	Estate	Intc	Interchange	Pl	Place	Wr	Water
Com	Community	Ex	Exhibition	Junc	Junction	Prec	Precinct	Yd	Yard

Index of towns, villages, townlands, streets, hospitals, industrial estates, railway stations, schools, shopping centres, universities and places of interest

Abb–Alb

A

Abbey Bsns Ctr BT36.... 133 E1
Abbey Cres BT37........ 133 F3
Abbeycroft Dr BT37..... 134 A7
Abbeycroft Gdns BT37... 134 A7
Abbeycroft Rd BT37..... 134 A7
Abbey Ct BT37........... 134 A5
Abbeydale BT47......... 179 C6
Abbeydale Cl BT37...... 134 A4
Abbeydale Cres BT14... 119 E1
Abbeydale Ct BT14...... 136 D1
Abbeydale Dr BT14...... 136 D1
Abbeydale Gdns BT14... 136 D1
Abbey Dale Gdns BT14.. 136 D1
Abbeydale Parade BT14. 136 D1
Abbeydale Pk BT14..... 136 D1
Abbeydeen Manor BT37. 134 A4
Abbeyfield Pk BT41..... 187 C2
Abbey Gdns
  Antrim BT41........... 109 C1
  Belfast BT5.......... 146 E4
  ❶ Kells BT42........ 95 A6
Abbeyglen Cres BT37 ... 134 A7
Abbeyglen Dr BT37..... 134 A7
Abbeyglen Pk BT37..... 134 A7
Abbey Gn BT37.......... 128 E1
Abbeyhill Dr ❸ BT37.. 133 F7
Abbeyhill Pk BT37...... 133 F7
Abbeyhill Rd ❹ BT37.. 133 F7
Abbeyhill Way ❶ BT37. 133 F7
Abbey Pk
  Belfast BT5.......... 146 E4
  ❻ Londonderry BT48.. 178 E5
  Newtownabbey BT37.... 133 F3
Abbey Rd
  Antrim BT41.......... 109 D1
  Belfast BT5.......... 146 D4
Abbey Ret Pk BT36...... 133 D2
Abbey Ring BT18........ 139 C5
Abbey St
  Coleraine BT52 ...... 174 C3
  Londonderry BT48..... 178 E5
Abbey Trading Ctr BT37. 133 E1
Abbeyview BT41......... 187 B1
Abbeyville Gdns BT37... 134 A6
Abbeyville Pk BT37..... 134 A6

Abbeyville Pl BT37..... 134 A6
Abbeyville St BT37..... 134 A6
Abbots Cross BT37...... 133 F5
Abbots Cross Prim Sch ❷
  BT37................ 133 F5
Abbots Dr BT37........ 133 F5
Abbots Gdns BT37...... 133 F5
Abbots Rd BT37........ 133 F5
Abbots Wlk BT48....... 178 D5
Abbots Wood BT18...... 139 D5
Abercorn BT28......... 159 F3
Abercorn Ave BT55..... 173 D5
Abercorn Dr BT39...... 184 D5
Abercorn Pl ❾ BT48... 178 E4
Abercorn Rd BT48...... 178 E4
Abercorn St N BT12.... 188 A2
Abercorn St ❺ BT9.... 144 C2
Aberdeen St BT13...... 188 B4
Aberdelghy Golf Course
  BT27................ 160 E6
Aberdelghy Gr BT27.... 160 D5
Aberfoyle Cres BT48... 178 E8
Aberfoyle Cresent S
  BT48................ 178 E8
Aberfoyle Gdns BT10... 150 D2
Aberfoyle Pk BT10..... 150 D2
Abernethy Dr BT36..... 133 A7
Abernethy Gdns BT36... 133 A7
Abernethy Pk BT36..... 133 A7
Abetta Parade BT5..... 145 C4
Abingdon Dr BT12...... 188 B1
Abyssinia St BT12..... 188 B2
Acacia Ave BT47...... 179 C5
Academy Rd BT48...... 178 D7
Academy St
  Ballymena BT42....... 78 B2
  Belfast BT1.......... 189 A4
ACHADH EOCHAILLE
  (AHOGHILL) BT42..... 77 E2
ACHADH LÍ (AGHALEE)
  BT67................ 155 C2
Achill Rd BT44........ 60 F5
Acorn Bsns Ctr BT53... 175 F3
Acorn Integrated Prim Sch
  BT38................ 125 B3
Acravally❶ BT54....... 8 F3
Acreback Rd BT38...... 100 B1
Acton St
  ❶ Belfast BT13...... 144 A7
  Belfast BT13......... 188 A4
Adair Ave BT80........ 185 B4
Adair Cl BT80......... 185 B4
Adair Dr BT80......... 185 B4

Adair Gdns BT80........ 185 B4
Adair Pk BT80.......... 185 B4
Adair St ❹ BT48....... 178 E4
Adam Clarke Gdns BT56. 172 C1
Adam St ❶❻ BT15...... 144 D8
Adare Pk BT37......... 128 E1
Addison Pk BT28....... 159 C1
Adelaide Ave
  Belfast BT9.......... 151 A8
  Coleraine BT52....... 174 D3
  Londonderry BT47..... 179 C5
  ❽ Whitehead BT38.... 100 D1
Adelaide Chase BT9.... 151 B8
Adelaide Ind Est BT12.. 144 A1
Adelaide Pk BT9....... 151 B8
Adelaide Pl ❷❺ BT38.. 100 D1
Adelaide St BT2....... 189 A2
Adelaide Sta BT12..... 151 A8
Adela Pl BT15......... 144 C7
Adela St BT15......... 144 C7
Adlon Cres BT28....... 159 E3
Adlon Gdns BT28....... 159 E3
Adlon Pk BT28......... 159 E3
Advantage Way BT13.... 143 C6
Aganageeragh❶ BT44... 47 A7
Agars Rd BT28......... 168 B8
Aghaboy❶ BT41........ 93 F2
Aghaboy Gdns BT41..... 187 B5
Aghacarnaghan❶ BT41.. 106 F4
Aghacarnan❶ BT28..... 147 A4
Aghacully❶ BT43...... 64 B1
Aghacully Rd BT43..... 64 A1
Aghadavy❶ BT28....... 156 D3
Aghadolgan❶ BT28..... 120 E3
Aghadolgan Rd BT28.... 120 F4
Aghadowey❶ BT51...... 42 B5
AGHADOWEY BT51........ 42 C5
Aghadrumglasny❶
  BT67................ 165 D6
Aghafad Rd BT82....... 68 E3
Aghafatten❶ BT43..... 64 B2
AGHAGALLON BT67....... 164 F8
Aghagaskin❶ BT45..... 91 A1
Aghagaskin Rd BT45.... 183 E8
Aghagheigh❶ BT44..... 32 E7
Aghaleck❶ BT53....... 19 A4
Aghalee❶ BT67........ 155 E4
AGHALEE (ACHADH LÍ)
  BT67................ 155 C2
Aghalee Rd
  Craigavon BT67....... 155 A1
  Lisburn BT28......... 155 C6

Aghalislone (Upper
  Belfast)❶ BT28 ..... 148 F1
Aghalislone (Upper
  Massereene)❶ BT28.. 159 D7
Aghaloughan❶ BT41.... 107 D5
Aghalum❶ BT44........ 48 F3
Aghamore Pk BT47..... 177 F5
Aghanamoney❶ BT28... 121 B3
Aghancrossy❶ BT53... 28 C8
Aghanliss❶ BT28...... 121 C2
Aghanloo Ind Est BT49.. 23 C2
Aghanloo Rd BT49..... 23 B6
Aghansillagh❶ BT49... 40 B4
Aghanure Rd BT42..... 80 D8
Aghavary❶ BT42....... 93 A6
Aghaveagh❶ BT80..... 114 C1
Aghaveagh Rd BT80.... 114 C2
Aghermore Ave BT56... 172 D2
Aghermore Cl BT56.... 172 D2
Aghermore Cres BT56.. 172 D2
Aghermore Ct BT56.... 172 D2
Aghermore Dr BT56.... 172 D2
Aghermore Gdns BT56.. 172 D2
Aghermore Mews BT56.. 172 D2
Agherton Cl BT56..... 172 D2
Agherton Ct BT56..... 172 D2
Agherton Dr BT56..... 172 C3
Agherton Gdns
  Ballymoney BT53..... 175 E6
  Portrush BT56....... 172 D1
Agherton Halls BT56... 172 D1
Agherton La BT56..... 172 C1
Agherton Pk
  ❹ Ballymoney BT53.. 175 E6
  Portrush BT56....... 172 C2
Agherton Rd BT56..... 172 D1
Agherton Village BT52. 174 C3
Aghery Wlk BT17...... 149 F2
Aghnadarragh❶ BT29.. 120 F6
Aghnadore❶ BT42..... 79 D6
Aghnadore Rd BT42.... 79 E5
Aghnahough❶ BT28.... 159 B6
Aghnatrisk❶ BT26.... 168 D1
Aghnatrisk Rd BT26... 168 E1
Aghrunniaght❶ BT53.. 18 B3
Agincourt Ave BT7.... 144 E1
Agincourt St BT7..... 144 E2
Agivey Rd BT51....... 43 A3
Agnes Ave BT40....... 182 E5
Agnes Cl BT13........ 144 B7
Agnes St Ind Est BT13.. 144 B7
Agnes St
  Belfast BT13......... 188 B4

Agnes St continued
  Carrickfergus BT38... 131 B8
Agnew St BT40......... 182 D4
Agolagh❶ BT44........ 21 A1
Agolagh Hts BT44..... 21 A1
Agra St BT7.......... 144 E1
Agriculture and Food
  Science Ctr The BT9 ... 151 C4
Agriculture Showgrounds★
  BT53................ 175 B4
AHOGHILL (ACHADH
  EOCHAILLE) BT42..... 77 E2
Ahoghill Rd BT41...... 107 F8
Aigburth Pk BT41..... 145 D6
Aileach Rd BT48...... 176 B2
Aileach View BT48.... 177 A5
Ailesbury Cres BT7... 151 E7
Ailesbury Dr BT7..... 151 E8
Ailesbury Gdns BT7... 151 E7
Ailesbury Rd BT7..... 151 F7
Ailsa Gdns BT40...... 182 A7
Ailsa Terr BT55...... 173 C5
Ainsworth Ave BT13... 143 F6
Ainsworth Dr BT13.... 143 F6
Ainsworth Par BT13... 143 F7
Ainsworth Pass BT13.. 143 F6
Ainsworth St BT13.... 143 F6
Aird❶ BT57.......... 5 F6
Aird Cl BT41......... 187 B4
Airfield Hts BT11.... 143 A1
Airfield Rd
  Antrim BT41......... 105 F6
  Londonderry BT47.... 36 F7
  Magherafelt BT45.... 106 A4
Airfield Rd Lower BT47.. 36 E7
Airport Rd
  Belfast BT3......... 138 D1
  Belfast BT29........ 117 A5
  Londonderry BT47.... 37 A6
Airport Rd W BT3..... 139 C4
Airport Rd W Link BT3 . 139 A3
Aitnamona Cres BT11... 143 B1
Ajax Ct BT41......... 186 D6
Alanbrooke Ave ❶ BT27. 170 C8
Alanbrooke Pk Ind Est
  BT6................. 145 D1
Alanbrooke Rd BT6.... 145 D1
Alanvale Cresent BT47. 179 D5
Alanvale Pk BT54..... 8 D4
Alban Ret Pk BT42.... 181 C4
Albany Dr BT38....... 130 E8
Albany Pl BT13....... 188 B4
Albany Sq BT13....... 188 B4

Albertbridge Rd BT5 .... 145 B5
Albert Ct BT12 .... 188 C3
Albert Dr BT6............ 152 C8
Albert Pl BT43 .... 181 D5
Albert Rd BT38 .... 131 A7
Albert Sq BT1........... 189 B4
Albert St
  Belfast BT12 .... 188 B3
  Larne BT40 .... 182 C4
Albert Terr BT12 .... 188 B3
Albertville Dr 20 BT14... 144 B8
Albion La BT7 .... 189 A1
Albion St BT1 .... 188 C1
Alcrossagh❶ BT53..... 18 C1
Alderbrook BT47........ 36 E4
Alderbrook Gdns BT51 .. 174 B1
Alder Cl
  Castlereagh BT5 .... 146 C1
  Dunmurry BT17 .... 161 A8
ALDERGROVE BT29 .... 116 E3
Alderley La BT36........ 132 C5
Alderley Pl BT36........ 132 C5
Alder Pk BT41 .... 187 A4
Alder Rd BT48.......... 177 C8
Alderwood Hill BT8 ..... 152 A1
Aldfreck❶ BT38........ 100 A4
Aldorough❶ BT53..... 30 D4
Aldrin Pass BT48........ 178 D8
Alexander Ave BT27..... 170 C8
Alexander Gdns BT38 ... 125 D2
Alexander Pk
  Carrickfergus BT38 ..... 125 C2
  Maghera BT46......... 74 F5
Alexander Rd
  Belfast BT6........... 145 C1
  Carrickfergus BT38 ..... 125 C2
  Limavady BT49 .... 180 B6
Alexander St BT43 ...... 181 D5
Alexander Terr
  Limavady BT49 .... 180 C6
  ❶ Londonderry BT47 .. 179 A3
Alexandra Ave
  Ballymoney BT53....... 175 D5
  Belfast BT15 .... 137 C2
  ❹ Larne BT40......... 83 B3
Alexandra Cres BT40 ... 182 D5
Alexandra Gdns BT15 .. 137 C3
Alexandra Pk
  Antrim BT41........... 187 C1
  Ballymena BT43........ 181 D7
  Holywood BT18 .... 139 D5
Alexandra Pk Ave ❸
  BT15 .... 137 E1
Alexandra Pl
  Carrickfergus BT38 ..... 125 B2
  Holywood BT18 .... 139 D7
  Londonderry BT48..... 178 E4
Alford Pk ❷ BT5....... 146 E3
Alfred St Pl BT42....... 181 D3
Alfred St
  Belfast BT2........... 189 B4
  Londonderry BT47 ..... 179 A5
Alina Gdns BT17 .... 149 F2
Alla Cross Roads BT47 .. 69 B5
Allan Pk BT82.......... 67 E4
Alla Upper❶ BT47 .... 69 A5
Allenbrook Mews BT40... 83 B2
Allen Ct BT41........... 186 E3
Allen Pk Golf Course
  BT41 .... 108 E5
Alliance Ave BT14...... 136 E1
Alliance Cl BT14 .... 136 F2
Alliance Cres BT14...... 136 F1
Alliance Dr BT14....... 136 F2
Alliance Gdns BT14 .... 136 F2
Alliance Gr BT14....... 136 F2
Alliance Par BT14....... 136 F2
Alliance Pk BT14....... 136 F2
Alliance Rd BT14....... 136 E2
Allingham Cl BT48...... 176 A2
Allison's Hill BT42 ...... 95 A6
Alloa St ❶ BT14....... 144 B8
All Saints Prim Sch
  BT43................. 181 E6
Allworthy Ave BT14..... 137 C1
Alma Pl BT48........... 178 E4
Almond Dr BT17 .... 149 D2
Altaghoney❶ BT47.... 69 B2
Altaghoney Rd BT47.... 69 A2
Altagore❶ BT54 ...... 21 A3
Altananam Pk BT54 .... 8 C3
Altan Ave BT17 .... 149 C3
Altan Cl BT17 .... 149 C3
Altan Dr BT17.......... 149 D3
Altan Gdns ❺ BT17 ... 149 C3
Altan Gr ❹ BT17 ...... 149 C3
Altan Pk BT17 .... 149 C3
Altan Pl ❻ BT17 ...... 149 D3
Altan Wlk BT17 .... 149 D3
Altarichard❶ BT53.... 30 C6
Altarichard Rd BT53..... 29 F6
Altaveedan North❶ BT53. 30 D3
Altaveedan South❶ BT44. 30 D3
Altayaskey Prim Sch
  BT45................. 102 A3
Altcar Ct (Cúirt Allt an
  Chairthe) 37 BT5..... 145 A5
Altcar Pk BT48.......... 176 E4
Altduff❶ BT51 .... 41 A1
Altibrian❶ BT51 ...... 24 D7
Altigarron❶ BT14..... 119 B1
Altikeeragh❶ BT49 ... 24 C8
Altikeeragh La BT51..... 12 F1
Altikeeragh Rd BT49 ... 12 F1
Altilevelly❶ BT40 ..... 99 A6
Altinaghree Castle★ BT82 68 B4
Altinure Lower❶ BT47.. 70 B3
Altinure Pk BT47........ 70 B3

Altinure Rd BT47........ 69 F4
Altmagarran Rd BT47 ... 54 B1
Alt Min Ave BT8......... 152 B3
Altmore Cl BT41........ 187 B5
Altmore Gn BT37....... 133 F3
Altmore Lower❶ BT44 .. 32 E1
Altmore St BT44........ 65 F7
Altmore Upper❶ BT44 .. 32 B1
Altmore Wlk ❷ BT44.... 65 F8
Altmover Rd BT47....... 55 A4
Altnacreeva Ave BT8.... 151 C1
Altnacreeva Cl BT8..... 151 C1
Altnacreeve Pk BT36.... 133 E5
Altnafoyle ❸ BT48..... 176 B1
ALTNAGELVIN BT47..... 179 B2
Altnagelvin Area Hospl
  BT47................. 179 C3
Altnagelvin Hospl Sch &
  Tuition Ctr BT47....... 179 C3
Altnagelvin Ind Est BT47. 179 B2
Altnagelvin Pk BT47..... 179 C2
Altnahinch❶ BT44..... 46 F8
Altnahinch Rd
  Ballymena BT44........ 46 E7
  Ballymena BT53........ 30 B3
Altona Rd BT27......... 170 C7
Altona Rd E BT27....... 170 C7
Alton St (Sráid Loch Alt Áin)
  ❶ BT13............... 188 C4
Altrest Rd BT47......... 67 A7
Alveston Dr BT8 .... 163 E2
Alveston Pk BT8 .... 163 E2
Ambleside ❺ BT42..... 77 F7
Ambleside Cres BT28.... 159 C3
Ambleside Ct
  Belfast BT13........... 144 A7
  Lisburn BT28 .... 159 C3
Ambleside Mews BT28... 159 C3
Ambleside St BT13...... 144 A7
Amcomri St BT12....... 143 F4
Amelia Ct BT48......... 177 B5
Amelia Earhart Ctr The★
  BT48................. 177 B6
Amelia St BT2.......... 189 A2
Ampere St BT6 .... 145 A2
Ampertaine Prim Sch
  BT46................. 74 F6
Ampertaine Rd BT46.... 75 A5
Anadale Flats BT7 ...... 144 E1
Anahorish Prim Sch
  BT41................. 106 A8
AN BAILE MEÁNACH
  (BALLYMENA) BT43..... 181 F4
An Carn Enterprise Ctr
  BT46................. 74 A4
AN CHORR CHRÍOCHACH
  (COOKSTOWN) BT80.... 185 E5
AN CIONN BÁN
  (WHITEHEAD) BT38..... 100 C1
Ancluainglas BT46 ..... 74 C2
AN CUACH (COAGH)
  BT80................. 114 C3
Anderson Ave BT49 .... 180 D5
Anderson Cres
  Limavady BT49 .... 180 D4
  Londonderry BT47..... 179 A3
Anderson Ct
  Doagh BT39............ 111 A6
  ❸ Belfast BT5......... 145 A5
Anderson Pk
  Doagh BT39............ 111 A6
  Limavady BT49 .... 180 D4
Andersonstown❶ BT11.. 150 A7
Andersonstown Cres (Corrán
  Bhaile Andarsan) ❹
  BT11................. 143 C1
Andersonstown Dr ❶
  BT11................. 143 C1
Andersonstown Gdns ❷
  BT11................. 143 C1
Andersonstown Gr ❷
  BT11................. 150 C8
Andersonstown Leisure Ctr
  BT11................. 150 C7
Andersonstown Par ❸
  BT11................. 143 C1
Andersonstown Pk (Páirc
  Bhaile Andarsan) ❽
  BT11................. 143 D1
Andersonstown Pk S
  ❾ Belfast BT11........ 143 D1
  ❶ Belfast BT11........ 150 C8
Andersonstown Pk W
  BT11................. 143 C1
Andersonstown Rd (Bóthar
  Bhaile Andarsan) ❶.... 150 B7
  BT41................. 94 A5
Andraid Cl BT41........ 187 B5
Andraid Rd BT41........ 94 A5
Andrew Ave BT40 ...... 182 E5
Andrew's Ct BT13....... 143 F8
Angus St BT41.......... 109 B6
AN MHACH (EGLINTON)
  BT47................. 36 D5
Annacloy❶ BT26....... 168 F1
Annadale Ave BT7 ..... 151 F6
Annadale Cres BT7..... 151 D8
Annadale Dr BT7....... 151 E7
Annadale Flats BT7 .... 151 E8
Annadale Gdns BT7 .... 151 E7
Annadale Gn BT7 ...... 151 E7
Annadale Gr BT7....... 151 E8
Annadale La BT49...... 180 B5
Annadale Pk BT49 ..... 180 B5
Annaghavoggy❶ BT51.. 58 D3

Annaghdroghal La BT67.164 A7
Annagh & Meneysterlin❶
  BT45................. 90 A2
Annaghmore❶
  Antrim BT41........... 106 D5
  Cookstown BT80 ...... 115 A3
  Magherafelt BT45 ..... 105 D8
Annaghmore La BT80... 115 B3
Annaghmore Rd
  Antrim BT41........... 106 D5
  Castledawson BT45..... 91 C1
  Cookstown BT80 ...... 115 A3
  Magherafelt BT45 ..... 105 D8
Annahavil❶ BT45...... 113 E4
Annalee Ct BT14....... 144 B8
Anna's Pk❶ BT36..... 132 C3
Annavale Ave BT8...... 163 D3
Annavale Dr BT8....... 163 D3
Anneeter Beg❶ BT80.. 115 C3
Anneeter More❶ BT80.. 115 C3
Annesley Hall BT36..... 169 C1
Annesley St BT15 ...... 144 C7
Anneter La BT80....... 115 C3
Anneter Rd BT80....... 115 D2
Annsborough St BT13 .. 188 A4
Ann St
  Ballycastle BT54 .... 8 D3
  Belfast BT1 .... 189 B3
  Londonderry BT48..... 178 C3
AN SEANMHULLACH
  (CASTLEDAWSON) BT45.. 91 B2
AN SUAITREACH
  (SWATRAGH) BT46.... 74 D8
Anticur❶ BT44 .... 45 B2
Anticur Rd BT44....... 45 B1
Antigua Ct BT14 .... 144 A8
Antiville❶ BT40....... 182 A4
Antiville Rd BT40...... 182 A3
ANTRIM (AONTROIM)
  BT41................. 186 F4
Antrim Area Hospl BT41. 187 B8
Antrim Board centre
  BT41................. 186 C3
Antrim Castle Gdns★
  BT41................. 186 C5
Antrim Enterprise Agency
  BT41................. 187 C4
Antrim Forum BT41..... 186 C4
Antrim Gdns BT55...... 173 D8
Antrim Gram Sch BT41.. 186 E6
Antrim Pk BT53........ 175 F3
Antrim Prim Sch BT41 .. 186 E4
Antrim Rd
  Ballyclare BT39........ 111 A1
  Ballymena BT42........ 181 D2
  Belfast BT15 .... 137 C2
  Belfast BT29 .... 117 A7
  Lisburn BT28 .... 159 F3
  Newtownabbey BT36... 119 E7
  Templepatrick BT39.... 110 C2
Antrim St
  Carrickfergus BT38 ..... 131 A8
  Lisburn BT28 .... 160 A2
Antrim Sta BT41....... 186 E5
Antrim Stadium BT41... 186 C4
Antrim Tech Pk BT41... 187 A1
An Tsráid Nua (New St) ❸
  BT17................. 55 C2
Antynanum❶ BT44.... 64 F4
AN YOBAR MÓR
  (TOBERMORE) BT45 ... 89 E5
AONTROIM (ANTRIM)
  BT41................. 186 F4
Apollo Ave BT55........ 173 E4
Apollo Cres BT55....... 173 E4
Apollo Gdns BT55...... 173 E4
Apollo Rd
  Belfast BT12.......... 143 F1
  Portrush BT56......... 172 D5
Apollo Wlk BT55....... 173 E4
Appelyard The ❽ BT51... 26 A7
Applecross ❷ BT47 ... 36 E5
Appletee❶ BT42...... 94 B6
Appletee BT42......... 94 B6
Appleton Pk BT11...... 150 C6
Apsley St BT7.......... 189 A1
Aquaholics Dive Ctr
  BT56................. 172 B6
Aquinas Diocesan Gram Sch
  BT6................. 152 A8
Araboy❶ BT57......... 6 D3
Aranmore Ave BT48.... 178 B4
Arbour St ❸ BT14...... 137 B1
Archdale Dr BT8........ 151 D2
Archdale Pk BT8........ 151 D2
Arches Art Gall★ BT4 .. 145 C5
Arches Bsns Ctr BT4 ... 145 C5
Archvale Ave BT36..... 133 A6
Archvale Cres BT36..... 133 A6
Archvale Dr BT36....... 133 A6
Archvale Gdns BT36..... 133 A6
Archvale Pk BT36....... 133 A6
Arda Chluain Ard (Clonard
  Hts) ❸ BT13.......... 188 A3
Ardadoney❶ BT44..... 59 F5
Ardagh❶
  Ballycastle BT54 .... 19 B1
  Cookstown BT80 ...... 114 F5
Ardaghmore❶ BT53 ... 31 A8
Ardaghmore or Glentop❶
  BT53................. 31 A7
Ardán an Mhachaire Bhuí
  (Magheraboy Terr)
  BT47................. 55 E1
ARD AN CHLÉIBH
  (ARTICLAVE) BT51..... 13 C2
Ardane BT28........... 159 E1
Ardanlee BT48.......... 177 E8

Ardan Mews BT48...... 35 E7
Ardan Rd BT48......... 35 E8
Ardavon Pk BT15 ...... 137 D3
Ardbann Ave ❸ BT51... 59 C5
Ardbeg Dr BT51........ 174 A3
Ardboe Rd BT80........ 115 C1
Ardcaien BT48.......... 177 A4
Ardcairn BT47.......... 55 D2
Ardcame❶ BT82....... 67 E6
Ardcame Rd BT82...... 67 E5
Ardcaoin Ave BT17..... 149 B4
Ardcaoin Dr BT17...... 149 B4
Ardcaoin Gdns BT17.... 149 B4
Ardcaoin Gn BT17...... 149 C4
Ardcaoin Gr BT17...... 149 B4
Ardcaoin Pk BT17...... 149 B4
Ardcaoin Pl BT17...... 149 B4
Ardcaoin View BT17.... 149 B4
Ardcaoin Wlk BT17..... 149 B4
Ardcarn Dr BT5........ 146 F4
Ardcarn Gn BT5........ 146 F4
Ardcarn Pk BT5........ 146 F4
Ardcarn Way BT5...... 146 F4
Ardclinis❶
  Ballymena BT44........ 33 B1
  Ballymena BT44........ 49 B8
Ardcloon BT37......... 133 F3
Ardean❶ BT80......... 115 D2
Ardeen Ave BT37....... 133 F3
Ardeen Gdns ❷ BT37 .. 133 F3
Ardenlee Ave ❷ BT6.... 145 A2
Ardenlee Cl ❸ BT6...... 145 A2
Ardenlee Cres BT6...... 145 A2
Ardenlee Ct ❷ BT6..... 145 A2
Ardenlee Gdns BT6..... 145 B2
Ardenlee Gn BT7....... 145 A2
Ardenlee Par ❶ BT6.... 145 B1
Ardenlee Pk ❸ BT6..... 145 A2
Ardenlee Pl ❻ BT6...... 145 A2
Ardenlee Rise ❼ BT6.... 145 A2
Ardenlee St BT6........ 145 B1
Ardenlee Way ❹ BT6... 145 A2
Arden❶ BT47.......... 179 C5
Ardenvohr St BT6....... 145 B3
Ardenwood ❽ BT6..... 145 A2
Ardfarn Cl BT37........ 133 E3
Ardfoyle BT48.......... 178 D3
Ardgart Pl BT37........ 133 F3
Ardgarvan BT49........ 39 C4
Ardgarvan❶ BT49..... 180 E1
Ardgowan Dr BT5...... 145 C3
Ardgowan St BT6....... 145 B2
Ard Grange BT48....... 178 A8
Ardgreenan Cres ❶❹ BT4. 146 A5
Ardgreenan Dr BT4 .... 146 A5
Ardgreenan Gdns ❾
  BT4................. 146 A5
Ardgreenan Mount ❷
  BT4................. 146 A5
Ardgreenan Pl ❽ BT4... 146 A5
Ardground❶ BT47..... 68 E8
Ardground Rd BT47..... 52 D1
Ardicoan❶ BT44...... 20 F1
Ardihannon❶ BT57....5 E6
Ardilea Pk BT47........ 179 E3
Ardilea St BT14........ 144 A8
Ardina❶ BT51......... 13 C3
Ardina Rd BT51........ 13 C3
Ardinarive❶ BT47..... 55 A7
Ardis Ave BT28......... 160 B4
Ardkeen Cres BT6...... 145 E1
Ardkill❶ BT47......... 51 F3
Ardkill Rd BT47........ 51 F3
Ardlea Cres BT37....... 133 F3
Ardlee Ave BT18....... 139 D6
Ardlough❶ BT47...... 179 E3
Ardlough Rd BT47...... 179 E3
Ardmillan BT15........ 137 C3
Ardmillan Dr BT37..... 133 F3
Ardmillan Gdns ❹ BT37. 133 F3
Ardmonagh Gdns BT11. 143 C3
Ardmonagh Par BT11... 143 C3
Ardmonagh Way BT11.. 143 C3
Ardmoneen Ct BT45.... 183 C7
Ardmore❶
  Belfast BT29 .... 116 C3
  Limavady BT49 .... 39 E6
  Londonderry BT47..... 51 E5
Ardmore Ave
  Belfast BT10.......... 150 A5
  Holywood BT18 .... 139 F6
Ardmore Ct
  Belfast BT10.......... 150 C5
  Holywood BT18 .... 139 F7
Ardmore Dr
  Belfast BT10.......... 150 C5
  Portrush BT56......... 172 C5
Ardmore Hts BT18...... 139 F6
Ardmore Pk
  Belfast BT10.......... 150 B5
  Holywood BT18 .... 139 F7
Ardmore Pk S BT10..... 150 C5
Ardmore Rd
  Belfast BT29 .... 116 C3
  Drumahoe BT47........ 179 D1
  Holywood BT18 .... 139 F6
  Londonderry BT47..... 51 E6
Ardmore Terr BT18..... 139 F7
Ardmoulin Ave BT13.... 188 B3
Ardmoulin Cl BT13..... 188 B3
Ardmoulin Pl BT12..... 188 B3
Ardmoulin St BT12..... 188 B3
Ardmoulin Terr BT12.... 188 B3
Ardmoyle Pk BT44..... 32 D4
Ardnabrocky Dr BT47... 179 F2
ARDNABROCKY BT47... 179 D3

Ardnaclowney Dr ❼
  BT12................. 143 F4
Ardnaglass❶ BT41..... 92 F5
Ardnaglass Gdns BT41 .. 187 B5
Ard na Gran ❻ BT47.... 55 D2
Ardnagreena Gdns BT18. 139 D4
Ardnaguniog❶ BT47... 36 B3
Ard na Maine ❷ BT42... 78 A6
Ardnamoghill❶ BT82... 50 B6
Ardnamoyle Pk BT48... 177 A5
Ardnarea Cresent BT48.. 177 A2
Ardnargle❶ BT49...... 23 B1
Ardnashee BT48........ 176 F2
Ardnashee Pk BT48..... 176 F1
Ard na Smoll BT47...... 55 D2
Ard-Na-Va Rd BT12..... 143 E3
Ardoyne❶ BT14....... 136 F1
Ardoyne Ave BT14..... 137 A1
Ardoyne Rd BT14...... 136 E1
Ardpatrick Gdns BT5 ... 145 D1
Ardrannay Dr BT36..... 133 E6
Ardreagh❶ BT51...... 42 D6
Ardreagh Rd BT51...... 42 B5
Ards Dr BT37.......... 129 A1
Ards Pk BT37.......... 129 A1
Ardtrea Rd BT71....... 113 F1
Ardvarna Cres BT4..... 146 A7
Ardvarna Pk BT4....... 146 A7
Ardvarness❶ BT51..... 25 D4
Ardymagh Rd BT39..... 97 A7
Areema Dr BT17....... 149 F2
Argyle Bsns Ctr BT13... 188 B4
Argyle Ct BT13......... 188 A4
Argyle St BT48......... 178 E2
Argyle Terr BT48....... 178 E7
Argyll Ave BT40........ 182 A7
Argyll View BT40....... 182 A7
Ariel St BT13.......... 188 B4
Arindale BT67......... 167 B7
Arizona St BT11........ 143 C2
Arlee Mews BT4........ 139 B2
Arlington Dr BT10...... 150 A5
Arlington Pk BT10...... 150 A5
Armitage Ct BT4....... 145 C6
Armour Ave BT53...... 175 D4
Armoy Gdns BT37...... 133 F3
ARMOY (OIRTHEAR MAÍ)
  BT53................. 18 A1
Armoy Prim Sch BT53... 18 A1
Armstrong Dr BT53..... 175 D5
Arney Cl BT6.......... 152 B7
Arnon St (Sráid Earnáin) ❸
  BT13................. 188 C4
Arosa Parade BT15..... 137 C2
Arran Ave BT42........ 181 F3
Arran Ct (Cúirt Arann) ❹
  BT5................. 145 A5
Arran Gdns BT40....... 182 A6
Arran St
  Antrim BT41........... 186 D8
  ❷ Belfast BT5......... 145 A5
Artana St BT7......... 144 E2
Arthur Ave BT36....... 133 D1
Arthur Cottage★ BT42... 77 E6
Arthur La BT1 .... 189 A3
Arthur Pk BT36........ 133 D1
Arthur Pl BT1.......... 189 A3
Arthur Rd BT36........ 133 D1
Arthur Sq BT1.......... 189 A3
Arthur St BT1.......... 189 A3
Artibrannan❶ BT43.... 78 B6
ARTICLAVE (ARD AN
  CHLÉIBH) BT51....... 13 C2
Articlave Lower❶ BT51.. 13 C3
Articlave Upper❶ BT51.. 13 B2
Articrunaght North❶
  BT52................. 15 A3
Articrunaght South❶
  BT52................. 15 A2
Artidillon❶ BT51...... 13 A3
Artidillon Rd BT51..... 12 F2
Artidillon Rd Est BT51... 13 A2
Artiferrall❶ BT44...... 44 F7
Artiforty or Shanaghy
  Lower❶ BT53........ 43 C2
Artigoran❶ BT53...... 27 A3
ARTIKELLY BT49....... 23 C1
Artillery Rd BT52....... 174 D5
Artillery St BT48....... 178 E4
Artiloman❶ BT53...... 43 C1
Artimacormick❶ BT57... 6 C6
Artlone❶ BT41........ 107 B7
Artlone Rd BT41....... 107 B7
Artnacrea❶ BT44...... 62 A8
Artnagross❶ BT53..... 43 C1
Artnagullian❶ BT42.... 95 D4
Artoges Rd BT43....... 79 D7
Artresnahan❶ BT41.... 107 A6
Artwell Wlk BT12...... 188 B2
Ascaill Bheann Bradáin
  (Benbradagh Ave) ❷
  BT47................. 55 D2
Ascaill Chluanaí (Springfield
  Ave) BT12........... 143 F5
Ascot Cres BT28....... 159 E5
Ascot Gdns BT5....... 146 A2
Ascot Mews ❶ BT5.... 146 A2
Ascot Pk BT5.......... 146 A2
Ashbourne BT36....... 133 A7
Ashbourne Manor BT42. 78 C4
Ashbourne Pk
  Coleraine BT51........ 174 A2
  Lisburn BT27 .... 160 C5

Ashbrook Cres **3** BT4... 145 F7
Ashbrook Dr BT53... 27 B2
Ashbrooke Dr BT4... 145 F7
Ashbrook Pk
  Ballymoney BT53... 27 B2
  2 Limavady BT49... 180 C4
Ashburn Ave BT47... 179 C5
Ashburncourt BT49... 180 C5
Ashburne Mews BT7... 189 A1
Ashburn Pk BT47... 36 E4
Ashbury Cres **15** BT51... 26 A7
Ashbury Pk **16** BT51... 26 A7
Ashbury Rise **19** BT51... 26 A7
Ashby Glen BT51... 26 A7
Ashcroft BT47... 179 B1
Ashcroft Cl
  Lisburn BT28... 155 E8
  Londonderry BT47... 179 B2
Ashcroft Pk BT28... 170 A7
Ashcroft Pl **4** BT47... 179 A3
Ashcroft Way BT28... 155 E8
Ashdale
  Ballymena BT43... 181 F7
  Coleraine BT52... 174 F5
  Randalstown BT41... 108 A7
Ashdale Pk **3** BT49... 180 C4
Ashdale St BT5... 145 C5
Ashdene Dr BT15... 137 D2
Ash Dr **19** BT46... 74 D1
Ashes The BT40... 100 D3
Ashfield BT42... 79 C7
Ashfield Boys High Sch
  BT4... 146 A8
Ashfield Cres BT15... 137 C2
Ashfield Ct BT15... 137 C2
Ashfield Dr
  Belfast BT15... 137 D2
  Portrush BT56... 172 B4
Ashfield Gdns BT15... 137 D2
Ashfield Girls' High Sch
  BT4... 145 F8
Ashfield Rd BT47... 37 C5
Ashford Gn **1** BT4... 145 F7
Ashford Grange BT67... 164 A1
Ashford Lodge **6** BT36... 111 F1
Ashford Pk BT46... 70 E6
Ashglynne BT46... 74 D2
Ash Gn BT18... 139 D5
Ash Gr BT17... 161 A8
Ashgreen BT41... 187 A3
Ashgrove BT41... 187 C2
Ashgrove Cl BT67... 164 A1
Ashgrove Cres BT53... 175 F4
Ashgrove Dr BT67... 167 A8
Ashgrove Gdns BT67... 164 A1
Ashgrove Pk
  Belfast BT14... 137 A2
  Craigavon BT67... 167 A7
  Drumahoe BT47... 179 D2
  Lisburn BT28... 170 A7
  Magherafelt BT45... 183 E5
Ashgrove Prim Sch
  BT36... 133 A7
Ashgrove Rd BT36... 133 A6
Ashlamaduff **1** BT47... 56 F2
Ashlea Ave BT53... 175 F5
Ashlea Dr BT53... 175 F5
Ashlea Pk BT44... 76 D4
Ashlea Pl
  Ballymoney BT53... 175 F5
  Lisburn BT28... 170 A7
Ashlea Prim Sch BT47... 51 D6
Ashleigh BT45... 105 C2
Ashleigh Ct
  6 Belfast BT6... 145 A2
  Belfast BT29... 121 B5
Ashleigh Manor BT9... 144 B1
Ashleigh Pk
  9 Ballymena BT42... 78 C3
  Carrickfergus BT38... 130 F8
Ashley Ave BT9... 144 B2
Ashley Dr BT9... 144 B2
Ashley Gdns BT15... 137 D5
Ashley Lodge BT17... 149 F2
Ashley Mews BT9... 144 B2
Ashley Pk
  Ballymoney BT53... 28 B2
  Carryduff BT8... 163 E3
  Dunmurry BT17... 149 F2
  Newtownabbey BT36... 111 F2
Ashley Rd BT36... 111 F3
Ashmore Pl BT13... 188 A3
Ashmore St BT13... 188 A3
Ashmount Gdns BT27... 160 D1
Ashmount Gr BT4... 146 A7
Ashmount Pk
  2 Belfast BT4... 145 F7
  Lisburn BT27... 160 D1
Ash Pk BT43... 181 E7
Ash The BT80... 185 C2
Ashthorpe BT47... 179 B1
Ashton Ave BT10... 150 B5
Ashton Dr **1** BT52... 26 B7
Ashton Pk
  Belfast BT10... 150 B5
  2 Coleraine BT52... 26 B7
Ashvale Hts BT28... 147 C6
Ashvale Pk BT40... 84 E1
Ashville Pk BT41... 187 A3
Aspenburn BT41... 187 D2
Aspen Pk
  Belfast BT17... 149 E3
  Newtownabbey BT37... 133 E8
Aspen Wlk BT17... 149 E3

Aston Gdns BT4... 146 A5
Astoria Gdns **3** BT5... 146 A4
Asylum Rd BT48... 178 E6
Athol Ave E BT51... 174 B2
Athol Ave W BT51... 174 B2
Athol St BT12... 188 C2
Atlantic Ave
  Antrim BT41... 186 C6
  Ballycastle BT54... 8 E4
  Belfast BT15... 137 C1
  Carnlough BT44... 49 C2
  Portstewart BT55... 173 D7
Atlantic Cres **2** BT52... 174 D8
Atlantic Ct BT52... 174 C7
Atlantic Rd
  Coleraine BT52... 14 D5
  Portstewart BT55... 173 C1
Aubery St BT48... 178 E4
Auburn Dr BT45... 183 C5
Auburn St **3** BT17... 150 A2
Audley Ave BT28... 160 B4
Aughaboy BT44... 82 A8
Aughaboy Rd BT44... 65 E1
Aughalish BT41... 94 D2
Aughaloughan Rd BT41... 107 E5
Aughareamlagh BT44... 65 A7
Aughil **1** BT49... 11 F3
Aughlish **1**
  Cookstown BT80... 112 D3
  Londonderry BT47... 71 B2
Aughnabrack Rd BT14... 119 B5
Aughnacleagh BT44... 76 E8
Aughnadarragh Rd BT29 120 E6
Aughnadrumman **1**
  BT67... 166 E1
Aughnaholle BT54... 10 D1
Aughnahoy **1** BT44... 76 E2
Aughnahoy Rd BT44... 76 F2
Aughnamullan **1** BT29... 117 F2
Aughnasillagh **1** BT44... 21 B5
Aughrim **1** BT45... 105 D7
Aughrim La BT41... 106 A8
Aughrim Pk BT12... 188 C1
Aughrim Rd BT45... 183 E5
Aughrim Rd Ind Est
  BT45... 183 E5
Aughterclooney **1** BT42... 93 B7
Aughtermoy **1** BT82... 67 F3
Auglish Ct BT47... 179 E7
Ault alias Gowkstown **1**
  BT44... 65 F4
Ava Ave BT7... 144 E1
Ava Cres BT7... 151 E8
Ava Dr BT7... 151 E8
Ava Gdns BT7... 151 E8
Ava Hospl BT9... 144 B2
Ava Par **1** BT7... 144 E1
Ava St
  Belfast BT7... 151 E8
  Lisburn BT27... 170 C8
Avenue The BT38... 125 A1
Avish **1**
  Limavady BT49... 12 C2
  Londonderry BT47... 36 B3
Avish Gdns BT47... 179 B4
Avish La BT47... 36 B3
Avish Rd BT47... 36 C3
Avoca Cl BT11... 143 B3
Avoca Manor BT11... 143 A3
Avoca Pk Sh Ctr BT11... 150 B7
Avoca St BT14... 144 B4
Avonbrook Gdns BT52... 26 B7
Avon Ct BT41... 186 F3
Avondale
  Antrim BT41... 186 D7
  4 Coleraine BT52... 26 C7
Avondale Ave BT47... 179 C4
Avondale Dr BT39... 184 B4
Avondale Bsns Pk BT39 184 B3
Avondale St BT5... 145 C4
Avoniel Dr BT5... 145 C4
Avoniel Leisure Ctr BT5. 145 C4
Avoniel Par BT5... 145 C4
Avoniel Prim Sch BT5... 145 C4
Avoniel Rd BT5... 145 B4
Avonlea Gdns BT47... 133 F3
Avonmore Pk BT28... 169 F7
Avonorr Dr BT5... 145 C4
Avonvale BT4... 146 A8
Axe Factory★ BT44... 31 F3
Ayr St BT7... 137 E2
Azalea Gdns **6** BT17... 149 D7
Azamor St BT13... 188 A4

B

Babington Terr BT51... 13 B5
Bachelors Wlk BT28... 160 A1
Back **1** BT49... 22 E3
Back La The BT38... 131 A8
Back Rd BT27... 162 A2
Backwood Rd
  Craigavon BT67... 165 E4
  Moira BT67... 166 A3
BAILE AN CHAISTIL
  (BALLYCASTLE) BT54... 8 E4
BAILE AN DOIRE
  (BALLINDERRY) BT80... 114 F5
BAILE AN TUAIGHE
  (BALLINTOY) BT54... 7 C7
BAILE EACHAIDH
  (BELLAGHY) BT45... 91 E5
BAILE GEITHLIGH
  (BALLYGALLEY) BT40... 83 A8
BAILE MONAIDH
  (BALLYMONEY) BT53... 175 B3

BAILE NA CROISE
  (DRAPERSTOWN) BT45... 89 A3
BAILE NA MAINSTREACH
  (NEWTOWNABBEY)
  BT36... 133 C7
BAILE RAGHNAILL
  (RANDALSTOWN)
  BT41... 107 E7
BAILE UÍ CHEALLAIGH
  (BALLYKELLY) BT49... 38 B7
BAILE UÍ CHINNÉIDE
  (GRACEHILL) BT42... 78 A3
Bainesmore Dr BT13... 143 F6
Bain's Pl BT7... 189 A2
Baird Ave BT38... 125 B2
Baird Cl BT38... 125 B2
Baird Cres BT38... 125 B2
Bairds Brea★ BT36... 119 B7
Baird Wlk BT38... 125 B2
Balbane Pass BT48... 178 B5
Baldrick Cresent BT48... 178 D7
Balfour Ave
  Belfast BT7... 189 B1
  Whitehead BT38... 127 A8
Balholm Dr BT14... 143 F8
Balkan St BT12... 188 B3
Ballaghalare **1** BT82... 67 B3
Ballaghbeddy **1** BT53... 43 C5
Ballaghbeg **6** BT11... 143 B1
Ballaghmore **1** BT53... 28 B5
Ballaghmore Ave BT57... 5 C4
Ballaghmore Ct **2** BT57... 5 C4
Ballaghmore Pk BT57... 5 C4
Ballaghmore Rd BT57... 5 C4
Ballantrae Wlk BT40... 83 B5
Ballarat Ct **4** BT6... 145 A4
Ballarat St
  1 Belfast BT6... 145 A4
  Belfast BT6... 189 C2
Ballealy North **1** BT41... 107 F5
Ballealy South **1** BT41... 108 A4
BALLEE BT42... 78 F2
Ballee Com High Sch
  BT42... 78 E2
Ballee Dr BT42... 181 E1
Ballee Link Rd BT42... 78 F1
Ballee Prim Sch BT42... 181 E1
Ballee Rd W BT42... 78 E1
Ballee Way BT42... 181 E1
Balleny **1** BT53... 18 A3
Balleyhenry Prim Shool
  BT36... 132 E7
Ballinahone **1** BT53... 29 C5
Ballindam **1** BT44... 21 A2
Ballinderry **1**
  Lisburn BT28... 155 D8
  Magherafelt BT45... 90 C4
BALLINDERRY (BAILE AN
  DOIRE) BT80... 114 F5
Ballinderry Bridge Rd
  BT80... 114 C3
Ballinderry Gdns **2**
  BT28... 159 D1
Ballinderry Pk BT28... 159 E1
Ballinderry Prim Sch
  BT28... 155 D8
Ballinderry Rd
  Cookstown BT80... 114 F4
  Craigavon BT67... 155 C3
  Lisburn BT28... 157 B6
Ballinderry Rd Ind Est
  BT28... 159 D1
Ballindreen Irish **1** BT52 . 26 F7
Ballindreen Rd
  Ballymoney BT53... 15 D1
  Coleraine BT52... 27 A8
Ballindreen Scotch **1**
  BT52... 27 A7
Ballindrum **1** BT45... 114 A6
Balliniska Bsns Pk BT48 176 D2
Ballinlea Lower **1** BT54... 7 B2
Ballinlea Rd
  Ballycastle BT54... 7 C3
  Ballymoney BT53... 28 F7
Ballinlea Upper **1** BT54... 7 B3
Ballinloughan **1** BT54... 10 D2
Ballinrees **1** BT51... 25 B6
Ballinrees La BT51... 25 B6
Ballintaggart **1** BT51... 26 D3
Ballinteer Rd BT51... 25 D7
Ballintemple **1** BT51... 57 B7
Ballintine **1** BT27... 170 B6
Ballintoy **1** BT54... 7 C7
BALLINTOY (BAILE AN
  TUAIGHE) BT54... 7 C7
Ballintoy Demesne **1** BT54. 7 B7
Ballintrae **1** BT57... 5 B4
Ballintrae Pk BT57... 5 C4
Balloo **1**
  Antrim BT41... 117 A8
  Larne BT40... 100 D7
Balloonigan **1** BT67... 166 F1
Balloughry Hill Rd BT48... 50 D6
Balloughry Prim Sch BT48. 50 D6
Balloughry Rd BT48... 50 C5
Ballsallagh **1** BT43... 63 D8
Ballure
  Ballymena BT44... 20 E1
  Ballymoney BT53... 30 A7
Ballure Hts BT44... 46 B6
Ballyagan **1**
  Ballymena BT44... 32 E8
  Coleraine BT51... 42 C1
Ballyagan Rd BT51... 42 C2
Ballyaghagan **1** BT36... 119 F4
Ballyaghagan Nature
  Reserve★ BT36... 136 E7

Ballyagheran Ct BT56... 172 D1
Ballyaghlis **1** BT27... 161 E3
Ballyaghran Pk BT56... 172 D1
Ballyalbanagh **1** BT39... 97 C5
Ballyalbanagh Rd BT39... 97 D4
Ballyallaght **1** BT57... 6 A5
Ballyalton Pk BT37... 128 E1
Ballyalton Wlk BT37... 128 F1
Ballyarnett Ctry Pk★
  BT48... 177 B6
Ballyarnett Pk BT48... 177 B7
Ballyarnett Rd BT48... 176 F2
Ballyarnett Village BT48. 177 A7
Ballyarnot **1** BT41... 117 B8
Ballyarnott Rd BT41... 109 C1
Ballyartan **1**
  Coleraine BT52... 174 F6
  Londonderry BT47... 68 F7
Ballyarton Rd BT47... 68 F6
Ballyavelin **1** BT49... 39 F6
Ballyavelin North **1** BT49. 40 A6
Ballyavelin **1** BT49... 39 D5
Ballybeeny Rd BT52... 50 C1
Ballybeg **1** BT42... 77 D2
Ballybeg La BT45... 114 F8
Ballybeg Rd BT42... 77 D2
Ballybentragh **1** BT39... 110 C3
Ballybentragh Rd BT41... 110 B3
Ballyberidagh North **1**
  BT54... 9 A1
Ballyberidagh South **1**
  BT54... 9 A1
Ballybogey Old Rd
  Ballymoney BT53... 15 D2
  Portrush BT56... 4 F2
Ballybogey Rd BT53... 175 A8
Ballybogie BT47... 51 E5
Ballybog Rd BT17... 160 F8
Ballybogy **1** BT44... 46 B1
BALLYBOGY BT53... 15 D1
Ballybogy **1** BT53... 15 E1
Ballybogy Hill BT44... 46 B1
Ballybogy Rd BT44... 62 B8
Ballyboley **1**
  Ballyclare BT39... 97 F6
  Larne BT40... 83 B4
Ballyboley Rd BT40... 182 A4
Ballybollen **1** BT42... 93 C6
Ballybollen Rd BT42... 93 C5
Ballybought **1** BT36... 119 E6
Ballyboylands Lower **1**
  BT53... 28 C4
Ballyboylands Upper **1**
  BT53... 28 D3
Ballybracken **1** BT39... 96 C2
Ballybracken Rd BT39... 110 E8
Ballybrack **1** BT44... 32 C6
Ballybraddin **1** BT44... 30 C2
Ballybrakes **1** BT53... 175 B2
Ballybrakes Bsns Pk
  BT53... 175 B2
Ballybrakes Rd BT53... 175 A3
Ballybregagh **1** BT53... 29 D8
Ballybriest **1** BT80... 102 E4
Ballybriest Rd BT80... 102 E4
Ballybrissell **1** BT49... 23 D5
Ballybritain **1** BT51... 42 B7
Ballycaghan **1** BT51... 41 E8
Ballycairn **1** BT67... 155 A3
Ballycairn Cl BT67... 155 B1
Ballycairn Ct BT67... 155 B2
Ballycairn Dr BT8... 151 C1
Ballycairn Rd
  Coleraine BT51... 174 A6
  Craigavon BT67... 155 B3
Ballycalket **1** BT39... 111 B4
Ballycallaghan **1** BT47... 68 C6
Ballycanal **1** BT67... 166 D3
Ballycanice Mews BT47... 36 F5
Ballycarn **1** BT8... 162 B5
Ballycarrickmaddy **1**
  BT28... 158 B8
BALLYCARRY BT38... 100 B2
Ballycarry **1** BT54... 3 B6
Ballycarry North West **1**
  BT38... 99 F3
Ballycarry Prim Sch
  BT38... 100 A3
Ballycarry Sta BT40... 100 C3
Ballycarton **1** BT49... 23 B6
Ballycastle **1** BT49... 23 B4
BALLYCASTLE (BAILE AN
  CHAISTIL) BT54... 8 E4
Ballycastle Ct **13** BT14... 144 B8
Ballycastle Golf Club BT54. 8 E4
Ballycastle High Sch BT54. 8 D4
Ballycastle Mus★ BT54... 8 D3
Ballycastle Prim Sch BT54. 8 D3
Ballycastle Rd BT52... 174 E4
Ballycastle Rd Ind Est
  BT52... 174 E3
Ballyclaber **1** BT52... 14 F1
Ballyclan BT29... 116 D2
Ballyclan Rd BT29... 116 D2
Ballyclare **1** BT39... 184 B5
BALLYCLARE (BEALACH
  CLÁIR) BT39... 184 E4
Ballyclare Golf Club BT39. 97 A2
Ballyclare High Sch
  BT39... 184 B5
Ballyclare Prim Sch
  BT39... 184 C5
Ballyclare Rd
  Doagh BT39... 111 A6
  Newtownabbey BT36... 132 F6
  Templepatrick BT39... 110 D2

Ballyclare Sec Sch BT39. 184 B4
Ballyclare St **2** BT14... 137 B1
Ballyclaverty **1** BT39... 110 C7
Ballyclogh **1** BT44... 21 A3
Ballyclogh **1** BT28... 147 E1
Ballycloghan **1**
  Antrim BT41... 107 C4
  Ballymena BT43... 62 F1
  Belfast BT8... 146 C6
Ballycloghan Rd BT43... 63 A2
Ballyclogh **1**
  BT57... 15 F6
Ballyclogh (Centre) **1**
  BT57... 15 F6
Ballyclogh (North) BT57... 5 D2
Ballyclogh (North Centre) **1**
  BT57... 5 D1
Ballyclogh Rd BT57... 16 A3
Ballyclogh (South) **1**
  BT57... 15 F5
Ballyclogh (South Centre) **1**
  BT57... 15 F5
Ballyclose St BT49... 180 A6
Ballyclosh **1** BT43... 78 B6
Ballyclosh La BT43... 78 B6
Ballyclough BT51... 26 A1
Ballyclough Rd BT28... 158 E8
Ballycoan Rd BT8... 162 E8
Ballycolin Rd
  Belfast BT17... 148 F6
  Lisburn BT28... 141 E1
Ballycollin **1** BT17... 149 A6
Ballycomlargy **1** BT45... 104 C5
Ballyconagan **1** BT54... 3 A6
Ballyconnelly **1** BT42... 77 C5
Ballyconnelly Rd BT42... 77 C6
Ballyconnelly Terr BT42... 77 C5
Ballycoos **1** BT40... 66 B1
Ballycoose Rd BT40... 82 F8
Ballycor **1** BT39... 97 D2
Ballycormick **1** BT53... 175 A6
Ballycormick Pk BT53... 175 A6
Ballycorr Gdns BT39... 184 C6
Ballycorr Gr BT39... 97 D2
Ballycorr Mews BT39... 184 C6
Ballycorr Rd BT39... 184 D7
Ballycowan **1**
  Ballymena BT42... 94 E3
  Belfast BT8... 162 E6
Ballycowan Rd BT42... 94 E7
Ballycraig **1** BT53... 44 B1
Ballycraig Lower **1** BT56... 4 D3
Ballycraig Upper **1** BT56 .. 4 E2
Ballycraigy **1**
  Antrim BT41... 187 C3
  Larne BT40... 182 A3
  Newtownabbey BT36... 111 D2
Ballycraigy Dr BT41... 187 B2
Ballycraigy Gdns **27**
  BT36... 111 F1
Ballycraigy Pk
  29 Newtownabbey BT36... 111 F1
  Newtownabbey BT36... 132 F8
Ballycraigy Prim Sch
  BT41... 187 B2
Ballycraigy Rd
  Antrim BT41... 187 C3
  Larne BT40... 182 B7
  1 Newtownabbey BT36... 132 E8
Ballycraigy Rd N BT36... 111 C2
Ballycraigy Rd S BT36... 111 C1
Ballycraigy Ring BT40... 182 A6
Ballycraigy Way BT36... 111 F1
Ballycranny Dr BT51... 174 A5
Ballycreen Dr BT28... 159 E1
Ballycregagh **1** BT44... 62 A8
Ballycregagh Lower **1**
  BT53... 29 A6
Ballycregagh Rd BT44... 62 A8
Ballycregagh Upper **1**
  BT53... 29 C6
Ballycreggy **1** BT42... 79 A2
Ballycreggy Rd BT42... 79 B2
Ballycronan Beg **1** BT40... 84 B3
Ballycronan More **1** BT40 84 B2
Ballycrum **1** BT49... 40 D7
Ballycullo Tom of the Tae-
  End★ BT17... 149 C7
Ballycushan **1** BT39... 110 D3
Ballydarrog **1** BT49... 38 E3
Ballydawley **1** BT45... 114 A4
Ballydawley alias
  Crosspatrick **1** BT45... 114 A5
Ballydawley Rd BT45... 114 A4
Ballydermot **1** BT45... 91 E4
Ballydermot La BT45... 91 E4
Ballydermot Rd BT45... 91 F3
Ballydevit Rd BT51... 42 C6
Ballydevitt **1** BT51... 42 D6
Ballydivity **1** BT53... 16 B1
Ballydollaghan **1** BT8... 162 F8
Ballydollan **1** BT29... 121 D8
Ballydonaghy Rd
  Belfast BT29... 140 D8
  Crumlin BT29... 117 B1
Ballydonegan **1** BT47... 70 F2
Ballydonnell **1** BT45... 115 B7
Ballydonnelly **1**
  Antrim BT41... 107 A8
  Ballymena BT44... 60 A5
Ballydonnelly La BT44... 59 F5
Ballydonnelly Rd BT41... 107 B8
Ballydown **1** BT40... 84 B1
Ballydownfine **1** BT11... 143 B1
Ballyduff Gdns BT36... 128 D1
Ballyduff Prim Sch BT36. 128 C1
Ballyduff Rd BT36... 133 B8
BALLYDUGGENNAN Villas
  BT41... 106 E5

BALLYDULLAGHAN BT51 . . . . 58 B4
Ballydunmaul❶ BT41 . . . . 107 C8
Ballydunmaul Rd BT41 . . 107 C8
Ballydurnian❶ BT54 . . . . . . 8 C1
Ballyearl❶ BT36 . . . . 111 E3
Ballyearl Cl ⓫ BT36 . . . . . 111 F1
Ballyearl Cres ㉑ BT36 . . 111 F1
Ballyearl Ct ⓯ BT36 . . . . . 111 F1
Ballyearl Dr BT36 . . . . . . 111 F1
Ballyearl Gn ⓳ BT36 . . . . 111 F1
Ballyearl Leisure Ctr
  BT36 . . . . 111 F2
Ballyearl Rd BT36 . . . . . . 111 F3
Ballyearl Rise ⓴ BT36 . . . 111 F1
Ballyearl Terr ⓭ BT36 . . . 111 F1
Ballyearl Way BT36 . . . . . 111 F1
BALLYEASTON BT39 . . . . . . 97 D2
Ballyeaston Rd BT39 . . . 184 C7
Ballyedward❶ BT40 . . . . . . 83 B1
Ballyeglish❶ BT28 . . . . . . 114 C8
Ballyeglish Rd BT45 . . . . 114 C8
Ballyellough BT28 . . . . . . 158 B5
Ballyfad❶ BT44 . . . . 32 B3
Ballyfinaghy❶ BT10 . . . . 150 C4
Ballyfore❶ BT36 . . . . 98 E3
Ballyfore Ave BT36 . . . . . 128 D1
Ballyfore Gdns BT36 . . . 128 C1
Ballyfore Par BT36 . . . . . 128 C1
Ballyfore Pk BT36 . . . . . . 128 C1
Ballyfore Rd
  Larne BT40 . . . . 98 E4
  Newtownabbey BT36 . . . 128 C1
Ballyforlea❶ BT45 . . . . . . 113 C5
Ballyforlea Rd BT45 . . . . 113 C5
Ballygallagh❶ BT39 . . . . 184 D3
Ballygalley❶ BT40 . . . . . . 83 B8
BALLYGALLEY (BAILE
  GEITHLIGH) BT40 . . . . . 83 A8
Ballygalley Castle★ BT40. 83 B8
Ballygallin❶ BT52 . . . . 14 B4
Ballygallin Pk BT52 . . . . 174 D8
Ballygan Lower❶ BT53 . . . 27 B4
Ballygan Upper❶ BT53 . . . 27 A4
Ballygarvey❶ BT43 . . . . . . 79 A7
Ballygarvey Rd BT43 . . . 181 E8
Ballygawley❶ BT51 . . . . . . 42 C5
Ballygawley Rd BT51 . . . . 42 D4
Ballygawn❶ BT44 . . . . 66 B2
BALLYGELAGH VILLAGE
  BT56 . . . . 172 E6
Ballygelly❶ BT42 . . . . 80 B5
Ballygelly Rd BT42 . . . . . . 80 B5
Ballygilbert❶ BT44 . . . . . . 66 B3
Ballygillen Beg❶ BT80 . . 114 F6
Ballygillen More❶ BT80 . 114 E7
Ballygillen Rd BT80 . . . . 114 F6
Ballygill Middle❶ BT54 . . . 2 D6
Ballygill North❶ BT54 . . . .2 E7
Ballygill South❶ BT54 . . . . 2 D6
Ballyginniff❶ BT29 . . . . . 116 D5
Ballyginniff Rd BT29 . . . 116 D6
Ballyglosh La BT43 . . . . . 78 B6
Ballygobbin❶ BT53 . . . . . 175 A8
Ballygolan❶ BT36 . . . . . . 133 C1
Ballygolan Intake❶
  BT36 . . . . 137 F8
Ballygolan Prim Sch
  BT36 . . . . 137 D8
Ballygomartin❶ BT13 . . . 136 A1
Ballygomartin Dr BT13 . . 143 D6
Ballygomartin Ind Pk
  BT13 . . . . 143 C6
Ballygomartin Rd BT13 . . 143 E7
Ballygomartin Rd BT13 . . 143 C5
Ballygonny Beg BT45 . . . 114 B2
Ballygonny More❶
  BT45 . . . . 114 A3
Ballygonny Rd E BT45 . . 113 F2
Ballygonny Rd W BT45 . . 114 B3
Ballygore Rd BT41 . . . . . 187 B5
Ballygortgarve❶ BT29 . . . 117 A1
Ballygowan❶
  Ballyclare BT39 . . . . 96 B3
  Belfast BT17 . . . . 161 D5
Ballygowan (Ballynure)❶
  BT39 . . . . 98 C4
Ballygowan (Raloo)❶
  BT40 . . . . 98 D6
Ballygowan Rd
  Ballyclare BT39 . . . . 98 C6
  Ballymena BT42 . . . . 96 A3
  Belfast BT5 . . . . 153 B4
Ballygroll❶ BT47 . . . . 52 E7
Ballygroll Rd BT47 . . . . . . 52 D7
Ballygrooby❶ BT41 . . . . . 108 B7
Ballygrooby La BT45 . . . 104 E1
Ballygrooby Rd BT45 . . . 114 B7
Ballygrooby Rdbt BT41 . 108 B6
Ballygroogan❶ BT80 . . . . 112 D1
Ballygruby❶ BT45 . . . . . . 114 A8
Ballygudden❶ BT47 . . . . . 36 F4
Ballygudden Rd BT47 . . . . 36 F5
Ballyguddin❶ BT47 . . . . . . 55 C3
Ballyguddin Rd BT47 . . . . 55 B3
Ballygurk❶ BT45 . . . . 114 C7
Ballyhackamore❶ BT5 . . 145 E4
BALLYHACKAMORE BT5 . . 146 A3
Ballyhacket Glenahorry❶
  BT49 . . . . 12 E2
Ballyhacket Lisawilling❶
  BT49 . . . . 12 D1
Ballyhacket Magilligan❶
  BT49 . . . . 12 E2
Ballyhackett❶ BT40 . . . . . 82 F7

Ballyhacket Toberclaw❶
  BT51 . . . . 12 F2
Ballyhackett Prim Sch
  BT49 . . . . 12 F1
Ballyhagan Rd BT46 . . . . . 89 E7
Ballyhamage❶ BT39 . . . . 110 F6
Ballyhamage BT39 . . . . . 110 F6
Ballyhampton❶ BT40 . . . . . 83 B3
Ballyhampton Ct BT40 . . . 83 B2
Ballyhampton Rd BT40 . . 182 A3
Ballyhampton Rd N BT40 . 83 B3
Ballyhanedin❶ BT47 . . . . . 70 C7
Ballyhanedin Rd BT47 . . . 70 C7
Ballyhanna❶ BT49 . . . . . . 23 E5
Ballyhanwood❶ BT5 . . . . 153 F8
Ballyhanwood Rd BT5 . . . 146 E1
Ballyharigan❶ BT47 . . . . . 54 E3
Ballyharry❶ BT40 . . . . . . 100 C6
Ballyhartfield❶ BT39 . . . 110 F4
Ballyhartfield Rd BT39 . . 110 F3
Ballyharvey Lower❶
  BT41 . . . . 117 D8
Ballyharvey Rd BT41 . . . 117 D8
Ballyharvey Upper❶
  BT41 . . . . 117 C8
Ballyheather Rd BT82 . . . . 67 B5
Ballyheifer❶ BT45 . . . . . . 183 D8
Ballyheifer Rd BT45 . . . . 183 C8
Ballyhemlin❶ BT57 . . . . . . .5 C2
Ballyhenry❶ BT36 . . . . . . 111 F1
Ballyhenry Ave BT36 . . . 132 D7
Ballyhenry Cres ❺ BT36 . 132 E7
Ballyhenry Dr BT36 . . . . 132 D7
Ballyhenry East❶ BT49 . . . 23 A5
Ballyhenry Gdns BT36 . . 132 D7
Ballyhenry Gr ❶ BT36 . . . 132 E7
Ballyhenry Par BT36 . . . . 132 D7
Ballyhenry Pk ❷ BT36 . . . 132 E7
Ballyhenry Rd BT36 . . . . 132 D7
Ballyhenry West❶ BT49 . . 23 A5
Ballyhibistock Lower❶
  BT53 . . . . 16 B3
Ballyhibistock Upper❶
  BT53 . . . . 16 B3
Ballyhill❶ BT38 . . . . 99 F1
Ballyhill La BT29 . . . . 118 C3
Ballyhill Lower❶ BT29 . . . 118 C3
Ballyhill Rd BT14 . . . . 136 A5
Ballyhill Upper❶ BT29 . . . 118 D3
Ballyholly❶ BT47 . . . . 53 D3
Ballyhome❶ BT57 . . . . 5 A1
Ballyhome Lower❶ BT57 . . 15 C6
Ballyhome Rd BT52 . . . . . 15 B6
Ballyhone❶
  Coleraine BT51 . . . . 57 B3
  Larne BT40 . . . . 99 C6
Ballyhone Rd
  Carrickfergus BT38 . . . . . 99 E2
  Larne BT40 . . . . 99 B6
Ballyhowne❶ BT39 . . . . . 111 C5
Ballyhunsley North❶
  BT57 . . . . 15 F4
Ballyhunsley South❶
  BT57 . . . . 16 A3
Ballyhuriman❶ BT44 . . . . . 32 C1
Ballyhutherland❶ BT44 . . . 61 F7
BALLYKEEL BT42 . . . . 181 F3
Ballykeel❶
  Craigavon BT67 . . . . 165 B7
  Larne BT40 . . . . 82 F3
  Portrush BT56 . . . . 4 E3
Ballykeel Bsns Ctr BT42 . 181 F3
Ballykeel Rd
  Craigavon BT67 . . . . 165 C2
  Newtownards BT23 . . . . . 153 C1
Ballykeel❶ BT49 . . . . 38 D6
Ballykelly❶
  Limavady BT49 . . . . 38 C8
  Lisburn BT28 . . . . 156 B1
BALLYKELLY (BAILE UÍ
  CHEALLAIGH) BT49 . . . . 38 B7
Ballykelly Level (Intake)❶
  BT49 . . . . 22 C1
Ballykelly Prim Sch BT49 . 38 D6
Ballykelly Rd
  Ballykelly BT49 . . . . 38 D7
  Limavady BT49 . . . . 180 A5
Ballykennedy❶
  Ballymena BT42 . . . . 78 B2
  Belfast BT29 . . . . 118 B1
Ballykennedy Rd
  Ballymena BT42 . . . . 78 A2
  Belfast BT29 . . . . 118 B2
Ballykenver❶ BT53 . . . . . . 18 A3
Ballykenver Rd BT53 . . . . 28 F8
Ballyknock❶
  Ballymoney BT53 . . . . 29 F3
  Maghera BT46 . . . . 73 F4
Ballyknockan Ave ❶
  BT28 . . . . 159 D1
Ballyknockan Pk BT28 . . . 169 D8
Ballyknock La BT46 . . . . . . 74 A3
Ballyknock Little❶ BT44 . . 30 A3
Ballyknock Rd BT46 . . . . . 74 B2
Ballylacky❶ BT28 . . . . 156 E3
Ballylagan❶
  Ballyclare BT39 . . . . 98 C2
  Coleraine BT51 . . . . 26 E2
Ballylagan Rd
  Ballyclare BT39 . . . . 122 D8
  Coleraine BT52 . . . . 14 F5
Ballylame❶ BT46 . . . . 58 A3
Ballylame Rd
  Coleraine BT51 . . . . 57 F3
  Maghera BT46 . . . . 58 A3
Ballyleaghry Rd BT49 . . . . 39 D3
Ballyleagry❶ BT49 . . . . . . 39 E3

Ballyleckan❶ BT57 . . . . 5 C2
Ballyleese Pk BT56 . . . . . 172 D2
Ballyleighery Upper❶
  BT49 . . . . 23 D7
Ballylenaghan Ave BT8 . . 152 C1
Ballylenaghan Pk BT8 . . . 152 B2
Ballylenaghan Pk ❷
  BT8 . . . . 152 B1
Ballylenaghan Rd ❶
  BT8 . . . . 152 B1
Ballylenaghan Upper❶
  BT8 . . . . 151 F3
Ballylenully❶ BT41 . . . . . 107 A7
Ballylesson❶ BT42 . . . . . . 79 A1
BALLYLESSON BT8 . . . . . . 162 B7
Ballylesson❶ BT40 . . . . . . 99 C7
Ballylesson Rd
  Ballymena BT42 . . . . 94 D8
  Belfast BT8 . . . . 151 B2
  Larne BT40 . . . . 99 D7
  Lisburn BT27 . . . . 161 E4
Ballylifford❶ BT80 . . . . . . 115 A6
Ballylifford Prim Sch
  BT80 . . . . 115 A6
Ballylig❶
  Ballycastle BT54 . . . . 18 D6
  Ballymena BT44 . . . . 45 D4
  Larne BT40 . . . . 99 F7
Ballylig (Intake) BT40 . . . 100 A7
Ballyligpatrick❶ BT42 . . . 80 C8
Ballylig Rd
  Ballymena BT43 . . . . 79 E8
  Larne BT40 . . . . 99 E7
Ballylinney Rd BT39 . . . . 184 D1
Ballylinny❶
  Ballyclare BT39 . . . . 184 B2
  Bushmills BT57 . . . . 5 E6
BALLYLINTAGH BT51 . . . . . 26 A2
Ballylintagh Rd BT51 . . . . 26 B2
Ballyloghan Rd BT45 . . . 113 E3
Ballyloghan❶ BT40 . . . . . . 83 B3
Ballyloran Ind Est ⓵
  BT40 . . . . 83 D3
Ballylough❶
  Ballymena BT44 . . . . 45 A8
  Bushmills BT57 . . . . 5 E1
Ballyloughan❶
  Ballymena BT43 . . . . 181 C7
  Magherafelt BT45 . . . . . 113 E4
Ballyloughan Brow BT43 . 181 C8
Ballyloughan Hts BT43 . . 181 B7
Ballyloughan Pk BT43 . . . 181 B8
Ballylough Beg BT57 . . . . 16 B6
Ballylough More❶ BT57. . 16 A6
Ballylougry❶ BT48 . . . . 50 D6
Ballylumford❶ BT40 . . . . . 84 A2
Ballylumford Power Sta
  BT40 . . . . 84 A2
Ballylumford Rd BT40 . . . 84 A2
Ballylummin❶ BT42 . . . . . . 77 D1
Ballylummin Pk BT42 . . . . 77 F1
Ballylummin Rd BT42 . . . . 93 B8
Ballylurgan❶ BT41 . . . . . . 94 B2
Ballylurgan Rd BT41 . . . . 108 C8
Ballymacaldrack❶ BT44 . . 44 F3
Ballymacallion❶ BT47 . . . . 56 E6
BALLYMACARRET BT5 . . . 145 C5
Ballymacarret Intake❶
  BT3 . . . . 145 B7
Ballymacarrett Recn Ctr
  BT4 . . . . 145 C5
Ballymacarrett Walkway
  BT4 . . . . 145 C5
Ballymacash Dr BT28 . . . 159 D4
Ballymacash Pk BT28 . . . 159 E4
Ballymacash Prim Sch
  BT28 . . . . 159 C4
Ballymacash Rd BT28 . . . 159 B4
Ballymacbrennan❶
  BT27 . . . . 171 E5
Ballymacdoe❶ BT44 . . . . . 32 E4
Ballymacfin❶ BT53 . . . . . . 16 F2
Ballymacfin Rd BT53 . . . . 16 F3
Ballymacilcurr❶ BT47 . . . . 74 E3
Ballymacilcurr Rd BT46 . . 74 E2
Ballymacilhoyle❶ BT29 . . 116 A3
Ballymacilrany❶ BT67 . . . 155 A5
Ballymacilroy❶ BT41 . . . . 93 E6
Ballymaclanigan❶ BT47 . . 53 B3
Ballymaclary❶ BT49 . . . . . 12 A4
Ballymaclary House★
  BT49 . . . . 12 A3
Ballymaclose❶ BT28 . . . . 121 A1
Ballymacmary❶ BT29 . . . 116 C1
Ballymacombs Beg❶
  BT45 . . . . 91 F8
Ballymacombs La BT45 . . 91 F8
Ballymacombs More❶
  BT45 . . . . 92 A8
Ballymacombs Rd BT45 . . 91 F7
Ballymaconaghy❶
  Belfast BT6 . . . . 145 C2
  Castlereagh BT6 . . . . . . 152 C6
Ballymaconaghy Mews
  BT8 . . . . 152 D3
Ballymaconaghy Rd BT8 . 152 D3
Ballymaconnelly❶ BT44. . 59 F7
Ballymaconnelly Rd BT44 . 59 F7
Ballymacoss❶ BT28 . . . . . 159 C3
Ballymacpeake Lower❶
  BT44 . . . . 75 F4
Ballymacpeake Rd BT44 . . 75 F4
Ballymacpeake Upper❶
  BT45 . . . . 91 D8
Ballymacpherson❶
  BT45 . . . . 104 B7

Ballymacran❶ BT49 . . . . . . 22 E3
Ballymacrea Lower❶ BT56 .4 D2
Ballymacrea Rd BT56 . . . . . 4 D2
Ballymacrea Upper❶ BT56 .4 E2
Ballymacrevan❶
  Belfast BT28 . . . . 120 E8
  Lisburn BT28 . . . . 120 F3
Ballymacricket❶ BT29 . . . 121 B4
Ballymacrickett Prim Sch
  BT29 . . . . 121 B4
Ballymacrea Rd BT42 . . . . 94 F5
Ballymacward Lower❶
  BT28 . . . . 147 D8
Ballymacward Prim Sch
  BT28 . . . . 147 F8
Ballymacward Rd
  Belfast BT29 . . . . 141 A3
  Lisburn BT28 . . . . 141 B2
Ballymacward Upper❶
  BT28 . . . . 141 B2
Ballymadigan❶ BT51 . . . . 13 A3
Ballymadigan Rd BT51 . . . 13 A3
Ballymagarry❶
  Belfast BT13 . . . . 143 D6
  Portrush BT56 . . . . .4 F2
Ballymagarry La BT13 . . . 143 C7
Ballymagarry Rd BT56 . . . . 4 F3
Ballymaghan❶
  Belfast BT4 . . . . 146 B8
  Holywood BT18 . . . . 139 D1
Ballymaglin❶ BT49 . . . . . . 23 C6
Ballymagland❶ BT49 . . . . 11 D4
Ballymagowan❶ BT48 . . . . 34 E1
BALLYMAGOWAN BT48 . . . 178 B4
Ballymaguigan❶ BT45 . . . 105 E6
Ballymaguigan Rd BT45 . . 105 D6
Ballymaguire Rd BT71 . . . 113 E1
Ballymakeever❶ BT47 . . . . 55 F4
Ballymarlagh❶ BT42 . . . . . 79 B2
Ballymartin❶ BT39 . . . . . . 110 F3
Ballymartin Rd BT39 . . . . 110 F3
Ballymather Lower❶
  BT29 . . . . 118 C6
Ballymather Rd BT29 . . . . 118 D4
Ballymather Upper❶
  BT29 . . . . 118 D4
Ballymatoskerty❶ BT41 . . 93 A1
Ballymatoskerty Rd
  BT41 . . . . 107 A8
Ballymave❶ BT28 . . . . 157 E6
Ballymena❶ BT43 . . . . 63 D3
Ballymena Acad BT43 . . . 181 B4
BALLYMENA (AN BAILE
  MEÁNACH) BT43 . . . . . 181 F4
Ballymena Bsns
  Development Ctr BT42 . . 78 A3
Ballymena Ct ⓲ BT14 . . . 144 B8
Ballymenagh❶
  Coleraine BT51 . . . . 41 C7
  Cookstown BT80 . . . . . . 185 F7
Ballymenagh Rd BT51 . . . 58 B5
Ballymena Golf Club
  BT42 . . . . 79 C6
Ballymena Mus★ BT43 . . 181 D6
Ballymena Prim Sch
  BT43 . . . . 181 C6
Ballymena Rd
  Antrim BT41 . . . . 186 C8
  Ballyclare BT39 . . . . 110 D8
  Ballymena BT44 . . . . 49 C1
  Ballymoney BT53 . . . . . . 175 F4
  Cullybackey BT43 . . . . . . 78 A6
  Larne BT40 . . . . 182 A3
  Portglenone BT44 . . . . . . 76 D4
Ballymena Sta BT53 . . . . 181 C4
Ballymenoch Pk BT18 . . . 139 E8
Ballyminstra❶ BT42 . . . . . 78 A1
Ballyminymore❶ BT29 . . 121 D6
Ballyminymore Rd BT29 . 121 D6
Ballymiscaw❶ BT16 . . . . . 146 F7
Ballymiscaw Rd BT18 . . . 146 E8
Ballymisert❶ BT4 . . . . 145 F7
Ballymoghan Beg❶
  BT45 . . . . 104 E4
Ballymoghan La BT45 . . . 105 A4
Ballymoghan More❶
  BT45 . . . . 104 F4
Ballymoghan Rd BT45 . . . 183 B1
Ballymonan❶ BT47 . . . . . . 56 A1
Ballymoney❶
  Coleraine BT51 . . . . 13 B2
  Larne BT40 . . . . 84 F1
  Limavady BT49 . . . . 23 D3
BALLYMONEY
  Londonderry BT47 . . . . . . 54 B2
  Ballymoney BT53 . . . . . . 175 B3
Ballymoney High Sch
  BT53 . . . . 175 E4
Ballymoney Ind Christian Sch
  BT53 . . . . 175 C6
Ballymoney Model Prim Sch
  BT53 . . . . 175 B4
Ballymoneymore❶ BT29 . 121 F6
Ballymoney Mus★ BT53 . 175 C4
Ballymoney Rd BT43 . . . . 181 A7
Ballymoney St
  Ballymena BT43 . . . . 181 D5
  ❸ Belfast BT14 . . . . 144 B8
Ballymontenagh❶ BT42 . . 93 E8
Ballymontenagh Rd BT42 . 93 E8
Ballymore❶ BT49 . . . . 39 A4
Ballymore Ave BT49 . . . . . 39 B4
Ballymore Pk BT48 . . . . . 178 B5
Ballymote❶ BT29 . . . . 121 C5
Ballymote Rd BT29 . . . . . 121 C4
Ballymoy❶ BT57 . . . . 6 A6

Ballymoyle❶ BT80 . . . . . . 114 D5
Ballymoyle Rd BT80 . . . . 114 D5
Ballymuckleheany❶
  BT45 . . . . 104 D4
Ballymuckvea❶ BT42 . . . . 94 D5
Ballymulderg Beg❶
  BT45 . . . . 105 B3
Ballymulderg More❶
  BT45 . . . . 105 B4
Ballymuldrogh❶ BT40 . . . 100 D7
Ballymulholland❶ BT49 . . 11 C3
Ballymullan❶ BT27 . . . . . . 160 E1
Ballymullan Rd BT27 . . . . 170 F7
Ballymulligan❶ BT45 . . . . 105 A1
Ballymulligan Rd BT45 . . 183 F1
Ballymullock❶ BT40 . . . . . 83 A4
Ballymullock Rd BT40 . . . 83 A6
Ballymully❶ BT49 . . . . 39 C4
Ballymultimber❶ BT49 . . . 11 C1
Ballymultrea❶ BT45 . . . . 115 B8
Ballymurphy❶
  Belfast BT12 . . . . 143 D4
  Dungannon BT71 . . . . . . 114 F4
Ballymurphy Cres BT12 . . 143 C4
Ballymurphy Dr BT12 . . . 143 C4
Ballymurphy Parade
  BT12 . . . . 143 C4
Ballymurphy Rd BT12 . . . 143 D3
Ballymurphy St BT12 . . . 143 C4
Ballymurphy Women's Ctr
  BT12 . . . . 143 C4
Ballymurphy❶ BT39 . . . . 118 E6
Ballymurphy Rd BT39 . . . 118 F8
Ballynabwee❶ BT47 . . . . . 67 A6
Ballynacaird❶ BT42 . . . . . 80 F7
Ballynacally Beg❶ BT51. . 41 F6
Ballynacally More❶ BT45 . 41 E6
Ballynacally Rd BT51 . . . . 41 E6
Ballynacanon❶ BT51 . . . . . 25 E3
Ballynacloy Rd BT28 . . . . 140 A1
Ballynacooley❶ BT41 . . . 107 C2
Ballynacooley Rd BT41 . . 107 C2
Ballynacraig❶ BT51 . . . . . 121 F5
Ballynacraig Gdns BT48 . 177 A2
Ballynacraigy❶ BT41 . . . . 107 C2
Ballynacree Ave BT53 . . . . 27 B2
Ballynacree Beg❶ BT53 . . 27 C1
Ballynacree Dr BT53 . . . . . 27 B2
Ballynacree More❶ BT53. 27 B1
Ballynacross❶
  Magherafelt BT45 . . . . . . 90 E7
  Strabane BT82 . . . . 68 E3
Ballynacross Rd
  Maghera BT46 . . . . 90 E7
  Magherafelt BT45 . . . . . . 90 F6
  Strabane BT82 . . . . 68 E4
Ballynadolly❶ BT28 . . . . . 147 C3
Ballynadrentagh❶ BT29 . 116 F2
Ballynadrentagh Rd
  BT29 . . . . 117 A2
Ballynafeigh❶ BT53 . . . . . 28 F8
BALLYNAFEIGH BT6 . . . . . 152 A8
Ballynafey❶ BT41 . . . . . . 107 A5
Ballynafey Rd BT41 . . . . . 107 A6
Ballynafie❶ BT44 . . . . 77 A3
Ballynafie Hill BT44 . . . . . 77 B3
Ballynafie Rd BT44 . . . . . . 77 B2
Ballynagabog❶ BT7 . . . . . 144 F1
Ballynagalliagh❶ BT48 . . 176 D6
Ballynagard❶
  Ballycastle BT54 . . . . 3 A6
  Londonderry BT48 . . . . . 177 D8
Ballynagard Cres BT48 . . 177 E7
Ballynagard Rd
  Ballycastle BT54 . . . . 9 B2
  Londonderry BT48 . . . . . 177 D7
Ballynagarrick❶ BT53 . . . 163 A1
Ballynagarrick Rd BT8 . . 162 F3
Ballynagarve❶ BT45 . . . . 105 C6
Ballynagarve Rd BT45 . . . 105 D4
Ballynagashel❶ BT53 . . . . 43 B4
Ballynageeragh❶ BT29 . . 116 D4
Ballynaghten❶ BT28 . . . . 156 B2
Ballynagilly❶ BT80 . . . . . . 102 D1
Ballynagilly La BT80 . . . . 112 C8
Ballynagilly Rd BT80 . . . . 102 C1
Ballynagog❶ BT54 . . . . 9 A4
Ballynag Lower❶ BT52. . . 26 E8
Ballynagor❶ BT53 . . . . 16 F1
Ballynagowan Rd BT45 . . 104 B8
Ballynag Upper❶ BT52 . . . 26 E8
Ballynahatty❶ BT8 . . . . . . 151 A1
Ballynahatty Rd BT8 . . . . 162 B8
Ballynahaville❶ BT44 . . . . 32 C3
Ballynahery❶ BT49 . . . . . . 39 E7
Ballynahinch Rd
  Carryduff BT8 . . . . 163 D1
  Lisburn BT27 . . . . 170 D7
Ballynahone❶ BT45 . . . . . 113 F2
Ballynahone Beg BT46 . . . 90 A7
Ballynahone More❶
  BT45 . . . . 90 C5
Ballynahone Rd BT46 . . . . 90 C6
Ballynalargy❶ BT67 . . . . . 167 D8
Ballynaleney❶ BT41 . . . . . 107 A2
Ballynaloob❶ BT44 . . . . . . 45 B6
Ballynaloob Rd BT44 . . . . 45 B5
Ballynalough❶ BT39 . . . . 118 E6
Ballynalougher❶ BT44 . . . 32 D3
Ballynamaddy❶ BT44 . . . . 61 F6
Ballynameen❶ BT51 . . . . . 58 A7
Ballynameen Ave ❻ BT51 . 58 A8

Ballynameen Rd BT51 .... 58 A6
Ballynamenagh North or
Cummingstown❶ BT53 . 28 A4
Ballynamore❶ BT47 .... 52 C5
Ballynamore Rd BT47 .... 52 C5
Ballynamullan❶ BT41 ..106 D3
Ballynamullan Rd BT41 ..107 A3
Ballynanaghten❶ BT67 ..166 C7
Ballynargan❶ BT80 .... 114 B1
Ballynargan Rd
 Cookstown BT80 ......114 B1
 Dungannon BT71 ......113 F1
Ballynarrig Rd BT49 ..... 38 F3
Ballynarry❶ BT39 ...... 98 E3
Ballynarry Lower BT57 . 16 A5
Ballynarry Rd BT53 ..... 16 A4
Ballynarry Upper BT53 . 16 A3
Ballynashallog❶ BT48 . 177 C4
Ballynashallog Gdns
 BT48 ....177 A2
Ballynashee❶ BT45 ..... 97 A6
Ballynashee Rd BT39 .... 97 A6
Ballynasilloe Ave BT48 .. 177 A2
Ballynastraid❶ BT57 .... 6 F5
Ballyneaner❶ BT82 ..... 68 E4
Ballynease-Helton❶
 BT44 ....76 C2
Ballynease-MacPeake❶
 BT44 ....76 D1
Ballynease Prim Sch
 BT44 ....76 C1
Ballynease Rd
 Ballymena BT44 ...... 76 C2
 Magherafelt BT45 ..... 91 F6
Ballynease-Strain❶ BT44 76 C1
Ballyneill Beg❶ BT45 .. 114 F8
Ballyneill More❶ BT45 . 105 C1
Ballyneill Rd BT45 ..... 105 C1
Ballynenagh❶ BT45 .... 104 F1
Ballyness❶
 Bushmills BT57 .... 5 D2
 Coleraine BT51 .... 26 B6
 Londonderry BT47 ..... 56 C7
Ballyness Pk
 ❶ Bushmills BT57 ..... 5 D3
 Coleraine BT51 .... 26 B6
Ballynewy❶ BT80 ..... 114 B6
Ballynian❶ BT46 .... 58 D1
Ballynian La BT46 ...... 74 F8
Ballynocker❶ BT45 ..... 91 B3
Ballynoe❶
 Antrim BT41 ....109 E7
 Ballycastle BT54 ...... 3 B5
Ballynoe La BT41 ......109 E7
Ballynoe Rd
 Antrim BT41..........187 D8
 Ballymena BT42....... 95 F1
Ballynulto❶ BT42 ..... 80 B3
Ballynulto Rd E BT42 .... 96 C8
Ballynulto Rd W BT42 .. 80 B4
BALLYNURE BT39 ...... 97 F2
Ballynure❶ BT45 ...... 89 A7
Ballynure La BT45....... 89 A7
Ballynure Prim Sch BT39 . 97 F2
Ballynure Rd BT39 ..... 184 D5
Ballynure St
 ❶ Belfast BT14.......137 B1
 Belfast BT14 ....144 B8
Ballyoan❶ BT47 .... 35 F3
Ballyoglagh❶ BT53 ..... 6 E1
Ballyoglagh Loughlynch❶
 BT53 ....17 A6
Ballyore❶ BT47....... 50 E5
Ballyore Dr BT47 ...... 50 F5
Ballypalady❶ BT39 .... 111 A4
Ballypalady Rd BT39 .... 111 C3
Ballypatrick❶
 Ballycastle BT54 ...... 20 A5
 Ballymoney BT53...... 175 A4
Ballypitmave❶ BT29 ... 121 E4
Ballypitmave Rd BT28 .. 147 B6
Ballypollard❶ BT40 .... 99 E6
Ballypollard Rd BT40 .... 99 F6
Ballyportery North❶
 BT44 ....45 C8
Ballyportery Rd BT44.... 45 C8
Ballyportery South❶
 BT44 ....45 E6
Ballyprior Beg❶ BT40 .. 84 C3
Ballyprior More❶ BT40 . 84 D1
Ballyquillan Rd BT29 ... 116 E4
Ballyquillin❶ BT29 .... 116 F4
Ballyquin❶ BT49....... 39 D2
Ballyquin Rd
 Limavady BT49 ....180 D2
 Londonderry BT47 ..... 55 D4
Ballyrashane❶ BT52 ... 15 B2
Ballyrashane Rd BT52 .. 15 C2
Ballyratahan Lower❶
 BT53 ....16 D1
Ballyratahan Upper❶
 BT53 ....28 B8
Bally Rd BT43.......... 78 F7
Ballyreagh❶
 Ballymena BT44........ 62 A5
 Portstewart BT55 ..... 173 B4
Ballyreagh Bsns Pk
 BT80 ....185 B1
Ballyreagh Castle★
 BT55 ....173 A5
Ballyreagh Golf Course
 BT56 ....172 F7
Ballyreagh Ind Est BT80 . 185 B1

Ballyreagh Lower❶ BT54.. 9 C4
Ballyreagh Mews BT55 .. 173 A5
Ballyreagh Pk BT55 .... 173 A4
Ballyreagh Rd
 Ballymena BT44........ 62 A4
 Portrush BT56........ 172 E7
 Portstewart BT55 ..... 173 A5
Ballyreagh Upper❶ BT54.. 9 C4
Ballyrickard Beg❶ BT40 .. 98 F7
Ballyrickard More❶ BT40 98 E7
Ballyrickard Rd BT40.... 98 E5
Ballyriff❶ BT45 .... 105 B2
Ballyriff Rd BT45....... 105 B3
Ballyrisk Beg❶ BT49.... 23 F1
Ballyrisk More❶ BT49.. 23 F2
Ballyrobert Cross Roads
 BT39 ....111 C4
Ballyrobert Rd BT39 ... 184 A1
Ballyrobin❶
 Antrim BT41..........117 F7
 Ballymoney BT53...... 28 D6
Ballyrobin Rd
 Antrim BT41..........117 E7
 Ballyclare BT39 ...... 110 A1
Ballyrock Irish❶ BT53... 15 E3
Ballyrock North❶ BT57 . 15 E5
Ballyrock Rd BT57 ..... 15 E5
Ballyrock Scotch❶ BT57 . 15 E5
Ballyrock South❶ BT53 . 15 E4
BALLYROGAN BT51 .... 41 C2
Ballyrogan❶ BT51 ..... 41 C2
Ballyrogan Rd BT51 .... 57 C8
Ballyrogully❶ BT45 .... 114 D8
BALLYRONAN BT45 .... 105 E2
Ballyronan Beg❶ BT45.. 105 E1
Ballyronan More❶ BT45 105 D3
Ballyronan Pk BT37 .... 133 E3
Ballyronan Rd BT45 .... 183 E4
Ballyrorey Hill BT36 .... 133 D1
Ballyrory❶ BT47 .... 69 E4
Ballyrory Rd BT47 ...... 69 E5
Ballyrushboy❶ BT5 .... 145 D2
Ballyrutherford❶ BT40 .. 66 D1
Ballyryland❶ BT40 ..... 99 B6
Ballysallagh Rd BT43... 47 D1
Ballysally❶ BT52 ..... 174 C8
Ballysally Prim Sch
 BT52 ....174 D7
Ballysally Rd BT52 ..... 174 D8
Ballysavage❶ BT41 .... 110 A5
Ballysavage Rd BT39 ... 110 B5
Ballyscolly❶ BT28 ..... 156 F7
BALLYSCULLION BT49 ... 11 D1
Ballyscullion East❶ BT41 . 92 D4
Ballyscullion La BT45 ... 92 A6
Ballyscullion Rd
 Bellaghy BT45 .... 91 F5
 Magherafelt BT45 ..... 92 A5
Ballyscullion Rd E BT41.. 92 D4
Ballyscullion Rd W BT41.. 92 D5
Ballyscullion West❶
 BT45 ....92 B5
Ballysculty❶ BT41 .... 117 F6
Ballysculty Rd BT41 ... 117 E7
Ballysessy❶ BT29..... 121 A6
Ballyshanaghill❶ BT29 . 120 F7
Ballyshasky❶ BT47 .... 51 E6
Ballysillan❶ BT14..... 136 D4
Ballysillan Ave BT14.... 136 D4
Ballysillan Cres BT14 ... 136 E4
Ballysillan Dr BT14 .... 136 E4
Ballysillan Leisure Ctr
 BT14 ....136 E2
Ballysillan Lower❶
 BT14 ....119 E1
Ballysillan Pk BT14 .... 136 E4
Ballysillan Prim Sch
 BT14 ....136 E4
Ballysillan Rd BT14 .... 136 E3
Ballysillan Upper❶
 BT14 ....119 D3
BALLYSKEAGH BT27 ... 161 A6
Ballyskeagh❶ BT27 ... 161 A7
Ballyskeagh Rd
 Belfast BT17 ....161 B6
 Strabane BT82....... 67 A1
Ballysnod❶ BT40 ..... 83 C1
Ballysnod Rd BT40 .... 182 B2
Ballyspallan❶ BT49 .... 38 D8
Ballystrone❶ BT51 .... 25 C6
Ballystrone Coverts❶
 BT51 ....25 B7
Ballystrone Rd BT51 ... 25 C6
BALLYSTRUDDER BT40 .. 100 D3
Ballystrudder Gdns
 BT40 ....100 D3
Ballystrudder Rd BT40 .. 100 D3
Ballytaggart❶ BT53.... 29 B4
Ballytaylor❶ BT57 ..... 5 D4
Ballyteerim❶ BT44 .... 21 A3
Ballytober❶ BT40..... 82 F5
Ballytober East❶ BT53 .. 5 C2
Ballytober La BT40 .... 100 B8
Ballytober Prim Sch BT57 . 5 C1
Ballytober Rd
 Bushmills BT57 .... 5 B2
 Larne BT40 .... 83 B5
Ballytober West❶ BT57 .. 5 B2
Ballytresna❶ BT41 .... 93 F1
Ballytromery❶ BT29 ... 121 A8
Ballytromery Rd ❷ BT29 117 B1
Ballytunn❶ BT53 ...... 60 A8
Ballytweedy❶ BT41 ... 118 B7
Ballyutoag❶ BT14 .... 119 B3
Ballyutoag Hill BT14 ... 119 A3
Ballyutoag Rd BT14 ... 136 A6
Ballyvaddy❶ BT44 .... 65 B5
Ballyvaddy Rd BT44 .... 65 B6

Ballyvallagh❶ BT40 .... 99 A3
Ballyvallagh Rd
 Ballyclare BT39 ...... 98 E3
 Larne BT40 .... 99 A4
Ballyvanen❶ BT28 .... 120 D3
Ballyvannon Rd BT28... 120 E4
Ballyvaston❶ BT36 .... 119 E5
Ballyveely❶ BT54....... 8 E1
Ballyveely Lower❶ BT53 . 29 E3
Ballyveely Rd
 Ballymena BT44....... 45 E4
 Ballymoney BT53 ..... 29 E3
Ballyveely Upper❶ BT44 . 29 F2
Ballyvelligan❶ BT44 ... 49 D6
Ballyvelton❶ BT52..... 26 E8
Ballyvelton Lower❶ BT52 15 A1
Ballyvelton Rd BT52.... 26 F8
Ballyvelton Upper❶ BT52 15 A1
Ballyvennaght❶ BT54... 20 C6
Ballyvennaght Rd BT54... 9 D2
Ballyvennox❶ BT51..... 25 D6
Ballyvernstown❶ BT40 .. 99 B8
Ballyvernstown Rd BT40 .. 99 A7
Ballyversall❶ BT52 .... 15 B4
Ballyversal Rd BT52..... 15 B4
Ballyvesey❶ BT36 .... 119 D8
Ballyvesey Ct ❸❽ BT36 . 111 F1
Ballyvesey Pk ❷❸ BT36 . 111 F1
Ballyvesey Rd BT36 .... 111 C1
Ballyvesey Rise ❷❹ BT36 . 111 F1
Ballyvollen❶ BT29 .... 120 F6
Ballyvooly❶ BT44...... 32 D6
Ballyvorally❶ BT28 .... 120 F5
Ballyvoy❶ BT54......... 9 B3
Ballywatermoy Crankill❶
 BT43 ....61 F3
Ballywatermoy Rd BT44 . 61 D2
Ballywatt East❶ BT53 .. 15 D4
Ballywattick Lower❶
 BT53 ....27 C3
Ballywattick Middle❶
 BT53 ....27 C4
Ballywattick Upper❶
 BT53 ....27 C4
Ballywatt Leggs❶ BT52 . 15 C4
Ballywatt Rd BT52 ..... 15 C5
Ballywatt West❶ BT52 .. 15 C4
Ballywee❶ BT39 ...... 110 C6
Ballyweeny❶ BT44..... 45 F6
Ballyweeny Rd BT44.... 45 F6
Ballywee Rd BT39 ..... 110 B6
Ballywildrick Lower❶
 BT51 ....13 C1
Ballywildrick Upper❶
 BT51 ....25 A8
Ballywillan Rd
 Larne BT40 .... 99 C5
 Portstewart BT55 ..... 173 F5
Ballywillen Cres BT55 .. 173 F5
Ballywillen Pk BT55 .... 173 F5
Ballywillin❶
 Coleraine BT51 .... 42 C6
 Larne BT40 .... 83 A7
 Portstewart BT55 ..... 173 F4
Ballywillin Bog❶ BT52 .. 14 D5
Ballywindelland Lower❶
 BT53 ....27 A4
Ballywindelland Rd BT53 . 27 A5
Ballywindelland Upper❶
 BT53 ....27 A4
Ballywonard❶ BT36 ... 119 E6
Ballywoodock❶
 Ballyclare BT39 ...... 110 A8
 Coleraine BT51 .... 12 F3
Ballywoodock Rd
 Ballyclare BT39 ...... 110 A8
 Coleraine BT51 .... 13 A3
Ballywoolen❶ BT51 .... 13 C4
Ballywoolen House★
 BT51 ....13 C4
Ballywoolen Rd BT51 ... 13 D3
Balmoral Ave
 Ballymena BT43........ 181 C4
 Belfast BT9 .... 150 F6
 Londonderry BT48 .... 176 F2
 Whitehead BT38 ..... 127 A8
Balmoral Bsns Pk BT12.. 143 F1
Balmoral Ctr BT9 ..... 150 E7
Balmoral Dr BT9 ...... 150 F6
Balmoral Est BT12 .... 150 E8
Balmoral Gdns BT9 .... 150 F6
Balmoral Golf Club BT9 . 150 C6
Balmoral High Sch BT10 150 B5
Balmoral Link BT12 .... 150 F7
Balmoral Pk BT10...... 150 F5
Balmoral Rd BT12 ..... 150 F7
Balmoral Sta BT9 ..... 150 E6
BALNAMORE BT53 .... 27 C1
Balnamore Prim Sch
 BT53 ....27 B2
Balnamore Rd BT53 ... 175 A3
Balteagh Rd BT51...... 25 B4
Baltic Ave BT15 .... 137 C1
Bamber Ave BT43 ..... 181 A4
Bamber Pk BT43 ...... 181 A4
Banagher Rd BT47 ..... 71 C4
Banbury St BT4 .... 145 C6
Bancran Globe❶ BT45 .. 88 B3
Bancran Rd BT45 ...... 88 C3
Bandon Ct ❶❻ BT14 ... 144 B8
Bangor Rd BT18 ...... 139 E7
Bankfield Dr ❸ BT80 ... 114 C3
Bankhall Rd BT40 ...... 99 F4
Bankheads La BT40 ... 182 E5
Bankmore St BT7 ..... 189 A2
Bank Pl BT48 .... 178 F5
Bank Rd BT40......... 182 D3

Bank Sq & La ❶❶ BT46 ... 74 D1
Bank St BT1 .... 189 A3
Bannagh Cnr BT6 ..... 152 B7
Bann Bridge BT52..... 174 C3
Bannbrook Lower❶ BT51 13 F3
Bannbrook Upper❶ BT51. 13 F3
Bann Ct ❶❾ BT14 .... 144 B8
Bann Dr BT47......... 179 B4
Bannfield Rd BT52..... 175 B2
Bann La BT29 .... 121 D5
Bann Rd
 Ballymena BT44....... 59 E6
 Ballymoney BT53...... 175 B1
Bannside BT41........ 106 C8
Bannvale BT51 .... 174 B5
Bann View❶ BT51 ..... 59 E3
Bannview Pk BT53 .... 175 B2
Bantry Rd BT48 ...... 176 B1
Bantry St ❼ BT13 .... 143 F5
Bapaume Ave BT6 .... 152 C8
Baraghilly❶ BT44..... 48 C6
Baran❶ BT49.......... 40 F5
Baranailt❶ BT49...... 38 C2
Baranailt Pk ❸ BT47 ... 69 C8
Baranailt Rd
 ❶ Claudy BT47 ...... 69 C8
 Limavady BT49 ...... 180 A5
 Londonderry BT47 .... 53 F5
Barard❶ BT44........ 31 F1
Barhallive❶ BT53 ..... 30 A6
Barkley Ct BT53....... 28 B2
Barley Hill BT27 ...... 160 D2
Barleywood Mill BT28 .. 160 B8
Barmeen❶ BT44...... 20 F1
Barmouth Rd BT51 .... 13 C4
Barnagaw❶ BT51 ..... 58 D4
Barnailt Rd
 Claudy BT47......... 69 C8
 Londonderry BT47 .... 53 B2
Barnakilly❶ BT49 ..... 38 A6
Barna Sq BT37........ 133 E3
Barnes Rd BT47....... 70 C2
Barnet Rd BT3 .... 144 F8
Barnett's Chase BT5 ... 146 C4
Barnett's Cres BT5..... 146 C4
Barnett's Ct BT5...... 146 D4
Barnett's Ct Mews BT5 . 146 C4
Barnett's Gn BT5 ..... 146 D4
Barnett's Lodge BT5.... 146 D4
Barnett's Rd BT5....... 146 C4
Barnfield Cotts BT28 ... 149 B1
Barnfield Grange N
 BT28 ....149 B1
Barnfield Grange S BT28 149 B1
Barnfield Rd
 Dunmurry BT28 ...... 160 B8
 Lisburn BT28 .... 149 A2
Barnish❶
 Antrim BT41..........108 D7
 Ballycastle BT54 ...... 9 A3
 Ballymena BT42....... 96 A4
Barnish Prim Sch BT54... 9 B3
Barnish Rd
 Antrim BT41..........108 D7
 Ballymena BT42....... 95 F4
Barn Mills BT38 ...... 125 C4
Barn Oak La BT5....... 146 D4
Barn Rd BT38 .... 125 C1
Barnside Rd BT51 ..... 58 D4
Barnwall Pl BT47 ..... 179 A4
Baroda Dr ❺ BT7 ..... 144 E1
Baroda Parade ❻ BT7 .. 144 E1
Baroda St BT7 .... 144 E1
Baronet St BT48 ...... 178 F7
Baronscourt Ave BT8... 163 E4
Baronscourt Cl BT8 .... 163 D4
Baronscourt Dr BT8 .... 163 D4
Baronscourt Gdns BT8 .. 163 E4
Baronscourt Glen BT8... 163 E4
Baronscourt Hts BT8 ... 163 E4
Baronscourt La BT8 .... 163 E4
Baronscourt Link BT8 .. 163 D4
Baronscourt Mews BT8 . 163 D4
Baronscourt Pk BT8 .... 163 D4
Baronscourt Rd BT8.... 163 D4
Barons Ct BT45 ...... 183 C7
Barrack Rd BT45 ..... 105 E5
Barrack St
 Belfast BT12 ....188 C3
 Londonderry BT48 .... 178 E4
Barra Dr BT42 .... 181 E3
Barran❶ BT82 .... 67 C1
Barra St BT41......... 186 D8
Barr-Cregg BT47 ..... 69 B8
Barr Cregg❶ BT47 .... 53 A4
Barrington Gdns BT12... 188 B1
Barron Rd BT82....... 67 C2
Barrs La BT48......... 176 A1
Barry St BT48 .... 178 F8
Barscourt BT27 ...... 160 B5
Bartins Bay Rd BT47 ... 120 H3
Bashfordsland BT38.... 125 D4
Baskin St ❼ BT5 ..... 145 B5
Bates Pk BT38 .... 129 F2
Bathgate Dr ❻ BT4 ... 145 E6
Bath Rd BT55......... 173 D8
Bath St BT55.......... 173 D7
Batley St BT5 .... 145 D4
Battenberg St BT13 ... 188 A4
Battery Rd BT80 ..... 115 B2

Bawn Ct BT49......... 38 C7
Bawnmore BT45 ...... 91 E6
Bawnmore Gr ❶ BT36.. 133 E1
Bawnmore Pk BT36.... 133 E1
Bawnmore Pl
 ❷ Newtownabbey BT36.. 133 E1
 Strathfoyle BT47 ..... 177 F6
Bawnmore Rd BT9 .... 151 A7
Bawnmore Terr ❸ BT36. 133 E1
Bay❶ BT44........... 32 F1
Bayhead Pk BT57 ..... 5 C4
Bayhead Rd BT57...... 5 B4
Baylands BT40........ 182 F4
Bay Pk BT40.......... 182 F4
Bay Rd
 Belfast BT29 ....120 D8
 Carnlough BT44 ..... 49 C3
 Cushendun BT44 ..... 21 A2
 Larne BT40 .... 182 F4
 Londonderry BT48 .... 177 A1
Bay Rd Ind Est
 Larne BT40 .... 182 F3
 Londonderry BT48 .... 177 B1
Bay Rd Pk★ BT48...... 177 C1
Bayswater BT47....... 179 C7
Bayview Ind Pk BT3.... 138 A3
Bayview Pk
 Ballymena BT44....... 32 F4
 Craigavon BT67 ..... 154 A6
 Londonderry BT47 .... 179 C7
Bayview Rd BT54....... 8 F5
BBC Blackstaff House★
 BT2 ....189 A2
Beachlands BT44 ..... 49 C2
Beach Rd
 Portballintrae BT57 ... 5 C5
 Whitehead BT38 ..... 127 A4
Beafort Dr BT47 ..... 179 D4
Beaghmore Stone Circles,
 Alignments & Cairns★
 BT80 ....101 D1
Beagh Rd BT46 ...... 74 E2
Beaghs❶ BT53 .... 31 B5
Beagh (Spiritual)❶ BT46. 90 D8
Beagh (Temporal)❶
 BT46 ....74 E2
Beagh Terr BT46...... 90 E8
Beaghville Dr BT55.... 173 C5
BEALACH CLÁIR
 (BALLYCLARE) BT39 ... 184 E4
Bealachmor ❽ BT48 ... 176 B2
Bealachmor Lower ❼
 BT48 ....176 B2
BÉAL FEIRSTE (BELFAST)
 BT1 ....189 C2
Bean Fort★ BT41 ..... 108 F1
Beanstown Rd BT28 ... 159 C6
Beardiville❶ BT57 .... 15 C5
Bearnagh Dr BT11 .... 150 B8
Bearnagh Glen BT11 ... 143 C1
Beattie Pk Central BT17. 150 A4
Beattie Pk N BT17...... 150 A2
Beattie Pk S BT17...... 150 B1
Beaufort Ave BT8 ..... 151 F3
Beaufort Cres BT8 .... 151 F3
Beaufort Dr BT47 ..... 179 D4
Beaufort Gdns BT8..... 151 F3
Beaufort Gr BT8 ...... 151 F3
Beaufort Pk BT8 ...... 152 A3
Beaumont Hill BT43 ... 181 B6
Beaver Cres BT46 ..... 74 C1
Beaver Dr ❷ BT46 .... 74 C1
Beckeley Deane BT38 .. 129 D4
Beckett Ave BT53 .... 175 A6
Beckett Cl BT53....... 175 A6
Beckett Ct BT53....... 175 A6
Beckett Dr BT53....... 175 A6
Beckett Pk BT53 ..... 175 A6
Bedford St BT2 .... 189 A2
Beech Ave BT52 ..... 174 C8
Beech Cres BT28 ..... 159 E3
Beechcroft BT53 ..... 175 B6
Beechdene Dr BT28 ... 159 F4
Beechdene Gdns BT28 . 159 F4
Beechdene Pk BT28 ... 159 F3
Beech Dr
 Ballymena BT43........ 181 E8
 Carrickfergus BT38 ... 130 F8
Beech End BT18 ...... 139 C5
Beeches Manor The
 BT28 ....147 D5
Beeches The
 Ballymena BT42....... 181 A3
 Castlereagh BT8 ..... 151 E2
 Crumlin BT29........ 121 A8
 Drumahoe BT47...... 179 F1
 ❽ Larne BT40........ 83 D4
 Maghera BT46....... 74 F5
 Newtownabbey BT36... 132 D3
Beechfield
 Antrim BT41..........186 F6
 Ballyclare BT39 ...... 110 A4
Beechfield Ave BT38 ... 125 A4
Beechfield Cl
 Ballymena BT42....... 181 B4
 Carrickfergus BT38 ... 125 A4
Beechfield Ct
 ❸❺ Belfast BT5 ...... 145 A5
 Coleraine BT52 ...... 174 F5
Beechfield Lodge BT67. 155 C3
Beechfield Manor BT67. 155 C3
Beechfield Pk
 Coleraine BT52 ...... 174 F5
 Lisburn BT28........ 169 C8
Beechfield Prim Sch ❸❽
 BT5 ....145 A5
Beechfield St
 Belfast BT5 .... 145 A5
 ❸❹ Belfast BT5....... 145 A5

Beech Gn BT39 . . . . 110 F6
Beech Gr
Ballymena BT43. . . . . 181 F8
Dunmurry BT17 . . . . 160 F8
[7] Larne BT40. . . . . 83 B3
Beechgrove
Antrim BT41. . . . . 187 C3
Kilrea BT51 . . . . 59 B5
Lisburn BT27 . . . . 160 B4
Beechgrove Ave
Castlereagh BT6 . . . . 152 B5
Craigavon BT67 . . . . 164 F7
Beechgrove Cres
Castlereagh BT6 . . . . 152 C6
Newtownabbey BT36. . . . . 128 A1
Beechgrove Dr
Castlereagh BT6 . . . . 152 B6
Craigavon BT67 . . . . 164 F7
[3] Newtownabbey BT36 . . 128 A1
Beechgrove Gdns
Castlereagh BT6 . . . . 152 B6
Newtownabbey BT36. . . . . 128 A1
Beechgrove Hts BT45 . . . 183 B6
Beechgrove Manor BT43 181 F7
Beechgrove Pk
Castlereagh BT6 . . . . 152 B6
Craigavon BT67 . . . . 164 E8
Beechgrove Rise BT6 . . . 152 C6
Beechgrove Sch BT43 . . . 181 F8
Beech Hill BT53. . . . . 175 B5
Beech Hill Gdns BT28 . . . 159 D5
Beech Hill Pk BT28. . . . . . 159 E4
Beechill Ave BT8. . . . . 152 B2
Beechill Ct BT8 . . . . 152 A2
Beechill Gr BT28 . . . . 160 B8
Beechill Ind Pk BT8. . . . . 151 F2
Beechill Pk BT8. . . . . 152 A3
Beechill Pk Ave BT8. . . . . 152 A2
Beechill Pk E BT8 . . . . 152 B3
Beechill Pk N BT8. . . . . . . 152 B3
Beechill Pk S BT8. . . . . . . 152 B2
Beechill Pk W BT8 . . . . . . 152 A3
Beechill Rd BT8. . . . . 151 F3
Beechland Dr
[2] Ballymena BT44 . . . . 76 B4
Lisburn BT28 . . . . 170 A7
Magherafelt BT45 . . . . 183 E5
Beechland Gdns [4] BT44 . 76 B4
Beechland Pk [3] BT44. . . . 76 B4
Beechland Pk E Lay [1]
BT44 . . . . 76 B4
Beechland Pl BT45 . . . . . . 183 E5
Beechland Rd BT45 . . . . . 183 E5
Beechlands BT9 . . . . 151 C8
Beechland Way BT28. . . . 170 A7
Beechland Wlk BT28 . . . . 170 A7
Beechlawn Ave BT17 . . . . 150 B2
Beechlawn Pk BT17 . . . . . 150 B3
Beechliegh Pk BT47. . . . . . 36 E5
Beechmount BT47 . . . . 70 E6
Beechmount Ave BT12 . . 143 F4
Beechmount Cl [2] BT12 . 143 F4
Beechmount Cres BT12 . 143 E4
Beechmount Dr BT12 . . . 143 F3
Beechmount Gdns BT12 . 143 E4
Beechmount Gr BT12 . . . 143 F4
Beechmount Leisure Ctr
BT12 . . . . 143 E3
Beechmount Parade
BT12 . . . . 143 E4
Beechmount Pass [3]
BT12 . . . . 143 F4
Beechmount Pk
Belfast BT10 . . . . 150 D5
Randalstown BT41. . . . . . . 108 A7
Beechmount Rd BT8 . . . . 163 E8
Beechmount St [8] BT12 . 143 F4
Beechmount Wlk [6]
BT12 . . . . 143 F4
Beechnut Pl [8] BT14 . . . . 144 B8
Beechpark St [7] BT14 . . . 144 B8
Beech Pk
Belfast BT6 . . . . 152 D8
Drumahoe BT47. . . . . 179 F1
Lisburn BT27 . . . . 160 B4
Beech Rd
Limavady BT49 . . . . 40 A2
Londonderry BT47. . . . . 55 A5
Beech Tree Ct BT17 . . . . . 149 F1
Beechvale BT42. . . . . 79 C7
Beechview BT39 . . . . 184 C4
Beechview Gdns [5] BT51 . 59 C5
Beechview Pk BT12 . . . . . 143 E3
Beechway BT80. . . . . 185 D6
Beechwood Ave
Ahoghill BT42 . . . . 77 F2
Ballycastle BT54 . . . . 8 D4
Ballymena BT42. . . . . 181 B2
Londonderry BT48. . . . . . . 178 C6
Moira BT67 . . . . 166 B2
Newtownabbey BT37. . . . . 133 F4
Beechwood Cres
Londonderry BT48. . . . . . . 178 C6
Moira BT67 . . . . 166 A2
Beechwood Ct
Castlereagh BT8 . . . . 151 F2
Moira BT67 . . . . 166 A1
Beechwood Dr
[6] Ahoghill BT42. . . . . 77 F2
Ballymoney BT53. . . . . 27 B2
Beechwood Gdns BT67. . 166 B2
Beechwood Gr
Castlereagh BT8 . . . . 151 F2
Lisburn BT28 . . . . 159 D4
Beechwood Mews BT8 . . 151 F2
Beechwood Pk
Moira BT67 . . . . 166 A1
Strathfoyle BT47 . . . . 177 F5
Beechwood St
Belfast BT5 . . . . 145 D4
[5] Londonderry BT48 . . . . 178 D5
BeerhillⓉ BT53 . . . . 16 B1
Beersbridge Rd BT5. . . . . 145 D4
Beit St BT12 . . . . 188 B1
BelaghertyⓉ BT45 . . . . . . 105 D1
Belair St BT13 . . . . 143 F6
Beleevna-MoreⓉ BT79. . 101 E1
Belemont Rd BT51 . . . . . . 173 A1
Belfast Airport Conservation
Area★ BT3. . . . . 139 A5
BELFAST (BÉAL FEIRSTE)
BT1 . . . . 189 C3
Belfast Bible Coll BT17 . . 150 B1
Belfast Boys Model Sch
BT14. . . . . 136 F5
Belfast Castle (Cave Hill
Visitor Centre)★ BT36. . 137 B7
Belfast Central Sta BT7 . 189 C2
Belfast City Hospl BT9 . . 188 C1
Belfast Harbour Ind Est
BT3. . . . . 138 C4
Belfast High Sch BT38 . . 129 E1
Belfast Inst of FE & HE
BT2. . . . . 189 A2
Belfast Inst of FE & HE
(Whiterock Building)
BT12. . . . . 143 D3
Belfast Int Airport BT29 . 117 B5
Belfast Lough Reserve★
BT3. . . . . 138 E4
Belfast Model Sch for Girls
BT14. . . . . 137 A3
Belfast Print Workshop
Gall★ BT1. . . . . 189 B4
Belfast Rd
Antrim BT41. . . . . 186 F3
Ballyclare BT39 . . . . 110 F2
Belfast BT8 . . . . 163 F1
Belfast BT29 . . . . 140 A1
Carrickfergus BT38 . . . . . 130 B5
Holywood BT18 . . . . 139 C5
Larne BT40 . . . . 98 D8
Lisburn BT27 . . . . 160 C2
Newtownabbey BT36. . . . . 132 B5
Belfast Royal Acad [5]
BT14 . . . . 137 C1
Belfast Royal Acaemy
BT14. . . . . 144 C8
Belfast Welcome Ctr
BT1 . . . . 189 A3
Belfast Zoo★ BT36. . . . . 133 B1
Belfield Pk BT48 . . . . 176 C1
Belford Pk BT53 . . . . 175 D5
BelgarrowⓉ BT51. . . . . 24 F7
Belgrano [3] BT42. . . . . 77 E2
Belgrave Pk BT47 . . . . 179 D4
Belgrave St BT13 . . . . 188 B4
Belgravia Ave BT9 . . . . . . 144 B2
Belagherty Rd BT45 . . . . 115 A8
BellaghyⓉ BT44 . . . . 45 C1
BELLAGHY (BAILE
EACHAIDH) BT45. . . . . 91 E5
Bellaghy Bawn★ BT45. . . . 91 F5
Bellaghy Cres BT44 . . . . . . 44 F4
Bellaghy Pk BT44 . . . . 44 F4
Bellaghy Prim Sch BT45. . 91 F6
Bellaghy Rd BT44 . . . . 61 C8
Bellahill Rd BT38 . . . . 125 E8
BellairⓉ BT44 . . . . 65 D8
Bellair Pk BT40 . . . . 182 A6
BellanyⓉ BT51 . . . . 13 F2
Bellany Rd BT51 . . . . 13 F3
BellarenaⓉ BT49 . . . . 22 F6
Bellarena Prim Sch BT49. 23 A7
Bellarena Sta BT49. . . . . . . 23 B8
BellassesⓉ BT52. . . . . 174 F3
Bell Cl BT13 . . . . 144 A7
BelleeⓉ BT43 . . . . 62 C2
Bellemont MoreⓉ BT52 . . 14 C5
BelleviewⓉ BT46 . . . . 58 B2
Belleville BT42. . . . . 181 D1
BellevueⓉ BT51 . . . . 42 B6
Bellevue Dr
Lisburn BT28 . . . . 160 A2
Newtownabbey BT36. . . . . 133 B2
Bellevue Manor BT36 . . . 133 B3
Bellevue Pk
Lisburn BT28 . . . . 160 A2
Newtownabbey BT36. . . . . 133 B2
Bellevue Pl BT39. . . . . 184 D4
Bellevue St
Ballyclare BT39 . . . . 184 D4
Belfast BT13 . . . . 188 A4
Bellfield Hts BT12. . . . . . . 143 B3
Bellhouse La BT52 . . . . . . 174 C4
Bellipar Pk BT47. . . . . 55 C3
Bellisk Dr BT44 . . . . 32 D4
Bellisk or WaterfordⓉ
BT44 . . . . 32 E3
Bellisk Pk BT44 . . . . 32 E4
BellisleⓉ BT53 . . . . 28 C7
Bellisle Rd BT53 . . . . 28 D7
Bellmount BT44. . . . . 60 B5
Bells Hill
Limavady BT49 . . . . 180 D6
Magherafelt BT45 . . . . 105 D7
Bells La BT27 . . . . 160 D6
Bell Steel Shops Rd
BT17 . . . . 149 C3
Bell Twrs BT7. . . . . 151 F7
BelluryⓉ BT51. . . . . 58 C8
BELMONT BT4. . . . . 146 B5
Belmont Ave [2] BT4. . . . . 145 F5
Belmont Ave W BT4. . . . . 145 F5
Belmont Church Rd BT4. 145 F6
Belmont Cl [1] BT4 . . . . . . 145 F5
Belmont Cres BT48. . . . . . 177 A2
Belmont Ct [3] BT4 . . . . . . 145 F6
Belmont Dr
Belfast BT4 . . . . 146 A5
Lisburn BT28 . . . . 159 E5
Londonderry BT48 . . . . 177 A2
Belmont Gr BT28. . . . . 159 E5
Belmont Grange BT4. . . . . 145 F5
Belmont House Sch [1]
BT48 . . . . 176 F2
Belmont Hts BT41. . . . . . . 187 A2
Belmont Mews [11] BT4. . . 145 E6
Belmont Pk
[7] Belfast BT4 . . . . 146 A5
Londonderry BT48. . . . . . . 176 F2
Belmont Pl BT52. . . . . 174 D5
Belmont Prim Sch BT4. . 145 F5
Belmont Rd
Antrim BT41. . . . . 186 E2
Belfast BT4 . . . . 145 E5
Lisburn BT28 . . . . 159 E5
Belmore Gdns BT37 . . . . . 133 E3
BelraughⓉ BT51. . . . . 41 B5
Belraugh Rd BT51. . . . . 56 E8
Belshaws Rd BT28 . . . . . . 120 F2
Belsize La BT27. . . . . 160 B4
Belsize Pk BT27. . . . . 160 B4
Belsize Rd BT27. . . . . 160 B4
Beltoy Ct BT38. . . . . 125 F3
Beltoy (Glynn)Ⓣ BT40. . . . 99 D4
Beltoy (Raloo)Ⓣ BT40. . . . 99 D3
Beltoy Rd BT38 . . . . 125 E4
Belt Rd BT47. . . . . 179 B2
Belvedere Ave BT51. . . . . . 13 B4
Belvedere Manor BT9 . . . 151 B8
Belvedere Pk
Belfast BT9 . . . . 151 D7
Castlerock BT51 . . . . 13 B4
[5] Londonderry BT48 . . . . 176 C1
Belview Ave BT48 . . . . . . 178 E4
Belvoir Cl BT8 . . . . 151 C2
Belvoir Cres
Castlereagh BT8 . . . . 151 D2
Lisburn BT28 . . . . 169 F8
Belvoir Dr BT8. . . . . 151 C2
Belvoir Pk
Lisburn BT28 . . . . 169 F8
Londonderry BT48. . . . . . . 177 F8
Belvoir Pk Hospl BT8 . . . 162 D8
Belvoir Pk Prim Sch
BT8. . . . . 151 D2
Belvoir Rd BT8. . . . . 151 F3
Belvoir St BT5 . . . . 145 B5
Benares St [6] BT13 . . . . . 143 F5
Benbane Pk BT57 . . . . 5 B4
Benbradagh Ave (Ascaill
Bheann Bradáin) [2]
BT47 . . . . 55 D2
Benbradagh Gdns BT11 . 150 B8
Benbradagh Resource Ctr
BT49. . . . . 180 C5
Benbragagh Ave BT49. . . 180 B4
Benburb St BT12. . . . . 188 A1
Bencrom Pk BT37. . . . . . . 133 E3
Bendigo St BT6. . . . . 189 C1
BendooraghⓉ BT53. . . . . . . 43 C8
BENDOORAGH BT53. . . . . . 43 D8
Bendooragh Rd BT53. . . . . 43 D1
Ben Eden Ave BT15 . . . . . 137 D6
Ben Eden Ct BT15. . . . . . . 137 D6
Ben Eden Gn BT15 . . . . . . 137 D6
Ben Eden Pk BT15 . . . . . . 137 D6
Benevenagh Ave BT49. . . 180 B5
Benevenagh Gdns BT48 . 178 B4
Benford Pk BT27. . . . . 170 D8
Bengore Gdns BT40. . . . . 182 A5
Ben Madigan Hts BT36 . . 133 C1
Ben Madigan Pk BT36. . . 133 C1
Ben Madigan Pk S BT36 . 133 C1
Ben Madigan Prep Sch
BT15. . . . . 137 C7
Benmore Ct BT10 . . . . 150 D4
Benmore Dr BT10. . . . . . . 150 D3
Benmore Pk BT43. . . . . 47 C3
BennareesⓉ BT51 . . . . 12 E4
Bennett Dr [10] BT14 . . . . 137 B1
BenoneⓉ BT49 . . . . 12 A4
Benone Ave BT49 . . . . 12 B4
Benraw Gn BT11. . . . . 150 C8
Benraw Rd BT11 . . . . 150 C8
Benson Pk BT28 . . . . 159 F1
Bensons Rd BT28 . . . . 159 A7
Benson St BT28. . . . . 159 E1
Bentham Dr BT12. . . . . . . 188 B1
Bentinck St [7] BT15. . . . . 144 E8
Bentley Terr [3] BT47. . . . 179 A5
BentraⓉ BT38 . . . . 100 C1
Bentra Municipal Golf
Course BT38. . . . . 100 C2
Bentrim Ct BT28 . . . . 159 F2
Bentrim Link Rd BT28 . . . 159 F2
Benvarden Ave BT47 . . . . 179 A4
BenvardinⓉ BT53. . . . . 15 F1
Benvardin Rd BT53. . . . . . . 15 E1
Benview Ave BT14 . . . . . . 136 E4
Benview Dr BT14. . . . . 136 E4
Benview Est BT48 . . . . 176 A5
Benview Pk BT14 . . . . 136 E3
Benview Rd BT48 . . . . 176 A5
Benvisteen Pk BT28 . . . . . 169 D8
Benwee Pk BT11. . . . . 149 F6
Beragh Hill Rd BT48. . . . . 176 E7
Beraghmore Rd BT48 . . . . 176 E6
Beresford Ave BT52 . . . . . 174 D2
Beresford Rd BT52. . . . . . 174 C3
Berkeley Rd BT3. . . . . 144 F7
Berkley Ct
Castlereagh BT8 . . . . 151 F3
Berkley Ct *continued*
[1] Crumlin BT29 . . . . 117 B1
Berkley Dr BT38 . . . . 124 F3
Berkley Rd BT38 . . . . 124 E3
Berlin St BT13 . . . . 188 A4
Berne Ave BT56. . . . . 172 A3
Berne Rd BT55. . . . . 172 A3
Bernice Rd BT39 . . . . 119 A7
Berryburn Gdns BT47 . . . . 51 F5
Berry Cres BT37 . . . . 129 A3
Berry Dr BT37 . . . . 129 A2
Berryfields Pk BT53. . . . . 175 D6
Berryfields Rd BT37. . . . . 129 A3
Berryhill Rd BT82 . . . . 67 B3
Berry La BT37 . . . . 129 A3
Berry Pk BT37 . . . . 129 A2
Berry St BT1. . . . . 189 A3
Berwick Hts BT67 . . . . 166 C1
Berwick Rd BT14. . . . . 136 F1
Berwick View BT67 . . . . . 166 C1
Berwick View Spine Rd
BT67 . . . . 166 D1
Bessfield Ave BT38. . . . . . 125 A4
Bessfield Cl BT38 . . . . 125 A4
Bessfield Pk BT38. . . . . . . 125 A4
Best's Hill BT8. . . . . 151 E1
Best's Hill Ct BT8 . . . . 151 E1
Best's Hill Glen BT8. . . . . . 151 F1
Best's Hill La BT8 . . . . 151 E1
Best's Hill View BT8. . . . . . 151 F1
Bethany St [5] BT4 . . . . . . 145 F5
Betts Rd BT49 . . . . 39 F1
Beverley Ave BT36 . . . . . . 128 A1
Beverley Cres [4] BT36. . . 128 A1
Beverley Dr [3] BT36. . . . . 133 A8
Beverley Gdns
[2] Londonderry BT47 . . . . 179 C4
[1] Newtownabbey BT36 . 133 A8
Beverley Gr BT36 . . . . 128 A1
Beverley Pk BT36 . . . . 133 A8
Beverley Rd BT36 . . . . 128 A1
Beverley Sh Ctr BT36. . . . 128 A1
Beverly St BT13. . . . . 188 B4
Big FrossesⓉ BT44 . . . . . . 61 E8
Big GlebeⓉ BT51 . . . . 13 A2
BighouseⓉ BT54. . . . . 9 F4
Big TroskⓉ BT44 . . . . 49 A4
Bigwood Rd
Londonderry BT47. . . . . 51 E3
Strabane BT82. . . . . 67 E8
Bilston Rd BT14. . . . . 136 D2
BinabananⓉ BT44 . . . . 49 C6
Bingnian Dr BT11 . . . . 150 B8
Bingnian Way [2] BT11. . . 150 B8
BinnⓉ BT47 . . . . 69 D7
BinnellyⓉ BT82. . . . . 67 D4
Binnelly Rd BT82. . . . . 67 D3
Birch Dale BT36 . . . . 132 D8
Birch Dr BT18 . . . . 139 D7
Birches The
Carrickfergus BT38. . . . . . 124 E1
Doagh BT39. . . . . 110 F6
Birch Gn
Dunmurry BT17. . . . . 160 F8
Newtownabbey BT36. . . . . 132 D8
Birchgrove BT80. . . . . 185 E3
Birch HillⓉ BT41 . . . . 187 A6
Birchill Ave BT41 . . . . 186 F6
Birchill Pk BT41 . . . . 187 A5
Birchill Rd BT41 . . . . 187 C7
Birchill Rd S BT41. . . . . . . 187 A6
Birch La BT36. . . . . 132 D8
Birch Mdw BT36 . . . . 132 D8
Birchmount [4] BT36 . . . . 128 A2
Birch Rd BT47 . . . . 52 C4
Birch View BT36 . . . . 132 D8
Birchwood
Bellaghy BT45 . . . . 91 E5
Lisburn BT28 . . . . 159 D4
Birchwood Pk [2] BT45 . . 105 A1
Birmingham Rd BT36. . . . 132 B5
Birren Rd BT47 . . . . 72 C5
Bishop St Without BT48 . 178 D4
Bishop's House & Bawn
(ruin)★ BT38 . . . . 126 C3
Bishops Rd BT49. . . . . 23 E7
Bishop St [3] BT48. . . . . . . 178 E4
Bishop's Well★ BT44. . . . . 76 E4
Black BraeⓉ BT47 . . . . 36 B7
Blackbrae Rd BT47. . . . . . . 36 B7
Black BraesⓉ BT47 . . . . . . 37 C2
Black Brea (Intake)Ⓣ
BT47 . . . . 36 B8
Blackburn Cres BT47. . . . 179 C4
BlackcaveⓉ BT40. . . . . 182 C8
Blackcave Cres BT40. . . . . . 83 D6
Blackcave Gdns BT40 . . . 182 D6
Blackcave Manor BT40. . . 182 C8
Blackcave N BT40. . . . . . . 182 C8
Blackcave Pk BT40. . . . . . 182 D7
Blackcave SouthⓉ BT40 182 D8
BlackfallsⓉ BT47 . . . . 54 F6
BlackheathⓉ BT51. . . . . 41 F8
Black HillⓉ BT38 . . . . 99 E2
Blackhill Rd BT47 . . . . 36 C3
Black MountainⓉ BT17 . 142 E3
Black Mountain Gr BT13 143 D5
Black Mountain Parade
BT13 . . . . 143 D5
Black Mountain Pk BT13 143 D5
Black Mountain Pl BT13 143 D5
Black Mountain Prim Sch
BT13. . . . . 143 C5
Black Mountain Way
BT13 . . . . 143 D5
Black Mountain Wlk
BT13 . . . . 143 C6
Blackpark Rd BT41. . . . . . 106 A8
Black Pk Rd BT54 . . . . 9 B4
Blackrock Pk
Coleraine BT51 . . . . 59 B5
Portstewart BT55 . . . . 173 C5
Blackrock Rd
Antrim BT41. . . . . 107 F4
Coleraine BT51 . . . . 58 E6
Omagh BT79 . . . . 101 C2
Portstewart BT55 . . . . 173 C5
Black Rock Rd BT51. . . . . . 59 B5
Blacks Gr BT43 . . . . 181 E8
Black's Rd BT11 . . . . 149 F6
Blackstaff Rd BT11. . . . . . 150 D8
Blackstaff Sq BT2. . . . . . . 189 A2
Blackstaff Way BT11 . . . . 150 D8
Blackstone Pk BT47. . . . . . 50 D3
Blackstone Rd BT44. . . . . . 60 C1
Blackstown Rd BT29 . . . . 116 F2
Blackthorn Ct BT52 . . . . . 174 F5
Blackthorn Dr BT37 . . . . . 128 F2
Blackthorn Grange [2]
BT37 . . . . 128 F2
Blackthorn Manor BT47 . 179 F6
Blackthorn Mews [3]
BT37 . . . . 128 F2
Blackthorn Pk BT38. . . . . 124 F1
Blackthorn Rd BT37. . . . . 128 F2
Blackthorn Way
Newtownabbey BT36. . . . . 128 E2
Randalstown BT41. . . . . . . 107 F8
Blackwater Ind Est BT36 132 A6
Blackwater Rd BT36. . . . . 132 B7
Blackwater Way BT12 . . . 188 B2
Blackwood St [2] BT7. . . . 144 E1
Bladon Ct BT9 . . . . 151 C6
Bladon Dr BT9. . . . . 151 C6
Bladon Pk BT9. . . . . 151 B6
BlaghⓉ BT52. . . . . 14 F4
Blagh Rd BT52. . . . . 14 F5
Blakeley Terr BT12. . . . . . 188 C2
Blakes LowerⓉ BT51. . . . . . 13 D2
Blakes Rd BT51 . . . . 25 C8
Blakes UpperⓉ BT51. . . . . . 13 D1
Blaney St BT13 . . . . 144 B7
BlarisⓉ BT27 . . . . 169 D6
Blaris Ind Est BT27. . . . . 170 B7
Blaris Old Burial Gd★
BT27. . . . . 169 D6
Blaris Pk BT28. . . . . 169 F7
Blaris Rd BT27. . . . . 169 B5
Bleach Gn BT14. . . . . 136 D3
Bleach Gn Ave BT37. . . . . 133 F6
Bleach Gn (Bóithrín an
Tuair) BT47 . . . . 55 D1
Bleachgreen Ct BT37. . . . 134 A6
Bleachroad BT47. . . . . 55 D1
BleerickⓉ BT41. . . . . 187 B4
Bleerick Dr BT41. . . . . 187 B4
Blenheim Dr
Belfast BT6 . . . . 145 D1
Carryduff BT8 . . . . 163 D3
Blenheim Pk BT8 . . . . 163 D3
Blenheim Pk S BT8 . . . . . 163 D3
Bligh's Gdns BT48 . . . . . . 178 C5
Bligh's La BT48 . . . . 178 A5
Blondin St BT12. . . . . 188 C1
Bloomdale St BT5. . . . . . . 145 C5
Bloomfield Ave BT5. . . . . 145 D4
Bloomfield Collegiate Sch
BT5. . . . . 146 A4
Bloomfield Commercial Ctr
BT5. . . . . 145 C4
Bloomfield Cres [3] BT5 . 145 C4
Bloomfield Ct [1] BT5. . . . 145 C4
Bloomfield Dr BT5 . . . . . . 145 C4
Bloomfield Gdns BT5. . . . 145 D3
Bloomfield Par BT5. . . . . . 145 C4
Bloomfield Pk
Belfast BT5 . . . . 145 D3
Londonderry BT48. . . . . . . 176 E4
Bloomfield Pk W [1] BT5 145 D3
Bloomfield Rd BT5. . . . . . 145 D4
Bloomfield St [2] BT5. . . . 145 C4
Blucher St BT48 . . . . 178 D5
Bluebell Ave BT47 . . . . 67 A8
Bluebell Hill Gdns BT48 . 178 D4
Bluefield Cl BT38 . . . . 125 D4
Bluefield Dr BT38. . . . . 125 C3
Bluefield Gdns BT38 . . . . 125 D3
Bluefield Pk BT38. . . . . 125 D3
Bluefield Rd BT38. . . . . 125 D3
Bluefield Way BT38 . . . . . 125 D3
Blythefield Prim Sch
BT12. . . . . 188 B1
Blythe St BT12. . . . . 188 C1
Boating Club La BT48 . . . 178 E6
BogaghⓉ BT47 . . . . 50 F3
Bogashen Rd BT44. . . . . . . 75 F2
Boghead Bridge Rd
BT67 . . . . 154 E7
BoghilboyⓉ BT51. . . . . 42 E1
BoghillⓉ BT52. . . . . 14 E3
Boghill Rd
Coleraine BT52 . . . . 174 F7
Newtownabbey BT36. . . . . 132 B3
Bog Mdws Nature Reserve★
BT12. . . . . 143 F2
Bog Rd
Ballymena BT42. . . . . 79 B4
Lisburn BT27 . . . . 168 F5
BOGSIDE BT48 . . . . 178 D5
BogtownⓉ BT51 . . . . 13 B4
BoighⓉ BT47. . . . . 55 B7
Bóithrín an Tuair (Bleach
Gn) BT47. . . . . 55 D1

BOLEA BT49 23 F2
Bolea BT49 24 A3
Bolea Pk BT49 23 F2
Bolea Rd BT49 23 D1
Boleran BT51 41 C4
Boleran Pk BT51 41 C4
Boleran Rd BT51 41 D4
Bolie BT47 37 E3
Bolies BT47 178 D1
Boltnaconnell BT29 118 B3
Boltnaconnell Rd BT29 118 A3
Bombay St BT13 188 A3
Bonamargy BT54 8 F2
Bonds Glen Rd BT47 68 C7
Bonds Hill BT47 179 A5
Bonds Pl BT47 179 A5
Bonds St BT47 179 A5
Boneybefore BT38 125 D1
Boneyclassagh BT57 5 B4
BONNANABOIGH BT47 55 B6
Bonnytober BT44 49 B1
Boodle's La BT14 136 C3
Boomhall Pk★ BT48 177 B2
Bootle St BT13 144 A7
Bootown BT53 27 C6
Botanic Ave BT7 189 A1
Botanic Ct BT9 144 D1
Botanic Prim Sch BT9 144 D1
Botanic Sta BT7 189 A1
Bóthar Bhaile Andarsan (Andersonstown Rd) BT11 150 B7
Bóthar Chluanaí (Springfield Rd) BT12 188 A3
Bóthar Dhoire na Bhflatha (Dernaflaw Rd) BT47 54 F3
Bóthar na Bhfál (Falls Rd) BT12 188 A2
Bóthar na Carraige Bric (Craigbrack Rd) BT47 37 A4
Bóthar Thulach Forde (Mountforde Rd) 23 BT5 145 A5
Bóthar Tullach Phoitinséir (Mountpottinger Rd) 7 BT5 145 A5
Bottom BT43 181 F7
Boucher Bsns Ctr BT12 144 A1
Boucher Cres BT12 150 E8
Boucher Ctr The BT12 150 E8
Boucher Pl BT12 150 F8
Boucher Rd BT12 150 E7
Boucher Ret Pk BT12 143 F1
Boucher Way BT12 143 F1
Boulevard BT52 174 C6
Boulevard The BT7 151 E7
Boundary St BT13 188 C4
Boundary Way BT13 188 C4
Boundary Wlk BT13 188 C4
Bourlon Rd BT41 186 F3
Bovagh BT51 42 E3
Bovally BT49 180 E4
Bovally Rd BT49 180 E4
Boveagh BT45 103 E8
BOVEDY BT51 58 E4
Bovedy BT51 58 F4
Bovedy Rd BT51 58 F2
Bovedy Terr Cross Roads BT51 58 F6
Boveedy Rd BT51 58 F4
Bovevagh BT47 54 F7
BOVEVAGH BT47 55 B6
Bovevagh Rd BT47 54 D7
Boviel BT47 56 B1
Boviel Rd BT47 72 C8
Bovolcan BT28 147 F5
Bowmans Rd BT45 91 B1
Bowness St 1 BT13 144 A7
Bow St Mall BT28 160 A1
Bow St BT28 160 B1
Boyds Rd BT44 45 C3
Boyd St BT13 188 C4
Boydstown BT40 98 C8
Boyland Rd BT53 28 C2
Boyne Bridge BT12 188 C2
Boyne Ct BT12 188 C1
Boystown BT51 42 B2
Bracaghreilly BT46 73 E1
Brackagh
Cookstown BT80 102 F1
Magherafelt BT45 102 E7
Brackagh La BT45 103 E6
Brackaghlislea BT45 89 C1
Brackagh North BT79 101 B7
Brackagh Rd BT45 103 F7
Brackaghreilly Rd BT46 89 D8
Brackagh Slieve Gallion BT45 103 E5
Brackalislea Prim Sch BT45 89 C1
Brackalislea Rd BT45 103 B8
Bracken Ave BT41 187 B2
Brackenberg Ave BT38 100 A2
Brackenberg Dr BT38 100 A2
Brackenberg Rd BT38 100 A2
Bracken Burn BT41 107 F8
Bracken Dale BT36 133 B8
Bracken Dr BT37 133 F4
Brackenhill BT28 121 B1
Bracken Mews BT36 133 C8
Bracken Pk BT48 176 D4
Bracken Ridge BT38 130 C6
Bracken Ridge Cl BT38 130 D7
Brackenridge Gdns BT38 130 D6
Brackenridge Gn BT38 130 C7
Brackens The BT36 133 B8
Brackenvale Bsns Pk BT8 163 C6
Bracken View
Newtownabbey BT36 133 C8
Portglenone BT44 76 D5
Bracken Way 4 BT37 133 F4
Brackenwood Cres BT8 163 C8
Brackenwood Dr BT8 163 C8
Brackenwood La BT17 150 D1
Brackfield BT47 52 D3
Brackley Hts 6 BT42 77 F7
Brackley Manor 1 BT42 77 F7
Bracknamuckley BT44 76 E7
Brackney BT53 8 F2
Bradbury Pl BT7 189 A1
Braden Glen BT37 133 D4
Braden Hts BT37 133 D4
Bradford Ct 4 BT8 152 A6
Bradford Gdns BT38 125 B5
Bradford Hts BT38 125 B5
Bradford Pl 2 BT8 152 A6
Bradford Sq BT1 189 B4
Bradley Pk
Draperstown BT45 89 A3
Londonderry BT48 176 F4
Bradleys Pass BT48 176 F4
Brae BT43 63 B6
Braefield 3 BT47 69 B8
Braehead Rd BT48 178 A2
Brae Hill Cres BT14 136 D3
Brae Hill Link 1 BT14 136 D3
Brae Hill Par BT14 136 D3
Brae Hill Pk BT14 136 D3
Brae Hill Rd BT14 136 D3
Brae Hill Way BT14 136 D3
Braemar Ct BT36 132 E6
Braemar St 10 BT12 143 F3
Braepark Rd BT39 97 C5
Brae Rd BT43 63 A6
Braeside Ave BT37 128 D1
Braeside Dr BT36 128 D1
Braeside Gdns BT41 186 F3
Braeside Gr BT5 146 A1
Braeside Pk BT36 128 D1
Braetown BT42 81 D2
Braid Prim Sch BT43 64 C2
Braid River Bsns Pk BT42 181 C3
Braidside Integrated Prim Sch BT43 181 F8
Braid Valley Hospl BT43 181 D6
Braidwater Gdns 2 BT42 79 C7
Braidwater Ret Pk BT43 181 D3
Braken Hill Rd BT28 156 C8
Bramble Ave BT36 128 F3
Bramble Glen BT37 129 A2
Bramble Grange BT37 128 F3
Bramble Pk BT36 128 F3
Bramble Rd BT37 128 F3
Brambles The
Ballymoney BT53 28 B8
Coleraine BT52 174 C8
Lisburn BT28 159 C3
Magherafelt BT45 183 D7
Randalstown BT41 108 A7
Bramble Way BT36 132 D8
Bramblewood
Craigavon BT67 167 A7
Crumlin BT29 121 C8
Brambling Cl BT28 159 E4
Bramcote St BT5 145 D4
Bramhall Cres BT47 179 E5
Branch Rd
Antrim BT41 107 F8
Carnlough BT44 49 C3
Londonderry BT48 176 C2
Branch The
Ballymena BT42 97 B8
Londonderry BT48 176 C3
Brandon Parade BT4 145 D6
Brandon Terr BT4 145 D6
Brandra St BT4 145 D6
Brandywell Ave 2 BT48 178 D4
Brandywell Rd BT48 178 D4
Brandywell Sports Ctr BT48 178 C3
Braniel BT5 153 B8
BRANIEL BT5 146 A1
Braniel Cres BT5 146 A1
Braniel Pk BT5 146 A1
Braniel Prim Sch BT5 146 B1
Braniel Rd BT27 171 C7
Braniel Way 7 BT5 146 A1
Brankins Island Rd BT67 154 B8
Brankinstown Rd BT67 154 E5
Branson Pk BT49 180 E4
Brantwood Gdns BT41 187 A3
Brantwood St BT15 137 D1
Brassey St BT12 188 B2
Bratwell BT51 24 E7
Bratwell Rd BT51 24 E7
Bravallen BT53 175 E1
Bravallen Rd BT53 175 D2
Bray Cl BT13 143 F8
Bray Ct BT13 143 F8
Bray St BT13 143 F7
Breach Cl 12 BT5 145 B4
Bread St BT12 188 B3
Bready Jubilee Prim Sch BT82 50 A1
Brecanlea BT47 69 B8
Brecart BT41 106 D8
Brecart Rd BT41 106 D7
Breckagh
Ballymena BT43 64 A3
Ballymoney BT53 28 D4
Breckenhill Rd BT39 96 D4
Breda Ave BT8 152 A4
Breda Cres BT8 152 A4
Breda Dr BT8 152 B4
Breda Gdns BT8 152 A4
Breda Parade BT8 152 A4
Breda Pk
Castlereagh BT8 152 A4
Drumahoe BT47 179 F1
Breda Rd BT8 152 A4
Breda Terr BT8 152 A3
Breen BT53 19 A1
Breen Ct BT37 128 E2
Breezemount Manor BT38 125 E3
Bregagh Rd BT53 29 D7
Brenda Pk BT11 150 B7
Brenda St BT5 145 C3
Brennan Ct BT45 183 E6
Brentwood Pk
Castlereagh BT5 145 F1
1 Londonderry BT48 176 C1
Brerton Cres BT8 151 E2
Brerton Gr BT8 151 E2
Bresk Hill 1 BT36 133 D1
Brettens Walls BT41 187 B8
Brewery La BT80 185 D5
Brewsters Cl 4 BT48 178 E6
Brian's Well Ct BT17 149 C4
Brian's Well Rd BT17 149 C4
Brianville Pk BT14 137 A5
Briarcourt BT37 128 F2
Briar Cres BT37 128 F2
Briarhill BT41 186 D2
Briar Hill BT8 152 C3
Briar Hill Cl 5 BT8 152 C3
Briar Hill (Cnoc na Ndriseacha) 4 BT47 37 C5
Briar Pk BT37 128 F2
Briarwood Pk BT5 146 D2
Brickfield The BT49 180 C7
Brickhill Pk
10 Newtownabbey BT36 111 F1
Newtownabbey BT36 128 A2
Brickkilns BT47 51 A6
Bridewell Dr BT38 125 A1
BRIDGE END 34 D6
Bridge End
Belfast BT5 189 C3
5 Magherafelt BT45 114 C3
Bridge End Rd
Ballyclare BT39 110 E3
Carrickfergus BT38 126 A8
Bridge End Sta BT3 145 A6
Bridgehouse Ct BT49 38 C7
Bridgend Rd BT45 114 B3
Bridge Pk BT39 110 C2
Bridge Rd
Ballyclare BT39 110 F8
Ballymena BT44 61 A7
Craigavon BT67 167 C1
Dunloy BT44 44 F4
Newtownabbey BT37 128 D1
Bridge Ret Pk BT42 181 F2
Bridger St BT45 113 E7
Bridge St
Antrim BT41 186 D4
Ballymena BT42 181 D3
Belfast BT1 189 A3
4 Bushmills BT57 5 D3
Carnlough BT44 49 C2
Castledawson BT45 91 C2
Coleraine BT52 174 C3
Cushendall BT44 32 D4
Garvagh BT51 58 A8
Kilrea BT51 59 C5
Larne BT40 182 C3
Lisburn BT27 160 D3
Lisburn BT28 160 B1
Londonderry BT48 178 F5
Randalstown BT41 108 A7
Rasharkin BT44 60 B6
Bridgewater BT47 179 E8
Brigade Rd BT47 179 C6
Brigadie Ave BT43 181 F7
Brigadie Cres BT43 181 F7
Brigadie Gdns BT43 181 F7
Brighton St 9 BT12 143 F4
Bright St 21 BT5 145 B5
Brishey BT47 56 B3
Brisland Rd BT47 37 A6
Bristol Ave BT15 137 D5
Bristol Ct BT51 174 A6
Bristow Dr BT5 146 E2
Bristow Pk BT9 150 F5
Britannic Dr BT12 188 C1
Britannic Pk BT12 188 C1
Britannic Terr BT12 188 C1
British Rd BT29 116 F5
Britton's Ct BT12 143 D4
Britton's Dr BT12 143 D4
Britton's Parade BT12 143 D3
Broadacres 5 BT39 110 C2
Broadbridge Prim Sch BT47 36 E5
Broadlands BT38 125 C4
Broadlands Dr BT38 125 C4
Broadlands Gdns BT38 125 D4
Broadlands Pk BT38 125 D4
Broad Rd BT49 180 E6
Broadwater Pk BT67 155 C2
Broadway
Belfast BT12 143 F3
Larne BT40 182 D3
Broadway Ave
Ballymena BT43 181 D4
Carrickfergus BT38 130 F7
Broadway Ct BT12 143 F3
Broadway Ind Est BT12 188 A1
Broadway Parade BT12 144 A2
Broagh BT45 91 A4
Broagh Rd BT45 91 A4
Brocagh Rd BT47 52 F8
Brockagh
Coleraine BT51 57 A6
Londonderry BT47 52 F8
BROCKAGHBOY BT51 57 C6
Brockagh Rd BT47 53 B7
Brockaghs BT54 31 D7
Brockish Cargin BT41 106 D6
Brocklamont BT42 181 B3
Brocklamont Cres BT42 181 A2
Brocklamont Pk BT42 181 A4
Broglasco BT49 22 E1
Broharris BT49 22 E1
Broighter BT49 22 E2
Broighter Ct BT47 179 E7
Broighter Rd BT49 38 E8
Brokagh Rd BT51 57 C6
Brokerstown Rd BT28 159 B3
Bromley St BT13 144 A7
Brompton Ct BT47 179 D4
Brompton Pk BT14 143 F8
Brone Park BT51 42 C3
Brone Pk BT51 42 C3
Brone Rd BT51 42 C3
Brook Ave BT38 125 B1
Brook Cres BT38 125 B1
Brookdale Cres BT48 176 E5
Brookdale Ct BT48 176 E4
Brookdale Pk BT48 176 E4
Brooke Activity Ctr BT17 149 E2
Brookeborough Ave BT38 125 D2
Brookeborough Squa 2 BT28 159 D3
Brooke Cl BT11 150 A6
Brooke Cres BT11 150 A5
Brooke Ct BT10 150 A5
Brooke Dr BT11 150 A5
Brooke Manor BT11 150 A5
Brooke Pk
Ballymena BT42 181 E2
Belfast BT10 150 A5
Brookfield BT47 50 D3
Brookfield Gdns 5 BT42 77 E2
Brookfield Hts 1 BT39 96 F1
Brookfield Pk BT49 39 B2
Brookfield Pl BT14 143 F8
Brookfield Rd BT39 96 F1
Brookfield Sch BT27 169 B3
Brookfield Specl Sch BT67 167 B4
Brookfield St BT14 143 F8
Brookfield Wlk BT14 143 F8
Brook Gn
Carrickfergus BT38 125 B1
Coleraine BT52 174 D5
Brookhill
Londonderry BT48 177 B5
Randalstown BT41 107 F8
Brookhill Ave BT14 137 C1
Brooklands
Ahoghill BT42 77 F2
Magherafelt BT45 183 C7
Brooklands Cl 20 BT38 100 D1
Brooklands Cres BT38 100 C1
Brooklands Dr 13 BT38 100 D1
Brooklands Gdns BT38 100 C1
Brooklands Grange BT17 149 E4
Brooklands Pk BT38 100 C1
Brookland St BT9 151 A8
Brookland View 2 BT39 96 F1
Brookleigh Hts BT43 181 B6
Brooklodge BT28 155 D7
Brooklyn Pk BT47 36 F5
Brooklyn Pl BT55 173 D5
Brook Mdw BT39 110 F6
Brookmill Way BT14 136 D4
Brookmount Rd
Lisburn BT28 158 D2
Magherafelt BT45 115 A7
Brookmount St BT13 188 A4
Brook Pk BT55 173 D4
Brook Rd BT82 67 E2
Brook St
Coleraine BT52 174 D4
Holywood BT18 139 E7
Londonderry BT48 178 D3
Brookvale
Antrim BT41 187 B5
Broughshane BT43 79 D7
Brookvale Ave BT14 137 B1
Brookvale Dr BT14 137 C1
Brookvale Par 11 BT14 137 B1
Brookvale Rise 1 BT28 160 A1
Brookvale St BT14 137 B1
Brookvale Terr BT55 173 C5
Brookview Glen BT47 36 E4
Brookville BT53 29 B5
Brookville Ct BT14 137 C1
Broombeg BT54 8 D2
Broombeg 1 BT54 8 D3
Broomhill BT41 187 B2
Broomhill Ave BT47 179 C7
Broomhill Cl BT9 151 B6
Broomhill Ct
Belfast BT9 151 B6
Londonderry BT47 179 C7
Broomhill Mews BT47 179 C7
Broomhill Pk
Belfast BT9 151 B6
Coleraine BT51 174 A1
Broomhill Pk Central BT9 151 C6
Broom-More BT54 18 F6
Broom Pk BT17 149 D1
Broom Pk Hts 7 BT17 149 D2
Broom St BT13 143 F7
Brougham St BT15 144 E8
Broughanlea BT54 8 F4
Broughanore BT44 45 C5
Broughderg BT79 101 A3
Broughderg Rd BT79 101 A3
Broughdone BT43 77 F8
Broughdone La BT43 77 F8
Broughgammon BT54 7 D3
Broughmore
Ballycastle BT54 19 C6
Lisburn BT28 168 A5
Brough Rd BT45 91 E1
BROUGHSHANE (BRUACH SHEÁIN) BT42 79 D7
Broughshane Lower BT42 79 A5
Broughshane Prim Sch 5 BT42 79 C7
Broughshane Rd BT43 181 E6
Broughshane St BT43 181 D5
Broughshane Upper BT42 79 C6
Broughton Gdns BT7 145 A1
Broughton Pk BT7 145 A1
Browndod
Ballyclare BT39 96 A1
Larne BT40 98 F8
Browndod Rd
Ballyclare BT39 110 A8
Larne BT40 99 A7
Brown Dr BT46 74 D1
Brownhill BT82 67 B1
Browning Dr BT47 178 F6
Brown Knowes BT47 52 B6
Brownlee Prim Sch BT27 160 B2
Browns Bay Dr BT40 84 B4
Browns Bay Rd BT40 100 C7
Brown's Pk BT18 139 F8
Browns Rd BT36 111 B1
Brown's Row BT1 189 A4
Browns Sq BT13 188 C4
Brown St BT13 188 C4
BRUACH SHEÁIN (BROUGHSHANE) BT42 79 D7
Bruce Pk BT51 13 A5
Bruce's Castle★ BT54 3 C6
Bruce St BT2 189 A2
Brucevale Ct 2 BT14 144 C8
Brucevale Pk BT14 144 C8
Brunswick Rd BT47 179 E5
Brunswick St BT2 189 A2
Brunswick Superbowl BT48 176 E1
Bruslee BT39 111 E6
Brussels St 8 BT13 144 A7
Brustin Brae Rd BT40 182 A7
Brustin Lee BT40 83 B8
Bryansford Pl 23 BT6 145 A3
Bryan St
Ballymena BT43 181 D4
Larne BT40 182 C4
Bryantang BT39 98 B2
Bryantang Rd BT39 110 E7
Bryson Ct
25 Newtownabbey BT36 111 F1
26 Belfast BT5 145 A5
Bryson Gdns
30 Newtownabbey BT36 111 F1
29 Belfast BT5 145 A5
Bryson Pk 30 BT36 111 F1
Bryson Sq 28 BT36 111 F1
Bryson St BT5 145 A5
BUCKNA BT42 80 C8
Buckna BT42 81 A8
Buckna Rd
Ballymena BT42 79 E7
Broughshane BT42 79 D7
Budore BT29 141 B7
Budore Rd
Belfast BT14 118 E1
Belfast BT29 141 C8
Lisburn BT28 140 F1
Buick Meml Prim Sch 4 BT42 77 F6
Bullaun Stone★ BT38 126 C3
BUN ABHANN DALLA (CUSHENDALL) BT46 32 E4
BUN ABHANN DUINNE (CUSHENDUN) BT44 21 B1
Bunbeg Pk BT11 149 E7
Buncrana Gdns BT11 149 E7
Buncrana Rd BT48 176 A5
Bunley Rd BT36 132 B6
Bunnamayne 34 D5
Bunowen BT82 67 F4
Bunscoil Bheann Mhadagain 12 BT14 137 B1
Bunscoil Cholmcille BT48 177 A4
Bunscoil Phobal Feirste Sch 4 BT11 150 A7
Bunshanacloney BT53 17 F3
Burandell Manor BT28 159 F5
Burleigh Dr BT38 130 E8
Burleigh Wlk BT38 124 E1
Burmah St BT7 144 E1
Burnaby Ct BT12 188 B2
Burnaby Pk BT12 188 B2
Burnaby Pl BT12 188 B2
Burnaby Way BT12 188 B2
Burnaby Wlk BT12 188 B2
Burnally BT49 23 A1
Burnally Rd BT49 22 F1

Burnavon Arts & Cultural
Ctr★ BT80. . . . . .185 C5
Burnbank BT80 . . . . .185 C6
Burn Brae BT57 . . . . .6 B6
Burn Brae Cres BT80 . . .185 C5
Burnet Ave BT37 . . . . . . .128 F2
Burnet Cl **7** BT37 . . . . . .128 F2
Burnet Dr BT37 . . . . .128 F2
Burnet Pk BT37 . . . . .128 F2
Burney's La BT36 . . . . . . .132 E5
Burney's Mews BT36 . . . .132 E6
Burnfield House Golf Club
BT37. . . . . .128 C3
BURNFOOT 34 B8
Burnfoot Prim Sch BT47. . 55 C6
Burnquarter⊕ BT47. . . . . 44 B7
Burnquarter La BT53. . . . 44 B7
Burnquarter Rd BT53. . . . 44 D7
Burn Rd
Ballyclare BT39 . . . . . . .110 E5
Coleraine BT52 . . . . . . .174 D8
Cookstown BT80 . . . . . .185 C5
BURNSIDE
Antrim BT41. . . . . .109 F4
Ballyclare BT39 . . . . . . .110 F8
Burnside⊕
Ballymena BT44. . . . . . . 49 D6
Ballymena BT53. . . . . . . 43 E8
Burnside BT56 . . . . .172 B3
Burnside Ave BT8 . . . . . .152 B3
Burnside Ct **8** BT39. . . . . 96 F1
Burnside Gdns BT47 . . . .179 D5
Burnside La BT38 . . . . . .100 A4
Burnside Manor BT48 . . . 50 C8
Burnside Mews BT56. . . .172 C3
Burnside Pk
5 Ballyclare BT39 . . . . . 96 F1
1 Ballyclare BT39 . . . .110 F8
Ballymena BT53. . . . . . . 27 B1
Castlereagh BT8 . . . . . .152 B3
Coleraine BT51 . . . . . . .174 B1
Burnside Rd
Antrim BT41. . . . . .109 F3
Ballyclare BT39 . . . . . . .110 F8
Ballymena BT42. . . . . . . 80 F8
Portstewart BT55 . . . . . .172 B2
Burnthill Ave **8** BT36 . .132 F7
Burnthill Cres BT36 . . . .132 F7
Burnthill Dr **3** BT36 . . .132 F7
Burnthill Gdns BT36 . . . .132 F7
Burnthill Pk **4** BT36 . . .132 F7
Burnthill Rd BT36 . . . . . .132 F7
Burntollet Way BT16 . . . .152 B8
Burn View **8** BT41. . . . . .107 F7
Burnview Dr BT8. . . . . . . .163 D5
Burren Beg⊕ BT49. . . . . . 12 E4
Burren More⊕ BT49 . . . . 12 E3
Burrenmore Rd BT49. . . . 12 E3
Burren Way BT6 . . . . . . .152 B8
BURT 34 A6
Bush⊕ BT41. . . . . .187 B8
Bushbank⊕ BT53. . . . . . . 28 F7
Bush Cres **5** BT57. . . . . . . .5 E3
Bushfield Mill BT47 . . . . . 70 B3
Bushfield Rd BT67 . . . . . .167 F7
Bushfoot Ave BT57 . . . . . . .5 C4
Bushfoot Dr BT57 . . . . .5 D5
Bushfoot Golf Links BT57. . 5 D5
Bushfoot or Lissanduff⊕
BT57 . . . . .5 D4
Bushfoot Pk BT57 . . . . .5 D4
Bushfoot Rd BT57 . . . . .5 D4
Bush Gdns
Bushmills BT57 . . . . .5 E2
Londonderry BT47. . . . . .179 B4
Bushmills Distillery★ BT57 5 E3
BUSHMILLS (MUILEANN NA
BUAISE) BT57. . . . . .5 D3
Bushmills Prim Sch BT57. . 5 D3
Bushmills Rd
Coleraine BT52 . . . . . . .174 D5
Portstewart BT55 . . . . . .173 F6
Bushmills Sta BT57 . . . . . .5 D4
Bush Pk BT41. . . . . .186 F6
Bush Rd
Antrim BT41. . . . . .187 A8
Ballymoney BT53. . . . . . 28 C7
Bushtown BT51 . . . . 26 A6
Bushtown Rd BT51 . . . . . . 25 F5
Bushvale⊕ BT53. . . . . 29 B5
Bush Valley Prim Sch
BT53 . . . . 28 E8
Buskin Way BT51 . . . . . . .174 B1
Butcher St BT48. . . . . . . .178 E5
Bute Gdns BT47. . . . . . . .182 A7
Butler Cres BT47. . . . . . . .177 F5
Butler's Wharf BT47 . . . . .70 B3
Buttermilk Loney BT14 . . .136 D4
Byrestown Rd BT42 . . . . . 95 A8
Byron Pl Mews BT18 . . . .139 C7

C

Cabin Hill Gdns BT5. . . . .146 C4
Cabin Hill Mews BT5 . . . .146 C4
Cabin Hill Pk BT5 . . . . . .146 B4
Cabin Hill Prep Sch BT4. 146 B5
Cable Rd BT51 . . . . .100 C1
Cable St BT48 . . . . .178 D5
Cabra Cl BT53 . . . . 43 C8
Cabragh⊕
Ballymena BT43. . . . . . . 62 A1
Ballymoney BT53. . . . . . 43 D7
Magherafelt BT45 . . . . . 91 A5
Cabragh or Cavanmore⊕
BT57 . . . . 16 C6
Cabragh Rd BT57 . . . . 16 D5

Cabra Rd BT26. . . . . .170 F1
Caddy⊕ BT41. . . . . 94 A3
Caddy Rd BT41. . . . . 93 F2
Cadger Rd BT8 . . . . .163 F4
Cadogan Pk BT9 . . . . .151 B8
Cadogan St BT7 . . . . .144 E2
Cadogan Pk BT47. . . . . . .179 D4
Cafe La **4** BT53. . . . . . . .175 C4
Caheny BT51 . . . . 42 F3
Caherty⊕ BT42. . . . . 79 C5
Caherty Rd BT42. . . . . 79 C5
Cahery⊕ BT49. . . . . 39 E8
Cahore⊕ BT45. . . . . 89 A1
Cahore Hts BT45 . . . . 89 A3
Cahore Rd
Draperstown BT45. . . . . 89 A3
Magherafelt BT45 . . . . .103 A8
Cahore Terr BT45 . . . . 89 A3
Cairnafinn Ave BT49 . . . .180 D5
Cairnbeg Cres BT40 . . . .182 C8
Cairnbeg Pk BT40. . . . . . .182 C8
Cairnburn Ave BT4. . . . . .146 B8
Cairnburn Cres BT4 . . . . .146 B7
Cairnburn Dr BT4 . . . . . . .146 B7
Cairnburn Gdns BT4 . . . .146 B7
Cairnburn Grange BT4 . . .146 A7
Cairnburn Pk BT4. . . . . . .146 B7
Cairnburn Rd BT4. . . . . . .146 A7
Cairndale Hts BT40 . . . . .182 C7
Cairncastle Prim Sch
BT40. . . . . 83 A8
Cairncastle Rd BT40 . . . . 83 A8
Cairn Ct BT51. . . . . .174 B6
Cairndale BT13 . . . . .136 C5
Cairndhu Golf Club BT40 . 83 C8
Cairn Gdns
Coleraine BT51 . . . . . . .174 B6
6 Crumlin BT29 . . . . .117 B1
Cairngorm Cres **3** BT36. 132 F6
Cairngorm Dr BT40 . . . . .182 A5
Cairn Gr BT40 . . . . .182 D8
Cairnhill BT51 . . . . .174 A6
Cairnhill Cres BT40 . . . . . 83 B8
Cairnhill Manor BT44 . . . 49 C3
Cairnhill Pl BT38. . . . . . . .125 A3
Cairnhill Rd BT39 . . . . . . .118 D7
Cairn Hill Rd BT29 . . . . . .121 F4
Cairnmore Ave BT28 . . . .159 E3
Cairnmore Cres BT28 . . .159 E3
Cairnmore Dr BT28 . . . . .159 E3
Cairnmore Pk BT28 . . . . .159 E3
Cairnmount Pk BT51 . . . .174 B6
Cairn Rd
Carrickfergus BT38 . . . . 99 A1
Coleraine BT51 . . . . . . .174 B6
CAIRNSHILL BT8. . . . . . . .152 B2
Cairnshill Ave BT8 . . . . . .152 B2
Cairnshill Cl BT8 . . . . . . .152 C3
Cairnshill Cres BT8 . . . . .152 B2
Cairnshill Ct **3** BT8 . . . .152 B1
Cairnshill Dr BT8 . . . . . . .152 B3
Cairnshill Gdns BT8 . . . . .152 B3
Cairnshill Gn BT8 . . . . . . .152 B3
Cairnshill Pk BT8 . . . . . . .152 B3
Cairnshill Prim Sch BT8. 152 B3
Cairnshill Rd BT8 . . . . . . .152 B2
Cairns Rd BT44 . . . . 32 D5
Cairns St BT12. . . . . .188 A4
Cairns The BT4 . . . . .146 A6
Cairn The BT36 . . . . .133 E3
Cairnvale BT51 . . . . .174 B6
Cairnvale Pk BT51 . . . . . .174 B6
Cairo St BT7. . . . . .144 E2
Caldanagh⊕ BT44 . . . . . . 44 F5
Caldwell Dr **3** BT55. . . . .173 D4
Caldwell Pk BT55. . . . . . .173 D4
Caldwellstown⊕ BT44 . . . 45 E3
Caledon Ct BT13 . . . . . . .143 F6
Caledon St BT13 . . . . . . .143 F6
Calgach Her Ctr **10** BT48. 178 E5
Calhame⊕
Ballyclare BT39 . . . . . . .122 A7
Ballymena BT44. . . . . . . 32 B5
Calhame Rd BT39 . . . . . .122 B8
Calheme⊕ BT53. . . . . 28 C2
Calhome Rd BT47. . . . . . . 55 A8
California Cl BT13 . . . . . .188 C4
Callan Way BT16 . . . . . . .152 B8
Callender St BT1. . . . . . . .189 A3
Callisnagh⊕ BT44 . . . . . . 32 C8
Calmore BT45 . . . . 89 E4
Calmore Pk **1** BT45. . . . . 89 F5
Calmore Rd BT45 . . . . 89 E5
Calvert Rd BT29. . . . . . . .118 D2
Calvin St BT5 . . . . .145 B4
Calwell Pk BT38 . . . . .100 A4
Cam⊕ BT51. . . . . 24 F1
Caman Cres BT54 . . . . .8 C4
Caman Dr BT54 . . . . .8 C4
Caman Pk BT49. . . . . 38 C7
Camberwell Ct BT15 . . . .137 C1
Camberwell Rd BT43 . . . .181 D7
Camberwell Terr BT15 . . .137 C1
Cambourne Cres BT53 . . .175 C1
Cambourne Dr BT53 . . . . .175 C2
Cambourne Pk
Ballymoney BT53. . . . . .175 C1
Belfast BT9 . . . . .151 A4
Londonderry BT47. . . . . .179 C4
Cambrai Dr BT37. . . . . . . .134 A5
Cambrai Rd BT43. . . . . . . .181 B3
Cambrai St BT13 . . . . . . .143 F7
Cambridge Dr BT42 . . . . .181 B2
Cambridge House Gram Sch
BT42. . . . . .181 A1
Cambridge Pk BT52 . . . . .174 D8

Cambridge St **8** BT15. . .144 E8
Camden St BT9 . . . . .144 C2
Camelia Ct BT47 . . . . . . .178 F2
Cameron St BT39 . . . . . . .184 C5
Cameronian Dr BT5 . . . . .145 E2
Cameron Pk BT42. . . . . . . 78 C3
Cameron St BT7 . . . . .189 A1
Cam La BT51 . . . . 41 B8
Camlin Gdns BT29 . . . . . .117 B1
Camlin Pk BT29 . . . . .121 B8
Camlough Pl BT6 . . . . . . .152 E8
Camnish BT47 . . . . 55 D5
Camnish Rd BT47 . . . . 55 D5
Camon BT54 . . . . .8 C4
Campbell Cl BT28 . . . . . . .168 E6
Campbell Coll BT4 . . . . . .146 C6
Campbell Ct
6 Belfast BT15 . . . . . .146 A5
Lisburn BT28 . . . . .168 E6
Campbell Pk Ave **1** BT4. 146 A5
Campbell Rd BT36 . . . . . .128 A1
Campbells Town⊕ BT51. . 58 F2
Campbell's Town⊕ BT51 . 58 F2
Campbelltown **2** BT45. . . 89 A3
Campbelltown⊕ BT44 . . . 49 C3
Camden Pk BT38 . . . . . . .124 F4
Camphill Pk BT42. . . . . . .181 C1
Camphill Prim Sch BT42 .181 C1
Campion Ct BT47 . . . . . . .178 F2
CAMPSEY BT47 . . . . 36 C5
Campsey Upper⊕ BT47. . 36 C5
Campsie Bsns Pk BT47 . . 36 D5
Campsie Ind Est BT47. . . 36 D6
Camross Pk
3 Belfast BT9 . . . . . . .144 C2
Newtownabbey BT37. . .133 E3
Camus⊕ BT51 . . . . 26 C4
Camus La BT51. . . . . 26 C4
Camus Macosquin Glebe⊕
BT51. . . . . 26 C6
Canada St **2** BT6 . . . . . .145 A3
Canal St BT27. . . . . .160 C1
Canberra St BT36. . . . . . .132 E5
Candahar St BT7. . . . . . . .144 E1
Caneese⊕ BT80 . . . . .113 A8
Caneese Rd BT80 . . . . . . .113 B8
Canmore Cl BT13 . . . . . . .188 A3
Canmore Gr BT13 . . . . . . .188 A4
Canmore St BT13 . . . . . . .188 A4
Canning Gr **4** BT29 . . . .117 A1
Canning Pl **9** BT15 . . . . .144 E8
Canning's Ct BT13 . . . . . .188 B4
Canterbury Pk BT47. . . . .179 E6
Canton Ct BT6 . . . . .145 B4
Caoran-Dubh BT47. . . . . . 55 D2
Capall Ct BT48. . . . . .176 F5
Capanagh⊕ BT42. . . . . . . 81 F5
Cape Castle⊕ BT54 . . . . . 18 C5
Capecastle Rd BT54. . . . . 18 C6
Cappagh Ave BT56 . . . . . .172 D1
Cappagh Beg⊕ BT56. . . .172 D1
Cappagh Gdns BT6. . . . . .152 B8
Cappagh Gr⊕ BT56 . . . . .172 D1
CAPPAGH MORE⊕ BT56 .172 D1
Cappaghmore Manor
BT56. . . . . .172 D1
Cappagh Pk BT56 . . . . . . .172 D1
Cappagh Rd BT56 . . . . . . .172 D1
Cappagh Rd BT56 . . . . . . .172 C2
Capstone St BT12 . . . . . .150 F7
Captain St Lower BT51 . . .174 B3
Captain St Upper BT51 . . .174 B4
Captain Shutt Gdns **3**
BT55. . . . . .173 E5
Caradale Pk BT48 . . . . . .176 C1
Caranbane⊕ BT47 . . . . . . 69 D4
Carbalintober⊕ BT51. . . . 58 A5
Carbullion⊕ BT49 . . . . . . 23 B3
Carclinty Rd BT42 . . . . . . 77 E8
Carclunty⊕ BT42 . . . . 61 A3
Cardigan Dr BT14. . . . . . .137 A2
Cardonaghy⊕ BT42. . . . . 77 F5
Cardonaghy Rd BT42. . . . 77 F4
Carew St BT7 . . . . .145 C4
Carey Isle⊕ BT44 . . . . .9 A3
Careymill BT54 . . . . .9 A3
Carey Mill⊕ BT54 . . . . .9 A3
CARGAN BT43 . . . . 47 C3
Cargill St BT13. . . . . .188 C4
Cargin⊕ BT41. . . . . .106 F5
Cargin Rd BT41. . . . . .106 D3
Carhill Ct **5** BT51. . . . . . . 58 A5
Carhill Prim Sch BT51. . . . 58 A5
Carhill Rd BT51 . . . . 57 F7
Carickmore Rd BT54 . . . . . .9 A4
Carlan Cl **3** BT37 . . . . . .133 E3
Carlane⊕ BT41. . . . . .106 E3
Carlane Cres BT41 . . . . . .106 D7
Carlane Prim Sch BT41. . .106 E3
Carlane Rd BT41. . . . . . . .106 F3
Carlaragh⊕ BT49 . . . . 38 F5
Carlaragh Rd BT49 . . . . . . 38 F4
Carleton Ct **5** BT48. . . . .176 B2
Carlingford St BT6 . . . . . .145 B3
Carlin Terr BT47 . . . . .179 A4
Carlisle Parade BT15. . . .144 D7
Carlisle Rd
Ballyclare BT39 . . . . . . .110 F2
Belfast BT15 . . . . .144 D7
Londonderry BT48. . . . . .178 F5
Carlisle Terr BT15. . . . . . .144 D7
Carlow St BT13 . . . . .188 B4
Carlton Hills BT8. . . . . . . .163 D4
Carmacmoor⊕ BT42. . . . 77 F1
Carmagrim **1** BT44 . . . . . 77 A1
Carmagrim Rd BT42. . . . . 92 F8
Carmavy La BT41 . . . . . . .118 A6

Carmavy Rd
Antrim BT41. . . . . .117 D6
Belfast BT29 . . . . .118 C6
Carmean⊕ BT45 . . . . . . .104 C4
Carmean La BT45 . . . . . . .104 C4
Carmean Rd BT45 . . . . . .104 C5
Carmeen Dr BT47. . . . . . .133 D4
Carmel St BT7 . . . . .144 D2
Carmond Dr BT40. . . . . . .182 B4
Carmoney⊕ BT47. . . . . . . 36 C4
Carmoney Rd BT47. . . . . . 35 F4
Carmorn⊕ BT41. . . . . . . .107 A4
Carmorn Rd BT41. . . . . . .106 F4
Carn⊕ BT47. . . . . 35 F2
Carnaboy⊕ BT52 . . . . 15 B4
Carnafarn⊕ BT47. . . . . . . 51 B3
Carnaff⊕ BT53 . . . . 16 C2
Carnagall⊕ BT44 . . . . 46 A5
Carnageeragh⊕ BT53 . . . 29 A3
Carnagh BT80 . . . . .115 A6
Carnaghliss⊕ BT14 . . . . .118 E3
Carnaghliss Rd BT29 . . . .140 D8
Carnaghts⊕ BT42 . . . . . . 94 E7
Carnaghts Prim Sch BT42 94 D7
Carnagribban⊕ BT82. . . . 68 B3
Carnahagh⊕ BT44. . . . . . 32 C4
Carnakilly Lower⊕ BT47 . 37 A2
Carnakilly Upper⊕ BT47 . 36 F3
Carnalbanagh⊕
Ballymena BT44. . . . . . . 65 A1
Portstewart BT55 . . . . . . 14 A4
Carnalbanagh East⊕
BT67 . . . . .166 C2
Carnalbanagh Prim Sch
BT44. . . . . 65 A1
Carnalbanagh Rd BT44 . . 65 B2
Carnalbanagh West⊕
BT67 . . . . .166 B2
Carnalea Pl **3** BT15. . . . .144 E8
Carnalridge⊕ BT51 . . . . .173 C3
Carnalridge Prim Sch
BT55 . . . . .173 D2
Carnamaddy⊕ BT45. . . . . 20 B1
Carnaman Rd BT45. . . . . . 91 C7
Carnamena Ave BT6 . . . .152 D8
Carnamena Gdns **1** BT6 152 D8
Carnamenagh⊕ BT44 . . . 46 B6
Carnamenagh Rd BT44 . . 46 A5
Carnamena Pk **2** BT6. . .152 D8
Carnamona Ct **4** BT11 . .143 B1
Carnamoney⊕ BT45 . . . . 88 F7
Carnamoney La BT45. . . . 89 B7
Carnamuck⊕ BT5. . . . . . .145 F1
Carnamuff⊕ BT49 . . . . . . 37 F3
Carnamuff Rd BT49 . . . . . 37 F3
Carnanbane⊕ BT47 . . . . . 71 D4
Carnanbane Rd BT47. . . . 71 D7
Carnanee⊕
Ballyclare BT39 . . . . . . .111 A2
Ballymena BT44. . . . . . . 32 D3
Portstewart BT55 . . . . . . 14 A4
Carnanee Rd BT39 . . . . . .111 A2
Carnaneigh⊕ BT44 . . . . . 21 A5
Carnanmore Pk BT17. . . .149 F5
Carnanreagh⊕ BT57 . . . . . .6 A3
Carnanreagh Rd BT47 . . . 69 B1
Carnan St BT13 . . . . .188 A4
Carnany Ave BT53 . . . . . .175 C4
Carnany Ct BT53 . . . . 28 A2
Carnany Dr BT53. . . . . 28 A2
Carnany Gdns BT53 . . . . .175 C4
Carnany Lower⊕ BT53 . . .175 C4
Carnany Pk BT53. . . . . . . .175 C4
Carnany Upper⊕ BT53 . . 28 B2
Carnasheeran⊕ BT44 . . . 32 D7
Carnave⊕ BT44. . . . . 65 D6
Carnbane⊕ BT27 . . . . . . .169 E2
Carnbane Rd BT27 . . . . . .169 E2
Carnbank BT39 . . . . .111 A1
Carnbeg⊕ BT44 . . . . 45 D3
Carnbeg Ave BT41 . . . . . .186 B8
Carnbeg Mdws BT41. . . . .186 A8
Carnbore⊕ BT53. . . . . 16 F4
Carnbore Rd
Ballymoney BT53. . . . . . 16 E6
Bushmills BT57 . . . . .5 F2
Carnbrae Ave BT8. . . . . . .152 C3
Carnbrae Pk BT8. . . . . . . .152 C3
Carnbrock Cl BT41. . . . . . .187 A5
Carnbuck⊕ BT44 . . . . 46 F6
Carnburn Pk BT43 . . . . . .181 A7
Carnburn Rd BT43 . . . . . .181 A7
CARNCASTLE BT40. . . . . . 82 F8
Carncaver Rd
1 Belfast BT6 . . . . . . .145 E1
Belfast BT6 . . . . .152 E8
Carncoagh⊕ BT43 . . . . . . 62 E3
Carncoagh Rd BT43 . . . . . 62 E3
Carncoggy⊕ BT53. . . . . . . 16 B2
Carncolp⊕ BT57. . . . . .6 B6
Carncome⊕ BT42 . . . . . . 95 C5
Carncome Rd BT42. . . . . . 95 C5
Carncoole Pk BT14. . . . . .137 A5
Carncose⊕ BT45. . . . . . . .103 F5
Carncose Rd BT45 . . . . . .104 A5
Carn Cres **17** BT36 . . . . .111 F1
Carncullagh Lower⊕
BT53 . . . . 28 C8
Carncullagh Middle⊕
BT53 . . . . 28 D8
Carncullagh Rd BT53. . . . 28 E8
Carncullagh Upper⊕
BT53 . . . . 28 E8
Carndaisy⊕ BT45 . . . . . . .103 E3
Carndaisy Rd BT45. . . . . .103 F2
Carndale Mdws BT43. . . .181 B5

Carndougan⊕ BT51. . . . . 26 E2
Carn Dr **16** BT36. . . . . . . .111 F1
Cardnuff⊕
Ballycastle BT54 . . . . .8 B5
Larne BT40 . . . . 83 D1
Carnduff Dr BT43 . . . . . . .181 D4
Carnduff Pk BT54. . . . . .8 B4
Carnduff Rd BT40 . . . . 99 B8
Carneal⊕ BT40 . . . . 99 B4
Carneal Cl BT40. . . . . .182 A6
Carneal Rd BT40 . . . . 99 C3
Carnearney⊕ BT42 . . . . . 77 E1
Carnearney La
Antrim BT41. . . . . .109 D8
Ballymena BT42. . . . . . . 95 E1
Carnearney Rd BT42 . . . . 95 E1
Carnearny⊕ BT42. . . . . . . 95 E1
Carneatly⊕
Ballycastle BT54 . . . . .8 A2
Carneety⊕ BT51. . . . . 13 B3
Carnegie Bsns Ctr BT12 .188 D1
Carnegie Ctr Mus & Arts **10**
BT40 . . . . .182 C4
Carn End BT18. . . . . .139 D5
Carnet⊕ BT49 . . . . 39 F5
Carneybaun Dr BT55 . . . .173 E4
Carneybaun Pk BT55. . . .173 E4
Carneybaun Rd BT55. . . .173 F4
Carney Cres BT6 . . . . . . .152 E8
Carney Hill⊕ BT53 . . . . . . 59 D8
Carnfeogue⊕ BT53. . . . . . 17 C1
Carnfinton⊕ BT44 . . . . . . 60 B6
Carnfinton Pk BT44. . . . . . 60 B6
Carnforth St BT5. . . . . . . .145 B5
Carnfunnock⊕ BT40 . . . . 83 B7
Carnglass Beg⊕ BT53. . . 15 C3
Carnglass More⊕ BT52 . . 15 C3
Carn Gn **22** BT36. . . . . . . .111 F1
Carn Gr BT43 . . . . .181 A7
Carngraney Rd BT39 . . . .118 F8
Carngranny⊕ BT41 . . . . .108 E6
Carnhill BT48 . . . . .176 F3
Carn Hill BT48 . . . . .176 E3
Carnhill Ave BT36 . . . . . .133 A8
Carnhill Cres BT36 . . . . .133 A7
Carnhill Dr BT36 . . . . . . .133 A7
Carnhill Gdns BT36 . . . . .133 A7
Carnhill Gr BT36 . . . . . . .133 B8
Carnhill Parade BT36 . . .133 A7
Carnhill Rd BT36 . . . . . . .133 A8
Carnhill Wlk BT38. . . . . . .125 A2
Carniny⊕ BT43 . . . . .181 A6
Carniny Ct BT43 . . . . .181 B5
Carniny Prim Sch BT43. . .181 A6
Carniny Rd BT43 . . . . .181 A6
Carnkeeran⊕ BT43 . . . . . 79 F8
Carnkilly Lower⊕ BT29 . .121 B4
Carnkilly Upper⊕ BT29. . .121 C4
Carnkirk⊕ BT57 . . . . .6 A4
Carnkirn⊕ BT53 . . . . 17 D3
CARNLACH (CARNLOUGH)
BT44. . . . . 49 D3
Carnlea⊕
Ballyclare BT39 . . . . 96 F5
Ballymena BT44. . . . . . . 61 F4
Carnlea Rd
Ballyclare BT39 . . . . 97 A3
Ballymena BT44. . . . . . . 61 F3
Carnlea Rd N BT39 . . . . . . 96 E6
Carnlelis⊕ BT53 . . . . 17 C6
Carnlelis Rd
Ballymoney BT53. . . . . . 17 C5
Bushmills BT57 . . . . .7 A2
CARNLOUGH (CARNLACH)
BT44. . . . . 49 D3
Carnlougherin⊕ BT67. . . .167 E5
Carnlougherin Rd BT67 . .167 E5
Carnlough North⊕ BT44 . 49 C3
Carnlough Prim Sch BT44 49 D2
Carnlough Rd BT43 . . . . . 79 F8
Carn Manor The BT47. . . .179 F6
CARN MONAIDH
(CARNMONEY) BT36. . .133 A8
Carnmoney⊕ BT36. . . . . .133 A7
Carnmoney Bog BT36 . . .119 F7
CARNMONEY (CARN
MONAIDH) BT36. . . . . .133 A8
Carnmoney Glebe⊕
BT36. . . . . .133 A6
Carnmoney Prim Sch
BT36. . . . . .133 A8
Carnmoney Rd BT36 . . . .132 F6
Carnmoney Rd N BT36 . . .128 A1
Carnmoon⊕
Ballycastle BT54 . . . . .8 B5
Ballymoney BT53. . . . . . . .6 C1
Carn-More⊕ BT44. . . . . . . 62 A6
Carnmore Pl BT12 . . . . . .143 C4
Carnmoyne **4** BT42. . . . . 77 E2
Carn Neill Pk BT44 . . . . . . 32 D2
Carnowry⊕ BT49 . . . . 12 C3
Carnrallagh⊕ BT51 . . . . . 42 D5
Carnralla Pk BT51. . . . . . .174 A5
Carnrawsy Wlk BT38 . . . .124 E1
Carn Rd BT29 . . . . .118 E3
Carnreagh⊕ BT47 . . . . . . 69 D1
Carnreagh Bend BT37. . . .134 E7
Carnrig Fort★ BT53. . . . . . 17 D1
Carn Rise BT36 . . . . .111 F1
Carnroe BT29 . . . . .118 E3
Carnsampson⊕ BT54 . . . . .8 A3
Carnside⊕ BT57. . . . . .5 F6

Carnspindle❶ BT40 . . . . 84 C1
Carnstroam Rd BT42 . . . . . 80 E7
Carnstroan❶ BT42 . . . . . . 80 E6
Carnstron La BT42 . . . . . . 80 D6
Carntall Ct **28** BT36 . . . . . 111 F1
Carntall Rd BT36 . . . . 128 A4
Carntall Rise **33** BT36 . . . . 111 F1
Carntall View **33** BT36 . . . . 111 F1
Carntall Way **34** BT36 . . . . 111 F1
Carntogher Rd BT28 . . . . . 159 F1
Carnvale BT43 . . . . 181 B5
Carnvale Cl BT43 . . . . 181 B5
Carn View BT43 . . . . 74 D8
Carnview Pk BT43 . . . . . . 181 A6
Carnvue Ave BT36 . . . . . . 132 F8
Carnvue Cres BT36 . . . . . . 133 A8
Carnvue Ct **8** BT36 . . . . . 133 A8
Carnvue Dr BT36 . . . . 132 F8
Carnvue Gdns **2** BT36 . . . 132 F8
Carnvue Pk **1** BT36 . . . . . 132 F8
Carnvue Rd BT36 . . . . 132 F8
Carn Way **18** BT36 . . . . . . 111 F1
Carolan Rd BT7 . . . . 151 F7
Carol Gdns **7** BT36 . . . . . 133 A8
Carolhill Dr BT4 . . . . 145 F7
Carolhill Gdns BT4 . . . . . 145 F7
Carolhill Pk
  Ballymena BT42 . . . . 181 C1
  Belfast BT4 . . . . 145 F7
  Newtownabbey BT36 . . . . 132 D5
Carolhill Rd BT36 . . . . . . 132 D5
Carolina St BT13 . . . . 188 A4
Carol Pk BT36 . . . . 133 A8
Carracloghy❶ BT53 . . . . . . 17 C1
Carragh Rd BT57 . . . . 15 E5
Carraigard BT44 . . . . 176 C3
CARRAIG FHEARGHAIS
  (CARRICKFERGUS)
  BT38 . . . . 124 F2
Carrakeel❶ BT47 . . . . 36 A5
Carrakeel Dr BT47 . . . . 35 F5
Carraloan (Glebe)❶
  BT45 . . . . 105 B6
Carraloan Rd BT45 . . . . . . 105 C5
Carran❶ BT49 . . . . 180 E2
Carranbane Wlk BT48 . . . . 177 A5
Carranroe❶ BT51 . . . . 43 A2
Carravinally❶ BT54 . . . . 3 A3
Carravindoon❶ BT54 . . . . . . 3 B3
Carrawcroey Rd BT53 . . . . . 7 A1
Carriagecourt BT49 . . . . . . 11 D2
Carrick❶ BT49 . . . . 39 B2
Carrick-a-Rede Rope
  Bridge★ BT54 . . . . 7 E7
Carrickatane❶ BT82 . . . . . . 67 D7
Carrickatane Rd BT82 . . . . . 67 D7
Carrick Ave BT49 . . . . 39 B2
Carrickbeg Ave BT56 . . . . 172 C4
Carrickburn Dr BT38 . . . . . 125 D2
Carrickburn Rd BT38 . . . . . 125 D2
Carrick East❶ BT49 . . . . . . 39 C3
Carrickfergus❶ BT38 . . . . . 131 A7
CARRICKFERGUS (CARRAIG
  FHEARGHAIS) BT38 . . . . 124 F2
Carrickfergus Central Prim
  Sch BT38 . . . . 130 F8
Carrickfergus Coll BT38 . . 124 F2
Carrickfergus Golf Club
  BT38 . . . . 125 A1
Carrickfergus Gram Sch
  BT38 . . . . 124 F2
Carrickfergus Ind Ctr
  BT38 . . . . 130 D8
Carrickfergus Leisure
  Complex BT38 . . . . 130 F7
Carrickfergus Leisure Ctr
  BT38 . . . . 131 B8
Carrickfergus Marina &
  Harbour (Conference
  Centre) BT38 . . . . 131 A6
Carrickfergus Model Prim
  Sch BT38 . . . . 130 F7
Carrickfergus Rd
  Ballyclare BT39 . . . . 98 C2
  Ballynure BT39 . . . . 97 F2
  Larne BT40 . . . . 182 C2
Carrickfergus Sta BT38 . . 131 A8
Carrickfern Gdns BT38 . . . 129 E3
Carrick Hill (Cnoc na
  Carraige) BT13 . . . . . . 189 A4
Carrickhugh❶ BT47 . . . . . . 37 F7
Carrickmore❶ BT39 . . . . . . 39 D3
Carricknakielt❶ BT46 . . . . . 90 D7
Carricknakielt La BT45 . . . . 90 D6
Carricknakielt Rd
  Maghera BT46 . . . . 90 C8
  Magherafelt BT45 . . . . . . 90 D8
Carrickreagh Gdns BT48 . . 178 B4
Carrick Rocks❶ BT49 . . . . . 39 C3
CARRIGANS BT48 . . . . . . 50 A4
Carrigart Ave BT11 . . . . . . 149 E7
Carrington St BT6 . . . . . . 189 C1
Carrisbrook Gdns BT27 . . . 160 B6
Carrivcashel❶ BT53 . . . . . . 29 E6
Carrive❶ BT44 . . . . 81 E7
Carrivemurphy BT44 . . . . . 49 A8
Carrivereagh❶ BT44 . . . . . . 49 B5
Carrowcarragh❶ BT44 . . . . 45 A3
Carrowcladagh❶ BT51 . . . . 57 B5
Carrowclare❶ BT49 . . . . . . 22 D4
Carrowclare Rd BT49 . . . . . 22 D4
Carrowcloghan❶ BT54 . . . . 17 F6
Carrowcowan❶ BT43 . . . . . 63 A8
Carrowcrin❶ BT53 . . . . 29 F5
Carrowcrin Rd BT53 . . . . . 29 E7

Carrowcroey❶ BT54 . . . . 7 B1
Carrowcroey Rd
  Ballycastle BT54 . . . . 7 B1
  Ballymoney BT53 . . . . 6 F1
Carrowdoon Rd BT44 . . . . . 45 A4
Carrowlaverty❶ BT53 . . . . . 30 A8
Carrowmenagh❶
  Limavady BT49 . . . . 22 D5
  Maghera BT46 . . . . 74 B4
Carrowmenagh La BT46 . . . 74 B3
Carrowmuddle❶ BT49 . . . . . 22 F5
Carrownamaddy❶ 34 B6
Carrowoaghtragh❶ BT79 . . . 86 F3
Carrowreagh❶
  Ballymoney BT53 . . . . . . 17 D4
  Bushmills BT57 . . . . 6 B7
  Coleraine BT51 . . . . 42 B1
  Limavady BT49 . . . . 22 E4
Carrowreagh Mountain
  BT57 . . . . 6 B8
Carrowreagh Pk BT47 . . . . 50 E5
Carrowreagh Prim Sch
  BT53 . . . . 43 F5
Carrowreagh Rd
  Ballymoney BT53 . . . . . . 17 E3
  Coleraine BT51 . . . . 42 F1
Carrowroad BT47 . . . . 72 C7
Carrs Glen La BT14 . . . . . 136 F4
Carr's Glen Linear Pk★
  BT14 . . . . 119 F3
Carrs Glen Pk BT14 . . . . . 136 E4
Carrs Glen Prim Sch
  BT14 . . . . 119 F2
Carr's Glen Prim Sch
  BT14 . . . . 136 F3
Carrydarragh❶ BT45 . . . . . 103 F1
Carrydarragh Rd
  Cookstown BT80 . . . . . . 113 B8
  Magherafelt BT45 . . . . . 103 F1
  Moneymore BT45 . . . . . 113 E8
Carrydoo❶ BT49 . . . . 24 A2
Carryduff❶ BT8 . . . . 163 D4
Carryduff Bsns Pk BT8 . . . 163 E3
CARRYDUFF (CEATHRÚ
  AODHA DHUIBH) BT8 . . 163 C3
Carryduff Prim Sch BT8 . 163 E3
Carryduff Sh Ctr The
  BT8 . . . . 163 D2
Carse Rd BT49 . . . . 22 E1
Carson Ct **4** BT28 . . . . . . 159 D3
Carson St BT40 . . . . 182 C4
Carsonville Dr BT46 . . . . . . 74 F5
Carthall Cres BT51 . . . . . . 174 A4
Carthall Manor BT51 . . . . . 174 A3
Carthall Pk BT51 . . . . 174 A4
Carthall Rd BT51 . . . . 174 A4
Carwood Ave BT36 . . . . . . 132 E8
Carwood Cres BT36 . . . . . 132 E8
Carwood Dr BT36 . . . . 132 E7
Carwood Gdns BT36 . . . . . 132 E8
Carwood Parade BT36 . . . . 132 E8
Carwood Pk BT36 . . . . 132 F7
Carwood Pk S BT36 . . . . . 132 F7
Carwood Way **8** BT36 . . . . 132 E7
Casaeldona Cres BT6 . . . . 152 F8
Casaeldona Dr **1** BT6 . . . . 152 F8
Casaeldona Gdns BT6 . . . . 152 E8
Casaeldona Pk BT6 . . . . . 152 E8
Casaeldona Rise BT6 . . . . 152 F8
Casements Brae BT40 . . . . 182 C3
Casement St BT42 . . . . . . 181 D3
Casements View BT40 . . . . 182 C3
Cashel❶
  Coleraine BT51 . . . . 25 C1
  Londonderry BT47 . . . . . 72 C8
Cashelbane Cairn★ BT82 . . 68 F2
Cashel Cl BT37 . . . . 128 E1
Cashel Dr BT37 . . . . 128 E1
Cashelhill BT48 . . . . 176 E5
Cashelmore Pk BT48 . . . . . 178 B8
Cashel Rd
  Ballymena BT42 . . . . 80 A7
  Coleraine BT51 . . . . 41 C8
Casheltown❶ BT42 . . . . . . 92 F8
Casheltown Rd BT44 . . . . . 92 E8
Cashlan❶ BT44 . . . . 31 E6
Castle Arcade BT1 . . . . . 189 A3
Castle Ave
  Belfast BT15 . . . . 137 D6
  Moira BT67 . . . . 166 B2
  Randalstown BT41 . . . . . 108 A7
Castle Bawn The★ BT55 . . . 5 C1
Castlebay Ave BT8 . . . . . . 151 E3
Castlebrook Ave BT38 . . . . 98 A2
Castlebrook La **1** BT39 . . . 98 A2
Castleburn Ave BT38 . . . . 125 E3
Castleburn Dr BT38 . . . . . 125 E2
Castleburn Pk BT38 . . . . . 125 E2
Castleburn Rd BT38 . . . . . 125 D3
Castle Carra★ BT44 . . . . . . 21 A2
CASTLECAT BT57 . . . . . . 16 B6
Castlecat Rd BT57 . . . . . . 16 B5
Castlecatt Rd **1** BT53 . . . . 28 B8
Castle Chichester★
  BT40 . . . . 100 E1
Castlecoole Lodge BT8 . . . 151 E2
Castlecoole Pk BT8 . . . . . 151 E2
Castlecoole Wlk BT8 . . . . 151 E3
Castle Cres BT45 . . . . 91 D1
Castlecroft **2** BT53 . . . . . 175 C4
Castle Ct
  Castledawson BT45 . . . . . 91 D1
  Castlereagh BT6 . . . . . . 152 F8
  Cookstown BT80 . . . . . . 185 D2
Castle Ctr BT80 . . . . 186 D4
Castle Ctr Sh Ctr BT1 . . . 189 A3

CASTLEDAWSON (AN
  SEANMHULLACH) BT45 . . 91 B2
Castledawson Bypass
  BT45 . . . . 91 D1
Castledawson Prim Sch 6
  BT45 . . . . 91 C2
Castledawson Rd BT45 . . . 183 E7
Castle Demesne BT44 . . . . 65 E8
Castle Demesne Link
  BT43 . . . . 181 E4
Castledillon Rd BT8 . . . . . 151 E2
Castle Dr
  Belfast BT15 . . . . 137 D5
  5 Castledawson BT45 . . . 91 C1
  3 Randalstown BT41 . . . 108 A7
Castle Erin Rd BT55 . . . . . 173 D7
Castle Gdns
  Ballymena BT42 . . . . 181 D3
  Belfast BT15 . . . . 137 D5
  Limavady BT49 . . . . 180 D5
Castle Gn **3** BT39 . . . . . . 98 A2
Castlegore❶ BT42 . . . . 95 E7
Castle Grange BT5 . . . . . . 153 A8
Castlehill Ave BT53 . . . . . 175 D6
Castlehill Cl BT53 . . . . . . 175 D6
Castlehill Cres **1** BT53 . . . 175 E6
Castlehill Ct BT53 . . . . . . 175 D5
Castlehill Dr
  Ballymoney BT53 . . . . . . 175 D6
  Belfast BT4 . . . . 146 C6
Castle Hill Farm BT5 . . . . 153 A8
Castlehill Gdns BT53 . . . . 175 D6
Castlehill Gr BT53 . . . . . . 175 D6
Castlehill Manor BT4 . . . . 146 C6
Castlehill Pk
  3 Ballymoney BT53 . . . 175 E6
  Belfast BT4 . . . . 146 C5
Castlehill Pk W BT4 . . . . . 146 C5
Castlehill Pl BT53 . . . . . . 175 D6
Castlehill Rd BT4 . . . . 146 C5
Castlehill Terr BT53 . . . . . 175 D6
Castlehill View BT53 . . . . 175 D6
Castlehill Way **2** BT53 . . . 175 E6
Castlehume Gdns BT8 . . . . 151 E2
Castlekaria Manor BT4 . . . 146 D6
Castle La
  Ballymena BT44 . . . . 65 E7
  Belfast BT1 . . . . 189 A3
  4 Castledawson BT45 . . . 91 C1
Castle Lodge BT41 . . . . . . 108 B7
Castle Manor
  Antrim BT41 . . . . 186 D3
  2 Ballynure BT39 . . . . . 98 A2
Castlemara Dr BT38 . . . . . 125 A2
Castlemara Wlk BT38 . . . . 125 A2
Castlemellan❶ BT82 . . . . . 67 D6
Castle Mews BT6 . . . . 152 F8
Castlemore Ave BT6 . . . . . 152 E7
Castlemore Pk BT6 . . . . . 152 E7
Castlenagree❶ BT57 . . . . . . 6 A4
Castlenagree Rd BT57 . . . . 5 F2
Castle Oak BT45 . . . . 91 C1
Castleorr Manor BT4 . . . . 146 C6
Castle Park BT44 . . . . 21 B2
Castle Pk
  Antrim BT41 . . . . 186 C6
  Ballymena BT44 . . . . 21 B2
  Belfast BT15 . . . . 137 B5
  Eglinton BT47 . . . . 36 E5
  Limavady BT49 . . . . 180 D6
  Tobermore BT45 . . . . . . 89 E5
Castle Pl
  Belfast BT1 . . . . 189 A3
  Coleraine BT51 . . . . 174 B3
Castlequarter BT44 . . . . . 29 E1
Castlereagh Ind Est BT6 . . 145 C1
Castle Rd
  Antrim BT41 . . . . 186 A5
  Ballyclare BT39 . . . . 98 B3
  Ballynure BT39 . . . . 97 F2
  Bushmills BT57 . . . . 15 D5
  Carrickfergus BT38 . . . . 125 C2
  5 Castledawson BT45 . . . 91 C1
  Cookstown BT80 . . . . . . 185 E2
CASTLEREAGH BT6 . . . . 145 D1
Castlereagh❶ BT6 . . . . . . 152 E7
Castlereagh Coll of Further
  Ed BT6 . . . . 145 C1
Castlereagh Ind Est BT6 . 145 C1
Castlereagh Parade BT5 . . 145 C3
Castlereagh Pl BT5 . . . . . 145 A4
Castlereagh Rd BT6 . . . . . 145 D2
Castle Robin★ BT28 . . . . . 148 D2
Castlerobin Rd BT8 . . . . . 151 E3
CASTLEROCK BT51 . . . . . 13 B5
Castlerock Golf Club
  BT51 . . . . 13 C5
Castlerocklands BT38 . . . . 130 F6
Castlerocklands BT38 . . . . 130 E6
Castlerock Rd BT51 . . . . . 174 A5
Castlerock Sta BT51 . . . . 13 B4
CASTLEROE BT51 . . . . . . 26 B6
Castleroe Prim Sch BT51 . 26 B6
Castleroe Rd BT52 . . . . . . 174 C1
Castle St
  Antrim BT41 . . . . 186 D4
  Ballycastle BT54 . . . . 8 D3
  Ballymena BT43 . . . . . . 181 D4
  Ballymoney BT53 . . . . . . 175 C3
  Belfast BT1 . . . . 189 A3
  Bellaghy BT45 . . . . 91 F5
  Lisburn BT27 . . . . 160 B1
  6 Londonderry BT48 . . . 178 E5
  5 Castleton **4** BT39 . . . 110 C2
  Castleton Ave **2** BT15 . . 137 E1

Castleton Gdns BT15 . . . . 137 C1
Castleton Pk BT56 . . . . . . 172 B5
Castletoodry❶ BT51 . . . . . . 14 A2
Castletown❶
  Ballyclare BT39 . . . . 98 B3
  Whitehead BT38 . . . . . . 100 D1
Castletown Pk **4** BT39 . . . 98 A2
Castletown Rd BT39 . . . . . 98 B2
Castleview Pk
  Londonderry BT48 . . . . . 177 A3
  Portstewart BT55 . . . . . 173 F4
Castleview Rd
  Belfast BT5 . . . . 146 C4
  Whitehead BT38 . . . . . . 100 D1
Castleview Terr **3** BT4 . . . 145 F5
Castle Villas BT80 . . . . . . 185 E3
Castlevue Gdns BT67 . . . . 166 B2
Castlevue Pk BT67 . . . . . . 166 B2
Castlewarren❶ BT82 . . . . . 68 A7
Castlewarren Rd BT82 . . . . 67 F6
Castle Way BT41 . . . . 186 D4
Castle Wlk BT51 . . . . 13 B4
Castlewood Ave BT52 . . . . 26 B7
Castlewood Manor BT10 . . 150 B5
Castor Bay Rd BT67 . . . . . 164 A1
Castruse❶ 34 B1
Catherine Ct BT36 . . . . . . 137 E8
Catherine St N BT2 . . . . . 189 B2
Catherine St
  Belfast BT2 . . . . 189 B2
  Limavady BT49 . . . . 180 A5
Caulhame❶ BT51 . . . . 58 D8
Caulside❶ BT41 . . . . 187 D4
Caulsidedrive BT41 . . . . . 187 D4
Caulside Pk BT41 . . . . 187 D3
Causeway End Gdns
  BT28 . . . . 159 D2
Causeway End Rd **2** BT28 . 159 D2
Causeway End Rd BT28 . . . 159 C1
Causeway Hospl BT52 . . . . 174 F2
Causeway Inst BT53 . . . . 175 C5
Causeway Inst of FE
  (Coleraine Campus) The
  BT52 . . . . 174 C4
Causeway Manor BT28 . . . 159 D2
Causeway Mdws BT28 . . . 159 D2
Causeway Rd BT57 . . . . 5 F7
Causeway St BT55 . . . . . . 173 E7
Causeway View
  Portballintrae BT57 . . . . . 5 D4
  Portstewart BT55 . . . . . 173 D7
Causeway View La BT55 . . 173 C8
Cavalier Ct BT41 . . . . 186 D5
Cavan❶ 5 F1
Cavancreagh❶ BT82 . . . . . 67 C6
Cavancreagh Rd BT47 . . . . 67 C6
Cavanmore Gdns BT11 . . . 150 A7
Cavanreagh❶ BT45 . . . . . . 88 A1
Cavanreagh Rd BT45 . . . . 102 B8
Cavehill Ctry Pk★ BT36 . . . 136 F7
Cave Hill Ctry Pk★ BT36 . . 137 B7
Cavehill Prim Sch BT15 . . 137 B5
Cavehill Rd BT15 . . . . 137 B4
Cavendish Ct (Cúirt
  Chaibhendis) 10 BT12 . . 143 F5
Cavendish Sq BT12 . . . . . 188 A2
Cavendish St BT12 . . . . . . 188 A2
Cave Rd BT44 . . . . 21 A1
CAW BT47 . . . . 179 D7
Cawhill Pk BT47 . . . . 179 E7
Cawnpore St BT13 . . . . . . 188 C4
Caw Pk BT47 . . . . 179 C7
CEATHRÚ AODHA DHUIBH
  (CARRYDUFF) BT8 . . . . 163 C3
Cedar Ave
  Ballycastle BT54 . . . . 8 D4
  Belfast BT15 . . . . 137 B2
  Magherafelt BT45 . . . . . 183 B6
Cedar Dr BT54 . . . . 8 D4
Cedar Gr
  Belfast BT4 . . . . 139 B2
  6 Coleraine BT51 . . . . . 26 A7
Cedarhill BT41 . . . . 187 D3
Cedar Hill
  1 Newtownabbey BT36 . 111 F1
  Newtownabbey BT36 . . . 132 E8
Cedar Hts BT80 . . . . 185 E7
Cedarhurst Ct BT8 . . . . . . 152 A2
Cedarhurst Rd BT8 . . . . . . 151 F2
Cedarhurst Rise BT8 . . . . 151 F3
Cedar Lodge Sch BT36 . . . 137 D8
Cedarmount BT41 . . . . . . 186 D2
Cedar Pk
  Carrickfergus BT38 . . . . 130 E8
  Carrickfergus BT38 . . . . 130 E8
Cedar Pl BT52 . . . . 174 D5
Cedar St BT48 . . . . 178 D7
Cedars The **4** BT41 . . . . . 186 A6
Cedric St BT40 . . . . 182 A4
Céide Chlann Aodha Buí
  (Clandeboye Dr) 31
  BT5 . . . . 145 A4
Céide Chluanaí (Springfield
  Dr) 9 BT12 . . . . 143 F5
Céide na Seileastar (Iris Dr)
  4 BT12 . . . . 143 F5
Céide Thulach Forde
  (Mountforde Dr) 16
  BT5 . . . . 145 A5
Celandine Ct BT47 . . . . . . 178 F2
Celtic Ct BT48 . . . . 178 A4
Cemetery Rd BT80 . . . . . . 185 C3
Cennick Gr BT42 . . . . 78 B3
Cennick Rd BT42 . . . . 78 B2
Centaur Ct **2** BT41 . . . . . 186 D4

Central Ave
  Cookstown BT80 . . . . . . 185 C5
  Portrush BT56 . . . . 172 B5
Central Dr BT48 . . . . 178 B4
Central Pk BT41 . . . . 187 A5
Central Pk Ind Est BT36 . . 132 B6
Cesnor Pk BT41 . . . . 125 D2
Ceylon St BT13 . . . . 143 F6
Chadolly St **14** BT5 . . . . . 145 B5
Chadwick St BT9 . . . . 144 A1
Chaine Ct BT41 . . . . 187 B2
Chaine Meml Rd BT40 . . . 182 F4
Chaine Wlk BT41 . . . . 187 C2
Chamberlain St
  19 Belfast BT5 . . . . 145 B5
  3 Londonderry BT48 . . . 178 E5
Chambers St BT7 . . . . 189 A1
Channel Commercial Pk
  . . . . 145 B8
Channing St BT5 . . . . 145 C3
Chapel Ct BT80 . . . . 185 D4
Chapel Hill BT28 . . . . 160 A1
Chapel La BT1 . . . . 189 A3
Chapel Rd
  Ballymena BT44 . . . . 32 C4
  Belfast BT29 . . . . 120 F4
  Cookstown BT80 . . . . . . 185 D3
  Craigavon BT67 . . . . . . 155 E4
  Dungiven BT47 . . . . 55 D1
  Lisburn BT28 . . . . 156 C3
  Londonderry BT47 . . . . . 179 A4
Chapel Rd Prim Sch
  BT47 . . . . 179 A4
Chapel Sq BT52 . . . . 174 D3
Chapel St BT80 . . . . 185 D4
CHAPELTOWN BT41 . . . . 94 F3
Chapeltown Rd BT41 . . . . 94 E3
Charles Dr BT39 . . . . 184 C6
Charles Legg Dr **2** BT38 . 129 C1
Charles St S BT12 . . . . . . 188 C2
Charles St BT53 . . . . 175 C5
Charleville Ave **1** BT9 . . . 151 A8
Charleville St BT13 . . . . . 144 B7
Charley Meml Prim Sch
  BT17 . . . . 161 C7
Charlotte St
  Ballymoney BT53 . . . . . . 175 B4
  Belfast BT7 . . . . 189 B1
Charnwood Ave BT15 . . . . 137 B3
Charnwood Ct BT15 . . . . . 137 C3
Charnwood Pk BT52 . . . . . 26 B7
Charters Ave **2** BT5 . . . . 146 D2
Chartwell Pk BT8 . . . . . . 152 B3
Chase The BT39 . . . . 110 C4
Chater St BT4 . . . . 145 C5
Chathamhall❶ BT53 . . . . . 17 D2
Chatham Rd BT53 . . . . . . 17 D2
Chatsworth Gdns BT28 . . . 159 E5
Chatsworth St BT5 . . . . . 145 B4
Cheadle Pk BT47 . . . . . . 179 D4
Chelmsford Pl BT40 . . . . . 182 F4
Chelsea St BT4 . . . . 145 C6
Cheltenham Gdns BT6 . . . 152 A7
Cheltenham Pk BT6 . . . . . 152 A7
Chemical St (Sráid na
  gCeimiceán) 15 BT5 . . . 145 A5
Cherryburn Gdns BT47 . . . 179 C5
Cherryburn Rd BT39 . . . . 118 D2
Cherry Cl BT17 . . . . 149 E3
Cherry Ct BT17 . . . . 149 E3
Cherry Dr
  Belfast BT17 . . . . 149 E3
  5 Eglinton BT47 . . . . . . 36 E5
Cherry Gdns
  Ballymoney BT53 . . . . . . 175 E3
  Belfast BT17 . . . . 149 E3
Cherry Gr **2** BT47 . . . . . . 55 C2
Cherryhill
  Belfast BT9 . . . . 151 C8
  4 Maghera BT46 . . . . . 74 C1
Cherryhill Rd BT41 . . . . . 109 F5
Cherry La BT28 . . . . 159 E4
Cherrylands BT36 . . . . . . 133 E8
Cherrymanor BT51 . . . . . . 26 B6
Cherry Mdws BT36 . . . . . 132 E5
Cherry Mews BT17 . . . . . 149 F3
Cherrymount BT36 . . . . . 128 A2
Cherry Pk
  Belfast BT17 . . . . 149 E3
  Coleraine BT51 . . . . 26 B6
Cherry Pl BT52 . . . . 174 C5
Cherry Rd BT17 . . . . 149 F3
Cherry Tree BT5 . . . . 146 C4
Cherry Tree Wlk BT5 . . . . 146 B3
Cherry Vale BT28 . . . . . . 170 A7
Cherryvale Ave
  Magherafelt BT45 . . . . . . 90 B1
  Newtownabbey BT36 . . . 132 E5
Cherryvale Dr BT36 . . . . . 132 E5
Cherryvale Pk BT36 . . . . . 132 E5
Cherryvalley BT5 . . . . . . 146 B3
Cherryvalley Gdns BT5 . . . 146 C3
Cherryvalley Gn BT5 . . . . 146 B3
Cherryvalley Pk BT5 . . . . 146 B3
Cherryvalley Pk W BT5 . . . 146 C2
Cherryvalley Rd BT29 . . . 120 F8
Cherryville St BT6 . . . . . . 145 B3
Cherry Wlk BT17 . . . . 149 E3
Cherry Wlk The BT38 . . . . 124 F1
Chesham Cres BT6 . . . . . . 145 B2
Chesham Dr BT6 . . . . 145 A2
Chesham Gdns **2** BT6 . . . 145 B2
Chesham Gr BT6 . . . . 145 A2
Chesham Parade BT6 . . . . 145 A2
Chesham Pk BT6 . . . . 145 A2
Chesham Terr **1** BT6 . . . . 145 B2
Chesney Cres BT44 . . . . . . 76 C4

Chester Ave
5 Whitehead BT38......**100** D1
Whitehead BT38......**127** B8
Chesterfield Pk BT6...**152** A6
Chestnut Dr BT47......**179** E1
Chestnut Gdns 6 BT14..**137** B1
Chestnut Glen BT29...**121** B5
Chestnut Gr
Ballymoney BT53......**175** F3
Belfast BT15......**137** C4
Chestnut Hill
Dunmurry BT27......**160** C8
Newtownabbey BT37...**134** C7
Chestnut Hill Rd BT67..**166** C6
Chestnut Hollow BT27..**160** C8
Chestnut Lodge BT27...**162** B2
Chestnut Pk BT17......**149** E3
Chestnut Way 9 BT40...**83** B3
Cheston St BT38......**131** A7
Cheviot Ave BT4......**145** D5
Cheviot St BT4......**145** D5
Chichester Ave
Belfast BT15......**137** B4
Castledawson BT45......**91** D1
Chichester Cl 2 BT15..**137** C4
Chichester Ct 1 BT15..**137** C4
Chichester Gdns BT15..**137** B4
Chichester Mews BT15..**137** B4
Chichester Pk 28 BT38..**100** D1
Chichester Pk Central
Ballymena BT42......**181** E2
Belfast BT15......**137** B3
Chichester Pk E BT42...**181** E2
Chichester Pk N BT15...**137** B4
Chichester Pk S BT15...**137** B3
Chichester Pk W BT42..**181** E2
Chichester Rd BT15......**137** B4
Chichester Sq BT38......**124** F1
Chichester St BT1......**189** B3
Chief St BT13......**143** F7
Chilton Rd BT38......**125** C2
Chippendale Ct BT10...**150** D3
Chippendale Gdns BT10 **150** D3
Chippendale Pk BT48...**176** C1
Chism Ct BT40......**182** A3
Chiswick Wlk BT43......**181** D7
Chlorine Gdns BT9......**144** C1
Chobham St BT5......**145** F6
Christ Church Cath BT27 **160** B1
Christian Brothers Gram Sch
BT11......**143** A1
Christian Brothers Sch
BT11......**143** A1
Christian Pl BT12......**188** B3
Christies Building Ctr
BT48......**176** E1
Christine Dr BT36......**128** B2
Christine Gdns BT36...**128** B2
Christine Gr BT36......**128** B2
Christine Pk BT36......**128** B2
Christine Rd BT36......**128** B2
Christ the Redeemer Prim
Sch BT17......**149** C2
Church Ave
Carryduff BT8......**163** D3
Dunmurry BT17......**150** A2
Holywood BT18......**139** E7
Newtownabbey BT37......**129** B1
Church Brae BT47......**179** C2
Church Cres BT36......**133** A5
Church Ct BT18......**139** E6
Church Dr BT36......**133** A5
Churchfield BT4......**9** A2
Church Field BT46......**75** C6
Churchfield Rd BT54......**8** F3
Church Glen BT28......**160** C8
Church Gn BT18......**139** D6
Church Hill
Dunmurry BT27......**160** E6
Holywood BT18......**139** D7
Church Hill 1 BT82...**67** F6
Churchhill Ave BT44...**45** F2
Churchill Cres BT44......**60** B6
Churchill Dr BT38......**125** D2
Churchill Rd BT40......**182** A5
Churchill St BT15......**144** C7
Church La
Antrim BT41......**93** B4
Ballymena BT44......**60** C5
Ballymoney BT53......**175** C4
Belfast BT1......**189** B4
Cushendun BT44......**21** A2
2 Lisburn BT28......**160** B1
Lisburn BT28......**168** B6
Churchland 1 BT51...**25** F8
Churchland Cl BT4......**139** B2
Churchland La BT51......**174** A1
Churchlands BT38......**100** B3
Churchlands Rd BT51...**174** B2
Church Mdw
Ballymena BT44......**60** B5
Londonderry BT47......**179** C5
Church Pass
Portrush BT56......**172** B5
Portstewart BT55......**173** D7
Church Pk BT36......**133** A5
Church Quarter 1 BT54...**3** A6
Church Rd
Antrim BT41......**107** C7
Ballycastle BT54......**8** C3
Ballyclare BT39......**97** E2
Ballymena BT42......**96** D8
Ballymoney BT53......**18** A1
Belfast BT8......**152** A5
Carryduff BT8......**163** D2
Castlereagh BT6......**152** F7
Drumahoe BT47......**179** D2
Holywood BT18......**139** E7

Church Rd continued
Larne BT40......**182** C3
Londonderry BT47......**179** C1
Newtownabbey BT36......**133** A5
4 Randalstown BT41......**108** A7
Church St
Ahoghill BT42......**77** E2
Antrim BT41......**186** D4
Ballymena BT43......**181** D4
3 Ballymoney BT53......**28** B8
Ballymoney BT53......**175** C4
Belfast BT1......**189** A4
6 Bushmills BT57......**5** E3
1 Claudy BT47......**69** C8
Coleraine BT52......**174** C3
Cookstown BT80......**185** D3
Kilrea BT51......**59** C5
Limavady BT49......**180** B6
Maghera BT46......**74** D1
Magherafelt BT45......**183** D6
Portrush BT56......**172** B5
Rasharkin BT44......**44** D4
Church Tamlaght 1 BT44..**60** C5
Churchtown 1 BT51......**57** D8
CHURCHTOWN BT80......**112** F7
Churchtown La BT51......**58** F1
Churchtown Prim Sch
BT80......**112** F7
Churchtown Rd
Coleraine BT51......**57** E8
Cookstown BT80......**112** F7
Church View
Holywood BT18......**139** D6
11 Randalstown BT41......**107** F7
9 Randalstown BT41......**108** A7
Strabane BT82......**67** E3
Tobermore BT45......**89** E5
Church View Mews
BT18......**139** D7
Churchview Pk 5 BT51..**25** E5
Church Way
7 Larne BT40......**182** C4
Newtownabbey BT36......**133** A5
Churchwell La BT45......**183** D6
Church Wynd BT5......**146** D1
Cicero Gdns BT6......**145** D2
Cidercourt Dr 2 BT29..**117** A1
Cidercourt Pk BT29......**117** A1
Cidercourt Rd BT29......**121** A8
CILL RIA (KILREA) BT51...**59** C5
Circular Pk BT43......**181** C6
Circular Rd
Ballymena BT43......**181** C6
Belfast BT4......**145** F7
Castlerock BT51......**13** B4
Coleraine BT52......**174** C3
Larne BT40......**182** D3
Londonderry BT48......**178** A4
Moneymore BT45......**113** C8
Newtownabbey BT37......**134** B8
City Bsns Pk BT17......**160** E8
City Hospl Sta BT12......**188** C1
Citylink Bsns Pk BT12...**188** C3
City of Derry Airport BT47 **36** F7
City Way BT12......**188** C1
Civic Amenity Ctr BT7...**189** A1
Clady 1 BT44......**20** E2
CLADY BT44......**76** C4
Clady Manor 6 BT44...**76** B4
Clady Rd
Antrim BT41......**109** F1
Ballyclare BT39......**118** A8
5 Ballymena BT44......**76** B4
Cladytown Rd BT43......**61** E2
Clagan 1
Coleraine BT52......**42** F4
Cookstown BT80......**103** A1
Limavady BT49......**23** A7
Londonderry BT47......**70** A5
Clagan Pk BT51......**42** F4
Clagan Rd BT47......**70** A6
Claggan 1 BT80......**113** A5
CLAGGAN BT80......**115** C1
Claggan 1 BT71......**113** F1
Claggan Dr BT80......**185** D7
Claggan La BT80......**185** D7
Claggan North 1 BT82..**68** C2
Claggan Pk BT80......**185** D7
Claggan Rd
Cookstown BT80......**112** E8
Londonderry BT47......**70** A4
Claires Hill BT33......**175** E6
Clampernow 1 BT47......**50** E3
Clampernow Rd BT47...**50** E2
Clanbrassil Rd BT37......**135** B1
Clanbrassil Terr BT37...**135** B1
Clanchattan St 5 BT15..**137** D1
Clandeboye Dr (Céide
Chlann Aodha Buí) 31
BT5......**145** A4
Clandeboye Gdns (Gairdíní
Chlann Aodha Buí) 30
BT5......**145** A5
Clandeboye St BT5......**145** B4
Clanmorris St BT15......**144** B8
Clanroy Par BT4......**145** E5
Clanterkee 1 BT47......**36** D7
Clara Ave BT5......**145** D4
Clara Cres Lower 2
BT5......**145** D4
Clara Cres Upper 3
BT5......**145** D4
Claragh 1 BT51......**59** B6
Claragh Hill Cres BT51..**59** C5
Claragh Hill Ct BT51......**59** C6
Claragh Hill Dr BT51......**59** C5

Claragh Hill Pk BT51......**59** C5
Claragh Hill Rd BT51......**59** C6
Clara Pk BT5......**145** F3
Clara Rd BT5......**145** F3
Clara St BT5......**145** B3
Clara Way BT5......**145** D4
Clarawood Cres BT5......**145** F3
Clarawood Dr BT5......**145** F3
Clarawood Gr BT5......**145** F3
Clarawood Pk BT5......**145** F2
Clarawood Sch BT5......**145** F3
Clare
Antrim BT41......**93** F5
Ballycastle BT54......**8** C4
Cookstown BT80......**112** A3
Moira BT67......**166** D1
Clare Ave BT54......**8** D4
Clare Gdns
Belfast BT15......**136** E4
Newtownabbey BT37......**133** E3
Clare Glen BT14......**136** E4
Clarehill 1 BT51......**42** E7
Clare Hill
Ballymena BT42......**78** E2
Belfast BT14......**136** E4
Clarehill Cotts BT18......**139** C4
Clarehill Ct BT28......**159** D2
Clarehill La BT18......**139** C4
Clarehill Mews BT18......**139** C6
Clarehill Pk BT51......**42** E6
Clarehill Rd BT67......**166** D1
Clare Hts
Ballycastle BT39......**184** A5
Belfast BT14......**136** E4
Clare La BT80......**113** B2
Claremont Ave BT67......**166** C1
Claremont Cres BT67......**166** C1
Claremont Ct BT67......**166** C1
Claremont Dr BT67......**166** C1
Claremont Mews 2 BT9..**144** C2
Claremont Pk BT67......**166** C1
Claremont St
4 Belfast BT9......**144** C2
3 Londonderry BT48......**178** E7
Clare Mountain BT54...**19** A4
Clarence Ave 6 BT48...**178** E7
Clarence Ct BT51......**174** B2
Clarence Pl Mews BT1...**189** B2
Clarence St W BT2......**189** A2
Clarence St
Ballymena BT43......**181** C5
Belfast BT2......**189** A2
Clarendon Ave BT5......**145** D3
Clarendon Rd BT1......**189** B4
Clarendon St BT48......**178** E6
Clare Rd BT54......**8** C5
Clare St 4 BT54......**8** D3
Clareville Ave BT39......**184** B5
Clareville Pk BT39......**184** B5
Clareville Wlk BT39......**184** A5
Clark Ave BT46......**74** D1
Clarke Ct BT41......**186** D4
Clarkes Ct BT45......**90** F8
Clarke's La BT1......**189** A4
Clark Lodge Rd BT36...**119** B8
Clatteryknowes 1 BT42..**96** A8
Claudy 1 BT47......**53** A2
CLAUDY (CLÓIDIGH)
BT47......**69** C8
Claughey 1 BT53......**43** F6
Clearwater BT47......**179** D8
Cleaver Ave BT9......**151** B8
Cleaver Ct BT9......**151** B8
Cleaver Gdns BT9......**151** C7
Cleaver Pk BT9......**151** B7
Cleggan 1
Ballycastle BT54......**7** B6
Ballymena BT44......**32** B8
Ballymoney BT53......**17** B4
Clegnagh 1
Ballycastle BT54......**7** B6
Ballymena BT44......**32** B8
Ballymoney BT53......**18** F3
Clementine Dr BT12......**188** C1
Clementine Gdns BT12..**188** C1
Clementine Pk BT12......**188** C1
Clementshill 1 BT39......**111** E8
Clevely Pk BT8......**152** B3
Clifton Cres BT14......**137** B1
Cliftondene Cres BT14..**136** F2
Cliftondene Gdns BT14..**136** F2
Cliftondene Pk BT14......**136** F2
Clifton Dr BT14......**137** B1
Cliftonpark Ave
1 Belfast BT14......**137** C1
Belfast BT14......**144** B8
Clifton Pk BT52......**174** F4
Clifton Pk Ct 1 BT14...**144** C8
Clifton St
Belfast BT13......**144** C7
Londonderry BT47......**179** A4
Cliftonville 1 BT14......**137** B2
Cliftonville Ave
Belfast BT14......**137** B1
1 Londonderry BT47......**179** B5
Cliftonville Dr 7 BT14..**137** B1
Cliftonville Golf Club
BT14......**137** A3
Cliftonville Parade 8
BT14......**137** B1
Cliftonville Prim Sch
BT14......**137** B1
Cliftonville Rd BT14......**137** A2
Cliftonville St BT14......**137** B1
Clintagh 1 BT51......**41** E8
Clintagh La BT51......**41** E8

Clinton Ville Gdns BT51..**41** F1
Clinty 1 BT43......**78** D8
Clinty Rd BT43......**78** C8
Clipperstown Sta BT38...**130** F8
Cliveden Cres BT8......**152** B4
Cloane 1 BT45......**88** E7
Cloane La BT45......**88** F6
Cloane Rd BT45......**88** F6
Cloch-na-Larty ★ BT38...**129** E2
CLOGH BT44......**62** B7
Cloghan 1 BT45......**40** A3
Cloghan Cres BT5......**146** E4
Cloghanduff 1 BT39......**110** E2
Cloghan Gdns BT10......**150** E3
Cloghanmurry 1 BT54...**18** C6
Cloghan Pk BT5......**146** E4
Cloghan Rd BT49......**39** F3
Cloghastucan or White
Lady ★ BT44......**33** E1
Cloghboy 1 BT82......**50** A1
Cloghboy Rd BT82......**50** A1
Cloghcor 1 BT54......**48** A3
Cloghcorr 1 BT54......**7** E4
Clogher 1
Ballymena BT43......**78** E8
Lisburn BT28......**159** E1
Clogher Anderson BT57..**5** E3
Clogher Ct 4 BT57......**5** E3
Clogher North 1 BT57...**5** E3
Clogher Rd
Ballymena BT43......**78** E7
Bushmills BT57......**5** F4
Clogher South 1 BT57...**5** F3
Cloghfin 1
Larne BT40......**100** D3
Londonderry BT47......**54** D2
Cloghgaldanagh 1 BT44..**62** C7
Cloghglass 1 BT44......**32** D5
Cloghinarney 1 BT42...**80** D3
CLOGH MILLS 1 BT44...**45** E2
Clogh Mills 1 BT44......**45** F2
Cloghnagalla Chambered
Grave ★ BT47......**72** D8
Cloghog 1 BT80......**113** C2
Cloghogle 1 BT82......**50** C1
Cloghog Rd BT80......**185** F4
Cloghogue 1 BT41......**93** F7
Cloghole 1 BT47......**36** B7
Cloghole Rd BT47......**36** A4
Cloghornagh 1 BT47......**86** E6
Cloghs 1 BT44......**32** A4
Cloghy East 1 BT44......**32** B6
Cloghy West 1 BT44......**32** A8
CLÓIDIGH (CLAUDY)
BT47......**69** C8
Cloint 1 BT53......**43** C5
Clonallon Ct BT4......**145** F6
Clonallon Gdns BT4......**145** F6
Clonallon Pk BT4......**145** F6
Clonallon Sq 4 BT4......**145** F6
Clonard Cres (Corrán
Chluain Ard) 5 BT13...**188** A3
Clonard Ct BT13......**188** A3
Clonard Gdns BT13......**188** A3
Clonard Hts (Arda Chluain
Ard) 3 BT13......**188** A3
Clonard Monastry BT13...**188** A3
Clonard Pl (Plás Chluain
Ard) 1 BT13......**188** A3
Clonard Rise (Mala Chluain
Ard) 4 BT13......**188** A3
Clonard St BT13......**188** A3
Clonaslea BT37......**129** A2
Clonaver Cres N BT4......**145** F7
Clonaver Cres S BT4......**145** F6
Clonaver Dr BT4......**145** F6
Clonaver Pk BT4......**145** F7
Clonavon Rd BT43......**181** D4
Clonavon Terr 2 BT43..**181** C4
Clonbeg Dr BT37......**133** B3
Clonboy 1 BT41......**107** E7
Clonboy Wlk
9 Randalstown BT41......**107** F7
8 Randalstown BT41......**108** A7
Cloncool Pk BT48......**177** E8
Clondara Parade BT12..**143** E2
Clondara St BT12......**143** E2
Clondermot 1 BT47......**51** C6
Clondermot Rd BT47......**179** B3
Clonduff Dr BT6......**152** E8
Cloneen Cres BT46......**74** D2
Cloneen Dr
Ballymoney BT53......**175** D5
Moneymore BT45......**113** F8
Cloneen Manor BT46...**74** D2
Clonelly Ave BT11......**150** A8
Clonetrace 1 BT43......**63** C5
Clonetrace Rd BT43......**79** D8
Clonevin Pk BT28......**160** A2
Cloney 1 BT43......**20** F1
Cloney The BT44......**65** D6
Clonfadan Cres BT12...**188** C3
Clonfadan St BT12......**188** C3
Clonkeen 1 BT41......**93** B1
Clonkeen Hill BT41......**93** B2
Clonkeen Rd BT41......**107** C8
Clonlee Dr BT4......**145** E5
Clonliff Pk BT48......**35** F7
Clonmakane 1 BT47......**37** A1
Clonmakane Ct BT47......**179** E7
Clonmeen Dr BT47......**177** F5
Clonmore Gn BT37......**133** D4
Clonmore Manor BT27..**160** C5
Clonney St BT12......**143** E4
Clon Rd BT47......**36** F1
Clonreagh 1 BT44......**48** D2

Clonsilla Dr 3 BT51......**25** E5
Clontara Pk BT27......**160** B6
Clontarriff Rd BT6......**156** C6
Clontifinnan Rd BT53......**29** C7
Clontonacally Rd BT6...**152** F1
Clontyferagh 1 BT80...**112** A3
Clontyfinnan East 1 BT53..**29** C8
Clontyfinnan West 1
BT53......**29** B7
Clonvara BT37......**129** B1
Cloona Ave BT17......**149** E5
Cloona Cres BT17......**149** E5
Cloona Pk BT17......**149** E5
Cloonavin Gn BT52......**174** C6
Cloonavin Pk BT52......**174** C6
Clooney 1
Bushmills BT57......**5** A3
Limavady BT49......**11** F2
CLOONEY BT47......**179** B5
Clooney 1 BT45......**90** A5
Clooney Pk E BT47......**179** B6
Clooney Pk W BT47......**179** B6
Clooney Rd
Ballymena BT42......**93** A7
Greysteel BT47......**37** D5
Limavady BT49......**38** A7
Londonderry BT47......**179** C7
Magherafelt BT45......**90** C5
Tobermore BT45......**89** F5
Clooneyville Ave 1
BT47......**179** A6
Cloonty 1 BT53......**16** C5
Cloreen Pk BT9......**144** C1
Close The
4 Ballymena BT42......**78** C4
Belfast BT10......**150** D3
Holywood BT18......**139** F8
Lisburn BT27......**170** C8
Clós Ghort na Sí BT48...**177** A4
Clós na Carriage Báine
(Whiterock Cl) BT12...**143** C3
Clós na Trá (Strand Cl) 9
BT5......**145** A6
Clós Pholaird (Pollard Cl) 2
BT12......**143** F5
Clotworthy Arts Ctr ★
BT41......**186** C4
Cloughanduff Rd BT39..**110** D3
Cloughfern Ave BT37...**133** F8
Cloughfin 1 BT45......**89** F3
Cloughglass 1 BT48......**178** E8
Cloughlands BT38......**125** E2
Cloughlin La BT39......**184** A6
Cloughmills Prim Sch
BT44......**45** F2
Cloughmore Rd BT36...**132** B6
Cloughogue Rd BT41...**106** C3
Cloughs Rd BT44......**32** A4
Cloughs Upper 1 BT44..**32** B4
Cloughwater Rd BT43...**62** C4
Clovelly St BT13......**143** E5
Clover Hill BT49......**23** A2
Cloverhill Ave
Drumahoe BT47......**179** F1
Lisburn BT27......**170** C8
Cloverhill Gdns BT4......**146** D6
Cloverhill Pk
Belfast BT4......**146** D7
Coleraine BT51......**174** A1
Cloverhill Rd
Cookstown BT80......**114** F6
Magherafelt BT45......**114** F7
Clover La BT67......**167** B4
Clovervale BT49......**180** E4
Clowney St BT12......**143** F4
Cloyfin Bsns Pk BT52......**174** F7
Cloyfin North 1 BT52...**15** A4
Cloyfin Pk BT52......**174** E6
Cloyfin Rd BT52......**174** E6
Cloyfin South 1 BT52...**15** A3
Cloyne Cres BT37......**128** E1
Cluain Mor Ave BT12...**143** F5
Cluain Mor Cl BT12......**143** E5
Cluain Mor Dr BT12......**143** F4
Cluain Mor La BT12......**143** E5
Cluain Mor Pk BT12......**143** E4
Cluan Pl BT5......**145** A4
Clubhill 1 BT51......**42** A2
Cluntirriff 1 BT28......**156** C6
Cluntoe (Quin) 1 BT80..**115** C2
Cluntoe (Richardson) 1
BT80......**115** D1
Cluntydoon 1 BT80......**112** B6
Cluntyganny 1 BT80......**112** C6
Cluntygeeragh 1 BT47..**72** D5
Clyde Ct (Cúirt Chluaidh) 1
BT5......**145** A5
Clyde Streeet BT48......**178** E6
Clyttaghan 1 BT54......**20** A1
Cnoc na Carraige (Carrick
Hill) BT13......**189** A4
Cnoc na Ndriseacha (Briar
Hill) 4 BT47......**37** C5
Coachmans Ct BT56......**172** C3
Coachmans Rise BT26...**169** B2
Coachmans Way BT26...**169** B1
Coach Row BT43......**181** D3
Coagh 1 BT80......**114** D3
COAGH (AN CUACH)
BT80......**114** C3
Coagh Prim Sch 6 BT80 **114** C3
Coagh Rd BT80......**185** F5
Coagh St BT80......**185** D6
Coar's La BT1......**189** A4

Coastguard Rd
Larne BT40 . . . . **182** F3
Portballintrae BT57 . . . . . . **5** C5
Coastguard Rd S BT40. . . **182** F2
Coast Rd
Ballymena BT44. . . . . **65** F8
Cushendall BT44. . . . . **32** E3
Larne BT40 . . . . **182** D7
Coates Ave BT38 . . . . . . **125** B2
Coates Gdns BT38. . . . . **125** B2
Coburg St BT6. . . . . **145** A3
Cochranstown Rd BT29. . **140** C5
Cockhill Rd
Ballymena BT42. . . . . **94** C7
Lisburn BT27 . . . . **168** B2
Cockle Row BT40 . . . . . . **182** D4
Cockpit Brae 2 BT53 . . **175** D4
Coey Cl 2 BT40. . . . . . . **83** B2
Coggrey BT39 . . . . **97** A1
Cogry Hill BT39 . . . . **110** F8
Cogry Manor 5 BT39 . . **110** F8
Cogry Rd BT39 . . . . **184** A7
Cogry Rise BT39 . . . . . . **110** F8
Cogry Sq 4 BT39 . . . . . **110** F8
COILL NA BAICE
(CULLYBACKEY) BT42 . . **77** F6
COINNIRE (CONNOR)
BT42 . . . . **95** B5
Colane Mdws BT67. . . . . **164** E7
Colane Rd BT67. . . . . . . **164** E7
Colby Ave BT48 . . . . **177** B5
Colby Pk BT8 . . . . **152** B4
Colchester St BT12. . . . . **188** B1
Coldagh BT53. . . . . **27** C2
Coldagh Hill BT53. . . . . . **27** C3
Colebreene Lower
BT52 . . . . **26** E4
Colebreene Upper BT53 **26** F3
Colenso Ct BT9 . . . . **144** D1
Colenso Parade BT9 . . . **144** D1
Coleraine Academical
Institution BT51 . . . . . **174** B5
Coleraine Coll BT51. . . . . **174** A3
COLERAINE (CÚIL RAITHIN)
BT52 . . . . **174** B5
Coleraine Ent Ctr BT52. . **174** F7
Coleraine High Sch
BT52. . . . . **174** E3
Coleraine Leisure Ctr
BT52. . . . . **174** D3
Coleraine Rd
Ballycastle BT54 . . . . **8** C3
Ballymoney BT53. . . . . . . **175** B5
Maghera BT46 . . . . **74** D1
Portrush BT56 . . . . **172** C3
Portstewart BT55 . . . . . . **173** D3
Coleraine St BT51. . . . . . **59** C5
Coleraine Sta BT52 . . . . . **174** D4
Coleraine & Suburbs
BT52 . . . . **174** E3
Coleshill Gdns BT8. . . . . **151** E3
Colinbrook Ave 7 BT17 **149** D6
Colinbrook Cl 5 BT17 . . **149** D6
Colinbrook Cres BT17 . . **149** D6
Colinbrook Dr BT17 . . . . **149** D6
Colinbrook Gdns 2
BT17 . . . . **149** D6
Colinbrook Gn 6 BT17 . . **149** D6
Colinbrook Main S BT17 **149** D6
Colinbrook Pk 1 BT17 . . **149** D6
Colindale Pk BT17 . . . . . . **149** F3
Colin Glen Forest Pk Ctr ★
BT17. . . . . **149** E6
Colinglen Pk BT17 . . . . . **149** C8
Colinglen Rd BT17 . . . . . **149** B4
Colinmill BT17 . . . . **149** D5
Colinpark St BT12. . . . . . **143** F5
Colin Rd BT17 . . . . **149** D5
Colinvale BT17 . . . . **149** D6
Colinvalley Golf Course
BT17. . . . . **149** F4
Colinview St BT12. . . . . . **143** F5
Colinward St BT12 . . . . . **143** F5
Colinwell Rd BT17 . . . . . **149** B6
College Ave
Belfast BT12 . . . . **188** C3
Londonderry BT48. . . . . . **178** E7
College Ct BT1. . . . . **189** A3
College Dr BT7 . . . . **151** E7
College Gdns BT9. . . . . . **144** C2
College Glen BT48 . . . . . **176** D3
College Gn BT7 . . . . **144** D2
College Mews BT52 . . . . **174** D6
College Pk
Belfast BT7 . . . . **144** D2
Coleraine BT51. . . . . **174** A6
College Pk Ave BT7 . . . . **144** D2
College Pk E BT7 . . . . . . **144** D2
College Pl N BT12. . . . . . **188** C3
College St Mews BT1 . . **189** A3
College Sq E BT1 . . . . . . **189** A3
College Sq N BT12 . . . . . **188** C3
College St BT12. . . . . . . **189** A3
College Terr BT48. . . . . . **178** E7
College Wlk BT38 . . . . . . **125** C3
Colligan St BT13 . . . . . . **188** A2
Collinbridge Cl BT36 . . . **132** F4
Collinbridge Dr BT36. . . **132** F3
Collinbridge Gdns BT36 **132** F3
Collinbridge Pk BT36. . . **132** F4
Collinbridge Rd BT36 . . **133** A3
Collin Gdns BT11 . . . . . . **150** B8
Collingwood Ave BT7 . . **144** E2

Collingwood Rd 9 BT7. . **144** E1
Collin Hts BT38 . . . . **124** D2
Collin Rd
Ballyclare BT39 . . . . **96** F4
Ballymena BT42. . . . . **96** D6
Collins BT51 . . . . **26** C1
Collinvale BT39 . . . . **184** D4
Collinview BT39 . . . . **184** D5
Collinview Ave BT39 . . . **184** E5
Collinview Dr BT39. . . . . **184** E5
Collinview Gr BT39. . . . . **184** E5
Collinward BT36 . . . . . . **133** A3
Collinward Ave BT36 . . . **133** B4
Collinward Cres BT36 . . **133** A5
Collinward Dr BT36 . . . . **133** B5
Collinward Gdns BT36. . **133** B5
Collinward Gr BT36 . . . . **133** B5
Collinward Pk BT36 . . . . **133** A4
Collinwood BT43. . . . . . **181** B6
Collinwood Cl BT43 . . . . **181** A7
Collnasillagh La
Londonderry BT47. . . . . . **73** C1
Magherafelt BT45 . . . . . . **89** A8
Collon La BT48 . . . . **176** D3
Colman Ave BT53 . . . . . . **16** C5
Colonsay Pk BT42. . . . . . **181** F4
Coltrim BT45 . . . . **113** D7
Coltrim Cross Roads
BT45 . . . . **113** D7
Coltrim La BT45. . . . . . . **113** D6
Columbia Pk BT47 . . . . . **54** C2
Columbia St BT13. . . . . . **143** F8
Colvil St BT4. . . . . **145** D6
Comber Ct (Cúirt an
Chomair) 25 BT5 . . . . . **145** A5
Comber Gdns (Garraithe an
Chomair) 28 BT5 . . . . . **145** A5
Combermere St BT2 . . . **188** C1
Comber Rd
Carryduff BT8 . . . . **163** E3
Lisburn BT27 . . . . **171** C2
Commercial Ct BT1 . . . . **189** A4
Commercial Way BT36 . . **132** C6
Commons BT38 . . . . **99** A1
Commons Brae BT8 . . . . **152** A3
Commons The BT43. . . . . **79** D7
Community Wlk BT53 . . . **17** B4
Conagher Rd BT53 . . . . . **27** E8
Concorde Pk BT42 . . . . . **181** C1
Condiere Ave BT42. . . . . **95** B5
Conduit St BT7 . . . . **189** A1
Coneyburrow BT47. . . . . **177** F5
Coney Rd BT48 . . . . **35** F8
Coney Ville BT48. . . . . . . **35** F7
Conifer Ave BT47 . . . . . . **179** C5
Coniston Cl 2 BT13. . . . . **144** A7
Connaughtliggar Rd BT44 **76** F3
Connaught Rd BT41. . . . **108** A8
Connaught St BT12 . . . . **188** B1
Connell St BT49. . . . . . . **180** B5
Conneywarren BT14. . . . **136** C4
CONNOR (COINNIRE)
BT42 . . . . **95** B5
Connor Rd
Ballyclare BT39 . . . . **110** B6
Ballymena BT42. . . . . . . **109** F8
Connors Rd BT47 . . . . . . **36** B5
Connsbank Rd BT3. . . . . **145** C7
Connsbrook Ave BT4. . . . **145** D6
Connsbrook Dr BT4 . . . . **145** D6
Connsbrook Pk BT4. . . . . **145** D5
Connswater Gr 3 BT4 . . **145** C6
Connswater Ind Est BT5 **145** C4
Connswater Link BT5 . . . **145** C5
Connswater Mews 2
BT4 . . . . **145** C6
Connswater Ret Pk BT5 . . **145** C4
Connswater Sh Ctr BT5 **145** C5
Connswater St BT4 . . . . . **145** C5
Conogher BT53. . . . . **27** F7
Conogher Cross Roads
BT53 . . . . **27** F6
Conor Rise BT11 . . . . . . **150** A7
Constance St 1 BT5 . . . **145** B4
Convention Ave BT56 . . **172** B5
Convention Ct BT4 . . . . . **145** B5
Convent Rd BT80 . . . . . . **185** C4
Conway Ct BT13 . . . . . . **188** A4
Conway Ind Est BT13. . . **188** A3
Conway La BT17 . . . . . . **160** E7
Conway Link BT13 . . . . . **188** A3
Conway Pk BT47 . . . . . . **51** E6
Conway Sq BT13 . . . . . . **188** A3
Conway St
Belfast BT13 . . . . **188** A3
1 Lisburn BT27 . . . . . . **160** B2
Conway Wlk BT13. . . . . . **188** A4
Conyngham St 10 BT45. . **113** E8
Cooke Ave 14 BT46. . . . . **74** C1
Cooke Cres BT80. . . . . . **185** D3
Cooke Cl BT7 . . . . **189** B1
Cooke Mews BT7 . . . . . . **189** B1
Cooke Pl BT7 . . . . **189** B1
Cooke St
Belfast BT7 . . . . **189** B1
Londonderry BT48. . . . . . **178** D4
Cookstown BT80 . . . . . . **185** D6
COOKSTOWN (AN CHORR
CHRÍOCHACH) BT80 . . **185** E5
Cookstown Ent Ctr BT80 **185** B2
Cookstown High Sch
BT80. . . . . **185** E5
Cookstown Leisure Ctr
BT80. . . . . **185** D4
Cookstown Prim Sch
BT80. . . . . **185** D5
Cookstown Rd BT45. . . . **113** D7

Coolafinney Rd BT47. . . . **36** E5
Coolafinny BT47. . . . . . . **36** D5
Coolagh BT47. . . . . **37** E6
Coolagh Rd
Londonderry BT47. . . . . . **37** E2
Maghera BT46 . . . . **89** E8
Coolaveely BT54 . . . . **19** C6
Coolcoscreaghan BT51. **57** B3
Cooldarragh Pk BT14 . . **137** A4
Cooldarragh Pk N BT14 **137** B4
Coolderry Gdns BT37. . . **133** C4
Coolderry North BT52. . **26** F5
Coolderry South BT52. . **26** E4
Coole BT53 . . . . **16** D3
Coleen Pk
Londonderry BT48. . . . . . **35** E7
Newtownabbey BT37. . . . **134** B8
Coole Gn BT51. . . . . **174** B2
Coolehill Cres BT36 . . . . **132** F6
Coolehill Pk BT36. . . . . . **132** F6
Coole Pk BT36. . . . . **133** A6
Coolessan Drumrane
BT49. . . . . **180** A2
Coolessan Wlk BT49. . . . **180** C3
Coolfin St BT12 . . . . **188** B1
Coolhill BT51. . . . . **42** F2
Coolkeeghan BT53. . . . . **57** F4
Coolkeeghan Rd BT53 . . **57** E4
Coolkeenaght BT49. . . . **37** F6
Coolkeeragh BT47. . . . . **35** F6
Coolkeeragh Rd BT47. . . **35** F6
Coolkeeran BT53 . . . . . . **30** A4
Coolkeeran Rd
Ballymena BT44. . . . . **30** A2
Ballymoney BT53. . . . . . . **29** F7
Coolkenny BT54 . . . . **7** F1
Coolmaghery BT47. . . . . **50** D2
Coolmaghra BT53 . . . . . . **7** F6
Coolmount Ave BT80. . . **185** C8
Coolmount Dr BT80 . . . . **185** C7
Coolnacolpagh BT47. . . . **53** C1
Coolnafranky BT80. . . . **185** E4
Coolnafranky Pk BT80. . **185** E3
Coolnagoppoge BT54 . . **9** F2
Coolnahavil BT80 . . . . . . **185** E3
Coolnamonan BT47. . . . **70** E4
Coolnasallagh Rd BT47. . **72** B8
Coolnasilla Ave BT11. . . **150** B8
Coolnasilla Cl 1 BT11. . **150** B8
Coolnasilla Dr BT11. . . . **150** B8
Coolnasilla Gdns BT11 . **150** B8
Coolnasillagh
Coleraine BT51 . . . . **40** F3
Magherafelt BT45 . . . . . . **73** C1
Coolnasillagh Rd
Coleraine BT51 . . . . **41** B3
Maghera BT46 . . . . **89** B8
Coolnasilla Pk BT11 . . . **143** B1
Coolnasilla Pk E
8 Belfast BT11. . . . . . . **143** B1
Belfast BT11 . . . . **150** B8
Coolnasilla Pk S
7 Belfast BT11. . . . . . . **143** B1
Belfast BT11 . . . . **150** B8
Coolnasilla Pk W BT11 . **150** B8
Coolpark Ave BT8. . . . . . **152** B4
Coolranny BT54. . . . . . . **21** A6
Coolreaghs BT80. . . . . . **185** F5
Coolreaghs Cres BT80. . **185** F5
Coolreaghs Rd BT80 . . . **185** C6
Coolsaragh BT45. . . . . . **89** F2
Coolsara Pk BT28 . . . . . **160** A2
Coolshannagh Pk 1
BT37 . . . . **133** E5
Coolshinney Cl BT45. . . . **183** B4
Coolshinney Hts BT45. . **183** B4
Coolshinney Pk BT45. . . **183** B3
Coolshinney Rd BT45. . . **183** B3
Coolshinney BT45. . . . . . **183** B2
Coolsythe BT41. . . . . **93** E3
Coolsythe Rd BT41. . . . . **93** E2
Coolsythe Wlk BT41. . . . **108** A8
Coolvenny Rd BT51 . . . . **26** A3
Coolyvenny BT51. . . . . . **26** C2
Coolyvenny Rd BT51. . . . **26** E2
Coombe Hill Pk BT14. . . **136** F4
Cooneen Way BT6 . . . . . **152** B8
Coopers La BT40. . . . . . **182** C4
Cooper The BT27 . . . . . **162** E1
Coose Quarter BT51. . . . **41** B3
Copeland Cres BT47 . . . . **38** D7
Copeland Pk BT51 . . . . . **174** A2
Copeland View Terr
BT38 . . . . **124** F4
Copperfield Ct BT67 . . . **167** A8
Copperfield Dr BT47 . . . . **179** E5
Copperfield Mews BT47 **179** E5
Copperfields BT67 . . . . . **167** A8
Copperthorpe BT47. . . . . **179** F2
Copperwood Ave BT38 . . **125** B5
Copperwood Cl BT38. . . **125** C5
Copperwood Cres BT38 **125** B5
Copperwood Dr BT38 . . **125** C5
Copperwood Rd BT38 . . **125** C5
Copperwood Way BT38. . **125** C6
Copperwood Wlk BT38. . **125** C5
Coral Cl BT53 . . . . **43** B4
Coral Cres BT41 . . . . . . **186** C5
Corbally
Ballymena BT42. . . . . **78** A4
Belfast BT29 . . . . **116** F7
Coleraine BT52 . . . . **4** E1
Corbally Ave BT44 . . . . . **186** F4
Corbally Pk BT41 . . . . . . **186** F4
Corbally Rd
Ballymena BT42. . . . . **77** F4
Belfast BT29 . . . . **116** E6
Coleraine BT52 . . . . **4** E1

Corby Dr BT28 . . . . **159** E4
Corby Way BT28 . . . . . . **150** B8
Cordarragh BT45 . . . . . . **89** A4
Corick
Londonderry BT47. . . . . . **72** F6
Magherafelt BT45 . . . . . . **102** F6
Corick Rd
Londonderry BT47. . . . . . **72** C8
Magherafelt BT45 . . . . . . **102** E6
Corkermain BT40 . . . . . . **82** F8
CORKEY BT44 . . . . **46** B7
Corkey Middle BT44. . . . **46** C8
Corkey North BT44. . . . . **30** C1
Corkey Rd BT44. . . . . . . **46** B6
Corkey South or Little
BT44 . . . . **46** D8
Cormac Rd BT28 . . . . . . **156** F8
Cormanagh Ct BT55. . . . **173** E4
Cormorant Pk
Carrickfergus BT38. . . . . **125** A8
Castlereagh BT5 . . . . **153** A8
Cornaclery BT51. . . . . . . **57** F4
Cornakilly BT47. . . . . **85** E5
Cornakinnegar BT67. . . . **164** C2
Cornakinnegar Rd BT67. **164** C5
Cornamoney BT47. . . . . . **54** D2
Cornamuclagh BT51. . . . **42** F5
Corndale Upper BT49 . . **23** A1
Cornmarket BT1. . . . . . . **189** A3
Cornshell Fields BT48. . **177** A5
Cornwall Cl BT47. . . . . . **187** C5
Coronation Cres BT38. . **125** C2
Coronation Dr BT37. . . . **129** B1
Coronation Gdn BT27 . . **169** B4
Coronation Pk BT44. . . . **62** B7
Coronation Rd BT38. . . . **125** C2
Corporation Sq BT15. . . **189** B4
Corporation St
Belfast BT1 . . . . **189** B4
2 Londonderry BT48 . . . . **178** E4
Corpus Christi Coll BT12 **143** E4
Corramore Rd BT79 . . . . **85** F1
Corrán Bhaile Andarsan
(Andersonstown Cres) 4
BT11 . . . . **143** C1
Corrán Chluain Ard (Clonard
Cres) 5 BT13 . . . . . . **188** A3
Corrán Chluanaí (Springfield
Cres) 8 BT13 . . . . . . **143** F5
Corran Integrated Prim Sch
BT40. . . . . **182** C8
Corran Manor BT40 . . . . **182** E4
Corrán na Tíre Thiar
(Westland Cres) 1
BT47 . . . . **37** C5
Corratary BT79 . . . . **86** D2
Correen BT43 . . . . **63** B2
Corrib Ave BT11. . . . . . . **149** F7
Corrib Ct BT48 . . . . **176** B3
Corrina Ave BT17. . . . . . **149** E4
Corrina Pk BT17 . . . . . . **149** E4
Corrody BT47 . . . . **51** B6
Corrody Dr BT47 . . . . . . **179** A3
Corrody Rd BT47. . . . . . **178** F1
Corrstown BT55 . . . . . . **173** E5
Corrstown Pk BT55. . . . . **173** E4
Corrstown Rd BT28 . . . . **156** E3
Corry Link BT3. . . . . **144** F7
Corrymellagh BT44 . . . . **21** B4
Corry Pl BT15. . . . . **144** F7
Corry Rd BT3 . . . . **144** F7
Corvally BT53 . . . . **19** A4
Cosgrave St 17 BT15 . . . **144** D8
Cosgrave St 19 BT15 . . . **144** D8
Coshkib BT44. . . . . **32** D6
Coshowen
7 Dungiven BT47. . . . . . **55** D2
Londonderry BT47. . . . . **178** D3
Coshquin BT48 . . . . **34** E4
Coshquin Rd BT48 . . . . . **176** A4
Cossack Ct BT41. . . . . . **186** E5
Cotlands Gn BT17. . . . . . **149** C4
Cotswold Ave
Castlereagh BT8 . . . . **152** B3
Londonderry BT47. . . . . **179** C4
Cottage Gdns
Limavady BT49 . . . . **40** A2
Lisburn BT28 . . . . **159** D5
Cottage Hospl BT43. . . . **181** D6
Cottage Pk 3 BT47 . . . . . **36** E5
Cottage Row BT47. . . . . . **36** E5
Cotts The BT41. . . . . **107** F8
Coulson Ave BT28. . . . . . **170** B8
Councillors Rd BT38 . . . . **123** C5
Courtauld Way BT47 . . . . **36** C6
Courtrai St BT13 . . . . . . **144** A7
Covehill Pk BT52. . . . . . . **174** C6
Coyle St BT7 . . . . **189** B1
Cozies BT57 . . . . **16** D6
Cozies Rd BT57 . . . . **16** C6
Crabarkey BT47 . . . . **53** B1
Cragfergus Ave 1 BT38 . **125** A3
Cragfergus Gr BT38. . . . **125** A4
Craig
35 D8
Ballymena BT44. . . . . **32** A5
Bushmills BT57 . . . . **6** A1
Limavady BT49 . . . . **12** A3
Craigaboney BT57. . . . . . **5** C3
Craigaboney Rd BT57. . . **5** C2
Craigadick BT46. . . . . . . **90** A8
Craigadick Pk BT46. . . . . **74** C1
Craigadick Rd BT46. . . . . **89** F7

Craigadoo La BT42 . . . . . **79** D3
Craigadoo Rd BT42 . . . . . **79** E1
Craighulliar BT52. . . . . . . **.4** C1
Craighulliar Rd BT52 . . . . **4** D1
Craigalappan BT54 . . . . . **7** A4
Craigalappin Rd BT54 . . . **7** A4
Craigall BT51. . . . . **58** F7
Craiganboy BT40. . . . . . . **99** D8
Craiganboy Pk 5 BT40. . **99** C8
Craiganee
Ballycastle BT54 . . . . **7** C5
Larne BT40 . . . . **99** D5
Craiganee Rd BT40. . . . . **99** D5
Craigarogan BT36. . . . . . **119** B7
Craigarogan Pk BT36 . . . **119** B8
Craigatempin BT53 . . . . . **28** E2
Craigatempin Rd BT53 . . **28** E2
Craigatoke Rocks BT47. **53** C5
CRAIGAVOLE BT46. . . . . . **58** B3
Craigavon Bridge BT48. . **178** F4
Craigavon Dr BT38 . . . . . **125** D2
Craigban BT54. . . . . **19** C5
Craigbrack BT47 . . . . **37** A3
Craigbrack Prim Sch
BT47. . . . . **37** A3
Craigbrack Rd
Londonderry BT47. . . . . . **37** A2
Londonderry BT47. . . . . . **53** A8
Craigburn BT41. . . . . **187** C2
Craig Cres BT28 . . . . **169** F8
Craig Ct BT43. . . . . **181** C5
CRAIGDARRAGH BT47. . . **69** F7
Craigdarragh Pk BT38. . . **125** D2
Craigdunloof BT43. . . . . **47** B2
Craigdunloof Rd BT43 . . **47** A1
Craigfad
Ballycastle BT54 . . . . **9** D4
Ballymena BT44. . . . . **62** D7
Craigfaddock BT44. . . . . **62** B7
Craigfad Dr BT41. . . . . . **187** A5
Craigfad Rd BT54 . . . . . . **9** C4
Craig Gdns 3 BT28 . . . . **169** F8
Craighill BT41 . . . . **187** B2
Craiginorne BT40. . . . . . . **98** C7
Craiglands Dr 5 BT36. . . **111** F1
Craiglands Manor 7
BT36. . . . . **111** F1
Craiglea Gdns BT51. . . . . **59** C5
Craiglea Glebe BT51 . . . . **41** F8
Craigmacagan BT54. . . . . **.3** B4
CRAIGMORE BT41. . . . . . **107** C7
Craigmore BT51. . . . . **41** B7
Craigmore BT46. . . . . **74** C2
Craigmore BT46. . . . . **73** B3
Craigmore Hts BT41. . . . . **74** C2
Craigmore Pk BT41 . . . . **186** F4
Craigmore Rd
Antrim BT41. . . . . **107** D8
Coleraine BT51 . . . . **40** F7
Lisburn BT28 . . . . **159** F1
Magherafelt BT45 . . . . . . **103** F4
Craigmore Way BT7. . . . **189** A1
Craignagat BT44. . . . . . . **48** C6
Craignageeragh BT42 . . **77** D4
Craignageeragh Rd BT44. **77** C3
Craignahorn BT52. . . . . . **14** F5
Craignamaddy
Ballymoney BT53. . . . . . . **.6** C1
Coleraine BT51 . . . . **25** A2
Craigowen Rd BT38 . . . . **125** D2
Craig Quartier BT51. . . . **59** E1
Craigroe BT51. . . . . **40** F8
Craigroryoge BT51. . . . . **25** B2
Craigs
Ballymena BT42. . . . . **61** B1
Cookstown BT80 . . . . . . **112** C5
Craig's Cl BT38 . . . . **125** D5
Craig's Gn BT38. . . . . . . **125** D6
Craigs Rd
Ballymena BT42. . . . . **77** D8
Cookstown BT80 . . . . . . **112** B5
Craig's Rd BT38. . . . . . . **125** D5
Craigstown Ind Est BT41 . **94** D1
Craigstown Mdw BT40 . . **99** E6
Craigstown Rd
Antrim BT41. . . . . **108** B8
Ballymena BT42. . . . . **95** C6
Craigs Upper or Irish
Craigs BT53. . . . . **44** C2
Craigtara BT18 . . . . **139** D6
Craigtown BT47. . . . . **50** E1
Craigtown La BT56. . . . . **172** F5
CRAIGTOWN MORE
BT55 . . . . **173** A2
Craig Vara BT55 . . . . **173** D7
CRAIGVILLE BT40 . . . . . . **182** A6
Craigwarren BT43. . . . . . **62** D1
Craigy Hall BT41. . . . . . **187** E8
Craigyhill BT40. . . . . **182** B5
Cranagh Rd BT51 . . . . . . **13** F3
Cranberry Pk 17 BT51 . . **26** A7
Cranboreghts 18 BT51. . **26** A7
Cranbourne Glen BT40 . . **83** B5
Cranbourne View BT40. . **83** B5
Cranbrock Dr BT41. . . . . **187** A5
Cranbrook Ct BT14. . . . . **136** F1
Cranbrook Gdns BT14. . . **136** F1
Craneystown Rd BT28 . . **157** F8
Cranfield
Antrim BT41. . . . . **107** D3
Cookstown BT80. . . . . . . **113** B3
Cranfield Cross ★ BT41 . **107** D3
Cranfield Ct BT56 . . . . . **172** C4
Cranfield Gdns BT10 . . . **150** D3
Cranfield Rd BT41. . . . . **182** A5
Cranford Cres BT47 . . . . **179** C4

Crankill Rd BT43 . . . . 181 A8
Cranlee Pk BT48 . . . . . 35 E7
Cranmore Ave BT9 . . . . . 151 A7
Cranmore Gdns BT9 . . . . 151 A7
Cranmore Integrated Prim
Sch BT10 . . . . 150 C6
Cranmore Pk
Belfast BT9 . . . . 151 A7
4 Coleraine BT51 . . . . . 25 F7
Crannie Ave BT44 . . . . . 49 C3
Cranny❶ BT45 . . . . . . 104 B5
Cranny La BT45 . . . . . . 104 A5
Cranny View BT44 . . . . . 49 C3
Cranog Pk BT47 . . . . . . 177 E5
Craven St BT13 . . . . . . 188 B4
Crawford Pk BT5 . . . . . 152 F7
Crawfordsburn 7 BT46 . . 74 D1
Crawfordsburn Dr 6
BT46 . . . . 74 D1
Crawfordsburn Rd BT39 . . 96 D1
Crawford Sq
Limavady BT49 . . . . . . 180 C6
Londonderry BT47 . . . . 178 E7
Crawfordstown Rd BT44 . . 76 F6
Creagh❶ BT41 . . . . 93 E5
Creaghan Glebe❶ BT82 . . 67 F4
Creaghcor❶ BT82 . . . . . 50 A2
Creagh Hill BT45 . . . . . . 91 F1
Creagh Rd
Antrim BT41 . . . . 106 B7
4 Magherafelt BT45 . . . 106 A8
Creamery Rd BT52 . . . . . 15 A3
Crea Rd BT41 . . . . 93 E6
Creavery Prim Sch BT41 . 108 F8
Crebarkey Rd BT47 . . . . . 72 A7
Crebilly❶ BT42 . . . . 79 B4
Crebilly Rd BT42 . . . . . . 181 F3
Credenhill Pk BT17 . . . . 149 E3
Creenagh❶ BT67 . . . . . 167 C3
Creeslough Ct BT11 . . . . 149 E7
Creeslough Pk BT11 . . . . 149 E7
Creevagh❶ BT80 . . . . . 112 C7
Creevagh La BT80 . . . . . 112 D7
Creevagh Lower❶ BT48 . . 50 E8
Creevagh Rd
Cookstown BT80 . . . . . 112 A7
Londonderry BT48 . . . . 178 A2
Creevagh Upper❶ BT48 . 50 D8
Creevamoy❶ BT42 . . . . . 80 A6
Creevamoy Rd BT42 . . . . 79 E6
Creeve❶
Antrim BT41 . . . . 107 D4
Cookstown BT80 . . . . . 112 D8
Creevedonnell❶ BT47 . . . 51 B2
Creeve Pl BT28 . . . . . . 159 F1
Creeve Rd BT41 . . . . . . 107 D5
Creevery❶ BT41 . . . . . . 109 A8
Creevery Rd BT41 . . . . . 108 F8
Creeve The BT51 . . . . . 174 B2
Creeve Wlk BT11 . . . . . 150 C8
Creevy Ave BT5 . . . . . . 146 B1
Creevy Rd BT27 . . . . . . 171 E2
Creevy Way BT5 . . . . . . 146 B1
CREGAGH❶ BT6 . . . . . 152 B8
Cregagh❶ BT6 . . . . . . 152 D7
Cregagh Ct BT6 . . . . . . 145 B1
Cregagh Pk BT6 . . . . . . 152 C7
Cregagh Pk E BT6 . . . . 152 C7
Cregagh Prim Sch BT6 . . 152 B8
Cregagh Rd
Ballymoney BT53 . . . . . 29 B5
Belfast BT6 . . . . 152 D7
Cregagh St BT6 . . . . . . 145 B2
Cregagh View BT44 . . . . 21 A1
Cregan❶ BT47 . . . . 37 B6
Cregcattan (part of
Galdanagh) BT44 . . . . 65 A7
Cregg❶ BT47 . . . . 69 B8
Creggan❶
Antrim BT41 . . . . 107 E4
Ballymena BT44 . . . . . 48 E4
Londonderry BT48 . . . . 178 A6
Cregganboy❶ BT54 . . . . 8 B6
Creggan Broadway BT48 . 178 C5
Creggan Hts BT48 . . . . 178 B5
Creggan Prim Sch BT41 . 107 D4
Creggan Rd
Antrim BT41 . . . . 107 E3
Londonderry BT48 . . . . 178 C8
Creggan St Mews BT48 . . 178 D6
Creggan St BT48 . . . . . 178 D6
Cregglea 2 BT47 . . . . . 69 C8
Cregg Mor Dr 5 BT47 . . 69 B8
Cregg Rd BT47 . . . . 69 B7
Creightons Rd BT17 . . . . 149 E2
Crescent Arts Ctr & the
Fenderesky Gall★ BT7 . 189 A1
Crescent Bsns Pk BT28 . 159 D1
Crescent Gdns
Belfast BT7 . . . . 189 A1
Larne BT40 . . . . 182 B3
Crescent Link BT47 . . . . 179 B3
Crescent Link Ret Pk
BT47 . . . . 179 F6
Crescent Rd BT47 . . . . . 179 B3
Crescent The
3 Ballymena BT42 . . . . 78 C4
Ballymoney BT53 . . . . . 175 D5
Belfast BT10 . . . . 150 C3
Carryduff BT8 . . . . . . 163 D3
Coleraine BT52 . . . . . 174 E4
Cookstown BT80 . . . . . 114 C3
Holywood BT18 . . . . . 139 D7
Londonderry BT48 . . . . 176 F4
Portrush BT56 . . . . . . 172 B5
Cressy Crib BT49 . . . . . 23 A4
Crevagh Pk BT48 . . . . . 50 E7
Crevenish Wlk BT8 . . . . 151 E3

Crevilly-Valley❶ BT42 . . 94 C6
Crevolea❶ BT51 . . . . . . 42 A7
Crevolea Rd BT51 . . . . . 42 A7
Crew❶
Belfast BT29 . . . . 121 D3
Maghera BT46 . . . . . . 74 F2
Crewe Dr BT46 . . . . 74 D1
Crewe Hill BT28 . . . . . 121 E3
Crewe Pk Rd BT29 . . . . 121 C3
Crewe Rd BT29 . . . . . . 121 C3
Crew Park❶ BT29 . . . . . 121 C3
Crew Rd BT46 . . . . 74 E2
Cricklewood Cres BT9 . . 151 D6
Cricklewood Pk
Belfast BT9 . . . . 151 D6
Londonderry BT47 . . . . 179 D4
Crievagh Prim Sch BT80 . 112 B7
Crimea Ct BT13 . . . . . . 188 B4
Crimea St BT13 . . . . . . 188 B4
Crindle❶ BT49 . . . . 22 F4
Croaghan❶
Coleraine BT51 . . . . . 25 A2
Limavady BT49 . . . . . . 23 C7
Croaghan Gdns BT11 . . . 150 B8
Croaghbeg❶ BT57 . . . . . 6 E3
Croaghmore❶ BT57 . . . . 6 F3
Croaghnabehy❶ BT57 . . . 59 D7
Crockahilly Rd BT47 . . . . 86 A8
Crockanidillish❶ BT44 . . 66 A7
Crockanroe❶
Ballymena BT44 . . . . . 45 A8
Coleraine BT51 . . . . . 57 D2
Crockdonnelloge❶ BT51 . 57 C2
Crockindollagh❶ BT51 . . 41 E4
Crockmore Rd BT47 . . . . 69 D1
Crock na Brock Rd BT47 . 54 B1
Crocknaconspody❶ BT51 . 57 C2
Crocknamack Rd BT55 . . 173 D5
Crocknamack St BT55 . . 173 E5
Crocknamohill Rd BT45 . 103 C8
Crocknamoyle❶ BT54 . . . 31 D8
Crockore❶ BT51 . . . . . . 57 C4
Crocus Rd BT47 . . . . . . 36 B1
Crocus St BT12 . . . . . . 188 A2
Croft Ave BT44 . . . . 49 C3
Croft Cl
Carnlough BT44 . . . . . 49 C3
Holywood BT18 . . . . . 139 F7
Croft Gdns BT18 . . . . . 139 F7
Croft Gr BT44 . . . . 49 C3
Croft Hill BT8 . . . . 152 C2
Croft House Ct BT5 . . . . 146 E3
Croft Hts BT40 . . . . 83 B8
Croftmanor BT40 . . . . . 83 B8
Croft Manor BT18 . . . . 139 F7
Croft Mdws BT18 . . . . . 139 F7
Crofton Glen BT18 . . . . 139 E7
Croft Pk
Holywood BT18 . . . . . 139 F7
Larne BT40 . . . . 83 B8
Croft Rd
Carnlough BT44 . . . . . 49 C3
Holywood BT18 . . . . . 139 F7
Larne BT40 . . . . 83 A7
Croft Rise BT18 . . . . . . 139 F7
Croft The 4 BT42 . . . . . 77 E2
Croghfern❶ BT37 . . . . . 133 F7
Cromac Ave BT7 . . . . . 189 B1
Cromac Pl BT7 . . . . . . 189 B1
Cromac Quay BT7 . . . . 189 B1
Cromac Sq BT2 . . . . . . 189 B2
Cromac St BT1 . . . . . . 189 B2
Cromaghs❶ BT53 . . . . . 18 C1
CROMGHLINN (CRUMLIN)
BT29 . . . . 117 A1
Cromie Pk BT56 . . . . . 172 D1
Cromkill❶
Ballymena BT42 . . . . . 94 D8
Londonderry BT47 . . . . 51 C2
Cromkill Ct BT47 . . . . . 179 A2
Cromkill Rd BT42 . . . . . 94 C8
Cromlech Cl BT56 . . . . 172 D1
Cromlech Ct BT56 . . . . 172 D1
Cromlech Gdns BT56 . . . 172 D1
Cromlech Mews BT56 . . . 172 D2
Cromlech Pk BT56 . . . . 172 D1
Crommelin Hill BT43 . . . 62 F8
Crommelin Pl BT28 . . . . 170 B8
Cromore Dr BT56 . . . . . 172 D4
Cromore Gdns BT48 . . . 178 B4
Cromore Pk BT56 . . . . . 172 D4
Cromore Rd
Coleraine BT52 . . . . . 174 C8
Portrush BT56 . . . . . . 172 F3
Cromwell Cl 2 BT27 . . . 160 D1
Cromwells Highway 1
BT27 . . . . 160 D1
Cromy & Taggarts Land❶
BT39 . . . . 110 C5
Crookedstone❶ BT41 . . . 117 C7
Crookedstone Rd BT29 . . 117 C6
Crooknahaya❶ BT43 . . . 63 C7
Crosby St BT13 . . . . . . 188 B4
Cross❶
Ballycastle BT54 . . . . . 9 D5
Ballymena BT42 . . . . . 79 F1
Ballymoney BT53 . . . . . 43 B7
Crossan❶ BT27 . . . . . . 171 D3
Crossan Rd BT27 . . . . . 171 C1
Crossan Wlk BT28 . . . . 169 E8
Crossballycormick❶
BT47 . . . . 52 A5
Crossbill Pl BT28 . . . . 159 E4
Crosscanley Glebe❶
BT51 . . . . 26 B1
Cross-Carved Stone★
BT53 . . . . 28 F4
Crosscollyer St BT15 . . . 137 D1

Crossgare❶ BT51 . . . . . 26 A3
Cross Glebe❶ BT52 . . . . 14 E2
Cross Gn BT38 . . . . . . 124 D1
Crosshead❶ BT47 . . . . . 52 A4
Crosshill❶
Ballymena BT42 . . . . . 80 D1
Belfast BT29 . . . . 117 B2
Crosshill Cah❶ BT51 . . . 41 E4
Crosshill Rd
Belfast BT29 . . . . 117 B3
Larne BT40 . . . . 183 D4
Crosshill View 6 BT42 . . 95 A5
Cross-Incised Stone★
BT44 . . . . 66 A1
Crosskennan❶ BT41 . . . 109 D6
Crosskennan Fort★
BT41 . . . . 109 D7
Crosskennan La BT41 . . 109 E7
Crosskennan Rd BT41 . . 187 D6
Crosskeys Rd
Antrim BT41 . . . . 92 F5
Ballymena BT42 . . . . . 93 B7
Cross La BT28 . . . . 168 E8
Crossland❶ BT51 . . . . . 58 C3
Crossland Ct BT13 . . . . 188 A4
Crossland Rd BT51 . . . . 58 D3
Crossland St BT13 . . . . 188 A4
Crossmakeever❶ BT51 . . 25 E1
Crossmakeever La BT51 . 25 D2
Crossmary❶ BT38 . . . . . 125 D6
CROSSNACREEVY BT5 . . 153 C3
Crossnadonnell Pk BT49 . 180 E5
Crossnadonnell Rd BT49 . 180 D5
Crossnarea❶ BT45 . . . . 113 E7
Cross Par BT7 . . . . 144 F1
Crosspartick Well★
BT45 . . . . 114 A4
Cross & Passion Coll 5
BT54 . . . . 8 D3
Crosspatrick Rd BT45 . . 113 F5
Crossreagh❶
Coleraine BT52 . . . . . 4 D1
Portrush BT56 . . . . . . 4 D1
Crossreagh Dr
Antrim BT41 . . . . 187 A5
Newtownabbey BT37 . . . 133 D4
Cross Roads Prim Sch
BT51 . . . . 59 A2
Cross St 8 BT47 . . . . . 179 A4
Crosstagherty❶ BT53 . . . 44 E8
Crown Entry BT1 . . . . . 189 A4
Cruckanim❶ BT47 . . . . . 56 E2
CRUMLIN (CROMGHLINN)
BT29 . . . . 117 A1
Crumlin Gdns BT13 . . . . 143 E8
Crumlin High Sch BT29 . 121 B8
Crumlin Prim Sch 11
BT29 . . . . 117 B1
Crumlin Rd
Belfast BT14 . . . . 143 E8
Belfast BT29 . . . . 121 A6
Lisburn BT28 . . . . 155 D8
Strabane BT82 . . . . . . 68 C4
Crushybracken❶ BT44 . . 60 E6
Crystal St BT5 . . . . . . 145 D4
Cuan Glas (Greenhaven)
BT47 . . . . 55 D1
Cuan Parade BT13 . . . . 143 E6
Cuba Wlk BT4 . . . . . . 145 B5
Cubbindall❶ BT53 . . . . . 28 D6
Cuckoo Rd BT47 . . . . . 52 E8
Cuilbane❶ BT51 . . . . . . 57 E6
Cuillin Hts BT40 . . . . . 182 B4
CÚIL RAITHIN (COLERAINE)
BT52 . . . . 174 E3
Cúirt Allt an Chairthe (Altcar
Ct) 37 BT5 . . . . 145 A5
Cúirt an Chomair (Comber
Ct) 25 BT5 . . . . 145 A5
Cúirt Andarsan (Anderson
Ct) 3 BT5 . . . . 145 A5
Cúirt Arann (Arran Ct) 4
BT5 . . . . 145 A5
Cúirt Bholcáin (Vulcan Ct) 12
BT5 . . . . 145 A5
Cúirt Chaibhendis
(Cavendish Ct) 10 BT12 . 143 F5
Cúirt Chluaidh (Clyde Ct) 1
BT5 . . . . 145 A5
Cúirt Maidrid (Madrid Ct) 6
BT5 . . . . 145 A5
Cúirt Mhaigh Rath (Moira Ct)
5 BT5 . . . . 145 A5
Cúirt Mhic Giolla Stoic
(Stockman's Ct) 1
BT11 . . . . 150 D8
Cúirt na Bhfáil (Falls Ct) 6
BT13 . . . . 188 A3
Cúirt Naoimh Maitiú (St
Matthew's Ct) 22 BT15 . . 145 A5
Cúirt Phluincéid (Plunkett
Ct) BT13 . . . . 189 A4
Cúirt Suí Forde (Seaforde Ct)
20 BT5 . . . . 145 A5
Cúirt Thulach Forde
(Mountforde Ct) 18
BT5 . . . . 145 A5
Cúirt Uí Bhríosáin (Bryson
Ct) 26 BT5 . . . . 145 A5
CULBANE BT44 . . . . . . 76 D1
Culbane❶ BT53 . . . . . . 29 D5
Culbane La BT51 . . . . . 57 E5
Culbane Rd BT44 . . . . . 76 D2
Culbidag❶ BT44 . . . . . . 32 D2
Culcavy Bridge BT26 . . 169 B1
Culcavy Rd BT26 . . . . . 169 B2
Culcavy❶ BT26 . . . . . . 169 B1
CULCAVY BT26 . . . . . . 169 C1

Culcrow❶ BT51 . . . . . . 42 F8
Culcrow Prim Sch BT51 . 42 E8
Culcrum❶ BT44 . . . . . . 45 D5
Culcrum Rd BT44 . . . . . 45 D4
Culdaff Gdns BT48 . . . . 178 B4
Culdaff Rd BT56 . . . . . 172 D6
Culdoo Lower❶ BT53 . . . 28 B1
Culdoo Upper❶ BT53 . . . 44 B8
Culdrum❶ BT51 . . . . . . 26 B1
Cullingtree Rd BT12 . . . 188 B2
Cullion❶
Londonderry BT47 . . . . 67 B8
Magherafelt BT45 . . . . 103 D7
Cullion Rd BT45 . . . . . 103 B6
Cullybackey❶ BT42 . . . . 78 A6
CULLYBACKEY (COILL NA
BAICE) BT42 . . . . . . 77 F6
Cullybackey Rd
2 Ahoghill BT42 . . . . . 77 E2
1 Ballymena BT43 . . . . 181 C4
Portglenone BT44 . . . . 76 E4
Cullybackey Rd Link BT42 77 F2
Cullybackey Sta BT43 . . 78 A6
Cullyburn Rd BT36 . . . . 128 C4
CULLYCAPPLE BT51 . . . 42 E5
Cullycapple Pk BT51 . . . 42 E5
Cullycapple Prim Sch
BT51 . . . . 42 E6
Cullycapple Rd BT51 . . . 42 E6
Cullyramer❶ BT51 . . . . 42 E2
Cullyrammer Rd BT51 . . 58 D8
Culmeglen BT37 . . . . . 134 B8
Culmore❶ BT44 . . . . . . 59 D6
CULMORE BT48 . . . . . . 35 E8
Culmore Gdns
Belfast BT9 . . . . 149 F8
5 Coleraine BT52 . . . . 26 B7
Culmore Lower❶ BT49 . . 23 A3
Culmore Pk BT48 . . . . . 177 A1
Culmore Point Rd BT48 . 177 F8
Culmore Prim Sch BT48 . 35 E7
Culmore Rd
Londonderry BT48 . . . . 34 G9
Londonderry BT48 . . . . 177 A1
Culmore Upper❶ BT49 . . 38 E5
CULNADY❶ BT46 . . . . . 75 A3
Culnady Prim Sch BT46 . 75 A4
Culnady Rd BT46 . . . . . 74 F4
Culnafay❶ BT41 . . . . . . 92 E6
Culnafay Rd BT41 . . . . . 92 E6
Culnafeigh Gn BT41 . . . 186 D7
Culnagrew❶ BT46 . . . . . 58 C1
Culnagrew Rd BT46 . . . . 58 B2
Culnaman❶ BT51 . . . . . 42 F1
Culnaman La BT51 . . . . 58 F8
Culramoney❶ BT53 . . . . 28 D5
Culramoney Rd BT53 . . . 28 D5
Culrath St BT52 . . . . . . 174 E4
CULTRA BT18 . . . . 135 B1
Cultra Ave BT37 . . . . . 135 B2
Cultra St 10 BT15 . . . . 144 E8
Culzean Glen BT40 . . . . 83 B5
Cumber❶ BT47 . . . . . . 69 C7
Cumber Claudy Prim Sch
BT47 . . . . 69 B8
Cumberland St BT13 . . . 188 A4
Cumberland Wlk BT13 . . 188 A4
Cumber Hts BT47 . . . . . 69 B6
Cumbrae Hts BT40 . . . . 83 B5
Cumbria Ct BT29 . . . . . 121 B8
Cumbria Lodge BT29 . . 121 B8
Cunningham Way BT41 . 186 E3
Cupar St Lower BT13 . . . 188 A3
Cupar St Upper (Sráid
Chúpar) 4 BT13 . . . . . 143 F5
Cupar Way BT13 . . . . . 188 A3
Curdian Rd BT46 . . . . . 75 C4
Curlew Way BT47 . . . . . 179 B5
Curr❶ BT45 . . . . 104 C8
Curragh❶
Ballymena BT44 . . . . . 21 A2
Coleraine BT51 . . . . . 26 F1
Maghera BT46 . . . . . . 75 A2
Curragh Hill BT44 . . . . . 49 C3
Curraghlane❶ BT42 . . . . 56 A2
Curraghmore Pk BT51 . . 57 D5
Curraghmore Rd BT51 . . 57 C4
Curragh Rd
Coleraine BT51 . . . . . 42 F8
Dungiven BT47 . . . . . . 55 E2
Limavady BT49 . . . . . . 11 D2
Londonderry BT47 . . . . 55 E3
Maghera BT46 . . . . . . 90 D8
Curragh Wlk BT48 . . . . 177 A5
Curramoney❶ BT53 . . . . 17 C6
Curran❶ BT45 . . . . 90 F3
Curran Bsns Pk BT40 . . . 182 F4
Curran & Drumaliss❶
BT40 . . . . 182 E4
Curran Rd
Larne BT40 . . . . 182 E4
Magherafelt BT45 . . . . 91 B2
Currells Ave BT43 . . . . . 79 A6
Currie Prim Sch BT15 . . 137 D1
Currish La BT44 . . . . . . 76 B8
Curr Rd BT45 . . . . 104 B8
Currudda❶ BT47 . . . . . 73 C5
Curryfree❶ BT47 . . . . . 51 B1
Curryfree Rd BT47 . . . . 51 B1
Currynierin❶ BT47 . . . . 51 B5
Curryshestkin❶
Ballymoney BT53 . . . . . 27 B3
Bushmills BT57 . . . . . . 6 D6
Curtis St BT1 . . . . 189 A4
Curzon St BT7 . . . . . . 144 E2
Cushendall❶ BT44 . . . . 32 E4

Cra–Dav 201

CUSHENDALL (BUN ABHANN
DALLA) BT45 . . . . . . 32 E4
Cushendall Rd
Ballycastle BT54 . . . . . 20 B5
Ballymena BT43 . . . . . 181 E8
Cushendun❶ BT44 . . . . 21 A2
CUSHENDUN (BUN ABHANN
DUINNE) BT44 . . . . . 21 B1
Cushendun GAC BT44 . . 21 A2
Cushleake Mountain
Middle❶ BT44 . . . . . 20 F5
Cushleake Mountain North❶
BT54 . . . . 20 D6
Cushleake Mountain South❶
BT54 . . . . 20 E4
Cushleake Rd BT44 . . . . 20 F2
Cushnahans Rd BT53 . . . 28 E1
Cussick St BT9 . . . . . . 144 B1
Custom House Sq BT1 . . 189 B4
Custom House St 4
BT48 . . . . 178 F5
Cuthbert St BT17 . . . . . 179 A3
Cuttings The BT42 . . . . 80 C8
Cutts The BT17 . . . . . . 160 D8
Cymric Dr BT40 . . . . . . 182 A4
Cypress Cl BT17 . . . . . 161 A8
Cypress Dr BT52 . . . . . 174 D5
Cypress Pk BT44 . . . . . 45 E3
Cyprus Ave BT5 . . . . . 145 E4
Cyprus Gdns BT5 . . . . . 145 F4
Cyprus Pk BT5 . . . . . . 145 E4
Cyprus Pl BT38 . . . . . . 124 F1

D

Daffodil La BT40 . . . . . 83 B8
Dagger Rd BT28 . . . . . 168 D8
Dairyholm BT38 . . . . . 100 A3
Dairyland❶ BT39 . . . . . 98 C1
Dairyland Rd BT39 . . . . 98 C1
Dairylands Rd BT39 . . . . 98 E1
Dairy St BT12 . . . . 143 F4
Dairyvale BT49 . . . . . . 180 E4
Daisy Dr BT49 . . . . 180 E4
Daisyfield Pk BT13 . . . . 178 C3
Daisyfield St BT13 . . . . 144 B7
Daisyhill Pk BT48 . . . . . 177 A4
Dalboyne Gdns BT28 . . 160 B3
Dalboyne Pk BT28 . . . . 160 B3
Dalebrook Ave BT11 . . . 150 A6
Dalebrook Pk BT11 . . . . 150 A6
Dales The BT80 . . . . . . 185 E6
Dalewood BT36 . . . . . . 132 D7
Dalriada Ave
Cushendall BT44 . . . . . 32 E4
Newtownabbey BT37 . . . 134 D8
Dalriada Cres BT44 . . . . 32 E4
Dalriada Dr
Cushendall BT44 . . . . . 32 E4
Newtownabbey BT37 . . . 134 C8
Dalriada Gdns
Ballycastle BT54 . . . . . 8 D3
Cushendall BT44 . . . . . 32 E4
Dalriada Hospl 19 BT54 . . 8 D3
Dalriada Pk BT44 . . . . . 32 E4
Dalriada Sch BT53 . . . . 175 B5
Dalry Pk BT5 . . . . 146 E3
Dalton St BT5 . . . . 189 C3
Dalway's Bawn★ BT38 . . 125 F7
Dalways Bawn Rd BT38 . 125 E6
Daly Cres BT48 . . . . . . 178 D6
Daly's Brae BT47 . . . . . 179 D2
Daly's Pk BT47 . . . . . . 179 C2
Damascus St BT7 . . . . . 144 E2
Damhead❶ BT52 . . . . . 26 F6
Damhead House★ BT51 . 13 C2
Damhead Prim Sch BT52 . 26 E6
Damhead Rd
Coleraine BT52 . . . . . 26 E6
Craigavon BT67 . . . . . 167 E3
Damhill Rd BT67 . . . . . 165 A1
Dandy St 4 BT36 . . . . 133 E1
Danesfort
Belfast BT9 . . . . 151 C7
Moira BT67 . . . . 165 F1
Danesfort Cres BT48 . . . 177 A3
Danes Hill❶ BT52 . . . . . 174 F8
Daneshill Rd BT52 . . . . 174 E6
Danns Row 3 BT6 . . . . 145 A4
Danny Boy Pl BT49 . . . . 180 E4
Dan's Rd BT42 . . . . . . 181 A2
Danube St BT13 . . . . . 144 A7
Daphne Gdns BT47 . . . . 179 C6
Daphne St BT12 . . . . . 188 B1
Darachean Rd BT28 . . . 120 E4
Darby St BT38 . . . . . . 125 A2
Dargan Cres BT3 . . . . . 137 F3
Dargan Dr BT3 . . . . . . 138 A3
Dargan Ind Pk BT3 . . . . 138 A3
Dargan Rd BT3 . . . . . . 137 F4
Darkfort Ct BT57 . . . . . 5 D5
Darkfort Dr BT57 . . . . . 5 C5
Darleen Pk BT44 . . . . . 177 A3
Dart Hill BT11 . . . . . . 150 C7
Dartress❶ BT51 . . . . . . 13 C1
Davagh Lower❶ BT79 . . 101 E3
Davagh Pk BT79 . . . . . 101 D3
Davagh Rd
Magherafelt BT45 . . . . 101 F5
Omagh BT79 . . . . 101 A3
Davagh Upper❶ BT79 . . 101 D4
David St BT13 . . . . . . 188 A3
Davison Villas BT45 . . . 91 C1
Davy's St BT38 . . . . . . 130 F7

Dawros Gdns BT48.....178 C5
Dawson St 15 BT15.....144 D8
Dayton St BT13.....188 C4
DC Bsns Pk BT11.....150 D8
Deacon St BT15.....137 D1
Deanby Gdns BT14.....137 A2
Deane Pk BT53.....18 A2
Deanery St BT48.....178 D4
Deanfield BT47.....179 A7
Dean Pk BT38.....125 A2
DEARBHÓG (DERVOCK)
  BT53.....28 C8
De Beere Ct BT10.....150 D3
Deburgh Sq 6 BT48.....178 D7
Deburgh Terr BT48.....178 D6
De Courcy Ave BT38.....125 C2
Decourcy St BT38.....131 A8
Deehan's Ind Est BT47.....51 E6
Deepstown BT53.....16 B2
Deerfin BT42.....79 E3
Deerfin Burn BT42.....79 A2
Deerfin Pk BT37.....133 D4
Deerfin Rd BT42.....79 E3
Deerfin Way BT43.....181 D6
Deer Park
  Antrim BT41.....116 F8
  Craigavon BT67.....120 B1
  Limavady BT49.....180 C1
Deerpark Dr BT14.....136 F2
Deer Park Farms BT44.....65 D2
Deerpark Gdns BT14.....136 E2
Deerpark Gr BT14.....137 A2
Deerpark Parade BT14.....136 F2
Deerpark Rd
  Ballyclare BT39.....110 E7
  Ballymena BT44.....81 E8
  Belfast BT14.....136 F2
  Larne BT40.....98 D8
  Magherafelt BT45.....91 F4
Deer Pk BT47.....179 C4
Dee St BT4.....145 B5
Deffrick BT53.....16 F3
Deghill Pk BT47.....52 C7
De Glin Pk 1 BT47.....69 B8
Dehra Gdns BT53.....175 E3
Dehra Gr BT4.....145 E6
Delacherois Ave BT27.....160 D2
De Lacy Ave BT38.....125 C2
De Lacy Dr BT38.....125 C2
Delamont Pk BT6.....152 E7
Delaware St 7 BT6.....145 A3
Delgany Ave BT8.....152 C3
Delhi Par BT7.....144 E1
Delhi St BT7.....144 E1
Delwood Pk BT47.....36 E4
Demesne
  Ballycastle BT54.....3 B5
  Larne BT40.....82 F2
Demesne Ave
  Ballymena BT43.....181 E4
  Holywood BT18.....139 E6
  Londonderry BT48.....178 C5
Demesne Banks BT51.....57 F8
Demesne Cl BT18.....139 E6
Demesne Gate BT18.....139 E6
Demesne Gdns BT48.....178 C5
Demesne Gr
  Holywood BT18.....139 E6
  Moira BT67.....166 C2
Demesne Manor BT18.....139 E6
Demesne Pk BT18.....139 E6
Demesne Pl BT49.....180 A6
Demesne Rd BT18.....139 E5
Demesne The BT15.....137 D4
Demesne Upper BT44.....65 D8
Demiville Ave BT27.....169 A5
Dempsey Pk BT53.....43 B4
Denewood Dr BT11.....143 C1
Denewood Pk BT11.....143 C1
Denmark St BT13.....188 C4
Dennet End BT6.....152 B8
Dennet Gdns BT47.....179 A4
Dennison Ind Est BT39.....184 B3
Denorrton Pk BT4.....145 E7
Department of Veterinary
  Sciences Queen's Univ
  Belfast BT16.....146 F6
Depot Rd BT3.....138 F1
Deramore Ave
  Ballymena BT43.....181 E7
  Belfast BT7.....151 E8
  Moira BT67.....166 A2
Deramore Cl
  Ballymena BT43.....181 E7
  1 Moira BT67.....166 A2
Deramore Cres
  Ballymena BT43.....181 E7
  2 Moira BT67.....166 A2
Deramore Ct BT9.....151 C5
Deramore Dr
  Ballymena BT43.....181 F7
  Belfast BT9.....151 B6
  3 Moira BT67.....166 A2
  Strathfoyle BT47.....177 F5
Deramore Gdns
  Ballymena BT43.....181 E7
  Belfast BT7.....151 E7
Deramore Pk
  Ballymena BT43.....181 F7
  Belfast BT9.....151 B6
  4 Moira BT67.....166 A2
Deramore Pk S BT9.....151 B5
Deramore St BT7.....151 E7
Deramore View BT80.....185 B6
Dereen Dr BT47.....177 F5

Derganagh BT45.....90 E6
Derganagh Rd BT45.....90 E6
Derg Cres BT47.....179 B4
Derg La BT45.....105 A4
Dergmore's Grave ★ BT45 88 D4
Derlett St 3 BT7.....144 E1
Dermont Ave BT36.....132 A5
Dermont Cres BT36.....132 A5
Dermont Rd BT36.....132 A4
Dermont Way BT36.....132 A5
Dermott Hill Dr BT12.....143 B4
Dermott Hill Gdns BT12.....143 B4
Dermott Hill Gn BT12.....143 B4
Dermott Hill Gr BT12.....143 B4
Dermott Hill Par BT12.....143 B4
Dermott Hill Pk BT12.....143 B4
Dermott Hill Rd BT12.....143 B4
Dermott Hill Way BT12.....143 B4
Dernaflaw Cotts BT47.....55 A2
Dernaflaw Rd (Bóthar Dhoire
  na Bhflatha) BT47.....54 F3
Dernagross BT51.....42 C5
Dernaveagh Rd BT43.....62 B1
Derramore Ave BT45.....183 D7
Derramore Ct 1 BT45.....183 D7
Derramore Dr 2 BT45.....183 D7
Derramore Gdns BT45.....183 D7
Derramore Pk 3 BT45.....183 D7
Derramore Way BT80.....185 B6
Derranmore Hts BT45.....183 D7
Derriaghy Prim Sch
  BT28.....160 B8
Derriaghy Rd BT28.....159 E5
Derriaghy Sta BT17.....160 E8
Derrin Pass BT11.....150 C8
Derrin Pl BT28.....159 F1
DERRYAGHY BT27.....160 C8
Derryard BT47.....55 C4
Derryarkin Lower BT47.....36 E3
Derryarkin Upper BT47.....36 F2
Derryash Rd BT67.....154 E3
Derry Beg BT49.....23 D1
Derrychrier BT47.....54 F1
Derrychrier Rd BT47.....71 C8
Derrychrin Prim Sch
  BT80.....114 F4
Derryclone Rd BT67.....120 H2
Derrycoole Pk 7 BT37.....133 E5
Derrycoole Way BT37.....133 D4
DERRYCRIN BT80.....114 F4
Derrycrin (Conyngham)
  BT80.....114 F3
Derrycrin Cotts BT80.....115 A4
Derrycrin Rd BT80.....114 F3
Derrycrummy BT80.....113 A6
Derrydorragh BT51.....25 E3
Derrydrummult BT67.....166 E3
Derryduff BT47.....55 E4
Derryganard BT45.....103 A3
Derrygarve BT45.....105 E7
Derrygarve Pk BT45.....105 F8
Derrygarve Rd BT45.....105 D8
Derrygonigan BT80.....113 E2
Derrygonigan Rd BT80.....113 E2
Derrygowan BT41.....107 C5
Derrygowan Rd BT41.....107 C5
Derry Hill BT37.....133 D5
Derryhirk BT67.....154 B1
Derryhirk Pk BT67.....154 C1
Derryhirk Rd BT67.....164 D8
Derryhollagh BT41.....107 C6
Derryhollagh Cotts BT41 107 C6
Derryhollagh La BT41.....107 B6
Derryhollagh Rd BT41.....107 D6
DERRYKEIGHAN BT53.....16 C2
Derrykillultagh BT28.....121 F2
Derrylane BT47.....55 A4
Derryloran alias Kirktown
  BT80.....185 A3
Derryloran Ind Est BT80 185 A1
Derryloran Pl BT80.....185 D3
Derrymore
  Coleraine BT51.....58 F8
  Craigavon BT67.....154 A4
Derry More BT67.....23 D2
Derrymore Ave BT36.....132 E6
Derrymore Rd
  Craigavon BT67.....120 H3
  Craigavon BT67.....154 A2
Derrynaflaw BT47.....55 A2
Derrynahone Rd BT67.....167 F4
Derrynaseer BT67.....164 F7
Derrynisk BT67.....167 C6
Derrynoyd La BT45.....88 C4
Derrynoyd Rd BT45.....88 C4
Derryola Bridge Rd
  BT67.....154 C7
Derryola Island La BT67 154 D8
Derryork BT47.....55 F5
Derryork Rd BT47.....55 D6
Derry Rd BT36.....132 E5
Derryview 5 BT47.....179 A3
Derryview Terr BT47.....178 F3
Derry Visitor & Convention
  Bureau ★ BT48.....178 F5
Derryvolgie Ave BT9.....151 B8
Derryvolgie Mews 6
  BT9.....144 B1
Derryvolgie Pk BT27.....160 C5
Derryware BT47.....55 D3
Dervock BT53.....28 B8
DERVOCK (DEARBHÓG)
  BT53.....28 C8
Dervock Mission Hall
  BT53.....28 B8
Dervock Pl BT47.....179 A4
Dervock St 4 BT47.....179 A4

Derwent St 18 BT4.....145 B5
Desertderrin BT53.....59 D8
Desertlyn Rd BT45.....104 A1
DESERTMARTIN (DÍSEART
  MHÁRTAIN) BT45.....90 B1
Desertmartin Prim Sch
  BT45.....90 B2
Desertmartin Rd
  Magherafelt BT45.....183 A7
  Tobermore BT45.....89 F5
Desmond Ave BT47.....69 B8
Desrtmartin Rd BT45.....104 B5
Devenagh Way BT43.....181 D6
Devenish Ct BT13.....188 A3
Devenish Dr BT37.....134 A8
Devon Cl BT41.....187 C5
Devon Ct BT41.....187 B4
Devon Dr BT4.....145 D6
Devon Par BT4.....145 D6
Devonshire Pl BT12.....188 B2
Devonshire Way BT12.....188 B2
Devon Sq BT41.....187 B5
Dewey St
  12 Belfast BT13.....144 A7
  Belfast BT13.....188 A4
Dh Christie Meml Prim Sch
  BT51.....174 B5
Dhu Varren BT55.....173 C5
Dhu Varren Cres BT13.....143 F6
Dhu Varren Ct BT55.....173 C5
Dhu Varren Gdns BT55.....173 C5
Dhu Varren Parade BT13 143 F6
Dhu Varren Pk
  Belfast BT13.....143 F6
  Portstewart BT55.....173 C4
Dhu Varren Pk S BT55.....173 C5
Dhu Varren Sta BT55.....173 C5
Dhu Varren Village BT55 173 C4
Diamond
  Londonderry BT48.....178 E5
  Portrush BT56.....172 B5
Diamond Arc 7 BT51.....59 C5
Diamond Ave BT10.....150 C5
Diamond Bsns Pk BT48. 176 E1
Diamond Ctr The BT45.. 183 D6
Diamond Gdns BT10.....150 C5
Diamond Gr BT10.....150 D5
Diamond La BT67.....154 F6
Diamond Prim Sch The
  BT42.....77 D5
Diamond The
  Ahoghill BT42.....77 E2
  2 Coleraine BT52.....174 C3
  Magherafelt BT45.....183 C6
Dickey's Fort ★ BT51.....58 A8
Dickey's Town BT44.....66 A7
Dickeystown Rd BT44.....65 F8
Dicksonshill BT43.....181 C4
Dill Ave BT27.....170 C8
Dillon's Ave BT37.....134 A6
Dillon's Ct BT37.....134 A6
Dill Pk BT48.....178 E8
Dill Rd BT6.....145 C1
Dirnan BT80.....103 B1
Dirnan Rd BT80.....103 C2
Dirraw BT53.....43 F3
Dirraw Rd BT53.....43 E3
Dirtagh BT79.....23 F4
Dirty La BT52.....174 C3
Disc Dr BT48.....176 C2
DÍSEART MHÁRTAIN
  (DESERTMARTIN) BT45.. 90 B1
Disert BT45.....88 E1
Disertowen BT47.....51 A3
Disertowen Rd BT47.....51 B2
Disert Rd BT45.....102 E6
Diskirt BT44.....48 C5
Disraeli Cl 2 BT13.....143 F7
Disraeli Ct 4 BT13.....143 F8
Disraeli St BT13.....143 F7
Disraeli Wlk 5 BT13.....143 F8
Distillery Brae 1 BT47..179 A4
Distillery Cl 8 BT47.....179 A4
Distillery Ct BT12.....188 B2
Distillery La 6 BT47.....179 A4
Distillery Rd BT57.....5 E3
Distillery St BT12.....188 B2
Distillery Wlk BT12.....188 B2
Divis BT17.....142 D6
Divis Ct BT12.....188 C3
Divis Dr BT11.....143 D2
Divismore Cres
  Belfast BT12.....143 C4
  Castlereagh BT8.....151 F1
Divismore Pk BT12.....143 C4
Divismore Way BT12.....143 C4
Divis Rd BT14.....141 E7
Divis St BT13.....188 B3
Divis Way BT28.....159 F1
Doagh BT39.....111 A6
DOAGH (DUMHACH)
  BT39.....111 A6
Doagh Prim Sch BT39...111 A6
Doagh Rd
  Ballyclare BT39.....184 B4
  Ballymena BT42.....95 D6
  Newtownabbey BT36.....133 E8
Doaghs Upper BT49.....11 F5
Dobbs Pk BT38.....130 F7
Dock St BT15.....144 E7
Doctors Rd BT42.....79 B2
Dog Kennel La BT28.....160 A3
Dogleap Mus ★ BT49.....39 C4
Dog Leap Rd BT49.....180 D1
Doherty Twr ★ BT48.....176 B7

Doire Beg BT11.....150 B7
DOIRE (LONDONDERRY)
  BT47.....179 A7
Doluskey BT45.....114 A8
Dominican Coll BT15.....137 D4
Dominican Voluntary Gram
  Sch BT56.....172 A4
Donaghbrook Ave BT53..175 D3
Donaghbrook Cres BT53 175 D3
Donaghbrook Dr BT53...175 D3
Donaghedy Rd BT82.....67 A6
Donaghy La BT40.....182 A3
Donagreagh BT47.....164 E1
Donal Casey Ct BT48.....176 C3
Donald Mound ★ BT29..121 D8
Donaldsons Ave BT38.....125 D1
Donalds Way BT38.....180 B5
Donard Dr BT28.....159 F1
Donard St BT6.....145 A3
Donegall Arc BT1.....189 A3
Donegall Ave
  Belfast BT12.....188 B1
  Whitehead BT38.....100 D1
Donegall Cl BT38.....100 D1
Donegall Cres BT38.....100 D1
Donegall Dr 26 BT38.....100 D1
Donegall Gdns
  Belfast BT12.....144 A2
  18 Whitehead BT38.....100 D1
Donegall La BT1.....189 A4
Donegall Par BT12.....144 A2
Donegall Pass BT7.....189 A1
Donegall Pk
  Belfast BT10.....150 D5
  12 Whitehead BT38.....100 D1
Donegall Pk Ave BT15...137 C6
Donegall Pl BT1.....189 A3
Donegall Quay BT1.....189 B4
Donegall Rd BT12.....188 A1
Donegall Rd Prim Sch
  BT12.....188 A1
Donegall Rise 14 BT38...100 D1
Donegall St Pl BT1.....189 A4
Donegall Sq BT38.....125 A4
Donegall Sq E BT1.....189 A3
Donegall Sq Mews BT2.. 189 A2
Donegall Sq N BT1.....189 A3
Donegall Sq S BT1.....189 A2
Donegall Sq W BT1.....189 A3
Donegall St BT1.....189 A4
Donegall Way
  Carrickfergus BT38.....125 A4
  11 Whitehead BT38.....100 D1
Donegall Wlk N 19 BT38 100 D1
Donegall Wlk S 21 BT38 100 D1
Donegal Pl BT48.....178 C4
Donegore BT41.....110 A4
Donegore Dr BT41.....186 F4
Donegore Gdns BT11.....149 F5
Donegore Hill BT41.....109 F7
Doneyshiel Rd BT44.....59 E5
Donnelly Pk BT53.....43 D3
Donnybrewer BT47.....36 D6
Donnybrewer Level
  (Intake) BT47.....36 D8
Donnybrewer Rd BT47.....36 D6
Donnybrook St BT9.....144 B1
Donore Cres BT41.....187 B4
Donore Ct BT15.....144 C8
Donovan Par BT6.....145 D2
Dooey BT57.....5 E5
Dooey Beg BT52.....14 C4
Dooey's Cairn ★ BT44.....45 A3
Doon BT45.....88 D3
Doonameenock ★ BT44.. 66 B4
Doonan BT44.....65 A6
Doonans BT53.....18 C2
Doonbeg Dr BT37.....133 D5
Doonbought BT44.....62 D5
Doonbought Rd BT44.....62 C5
Doon Cotts BT11.....149 F6
Doon End BT10.....150 D4
Doonfin BT54.....19 B3
Doonmore BT54.....2 D7
Doonmore Fort ★ BT54.. 9 D5
Doon Pk BT8.....163 E2
Doon Rd
  Belfast BT11.....149 F6
  Magherafelt BT45.....88 E3
Doorless BT80.....113 D1
Doory BT44.....48 C6
Dorchester Ave BT36....132 D7
Dorchester Cres BT36....132 D6
Dorchester Dr BT36.....132 D7
Dorchester Gdns BT36 ..132 D7
Dorchester Pk
  Belfast BT9.....151 A4
  Lisburn BT29.....159 E5
  Londonderry BT47.....179 C5
  Newtownabbey BT36.....132 D7
Dorchester St BT12.....188 B1
Doric Dr BT40.....182 A4
Dornan Rd BT28.....155 C8
Dorset Cl
  Antrim BT41.....187 C5
  21 Ballymena BT42.....78 C3
Dorset Ct BT41.....187 C5
Dorset Sq BT41.....187 B5
Doss Bay Rd BT41.....106 E3
Douglas BT42.....80 F3
Douglas Ave 3 BT39.....110 F8
Douglas Ct BT41.....145 E5
Douglasland BT39.....110 E8
Douglasland Rd BT39.....110 E8
Douglas Rd BT42.....96 D8
Doury Rd BT43.....181 C6
Doury Rd BT43.....181 D7
Dove Gdns BT48.....178 D5

Dover Ave BT40.....182 E5
Dover Pl BT13.....188 B4
Dover Rd BT36.....132 B5
Dover St BT13.....188 C4
Dover Wlk BT13.....188 C4
Dowgry BT44.....61 F8
Dowgry Rd BT44.....61 F8
Downey House Pre & Prep
  Sch BT6.....152 C7
Downfine Gdns BT11.....143 B2
Downfine Pk BT11.....143 C2
DOWNHILL BT51.....12 F4
Downhill BT51.....13 A4
Downhill Ave
  Castlereagh BT8.....151 D2
  Newtownabbey BT36.....128 C2
Downhill Est ★ BT51.....12 F4
Downhill Pk BT36.....128 C2
Downhill Wlk 5 BT8.....151 D2
Downing Pk BT56.....172 B2
Downing St BT13.....188 B4
Downkillybegs BT42.....94 A3
Downpatrick Gn BT37....128 F1
Downpatrick St 6 BT4...145 C6
Down Royal BT28.....168 C6
Downshire Ave BT38.....125 D1
Downshire Dr BT38.....125 D1
Downshire Gdns BT38...125 D2
Downshire Halt BT38.....125 D1
Downshire Mews BT18...139 D6
Downshire Par 1 BT6...152 C7
Downshire Pk Central 1
  BT6.....152 C7
Downshire Pk E BT6.....152 C7
Downshire Pk N BT6.....152 C7
Downshire Pk S BT6.....152 C7
Downshire Pl
  Belfast BT2.....189 A2
  Holywood BT18.....139 D6
Downshire Rd
  Belfast BT6.....152 C7
  Carrickfergus BT38.....125 C2
  Holywood BT18.....139 D6
Downshire Sec Sch
  BT38.....125 C3
Downview Ave BT15.....137 C6
Downview Cres
  Ballymoney BT53.....175 A6
  Newtownabbey BT38.....129 E5
Downview Dr
  Ballymoney BT53.....175 A6
  Belfast BT15.....137 C6
Downview Gdns
  Belfast BT15.....137 D6
  Newtownabbey BT38.....129 E5
Downview Lodge BT15 ..137 C7
Downview Mews BT15 ..137 D6
Downview Pk
  Ballymoney BT53.....175 B6
  Belfast BT15.....137 C6
  Newtownabbey BT38.....129 F5
Downview Pk W BT15 ...137 B6
Downview Pk W BT38.....129 E5
Dows Rd BT8.....162 B4
Drain BT82.....67 F3
Drains BT40.....83 C6
DRAINS BAY BT40.....83 D6
Drains Bog BT40.....82 E8
Drapersfield Rd BT80.....113 C1
DRAPERSTOWN (BAILE NA
  CROISE) BT45.....89 A3
Draperstown Rd BT45 ...89 C5
Dreen
  Ballymena BT44.....60 B4
  Londonderry BT47.....86 B8
Dreenan BT45.....75 D2
Dreenan La BT46.....75 C3
Dreenan Rd
  Belfast BT29.....117 C6
  Magherafelt BT45.....75 C1
Dreen Rd BT42.....77 D5
Dremont Rd BT49.....39 E2
Drenaveagh BT43.....78 D8
Drenia BT11.....150 A5
Drive The BT9.....151 C6
Droagh BT40.....83 C7
Droghed BT51.....42 F4
DROICHEAD THUAMA
  (TOOME) BT41.....106 C7
Dromain BT40.....83 B5
Dromain Dr BT41.....187 B4
Dromaine Dr BT40.....182 A6
Dromara Pk BT28.....169 E8
Dromara St BT7.....144 E2
Dromona La (Dromona Rd)
  BT43.....61 D1
Dromona Rd (Dromona La)
  BT43.....61 D1
Dromore
  Ballymena BT44.....32 D7
  Ballymena BT44.....61 D5
  Coleraine BT51.....26 B2
  Limavady BT49.....38 F5
  Magherafelt BT45.....90 B2
Dromore Ave BT49.....38 F5
Dromore Rd
  Carrickfergus BT38.....125 D2
  Magherafelt BT45.....90 C2
Dromore St BT6.....145 B2
Drones Rd
  Ballymena BT44.....45 C6
  Ballymoney BT53.....29 D3
Drum
  Cookstown BT80.....112 C2

Drum *continued*
Londonderry BT49 .... 54 D5
Drumacarney⊙ BT49 .... 38 E6
Drumachose Mews BT49 180 C5
Drumachose Pk BT49 ... 180 D4
Drumachose Prim Sch
  BT49 .... 180 C6
Drumack⊙ BT44 .... 60 D3
Drumack La BT44 ...... 60 D5
Drumack Rd BT44 ...... 60 E4
Drumaconey Hts BT49... 38 B6
Drumacony⊙ BT49 ..... 38 E6
Drumacrow⊙ BT51 ..... 42 A5
Drumacullin⊙ BT54 .... 19 E3
Drumad⊙ BT80 .... 114 D1
Drumadarragh⊙
  Ballyclare BT39 .... 96 E3
  Ballymena BT45 .... 45 E1
Drumadarragh Rd BT39. 96 D2
Drumaderry⊙ BT49 .... 23 C3
Drumadion⊙ BT44 ..... 31 F8
Drumad La BT80 .... 114 D1
Drumadooey⊙ E8
Drumadoon⊙
  Ballycastle BT54 .... 9 D3
  Ballymena BT44 .... 45 D3
Drumadoon Rd BT44 .... 45 D3
Drumadowney Rd BT39. 111 E7
Drumadragh⊙ BT52 .... 14 F4
Drumadragh BT52 ...... 14 F4
Drumad Rd BT80 .... 114 D1
Drumadreen⊙ BT49 .... 39 D1
Drumaduan⊙ BT52 .... 27 A6
Drumaduff⊙ BT49 ..... 55 E8
Drumaduff Rd BT49 .... 55 E8
Drumagarner⊙ BT51 ... 59 B4
Drumagarner Rd
  Coleraine BT51 .... 59 B4
  Maghera BT46 .... 75 B8
Drumagore⊙ BT47 .... 50 F2
Drumagorgan⊙ BT41 .. 187 F8
Drumagosker⊙ BT49 .. 39 F4
Drumagrove⊙ BT44 ... 62 C6
Drumagrove Rd BT44 .. 62 C7
Drumagully⊙ BT51 .... 12 F4
Drumagully Rd BT51 ... 12 E4
Drumahaman⊙ BT54.... 8 F3
Drumaheglis⊙
  Ballymoney BT53 ...... 27 A2
  Ballymoney BT53 ...... 27 B2
Drumahiskey⊙ BT53 ... 43 C8
Drumahiskey Rd BT53.. 43 C8
Drumahitt⊙ BT54 ...... 8 F2
DRUMAHOE BT47 ..... 179 F1
Drumahoe⊙ BT47 ..... 179 F1
Drumahoe Gdns BT40 .. 83 B2
Drumahoe Ind Est
  Drumahoe BT47 ...... 179 E2
  Larne BT40 .... 83 A2
Drumahoe Prim Sch
  BT47 .... 179 E1
Drumahoe Rd
  Drumahoe BT47 ...... 179 E2
  Larne BT40 .... 83 A2
Drumahorgan⊙ BT49 .. 11 D4
Drumakeely⊙ BT44 ... 61 E6
Drumaleet⊙ BT67 .... 154 E2
Drumalief⊙ BT49 ..... 23 E3
Drumalief Rd BT49 .... 23 E3
Drumanaway⊙ BT41 .. 93 E2
Drumane⊙ BT51 ...... 9 F5
Drumane Lower⊙ BT45. 92 A5
Drumane Rd
  Bellaghy BT45 .... 91 F5
  Magherafelt BT45 ...... 92 A4
Drumane Upper⊙ BT45. 91 F6
Drumankelly⊙ BT28 .. 147 F3
Drumankelly Rd BT28.. 147 F2
Drumaqueran⊙ BT53 .. 28 F3
Drumaquill⊙ BT53 .... 13 F1
Drumaquill Rd BT51.... 14 A1
Drumard⊙
  Ballymoney BT53 ..... 175 F8
  Coleraine BT51 .... 75 D8
  Cookstown BT80 ...... 112 D2
  Magherafelt BT45 ...... 89 B1
Drumard Cotts BT42 .. 181 A2
Drumard Cres BT28 ... 159 E2
Drumard Ct 3 BT28 ... 159 D2
Drumard Dr
  Coleraine BT51 ...... 174 B2
  Lisburn BT28 .... 159 D2
Drumard Grange BT28 . 159 D2
Drumard Hill BT45 .... 91 B7
Drumard La BT45 ..... 89 B1
Drumard Pk
  1 Lisburn BT28 ..... 159 D2
  Londonderry BT47 ... 176 A1
Drumard Prim Sch BT46. 75 D7
Drumard Rd
  Coleraine BT51 .... 59 B1
  Maghera BT46 .... 75 C7
  Magherafelt BT45 .... 103 A6
Drumaridly⊙ BT54..... 8 F3
Drumaroan⊙ BT54 .... 9 A4
Drumaroan Rd BT54 ... 9 A4
Drumart Cres BT28.... 155 D8
Drumart Dr BT8 .... 151 D2
Drumart Gdns BT8 .... 151 E2
Drumart Sq BT8 ...... 151 E2
Drumart Wlk 4 BT8 ... 151 D2
Drumavaddy⊙ BT44 ... 45 C6
Drumavalley BT49 ..... 11 C1
Drumavally⊙ 11 C2
Drumavoley⊙ BT54....8 E3

Drumavoley Pk BT54 .... 8 E3
Drumavoley Rd BT54.... 8 E3
Drumawillan Pk BT54 ... 8 C1
Drumawillin BT54........ 8 C2
Drumballydonaghy⊙
  BT49 .... 180 A8
Drumbally Fort★ BT45 .. 90 A2
Drumballyhagan⊙ BT46.. 89 E7
Drumballyhagan Clark⊙
  BT45 .... 89 E6
Drumbane⊙
  Coleraine BT51 .... 57 E3
  Craigavon BT67 ...... 166 B4
  Limavady BT49 .... 23 C4
Drumbane Gdns BT47 . 179 E2
Drumbane Rd
  Coleraine BT51 .... 57 D3
  Craigavon BT67 ...... 165 F6
  Londonderry BT47 ..... 55 C5
  Maghera BT46 .... 74 C8
Drumbare⊙ BT44 ..... 45 E1
Drumbare Rd BT44 .... 45 E1
DRUMBEG BT17 ...... 161 D6
Drumbeg⊙ BT51 ..... 161 C5
Drumbeg Ct BT28 .... 169 F7
Drumbeg Dr BT28 .... 169 E7
Drumbeg Rd BT17 .... 161 D5
Drumbest⊙ BT53 ..... 29 A1
DRUMBO BT27 .... 162 A3
Drumbo⊙ BT27 ...... 162 B1
Drumboe⊙ BT41 ..... 107 B5
Drumbog⊙ BT47 ..... 85 C7
Drumbolg Rd BT46 .... 75 C5
Drumbo Prim Sch BT27. 162 A2
Drumbo Rd BT27 ..... 161 E3
Drumcairn Cl BT8 .... 151 C1
Drumceatt Pk BT49 .. 180 B3
Drumcill Rd
  Craigavon BT67 ...... 158 A1
  Lisburn BT28 .... 157 F2
Drumcliffe Ave BT48 .. 178 D5
Drumcon⊙ BT44 ...... 60 E3
Drumconan⊙ BT47 .... 51 B4
Drumconready⊙ BT46 .. 89 C7
Drumconready Rd BT46. 89 C7
Drumconvis⊙ BT80 ... 114 E2
Drumconvis Rd BT80 .. 114 D2
Drumcor Gn BT37 .... 133 D4
Drumcovit⊙ BT47 .... 70 F7
Drumcraig Rd BT47 .... 50 F2
Drumcraw⊙ BT80 .... 113 C3
Drumcree Pl BT37 .... 133 D4
Drumcroon⊙ BT51 .... 25 F2
Drumcrottagh⊙ BT53 .. 17 C1
Drumcrow⊙
  Ballymena BT44 ...... 81 E3
  Magherafelt BT45 ..... 89 E6
Drumcrow Rd BT44 ... 81 C6
Drumcudree⊙ BT44 ... 32 E7
Drumcullen⊙ BT41 ... 107 A6
Drumdallagh⊙ BT53 .. 29 C5
Drumdalt Pk BT53 ... 175 D8
Drumderg⊙
  Antrim BT41 .... 106 E7
  Magherafelt BT45 ..... 88 B5
Drumderg Rd BT45 ... 88 C5
Drumearn⊙ BT80 .... 112 C5
Drumearn Rd BT80 ... 112 C4
Drumeen⊙ BT51 ...... 41 F1
Drumeen Dr BT51 .... 42 A2
Drumeen Rd BT45 .... 113 C7
Drumeeny⊙ BT54..... 8 F1
Drumeeny Rd BT45 ... 113 C8
Drumeil⊙ BT51 ...... 43 A5
Drumeil Rd BT51 ...... 43 A4
Drumenagh⊙ BT45 ... 105 E4
Drumenny (Conyngham)⊙
  BT80 .... 115 B2
Drumenny Rd BT80 ... 115 A3
Drumenny (Stewart)⊙
  BT80 .... 115 A2
Drumfane⊙ BT43 ..... 78 F6
Drumfane Motte★ BT43 . 78 F6
Drumfin⊙ BT43 .... 62 A3
Drumfin Rd BT43 ..... 62 A3
Drumfresky⊙ BT54 ... 31 E8
Drumgarrell⊙ BT80 .. 113 D3
Drumgarrel Rd BT80 .. 113 D3
Drumgavenny Lower⊙
  BT49 .... 40 A1
Drumgavenny Upper⊙
  BT49 .... 56 B8
Drumgesh⊙ BT49..... 39 F6
Drumgrass⊙ BT80 ... 112 F6
Drumgrass Rd BT80 .. 113 A6
Drumgurland⊙ BT40 .. 84 D2
Drumhamer BT38 .... 124 D2
Drumhappy Rd BT47 .. 56 A7
Drumhoy Ct BT38 .... 124 F2
Drumhoy Dr BT38 .... 124 F1
Drumimerick Rd BT51 . 59 D2
Druminagh⊙ BT44 .... 49 C1
Druminard⊙ BT80 ... 114 D6
Druminard Rd BT80 .. 114 D6
Drumkeen Manor 1
  BT38 .... 152 A6
Drumkeen Ret Pk BT8.. 152 A6
Drumkeeran⊙ BT41.... 94 E3
Drumkeeran Rd BT41 .. 94 E3
Drumkil Gdns 1 BT51. 59 C5
Drumkil Mews 2 BT51 . 59 C5
Drumlaheen Cres 3

Drumlamph Rd BT45 ... 91 D5
Drumlane⊙ BT46 ..... 75 E7
Drumlane Rd BT46 .... 75 D7
Drumlea Pk BT80 .... 185 B2
Drumleck Gdns BT48 . 178 A4
Drumleckney⊙ BT42 .. 79 F7
Drumlee⊙ BT53 ...... 43 F5
Drumlee Ave BT40 ... 182 B4
Drumlee Rd BT53 .... 43 E5
Drumlough Gdns BT28 . 169 D8
Drum Lower⊙ BT47 ... 54 F5
Drumman⊙ BT82 .... 67 D2
Drummaneny⊙ BT47... 36 F9
Drummans⊙ BT54 ... 18 E6
Drummans Middle⊙
  BT47 .... 11 D4
Drummaul⊙ BT41 .... 93 F4
Drummaul Pk 10 BT41.. 107 F7
Drummen⊙ BT45 .... 113 C7
Drummond⊙
  Cookstown BT80 ...... 113 C1
  Limavady BT49 .... 38 D7
Drummond Ct BT40 .. 182 C3
Drummond Pk
  Ballykelly BT49 .... 38 D7
  Belfast BT9 .... 150 F4
  Londonderry BT48 ... 177 B5
Drummuck⊙
  Ballymena BT42 ...... 80 A7
  Maghera BT46 .... 75 B2
Drummuck Rd BT46 ... 75 A4
Drumnacanon⊙ BT46.. 75 C6
Drumnacanon Rd BT46. 75 B7
Drumnacole⊙ BT44 ... 49 C1
Drumnacross⊙ BT44.. 49 C5
Drumnacross Lower⊙
  BT80 .... 112 B1
Drumnacross Rd BT80. 112 C1
Drumnacross Upper⊙
  BT80 .... 112 B2
Drumnacur⊙ BT44 ... 32 D7
Drumnadonaghy⊙ BT40. 82 F2
Drumnadonaghy Rd BT40. 82 F3
Drumnadreagh⊙ BT40. 100 A6
Drumnadrough⊙ BT36. 133 D3
Drumnafivey⊙ BT53 .. 29 A6
Drumnagee⊙ BT57 .... 6 D4
Drumnagee Rd BT57 .. 6 C5
Drumnagessan⊙ BT57 . 6 D4
Drumnaglea⊙ BT44 ... 45 D2
Drumnaglogh⊙ BT80 . 112 B5
Drumnagreagh⊙ BT44. 66 B5
Drumnagreagh Rd BT40. 82 F8
Drumnahay⊙ BT47 ... 85 E6
Drumnaheigh⊙ BT53 .. 17 D6
Drumnaheigh Rd BT54. 17 E6
Drumnahoe⊙
  Ballymena BT44 ...... 49 C3
  Larne BT40 .... 83 B2
Drumnakeel⊙ BT54 ... 9 C2
Drumnamallaght Cl
  BT53 .... 175 A4
Drumnamallaght Pk
  BT53 .... 175 A4
Drumnamallaght Rd
  BT53 .... 175 A3
Drumnamalta⊙ BT80 . 112 A5
Drumnamalta Rd BT80. 112 A5
Drumnashear⊙ BT82 .. 50 C3
Drumnasmear⊙ BT44.. 32 D8
Drumnasole⊙ BT44 ... 49 A7
Drumneechy⊙ BT47 ... 55 D7
Drumnykerne⊙ BT67 . 164 F1
Drumoolish⊙ BT46 ... 75 E5
Drumourne⊙ BT44 ... 49 A1
Drumourne Rd BT44 .. 49 B2
Drumragh End BT6 ... 152 B8
DRUMRAIGHLAND BT49. 38 F4
Drumrainey⊙ BT45 ... 90 F1
Drumramer⊙
  Ballymena BT42 ...... 93 C7
  Limavady BT49 .... 40 C8
Drumramer Rd BT42 .. 93 C7
Drumrane Rd
  Limavady BT49 ...... 180 A1
  Londonderry BT47 ..... 55 C4
Drumrankin⊙ BT44 ... 46 A6
Drumraw⊙ BT44 ..... 77 B5
Drumraw La BT44 .... 77 B5
Drumraymond⊙ BT41 . 92 D2
Drum Rd
  Ballymena BT42 ...... 94 F3
  Cookstown BT80 ..... 185 B2
  Londonderry BT47 ..... 54 E4
Drumreagh⊙ BT53 ... 29 E5
Drumroan⊙ BT53 .... 17 D3
Drumrot⊙ BT45 ...... 113 D5
Drumrot Rd BT45 .... 113 E6
Drumsamney⊙ BT45 .. 90 B3
Drumsamney Rd BT45.. 90 B3
Drumsaragh⊙ BT51 .. 58 F6
Drumsaragh Rd BT51.. 59 A4
Drumsill⊙ BT28 ..... 168 C8
Drumskea⊙ BT53 .... 43 D8
Drumskea Rd BT53 .. 175 A1
Drumslade⊙ BT52 ... 14 B4
Drumslade Rd BT52 .. 14 A4
Drumsough⊙ BT41 .. 108 D7
Drumsough Rd BT41 . 108 D8
Drumsteeple⊙ BT51 .. 26 D1
DRUMSURN BT49 .... 39 F2
Drumsurn Lower⊙ BT49. 40 A1
Drumsurn Rd
  Limavady BT49 ...... 40 A1
  Limavady BT49 ...... 180 F5
Drumsurn Upper⊙ BT49. 40 B2

Drumtara⊙ BT42 ..... 78 F2
Drumtarsey Rd BT51 . 174 B3
Drumullan Rd BT47 ... 113 F4
Drum Upper⊙ BT47... 54 E4
Drumvale Ave
  Ballymoney BT53 ..... 43 C8
  Cookstown BT80 ..... 185 C3
Drumvale Dr BT53 .... 43 C8
Drumvale Pk BT80 ... 185 B3
Drumvale Rd BT80 ... 113 D1
Drunkendult East⊙ BT53. 27 C5
Drunkendult West⊙ BT53. 27 C5
Dryburgh Gdns BT38 . 130 D6
Dub La BT9 .... 150 F3
Dublin Rd
  Antrim BT41 .... 186 D1
  Belfast BT7 .... 189 A1
Dublin St 8 BT6 ..... 145 A3
Ducarbit⊙ BT54 ..... 19 D3
Duck La BT51 .... 13 B4
Duddys Ct BT47 ..... 179 A5
Dudley St BT7 .... 144 E2
Dufferin Hospl BT9 .. 144 B2
Dufferin Rd BT3 ..... 144 F8
Duffield Pk BT13 .... 143 D6
Dufless Rd BT80 ..... 113 D1
Duke St Underpass BT47. 178 F4
Dukes La BT49 .... 38 C7
Duke St
  Ballymena BT43 ...... 181 D5
  33 Belfast BT5 .... 145 A5
  Londonderry BT47 ... 178 F4
Dullaghy⊙ BT51 ..... 58 D5
Dullaghy Rd BT51 ... 58 D6
Dullerton Rd BT47 ... 67 C4
DUMHACH (DOAGH)⊙
  BT39 .... 111 A6
DUNADRY⊙ BT41 .... 109 E1
Dunadry Manor BT41.. 110 A2
Dunadry Rd BT41 .... 109 E1
Dunady⊙ BT47 ...... 69 C3
Dunaff Gdns BT48 ... 178 C5
DUNAGHY BT53 ...... 28 B3
Dunaghy Wood BT43 .. 63 A7
Dunaird⊙ BT42 ...... 79 E7
Dunalis Lower⊙ BT51 . 25 B8
Dunalis Upper⊙ BT51. 25 C7
Dun-a-Mallaght Cl BT54. 8 E3
Dun-a-Mallaght Pk BT54. 8 E3
Dun-a-Mallaght Rd BT54.. 8 E3
Dunamoney⊙ BT45 .. 183 F5
Dunamoy⊙ BT39 .... 97 A2
Dunamoy Dr BT41 ... 110 A1
Dunamoy Motte★ BT39. 97 A3
Dunamoy Rd BT39 ... 96 F2
Dunamuggy⊙ BT39 .. 110 C7
Dunanney⊙ BT36 ... 133 C5
Dunanney Rd BT36 .. 133 D5
Dunard Pk BT45 ..... 183 C4
Dunarnon⊙ BT45 .... 104 D6
Dunarnon Rd BT45 .. 183 A5
Dunarragan⊙ BT44 .. 65 F5
Dunaverny⊙ BT53 ... 28 A5
Dunbar Link BT1 .... 189 B4
Dunbar St BT1 ...... 189 B4
Dunbeg⊙ BT49 ...... 24 D2
Dunblane Ave BT14 .. 136 F2
Dunboe Cres BT51 ... 13 B2
Dunboe Ct BT51 ..... 13 B2
Dunboe Gdns BT51.... 13 C2
Dunboe House★ BT51 . 13 D2
Dunboe Rd BT51 .... 25 A8
Dunboyne Ave BT40 . 182 C5
Dunboyne Gdns 2 BT40. 182 C5
Dunboyne Gr BT40 .. 182 C5
Dunboyne Pk
  Belfast BT13 .... 143 D5
  Eglinton BT47 .... 36 E4
  Larne BT40 .... 182 C5
Dunbrock⊙ BT49 .... 38 A3
Dunbrock Rd BT49 ... 38 A4
Duncairn Ave 4 BT15 . 144 C8
Duncairn Bsns Pk BT15. 144 D8
Duncairn Gdns
  4 Belfast BT15 ...... 137 C1
  Belfast BT15 .... 144 D7
Duncairn Parade BT15. 144 D7
Duncansland⊙ BT39 . 110 D8
Duncans Rd BT28 ... 159 F4
Duncastle Pk BT47 ... 50 F5
Duncastle Rd
  Londonderry BT47 ..... 50 F2
  Strabane BT82 .... 67 B6
DUNCLUG BT43 ...... 181 D7
Dunclug Coll BT43 .. 181 D7
Dunclug Gdns BT43 . 181 D8
Dunclug Pk BT43 .... 181 D8
Dunclug Prim Sch BT43. 181 D7
Duncoole BT14 ...... 137 A5
Duncreggan Rd BT48. 178 E8
Duncrue Cres BT3 ... 137 F3
Duncrue Ind Est BT3 . 137 F3
Duncrue Link BT3 ... 137 F3
Duncrue Pass BT3 ... 137 F3
Duncrue Pl BT3 ...... 137 F2
Duncrue Rd BT3 ..... 137 F3
Duncrue St BT15 .... 144 E8
Duncrun⊙ BT49 ..... 11 E1
Duncrun Rd BT49 .... 23 B7
Dundarave Pk 3 BT57. 5 E4
Dundarave Rd BT57 ... 5 E4
Dundee St BT13 ..... 188 A4
Dundela Ave BT4 .... 145 E5
Dundela Cl BT4 ...... 145 E5
Dundela Cres BT4 ... 145 E5
Dundela Flats BT4 ... 145 E5
Dundela Gdns BT4 .. 145 E5

Dundela Inf Sch BT4 ... 145 E5
Dundela Pk BT4 ..... 145 D5
Dundela St BT4 ..... 145 E5
Dundela View BT4 ... 145 E5
Dunderg⊙ BT51 ..... 25 F6
Dunderg Pk 2 BT51 .. 25 E6
Dunderg Rd BT51 ... 25 E6
Dundermot Motte★ BT44. 61 D6
Dundesert⊙ BT29 ... 117 D2
Dundesert Rd BT29 .. 117 E3
Dundonald Int Ice Bowl
  BT5 .... 146 F3
Dundooan⊙ BT52 ... 14 D4
Dundooan Pk BT52 . 174 D8
Dundooan Rd BT52 . 174 A8
Dundrean⊙ 34 F7
Dundrean Pk BT48 .. 176 E4
Dundressan⊙ BT40 .. 84 C3
Dundrod⊙ BT29 .... 140 D7
DUNDROD⊙ BT29 ... 140 D8
Dundrod Ct BT28 ... 169 E8
Dundrod Rd
  Belfast BT29 .... 140 C8
  Lisburn BT28 .... 169 E8
Dundrod Wlk BT28 .. 169 F8
Dundrum BT48 ...... 176 C1
Duneane Cres BT41 . 106 D6
Duneane⊙ BT41 .... 106 F8
Duneane Prim Sch BT41. 107 A7
Duneane Rd BT41 .. 106 F8
Duneaney⊙ BT44 ... 61 A6
Duneany⊙ BT44 .... 61 A6
Duneany Motte★ BT44. 61 B6
Duneany Rd BT44 ... 60 C6
Duneden Pk BT14 ... 136 F1
Duneight⊙ BT27 .... 170 E4
Duneira Pk BT41 .... 182 B4
Duneoin Rd BT42 .... 77 B8
Dunfane Ave BT43 .. 181 E7
Dunfane Cres BT43 . 181 E7
Dunfane Gdns BT43 . 181 F7
Dunfane Pk BT43 .... 181 E8
Dunfane Sch BT43 .. 181 E8
Dunfield Terr BT47 .. 178 F3
Dungall⊙ BT43 ..... 62 B3
Dungall Motte★ BT43 . 62 B3
Dungannon Rd BT80. 185 D2
DÚN GEIMHIN (DUNGIVEN)⊙
  BT47 .... 55 C2
Dungiven⊙ BT47 .... 55 D2
DUNGIVEN (DÚN GEIMHIN)⊙
  BT47 .... 55 C2
Dungiven Prim Sch BT47. 55 D1
Dungiven Rd BT47 .. 179 B4
Dunglady⊙ BT46 .... 75 B5
Dunglady Fort★ BT46 . 75 B5
Dunglady Rd BT46 ... 75 B6
Dungloe Cres BT11 . 149 E8
Dungonnell⊙
  Ballymena BT43 ...... 47 E2
  Belfast BT29 .... 116 F6
Dungonnell Rd
  Ballymena BT43 ...... 47 E2
  Belfast BT29 .... 116 E5
Dungorbery⊙ BT53 .. 28 E3
Dungorkin⊙ BT47 ... 53 B1
Dungullion⊙ BT47 ... 37 B5
Dungullion Rd BT47.. 37 B4
Dunhill Rd BT51 .... 174 B1
Dunhin Motte★ BT41. 108 B4
Dunhugh⊙ BT47 .... 50 F6
Dunhugh Rd BT47 ... 50 F6
Dunineny Castle★ BT54. 8 D5
Dunkeld Ave BT48 .. 177 A3
Dunkeld Gdns BT14 . 136 F2
Dunlade Glebe⊙ BT47. 37 C1
Dunlade Rd BT47 .... 37 D3
Dunlambert Ave BT15. 137 D4
Dunlambert Dr BT15 . 137 D4
Dunlambert Gdns BT15. 137 D4
Dunlambert Pk BT15 . 137 D4
Dunleath Ave BT80 . 185 D3
Dunlewey St BT13 .. 188 A3
Dunlogan⊙ BT53 .... 87 F6
Dunlogan Rd BT45 .. 88 B6
DUNLOY⊙ BT44 ..... 44 F4
Dunloy⊙ BT44 ...... 44 F4
Dunloy Gdns BT37 . 133 C4
Dunluce Ave
  Belfast BT9 .... 144 B2
  Portstewart BT55 ... 173 D6
Dunluce Castle★ BT57. 5 A4
Dunluce Cotts 2 BT57. 5 D3
Dunluce Ct
  7 Bushmills BT57 .... 5 E3
  Londonderry BT48 .. 176 B3
Dunluce Ctr 8 BT55 . 173 D6
Dunluce Manor 3 BT57. 5 D3
Dunluce Pk
  Ballymena BT42 ..... 181 A1
  Portballintrae BT57 .. 5 C4
Dunluce Rd
  Bushmills BT57 .... 5 B4
  Portrush BT56 .... 4 D2
  Portstewart BT55 ... 173 F5
Dunluce Sch BT55 ... 5 D3
Dunluce St 8 BT40 . 182 C4
Dunluskin Cres BT38 . 125 A3
Dunluskin Gdns BT38. 125 A3
Dunmakelter⊙ BT54 . 19 E8
Dunman⊙ BT80 ..... 113 B5
Dunminning⊙ BT44 .. 61 C3
Dunminning Rd BT42.. 77 E8

E

Dunmisk Pk BT11 . . . . . . 150 C8
Dunmisk Wlk BT11 . . . . . 150 C8
Dunmore
  Cookstown BT80 . . . . . . 102 E2
  Limavady BT49 . . . . 24 C4
  Strabane BT82 . . . . 50 B5
Dunmore Ave BT15 . . . . 137 D2
Dunmore Cl BT80 . . . . . 185 D6
Dunmore Cres
  Belfast BT15 . . . . 137 C2
  Cookstown BT80 . . . . . . 185 D6
Dunmore Dr BT15 . . . . . 137 C2
Dunmore Gdns BT48 . . . 178 C6
Dunmore Ind Est BT15 . . 137 C2
Dunmore La BT80 . . . . . 103 A1
Dunmore Mews BT15 . . . 137 D2
Dunmore Pk
  Belfast BT15 . . . . 137 D2
  Carrickfergus BT38 . . . . 130 B6
  Cookstown BT80 . . . . . . 185 D7
Dunmore Pl BT49 . . . . . 180 B5
Dunmore St BT52 . . . . . 174 C3
Dunmoyle St BT13 . . . . . 143 F6
DÚN MUIRIGH (DUNMURRY)
  BT28 . . . . 149 B2
Dunmull ★ BT52 . . . . 15 B5
Dunmurray Halt BT17 . . 150 A3
Dunmurry
  Dunmurry BT17 . . . . 149 E2
  Magherafelt BT45 . . . . . . 88 D3
DUNMURRY (DÚN MUIRIGH)
  BT28 . . . . 149 B2
Dunmurry Golf Club
  BT10 . . . . 150 C2
Dunmurry High Sch
  BT17 . . . . 160 F7
Dunmurry Ind Est BT17 . 160 D8
Dunmurry La BT17 . . . . . 150 C2
Dunmurry Lodge BT10 . . 150 A4
Dunmurry Prim Sch
  BT17 . . . . 150 A1
Dunnabraggy BT45 . . . . . 88 D6
Dunnabraggy BT45 . . . . 113 C6
Dunnabraggy Rd BT45 . . 113 C7
Dunnalong BT82 . . . . 50 B3
Dunnalong Rd
  Londonderry BT47 . . . . . . 50 C3
  Strabane BT82 . . . . 50 A2
**DÚN NA MANACH
  (DUNNAMANAGH) BT82** . . 67 D4
Dunnamanagh BT82 . . . . 67 E3
Dunnamanagh Castle ★
  BT82 . . . . 67 E4
**DUNNAMANAGH (DÚN NA
  MANACH) BT82** 67 D4
Dunnavenny BT51 . . . . . . 57 D5
Dunnyboe Rd BT82 . . . . . 67 E2
Dunnygarron BT43 . . . . . 78 A8
Dunnygarron Rd BT43 . . . 78 A8
Dunnyvadden BT42 . . . . . 79 D2
Dunore BT44 . . . . 32 C8
Dunowen Gdns BT14 . . . 137 A2
Dunowen Pass BT37 . . . 133 D5
Dunraven Ave BT5 . . . . 145 D3
Dunraven Cres BT5 . . . . 145 D3
Dunraven Ct BT5 . . . . . 145 D4
Dunraven Dr BT5 . . . . . 145 D3
Dunraven Gdns BT5 . . . 145 D3
Dunraven Par BT5 . . . . 145 D3
Dunraven Pk
  Belfast BT5 . . . . 145 D3
  Londonderry BT48 . . . . . 176 C1
Dunree Gdns BT48 . . . . 178 B5
Dunronan BT45 . . . . . . 104 D3
Dunronan Rd BT45 . . . . 104 E2
Dunseverick Ave BT8 . . 151 E2
Dunseverick Castle ★ BT57 6 C7
Dunseverick Pk BT47 . . 179 C2
Dunseverick Prim Sch
  BT57 . . . . 6 C6
Dunshammer ★ BT57 . . . . 6 C7
Dunsilly BT41 . . . . 109 A7
Dunsilly Rd BT41 . . . . . 108 F6
Dunsilly Rdbt BT41 . . . . 108 F7
Dunsona Ave BT37 . . . . 134 C8
Dunsona Dr BT37 . . . . . 134 C8
Dunsona Rd BT37 . . . . . 134 B8
Dunsuivnish Ave BT56 . . 172 D4
Dunsuivnish Dr BT56 . . . 172 E4
Dunsuivnish Grange
  BT56 . . . . 172 E4
Dunsuivnish Pk BT56 . . . 172 D4
Dunteige BT44 . . . . 66 A1
Duntibryan BT49 . . . . . . 89 C5
Duntibryan Rd BT45 . . . . 89 C5
Dunturky BT39 . . . . 97 F1
Dunvale BT43 . . . . 181 D8
Dunvale Pk BT48 . . . . . 178 E8
Dunvegan St BT6 . . . . . 189 C1
Dunverne Gdns BT47 . . . 36 E5
Dunville Pk BT12 . . . . . 188 A2
Dunville St BT13 . . . . . 188 A2
Dunwood Pk BT47 . . . . . 50 F6
Dunygarton Rd BT27 . . . 168 B2
Durham BT12 . . . . 188 C3
Durham Pk BT47 . . . . . 179 E5
Durhams Land BT39 . . . 110 C5
Durham St BT12 . . . . . 188 C2
Durnascallon BT45 . . . . 104 A7
Durnascallon Rd BT45 . . 104 A7
Durnish Rd BT41 . . . . . 186 D8

E

Eachlann na Trá (Strand
  Mews) 11 BT5 . . . . . . 145 A5
Eagle Terr BT27 . . . . . . 160 C2
Eagry BT57 . . . . 5 E3
Eagry Pk BT57 . . . . 5 E2
Ean Hill BT18 . . . . 139 D6
Earl Cl BT15 . . . . 144 D7
Earlford Hts BT36 . . . . . 128 A3
Earl Haig Cres 3 BT6 . . 145 B2
Earl Haig Pk BT6 . . . . . 145 B2
Earlscourt St BT12 . . . . 143 F4
Earl's Ct BT47 . . . . 179 D3
Earl's Ct The 4 BT4 . . . 145 F5
Earlsfort BT67 . . . . 166 A1
Earlswood Gr BT4 . . . . . 145 F5
Earlswood Pk BT4 . . . . 145 F5
Earlswood Rd BT4 . . . . 145 F5
Earlview Prim Sch 42
  BT36 . . . . 111 F1
East Antrim Inst of FE & HE
  (Felden Campus) BT36 . 133 E1
East Antrim Inst of FE & HE
  (Larne Campus) BT40 . . 182 C4
East Antrim Inst of FE & HE
  (Newtown Abbey Campus)
  BT37 . . . . 134 A5
East Ave BT47 . . . . 179 B3
East Ballymaclevennon 9
  BT52 . . . . 173 F1
Eastbank Rd BT8 . . . . . 163 D4
East Belfast Enterprise Pk 4
  BT4 . . . . 145 C5
East Bread St BT5 . . . . 145 C5
East Bridge St BT7 . . . . 189 C2
Eastburn Ave BT53 . . . . 175 E5
Eastburn Cres BT53 . . . 175 E5
East Burn Dr BT53 . . . . 175 E5
Eastburn Pk BT53 . . . . 175 E5
East Circular Rd BT80 . . 185 E6
East Crossreagh BT51 . . . 1 B5
East Down View BT27 . . 160 D2
Eastermeade Gdns BT53 . 175 C4
Eastermeade Pk BT53 . . 175 E4
East Glebe BT45 . . . . . . 92 A6
Eastleigh Dale 13 BT4 . . 146 A5
Eastleigh Pk BT4 . . . . . 145 F5
East Link BT18 . . . . . . 139 D5
Easton Ave BT14 . . . . . 137 B1
Easton Cres BT14 . . . . . 137 B1
East Park BT57 . . . . 15 D6
East Rd BT49 . . . . 39 D2
East Torr BT54 . . . . 10 B2
East Twin Rd BT3 . . . . . 138 C1
East Tyrone Coll of FE & HE
  BT80 . . . . 185 C5
Eastway BT48 . . . . 178 C5
East Way BT37 . . . . 133 E5
Eastway Gdns BT48 . . . 178 C5
Eaton Ct BT42 . . . . 79 A5
Eblana St BT7 . . . . 144 D2
Ebor Dr BT12 . . . . 144 A2
Ebor Parade BT12 . . . . 144 A2
Ebor St BT12 . . . . 188 A1
Ebrington Ctr & Waterside
  Theatre BT47 . . . . 179 B5
Ebrington Gdns
  Belfast BT4 . . . . 145 E5
  Londonderry BT47 . . . . 179 A5
Ebrington Pk BT47 . . . . 179 B7
Ebrington Prim Sch
  BT47 . . . . 179 B5
Ebrington St BT47 . . . . 179 A5
Eccles St BT13 . . . . . . 144 A7
Ecos Millennium
  Environmental Ctr ★
  BT42 . . . . 181 F4
Edanmount Pk BT48 . . . 178 C8
Eden
  Ballymena BT44 . . . . . . 75 A4
  Ballymena BT53 . . . . . . 43 C6
EDEN BT38 . . . . 125 E2
Eden BT47 . . . . 70 C3
Edenballymore BT48 . . . 178 C6
Edenbane BT51 . . . . 58 D7
Edenbane Rd BT51 . . . . . 58 C7
Edenbrook Cl 13 BT13 . . 144 A7
Edenbrooke Prim Sch
  BT13 . . . . 144 A8
Edenderry BT8 . . . . 143 F7
Edenderry Cl BT13 . . . . 144 A7
Edenderry Ind Est BT13 . 144 A7
Edenderry Rd BT8 . . . . 161 F8
Edenderry St 7 BT13 . . . 144 A7
Edenmore BT49 . . . . 39 D5
Edenmore Ct BT48 . . . . 178 E7
Edenmore Dr BT11 . . . . 150 A7
Edenmore Gdns BT49 . . 180 D4
Edenmore Rd BT49 . . . . 180 D4
Edenmore St BT48 . . . . 178 E7
Eden Pl BT48 . . . . 178 E5
Eden Prim Sch
  Ballymoney BT53 . . . . . 43 B6
  Carrickfergus BT38 . . . . 125 E3
Eden Rd
  Ballymena BT44 . . . . . . 75 A4
  Belfast BT5 . . . . 153 F6
  Londonderry BT47 . . . . . 70 D3
Edenreagh BT45 . . . . . . 91 E3
Edenreagh Beg BT47 . . . 36 C1
Edenreagh More BT47 . . 36 D4
Edenreagh Rd BT47 . . . . 52 B8
Eden Terr BT48 . . . . . . 178 E8
Edenturcher BT29 . . . . 121 A5
Edenturcher Rd BT29 . . 121 A5

Edenvale BT42 . . . . 95 B3
Edenvale BT49 . . . . . . 180 E3
Edenvale Ave BT38 . . . . 125 E3
Edenvale Cres BT4 . . . . 145 E6
Edenvale Ct
  1 Belfast BT4 . . . . 145 F6
  Lisburn BT28 . . . . 159 D3
Edenvale Dr 9 BT4 . . . . 145 E6
Edenvale Gdns
  5 Belfast BT4 . . . . 145 E6
  Lisburn BT28 . . . . 159 D4
Edenvale Gr 2 BT4 . . . . 145 E6
Edenvale Mdws BT17 . . 150 A3
Edenvale Pk
  Antrim BT41 . . . . 186 F5
  7 Belfast BT4 . . . . 145 E6
  Dunmurry BT17 . . . . . . 150 A3
Edenview Cres BT67 . . . 166 F7
Edenview Gdns BT67 . . . 166 F7
Edenview Way BT67 . . . 166 F7
Ederny Wlk BT38 . . . . . 124 F2
Ederowen Pk BT48 . . . . 176 E5
Edgar Ave BT8 . . . . . . 163 E3
Edgar Rd BT8 . . . . 163 E3
Edgar Rd Ind Est BT8 . . 163 E4
Edgar St BT5 . . . . 145 A5
Edgecumbe Dr BT4 . . . 145 F6
Edgecumbe Gdns BT4 . . 145 F6
Edgecumbe Pk BT4 . . . 145 F6
Edgecumbe View BT4 . . 145 F6
Edgehill Coll BT9 . . . . . 151 C8
Edgehill Pk BT27 . . . . . 170 B7
Edgewater
  Lisburn BT27 . . . . 170 B8
  Londonderry BT47 . . . . . 50 E5
Edgewater Bsns Pk BT3 . 138 B4
Edgewater Rd BT3 . . . . 138 B4
Edgewood Ct BT41 . . . . 186 F3
Edinburgh Ave BT18 . . . 139 E6
Edinburgh Dr BT80 . . . . 185 C6
Edinburgh Mews BT9 . . 144 B1
Edinburgh St BT9 . . . . . 144 A1
Edith St 2 BT5 . . . . . . 145 B4
Edlingham St BT15 . . . . 144 C8
Edmondstone Ave BT38 . 100 A2
Edmundcourt 2 BT45 . . . 89 F5
Edmund Rice Coll BT36 . 132 E4
Edmund Rice Prim Sch
  BT15 . . . . 144 C7
Edward Ave BT40 . . . . . 182 C4
Edward Dr BT38 . . . . . . 125 C1
Edward Rd 24 BT38 . . . 100 D1
Edward St
  Ballymena BT42 . . . . . 181 D3
  4 Ballymoney BT53 . . . 175 D4
  Belfast BT1 . . . . 189 A4
  Londonderry BT48 . . . . 178 E6
Edwina St BT13 . . . . . . 188 A4
Egeria St BT12 . . . . . . 188 B1
EGLANTINE BT27 . . . . . 169 C3
Eglantine Ave BT9 . . . . 144 B1
Eglantine Ct BT27 . . . . 169 E4
Eglantine Pk BT26 . . . . 169 B2
Eglantine Pl BT9 . . . . . 144 C1
Eglantine Rd BT27 . . . . 169 D4
EGLINTON (AN MHAGH)
  BT47 . . . . 36 D5
Eglinton La BT55 . . . . . 173 D6
Eglinton Pl 8 BT48 . . . . 178 E5
Eglinton Prim Sch 9
  BT47 . . . . 36 D5
Eglinton St BT55 . . . . . 173 D6
Eglinton Terr 2 BT48 . . . 178 D5
Eglish
  Ballycastle BT54 . . . . . . 9 B1
  Ballymena BT43 . . . . . . 62 F2
Eglish Cemy ★ BT45 . . . 114 C8
Eglish Cl 3 BT45 . . . . . 105 A1
Eglish Rd BT43 . . . . 62 C1
Egmont Gdns BT12 . . . . 188 B1
Eia St BT14 . . . . 137 C1
Eileen Gdns BT9 . . . . . 151 B8
Elagh More 9 BT47 . . . 176 B7
Elaghmore Pk BT48 . . . 176 E5
Elagh Rd BT48 . . . . . . 176 A6
Elaine St BT9 . . . . 144 D1
Elderburn 5 BT36 . . . . 128 A2
Elder Cres BT47 . . . . . 179 C6
Electra Rd BT47 . . . . . . 35 F6
Elesington Ct BT6 . . . . 145 C1
Elginny BT43 . . . . 63 C3
Elginny Rd BT43 . . . . . . 63 C3
Elgin St BT7 . . . . 144 E1
Elimgrove St 9 BT14 . . . 137 B1
Elizabeth Ave
  Carrickfergus BT38 . . . . 125 C1
  4 Larne BT40 . . . . 182 C4
Elizabeth Gdns BT39 . . . 184 C6
Elizabeth Pl BT53 . . . . . 16 F3
Elizabeth Rd BT18 . . . . 139 F6
Eliza St Cl BT27 . . . . . 189 B2
Eliza St Terr BT7 . . . . . 189 B2
Eliza St BT2 . . . . 189 B2
Ellanabough BT44 . . . . . 32 E3
Ellis St BT38 . . . . 130 F8
Elm Cl BT47 . . . . 51 D6
Elm Cnr 1 BT17 . . . . . 160 F8
Elm Ct BT36 . . . . 132 F3
Elmdale BT41 . . . . 187 C3
Elmfield Ave BT36 . . . . 133 A4
Elmfield Cres BT36 . . . . 133 A4
Elmfield Dr BT36 . . . . . 133 A4
Elmfield Pk BT36 . . . . . 133 A4
Elmfield Rd BT36 . . . . . 133 A5
Elmfield St BT14 . . . . . 143 F8
Elmgrove BT48 . . . . . . 176 F4
Elmgrove Prim Sch BT5 . 145 D3

Elm Pk
  Drumahoe BT47 . . . . . 179 E1
  Moneymore BT45 . . . . . 113 E8
Elm Rd BT82 . . . . 67 D2
Elms Pk BT52 . . . . 174 D7
Elm St BT7 . . . . 189 A1
Elmurst Pk BT43 . . . . . . 62 F7
Elmvale BT48 . . . . 177 E8
Elmvale St BT48 . . . . . 178 D4
Elmwood Ave BT9 . . . . 144 C2
Elmwood Dr BT38 . . . . 170 A8
Elmwood Gr 4 BT36 . . . 111 F1
Elmwood House Bsns Ctr
  BT9 . . . . 144 B2
Elmwood Mews BT9 . . . 144 C2
Elmwood Pk
  Carrickfergus BT38 . . . . 130 F8
  Lisburn BT27 . . . . 160 C3
  Carrickfergus BT38 . . . . 130 E8
Elmwood Rd BT48 . . . . 178 D5
Elmwood St BT48 . . . . 178 D4
Elsmere Hts BT5 . . . . . 146 E1
Elsmere Manor BT5 . . . 146 E2
Elsmere Pk BT5 . . . . . 146 E2
Elstree Ct BT4 . . . . . . 180 C7
Elswick St (Sráid Elswick)
  BT12 . . . . 143 F5
Elver Ave BT51 . . . . . . 106 D7
Elver Slip BT51 . . . . 43 A2
Emerald Dr BT38 . . . . . 125 E3
Emerald St 3 BT6 . . . . 145 A3
Emerson Gdns BT47 . . . 179 A5
Emerson St BT47 . . . . . 179 A5
Empire Dr BT12 . . . . . 188 A1
Empire Parade BT12 . . . 188 A1
Empire St BT12 . . . . . . 188 A1
Enagh
  Limavady BT49 . . . . . . 180 D4
  Londonderry BT47 . . . . 177 F4
Enagh Cres BT47 . . . . . 35 F4
Enagh Lower BT53 . . . . 27 D1
Enagh Pk BT49 . . . . . . 180 C3
Enagh Rd BT53 . . . . . . 27 D1
Enagh Upper BT53 . . . . 175 A1
Enfield Dr BT13 . . . . . . 143 F7
Enfield Gdns BT56 . . . . 172 B5
Enfield Parade BT13 . . . 143 F7
Enfield St
  Belfast BT13 . . . . 143 F7
  Portrush BT56 . . . . . . 172 B5
Englishtown BT51 . . . . . 26 A3
Enid Dr BT5 . . . . 145 F4
Enid Par BT5 . . . . 145 F4
Enkalon Ind Est BT41 . . 186 C6
Enniskeen Ave BT37 . . . 133 D5
Enniskillen BT71 . . . . . 114 A1
Ennismore Hall BT43 . . 181 C5
Ennis Pl BT14 . . . . 176 A2
Enterprise Ave BT56 . . . 172 B4
Enterprise Cres BT28 . . 159 C1
Enterprise Par BT56 . . . 172 B4
Epworth St
  Belfast BT5 . . . . 145 B4
  Londonderry BT48 . . . . 178 D7
Erganagh BT51 . . . . 59 A6
Erganagh Rd BT51 . . . . . 59 A7
Erinvale Ave
  Belfast BT10 . . . . 150 C3
  Londonderry BT47 . . . . 179 E5
Erinvale Dr BT10 . . . . . 150 C2
Erinvale Gdns BT10 . . . 150 C3
Erinvale Park BT53 . . . . 29 F5
Erinvale Pk BT10 . . . . . 150 D3
Erin Way BT7 . . . . 189 A1
Erne Gdns BT47 . . . . . 179 B4
Ernest St BT48 . . . . . . 178 D7
Erosmore Dr BT47 . . . . 179 D5
Errigal Ct 4 BT55 . . . . . 173 D4
Errigal Pk BT11 . . . . . . 150 B7
Erris Gr BT11 . . . . 149 F5
Erskine Pk BT39 . . . . . 184 B6
Erskine St 8 BT5 . . . . . 145 B5
Ervey BT47 . . . . 52 D4
Ervey Cross Roads BT47 . 52 D5
Ervey Ct BT47 . . . . 36 E1
Ervey Rd BT47 . . . . 52 D3
Esdale Pk 3 BT57 . . . . . 5 E3
Eshery BT44 . . . . 31 E2
Eskaheen View BT47 . . . 178 F3
Eskdale Gdns BT14 . . . 136 F1
Esker Gdns BT47 . . . . . 179 E7
Eskylane BT41 . . . . 95 A2
Eskylane Rd BT41 . . . . . 95 A2
Espie Way 2 BT6 . . . . . 145 E1
Espl The BT18 . . . . . . 139 D7
Essan BT53 . . . . 19 A4
Essex Gr BT7 . . . . 144 E2
Essex St BT38 . . . . . . 131 A7
Esther St BT15 . . . . . . 137 D1
Estoril Pk BT14 . . . . . . 136 F1
Ethel St BT9 . . . . 144 A1
Etna Dr BT14 . . . . 136 F1
Eureka Dr BT12 . . . . . . 188 C1
Eurocentre W BT48 . . . 176 F1
Euston Parade BT6 . . . . 145 B3
Euston St Prim Sch 9
  BT6 . . . . 145 B3
Euston St BT6 . . . . . . 145 B3
Euterpe St BT12 . . . . . 188 B1
Evelyn Ave BT5 . . . . . . 145 D4
Evelyn Gdns BT15 . . . . 137 B3
Everglades The BT54 . . . 8 D4
Eversleigh St 24 BT6 . . 145 A3
Everton Dr BT6 . . . . . . 152 C7
Evewilliam Pk BT15 . . . 137 C3
Evish BT51 . . . . 40 E2
Evishacrow BT43 . . . . . 47 D4
Evishagaran BT47 . . . . . 56 C2

Evishnablay BT43 . . . . . 63 C8
Ewing St BT5 . . . . 178 E3
Exchange Ave BT39 . . . 111 A6
Exchange Pl BT1 . . . . . 189 A4
Exchange Rd BT40 . . . . 182 A4
Exchange St W BT1 . . . 189 A4
Exchange St BT1 . . . . . 189 A4
Excise Wlk BT12 . . . . . 188 D2
Exorna BT51 . . . . 13 B3
Exorna La BT51 . . . . . . 13 B3
Exorna Pk BT51 . . . . . . 13 B3

F

Faburn Pk BT14 . . . . . 136 D2
Factory La BT80 . . . . . 185 C6
Factory St BT5 . . . . . . 145 C4
Fahan St BT48 . . . . . . 178 E5
Fairfax Ct BT14 . . . . . . 144 A8
Fairfield
  Ballymena BT42 . . . . . . 78 B3
  Lisburn BT27 . . . . 160 C4
  5 Maghera BT46 . . . . . 74 C1
Fairfield Rd BT46 . . . . . 172 C3
Fairfield Rise BT28 . . . . 159 C4
Fairfields 1 BT41 . . . . 186 E5
Fairhaven Pk BT38 . . . . 129 C4
Fairhead Rd BT54 . . . . . 9 D5
Fairhead View BT54 . . . . 8 D4
Fairhill BT46 . . . . 74 C1
Fair Hill
  Ballymena BT44 . . . . . . 32 C4
  Magherafelt BT45 . . . . 183 D5
Fairhill Cl BT80 . . . . . . 185 C5
Fairhill Cres BT36 . . . . 133 B7
Fairhill Dr BT36 . . . . . . 133 A8
Fairhill Gdns
  Belfast BT15 . . . . 137 D6
  9 Newtownabbey BT36 . 133 B8
Fairhill Gn 6 BT36 . . . . 133 B8
Fairhill Gr BT80 . . . . . 185 C4
Fairhill Ind Est BT45 . . 183 E5
Fairhill La BT43 . . . . . 181 D5
Fairhill Pk
  Belfast BT15 . . . . 137 D5
  4 Maghera BT46 . . . . . 74 C1
  Newtownabbey BT36 . . 133 B8
Fairhill Rd
  Cookstown BT80 . . . . . 185 B5
  Newtownabbey BT36 . . 133 A8
Fairhill Sh Ctr BT43 . . . 181 D5
Fairhill St
  Ballycastle BT54 . . . . . 8 D3
  Ballymoney BT53 . . . . . 18 A1
Fairhill Way BT15 . . . . 137 D6
Fairhill Wlk BT15 . . . . . 137 D5
Fairlands 3 BT42 . . . . . 95 E8
Fairlea Ct BT45 . . . . . 113 F8
Fairlea Hts BT45 . . . . . 113 F8
Fairman Pl BT48 . . . . . 178 D7
Fairtree Hill BT27 . . . . 160 C5
Fairview BT51 . . . . 58 C5
Fairview Ave
  Newtownabbey BT36 . . 128 B1
  Whitehead BT38 . . . . . 100 D2
Fairview Cres
  Carrickfergus BT38 . . . 125 C1
  Newtownabbey BT36 . . 128 B1
Fairview Dr BT36 . . . . . 128 B1
Fairview Gdns BT36 . . . 128 B1
Fairview La BT51 . . . . . 13 C2
Fairview Par BT36 . . . . 128 B1
Fairview Pk
  Carrickfergus BT38 . . . 125 C2
  Coleraine BT51 . . . . . . 13 C2
  Dunmurry BT17 . . . . . 160 D8
  Newtownabbey BT36 . . 128 B1
  Whitehead BT38 . . . . . 100 D2
Fairview Prim Sch BT39 . 184 B5
Fairview Rd
  Londonderry BT48 . . . . 176 E5
  Newtownabbey BT36 . . 128 C1
Fairview St BT13 . . . . . 144 C7
Fairview Way BT36 . . . . 128 B1
Fairway BT40 . . . . 182 A5
Fairway Ave BT9 . . . . . 150 F3
Fairway Cres BT9 . . . . 150 F3
Fairway Dr BT9 . . . . . . 150 F3
Fairway Gdns
  Belfast BT9 . . . . 150 E3
  Castlereagh BT5 . . . . . 146 B1
Fairways BT42 . . . . 79 C6
Fair Ways The BT51 . . . . 59 D5
Fairyhill BT42 . . . . 78 B4
Fairyknowe Dr BT36 . . . 133 B3
Fairyknowe Gdns BT36 . 133 C3
Fairyknowe Pk BT36 . . . 133 C3
Falcarragh Dr BT11 . . . 149 E2
Falcon Rd BT12 . . . . . 151 A8
Falgortreevy Rd BT46 . . 89 F8
Falgortreevy BT46 . . . . 89 F8
Fallagloon BT46 . . . . . 73 E1
Fallagloon Rd BT46 . . . 73 F1
Fallahogey Rd
  Coleraine BT51 . . . . . . 59 D4
  Maghera BT46 . . . . . . 75 F8
Fallahogy BT51 . . . . . . 75 F8
Fallinerlea BT44 . . . . . . 32 C4
Falloward BT47 . . . . . . 36 D2
Fallowfield Pk BT47 . . . 179 B1
Fallowlea 7 BT47 . . . . . 36 D4
Fallowlea Pk BT47 . . . . 179 E7
Fallowvee BT44 . . . . . . 33 B1
Falls Ct (Cúirt na Bhfál) 6
  BT13 . . . . 188 A3
Falls Leisure Ctr BT13 . . 188 B3
Falls Rd
  Belfast BT12 . . . . 143 E3

Falls Rd continued
Belfast BT12 . . . . 188 A2
Fallswater Dr BT12 . . . . . . 143 F3
Fallswater St BT12 . . . . . . 143 F3
Fallylea❶ BT46 . . . . 73 F3
Fallylea La BT46 . . . . 73 F2
Fallylea Rd BT46 . . . . 74 A2
Falmacrilly❶ BT44 . . . . . . 31 F6
Falnaglass❶ BT44 . . . . . . 32 C6
Falrusklin❶ BT44 . . . . . . 48 D7
Fanad Dr BT78 . . . . 178 B5
Fane St Prim Sch BT9 . . . 144 B2
Fane St BT9 . . . . 144 B2
Far Bellaghy❶ BT44 . . . . . 45 C1
Farkland❶ BT47 . . . . 54 B4
Farkland Rd BT47 . . . . 54 A3
Farland Way BT48 . . . . . . 176 A1
Farlough❶ BT41 . . . . 94 B3
Farlow❶ BT49 . . . . 22 F1
Farlow Ct BT47 . . . . 179 E7
Farlow Rd BT49 . . . . 38 F8
Farmhill BT41 . . . . 187 C2
Farmhill❶ BT52 . . . . 14 F1
Farmhill BT48 . . . . 176 B2
Farmhill La BT37 . . . . 135 B1
Farmhill Rd
Crumlin BT29 . . . . 117 B2
Newtownabbey BT37 . . . . 135 B1
Farmhurst Gn BT5 . . . . . . 146 C1
Farmhurst Way BT5 . . . . . 146 C1
Farmley Cres BT36 . . . . . 132 F5
Farmley Gdns BT36 . . . . . 132 F4
Farmley Mews BT36 . . . . . 132 F4
Farmley Pk BT36 . . . . 132 F5
Farmley Rd BT36 . . . . . . 132 F5
Farm Lodge BT43 . . . . . . 181 E5
Farm Lodge Ave BT43 . . . 181 E5
Farm Lodge Cl BT38 . . . . 129 C4
Farm Lodge Ct BT38 . . . . 129 C4
Farm Lodge Dr BT38 . . . . 129 C4
Farm Lodge Gdns BT38 . . 129 C4
Farm Lodge Gn BT38 . . . 129 C3
Farmlodge Pk BT38 . . . . . 129 D4
Farm Lodge Pk BT38 . . . . 129 D4
Farm Lodge Rd BT38 . . . . 129 C4
Farm Lodge Way BT38 . . . 129 C3
Farm Lodge Wlk BT38 . . . 129 C3
Farnham St BT7 . . . . 144 E2
Farranacushog❶ BT44 . . . . 62 B6
Farranalessary❶ BT53 . . . . 28 B5
Farranflugh Rd BT41 . . . . 108 E7
Farranlester❶ BT51 . . . . . . 14 A3
Farranmacallan❶ BT54 . . . . 10 C2
Farranmacallan Rd BT54 . . . 10 C2
Farranmacarter❶ BT54 . . . . 19 C6
Farranseer❶ BT51 . . . . 25 E6
Farranseer Pk BT51 . . . . . . 25 E5
Farranshane❶ BT41 . . . . . 187 C6
Farrantemple Fort* BT51 57 D7
Farrantemple Glebe❶
BT51 . . . . 57 D7
Far Reastown❶ BT51 . . . . . 59 B5
Farrenlester Rd BT51 . . . . 25 F7
Farren Pk BT48 . . . . 176 F1
Farren Rd BT53 . . . . 28 B5
Farrier Ct❸ BT53 . . . . . . 132 F5
Farringdon Ct BT14 . . . . . 136 E1
Farringdon Gdns BT14 . . . 136 F1
Farset Ent Pk BT12 . . . . . 143 E5
FARTOWN BT51 . . . . 81 C8
Fasagh❶ BT44 . . . . 44 E4
Fashoda St BT5 . . . . 145 C3
Fassagh Pk BT44 . . . . 44 F4
Father Mulvey Pk ❶
BT48 . . . . 178 D5
Faughan Cres BT47 . . . . . 179 E2
Faughanvale❶ BT47 . . . . . 37 E6
Faughanvale Prim Sch
BT47 . . . . 37 D6
Faughan Valley Golf Club
BT47 . . . . 36 A4
Faughan View Cres BT47 . 69 D8
Faughan View Pk BT47 . . 179 E2
Faughill❶ BT44 . . . . 32 D5
Faunoran Pk BT38 . . . . . . 129 F3
Faustina Ret Pk BT48 . . . 176 D3
Fawney❶
Londonderry BT47 . . . . . 52 B6
Strabane BT82 . . . . 67 F6
Fawney Rd BT47 . . . . 52 A5
Feather Bed Rd BT67 . . . . 154 C3
Federation St BT6 . . . . . . 145 A2
Feegarran❶ BT80 . . . . . . 112 C7
Feegarran Rd BT80 . . . . . 112 A8
Feegarren La BT80 . . . . . 112 C6
Feegarren Rd BT80 . . . . . 112 C6
Feegarren Rod BT80 . . . . 112 E5
Feehogue❶ BT41 . . . . . . 107 F7
Feenan Beg❶ BT45 . . . . . 113 E8
Feenan More❶ BT45 . . . . 113 D8
Feeny❶ BT47 . . . . 70 C7
FEENY BT47 . . . . 70 F6
Feeny Rd BT47 . . . . 70 F6
Feigh alias Dunseverick❶
BT57 . . . . 6 C7
Feigh Mountain❶ BT57 . . . 6 B8
Feigh Rd BT53 . . . . 29 A7
Felt St BT12 . . . . 188 C1
Fenagh❶ BT43 . . . . 78 B8
Fenagh Pk ❷ BT51 . . . . . 26 A7
Fenagh Rd BT43 . . . . 78 A7
Fenaghy❶ BT42 . . . . 78 A5
Fenaghy Cl BT42 . . . . 78 B3
Fenaghy Hts BT42 . . . . . . 78 B3
Fenaghy Pk BT42 . . . . . . 78 B3
Fenaghy Rd BT42 . . . . . . 78 A5

Fendale Pk BT43 . . . . 78 A6
Fennel Rd BT41 . . . . 186 A3
Fenton Cres BT44 . . . . . . 45 F3
Fenton Pk BT44 . . . . 45 F3
Fergleen Pk BT48 . . . . . . 176 D4
Fergus Ave BT38 . . . . . . 130 F8
Ferguson Dr
❹ Belfast BT4 . . . . 145 E6
Lisburn BT28 . . . . 159 B1
Ferguson Rd BT28 . . . . . . 159 B1
Fergusons Land❶ BT39 . . 110 D5
Ferguson St BT48 . . . . . . 178 E4
Fermoyle Dr BT51 . . . . . 174 A6
Fernabbey BT48 . . . . 176 E6
Fernabbey Cl BT48 . . . . . 176 E6
Fernabbey Dr BT48 . . . . . 176 E6
Fernabbey Pk BT48 . . . . . 176 E6
Fernagh❶ BT44 . . . . 60 C2
Fernagh Ave BT37 . . . . . 134 A6
Fernagh Ct BT37 . . . . . . 134 A6
Fernagh Dr BT37 . . . . . . 134 A6
Fernagh Gdns BT37 . . . . 134 A6
Fernagh Par BT37 . . . . . 134 A6
Fernagh Rd BT37 . . . . . . 133 F6
Fernbank Pk BT53 . . . . . . 29 D5
Fernbrae Gdns BT47 . . . . 179 E5
Fern Brook ❹ BT42 . . . . 95 A5
Fern Bsns Pk BT11 . . . . . 150 E8
Ferndale Ave
Lisburn BT27 . . . . 170 D8
Newtownabbey BT36 . . . 133 A7
Portrush BT56 . . . . 172 B2
Ferndale Cl BT48 . . . . . . 176 E6
Ferndale Cres ❺ BT36 . . 132 F7
Ferndale Ct
❹ Belfast BT9 . . . . 151 A8
Londonderry BT48 . . . . . 176 E6
Ferndale Dr
Londonderry BT48 . . . . . 176 E6
Newtownabbey BT36 . . . 132 F7
Ferndale Gdns ❻ BT36 . 132 F7
Ferndale Gr ❿ BT36 . . . 132 F7
Ferndale Par BT36 . . . . . 133 A7
Ferndale Pk
Londonderry BT48 . . . . . 176 E6
Newtownabbey BT36 . . . 133 A7
Portrush BT56 . . . . 172 B2
Fern Dr
❶ Kells BT42 . . . . 95 A5
Magherafelt BT45 . . . . . 183 B6
Fern Gr BT67 . . . . 164 E7
Ferngrove BT55 . . . . 173 E4
Ferngrove Ave BT67 . . . . 164 E7
Ferngrove Cres BT67 . . . . 164 E7
Ferngrove Dr BT67 . . . . . 164 E8
Ferngrove Manor BT67 . . 164 E7
Ferngrove Pk BT67 . . . . . 164 E7
Fernhill Cres BT51 . . . . . . 25 F7
Fernhill Hts BT13 . . . . . . 143 D8
Ferniskey Rd BT41 . . . . . . 94 F3
Ferniskey❶ BT42 . . . . . . 95 A4
Ferniskey Ct ❺ BT42 . . . . 95 A5
Ferniskey Gdns ❼ BT42 . . 95 A5
Ferniskey Pk ❽ BT42 . . . . 95 A5
Fernlea Gdns BT39 . . . . . 184 B4
Fernlea La BT36 . . . . 133 C8
Fernlea Pk BT36 . . . . 133 C8
Fernmount Pk BT53 . . . . . 18 A1
Fern Pk BT48 . . . . 176 E4
Fern Rd BT48 . . . . 176 E4
Fern Ridge BT36 . . . . 111 E1
Fernvale St BT4 . . . . 145 E7
Fernwood Pk BT41 . . . . . 187 B2
Fernwood St BT7 . . . . . . 151 E8
Ferris Ave BT40 . . . . 182 D5
Ferryquay Pl ❶ BT52 . . . 174 C3
Ferryquay St BT48 . . . . . 178 E5
Festival Pk BT80 . . . . . . 185 F4
Feumore❶ BT28 . . . . 120 C3
Feumore Rd BT28 . . . . . . 120 C3
Feystown Rd
Ballymena BT44 . . . . 65 F3
Larne BT40 . . . . 82 C8
FHIONNBHOITH (FINVOY)
BT53 . . . . 43 F3
Fiddlers Way BT49 . . . . . 180 D4
Fife St BT15 . . . . 137 E2
Fifth St BT13 . . . . 188 A4
Fifty Acres❶ BT39 . . . . . 110 D5
Filterbeds Rd BT28 . . . . . 121 F2
Finaghy Pk Central BT10 150 C4
Finaghy Pk N BT10 . . . . . 150 C5
Finaghy Pk S BT10 . . . . . 150 C5
Finaghy Prim Sch BT10 150 D4
Finaghy Rd N BT11 . . . . . 150 B6
Finaghy Rd S BT10 . . . . . 150 C4
Finaghy Sta BT10 . . . . . . 150 C5
Finbank Ct BT9 . . . . 150 E4
Finbank Gdns BT9 . . . . . 150 E4
Fincairn Rd
Drumahoe BT47 . . . . . . 179 F2
Londonderry BT47 . . . . . 51 F8
Finch Cl BT9 . . . . 150 F4
Finch Ct BT9 . . . . 150 F4
Finch Gdns BT9 . . . . 159 E4
Finch Pk BT9 . . . . 150 E4
Finchley Dr ❷ BT4 . . . . 146 B8
Finchley Gdns ❶ BT4 . . 146 B8
Finchley Gr BT38 . . . . . . 124 E3
Finchley Pk BT4 . . . . 146 B8
Finchley Vale BT4 . . . . . 146 B8
Formby Pk BT14 . . . . 136 E3

Finch Pl BT9 . . . . 150 F4
Finch Way BT9 . . . . 150 F4
Findon Gdns BT9 . . . . . . 150 F4
Findon Pl BT9 . . . . 150 F4
Fingals Ct BT13 . . . . 188 C3
Fingal St BT13 . . . . 143 F7
Finglen❶ BT47 . . . . 71 D1
Finlay Pk BT36 . . . . 137 E8
Finlaystown Rd BT44 . . . . 76 F4
Finmore Ct BT41 . . . . . . 145 B5
Finner Wlk BT37 . . . . 128 F1
Finn Gdns BT47 . . . . 179 B3
Finnis Cl BT9 . . . . 150 E4
Finnis Dr BT9 . . . . 150 E4
Finnobar BT80 . . . . 114 C3
Finn Sq BT13 . . . . 188 C3
Finsbury Ave BT8 . . . . . . 152 C2
Finsbury Cres BT8 . . . . . 152 C2
Finsbury Dr BT8 . . . . 152 C2
Finsbury Pk BT8 . . . . 152 B2
Finsbury St BT6 . . . . 145 B1
Finvola Pk ❶ BT47 . . . . . . 55 D2
FINVOY (FHIONNBHOITH)
BT53 . . . . 43 F3
Finvoy Rd
Ballymena BT44 . . . . 60 A7
Ballymoney BT53 . . . . . 175 C1
Finvoy St BT5 . . . . 145 D5
Finwood Cl BT9 . . . . 150 E4
Finwood Pk BT9 . . . . 150 E4
Fir Ave BT49 . . . . 39 F2
Firfields BT41 . . . . 186 C3
Firgrove La BT41 . . . . . . 187 A2
Firmount BT15 . . . . 137 C3
Firmount Cres BT18 . . . . 139 D3
Firmount Dr BT41 . . . . . 187 B3
Fir Pk BT42 . . . . 79 D7
Fir Rd BT48 . . . . 177 A6
Firs The BT28 . . . . 168 D6
First St BT13 . . . . 188 A3
Fisherwick Cres BT43 . . . 181 F5
Fisherwick Gdns BT43 . . 181 F6
Fisherwick Pl BT12 . . . . . 189 A2
Fish Loughan❶ BT52 . . . . 26 E6
Fitzroy Ave BT7 . . . . 144 E2
Fitzwilliam Ave BT7 . . . . 151 F8
Fitzwilliam St BT9 . . . . . 144 C2
Five Acres❶ BT53 . . . . . . 16 E2
Five Mile Straight
Maghera BT46 . . . . 74 A1
Magherafelt BT45 . . . . . 89 A7
Fivey Rd BT53 . . . . 28 F6
Flame - Gasworks Mus of
Ireland ❺ BT38 . . . . . 131 A7
Flanders❶ BT47 . . . . 55 B4
Flanders Rd BT47 . . . . . . 55 B4
Flax St BT14 . . . . 144 A8
Fleet St BT40 . . . . 182 F3
Fleetwood St BT15 . . . . . 144 C7
Fleming Fulton Prim Sch
BT9 . . . . 150 F3
Fletcher Ave BT48 . . . . . 178 F7
Floral Gdns BT36 . . . . . . 133 B3
Floral Pk BT36 . . . . 133 B3
Floral Rd BT36 . . . . 133 B3
Flora St BT5 . . . . 145 C4
Florence Ct BT13 . . . . . . 144 C7
Florence Pl BT13 . . . . . . 144 C7
Florence Sq BT13 . . . . . . 144 C7
Florence St ❶ BT47 . . . . 179 A5
Florenceville Ave BT7 . . . 151 F7
Florenceville Dr BT7 . . . . 151 F8
Florenceville Dr BT7 . . . . 151 F8
Florida St ❺ BT6 . . . . . . 145 A3
Florwnce Ct BT27 . . . . . . 169 B4
Flow Bog Rd BT28 . . . . . 148 A7
Flowerfield Arts Ctr*
BT56 . . . . 172 C2
Flowerfield Rd BT56 . . . . 172 C2
Flower Hill ❶ BT57 . . . . . . 5 D1
Flurry Bridge Enterprise Ctr
BT54 . . . . 9 D4
Flush Dr BT6 . . . . 152 A7
Flush Gdns BT6 . . . . 152 A8
Flush Gn BT6 . . . . 152 A7
Flush Pk
Belfast BT6 . . . . 152 A7
Lisburn BT28 . . . . 169 C8
Flush Pk Ind Est BT28 . . 169 C8
Flush Rd BT14 . . . . 136 A7
Fodnamona Ct ❺ BT11 . . 143 B1
Fogarty Cres ❶❺ BT54 . . . 8 C3
Folly The BT41 . . . . 187 A4
Forbidden Wlk BT53 . . . . 175 A5
Ford Ave BT53 . . . . 28 F7
Ford Rd BT44 . . . . 76 A4
Foreglen Rd BT47 . . . . . . 54 D2
Forest Glen BT29 . . . . . . 121 B6
Forest Gr BT8 . . . . 151 E2
Forest Hill BT9 . . . . 151 B5
Forest Lodge ❸ BT40 . . 182 C5
Forest Pk
Belfast BT17 . . . . 149 E3
Coleraine BT52 . . . . . . 174 C1
Londonderry BT48 . . . . . 178 C6
Forest Rd BT51 . . . . 57 F8
Forestside Sh Ctr BT8 . . 152 A5
Forest St BT12 . . . . 143 F5
Forfar St BT12 . . . . 143 F5
Forge Integrated Prim Sch
BT7 . . . . 151 F7
Forge Rd BT47 . . . . 51 D4
Forgetown Rd BT46 . . . . . 89 C6
Forge Town Rd BT45 . . . . 89 B5
Forglen Rd BT47 . . . . 52 D2
Foriff❶ BT44 . . . . 32 D2

Formil❶ BT47 . . . . 56 E4
Formoyle❶ BT51 . . . . 24 F5
Formoyle Rd BT51 . . . . . . 24 E5
Formullen❶ BT51 . . . . 24 F7
Formoyle❶ BT51 . . . . 24 F7
Formoyle St BT51 . . . . . . 26 A7
Forster Gn Hospl
Castlereagh BT8 . . . . . . 152 A5
Lisburn BT27 . . . . 171 A5
Forster St BT13 . . . . 144 B7
Fort Cres BT52 . . . . 26 B7
Fortfield Ave BT48 . . . . . 176 F3
Fortfield Pl BT15 . . . . . . 144 D8
Fort Gn BT41 . . . . 186 E7
Forthbrook Ct BT13 . . . . 143 E7
Forth Glen BT48 . . . . . . 185 A6
Forthill❶
Ballycarry BT38 . . . . . . 100 B2
Ballymena BT42 . . . . 95 D4
Fort Hill
Lisburn BT28 . . . . 160 B2
Tobermore BT45 . . . . . . 89 F5
Fort Hill Coll BT27 . . . . 160 D2
Forthill Dr
Cookstown BT80 . . . . . 185 B4
Newtownabbey BT36 . . . 133 C8
Forthill Gdns BT36 . . . . . 133 C8
Forthill Gr BT36 . . . . 128 C1
Forthill Pk
Ballymena BT42 . . . . . . 181 D1
Newtownabbey BT36 . . . 128 C1
Forthill Prim Sch BT27 . 160 C2
Forthill Rd BT38 . . . . 100 B1
Forthill Rise BT80 . . . . . 185 B4
Forth Par BT13 . . . . 143 E6
Forthriver Cl BT13 . . . . . 136 C1
Forthriver Cres BT13 . . . . 143 C8
Forthriver Dale BT13 . . . 136 C2
Forthriver Dr BT13 . . . . . 136 C1
Forthriver Gn BT13 . . . . 136 D1
Forthriver Link BT13 . . . . 136 D1
Forthriver Par BT13 . . . . 136 C1
Forthriver Pass BT13 . . . 143 D8
Forthriver Pk BT13 . . . . . 136 C2
Forth River Prim Sch
BT13 . . . . 143 E8
Forthriver Rd BT13 . . . . . 143 D8
Forthriver Way BT13 . . . . 143 D8
Fort Rd
Belfast BT8 . . . . 162 C5
Belfast BT29 . . . . 140 C4
Carrickfergus BT38 . . . . 126 B4
Coleraine BT51 . . . . 58 A8
Newtownabbey BT36 . . . 119 B8
Fortsandel Ave BT52 . . . . 26 B7
Fort St BT12 . . . . 143 F5
Fort The
Ballyclare BT39 . . . . . . 119 A8
Maghera BT46 . . . . 74 C2
Fort Town BT53 . . . . 27 D6
Fortuna St BT12 . . . . 188 B1
Fortview
Antrim BT41 . . . . 187 A4
Portballintrae BT57 . . . . . 5 C4
Fort View
Ballymena BT42 . . . . 94 D8
Magherafelt BT45 . . . . . 88 D6
Fort William❶ BT15 . . . . 137 C5
Fortwilliam Cres BT15 . . 137 E4
Fortwilliam Ct ❹ BT15 . . 137 C3
Fortwilliam Dr BT15 . . . . 137 C5
Fortwilliam Gdns BT15 . . 137 C4
Fortwilliam Golf Club
BT15 . . . . 137 D7
Fortwilliam Grange
BT15 . . . . 137 E4
Fortwilliam Ind Est BT3 . 138 A3
Fortwilliam Parade ❸
BT15 . . . . 137 D3
Fortwilliam Pk BT15 . . . . 137 D4
Fortwilliam Rdbt BT3 . . . 137 F4
Fortwilliam Terr BT48 . . . 177 A3
Foundry La BT39 . . . . . . 184 B5
Fountain Cl BT80 . . . . . . 185 D4
Fountain Ct BT80 . . . . . . 185 E4
Fountain Ctr BT1 . . . . . . 189 A4
Fountain Hill
Antrim BT41 . . . . 186 F3
❹ Londonderry BT47 . . 178 F4
Londonderry BT47 . . . . . 179 A4
Fountain La
Antrim BT41 . . . . 186 F3
Belfast BT1 . . . . 189 A3
Fountain Pl BT43 . . . . . . 181 C5
Fountain Prim Sch ❷⓪
BT48 . . . . 178 E4
Fountain Rd BT80 . . . . . 185 D4
Fountain St
Antrim BT41 . . . . 186 F3
Belfast BT1 . . . . 189 A3
Londonderry BT48 . . . . . 178 E4
Fountain The BT48 . . . . . 178 E4
Fountainville❶ BT51 . . . . 57 F8
Fountainville Ave ❻
BT9 . . . . 144 C2
Four Score Acre BT40 . . . 66 D1
Fourtowns Manor ❺
BT42 . . . . 77 F2
Fourtowns Prim Sch ❼
BT42 . . . . 77 E2
FOUR WINDS BT8 . . . . . 152 C4
Four Winds Ave BT8 . . . . 152 C4
Four Winds Dr BT8 . . . . . 152 C4
Four Winds Pk BT8 . . . . . 152 C4
Four Winds Sh Ctr BT8 . . 152 C4
Foxglove ❻ BT5 . . . . . . 145 C4
Foxhill
Ballymena BT43 . . . . . . 181 A6
Londonderry BT47 . . . . . 178 E2

Fal–Gal **205**

Fox's Glen BT67 . . . . . . 164 A1
Fox's Hill BT67 . . . . 164 A1
Foyle Ave BT47 . . . . 37 C6
Foyle Cres BT47 . . . . 50 F5
Foyle Ct BT14 . . . . 144 B8
Foyle Emb BT48 . . . . 178 E6
Foyle Hill ❸ BT47 . . . . . 133 C5
Foyle Hospice BT48 . . . 177 B3
Foyle Int Golf Ctr BT48 . 177 C7
Foyle Language Sch ❽
BT48 . . . . 178 E6
Foyle & Londonderry Coll
BT48 . . . . 178 E8
Foyle Pk
Londonderry BT48 . . . . . 178 D3
Portrush BT56 . . . . 172 C6
Foyle Rd BT48 . . . . 178 D3
Foyleside Sh Ctr ❽
BT48 . . . . 178 F5
Foyle Springs Rd ❷
BT48 . . . . 178 C8
Foyle St BT48 . . . . 178 F5
Foyle View❶ BT49 . . . . . 38 B8
Foyle View Pk (Páirc
Radharc an Fheabail)
BT47 . . . . 37 A5
Foyle View Sch BT48 . . 176 F2
Francis St
Ballymena BT42 . . . . . . 181 D3
Belfast BT1 . . . . 189 A3
Londonderry BT48 . . . . . 178 E6
Frankhill Dr BT13 . . . . . . 163 D3
Frankhill Pk BT8 . . . . . . 163 D3
Franklin St Pl BT2 . . . . . 189 A2
Franklin St BT2 . . . . 189 A2
Frank St ⓯ BT5 . . . . . . 145 B4
Fraser Ave BT47 . . . . 36 E4
Fraser Pass BT4 . . . . 145 A5
Frasier St BT3 . . . . 145 A6
Frazer Ave BT47 . . . . 36 E4
Frederick St BT1 . . . . . . 189 A4
Fredrick St ❼ BT48 . . . . 178 E5
Freehall Dunlop❶ BT51 . . 13 A4
Freehall or Moneyvennon❶
BT49 . . . . 23 D4
Freehall Rd
Castlerock BT51 . . . . . . 13 B4
Limavady BT49 . . . . 23 D4
Freehall Watson❶ BT51 . . 13 B4
Freemanston❶ BT39 . . . . 110 C6
Frencheshill BT44 . . . . . . 76 B5
Frenches Hill BT44 . . . . . 76 B5
Frenchpark St BT12 . . . . 144 A2
Freugh❶ BT51 . . . . 40 F2
Friars Ct BT51 . . . . 174 A6
Friary Ct BT9 . . . . 29 F4
Friary Rd BT53 . . . . 29 F4
Friel St ❶ BT48 . . . . 176 A2
Friendly Pl BT7 . . . . 189 B2
Friendly Row BT7 . . . . . . 189 B2
Friendly St BT7 . . . . 189 B2
Friendly Way BT7 . . . . . . 189 B2
Friends Sch BT28 . . . . . 160 B3
Frome St ⓭ BT5 . . . . 145 B5
Front Rd BT27 . . . . 162 B2
Frosses Rd
Ballymena BT44 . . . . 61 E7
Ballymoney BT53 . . . . . 175 D6
Fruithill❶ BT49 . . . . 180 F7
Fruithill Ct BT11 . . . . . . 150 C8
Fruithill Pk BT11 . . . . . . 150 C8
Fry's Hollow BT43 . . . . . 181 F7
Frys Rd BT43 . . . . 181 F8
Fulmar Ave
Carrickfergus BT38 . . . . 125 A3
Lisburn BT28 . . . . 159 D5
Fulmar Cres BT28 . . . . . 159 D4
Fulton Pk BT49 . . . . 180 E3
Fulton St BT7 . . . . 189 A1
Furze Rd BT29 . . . . 121 B4

G

Gables The
Castlereagh BT8 . . . . . . 152 B2
Randalstown BT41 . . . . 107 F6
Gaelscoil an Damba
BT12 . . . . 143 C5
Gaelscoil na Bhfal BT12 . 143 F3
Gaffikin St BT12 . . . . . . 188 C1
Gainsborough Dr BT15 . . 137 D1
Gairdíní Bholcáinin (Vulcan
Gdns) ⓭ BT5 . . . . . . 145 A5
Gairdíní Chlann Aodha Buí
(Clandeboye Gdns) �220
BT5 . . . . 145 A5
Galboly Lower❶ BT44 . . . 33 D1
Galboly Upper❶ BT44 . . . 33 C1
Galdanagh❶ BT44 . . . . . . 65 B8
Galdanagh Dr BT44 . . . . . 62 B7
Galdanagh Rd BT44 . . . . . 65 C8
Galgorm❶ BT42 . . . . 78 C3
Galgorm Cres ⓲ BT42 . . 78 C3
Galgorm Ct ⓭ BT42 . . . . 78 C3
Galgorm Dr ⓰ BT42 . . . . 78 C3
GALGORM (GALGORM)
Ballymena BT42 . . . . 78 C4
Ballymena BT42 . . . . 78 C4
Galgorm Gdns ⓾ BT42 . . 78 C3
Galgorm Hall ❹ BT42 . . . 78 B4
Galgorm Ind Est BT42 . . . 78 B4
Galgorm Lodge BT42 . . . . 78 C4
Galgorm Parks ❺ BT42 . . 78 C4
Galgorm Pk ⓫ BT42 . . . . 78 C3

Galgorm Rd
Ahoghill BT42 . . . . **77** F2
Ballymena BT42 . . . . . **181** A3
Galgorm St BT43 . . . . . **181** C4
Gallagh❶ BT41 . . . . . . **106** C5
Gallagh Rd BT41 . . . . . **106** D4
Gallanagh❶ BT41 . . . . . . **95** A2
Gallany❶ BT47 . . . . **71** B6
GALLIAGH BT48 . . . . . . **176** E5
Galliagh Pk BT48 . . . . **176** D4
Gallows Knowe❶ BT49 . . **24** B3
Gally Hill❶ BT41 . . . . . **109** B6
Galvally❶ BT56 . . . . . **172** D5
Galwally
  Belfast BT7 . . . . **151** F6
  Castlereagh BT8 . . . . **152** B5
Galwally Ave BT8 . . . . **151** E5
Galwally Mews BT8 . . . **151** F5
Galwally Pk BT8 . . . . . **152** A6
Galway St BT12 . . . . . . **188** C3
Gamble St BT1 . . . . . . **189** B4
Ganaby❶ BT53 . . . . **28** E4
Ganard La BT80 . . . . . **103** C2
Ganiamore Ave BT55 . . **173** E5
Gannet Way BT38 . . . . **125** A3
Gar❶ BT53 . . . . **27** B4
GARBHACHADH (GARVAGH)
  BT51 . . . . **58** A8
Garborgle❶
  Coleraine BT51 . . . . . . **13** F4
  Portstewart BT55 . . . . **14** A4
Garden Ave BT56 . . . . **172** B5
Garden City BT48 . . . . **177** A1
Garden City Lower BT48 **177** A1
Gardeners Rd BT27 . . . **171** A3
Garden Mews BT80 . . . **185** C6
Gardenmore Rd BT40 . . **182** C4
Gardenmore Rd BT17 . . **149** D2
Garden of Eden BT38 . . **125** E3
Garden Row ❶ BT17 . . . **149** D2
Garden St BT45 . . . . . . **183** C6
Gardenstreet Mews
  BT45 . . . . **183** C6
Garden Terr BT45 . . . . **183** C6
Garden Village BT41 . . **187** B2
Gardiner Pl BT13 . . . . . **188** C4
Gardiner St BT13 . . . . . **188** C4
Garfield Dr ❶ BT43 . . . **181** D5
Garfield Pl ❷ BT43 . . . **181** D5
Garland Ave BT8 . . . . . **152** C4
Garland Cres BT8 . . . . **152** C5
Garland Gn BT8 . . . . . **152** D4
Garland Hill BT8 . . . . . **152** C4
Garland Pk BT8 . . . . . . **152** C5
Garlandstown Rd BT29 . **121** D7
Garley Mews BT42 . . . . **181** A1
Garmoyle St BT15 . . . . **144** E7
Garnerville Dr
  ❷ Belfast BT4 . . . . . **139** A1
  Belfast BT4 . . . . **146** A8
Garnerville Gdns BT4 . . **146** B8
Garnerville Pk BT4 . . . **139** A1
Garnerville Rd BT4 . . . **139** A1
Garnock BT11 . . . . **150** A5
Garnock Hill BT10 . . . . **150** A4
Garn Rd BT47 . . . . **55** F6
Garraithe an Chomair
  (Comber Gdns) ❷❽ BT5 . **145** A5
Garraithe Suí Forde
  (Seaforde Gdns) ❶❾
  BT5 . . . . **145** A5
Garraithe Thulach Forde
  (Mountforde Gdns) ❶❼
  BT5 . . . . **145** A5
Garraithe Uí Bhríosáin
  (Bryson Gdns) ❷❾ BT5 . **145** A5
Garranard Manor BT4 . . **146** A7
Garranard Pk BT4 . . . . **146** A7
Garriffgeery❶ BT41 . . . **107** B5
Garrison Rd BT45 . . . . . **90** F3
Garron Cres
  Belfast BT10 . . . . . . **150** D4
  Larne BT40 . . . . **182** A5
Garron Hts BT38 . . . . . **124** D2
Garron Pk BT55 . . . . . **173** C4
Garron Rd BT44 . . . . . . **49** D7
Garry Dr BT53 . . . . . . **175** D5
Garryduff❶ BT53 . . . . . **44** D7
Garryduff Rd BT53 . . . **175** E4
Garryduff Prim Sch BT53 . **44** C6
Garrylaban Ct BT56 . . . **172** D3
Garrylaban Dr BT56 . . . **172** D3
Garrylaban Manor BT56 . **172** D3
Garrylaben❶ BT56 . . . . **172** D3
Garry Lower❶ BT53 . . . . **27** F6
Garry Upper❶ BT53 . . . . **27** F5
Garshooey BT82 . . . . . . **50** A8
Gartan Sq ❹ BT48 . . . . **178** D5
Gartford❶ BT44 . . . . . . **49** B1
Gartford La BT44 . . . . . **49** B1
Garton Way BT36 . . . . . **133** D1
Gartree❶ BT29 . . . . . . **120** B8
Gartree Pl BT11 . . . . . . **150** A8
Garvagh❶
  Coleraine BT51 . . . . . . **41** F1
  Omagh BT79 . . . . **86** A3
Garvagh Cres BT44 . . . . **76** E5
Garvagh Ct BT47 . . . . . **179** E7
GARVAGH (GARBHACHADH)
  BT51 . . . . **58** A8
Garvagh Gr BT44 . . . . . **76** E5
Garvagh High Sch BT51 . **57** F8
Garvagh Mus & Heritage Ctr
  ❽ BT51 . . . . **58** A8

Garvagh Prim Sch BT51 . . **42** A1
Garvagh Rd
  Dungiven BT47 . . . . . . **55** D2
  Maghera BT46 . . . . . . **58** B1
  Swatragh BT46 . . . . . . **74** D8
Garvaghy❶ BT44 . . . . . . **76** F4
Garvaghy Ave BT44 . . . . **76** E5
Garvaghy Cres BT44 . . . **76** E5
Garvaghy Hill BT44 . . . . **76** F5
Garvaghy Rd BT44 . . . . . **76** F4
Garves❶ BT44 . . . . **44** D3
Garvey Glen BT17 . . . . **149** D7
Garvey Manor BT11 . . . **149** D7
Garveywood BT43 . . . . **181** D8
Garyduff Rd Ind Est
  BT53 . . . . **175** F3
Gasyard Ctr* BT48 . . . **178** D4
Gate End BT53 . . . . . . **175** C3
Gateside❶ BT52 . . . . . . **14** E4
Gateside Ave BT39 . . . **184** C7
Gateside Cres BT39 . . . **184** B7
Gateside Dr BT39 . . . . **184** C8
Gateside Manor BT39 . . **184** B7
Gateside Park❶ BT52 . . . **14** E5
Gateside Pk BT39 . . . . **184** B7
Gateside Rd
  Coleraine BT52 . . . . . **174** F7
  Portrush BT55 . . . . . . **14** F6
Gault Pk BT53 . . . . . . **175** D5
Gaults Rd BT44 . . . . . . **47** F8
Gawn St BT4 . . . . **145** C5
Geary Rd BT5 . . . . **146** D2
Geeragh Pl BT10 . . . . . **150** D4
Gelvin Grange BT47 . . . **179** B2
Gelvin Rd BT47 . . . . **55** E7
General Steele Cl BT38 . . **100** A2
Geneva Gdns BT9 . . . . **151** D7
Genoa St BT12 . . . . . . **188** B2
Geoffrey St ❺ BT13 . . . **144** A7
George Ave
  Ballyclare BT39 . . . . . **184** B5
  Larne BT40 . . . . **182** A5
George Best Belfast City
  Airport BT3 . . . . **145** E8
George Cl BT39 . . . . . **184** C5
George Ct BT39 . . . . . . **97** F2
George Gdns BT39 . . . . **184** C5
Georges St ❶❶ BT48 . . **178** E4
George St ❶ BT43 . . . . **181** D4
Gettistown Rd BT51 . . . . **42** E2
Ghent Pl BT13 . . . . . . **144** A7
Giant's Cswy Sta BT57 . . .**5** E6
Giants Ring Earthwork &
  Chambered Grave*
  BT8 . . . . **162** A8
Giants Ring Rd BT8 . . . **151** B1
Giant's Sconce* BT51 . . **24** F6
Gibbons St BT47 . . . . . **179** C5
Gibson Pk Ave BT6 . . . **145** B2
Gibson Pk Dr BT6 . . . . **145** C2
Gibson Pk Gdns BT6 . . . **145** B2
Gibson St BT12 . . . . . . **188** B2
Gibsontown Rd BT39 . . . **118** C5
Gilbourne Ct BT5 . . . . . **146** C2
Gilky Hill❶ BT47 . . . . . . **69** E5
Gillistown❶ BT41 . . . . . **93** A5
Gillistown Rd BT41 . . . . **93** A5
Gills❶ BT51 . . . . **26** D3
Gilmore St BT42 . . . . . **181** D3
Gilnahirk❶ BT5 . . . . . . **153** E7
Gilnahirk Ave BT5 . . . . **146** C2
Gilnahirk Cres BT5 . . . **146** C2
Gilnahirk Dr BT5 . . . . . **146** C2
Gilnahirk Golf Club BT5 . **153** E7
Gilnahirk Prim Sch BT5 . **146** D2
Gilnahirk Rd
  ❶❶ Belfast BT4 . . . . **146** A5
  Belfast BT5 . . . . **153** E8
  ❹ Castlereagh BT5 . . **146** A1
Gilnahirk Rd W BT5 . . . **153** E8
Gilnahirk Rise BT5 . . . **146** C2
Gilnahirk Wlk BT5 . . . . **146** C2
Gipsy St BT7 . . . . **151** F8
Girona Ave BT55 . . . . . **173** E5
Girona Cres BT55 . . . . **173** E5
Girona Ct BT55 . . . . . . **173** E5
Girona Dr BT55 . . . . . . **173** E5
Girona Pk BT55 . . . . . . **173** E5
Girona Wreck Site* BT57 . .**5** F8
Glack❶ BT47 . . . . **38** B1
Glack Rd BT49 . . . . **38** C4
Glade The BT36 . . . . . **128** A3
Glandore❶ BT53 . . . . . . **43** D1
Glandore Ave BT15 . . . **137** C3
Glandore Gdns BT15 . . . **137** C3
Glandore Parade BT15 . . **137** D2
Glanisland Terr BT38 . . **129** D4
Glanleam Dr BT15 . . . . **137** C2
Glanroy Cres BT37 . . . . **133** E5
Glanroy Terr BT37 . . . . **133** E5
Glantane Dr BT15 . . . . **137** C3
Glantrasna Dr BT15 . . . **137** C2
Glanworth Dr BT15 . . . . **137** C3
Glanworth Gdns BT15 . . **137** C2
GLARRYFORD BT44 . . . . **61** D5
Glasakeeran❶ BT47 . . . . **53** C8
Glasgort❶ BT51 . . . . . . **43** A6
Glasgort Rd BT51 . . . . . **43** A6
Glasgow St
  Belfast BT15 . . . . . . **137** E2
  Londonderry BT48 . . . **178** E7
Glasgow Terr BT48 . . . . **178** E7
Glasmullen❶ BT44 . . . . . **48** C7
Glasmullen Rd BT44 . . . . **48** C7
Glassagh Pk BT48 . . . . **178** B5
Glassagh Rd BT48 . . . . **178** A4

Glassaneeran Lower❶
  BT53 . . . . **17** A4
Glassaneeran Upper❶
  BT53 . . . . **17** A5
Glassillan Ct BT38 . . . . **129** F3
Glassillan Gr BT38 . . . . **129** E3
Glassmullin Gdns BT11 . **150** B7
Glastonbury Ave BT15 . . **137** C5
Glasvey❶ BT49 . . . . . . **38** C6
Glasvey Cl BT17 . . . . . **149** D3
Glasvey Cres BT17 . . . . **149** E3
Glasvey Ct BT17 . . . . . **149** D4
Glasvey Dr
  Ballykelly BT49 . . . . . **38** B7
  Dunmurry BT17 . . . . . **149** D3
Glasvey Gdns ❶ BT17 . **149** D3
Glasvey Pk ❹ BT17 . . . **149** D3
Glasvey Rise BT17 . . . . **149** E3
Glasvey Sch BT49 . . . . . **38** C7
Glasvey Wlk BT17 . . . . **149** D3
GLEANN AIREAMH
  (GLENARIFF OR
  WATERFOOT) BT44 . . . **32** D2
Glebe❶
  Ballycastle BT54 . . . . . **3** B5
  Ballymena BT42 . . . . . **93** D8
  Ballymena BT44 . . . . . **32** E6
  Ballymoney BT53 . . . . **16** C3
  Ballymoney BT53 . . . . **18** B2
  Ballymoney BT53 . . . . **43** F1
  Ballymoney BT53 . . . . **175** D4
  Bushmills BT57 . . . . . . **5** D3
  Coleraine BT52 . . . . . **15** B2
  Cookstown BT80 . . . . **113** B5
  Larne BT40 . . . . **83** B2
  Limavady BT49 . . . . . **23** A7
  Limavady BT49 . . . . . **38** E8
  Londonderry BT47 . . . . **37** C4
  Londonderry BT47 . . . . **55** C5
  Maghera BT46 . . . . . . **74** D5
  Magherafelt BT45 . . . . **89** B4
  Portrush BT56 . . . . . . **4** D1
Glebe Ave
  Ballymoney BT53 . . . . **16** C2
  Coleraine BT52 . . . . . **174** E4
  Moira BT67 . . . . **166** B1
Glebe (Ballywillin)❶
  Portrush BT56 . . . . . . **4** D1
Glebecoole Ave BT36 . . **133** A5
Glebecoole Dr BT36 . . . **133** A6
Glebecoole Pk BT36 . . . **133** A5
Glebe Cotts BT42 . . . . . **77** E2
Glebe Cres BT67 . . . . . **166** B1
Glebe Ct BT40 . . . . **83** B2
Glebe (Derryloran)❶
  BT80 . . . . **185** B2
Glebe Gdns
  Moira BT67 . . . . **166** B1
  Newtownabbey BT36 . . **133** A5
Glebe Ind Est BT45 . . . **183** D6
Glebe Lodge BT36 . . . . **133** B6
Glebe Manor
  ❶ Ballymena BT42 . . . **77** E2
  Newtownabbey BT36 . . **133** B6
Glebe Pk
  Ballymoney BT53 . . . . **16** B2
  Moira BT67 . . . . **166** B1
  Rasharkin BT44 . . . . . **60** B5
Glebe Rd
  Antrim BT41 . . . . **93** D6
  Ballymena BT42 . . . . . **77** E1
  Coleraine BT51 . . . . . **57** F7
  Dunmurry BT17 . . . . . **150** A2
  Newtownabbey BT36 . . **132** E8
  Rasharkin BT44 . . . . . **60** B5
Glebe Rd E BT36 . . . . . **133** B5
Glebe Rd W BT36 . . . . **133** A6
Glebeview Pk BT51 . . . . **42** A1
Glebe Villas BT36 . . . . **133** A5
Glebe Way BT67 . . . . . **166** B1
Glebe Wlk BT28 . . . . . **169** F8
Glenaan❶ BT44 . . . . . . **31** E4
Glenaan Pk BT42 . . . . . **95** A5
Glenabbey Ave BT37 . . . **134** A7
Glenabbey Cres BT37 . . . **134** A7
Glenabbey Dr BT37 . . . . **134** A7
Glenaden Hill BT47 . . . **179** B2
Glenagherty Dr ❶❹ BT42 . **78** C3
Glenagoorland Rd BT82 . . **67** F7
Glenalina Cres BT12 . . . **143** C4
Glenalina Gn BT12 . . . . **143** C4
Glenalina Pass BT12 . . . **143** C4
Glenalina Pk BT12 . . . . **143** C4
Glenalina Rd BT12 . . . . **143** C4
Glenallen St BT5 . . . . . **145** B5
Glenalpin St BT2 . . . . . **189** A1
Glenamanus❶ BT55 . . . **173** C4
Glenann Ave BT17 . . . . **150** A1
Glenann Dr BT55 . . . . . **173** C4
Glenann Prim Sch BT44 . . **32** C5
Glenara Wood BT51 . . . . **26** C6
Glenard Brook BT14 . . . **137** B1
Glenariff Dr BT17 . . . . **150** A1
Glenariffe Cres BT43 . . **181** D6
Glenariff Mountain Lower❶
  BT44 . . . . **48** F7
GLENARIFF OR WATERFOOT
  (GLEANN AIREAMH)
  BT44 . . . . **32** D2
Glenariff Pk BT37 . . . . **134** B8
Glenariff Rd
  Ballymena BT44 . . . . . **47** E5
  Portstewart BT55 . . . **173** C4
GLENARM BT44 . . . . . . **65** E8
Glenarm Ave S BT55 . . **173** C4
Glenarm Castle* BT44 . . **65** E8

Glenarm Ct BT43 . . . . . **181** E6
Glenarm Demesne❶
  BT44 . . . . **65** E7
Glenarm Prim Sch BT44 . **65** E8
Glenarm Rd BT40 . . . . **182** E4
Glenarm Sq BT10 . . . . **150** E3
Glenarny❶ BT80 . . . . . **112** B1
Glenarny Rd BT80 . . . . **112** B1
Glenavie Pk BT44 . . . . **134** B8
Glenavna Manor BT37 . . **134** B7
Glenavon Gdns BT80 . . **185** C3
Glenavon Pk
  Cookstown BT80 . . . . **185** C3
  Newtownabbey BT37 . . **134** B8
Glenavy❶ BT29 . . . . . . **121** B5
GLENAVY BT29 . . . . . . **121** C6
Glenavy Gdns BT28 . . . **169** E8
Glenavy Rd
  Belfast BT29 . . . . . . **121** A7
  Craigavon BT67 . . . . **166** E6
  ❶ Crumlin BT29 . . . . **117** A1
  Lisburn BT28 . . . . . . **158** B8
Glenback❶ BT53 . . . . . **42** E8
Glenbane Ave ❷ BT37 . . **133** E5
Glenbank Cl BT17 . . . . **149** C4
Glenbank Ct BT17 . . . . **149** C4
Glenbank Dr
  Belfast BT14 . . . . . . **136** D2
  Dunmurry BT17 . . . . . **149** C4
Glenbank Gdns ❶ BT48 . **178** D8
Glenbank Parade ❶
  BT14 . . . . **136** D2
Glenbank Pk BT48 . . . . **178** D8
Glenbank Pl BT14 . . . . **136** D2
Glenbank Rd
  Ballycastle BT54 . . . . **19** B4
  Londonderry BT48 . . . **178** D8
Glenbawn Ave BT17 . . . **149** C4
Glenbawn Cl BT17 . . . . **149** C3
Glenbawn Cres BT17 . . . **149** C4
Glenbawn Ct BT17 . . . . **149** C4
Glenbawn Dr BT17 . . . . **149** C3
Glenbawn Link ❶ BT17 . **149** C3
Glenbawn Pl BT17 . . . . **149** C4
Glenbawn Sq BT17 . . . . **149** C4
Glenbawn Wlk BT17 . . . **149** C4
Glenbeg Ct ❼ BT52 . . . **26** B7
Glenbeigh Dr BT8 . . . . **152** B4
Glenbourne Ave BT36 . . **132** F5
Glenbracken Dr BT47 . . . **70** F6
Glenbrae BT28 . . . . . . **159** B3
Glen Brae BT18 . . . . . **139** F5
Glenbrae Gdns BT48 . . . **178** D8
Glenbrook BT44 . . . . . . **49** C1
Glenbrook Ave BT5 . . . **145** D4
Glenbrook House BT48 . . **178** E8
Glenbrook Pk ❸ BT52 . . **26** C7
Glenbrook Terr BT48 . . . **178** E8
Glenbroome Pk BT37 . . **134** C7
Glenbryn Dr BT14 . . . . **136** E1
Glenbryn Gdns BT14 . . . **136** E1
Glenbryn Parade BT14 . . **136** E1
Glenbryn Pk BT14 . . . . **136** E1
Glenbuck❶ BT44 . . . . . **44** F1
Glenbuck Rd BT44 . . . . . **60** E8
Glenburn Ave ❶ BT40 . . **99** C8
Glenburn Cres BT52 . . . **174** E6
Glenburn Ct BT17 . . . . **150** A1
Glenburn Dr ❷ BT40 . . . **99** C8
Glenburn Manor BT38 . . **125** B2
Glenburn Pk
  Ballymena BT43 . . . . . **181** E6
  Belfast BT14 . . . . . . **137** B4
  Magherafelt BT45 . . . **183** C5
Glenburn Pl BT45 . . . . **183** C6
Glenburn Rd
  Dunmurry BT17 . . . . . **150** A1
  Larne BT40 . . . . **99** C8
Glenburn Rd S BT17 . . . **150** B1
Glenburn Way BT49 . . . **180** C3
Glenbush Dr BT55 . . . . **173** C4
Glenbush Rd BT53 . . . . . **30** A5
Glencairn❶ BT13 . . . . . **136** C1
Glencairn Cres BT13 . . . **143** E8
Glencairn Dr BT36 . . . . **132** F6
Glencairn Pass BT13 . . . **136** C1
Glencairn Pk BT36 . . . . **132** E6
Glencairn Rd BT13 . . . . **143** C8
Glencairn St BT13 . . . . **143** E8
Glencairn Way BT13 . . . **136** C1
Glenchiel❶ BT79 . . . . . **85** C3
Glenchiel Rd BT79 . . . . **85** D2
Glen Cl
  Craigavon BT67 . . . . **167** B7
  ❺ Maghera BT46 . . . . **74** D1
Glencoe Dr BT55 . . . . . **173** D4
Glencoe Pk BT36 . . . . . **137** C8
Glencolin Ave BT11 . . . **149** E8
Glencolin Cl BT11 . . . . **149** E8
Glencolin Ct BT11 . . . . **149** E8
Glencolin Dr BT11 . . . . **149** E8
Glencolin Gr BT11 . . . . **149** E8
Glencolin Hts BT11 . . . **149** E8
Glencolin Manor BT11 . . **149** E8
Glencolin Pk BT11 . . . . **149** E8
Glencolin Rise BT11 . . . **149** E8
Glencolin Way BT11 . . . **149** E8
Glencolin Wlk BT11 . . . **149** E8
Glencollyer St BT15 . . . **137** D1
Glenconway❶ BT47 . . . . **54** C7
Glenconway Rd BT47 . . . **54** D5
Glencoole Pk BT36 . . . . **133** A6
Glencosh❶ BT82 . . . . . **67** C4
Glencosh Rd BT82 . . . . . **67** B4
Glencourt BT41 . . . . . . **107** F8

Glencraig BT41 . . . . . . **186** D8
Glencraig Cl BT36 . . . . **132** E8
Glencraig Gdns ❷ BT36 . **132** E8
Glencraig Hts ❹ BT36 . . **132** E8
Glencraig Rd BT36 . . . . **132** E8
Glencree
  Cookstown BT80 . . . . **185** D3
  ❸ Maghera BT46 . . . . **74** C1
Glencree Pk BT37 . . . . **134** B8
Glencregagh Ct BT6 . . . **152** B5
Glencregagh Dr BT6 . . . **152** B5
Glencregagh Pk BT6 . . . **152** B5
Glencregagh Rd BT6 . . . **152** B5
Glen Cres
  ❶❶ Belfast BT11 . . . **143** D1
  Craigavon BT67 . . . . **167** A7
  Newtownabbey BT37 . . **134** B8
  Portstewart BT55 . . . **173** D5
Glencroft Gdns BT36 . . **132** E8
Glencroft Rd BT36 . . . . **132** E8
Glen Ct
  ❼ Belfast BT11 . . . . **143** D1
  Lisburn BT27 . . . . . . **170** B2
Glencurb❶ BT51 . . . . . . **41** D7
Glendale BT10 . . . . . . **150** B4
Glendale Ave E BT8 . . . **152** B4
Glendale Ave N BT8 . . . **152** B4
Glendale Ave S BT8 . . . **152** B4
Glendale Ave W BT8 . . . **152** B4
Glendale Gdns BT41 . . . **107** F8
Glendale Main S BT10 . . **150** A4
Glendale Mews BT10 . . . **150** B4
Glendale Pk
  Castlereagh BT8 . . . . **152** A4
  Londonderry BT48 . . . **176** B3
Glendale Rd BT48 . . . . **176** D5
Glendara BT48 . . . . . . **178** C3
Glendarragh BT4 . . . . . **139** B2
Glendarragh Mews BT4 . **139** B2
Glendarragh Pk ❽ BT29 . **117** B1
Glendermere Hts BT36 . . **133** A7
Glendermott Prim Sch
  BT47 . . . . **51** E6
Glendermott Rd BT47 . . **179** A5
Glendermott Valley Bsns Pk
  BT47 . . . . **51** D6
Glenderowen❶ BT47 . . . **51** B5
Glendhu Gr ❶ BT4 . . . . **139** A1
Glendhu Manor BT4 . . . **139** A1
Glendhu Pk BT4 . . . . . **139** B1
Glendon Pk BT47 . . . . . **179** C2
Glendowen Ave BT17 . . **149** B3
Glendowen Cl BT17 . . . **149** B3
Glendowen Grange BT17 **149** B3
Glendowen Pk BT17 . . . **149** B3
Glendower St BT6 . . . . **145** B2
Glendun Cl BT55 . . . . . **173** C4
Glendun Cres ❶❶ BT52 . . **26** B7
Glendun Ct BT37 . . . . . **134** A7
Glendun Dr BT43 . . . . . **181** D6
Glendun Pk
  Ballymena BT43 . . . . . **181** D6
  Dunmurry BT17 . . . . . **150** A1
Glendun Rd
  Ballymena BT44 . . . . . **47** D2
  Cushendun BT44 . . . . **21** A1
Gleneagles
  Clogh Mills BT44 . . . . **45** F3
  Londonderry BT48 . . . **177** A2
Glen Ebor Hts BT4 . . . . **139** C1
Glen Ebor Pk BT4 . . . . **146** B8
Gleneden Pk BT37 . . . . **134** B8
Glenedra❶ BT47 . . . . . **87** D8
Glenedra Rd BT47 . . . . . **87** F8
Gleneen Pk BT47 . . . . . **179** C2
Glenelly Rd
  Magherafelt BT45 . . . . **88** A2
  Omagh BT79 . . . . **85** F2
Glenelly Villas BT45 . . . **89** A3
Glenelm Pk BT36 . . . . . **133** A4
Glenerin❶ BT79 . . . . . . **86** F5
Glenesk Gdns ❸ BT52 . . **26** B7
Glenfada Pk BT48 . . . . **178** E5
Glenfall Rd BT40 . . . . . **99** B7
Glenfarne Pl BT40 . . . . **182** A6
Glenfarne St BT13 . . . . **144** B7
Glenfearna Ave BT17 . . **149** C3
Glenfearna Gdns ❸
  BT17 . . . . **149** C3
Glenfearna Pk ❷ BT17 . **149** C3
Glenfearna Wood BT17 . **149** C3
Glenfern Dr ❾ BT52 . . . **26** B7
Glenfield Cl ❸ BT29 . . . **117** A1
Glenfield Wlk ❶ BT38 . . **124** E1
Glenford Rd BT40 . . . . . **99** B7
Glengad❶ BT53 . . . . . . **43** B5
Glengalliagh Pk BT48 . . **176** E3
Glengalliagh Rd BT48 . . **176** D4
Glengall Pk BT52 . . . . . **174** E1
Glengall St BT12 . . . . . **188** C2
Glengarry Pk BT37 . . . . **134** B8
Glen Gdns BT47 . . . . . **179** A3
Glengiven Ave BT49 . . . **180** C3
Glengoland Ave BT17 . . **149** E6
Glengoland Cres BT17 . . **149** E6
Glengoland Gdns BT17 . **149** E6
Glengoland Parade BT17 **149** E6
Glengoland Pk BT17 . . . **149** E6
Glengomna❶ BT45 . . . . **87** F3
Glengomna La BT45 . . . **88** C2
Glengomna Rd BT45 . . . **88** C2
Glengorm Ave
  ❹ Coleraine BT52 . . . **26** B7
  Coleraine BT52 . . . . . **174** E1
Glengormley High Sch
  BT36 . . . . **132** E2
Glengormley Integrated Sch
  BT36 . . . . **133** A5

Glengormley Prim Sch BT36 . . . 119 F7
Glengormly BT36 . . . 119 F7
Glengrainne Pk BT47 . . 70 A3
Glenhall BT51 . . . 26 D2
Glenhead BT42 . . . 81 C2
GLENHEAD BT49 . . . 38 D4
Glenhead Ave BT17 . . . 150 A1
Glenhead Rd
Ballymena BT42 . . . 82 A1
Larne BT40 . . . 97 F8
Limavady BT49 . . . 38 D4
Glenhill BT11 . . . 150 C8
Glenhill Rd 2 BT48 . . . 178 C8
Glenholm Ave BT8 . . . 152 B4
Glenholm Cres BT8 . . . 152 B4
Glenholm Dr BT8 . . . 152 B4
Glenholm Pk BT8 . . . 152 B4
Glenhoy Dr BT5 . . . 145 D3
Glenhugh BT42 . . . 77 D4
Glenhugh Cres BT8 . . . 152 A2
Glenhugh Pk
Ahoghill BT42 . . . 77 E2
Castlereagh BT8 . . . 152 A2
Glenhugh Rd BT42 . . . 77 E3
Glenhurst Dr BT36 . . . 137 D8
Glenhurst Gdns BT36 . . . 137 D8
Glenhurst Parade BT36 . . . 137 D8
Glenkeen BT51 . . . 41 D3
Glenkeen BT17 . . . 149 C4
Glenkeen
Limavady BT49 . . . 39 F7
Londonderry BT47 . . . 51 F5
Glenkeen Ct BT37 . . . 129 A1
Glenkeen Dr BT38 . . . 129 E3
Glenkeen Gdns BT37 . . . 129 A1
Glenkeen Hts BT41 . . . 107 F7
Glenkeen Manor BT37 . . . 129 B2
Glenkeen Pk BT37 . . . 129 B2
Glenkeen Rd BT51 . . . 42 E6
Glenkyle Ave BT36 . . . 128 B1
Glenkyle Cres BT36 . . . 128 B1
Glenkyle Dr 2 BT36 . . . 128 B1
Glenkyle Gdns BT36 . . . 128 B1
Glenkyle Gr 2 BT36 . . . 128 B1
Glenkyle Parade 3 BT36 . . . 128 B1
Glenkyle Pk BT36 . . . 128 B1
Glenkyle Pk Ave 1 BT36 128 B1
Glenlea Gr BT4 . . . 139 B1
Glenlea Pk
Belfast BT4 . . . 139 B1
Limavady BT49 . . . 180 C3
Glenleary BT51 . . . 26 B4
Glenleary Rd BT51 . . . 26 B5
Glenleslie BT44 . . . 46 C1
Glenleslie Rd BT44 . . . 62 C8
Glenloch Gdns BT4 . . . 139 B1
Glenloch Pk 11 BT52 . . . 26 B7
Glenlough
Ballymoney BT53 . . . 28 D1
Londonderry BT47 . . . 68 E7
Glenlough Rd BT53 . . . 44 C8
Glenluce BT4 . . . 139 B1
Glenluce Gn BT4 . . . 139 A1
Glenluce Wlk BT4 . . . 139 A1
Glenmachan Ave BT4 . . . 146 C7
Glenmachan Dr BT4 . . . 146 C8
Glenmachan Gr BT4 . . . 146 C7
Glenmachan Mews BT4 146 C8
Glenmachan Pk BT4 . . . 139 C1
Glenmachan Pl BT12 . . . 143 F2
Glenmachan Rd BT4 . . . 146 C8
Glenmachan St BT12 . . . 144 A2
Glenmakeeran BT54 . . . 19 F5
Glenmakeeran Rd BT54 9 C1
Glenmanus Pk BT55 . . . 173 C3
Glenmanus Rd BT55 . . . 173 C3
Glenmaquill BT45 . . . 90 E2
Glenmaquill Rd BT45 . . . 90 F3
Glenmeen Cl BT17 . . . 142 C2
Glen Mews BT39 . . . 184 D4
Glenmillan Dr BT4 . . . 146 B8
Glenmillan Rd BT4 . . . 146 B8
Glenmill Pk BT49 . . . 180 C3
Glenmore Activity Ctr *
BT27 . . . 160 D4
Glenmore Dr BT27 . . . 160 D4
Glenmore Gdns
Ballymoney BT53 . . . 175 C6
1 Coleraine BT52 . . . 26 C7
Limavady BT49 . . . 180 C4
Glenmore Rd BT47 . . . 179 C2
Glenmore St BT5 . . . 145 B5
Glenmore Wlk BT27 . . . 160 C4
Glenmount Dr BT37 . . . 133 E2
Glenmount Gr 1 BT37 . . . 133 E3
Glenmount Rd 2 BT37 . . . 133 E3
Glenmullion BT41 . . . 187 C8
Glenmullion Rd BT41 . . . 187 C8
Glenmurry Ct 5 BT11 . . . 143 C1
Glennagoorland Glebe
BT82 . . . 67 F8
Glennor Cres BT8 . . . 163 C2
Glennor Cres E BT8 . . . 163 C2
Glennor Cres W BT8 . . . 163 C2
Glenn Pk BT56 . . . 172 D4
Glenoak Ave BT8 . . . 117 B1
Glenoak Gdns BT29 . . . 117 C1
Glenocum BT43 . . . 63 D6
GLENOE BT40 . . . 99 B5
Glenone BT44 . . . 76 C4
Glenone Rd BT44 . . . 76 B4
Glenone Villas 1 BT44 . . . 76 B4
Glenowen BT44 . . . 45 B1
Glenowen Pk BT48 . . . 178 B6
Glen Parade BT11 . . . 143 D1

Glenpark BT47 . . . 54 C2
Glenpark St BT14 . . . 144 A8
Glenquilly Rd BT45 . . . 104 A3
Glenrandal Rd BT47 . . . 69 C3
Glenrandel BT47 . . . 36 E4
Glenravel Pk BT43 . . . 181 E4
Glenravel Prim Sch BT43. 62 F7
Glenravel Rd BT43 . . . 63 A8
Glenravel St BT15 . . . 144 D7
Glen Rd
Ballyclare BT39 . . . 184 F4
Ballymena BT44 . . . 48 C7
Belfast BT17 . . . 149 C8
Belfast BT29 . . . 121 A4
Castlereagh BT5 . . . 152 F8
Coleraine BT51 . . . 57 C5
Craigavon BT67 . . . 167 B7
Lisburn BT27 . . . 161 D1
Londonderry BT48 . . . 178 C7
Maghera BT46 . . . 74 A1
Newtownabbey BT37 . . . 134 B8
Portstewart BT55 . . . 173 A5
Glen Rd Hts BT11 . . . 142 F1
Glen Rise BT5 . . . 146 A1
Glen River Pk BT29 . . . 121 B6
Glenroan 1 BT79 . . . 85 A1
Glenroe Meghaberry
BT67 . . . 167 B7
Glenroe Pk BT47 . . . 55 D1
Glenroe Wlk BT49 . . . 180 C3
Glenrosa St BT15 . . . 144 D8
Glenross Pk 3 BT36 . . . 132 E8
Glenrush Gdns BT49 . . . 180 C3
Glensbrae Rd BT43 . . . 63 A5
Glenshane BT47 . . . 73 A3
Glenshane Bsns Pk BT47 . 55 D3
Glenshane Ent Ctr 12
BT47 . . . 55 D2
Glenshane Gdns
Belfast BT11 . . . 150 B7
4 Draperstown BT45 . . . 89 A3
Glenshane Pk
10 Draperstown BT45 . . . 89 A3
Newtownabbey BT37 . . . 134 C8
Glenshane Rd
Drumahoe BT79 . . . 179 E1
Londonderry BT47 . . . 179 C2
Maghera BT46 . . . 90 A8
Glensharragh Gdns BT6 . 152 D8
Glensharragh Pk 3 BT6 152 D8
Glenshesk Dr BT43 . . . 181 E4
Glenshesk Pk
Dunmurry BT11 . . . 150 A1
Portstewart BT55 . . . 173 C4
Glenshesk Rd BT54 . . . 8 F2
Glenside
Castlereagh BT6 . . . 152 C7
Larne BT40 . . . 99 C8
Glenside Ave BT27 . . . 162 A3
Glenside Brae BT49 . . . 180 C3
Glenside Dr 5 BT14 . . . 136 D2
Glenside Gdns 3 BT48 . . . 178 D8
Glenside Parade BT14. . . 136 D2
Glenside Pk
Belfast BT14 . . . 136 D2
Lisburn BT27 . . . 162 A3
Londonderry BT48 . . . 178 D8
Glenside Rd
Belfast BT17 . . . 149 B8
Londonderry BT48 . . . 178 D8
Glenstaghey BT54 . . . 7 E6
Glenstall Rd BT53 . . . 43 B8
Glenstaughey Rd BT54 . . . 7 E6
Glentaisie Dr BT54 . . . 8 D3
Glentaisie Pk BT55 . . . 173 C4
Glentask 1 BT57 . . . 5 B3
Glen The
Belfast BT15 . . . 137 C1
Craigavon BT67 . . . 164 F7
Glenties Dr BT11 . . . 149 E7
Glentop Rd BT44 . . . 19 B3
Glentoran Pl 14 BT6 . . . 145 A4
Glentoye Pk BT37 . . . 134 B8
Glenullin Rd BT51 . . . 57 A5
Glenvale
Ballymena BT44 . . . 61 A6
1 Maghera BT46 . . . 74 C1
Portstewart BT55 . . . 173 D5
Glenvale Cres BT55 . . . 173 D5
Glenvale Pk
Larne BT40 . . . 99 C8
4 Londonderry BT48 . . . 178 D8
2 Portstewart BT55. . . 173 D4
Glenvale Rd
Londonderry BT48 . . . 178 D8
Magherafelt BT45 . . . 92 B7
Glenvale St BT13 . . . 143 F7
Glenvara Ct BT51 . . . 26 B6
Glenvara Dr BT52 . . . 174 E7
Glenvarlock St BT5 . . . 145 C3
Glenvarna Ct 4 BT36 . . . 132 E7
Glenvarna Dr BT36 . . . 132 E7
Glenvarna Gn 6 BT36 . . . 132 E7
Glenvarna Sq 3 BT36 . . . 132 E7
Glenvarna Wlk 7 BT36. . . 132 E7
Glenveagh Dr BT11 . . . 149 E7
Glenveagh Pk BT11 . . . 149 D7
Glenveagh Sch BT9 . . . 150 F4
Glenview BT67 . . . 167 B7
Glen View
Coleraine BT51 . . . 57 C5
Maghera BT46 . . . 74 C1
Glenview Ave
Castlereagh BT5 . . . 153 A8
Holywood BT18 . . . 139 F6
Londonderry BT48 . . . 178 D8

Glenview Cl BT37 . . . 134 B7
Glenview Cres
Castlereagh BT5 . . . 152 F8
Newtownabbey BT37 . . . 134 B6
Glenview Dr
Castlereagh BT5 . . . 153 A8
Limavady BT49 . . . 180 C4
Newtownabbey BT37 . . . 134 B6
Glenview Gdns
Castlereagh BT5 . . . 153 A8
Newtownabbey BT37 . . . 134 B6
Glenview Hts BT5 . . . 153 A8
Glenview Pk
1 Castlereagh BT5 . . . 145 F1
Cushendun BT44 . . . 21 A1
Londonderry BT47 . . . 55 A5
Newtownabbey BT37 . . . 134 A6
Glenview Rd
Ballycastle BT54 . . . 19 C4
Ballymena BT44 . . . 81 E8
Holywood BT18 . . . 139 F6
Glenview St
Belfast BT14 . . . 144 A8
Londonderry BT48 . . . 178 D8
Glenview Way BT37 . . . 134 A6
Glenviggan BT45 . . . 101 D5
Glenviggan Rd BT45 . . . 101 F6
Glenville Cres BT37 . . . 134 B7
Glenville Ct BT37 . . . 134 B7
Glenville Ind Est BT37. . . 134 A7
Glenville Manor 2 BT37. 133 F7
Glenville or Leamore
BT44 . . . 32 D5
Glenville Parade BT37 . . . 134 B6
Glenville Pk BT37 . . . 134 B7
Glenville Rd
Ballymena BT44 . . . 32 D5
Newtownabbey BT37 . . . 133 F7
Glenville Terr BT46 . . . 74 F5
Glenville Way BT37 . . . 134 B6
Glenvista Rd BT48 . . . 178 D8
Glenwell Ave BT36 . . . 132 F4
Glenwell Cres BT36 . . . 132 F4
Glenwell Dr BT36 . . . 132 F4
Glenwell Gdns BT36 . . . 132 F4
Glenwell Gr BT36 . . . 132 F4
Glenwell Pk BT36 . . . 132 F4
Glenwell Rd BT36 . . . 132 F4
Glenwherry Pl 6 BT6 . . . 145 A4
Glenwhirry BT42 . . . 80 F1
Glenwhirry Ct BT37 . . . 134 A7
Glenwood
Ahoghill BT42 . . . 77 E3
Londonderry BT48 . . . 178 C7
Glenwood Ave BT52 . . . 174 F1
Glenwood Cl BT17 . . . 149 D4
Glenwood Copse BT17 . . . 160 E7
Glenwood Cres
Belfast BT17 . . . 149 D4
Cookstown BT80 . . . 185 D2
Glenwood Ct
Belfast BT17 . . . 149 D4
Larne BT40 . . . 83 B4
Lisburn BT28 . . . 159 C5
Glenwood Dr BT17 . . . 149 D4
Glenwood Gdns BT17 . . . 149 D4
Glenwood Gn
Belfast BT17 . . . 149 D4
Lisburn BT28 . . . 159 C5
Glenwood Pk BT17 . . . 160 E7
Glenwood Pl BT13 . . . 188 A4
Glenwood Prim Sch
BT13 . . . 188 A4
Glenwood Row BT17 . . . 160 F8
Glenwood St BT13 . . . 188 A4
Glenwood View BT17 . . . 149 D4
Glenwood Wlk BT17 . . . 149 D4
Gloonan BT42 . . . 78 A2
Gloonan Hill 2 BT42 . . . 77 F2
Gloonan Rd BT42 . . . 78 A2
Glore 1 BT44 . . . 65 D6
Gloucester Ave
Larne BT40 . . . 182 D5
3 Londonderry BT47 . . . 179 B5
Gloucester Cres BT55 . . . 172 A3
Gloucester St BT1 . . . 189 B3
Gloverstown Rd BT41 . . . 106 E7
Glrncairn BT27 . . . 170 B2
Glynn BT40 . . . 99 C8
GLYNN BT40 . . . 99 D8
Glynn Pk 6 BT37 . . . 133 E5
Glynn Pk Cl BT38 . . . 125 E3
Glynn Prim Sch BT40. . . 99 C8
Glynn Sta BT40 . . . 99 C8
Glynnview Ave BT40. . . 182 E4
Glynn Wlk BT38 . . . 124 E1
Gobbins Brae BT40 . . . 100 D6
Gobbins Path BT40 . . . 100 D3
Gobbins Rd BT40 . . . 100 D6
Gobnascale
Londonderry BT47 . . . 179 A3
Strabane BT82 . . . 67 C3
Gobrana 1 BT29 . . . 121 B7
Gobrana Rd BT29 . . . 121 B6
Gogarty Cl BT48 . . . 176 A2
Goldenview Rd BT38 . . . 129 E4
Goldsmith Ct 1 BT48 . . . 176 B2
Goles 1 BT79 . . . 87 C4
Goles Rd BT79 . . . 87 B4
Golf Course Rd BT17 . . . 149 F4
Golf View BT80 . . . 185 E3
Golfview Gdns BT49 . . . 180 A5
Goodland 1 BT54 . . . 9 F3
Good Shepherd Prim Sch
Belfast BT17 . . . 149 C5

Good Shepherd Prim Sch
continued
Londonderry BT47 . . . 179 B4
Good Shepherd Rd BT17 149 D6
Good Shepherds Glen
BT47 . . . 179 A4
Goorland Rd BT82 . . . 67 F7
Gooseberry Cnr BT67 . . . 154 A1
Gordansvale Dr BT40. . . 182 A3
Gordon St BT1 . . . 189 B4
Gordonville BT52 . . . 174 D3
Gordonville Pk BT53 . . . 175 E4
Gorman Cl BT38 . . . 129 E4
Gorran 1 BT51 . . . 41 F5
Gorran Prim Sch BT51. . . 42 A5
Gorran Rd BT51 . . . 41 F4
Gorse Rd
Londonderry BT47 . . . 69 A8
Strabane BT82 . . . 67 B5
Gort 1
Coleraine BT51 . . . 58 A7
Limavady BT49 . . . 23 B8
Gortaclare 1
Londonderry BT47 . . . 55 D6
Strabane BT82 . . . 68 B3
Gortaclare Rd BT82 . . . 67 F2
Gortaclee Rd BT44 . . . 32 D3
Gortaclee Rd BT44 . . . 32 D4
Gortacloghan 1 BT51 . . . 58 A5
Gortaghan BT41 . . . 107 C3
Gortagherty Upper 1
BT47 . . . 36 D4
Gortaghragan 1 BT44 . . . 32 C8
Gortagilly 1 BT45 . . . 104 D2
Gortagilly Rd BT45 . . . 104 D2
Gortahar 1 BT44 . . . 60 B7
Gortahar La BT44 . . . 60 B7
Gortahar Rd BT44 . . . 60 C7
Gortaheran 1 BT44 . . . 60 C1
Gortahurk 1 BT45 . . . 103 D8
Gortahurk Rd BT45 . . . 89 C2
Gortalowry 1 BT80 . . . 185 C3
Gortalowry Pk BT80 . . . 185 D2
Gortamaddy 1 BT54 . . . 8 C4
Gortamaddy or White Hall 1
BT54 . . . 8 B3
Gortamney 1 BT45 . . . 90 B4
Gortamney La BT45 . . . 90 A4
Gortanclochair Pk BT54. 8 D4
Gortanewry 1 BT45 . . . 104 A3
Gortateea 1 BT82 . . . 32 B2
Gortavea 1 BT82 . . . 50 A1
Gortcarney 1 BT44 . . . 49 B1
Gortclanny 1 BT44 . . . 59 E6
Gortconny 1 BT54 . . . 8 A4
Gortcorbies 1 BT49 . . . 24 B2
Gorteade 1 BT46 . . . 75 A6
Gorteade Pk BT46 . . . 74 F5
Gorteade Rd BT46 . . . 74 F7
Gortenny 1 BT47 . . . 36 E4
Gortfad 1
Ballymena BT44 . . . 76 E5
Coleraine BT51 . . . 57 E8
Gortfad Rd
Ballymena BT44 . . . 76 F6
Coleraine BT51 . . . 57 D8
Gortfin St BT12 . . . 143 F4
Gortfoyle Pl BT47 . . . 179 A4
Gortgare 1 BT47 . . . 37 C5
Gortgare Ave 3 BT47 . . . 37 C5
Gortgare Rd BT47 . . . 37 C5
Gortgarn 1
Antrim BT41 . . . 106 F6
Limavady BT49 . . . 23 E1
Londonderry BT47 . . . 56 A6
Gortgarn Rd BT49 . . . 39 F8
Gortgill 1 BT41 . . . 92 D1
Gortgole 1 BT44 . . . 76 C7
Gortgole Rd BT44 . . . 76 C7
Gortgran 1 BT51 . . . 13 E3
Gortgranagh 1 BT47 . . . 51 D5
Gortgrib 1 BT5 . . . 146 D2
Gortgrib Dr BT5 . . . 146 D2
Gortica 1 BT47 . . . 52 A7
Gortica Rd BT47 . . . 51 F7
Gorticloghan 1 BT52 . . . 15 B3
Gorticross 1 BT47 . . . 36 A2
Gorticross Rd BT47 . . . 52 B8
Gorticrum Irish 1 BT82. 67 A1
Gortilea 1 BT47 . . . 53 C3
Gortilea Rd BT47 . . . 69 E8
Gortileck 1 BT82 . . . 67 B2
Gortiles Cross Roads
BT47 . . . 53 C4
Gortin 1
Ballymena BT44 . . . 48 F3
Cookstown BT80 . . . 112 C4
Londonderry BT47 . . . 50 F4
Gortin Coolhill 1 BT51 . . . 43 A2
Gortin Fort * BT80 . . . 112 C4
Gortin Hill BT44 . . . 49 C3
Gortin Manor BT47 . . . 50 F4
Gortin Mayoghill 1 BT51 42 D4
Gortin Pk BT5 . . . 146 C3
Gortin Rd BT51 . . . 59 A8
Gortinreid 1 BT47 . . . 36 E2
Gortin Upper 1 BT51 . . . 42 D3
Gortinure 1
Londonderry BT47 . . . 51 A5
Maghera BT46 . . . 74 C5
Gortinure Rd BT47 . . . 51 A5
Gortin Way BT42 . . . 181 A1
Gortland Pk BT5 . . . 146 D2
Gortlands Mews 1 BT5. 146 D2
Gortlane 1 BT44 . . . 32 B1
Gortlane Dr BT38 . . . 129 E3

Gortmacrane 1 BT51 . . . 59 A4
Gortmacrane Rd BT51 . . . 58 F3
Gortmellan 1 BT47 . . . 67 C7
Gortmellon 1 BT47 . . . 67 B7
Gortmillish 1 BT53 . . . 18 D3
Gortmonly Rd
Londonderry BT47 . . . 67 A8
Strabane BT82 . . . 50 D2
Gortmore 1 BT29 . . . 12 B1
Gortmore Pk BT28 . . . 159 E2
Gortmore Pl BT47 . . . 177 F5
Gortnacapple 1 BT57 . . . 5 C3
Gortnacloghan Rd BT51. 57 F4
Gortnacor 1 BT47 . . . 167 F3
Gortnacor Lower 1 BT67 167 F3
Gortnacor Upper 1 BT67 167 F5
Gortnagallon 1 BT29 . . . 116 C1
Gortnagallon Rd BT29 . . . 116 C1
Gortnageeragh 1 BT43 . . . 63 B8
Gortnageeragh Glen BT43 47 C2
Gortnageeragh Rd BT43. 63 B8
Gortnagory 1 BT44 . . . 49 B4
Gortnagory Rd BT44 . . . 49 C3
Gortnagross 1
Cookstown BT80 . . . 112 D3
Londonderry BT47 . . . 55 F5
Gortnagross Lower or
Murroo 1 BT44 . . . 32 B3
Gortnagross Middle 1
BT44 . . . 32 B3
Gortnagross Rd
Cookstown BT80 . . . 112 C3
Limavady BT49 . . . 40 A1
Londonderry BT47 . . . 55 F6
GORTNAHEY BT47 . . . 54 F5
Gortnahey Beg 1 BT47 . . . 54 F5
Gortnahey More 1 BT47. 55 A5
Gortnahey Prim Sch BT47 54 F5
Gortnahey Rd BT47 . . . 54 F5
Gortnamaddy Pk 16 BT54. 8 C3
Gortnamona Ct BT11 . . . 143 B2
Gortnamona Hts BT11 . . . 143 B2
Gortnamona Pl BT11 . . . 143 B1
Gortnamona Rise BT11. 143 B2
Gortnamona View BT11 143 B2
Gortnamona Way BT11. 143 B2
Gortnamoney 1 BT49 . . . 23 B1
Gortnamoyagh 1 BT51. 57 B8
Gortnamoyagh Rd BT51. 57 A8
Gortnaran 1 BT47 . . . 69 A8
Gortnaran Rd
Londonderry BT47 . . . 69 A8
Strabane BT82 . . . 68 A5
Gortnari BT45 . . . 88 D5
Gortnarney 1 BT49 . . . 40 B3
Gortnarney Rd BT49 . . . 40 B1
Gortnaskey 1
Londonderry BT47 . . . 68 D6
Magherafelt BT45 . . . 89 B4
Gortnaskey Rd BT45 . . . 89 B4
Gortnee 1 BT57 . . . 5 C4
Gortnee Ct BT57 . . . 5 C4
Gortnee Dr BT57 . . . 5 C4
Gortnessy 1 BT47 . . . 36 C1
Gortnessy Rd BT47 . . . 36 C1
Gortnure Rd BT44 . . . 74 C5
Gortraney Rd BT28 . . . 155 E7
Gortrany 1 BT28 . . . 155 F7
Gort Rd BT80 . . . 115 A3
Gortreagh 1 BT80 . . . 112 D4
Gortree 1 BT47 . . . 36 A1
Gortree Rd BT47 . . . 52 A8
Gortscanlan 1 BT47 . . . 54 F6
Gortscreagan 1 BT47 . . . 69 E3
Gortscreagan Rd BT47. 69 E3
Gortstagherty Rd BT53. 44 F8
Gortycavan 1 BT51 . . . 25 B8
Gortycavan Rd BT51 . . . 25 B8
Gosheden 1 BT47 . . . 52 A2
Gosheden BT47 . . . 52 B3
Gosheden Rd BT47 . . . 52 B2
Gotha St BT6 . . . 145 A4
Goudy Bridge Rd BT67. 154 F2
Govan Dr 1 BT5 . . . 146 E3
Governor Rd BT48 . . . 179 F8
Governor's Bridge BT9. 151 D8
Governors Pl 4 BT38 . . . 131 C1
Governors Rd
3 Lisburn BT28 . . . 160 A1
Lisburn BT28 . . . 170 A1
Gowan Hts BT27 . . . 161 C6
Gow Hill BT45 . . . 91 F5
Grace Ave
Belfast BT5 . . . 145 D4
Larne BT40 . . . 83 B8
Grace Ave N BT40 . . . 83 B8
Gracefield BT42 . . . 78 B2
Gracefield Rd BT45 . . . 105 D7
GRACEHILL 1 BT53 . . . 17 D2
GRACEHILL (BAILE UÍ
CHINNÉIDE) BT42. . . 78 A3
Gracehill Rd BT53. . . 28 F5
Gracemount Pk BT8. . . 152 B2
Grace St BT2 . . . 189 B2
Grafton St BT48 . . . 178 D7
Graham Ct 2 BT67 . . . 166 C2
Graham Gdns
Belfast BT6 . . . 145 C1
Lisburn BT28 . . . 160 B1
Graham House Hospl
BT8 . . . 152 B1
Graham Ind Pk BT3 . . . 138 B3
Graham Rd BT40 . . . 83 B2
Graham St 3 BT27 . . . 160 C1

Grahamstown Pk BT39 . . **184** B5
Grahamstown Wlk BT39 . **184** B5
Graigcanon❶ BT51 . . . . . . **57** E3
Grainan Dr BT48 . . . . **176** F2
Grainan Pk BT48 . . . . **176** F3
Graingers Mill BT41 . . . . . **187** C1
Grainon Way BT4 . . . . . . **145** D5
Grampian Ave BT4 . . . . . . **145** D5
Granagh❶ BT44 . . . . **60** D7
Granaghan❶ BT46 . . . . . . **74** C7
Granagh Rd BT42 . . . . **77** D7
Granchester Pk BT47 . . . . . **36** F5
Grand Opera House★
BT12 . . . . **188** C2
Grand Parade BT5 . . . . . . **145** D2
Grand St BT27 . . . . **160** D2
Grange❶ BT45 . . . . **90** D3
Grange Ave
Ballymena BT42 . . . . . . **181** C2
Dunmurry BT17 . . . . . . **150** A3
❷ Londonderry BT47 . . . **179** D5
Magherafelt BT45 . . . . . **183** C8
Grange Beg❶ BT51 . . . . . . **13** D4
GRANGE CORNER BT41 . . . **93** B4
Grange Cotts BT41 . . . . . . **93** B4
Grange Ct BT45 . . . . **183** C7
Grange Dr
Ballyclare BT39 . . . . . . **184** A5
Ballymoney BT53 . . . . . **175** F4
Magherafelt BT45 . . . . . **183** C8
Grangefield BT41 . . . . **93** B4
Grange Gdns BT45 . . . . . **183** C8
Grangegorm Dr BT42 . . . . **181** B2
Grange Houses BT42 . . . . **181** B2
Grange La
Magherafelt BT45 . . . . . . **90** D2
Newtownabbey BT36 . . . **119** C2
Grangeleigh Ave BT42 . . . **181** C3
Grange Lodge BT41 . . . . . **187** B2
Grange Mdws BT41 . . . . . . **93** A4
Grange More❶ BT51 . . . . . **13** E4
Grangemore Pk
❶ Londonderry BT48 . . . **176** B1
Londonderry BT48 . . . . . **178** A8
Grange More Upper❶
BT51 . . . . **13** D2
Grange of Ballyrobert❶
BT39 . . . . **111** C3
Grange of Ballywalter❶
BT39 . . . . **111** B5
Grange of Carmavy❶
BT29 . . . . **118** B6
Grange of Inispollan
Mountain❶ BT54 . . . . . . **20** F3
Grange of Mallusk❶
BT36 . . . . **119** D7
GRANGE OF MALLUSK
BT36 . . . . **132** A5
Grange of Mountain❶
BT54 . . . . **20** E3
Grange of Umgall❶
BT39 . . . . **118** F5
Grange Park❶
Antrim BT41 . . . . **92** F4
Limavady BT49 . . . . **24** A6
Grange Pk
Ballyclare BT39 . . . . . . **184** B5
Dunmurry BT17 . . . . . . **150** A3
Limavady BT49 . . . . . . **180** B5
Magherafelt BT45 . . . . . **183** C8
Grange Rd
Antrim BT41 . . . . **92** F5
Ballyclare BT39 . . . . . . **110** D5
Ballymena BT42 . . . . . . **181** B3
Belfast BT29 . . . . **118** A5
Coleraine BT52 . . . . . . **174** E2
Cookstown BT80 . . . . . **185** D1
Magherafelt BT45 . . . . . . **90** D2
Granges Entry BT39 . . . . . **184** C5
Grange The
Antrim BT41 . . . . **187** B2
Ballyclare BT39 . . . . . . **110** C5
Ballymena BT42 . . . . . . **181** B2
Belfast BT4 . . . . **146** C7
Belfast BT29 . . . . **121** B6
Lisburn BT28 . . . . **159** C5
Newtownabbey BT37 . . . **134** D8
Grange Valley BT42 . . . . . **181** C2
Grange Valley Ave BT39 . . **184** B4
Grange Valley Cres BT39 . **184** B4
Grange Valley Dr BT39 . . . **184** B4
Grange Valley Gdns
BT39 . . . . **184** B4
Grange Valley Gn BT39 . . **184** B4
Grange Valley Gr BT39 . . . **184** B4
Grange Valley Pk BT39 . . . **184** B4
Grange Valley Way BT39 . **184** B4
Grangeville Dr BT10 . . . . . **150** C5
Grangeville Gdns BT10 . . . **150** C5
Grange Wlk BT39 . . . . . . **184** B5
Grangewood Ave BT42 . . . **181** B2
Grangewood Ct BT47 . . . . **179** D5
Grangewood Dr BT47 . . . . **179** D5
Grania's Well★ BT45 . . . . **113** F7
Grannagh BT49 . . . . **23** B2
Grannagh Pk BT49 . . . . . . **23** B2
Granny❶ BT45 . . . . **89** D4
Grannys Fort★ BT39 . . . . . **97** C5
Grannystown Rd BT44 . . . . **76** E7
Gransden Ct ❶❶ BT52 . . . **26** C7
Gransden Pk
❷❶ Coleraine BT52 . . . **26** C7
Eglinton BT47 . . . . **36** E4
Gransha❶
Larne BT40 . . . . **100** D6

Gransha continued
Londonderry BT47 . . . . . **177** E2
Gransha Ave BT11 . . . . . . **143** C1
Gransha Brae BT40 . . . . . **100** C6
Gransha Cres BT11 . . . . . . **143** C1
Gransha Dr BT11 . . . . **143** C1
Gransha Gdns BT11 . . . . . **143** C2
Gransha Gn BT11 . . . . **143** C2
Gransha Gr
❻ Belfast BT11 . . . . **143** C1
Newtownabbey BT37 . . . **133** E5
Gransha Hospl BT47 . . . . . **177** E1
Gransha Parade BT11 . . . . **143** C1
Gransha Pk
Belfast BT11 . . . . **143** C1
Londonderry BT47 . . . . . **177** D3
Gransha Rd BT23 . . . . **153** E2
Gransha Rise BT11 . . . . . . **143** C2
Gransha Way BT11 . . . . . . **143** C1
Grant Ave BT41 . . . . **107** F7
Granton Pk BT15 . . . . **146** E3
Grants La BT67 . . . . **154** C6
Granville Dr
Ballymena BT43 . . . . . . **181** E5
❶ Carrickfergus BT38 . . . **125** C1
Granville Manor ❷ BT42 . . **95** A6
Granville Pl BT12 . . . . **188** B2
Grasmere BT52 . . . . **174** F5
Grasmere Ct BT52 . . . . . . **174** F5
Grasmere Gdns BT15 . . . . **137** B4
Grassmere Pk BT38 . . . . . **125** E2
Gravelhill Rd
Lisburn BT28 . . . . **168** D6
Newtownabbey BT36 . . . **111** D1
Gravel La BT67 . . . . **154** D2
Graymount Cres BT36 . . . . **137** E8
Graymount Dr BT36 . . . . . **137** E8
Graymount Gdns BT36 . . . **137** D7
Graymount Gr BT36 . . . . . **137** E7
Graymount Parade BT36 . . **137** E8
Graymount Rd BT36 . . . . . **137** E8
Graymount Terr BT36 . . . . **137** E7
Gray's Ct BT15 . . . . **137** E7
Gray's La
Holywood BT18 . . . . . . **139** D7
Newtownabbey BT15 . . . **137** D7
Gray's Pk BT8 . . . . **151** D2
Gray's Pk Ave BT8 . . . . . . **151** D2
Grays Pk Dr BT8 . . . . **151** D2
Grays Pk Gdns ❸ BT8 . . . **151** D2
Great Deer Park ❶ BT44 . . **65** E4
Great George's St BT15 . . **144** D7
Great James St BT48 . . . . **178** E6
Great Northern Mall
BT12 . . . . **188** C2
Great Northern St BT9 . . . **151** A8
Great Patrick St BT1 . . . . **189** A4
Great Victoria St Sta
BT12 . . . . **188** C2
Great Victoria St BT2 . . . . **189** A2
Greenacre BT44 . . . . **44** F4
Green Acres
Cookstown BT80 . . . . . **185** C3
Newtownabbey BT36 . . . **133** A7
Greenaghan❶ BT44 . . . . . **48** D7
Greenan❶
Antrim BT41 . . . . **107** C5
Ballycastle BT54 . . . . . . **19** D2
Greenan BT11 . . . . **149** F8
Greenan❶ BT47 . . . . **36** B4
Greenane Cres BT10 . . . . **150** A5
Greenane Dr BT10 . . . . . . **150** A5
Greenan Rd
Antrim BT41 . . . . **107** C3
Ballycastle BT54 . . . . . . **19** C3
Greenavon Mews BT27 . . . **170** C8
Greenaway Dr BT52 . . . . . **174** D5
Greenbank
Carrickfergus BT38 . . . . **130** F8
Lisburn BT28 . . . . **160** B5
Greenburn Way BT27 . . . . **160** C7
Green Castle❶ BT36 . . . . **137** D8
Greencastle Cl BT36 . . . . **137** E7
Greencastle Pl BT15 . . . . **137** E7
Green Cres BT5 . . . . **146** A4
Green Dr BT40 . . . . **182** A6
Greenedge Ct ❶ BT38 . . . **131** B8
Green End BT37 . . . . **133** F4
Greenfield❶ BT51 . . . . . . **42** B6
Greenfield Pk BT47 . . . . . **177** F5
Greenfield Rd BT42 . . . . . **94** F5
Greenfields BT41 . . . . **108** A8
Greengage Cotts BT53 . . . **175** E5
Greengage La BT53 . . . . . **175** E5
Greenhall Highway BT51 . . **174** A3
Greenhall Manor BT51 . . . **174** A2
Greenhaven (Cuan Glas)
BT47 . . . . **55** D1
Greenhaw Ave BT48 . . . . **176** F3
Greenhaw Prim Sch
BT48 . . . . **176** F3
Greenhaw Rd BT48 . . . . . **177** A3
Greenhill❶ BT42 . . . . **80** B1
Greenhill Dr BT53 . . . . . . **175** C6
Greenhill Gdns BT36 . . . . **133** A6
Greenhill La BT14 . . . . . . **136** C3
Greenhill Pk
Coleraine BT51 . . . . . . **174** A5
Newtownabbey BT36 . . . **133** A6
Greenhill Rd
Ballymoney BT53 . . . . . **175** C7
Belfast BT14 . . . . **119** A2
Coleraine BT51 . . . . . . **174** A5
Newtownabbey BT36 . . . **133** A6
Greenisland Golf Club
BT38 . . . . **129** E5

GREENISLAND (INIS GLAS)
BT38 . . . . **129** F3
Greenisland Prim Sch
BT38 . . . . **129** E4
Greenisland Sta BT38 . . . . **129** E4
Green La BT27 . . . . **160** E5
Greenland❶ BT40 . . . . . . **182** B6
Greenland Cres BT40 . . . . **182** D6
Greenland Ct BT40 . . . . . **182** C5
Greenland Dr BT40 . . . . . **182** D5
Greenland Gdns BT40 . . . . **182** D6
Greenland Gr BT40 . . . . . **182** D6
Greenland Parade BT40 . . **182** A4
Greenland Rd BT40 . . . . . **182** C5
Greenland St BT13 . . . . . . **188** C4
Greenlea Gdns ❶ BT5 . . . **146** A1
Green Link
Larne BT40 . . . . **182** A6
Newtownabbey BT37 . . . **129** D1
Greenmill BT41 . . . . **187** B1
Greenmont Rd BT41 . . . . . **186** D1
Green Mound★ BT29 . . . . **121** E5
Green Mount ❸ BT5 . . . . **146** A1
Greenmount Ave
Ballymena BT43 . . . . . . **181** D5
❷❶ Coleraine BT51 . . . . **26** A7
Greenmount Campus
BT41 . . . . **109** B1
Greenmount Cres ❷ BT51 **25** F7
Greenmount Dr ❸ BT51 . . **25** F7
Greenmount Gdns
❷ Claudy BT47 . . . . **69** B8
Lisburn BT27 . . . . **170** C8
Greenmount Pk BT27 . . . . **170** C8
Greenmount Pl
❸ Ballymena BT43 . . . . **181** D5
❶❸ Belfast BT15 . . . . . **144** D8
Greenmount Rd
❶ Coleraine BT51 . . . . . **25** F7
Coleraine BT51 . . . . . . **174** A1
Greenmount Terr ❹
BT43 . . . . **181** D5
Greenore St BT5 . . . . **145** B3
Greenpark Ct BT41 . . . . . **186** C2
Greenpark Dr BT41 . . . . . **186** C2
Greenpark Gdns BT41 . . . **186** C2
Green Pastures BT8 . . . . . **163** C1
Green Pk BT38 . . . . **125** A1
Green Rd
Ballyclare BT39 . . . . . . **184** E4
Belfast BT5 . . . . **146** A4
Lisburn BT27 . . . . **170** D2
Londonderry BT47 . . . . . **51** F6
Green Rd Lower BT51 . . . . **25** C8
Green Rd Upper BT51 . . . . **13** E3
Greenshields Lower❶
BT53 . . . . **28** B4
Greenshields Upper❶
BT53 . . . . **28** C3
Green St BT38 . . . . **131** C8
Green The
Dunmurry BT17 . . . . . . **150** A3
Holywood BT18 . . . . . . **139** C5
Lisburn BT28 . . . . **159** F1
Maghera BT46 . . . . **74** F5
Greenvale BT41 . . . . **180** E3
Green Vale BT27 . . . . **161** B5
Greenvale Ave BT41 . . . . **186** E3
Greenvale Commercial Pk
BT80 . . . . **185** B3
Greenvale Dr
❷ Antrim BT41 . . . . **186** E3
Cookstown BT80 . . . . . **185** C4
Greenvale Gr ❶ BT41 . . . **186** E3
Greenvale Leisure Ctr
BT45 . . . . **183** D5
Greenvale Manor Ave
BT41 . . . . **186** E3
Greenvale Manor Cl
BT41 . . . . **186** E2
Greenvale Manor Ct
BT41 . . . . **186** E3
Greenvale Manor Gdns
BT41 . . . . **186** E2
Greenvale Manor Mews
BT41 . . . . **186** E2
Greenvale Pk
Antrim BT41 . . . . **186** E2
Magherafelt BT45 . . . . . **183** D4
Greenvale Pk Dale BT41 . . **186** F3
Greenvale Pk Glen BT41 . **186** F3
Greenvale Pk Lands
BT41 . . . . **186** F2
Greenvale Pk View BT41 **186** E2
Greenvale Pk Wood
BT41 . . . . **186** F2
Greenvale Rd BT41 . . . . . **186** E2
Greenvale St BT43 . . . . . **181** D4
Greenview BT43 . . . . **181** D6
Green View BT39 . . . . . . **110** C5
Greenview Ave BT41 . . . . **186** D2
Greenview Ct BT39 . . . . . **184** E5
Greenview Dr BT39 . . . . . **184** E5
Greenview Pk BT9 . . . . . . **150** F4
Greenview Pl BT41 . . . . . **186** D2
Greenview Way BT41 . . . . **186** D2
Greenville❶ BT53 . . . . . . **175** F6
Greenville Ave
Ballymoney BT53 . . . . . **175** E5
❶ Belfast BT5 . . . . **145** D4
Greenville Rd BT5 . . . . . . **145** C4
Greenville St BT5 . . . . . . **145** C4
Greenway BT6 . . . . **152** C8
Green Way BT40 . . . . **182** A5
Green Way Ave BT40 . . . . **182** A6
Green Wlk BT37 . . . . **133** F3

Greenwood
Lisburn BT27 . . . . **170** C8
Londonderry BT48 . . . . . **177** F8
Greenwood Ave
Ballyclare BT39 . . . . . . **184** E4
Belfast BT4 . . . . **146** A5
Prehen BT47 . . . . **178** C1
Greenwood Glen BT8 . . . . **151** F1
Greenwood Hill BT8 . . . . . **151** F1
Greenwood Pk
Ballymena BT44 . . . . . . **60** C4
❹ Belfast BT4 . . . . **146** A5
Carrickfergus BT38 . . . . **125** C3
Greenwood Prim Sch
BT4 . . . . **146** A5
Greer Pk Ave BT8 . . . . . . **151** E1
Greer Pk Dr BT8 . . . . **151** F1
Greer Pk Hts BT8 . . . . . . **151** F1
Greerstown or Cloghore❶
BT47 . . . . **51** A4
Gregg Gdns BT45 . . . . . . **91** F5
Gregg St Mews BT27 . . . . **160** C1
Greggs Quay BT5 . . . . . . **189** C3
Gregg St BT27 . . . . **160** C1
Gresham St BT1 . . . . **189** A4
Gresteel Beg❶ BT47 . . . . **37** B5
Gresteel More❶ BT47 . . . **37** C6
Greyabbey Gdns BT37 . . . **128** F1
Greycastle Manor BT6 . . . **152** F7
Grey Man's Well★ BT54 . . **9** E6
Greymount Cres BT47 . . . **179** D5
Greymount Rd BT53 . . . . . **43** F3
GREYSTEEL BT47 . . . . . . **37** C5
Greystone Cres BT53 . . . . **28** B8
Greystone Link BT41 . . . . **187** B3
Greystone Pk
Coleraine BT51 . . . . . . **174** B6
❶ Limavady BT49 . . . . . **180** C4
Greystone Prim Sch
BT41 . . . . **187** B3
Greystone Rd
Antrim BT41 . . . . **187** A3
Limavady BT49 . . . . . . **180** D5
Greystone Sh Mall BT41 . **187** B4
Greystown Ave BT9 . . . . . **150** D3
Greystown Cl BT28 . . . . . **166** F8
Greystown Pk BT10 . . . . . **150** D3
Grianan Ailigh★ **34** A4
Griffith Pk BT18 . . . . **177** B4
Grillagh BT46 . . . . **74** D4
Grillagh Hill BT46 . . . . **74** D4
Grillagh Rd BT46 . . . . **74** C5
Grillagh Wy BT6 . . . . **152** B8
Groarty Prim Sch BT48 . . . **176** B3
Groarty Rd BT48 . . . . **176** B3
Groganstown Rd BT17 . . . **148** F5
Groggan❶ BT41 . . . . **93** D2
Groggan Prim Sch BT41 . . **93** D2
Groggan Rd BT41 . . . . . . **93** C2
Groomsport St BT14 . . . . **144** B8
Grosvenor Ct BT12 . . . . . **188** B2
Grosvenor Gram Sch
BT5 . . . . **145** E2
Grosvenor Rd BT12 . . . . . **188** C2
Grosvenor Recn Ctr
BT12 . . . . **188** B2
Grousehill Pk BT40 . . . . . **179** B2
Grovefield Pl ❾ BT5 . . . . **145** A4
Grovefield St ❼ BT6 . . . . **145** A4
Grove Hts BT41 . . . . **181** A7
Grove L St BT15 . . . . **137** E1
Grovelea BT67 . . . . **155** C3
Grove Manor BT43 . . . . . **181** A7
Grovemount Ct BT47 . . . . **179** D2
Grovemount Pk BT47 . . . . **179** D2
Grove Pk
Ballymoney BT53 . . . . . **27** B2
Hillsborough BT26 . . . . **169** B1
Grove Pl
❹ Belfast BT15 . . . . . . **137** E1
Londonderry BT48 . . . . . **178** F4
Grove Prim Sch BT15 . . . **137** E2
Grove Rd
Ballymena BT43 . . . . . . **181** B7
Belfast BT29 . . . . **118** C5
Coleraine BT51 . . . . . . **58** C4
Grove St E BT5 . . . . **145** C3
Grovesend Gdns BT52 . . . **174** E7
Grove St BT27 . . . . **160** D2
Grove Terr BT46 . . . . **74** D1
Grove The
Holywood BT18 . . . . . . **139** D5
Lisburn BT27 . . . . **170** E4
Grove Tree N BT12 . . . . . **188** B3
Grove Tree S BT12 . . . . . **188** B2
Grove View BT29 . . . . . . **117** D5
Grove View❶ BT51 . . . . . **58** C7
Gruig❶ BT44 . . . . **32** B7
Gruig La BT44 . . . . **46** B4
Guasson Villas ❶ BT45 . . **105** C3
Guildhall St ❺ BT48 . . . . **178** F5
Gulf Rd BT53 . . . . **52** E2
Gulladuff❶ BT45 . . . . **90** F8
GULLADUFF BT45 . . . . . . **91** A8
Gulladuff Hill BT45 . . . . . . **90** F8
Gulladuff Rd
Maghera BT46 . . . . **90** D8
Magherafelt BT45 . . . . . **91** C7
Gunnel Hill BT36 . . . . . . **133** D1
Gweebarra Pk BT48 . . . . **176** C1
Gweedore Cres BT11 . . . . **149** E7
Gweedore Gdns BT11 . . . . **149** E7
Gweedore Pk BT11 . . . . . **149** D7

Haddington Gdns BT6 . . . **145** B1
Haddington Hill BT28 . . . . **159** C5
Haddockstown Rd BT28 . . **156** A7
Haig St BT5 . . . . **145** B2
Halcombe St ❷⓿ BT6 . . . **145** A4
Halfgayne❶ BT46 . . . . . . **74** B6
Halfgayne Rd BT46 . . . . . **74** B4
Halfpenny Gate Rd BT67 . **167** C3
Halftown❶ BT39 . . . . **96** B1
Halftown Rd BT27 . . . . . . **169** A5
Half Umry Balloo❶
BT41 . . . . **186** C3
Hallcourt Pk BT41 . . . . . . **186** F6
Hall Cres ❶ BT46 . . . . . . **74** D1
Halliday's Rd ❾ BT15 . . . **144** C8
Hall La
Londonderry BT47 . . . . . **51** F5
Magherafelt BT45 . . . . . **91** A8
Hall Rd BT52 . . . . **26** D8
Hall St BT46 . . . . **74** D1
Hallstown Rd BT28 . . . . . **157** B3
Halstein Dr BT5 . . . . **145** F4
Hambleden BT27 . . . . . . **161** B6
Hamel Dr BT6 . . . . **152** C8
Hamill Glen ❶ BT11 . . . . **150** A8
Hamill Gr BT11 . . . . **150** A8
Hamill Pk BT11 . . . . **150** A8
Hamill St BT12 . . . . **188** C3
Hamillstown La BT44 . . . . **92** E8
Hamilton Gdns BT28 . . . . **159** C2
Hamilton Pk BT53 . . . . . . **175** D5
Hamilton Pl BT55 . . . . . . **173** E6
Hamilton Pl La BT55 . . . . **173** E6
Hamilton Rd BT3 . . . . **145** B7
Hamilton St BT2 . . . . **189** B2
Hamilton St BT39 . . . . . . **184** C7
Hamlet Gdns BT39 . . . . . **184** B7
Hamlet Gr BT39 . . . . **184** C7
Hamlets The BT4 . . . . . . **146** B5
Hamlet Way BT39 . . . . . . **184** C6
Hamlet Wlk BT39 . . . . . . **184** C7
Hammond Farm BT67 . . . **167** A4
Hammond Rd BT28 . . . . . **166** F8
Hammond St BT45 . . . . . **113** B8
Hampstead Ct BT48 . . . . **177** A2
Hampstead Pk BT48 . . . . **177** A3
Hampton Coll ❻ BT9 . . . . **144** C4
Hampton Cres
Larne BT40 . . . . **182** A4
Londonderry BT47 . . . . . **179** C5
Hampton Ct
Carrickfergus BT38 . . . . **124** C4
Holywood BT18 . . . . . . **139** F6
Newtownabbey BT37 . . . **129** A1
Hampton Ct Mews BT37 . **129** A1
Hampton Dr BT7 . . . . **151** E6
Hampton Gr ❶ BT7 . . . . . **151** E8
Hampton Manor BT7 . . . . **151** F6
Hampton Manor Dr BT7 . . **151** E6
Hampton Parade BT7 . . . . **151** E6
Hampton Pk BT7 . . . . **151** F6
Hampton Pl ❷ BT7 . . . . . **151** E6
Hampton Strand ❸ BT7 . . **151** E6
Hancock St BT27 . . . . . . **160** C1
Haneda Pk BT47 . . . . **179** C1
Hanna C ❶ BT53 . . . . . . **175** C4
Hannaghglen Hts BT17 . . **149** E8
Hannahstown❶ BT17 . . . . **142** C3
Hannahstown Bsns Pk
BT17 . . . . **149** D8
Hannahstown Hill BT17 . . **149** D8
Hannahstown Rd BT28 . . **148** C3
Hannas Rd BT40 . . . . **83** B3
Hanna St ❹ BT15 . . . . . . **144** E8
Hanover Pl BT52 . . . . . . **174** C3
Hanover Sq BT80 . . . . . . **114** C3
Harberton Ave BT9 . . . . . **150** F5
Harberton Dr BT9 . . . . . . **150** F5
Harberton Pk
Ballymena BT43 . . . . . . **181** B7
Belfast BT9 . . . . **150** F5
Londonderry BT47 . . . . . **179** C3
Harberton Specl Sch
BT9 . . . . **150** F4
Harbour Highway The
BT40 . . . . **182** A2
Harbour Mus★ BT48 . . . . **178** F6
Harbour Pl BT56 . . . . **172** B6
Harbour Rd
Ballycastle BT54 . . . . . . **7** B7
Carnlough BT44 . . . . . . **49** C2
Portrush BT56 . . . . **172** B6
Portstewart BT55 . . . . . **173** C7
Harcourt Dr BT14 . . . . . . **137** B1
Hardcastle St BT7 . . . . . . **189** A1
Hardinge Pl ❸ BT15 . . . . **144** C7
Harding Meml Prim Sch
BT6 . . . . **145** B2
Harding St ❽ BT48 . . . . . **178** E4
Harkness Gdns BT47 . . . . **179** C4
Harkness Parade BT4 . . . **145** C6
Harland Dr BT4 . . . . **145** A5
Harland Rd BT4 . . . . **145** D5
Harland Tech Pk BT3 . . . . **145** B6
Harland & Wolff Shipyard
BT3 . . . . **145** B7
Harleston St BT9 . . . . . . **151** D7
Harmin Ave BT36 . . . . . . **132** E5
Harmin Cres BT36 . . . . . **132** E5
Harmin Dr BT36 . . . . **132** E5
Harmin Parade BT36 . . . . **132** F5
Harmin Pk BT36 . . . . **132** E5
Harmony Ct BT27 . . . . . . **160** C4
Harmony Hill BT27 . . . . . **160** C4

Harmony Hill Prim Sch
BT27 . . . . . 160 C4
Harmony Prim Sch BT13 143 C8
Harmony St BT2 . . . . 189 A2
Harpers Quay 5 BT47 . . 179 A4
Harperstown La BT42 . . . 77 F7
Harper St (Sráid Harper) 24
BT5 . . . . . 145 A5
HarphallⓉ BT44 . . . . 48 F2
Harpur's HillⓉ BT52 . . . 174 E4
Harpurs Hill Prim Sch
BT52 . . . . . 174 E4
Harrier Way BT39 . . . . 184 C5
Harrowgate St 5 BT12 . . 143 F4
Harrow St 8 BT7 . . . . 144 E1
Harrybrook St BT13 . . . . 144 B7
Harry's Rd BT26 . . . . 169 C2
HARRYVILLE BT42 . . . . 181 D2
Harryville BT56 . . . . 172 B5
Harryville Pk BT27 . . . . 170 B7
Harryville Prim Sch
BT42 . . . . . 181 E3
Hartford Pk BT52 . . . . 174 D6
Hartington St BT7 . . . . 189 A1
Hartswood BT29 . . . . 117 A1
Hartwell Pl 11 BT15 . . . . 144 D8
Harvest Mdws BT47 . . . . 37 D3
Harvey Ct 3 BT5 . . . . 145 B5
Harvey St BT48 . . . . 178 E5
Harwood Gdns BT38 . . . . 125 C3
Harwood Pk BT38 . . . . 125 C2
HassⓉ BT47 . . . . 55 E2
Hass Pk BT47 . . . . 55 D2
Hass Rd BT47 . . . . 55 D2
Hatfield St BT7 . . . . 144 E2
Hatmore Pk BT48 . . . . 178 C8
Hatton Dr BT6 . . . . 145 B3
Haughey's Row BT57 . . . . 5 E2
Havana Way BT14 . . . . 137 A1
Havana Wlk BT14 . . . . 137 A1
Havelock Pl BT44 . . . . 49 C3
Havelock St BT7 . . . . 189 B1
Hawbank Pk BT53 . . . . 28 F7
Hawkinge Ave BT40 . . . . 182 E5
Hawkin St BT48 . . . . 178 F4
Hawkswood BT41 . . . . 187 C3
Haw Rd BT57 . . . . 16 B6
Hawthorn Ave BT38 . . . . 130 F8
Hawthorn Bsns Ctr BT12 151 A8
Hawthornden BT41 . . . . 187 D2
Hawthornden Dr BT4 . . . . 146 B6
Hawthornden Gdns 1
BT4 . . . . . 146 B6
Hawthornden Pk BT4 . . . 146 B5
Hawthornden Rd BT4 . . . 146 B5
Hawthornden Way BT4 . . 146 B6
Hawthorne Gr 3 BT40 . . . 99 C8
Hawthorne Hill BT40 . . . 182 B5
Hawthorne La BT28 . . . . 160 A3
Hawthorne Manor BT45 . . 113 F3
Hawthorne Rd BT37 . . . . 128 D2
Hawthornes The BT52 . . . 14 C4
Hawthorne Terr BT48 . . . 178 D7
Hawthorne Way BT39 . . . 184 B4
Hawthorn Glen BT17 . . . 149 C8
Hawthorn Gr BT38 . . . . 124 F1
Hawthorn Hill BT17 . . . . 149 D8
Hawthorn Manor BT8 . . . 163 C2
Hawthorn Pk
Ballymena BT43 . . . . 181 E7
Dunmurry BT17 . . . . 149 F1
8 Londonderry BT47 . . . . 37 C5
Hawthorn Pl BT52 . . . . 174 F5
Hawthorn St BT12 . . . . 188 A2
Hawthorns The
Belfast BT10 . . . . 150 B4
Londonderry BT48 . . . . 176 D3
Hawthorn Terr
Coleraine BT52 . . . . 174 D4
Dunloy BT44 . . . . 44 F4
Hawthorn View BT17 . . . 149 C8
Hayesbank Pk BT47 . . . . 179 A4
Haymarket Arc BT1 . . . . 189 A4
Haypark Ave
Belfast BT7 . . . . 151 E7
Drumahoe BT47 . . . . 179 F1
Haypark Gdns BT7 . . . . 151 E7
Haywood Ave BT7 . . . . 151 E8
Haywood Dr BT7 . . . . 144 E1
Hazel Ave BT17 . . . . 160 F8
Hazelbank Dr BT47 . . . . 179 E1
Hazelbank Gdns BT51 . . . 174 A2
Hazelbank Mews BT51 . . 174 B3
Hazelbank Prim Sch BT42 80 C8
Hazelbank Rd
Ballymena BT42 . . . . 80 D8
Coleraine BT51 . . . . 174 A2
Drumahoe BT47 . . . . 179 F1
Hazelbrook BT45 . . . . 183 E4
Hazelbrook Dr BT14 . . . . 136 D4
Hazelburn Rd BT36 . . . . 128 A2
Hazeldene Ave BT45 . . . . 183 B7
Hazeldene Dr
4 Bushmills BT57 . . . . 5 E3
Coleraine BT52 . . . . 174 D7
Hazeldene Pk
Lisburn BT28 . . . . 159 E1
Magherafelt BT45 . . . . 183 B7
Newtownabbey BT36 . . . . 133 C2
Hazelfield St BT13 . . . . 144 B7
Hazel Gr BT45 . . . . 89 E5
Hazel Pk BT55 . . . . 173 E5
Hazelwood Ave
Belfast BT17 . . . . 149 E5
Prehen BT47 . . . . 178 C1
Hazelwood Cres BT43 . . . 62 D1
Hazelwood Dr BT43 . . . . 78 F8
Hazelwood Integrated Coll
BT36 . . . . . 137 D7
Hazelwood Integrated Prim
Sch 1 BT36 . . . . 133 C1
Hazelwood Pk BT36 . . . . 133 C2
Headlands Ave BT53 . . . . 28 B3
HeadwoodⓉ BT40 . . . . 98 B7
HeaglesⓉ BT53 . . . . 27 B7
Heagles Rd BT53 . . . . 27 B6
Heathdor Dr BT40 . . . . 83 B8
Heatherbell St BT5 . . . . 145 C4
Heather Cl BT41 . . . . 187 B3
Heatherdale Pk BT40 . . . 182 C7
Heather Dr
8 Eglinton BT47 . . . . 36 E5
Newtownabbey BT37 . . . . 133 F5
Heatherlea Ave BT56 . . . 172 C5
Heatherlea Dr BT40 . . . . 182 C7
Heatherlea Pl BT53 . . . . 175 E4
Heather Pk
Ballyclare BT39 . . . . 184 C4
Newtownabbey BT37 . . . . 133 F5
Heather Rd BT48 . . . . 176 E5
Heather St BT13 . . . . 143 F7
Heatherton Rise BT40 . . . 182 C7
HeathertownⓉ BT44 . . . . 45 C1
Heather Way BT40 . . . . 182 C7
HeathfieldⓉ BT51 . . . . 42 B3
Heathfield BT48 . . . . 177 B4
Heathfield Ct BT14 . . . . 137 A1
Heathfield Rd BT47 . . . . 69 E8
Heath Lodge Ave BT13 . . 143 C6
Heath Lodge Dr BT13 . . . 143 C6
Heathmount BT56 . . . . 172 B5
Hebron Hgts BT53 . . . . 43 F3
Hector St BT1 . . . . 189 A4
Hedgelea Ave BT37 . . . . 129 A3
Hedgelea Gr BT37 . . . . 129 A3
Hedgelea La BT37 . . . . 129 A3
Hedgelea Manor BT37 . . . 129 A3
Hedgelea Pk BT37 . . . . 129 A3
Hedgelea Rd BT37 . . . . 129 A3
Hedingham BT67 . . . . 166 A3
Heichbrae Airt (Tullyard
Way) BT6 . . . . 152 E8
Helens Dr BT67 . . . . 155 C3
Helens Lea BT5 . . . . 146 D2
Helens Pk BT67 . . . . 155 C2
Helen St
9 Crumlin BT29 . . . . 117 B1
Londonderry BT48 . . . . 178 D6
Helenswood BT17 . . . . 149 E5
Helgor Pk BT4 . . . . 145 F7
Helgor Pk Mews BT4 . . . 145 F7
Hempsonvale BT49 . . . . 180 E4
Hemp St BT4 . . . . 145 C5
Henderson Ave BT15 . . . 137 B4
Henderson Ct BT4 . . . . 139 B2
Hendra Ct BT52 . . . . 174 F4
Hendra Pk BT52 . . . . 174 F4
Henly Ave BT38 . . . . 124 E2
Henly Cl BT38 . . . . 124 E2
Henly Dr BT38 . . . . 124 E2
Henly Gdns BT38 . . . . 124 E2
Henly Gr BT38 . . . . 124 E2
Henly Hts BT38 . . . . 124 E3
Henly Pk BT38 . . . . 124 E2
Henly Rd BT38 . . . . 124 E2
Henrietta St
Belfast BT2 . . . . 189 B2
Londonderry BT48 . . . . 178 E4
Henry Pl BT15 . . . . 144 C7
Henry St
Ballymena BT42 . . . . 181 D3
Ballymoney BT53 . . . . 175 D4
Belfast BT1 . . . . 189 A4
12 Londonderry BT48 . . . 178 E4
Henryville Ct BT39 . . . . 184 E6
Henryville Lodge BT39 . . 184 E6
Henryville Manor BT39 . . 184 E6
Henryville Mdws BT39 . . 184 D6
Herat St BT7 . . . . 144 E1
Herbert Ave BT40 . . . . 182 D5
Herbert St
Belfast BT14 . . . . 143 F8
Carnlough BT44 . . . . 49 C3
Londonderry BT47 . . . . 179 A3
Herbison Fields BT43 . . . 181 E7
Herbison Pk BT43 . . . . 181 E7
Herdman Channel Rd
BT3 . . . . . 138 A2
Heritage Twr Mus★
BT48 . . . . . 178 E4
Hermitage
Hillsborough BT26 . . . . 169 B1
Moira BT67 . . . . 166 B2
Hermitage The
Belfast BT17 . . . . 161 C6
1 Randalstown BT41 . . . . 107 F7
Heron Rd BT3 . . . . 138 E3
Heronshaw 1 BT57 . . . . 5 E3
Heron View BT3 . . . . 138 F4
Heron Way BT47 . . . . 179 B5
Hertford Cres BT28 . . . . 169 D8
Hertford Sq BT28 . . . . 169 E8
Hervey Hill Rd BT51 . . . . 59 A2
Hesketh Gdns BT14 . . . . 136 E1
Hesketh Pk BT14 . . . . 136 E1
Hesketh Rd BT14 . . . . 136 E1
Heston Dr BT38 . . . . 124 F3
Hewitt Par BT5 . . . . 145 F4
Hewitt Rd BT48 . . . . 176 B3
Hezlett House★ BT51 . . . 13 B3
Hezlett Prim Sch BT51 . . . 13 B3
Higgins Ct BT38 . . . . 125 F2
Higginson's La BT40 . . . . 84 C3
Highburn Cres BT13 . . . . 143 D6
Highburn Gdns BT13 . . . . 143 D6
Highbury Gdns BT14 . . . . 136 F1
Highcairn Dr BT13 . . . . 143 D6
Highcliff Gdns BT13 . . . . 143 D6
Highdene Gdns BT13 . . . . 143 D6
Highfern Gdns BT13 . . . . 143 D6
Highfield Cres BT45 . . . . 183 C5
Highfield Dr
Belfast BT13 . . . . 143 D6
Coleraine BT51 . . . . 25 F7
Highfield Rd BT45 . . . . 183 C5
Highfields Ave BT28 . . . . 159 F5
Highfields Cl BT28 . . . . 159 F5
Highfields Cres BT28 . . . 159 F5
Highfields Ct BT28 . . . . 159 F5
Highfields Gr BT28 . . . . 159 F5
Highfields Pk BT28 . . . . 159 F5
Highfields Rd BT28 . . . . 159 F5
High Gate BT13 . . . . 143 D6
Highgate Cl 4 BT36 . . . . 119 C7
Highgate Dr 5 BT36 . . . . 119 C7
Highgate Manor 1
BT36 . . . . . 119 C7
Highgreen BT13 . . . . 143 D6
Highgrove BT27 . . . . 170 B2
Highgrove Ave BT39 . . . . 184 A4
Highgrove Ct BT39 . . . . 184 A4
Highgrove Dr BT39 . . . . 184 A4
Highland Par BT13 . . . . 143 D6
Highland Rd BT49 . . . . 38 D5
HighlandtownⓉ BT44 . . . . 49 C5
High Link BT13 . . . . 143 D5
HighmoorⓉ BT47 . . . . 52 E7
Highmoor Cross Roads
BT47 . . . . . 52 E8
Highmoor Rd BT47 . . . . 52 C7
Highpark Cres BT13 . . . . 143 D5
Highpark Cross BT13 . . . 143 D5
Highpark Dr BT13 . . . . 143 D6
High Pass BT13 . . . . 143 D5
High Pk BT48 . . . . 178 B3
High Rd BT56 . . . . 172 B6
High St Ct BT1 . . . . 189 B3
High Side BT13 . . . . 143 D5
High St
Antrim BT41 . . . . 186 D4
Ballymoney BT53 . . . . 175 C4
Belfast BT1 . . . . 189 B3
Carnlough BT44 . . . . 49 C2
Carrickfergus BT38 . . . . 131 A7
Cushendall BT44 . . . . 32 D4
8 Draperstown BT45 . . . . 89 A3
Holywood BT18 . . . . 139 D6
Larne BT40 . . . . 182 C4
Londonderry BT48 . . . . 178 E5
5 Moneymore BT45 . . . . 113 E8
Newtownabbey BT36 . . . . 137 E8
HightownⓉ BT40 . . . . 98 B8
Hightown Ave BT36 . . . . 132 C5
Hightown Cres BT36 . . . . 132 E4
Hightown Ct 2 BT36 . . . . 132 F5
Hightown Dr BT36 . . . . 132 E4
Hightown Gdns BT36 . . . . 132 E4
Hightown Industral Est
BT36 . . . . . 132 D5
Hightown Pk BT36 . . . . 132 E4
Hightown Rd BT36 . . . . 132 D4
Hightown Rise BT36 . . . . 132 E4
Highvale Gdns BT13 . . . . 143 D6
Highview Cres BT13 . . . . 143 D6
High Way BT13 . . . . 143 D6
HildenⓉ BT27 . . . . 160 D3
Hilden Brewery★ BT27 . . 160 D3
Hilden Cres BT27 . . . . 160 D2
Hilden Ct BT27 . . . . 160 D3
Hilden Integrated Prim Sch
BT27 . . . . . 160 E3
Hilden Rd BT27 . . . . 160 E4
Hilden Sta BT27 . . . . 160 D4
Hillburn Pk BT6 . . . . 152 D8
Hillcrest BT41 . . . . 187 A4
HillcrestⓉ BT47 . . . . 36 A4
Hillcrest Ave BT51 . . . . 174 B2
Hillcrest Cres BT36 . . . . 133 E7
Hillcrest Dr BT36 . . . . 133 E7
Hillcrest Gdns
Ballymoney BT53 . . . . 28 D2
Belfast BT5 . . . . 145 E4
Hillcrest Pk
1 Lisburn BT28 . . . . 159 E4
Newtownabbey BT36 . . . . 133 E7
Hillcrest Rd BT41 . . . . 117 E8
Hillcrest Villas BT37 . . . . 133 F7
Hill Croft Sch 1 BT37 . . . 133 F5
Hill Dr 3 BT36 . . . . 111 F1
Hillfoot St BT4 . . . . 145 D6
Hillfort Rd BT48 . . . . 176 A1
Hill Gn BT8 . . . . 152 B2
HILLHALL BT27 . . . . 160 F1
HillhallⓉ BT27 . . . . 161 C2
Hillhall Cl 5 BT27 . . . . 160 D1
Hillhall Gdns BT27 . . . . 160 D1
Hillhall Pk BT27 . . . . 160 D1
Hillhall Prim Sch BT27 . . 161 B1
Hillhall Rd BT27 . . . . 160 E1
Hillhampton BT47 . . . . 179 D6
HillheadⓉ BT44 . . . . 44 D5
Hill HeadⓉ BT51 . . . . 59 A5
HILL HEAD BT45 . . . . 91 D3
Hillhead Ave BT11 . . . . 150 A7
Hillhead Cotts
Antrim BT41 . . . . 91 F1
Belfast BT11 . . . . 150 A7
Hillhead Cres BT11 . . . . 150 A6
Hillhead Ct
Belfast BT11 . . . . 150 A7
3 Cullybackey BT42 . . . . 77 F6
Hillhead Dr BT11 . . . . 150 A6
Hillhead Hts 3 BT11 . . . . 150 A7
Hillhead Pk
Belfast BT11 . . . . 150 A7
Magherafelt BT45 . . . . 91 D2
Hillhead Rd
Antrim BT41 . . . . 106 B8
Ballyclare BT39 . . . . 184 E2
Belfast BT29 . . . . 147 A4
Carrickfergus BT38 . . . . 100 A4
Coleraine BT51 . . . . 58 F5
Lisburn BT28 . . . . 121 A1
Londonderry BT47 . . . . 55 A7
Magherafelt BT45 . . . . 105 F8
Hillhead Terr BT45 . . . . 91 D2
Hillman Cl 8 BT15 . . . . 144 D8
Hillman's Fancy BT52 . . . 174 D4
Hillman St 9 BT15 . . . . 144 D8
Hillman's Way BT52 . . . . 174 E4
Hillmount Ave BT39 . . . . 184 B5
Hillmount Cres BT45 . . . . 89 E5
Hillmount Ct BT10 . . . . 150 D3
Hillmount Gdns BT10 . . . 150 D3
Hillmount Rd BT42 . . . . 77 E8
Hill St Mews BT18 . . . . 139 D7
Hills Ave BT4 . . . . 145 D6
Hillsborough Bypass
BT27 . . . . . 169 E3
Hillsborough Dr BT6 . . . 145 C3
Hillsborough Gdns BT6 . . 145 C3
Hillsborough Old Rd
BT27 . . . . . 170 A6
Hillsborough Par BT6 . . . 145 C2
Hillsborough Rd
Belfast BT8 . . . . 163 B1
Craigavon BT67 . . . . 167 A2
Hillsborough BT26 . . . . 169 E1
Lisburn BT28 . . . . 170 A6
Moira BT67 . . . . 166 D2
Hillsbrough Rd 2 BT28 . . 160 A1
Hillside
Antrim BT41 . . . . 186 D2
Dunloy BT44 . . . . 44 F3
Portrush BT56 . . . . 172 B6
Hillside Ave BT44 . . . . 44 F3
Hillside Cres
Belfast BT9 . . . . 151 C6
Coleraine BT51 . . . . 174 B5
Lisburn BT28 . . . . 159 F2
Hillside Ct BT43 . . . . 181 A5
Hillside Dr
Ballymena BT43 . . . . 181 A6
Belfast BT9 . . . . 151 C6
Hillside Gdns
Belfast BT9 . . . . 151 C6
Lisburn BT28 . . . . 159 F2
Hillside Pk
Ballymena BT43 . . . . 181 A5
Belfast BT9 . . . . 151 C6
Dunloy BT44 . . . . 44 F3
1 Whitehead BT38 . . . . 100 D1
Hillside Rd
Ballycastle BT54 . . . . 18 D6
Ballymoney BT53 . . . . 18 B3
Coleraine BT51 . . . . 57 A6
Maghera BT46 . . . . 74 E6
Hillside Rise BT38 . . . . 100 D1
Hillside Terr BT26 . . . . 169 B2
Hillside View BT36 . . . . 133 E8
Hill St
Ballymena BT43 . . . . 181 D5
Belfast BT1 . . . . 189 B4
7 Crumlin BT29 . . . . 117 B1
5 Dunmurry BT17 . . . . 150 A2
Lisburn BT28 . . . . 170 B8
Hill The
Belfast BT10 . . . . 150 C3
Portrush BT56 . . . . 172 B6
Hillview Ave
Ballymoney BT53 . . . . 175 D5
Belfast BT5 . . . . 145 F4
Carrickfergus BT38 . . . . 124 D3
Lisburn BT27 . . . . 160 C5
Newtownabbey BT37 . . . . 133 F6
Prehen BT47 . . . . 178 D1
Hillview Ave W BT37 . . . 133 F6
Hillview Cres
Carrickfergus BT38 . . . . 124 D3
Larne BT40 . . . . 182 B3
Hillview Ct
6 Belfast BT14 . . . . 144 B8
Carrickfergus BT38 . . . . 124 D3
Hillview Dr
Carrickfergus BT38 . . . . 124 D3
Newtownabbey BT36 . . . . 132 F6
Hillview Ent Pk BT14 . . . 144 B8
Hillview Gdns
Carrickfergus BT38 . . . . 124 D3
Lisburn BT27 . . . . 160 C6
Hillview Gn BT38 . . . . 124 D3
Hillview Gr BT38 . . . . 124 D3
Hillview Pk
Ballymena BT44 . . . . 49 C1
Coleraine BT51 . . . . 174 A3
Dunloy BT44 . . . . 44 F4
Lisburn BT27 . . . . 160 C5
Newtownabbey BT36 . . . . 132 F6
Hillview Pl BT18 . . . . 139 E6
Hillview Rd
Belfast BT14 . . . . 144 B8
Carrickfergus BT38 . . . . 124 D3
Hillview Ret Pk BT14 . . . 144 A8
Hilton Ct BT44 . . . . 76 E5
Hilton Pk BT44 . . . . 76 E5
Hiltonstown Rd BT44 . . . . 77 A5
Hindsdale Pk BT6 . . . . 152 C7
Hinton Pk BT47 . . . . 179 B6
Hogarth St BT15 . . . . 144 D8
Holborn Hall BT27 . . . . 170 E7
HolestoneⓉ BT39 . . . . 110 E6
Holestone Cross Roads
BT39 . . . . . 110 E7
Holestone Rd BT39 . . . . 110 E7
Holland Cres BT5 . . . . 145 F4
Holland Dr BT5 . . . . 145 F4
Holland Gdns BT5 . . . . 145 F4
Holland Pk
Ballymena BT43 . . . . 181 D6
Belfast BT5 . . . . 145 F4
Hollies The BT38 . . . . 124 E1
Hollowburn Rd BT41 . . . . 187 B2
Hollow Rd BT40 . . . . 84 C1
Hollow Rd The BT67 . . . . 155 B4
Hollow The 6 BT42 . . . . 78 C4
Hollybank Bsns Pk BT39 110 D5
Hollybank Ct BT37 . . . . 128 F1
Hollybank Dr BT37 . . . . 133 F8
Hollybank Pk
Ballymena BT42 . . . . 181 D1
Newtownabbey BT37 . . . . 133 F8
Hollybank Prim Sch
BT37 . . . . . 128 F1
Hollybank Rd BT39 . . . . 110 C7
Hollybank Way BT37 . . . . 134 A8
Hollybrook
Ballymoney BT53 . . . . 43 C8
Craigavon BT67 . . . . 155 C3
Hollybrook Ave BT36 . . . . 132 D4
Hollybrook Cres BT36 . . . 132 C4
Hollybrook Ct BT36 . . . . 132 D4
Hollybrook Gdns BT36 . . . 132 D4
Hollybrook Gr BT36 . . . . 132 D4
Hollybrook Grange BT36 132 D4
Hollybrook Hts BT36 . . . 132 D3
Hollybrook Manor BT36 . 132 D4
Hollybrook Pk BT36 . . . . 132 D4
Hollybrook Rd
Antrim BT41 . . . . 94 A1
Newtownabbey BT36 . . . . 132 D4
Holly Bsns Pk BT11 . . . . 150 D8
Hollyburn BT28 . . . . 159 C3
Hollybush Gdns BT39 . . . 184 E5
Hollybush Prim Sch BT48 35 F8
Hollycroft Ave BT5 . . . . 145 D4
Hollygate Ave BT8 . . . . 163 D3
Hollygate Pk BT8 . . . . 163 D3
Hollyhall Rd BT48 . . . . 178 B6
Hollyhill Rd BT80 . . . . 112 D5
Holly La BT36 . . . . 132 D8
Holly Manor BT36 . . . . 132 D4
Hollymount
Belfast BT10 . . . . 150 D3
Dunmurry BT17 . . . . 160 F8
Hollymount Ct BT10 . . . . 150 D3
Hollymount Pk BT47 . . . . 179 A2
Hollyoaks BT47 . . . . 178 C1
Hollyvale 6 BT36 . . . . 128 A2
Hollywood Ave BT47 . . . . 179 C2
Holmdene Gdns BT14 . . . 136 F1
Holmes Ct BT2 . . . . 189 B2
Holmes St BT2 . . . . 189 A2
Holmlea Pk 10 BT47 . . . . 55 D2
Holybank 2 BT41 . . . . 107 F7
Holy Child Prim Sch
BT48 . . . . . 178 C5
Holy Child Prim Schools
BT11 . . . . . 150 C8
Holy Cross Boys' Prim Sch
BT14 . . . . . 143 F8
Holy Cross Girls Prim Sch
BT14 . . . . . 136 E2
Holy Family Prim Sch
Londonderry BT48 . . . . 176 C2
Magherafelt BT45 . . . . 183 E6
Holyrood BT9 . . . . 151 C8
Holy Rosary Prim Sch
BT7 . . . . . 151 E8
Holy Trinity Coll BT80 . . 185 C4
Holy Trinity Prim Sch
BT80 . . . . . 185 C4
Holy Trinity Prim Schools
BT11 . . . . . 143 B2
Holy WellⓉ BT41 . . . . 186 E8
Holy Well★ BT44 . . . . 76 E3
Holywell Hospl BT41 . . . 186 E8
HolywoodⓉ BT18 . . . . 139 E5
HOLYWOOD BT18 . . . . 139 E7
Holywood By-Pass BT18 139 D7
Holywood Golf Club
BT18 . . . . . 139 E5
Holywood Prim Sch
BT18 . . . . . 139 E7
Holywood Rd BT4 . . . . 145 D5
Holywood Sta BT18 . . . . 139 C7
Holywood Yacht Club
BT18 . . . . . 139 C7
Homefield PlaceⓉ BT57 . . . 4 F1
Homelands 2 BT41 . . . . 106 A8
Hood Ct BT41 . . . . 186 E5
Hopecroft BT29 . . . . 121 B5
Hopedene Ct BT4 . . . . 145 F5
Hopedene Mews BT4 . . . . 145 E5
Hopefield Ave
Belfast BT15 . . . . 137 B2
Portstewart BT55 . . . . 173 D5
Hopefield Cres BT55 . . . . 173 D5
Hopefield Ct 1 BT15 . . . . 137 C3
Hopefield Gdns BT55 . . . 173 E3
Hopefield Gr BT55 . . . . 173 E4
Hopefield Helipad BT52 . . 174 F1
Hopefield Pk BT55 . . . . 173 E3
Hopefield Rd BT55 . . . . 173 E3
Hope St
Ballymena BT43 . . . . 181 C4
Belfast BT12 . . . . 188 C2

Hope St *continued*
Larne BT40 . . . . 182 D3
Hopewell Ave BT13 . . . . . 144 B7
Hopewell Cres Link
BT13 . . . . 144 C7
Hopewell Pl BT13 . . . . . . 144 B7
Hopewell Sq BT13 . . . . . 144 C7
Horace St BT48 . . . . 178 F4
*Horizon House Childrens
Hospice* BT36 . . . . 133 B4
Hornbeam Rd BT17 . . . . 160 F7
Hornby Cres 21 BT4 . . . . 145 B5
Hornby Parade 22 BT5 . . 145 B5
Hornby St 17 BT4 . . . . . . 145 B5
Horn Dr BT11 . . . . 149 F6
Horse Pk Rd BT28 . . . . . 158 B5
Horse Pk The BT38 . . . . . 125 D1
Horseshoe BT14 . . . . 136 D4
Horseshoe Rd BT39 . . . . 111 D4
Hospital Rd
Belfast BT8 . . . . 162 D8
Castlereagh BT8 . . . . . 151 D1
Magherafelt BT45 . . . . 183 C7
Houston Cres 4 BT51 . . . . 58 A8
Houston Ct BT5 . . . . 145 F4
Houston Dr BT5 . . . . 145 E2
Houston Gdns BT5 . . . . . 145 E2
Houston Pk
Belfast BT5 . . . . 145 D2
Broughshane BT42 . . . . 79 C7
Houston Rd BT6 . . . . 153 C3
Howard Pl BT28 . . . . 160 A1
Howard St S BT7 . . . . . . 189 B1
Howard St BT12 . . . . 189 A2
Howe St BT13 . . . . 144 A7
Hoylake Pk BT14 . . . . . . 136 E3
Huey Cres 2 BT57 . . . . 5 E3
Hughenden Ave BT15 . . 137 B3
Hughes Ct BT6 . . . . 152 B8
*Hugh McPhelim O'Neill's
Tomb* ★ BT53 . . . . 30 F4
Hugh St BT9 . . . . 151 A8
Hugomont Ave BT43 . . . 181 E6
Hugomont Bsns Pk BT43 181 E6
Hugomont Dr BT43. . . . . 181 E6
Hugomont Pk BT43 . . . . 181 E6
Hugo St BT12 . . . . 143 E2
Huguenot Dr BT27 . . . . . 160 D2
Hulls La BT28 . . . . 169 B8
Humber Ct BT4 . . . . 145 B6
Hungry Hall 6 BT41 . . . . 187 D7
Hungry House La BT28 . . 147 B1
Hunterhouse Coll BT10. . 150 C3
Hunterlea 5 BT29 . . . . . . 117 A1
Hunter Pk BT12 . . . . 188 C1
Huntersbuoy BT40 . . . . . 182 B7
Hunters Glebe BT51 . . . . . 12 F2
Hunter's Glebe 1 BT51 . . . 12 F1
Hunters Pk BT45 . . . . 91 F6
Huntingdale BT39 . . . . . . 184 A4
Huntingdale Cres BT39 . 184 A3
Huntingdale Ct BT39 . . . 184 A3
Huntingdale Gn BT39 . . 184 A3
Huntingdale Gr BT39 . . . 184 A4
Huntingdale Grange
BT39 . . . . 184 A4
Huntingdale Lodge BT39 184 A4
Huntingdale Manor
BT39 . . . . 184 B4
Huntingdale Way BT39 . 184 A3
Hunt St BT4 . . . . 145 C5
Hurtletoot BT41 . . . . 187 D6
Hurtletoot Rd BT41 . . . . 187 E5
Huss Ct BT13 . . . . 188 B4
Huss Row BT13 . . . . 188 B4
Huston Rd BT36 . . . . 132 B5
Hutchinson St BT12 . . . . 188 C2
Hyacinth Ave BT49 . . . . . 38 C7
Hyde Bsns Pk BT48 . . . . 176 E1
Hydepark Cl BT36 . . . . . 132 A5
Hydepark Ind Est BT36 . 132 B6
Hydepark Industrial Est
BT36 . . . . 132 C6
Hydepark La BT36 . . . . . 119 C6
Hydepark Manor 2
BT36 . . . . 119 C7
Hydepark Rd BT36 . . . . 132 A4
Hyde Pk BT43 . . . . 181 D7
Hyndford St BT5 . . . . . . 145 C4
Iderown BT53. . . . . 17 C3

I

Ilford Ave BT6 . . . . 153 C3
Ilford Cres BT6 . . . . 153 C3
Ilford Dr BT6 . . . . 153 C3
Ilford Pk BT6 . . . . 153 B3
Ilford Rd BT6 . . . . 153 C3
Illanneyoon BT44 . . . . . . 44 E6
Illustrious Ct 3 BT41 . . 186 E5
Immaculate Conception Coll
BT47. . . . . 179 A2
Imperial Dr BT6. . . . . 145 A4
Imperial St BT6. . . . . 145 A3
Ina St BT4 . . . . 145 B6
Inchadoghill BT51 . . . . . 42 F6
Inchkeith Rd BT42 . . . . . 181 F3
Inchmarlo BT9. . . . . 151 A7
Inchmearing BT52 . . . . . 14 E5
Incholm Ave BT42 . . . . . 181 E3
Inch View BT48 . . . . 176 A1
Indiana Ave BT15 . . . . . 137 B3
India St BT7 . . . . 144 D2

Infirmary Rd BT48. . . . . . 178 E6
Ingledale Pk 3 BT14 . . . 136 E1
Ingledene 1 BT39 . . . . . 110 C2
Inglewood BT67 . . . . 164 B1
Inglewood Ave BT52 . . . . 26 B7
Inglewood Ct BT4 . . . . . 145 E7
Ingrams Rd BT28 . . . . . . 120 E5
Iniscarn BT45 . . . . 103 E6
Iniscarn Cl BT28 . . . . . . 159 E1
Iniscarn Cres BT48 . . . . 178 C5
Iniscarn Ct BT48 . . . . . . 178 C4
Iniscarn Pk BT28 . . . . . . 159 E1
Iniscarn Rd BT45. . . . . . . 103 F7
Inisconagher BT47 . . . . . 55 C6
INIS GLAS (GREENISLAND)
BT38 . . . . 129 F3
Inishgarry Pk BT41 . . . . 186 C5
Inishmore Cres BT11 . . . 150 A7
Inishmoyne Gn BT41 . . . 186 C5
Inishowen Cres BT56 . . . 172 C3
Inishowen Dr BT10. . . . . 150 E3
Inishowen Gdns BT48 . . 178 C6
Inishowen Pk
Ballymena BT43 . . . . . 181 A5
Portrush BT56 . . . . . . 172 C3
Inishrush BT44. . . . . 76 F5
INISHRUSH BT44. . . . . . . 76 A4
Inishrush Park (Mill Pk)
BT44. . . . . 76 A4
Inispollan BT44 . . . . 20 F1
Inisrush Rd BT44. . . . . . . 76 A4
Innis Ave BT37 . . . . 133 E4
Inniscarn BT37 . . . . 133 E5
Iniscarn Rd BT48 . . . . . 178 B4
Inniscoole Cl BT41 . . . . 186 C5
Inniscoole Pk BT36. . . . . 132 F6
Innisfayle Dr BT15 . . . . 137 D6
Innisfayle Gdns BT15 . . 137 D6
Innisfayle Pass BT15 . . . 137 D6
Innisfayle Pk
Belfast BT15 . . . . 137 B6
Lisburn BT28 . . . . 159 F2
Innisfayle Rd
Belfast BT15 . . . . 137 D6
Lisburn BT28 . . . . 159 F2
Innis Gdns BT28 . . . . . . 160 B4
Innisloughlin Rd BT67. . . 167 C2
Innis Pk BT37 . . . . 133 E4
Innisrush Gdns BT37 . . . 133 E4
Innis Wlk BT37. . . . . 133 E4
Inshaleen BT51 . . . . 42 B2
Inshamph BT43 . . . . 62 C4
Inshinagh BT53 . . . . 43 D7
Inshinagh La BT53 . . . . . 43 D8
Institution Pl BT12 . . . . 188 C3
Intake BT41. . . . . 106 B7
Intermediate Rd BT53 . . 175 E3
INVER BT40 . . . . 182 C3
Inverary Ave BT4. . . . . . 145 E8
Inverary Dr BT4. . . . . . . 145 E8
Inverary Hts BT40 . . . . . 182 C2
Inverary Rd BT40. . . . . . 182 C2
Inverary Valley BT40 . . . 182 C2
Inver Ave BT15. . . . . 137 B4
Inverbeg Ct BT40 . . . . . 182 B2
Inver Ct
Belfast BT4 . . . . 145 F4
Larne BT40 . . . . 182 C3
Inveresk Pk BT37 . . . . . 133 E4
Inver Gdn Mews BT40 . . 182 B3
Inver Hts BT40 . . . . 182 C2
Inverleith Dr BT40 . . . . . 145 E8
Invernook Dr BT4 . . . . . 145 E8
Invernook Pk BT4 . . . . . 145 E8
Inveroe Gdns BT48 . . . . 178 B4
Inver Pk BT18. . . . . 139 E5
Inver Rd BT40. . . . . 182 C3
Inver View BT40 . . . . . . 182 A3
Inverwood BT4 . . . . 145 E7
Inverwood Gdns BT4 . . . 145 F7
Iona Bsns & Enterprise Pk
BT48. . . . . 178 B3
Iona Ct
Coleraine BT52 . . . . . 174 D5
Londonderry BT48. . . . 178 D3
Iona Gdns
Ballymena BT42. . . . . 181 F3
Newtownabbey BT37. . 133 E4
Iona Pk
Londonderry BT48. . . . 178 D3
Newtownabbey BT37. . 133 E4
Iona Terr BT48. . . . . 179 A5
Ireton St BT7 . . . . 144 D2
Iris Cl BT12 . . . . 143 F4
Iris Ct BT12. . . . . 143 F4
Iris Dr
Belfast BT12 . . . . 143 F5
4 Belfast BT12. . . . . . 143 F4
Iris Gr BT12. . . . . 143 F4
Irish Gn St BT49 . . . . . . 180 B5
Irish Hill BT39 . . . . 122 C5
Irish Hill Rd
Ballyclare BT39 . . . . . 122 B2
Newtownabbey BT36. . 128 A8
Irish Omerbane BT44. . . 46 D3
Irish Quarter S BT38. . . . 131 A7
Irish Quarter W BT38. . . 131 A7
Irish Society's Prim Sch The
BT52. . . . . 174 C1
Irish St BT47. . . . . 179 A3
Irishtown BT41 . . . . 187 B6
Iris Mews BT12 . . . . 143 F4
Iris Terr BT48 . . . . 178 E4
Iris Wlk 1 BT12 . . . . . . 143 F4
Irragh BT54. . . . . 20 C2
Irragh La BT44. . . . . 20 D1

Irwell Ct BT12 . . . . 143 F3
Irwin Ave
Belfast BT4 . . . . 145 D5
Limavady BT49 . . . . . 180 B3
Irwin Cres
Belfast BT4 . . . . 145 E5
4 Claudy BT47. . . . . . 69 C8
Irwin Dr BT4. . . . . 145 D5
Irwinstown La BT28 . . . 121 B1
Isadore Ave BT13 . . . . . 143 E5
Ishlan Ct BT53 . . . . 175 B4
Islaharnan BT53 . . . . . . 29 D7
Islandahoe BT53 . . . . . . 16 C3
Islandarragh Rd BT54 . . 18 B6
Islandbane BT41 . . . . . . 187 E2
Islandbawn Dr
Antrim BT41 . . . . 187 B3
2 Belfast BT12. . . . . 143 F3
Islandbawn St 3 BT12 . 143 F3
Islandboy BT54 . . . . 7 D1
Islandboy Rd BT54 . . . . . 7 C1
Island Braddagh La BT57 . 5 A1
Island Carragh North
BT57. . . . . 15 F5
Island Carragh South
BT57. . . . . 15 F4
Island Civic Ctr Arts Centre ★
BT27. . . . . 160 C1
Island Effrick North
BT52. . . . . 14 F2
Island Effrick South
BT52. . . . . 15 A1
Island Flackey BT55 . . . 173 D1
Island – Heaghey BT52 . 14 F2
Island Kelly BT28 . . . . . 147 C5
Islandkelly Pk BT28 . . . 159 D5
Island MacAllan BT53 . . . 7 A1
Islandmagee Rd BT38 . . 100 D1
Islandmore BT53. . . . . . 28 F4
Islandmore Lower
BT55. . . . . 173 F2
Islandmore Upper BT52 14 F6
Islandnabracky BT43 . . 63 A7
Islandoo
Ballymoney BT53 . . . . 29 E7
Bushmills BT57 . . . . . . 6 A4
Island Pk BT38 . . . . 130 B3
Islandranny Rd BT57 . . . 6 D2
Island Rd
Ballycarry BT38. . . . . 100 B3
Ballymena BT42. . . . . 94 D4
Magherafelt BT45 . . . 90 C5
Island Rd Lower BT38 . . 100 B3
Islandreagh BT41 . . . . . 109 F2
Islandreagh Dr BT41 . . . 187 F1
Islandreagh Rd BT41 . . . 187 F1
Islandrose BT53. . . . . . . 16 D4
Islands of Carnmoon
BT57. . . . . 6 C2
Island St BT4 . . . . 145 B6
Islandstown BT43 . . . . . 62 E6
Islandstown Rd BT43 . . . 62 F5
Island Tasserty BT52 . . . 14 D5
Islandtasserty Rd BT52 . 14 D5
Island The BT45. . . . . . . 75 D2
Island Vardin BT52. . . . . 14 C5
Island View BT38 . . . . . 130 B4
Island Village BT40 . . . 100 D3
Islay St BT41 . . . . 186 D7
Isle Ct BT40 . . . . 182 C3
Islegorni BT44 . . . . 45 F5
Isle of Muck BT40 . . . . . 84 E3
Isle Rd
Bushmills BT57 . . . . . . 6 C2
Coleraine BT51 . . . . . 25 A5
Isles of Mount BT44 . . . 45 F5
Isles The BT41 . . . . 186 D6
Isoline St BT5. . . . . 145 C3
Issbawn or Upper
Gortnagross BT44 . . . 32 A2
Isthmus St BT6 . . . . 145 B4
Ivanhoe Ave BT8 . . . . . 163 D5
Ivan St
Belfast BT15 . . . . 137 E1
Lisburn BT28 . . . . 170 B8
Ivan Wilson Complex
BT51. . . . . 25 E6
Iveagh Cres BT12 . . . . . 143 F3
Iveagh Dr BT12 . . . . . . 143 F3
Iveagh Par BT12 . . . . . . 143 F3
Iveagh Pk
Greysteel BT47 . . . . . 37 C5
Prehen BT47 . . . . 178 C1
Iveagh St BT12. . . . . . . 143 F3
Iverna Cl BT12 . . . . 188 B1
Iverna St BT12 . . . . 188 B1
Ivy Ave BT82. . . . . 68 B4
Ivybank Rd BT45 . . . . . 113 C8
Ivy Hill BT28 . . . . 159 F8
Ivymead BT47. . . . . 179 D1
Ivy Terr BT48 . . . . 178 E4

J

Jackson Dr
Carrickfergus BT38 . . 125 E3
Magherafelt BT45 . . . . 90 F8
Jacksons Rd BT18. . . . . 139 C5
Jacquaeline Way BT48 . 178 D5
Jaffa St BT13 . . . . 144 B7
Jamaica Rd BT14 . . . . . 137 A1
Jamaica St BT14 . . . . . 136 F1
Jamaica Way BT14 . . . . 137 A1
James Craig Way 3
BT28 . . . . 159 D3
Jameson St BT7 . . . . . . 151 F8
James Pk BT41 . . . . . . 106 A8

James St S BT2 . . . . . . 189 A2
James St
Ballymena BT42 . . . . 181 D3
Coleraine BT52 . . . . . 174 D4
Cookstown BT80 . . . . 185 D5
Jane's Valley BT49 . . . . 180 E4
Jasmine Cnr 3 BT17 . . 149 D3
Jasmine Ct BT47 . . . . . 179 A3
Jasmine End 2 BT17 . . 149 D3
Jasmine Wlk BT17 . . . . 149 D3
Jeffrey Ave BT47 . . . . . 179 C6
Jellicoe Ave BT15 . . . . 137 D2
Jellicoe Dr
Belfast BT15 . . . . 137 D3
Holywood BT18 . . . . . 139 E6
Jellicoe Par BT15 . . . . . 137 D3
Jellicoe Pk 4 BT15 . . . 137 D3
Jenneys La BT28 . . . . . 157 F3
Jennings Dr BT37 . . . . . 128 F2
Jennings Pk BT37 . . . . . 128 F2
Jennymount St BT15 . . 137 E1
Jersey Ave BT27 . . . . . 160 B4
Jersey Pl 6 BT13 . . . . . 144 A7
Jerusalem St BT7 . . . . . 144 E2
Joanmount Dr BT14. . . . 136 F3
Joanmount Gdns BT14 . 136 F3
Joanmount Pk BT14 . . . 136 F3
Jocelyn Ave BT6 . . . . . . 145 B3
Jocelyn Gdns BT6 . . . . . 145 B3
Jocelyn St BT6 . . . . 145 A3
Jockeysquarter BT42. . . 81 B1
Joey Dunlop Leisure Ctr
BT53 . . . . 175 F2
John Field Pl BT48. . . . . 176 F2
John St
Ballymoney BT53 . . . . 175 C5
Belfast BT12 . . . . 188 C3
7 Randalstown BT41 . 108 A7
Johnston Cl BT43 . . . . 181 D7
Johnston Ct
Belfast BT5 . . . . 146 B4
Newtownabbey BT38. . 129 F3
Johnstone Cl BT38 . . . . 129 F3
Johnstone Rd BT12 . . . 188 A2
Johnston Pk BT29. . . . . 121 B5
Johnstonstown Rd BT43 62 D1
Johnston Way BT37 . . . 159 D3
Johnston Way BT37 . . . 159 D3
Jonesboro Pk BT5 . . . . 145 C3
Jordanstown Ave BT37 . 134 C8
Jordanstown Hts BT37 . 129 A2
Jordanstown Mews
BT37. . . . . 129 A1
Jordanstown Rd BT37 . . 134 C8
Jordanstown Rise BT37 . 129 A2
Jordanstown Sch BT37 . 129 C1
Jordanstown Sta BT37 . 129 B1
Josephine Ave BT49 . . . 180 B5
Josephine Terr BT49 . . . 180 B4
Joyce Ct 10 BT48 . . . . . 176 B2
Joymount BT38 . . . . . . 131 B8
Joy's Entry BT1 . . . . . . 189 B3
Joy St BT2 . . . . 189 B2
Jubilee Ave
Belfast BT15 . . . . 137 C2
Lisburn BT28 . . . . 169 F8
Jubilee Ct BT53 . . . . . . 175 C5
Jubilee Pk BT80 . . . . . . 185 D3
Jubilee Pl 1 BT28 . . . . 169 F8
Jubilee Rd
Belfast BT9 . . . . 144 B2
Maghera BT46 . . . . . . 75 A5
Jude St BT12 . . . . 188 B3
Judges Rd BT47 . . . . . . 177 F2
Julia St BT4 . . . . 145 B6
Junction One Outlet Ctr
BT41 . . . . 186 B7
Junction Rd
Antrim BT41. . . . . 108 D7
Ballyclare BT39 . . . . . . 98 A4
Juniper Ct 4 BT17 . . . . 149 D2
Juniper Pk
Dunmurry BT17 . . . . . 149 D2
Londonderry BT48. . . . 176 C1
Juniper Rise 5 BT17 . . 149 D2
Juniper St BT17 . . . . . . 149 D2
Juniper Way BT17 . . . . 149 D2
Jura St BT41 . . . . 186 D8

K

Kanestown La BT44 . . . . 65 B2
Kansas Ave BT15 . . . . . 137 B3
Kansas Ave Flats 2
BT15 . . . . 137 C3
Kashmir Rd BT13 . . . . . 188 A3
Kathleen Ct 9 BT5. . . . . 145 B5
Katrine Pk BT10 . . . . . . 150 D3
Kavanagh Ct 3 BT48. . . 176 B2
Keady
Limavady BT49 . . . . . 40 A8
Maghera BT46. . . . . . 74 F7
Keadycam BT79. . . . . . 87 B2
Keady Rd BT46. . . . . . 74 F7
Keadyville Ave BT15. . . 137 E2
Keady Way BT80 . . . . . 180 B5
Keans Hill Rd BT47 . . . . 36 C6
Keatley St 5 BT5. . . . . . 145 B5
Kebble BT54 . . . . 2 B6
Keeburn Ind Est BT38 . . 130 E8
Keeloges BT51 . . . . 26 F1
Keely BT51 . . . . 42 D7
Keely Gdns BT51 . . . . . 42 D7
Keenaght BT45 . . . . . . 103 D8
Keenaght Rd BT45 . . . . 103 D8
Kee Rd BT47 . . . . 36 E6
Keery Pk BT47 . . . . 50 D3
Keery Rd BT47 . . . . 50 D2

Kelburn Pk
7 Ballyclare BT39 . . . . 96 F1
Ballyclare BT39 . . . . . 110 F8
Kells Ave BT11 . . . . . . 149 F6
Kells & Connor Prim Sch
BT42 . . . . 95 A6
KELLS (NA CEALLA) BT42 . 95 A6
Kellswater Rd BT41 . . . . 94 B4
Kelvin Ct BT42 . . . . 181 A1
Kelvin Parade BT14 . . . 137 A2
Kemmil Hill Cl 5 BT41 . 107 F7
Kemmil Hill Gdns 6
BT41 . . . . 107 F7
Kemmil Hill Hts 7 BT41. 107 F7
Kemmil Hill Pk 4 BT41. . 107 F7
Kemp Pk BT54 . . . . 8 C4
Kenard Ave BT11. . . . . . 150 A8
Kenbaan Ct 5 BT5. . . . . 145 B4
Kenbaan St 6 BT5 . . . . 145 B4
Kenbane Ave BT52 . . . . 174 E7
Kenbane Cres BT42 . . . 181 A1
Kenbella Par BT15 . . . . 137 C3
Kendal St BT13 . . . . 188 B4
Kenilworth Ave BT28 . . 159 F5
Kenilworth Dr BT28 . . . 159 E5
Kenilworth Gr BT28 . . . 159 F5
Kenilworth Mews BT28. . 159 E5
Kenilworth Pk BT28. . . . 159 F5
Kenmara Pk BT54 . . . . . . 8 D4
Kenmare Pk
Belfast BT12 . . . . 188 C2
Londonderry BT48. . . . 176 C1
Kennedy Cl BT38 . . . . . 100 A2
Kennedy Dr BT27 . . . . . 160 B5
Kennedy Ctr BT11 . . . . 150 D8
Kennedy Pl 11 BT48 . . . 178 E4
Kennedy Sh Ctr BT11 . . 143 F1
Kennedy Way BT11 . . . 150 D8
Kennedy Way Ind Est
BT11 . . . . 150 E8
Kennel Bridge BT4 . . . . 146 B8
Kennelbridge Rd BT42 . . 79 B3
Kensington Ave BT5 . . . 145 C4
Kensington Cl BT27 . . . 170 C7
Kensington Ct BT5 . . . . 146 B3
Kensington Dr BT5. . . . . 146 C3
Kensington Gate BT5. . . 146 B2
Kensington Gdns BT5 . . 146 B2
Kensington Gdns S BT5. 146 B2
Kensington Gdns W BT5. 146 B2
Kensington Manor
Belfast BT5 . . . . 146 C2
15 Coleraine BT52. . . . 26 C7
Kensington Pk
Ballymena BT43. . . . . 181 D7
Belfast BT5 . . . . 146 B2
Lisburn BT27 . . . . 170 C8
Kensington Rd
Belfast BT5 . . . . 146 B2
Londonderry BT47. . . . 179 D5
Kensington St BT2 . . . . 189 A1
Kensingvale BT39 . . . . . 110 C4
Kent Ave BT40 . . . . 182 D5
Kent Ct BT41 . . . . 187 C5
Kenton Dr BT52 . . . . . . 174 D7
Kent St BT1 . . . . 189 A4
Kenvarra Pk BT52 . . . . 174 C6
Kernan Cl BT36 . . . . . . 133 D1
Kernan Dr 3 BT36. . . . . 133 D1
Kernyhill BT42. . . . . 96 B8
Kerohans La BT43. . . . . 181 D6
Kerrera Ct 2 BT14. . . . . 143 F8
Kerrera St 1 BT14. . . . . 143 F8
Kerrland Cres 3 BT5 . . 145 F4
Kerrsland Dr 1 BT5. . . . 145 F4
Kerrsland Mews BT5. . . 145 F4
Kerrsland Parade 2
BT5 . . . . 145 F4
Kerr St BT55 . . . . 173 C5
Kerryhill 20 BT42 . . . . . 78 C3
Kerrykeel Gdns BT11 . . 149 E7
Kerrymount Ave BT8 . . 152 B3
Kesh Rd BT27 . . . . 168 D3
Kestrel Grange BT17 . . 149 E5
Keswick St BT13 . . . . . 144 A7
Kew Gdns
Ballymena BT43. . . . . 181 D7
Castlereagh BT8 . . . . 152 B2
Kew Link BT43. . . . . . . 181 D7
Keylands Pl BT2 . . . . . . 189 A2
Kidds La BT28 . . . . 156 D4
Kilbeg Ct BT41. . . . . . . 186 F5
Kilbegs Bsns Pk BT41 . . 186 B8
Kilbegs Rd BT41 . . . . . 186 B8
Kilbeg Wlk BT41. . . . . . 187 A5
Kilbride BT39 . . . . 110 F8
Kilbride Central Prim Sch
BT39. . . . . 110 E8
Kilbride Cross Roads
BT39. . . . . 110 E9
Kilbride Gdns BT41 . . . 186 F4
Kilbride Gr 2 BT39 . . . . 110 F8
Kilbride Lodge 4 BT39. . 96 F1
Kilbride Rd BT39 . . . . . 110 F7
Kilbroney Bend BT6. . . . 152 C4
Kilburn Cres BT47. . . . . 179 C5
Kilburn St BT12. . . . . . . 188 A1
Kilcatten Rd BT47 . . . . . 68 F8
Kilcoan Beg BT40 . . . . 100 C7
Kilcoan More BT40. . . . 100 B8
Kilcoan Prim Sch BT40. . 100 C8
Kilcoobin BT57 . . . . 5 E4
Kilcoole Gdns BT14 . . . 136 F5
Kilcoole Pk BT14. . . . . . 136 F5
Kilcorig BT28 . . . . 158 D6
KILCORIG BT28 . . . . 158 C6
Kilcorig Rd BT28. . . . . . 158 C7

Kilcreen❶ BT47 . . . . 70 D2
Kilcreen Rd BT47 . . . . . . 70 D2
Kilcreeny❶ BT28 . . . . . 121 D2
Kilcreg❶ BT54 . . . . 8 D2
Kilcreg Pk BT54 . . . . 8 C3
Kilcronaghan Rd BT45 . . 89 F4
Kilcronagh Rd BT80 . . . 185 A1
Kilcross❶ BT28 . . . . . . 118 C4
Kilcross Rd BT29 . . . . . . 118 B5
Kilcrue Cross★ BT54 . . . . 8 A1
Kilculmagrandal❶ BT47 . 53 F1
Kilculmagrandal Rd BT47. 70 A7
Kilcurry❶ BT42 . . . . 92 F7
Kilcurry Rd BT44 . . . . . . 92 E7
Kildare St (Sráid Chill Dara)
 ❹ BT13 . . . . 188 C4
Kildoag❶ BT47 . . . . 68 C8
Kildoag Rd BT47 . . . . . . 68 C7
Kildollagh La BT52 . . . . . 26 D5
Kildowney❶ BT44 . . . . . . 61 E4
Kildowney Hill BT44. . . . . 61 D4
Kildowney Rd BT44 . . . . . 61 E5
Kildress Lower❶ BT80 . 112 C2
Kildress Upper❶ BT80 . . 112 C3
KILDRUM BT48 . . . . 50 B7
Kildrum Gdns BT48 . . . . 178 B3
Kildrum Lower❶ BT82 . . 50 A6
Kildrum Upper❶ BT82 . . 50 B8
Kileen (Dundonald)❶
 BT4 . . . . 146 D7
Kilfennan Link BT47. . . . 179 D5
KILFINNAN BT47. . . . . . 179 D5
Kilgad❶ BT42 . . . . 95 C8
Kilgad Cl ❷ BT42 . . . . . . 95 E8
Kilgad Rd BT42 . . . . 95 B7
Kilgavanagh❶ BT41. . . . 109 A8
Kilgavanagh Rd BT41. . . 109 A8
Kilgort❶ BT47 . . . . 69 E1
Kilgort Rd BT47 . . . . 69 E1
Kilgreel❶ BT39 . . . . . . 119 A8
Kilgreel Rd BT41 . . . . . . 186 F4
Kilhorne Gdns BT5 . . . . 146 B3
Kilhoyle❶ BT49. . . . . . . 40 C1
Kilhoyle Rd BT49. . . . . . 56 C1
Kilknock❶ BT41 . . . . . . 93 C4
Killagan Bend BT6 . . . . 152 B8
Killagan Rd BT44 . . . . . . 61 B7
Killaghy❶ BT67. . . . . . . 164 B4
Killaghy Rd BT67. . . . . . 164 A4
Killala Pk ❺ BT5 . . . . . . 176 C1
Killaleenan★ BT54 . . . . . . 9 D5
Killaloe BT38 . . . . 130 E8
Killaloo❶ BT47 . . . . 52 D2
Killane❶
 Ballymena BT42 . . . . . 77 F3
 Limavady BT49 . . . . . 180 C8
Killane Pk BT42 . . . . 77 F2
Killane Rd
 Ballymena BT42 . . . . . 77 F3
 Limavady BT49 . . . . . 180 C7
Killaney Ave BT28 . . . . . 169 F8
Killans Rd BT53. . . . . . . 43 C2
Killard Pl BT10. . . . . . . 150 D4
Killargus❶ BT44 . . . . . . 59 F6
Killary Rd BT48 . . . . . . 176 C2
Killberry BT45 . . . . 91 D4
Killcranny❶ BT51. . . . . . 14 A3
Killdrum❶ BT42 . . . . 94 E6
Killdrum Rd BT42 . . . . . . 94 E6
Killea❶ BT48 . . . . 50 C8
Killead Rd BT29 . . . . . . 117 C5
Killeague❶ BT51 . . . . . . 25 F1
Killeague Rd BT51 . . . . . 41 F8
Killealy❶ BT41 . . . . 117 D7
Killea Rd BT48 . . . . 50 C8
Killeaton Cres BT17. . . . 160 D8
Killeaton Pk BT17. . . . . 160 D7
Killeaton Pl BT17. . . . . 160 D7
Killeen (Holywood)❶
 BT4 . . . . 146 D7
Killeen Pk BT11. . . . . . 150 B7
Killelagh Pk BT46 . . . . . 74 D8
Killennan❶ BT47 . . . . . . 52 C6
Killennan Rd BT47 . . . . . 52 B6
Killenny❶ BT82 . . . . 67 E2
Killen St BT12 . . . . 188 C3
Killew Rd BT44 . . . . 72 C6
Killibleught❶ BT47. . . . . 55 B5
Killins North❶ BT53 . . . . 43 D2
Killins South❶ BT53 . . . . 43 D2
Killmakevitt Cres ❹ BT42 77 F7
Killmakevitt Dr BT42 . . . . 77 F7
Killmakevitt Rd ❶ BT42 . 77 F6
Killmakevitt Sq ❸ BT42 . 77 F7
Killough❶ BT67 . . . . . . 155 D1
Killoughag❶ BT44 . . . . . 32 C4
Killowen Cres BT28 . . . . 159 E3
Killowen Ct BT52 . . . . . 174 C3
Killowen Dr BT45 . . . . . 183 E5
Killowen Grange BT28. . 159 C5
Killowen Mews BT28 . . . 159 C4
Killowen Pk BT28 . . . . . 159 E4
Killowen Prim Sch
 Coleraine BT51 . . . . . 174 B2
 Lisburn BT28 . . . . . . 159 D3
Killowen St
 Belfast BT6 . . . . 145 B3
 Coleraine BT51 . . . . . 174 B3
Killtinny Rd BT51 . . . . . . 14 C4
Killultagh Rd BT28 . . . . 147 A1
Killunaght❶ BT47 . . . . . 70 F8
Killunaght Rd BT47 . . . . 71 A7
Killure❶ BT51 . . . . 25 F4
Killure Rd BT51 . . . . 25 F4
Killwaughter Castle (ruins)★
 BT40 . . . . 83 A2

Killybasky❶ BT80 . . . . 113 A7
Killybearn❶ BT80 . . . . 113 D2
Killybearn Rd BT80. . . . 113 E3
Killyberry Boyd❶ BT45. . 91 E5
Killyberry Downing❶
 BT45 . . . . 91 D3
Killyberry La BT45 . . . . . 91 D4
Killyblight Rd BT47. . . . . 55 A6
Killyboggin❶ BT45. . . . 104 C7
Killyboggin Rd BT45 . . . 104 C6
Killybready❶ BT49. . . . . 23 F3
Killycarn❶ BT42 . . . . . . 64 D5
Killycarn Rd BT42 . . . . . 64 C4
Killyclooney❶ BT44 . . . . 67 A4
Killyclooney Rd BT82. . . 67 B4
Killycolpy Rd BT71 . . . . 114 E1
Killycon Rd
 Ballymena BT44 . . . . . 76 A5
 Maghera BT46. . . . . . 75 F7
Killycoogan❶ BT44 . . . . 76 D8
Killycoogan Rd BT44 . . . 76 D8
Killycorr❶ BT47 . . . . 69 F7
Killycorr Ave BT47 . . . . . 69 F7
Killycowan❶ BT44 . . . . . 61 B4
Killycowan La BT41 . . . . 61 C6
Killycowan Rd BT44 . . . . 61 B5
Killycreen❶ BT44 . . . . . . 61 C7
Killycurragh❶ BT80. . . . 112 A7
Killycurragh Rd BT80. . . 112 A5
Killycurry Rd BT82 . . . . . 67 A4
Killydonnelly❶ BT44 . . . 61 A5
Killyfad❶ BT41 . . . . . . 107 B3
Killyfaddy❶ BT45 . . . . . 183 E2
Killyfaddy Rd BT45 . . . . 183 C4
Killyfast Rd BT41 . . . . . 107 B2
Killyfast❶ BT41 . . . . 93 A2
Killyflugh❶ BT43 . . . . . . 78 E7
Killyflugh Rd BT43 . . . . . 78 F7
Killygarn❶ BT44 . . . . . . 92 D8
Killyglen❶ BT40 . . . . . . 82 F4
Killyglen Link ❽ BT40. . . 83 B4
Killyglen Rd BT40 . . . . . 182 A6
Killygore❶ BT43 . . . . . . 62 E5
Killygore Rd BT43 . . . . . 62 E4
Killygreen Lower❶ BT51. 15 A5
Killygreen Upper❶ BT51. 15 A5
Killygullib Glebe❶ BT51. 58 F2
Killygullib Rd
 Maghera BT46. . . . . . 58 D1
 Swatragh BT46 . . . . . 74 E8
Killykergan❶ BT51. . . . . 42 B3
Killykergan Rd BT51 . . . . 42 B4
Killylaes❶ BT41 . . . . 92 F5
Killylane❶
 Ballyclare BT39 . . . . . 97 C8
 Londonderry BT47 . . . . 37 B4
Killyless❶ BT42 . . . . 77 C7
Killyless Rd BT42 . . . . . . 77 C7
Killymaddy❶ BT53 . . . . . 43 C4
Killymaddy Rd BT53 . . . . 43 C5
Killymallaght❶ BT47 . . . . 51 A1
Killymallaght Rd BT47. . . 67 B8
Killymallaght Rd T BT47 . 67 A7
Killymam❶ BT80 . . . . . 185 A7
Killymoon Cres BT80 . . . 185 D2
Killymoon Demesne❶
 BT80 . . . . 185 F1
Killymoon Golf Club The
 BT80. . . . . 185 D3
Killymoon Rd BT80. . . . 185 E3
Killymoon St BT80 . . . . 185 D3
Killymuck❶ BT80 . . . . . 115 B6
Killymuck Glebe❶ BT46 . 75 B7
Killymuck Rd
 Cookstown BT80 . . . . 115 B6
 Maghera BT46. . . . . . 75 A4
Killynaght❶ BT82. . . . . . 67 A2
Killynaght Rd BT82 . . . . . 67 A2
Killyneese❶ BT45 . . . . . 105 B8
Killyneese Rd BT45. . . . 105 C7
Killynether Gdns BT8. . . 151 C2
Killynumber❶ BT45 . . . . 90 A3
Killynure Ave BT8 . . . . . 163 E1
Killynure Cl ❸ BT8 . . . . 163 E2
Killynure Cres BT8 . . . . 163 E3
Killynure Gdns BT8 . . . . 163 D2
Killynure Pk ❷ BT8 . . . . 163 E1
Killynure Rd BT8. . . . . . 163 E1
Killynure Way ❶ BT8 . . . 163 E2
KILLYRAMER BT53 . . . . . 28 E3
Killyrammer Rd BT53. . . . 28 D3
Killyree❶ BT44 . . . . 62 C4
Killytoney BT45 . . . . 89 F4
Killyvalley Pk ❶ BT51 . . . 58 A8
Killyvalley Rd BT51. . . . . 58 B8
Killyvally❶ BT51 . . . . 58 B8
Killyveety❶ BT51 . . . . . . 13 B1
Killywool❶ BT47 . . . . 37 D2
Kilmaconnell❶ BT51 . . . . 26 A5
Kilmaconnell Rd BT51. . . 26 A5
Kilmahamogue❶ BT54 . . . 7 C2
Kilmahamogue Rd BT54 . . 7 C1
Kilmakee❶
 Ballyclare BT39 . . . . . 110 C1
 Dunmurry BT17 . . . . . 160 F8
Kilmakee Activity Ctr ❹
 BT17. . . . . 160 F8
Kilmakee Pk BT5 . . . . . 146 D2
Kilmakee Rd BT39 . . . . . 110 C1
Kilmandil❶ BT44 . . . . . . 45 D6
Kilmandil Rd BT44 . . . . . 45 D6
Kilmeen❶ BT53. . . . . 43 F1
Kilminioge❶ BT67 . . . . . 165 D3
Kilmore❶
 Ballymena BT44. . . . . 48 C8
 Craigavon BT67 . . . . 164 E5
Kilmore Cl BT13 . . . . . . 188 A3

Kilmore Hill Rd BT67 . . 164 C5
Kilmore Pk BT67 . . . . . 166 B2
Kilmore Rd
 Ballymena BT44. . . . . 32 D1
 Craigavon BT67. . . . . 164 F2
Kilmore Sq BT13 . . . . . 188 A3
Kilmory Gdns BT5 . . . . 146 E3
Kilmoyangey❶ BT53 . . . . 29 B2
Kilmoyle❶
 Ballymoney BT53 . . . . 15 E3
 Ballymoney BT53 . . . . 15 F1
 Ballymoney BT53 . . . . 17 E5
Kilmoyle Lower❶ BT53. . 27 D5
Kilmoyle Prim Sch BT53. 15 E1
Kilmoyle Rd BT53 . . . . . 15 E3
Kilmoyle Upper or
 Kirkmoyle❶ BT53. . . . 27 D5
Kilnacolpagh❶ BT42 . . . 64 E2
Kilnacolpagh Rd BT42. . . 80 D8
Kilnadore❶ BT44 . . . . . . 32 D4
Kilnadore Brae BT44 . . . 32 D4
Kilnadore Pk BT44 . . . . . 32 D4
Kilnadore Rd BT44 . . . . . 32 C3
Kilnappy❶ BT47 . . . . 36 A3
Kilnappy Rd BT47 . . . . . 52 B8
Kiln Gr BT82 . . . . 182 D5
Kilnhill BT43 . . . . 62 F7
Kilnhill❶ BT51. . . . . 25 B4
Kiln Pk BT39 . . . . 110 D2
Kiln Rd BT39 . . . . 111 E1
Kilns Rd BT54. . . . . 8 D3
Kilpatrick❶ BT54 . . . . 2 F7
Kilraghts❶ BT53 . . . . . . 28 F2
KILRAGHTS BT53 . . . . . 28 F3
Kilraughts Rd BT53 . . . . 175 E4
Kilrea❶ BT51 . . . . 59 C5
KILREA (CILL RIA) BT51 . 59 C5
Kilrea Ent Ctr BT51 . . . . 59 C5
Kilrea Golf Course BT51. 59 C4
Kilrea Prim Sch ❾ BT51. 59 C5
Kilrea Rd
 Ballymena BT44. . . . . 76 B6
 Coleraine BT51 . . . . . 58 A8
 Cullybackey BT42. . . . 77 F7
 Maghera BT46. . . . . . 75 A6
 Swatragh BT46 . . . . . 74 D8
Kilrea Sports Complex ❽
 BT51 . . . . 59 C5
Kilrobert❶ BT54 . . . . . . 19 B5
Kilronan Sch BT45 . . . . 183 C4
Kilroot Bsns Pk BT38 . . 126 A3
Kilross Prim Sch BT45. . 89 D4
Kiltcaltan❶ BT47 . . . . . . 52 E1
Kiltest❶ BT51 . . . . 40 F8
Kiltinny Beg❶ BT52 . . . . 14 C4
Kiltinny More❶
 Coleraine BT52 . . . . . 14 B4
 Portrush BT56 . . . . . 172 F1
Kiltinny Pk BT51 . . . . . . 25 C4
Kiltinny Rd BT56 . . . . . 172 F2
Kilton La BT40 . . . . 100 D4
Kilvillis❶ BT41 . . . . 92 E5
Kilvoragh Pk BT67 . . . . 164 B1
Kilwarlin Cres BT8 . . . . 151 C2
Kilwarlin Wlk BT8 . . . . . 151 C2
Kilwaughter❶ BT40 . . . . 82 F1
Kilwee Ind Est BT17. . . . 149 F5
Kimberley Dr
 Belfast BT7 . . . . 151 E8
 ❼ Newtownabbey BT36 133 A8
Kimberley Hill BT47. . . . 179 C4
Kimberley Pk ❷ BT36 . . 133 A8
Kimberley Rd BT36. . . . 133 A8
Kimberley St
 ❹ Belfast BT7 . . . . . 144 E1
 Belfast BT7 . . . . 151 E8
Kimona Dr BT4 . . . . . . 145 D6
Kimona St BT4. . . . . . . 145 D6
Kinallen Ct BT7 . . . . . . 144 E2
Kinallen St BT7 . . . . . . 144 E2
Kinbally❶ BT53 . . . . 28 C6
Kinbane Castle★ BT54 . . . 8 A6
Kinbane Way BT10 . . . . 150 D4
Kinbayne Brae BT38. . . 129 D3
Kinbayne Cres BT38. . . 129 D3
Kincora❶ BT42 . . . . 181 E1
Kincora Ave BT4 . . . . . 145 F5
Kincraig Pk BT36 . . . . . 133 C1
Kinculbrack❶ BT47 . . . . 69 E8
Kinedar Cres BT4 . . . . . 146 A5
Kingariff❶ BT53 . . . . . . 29 B7
Kingariff Rd BT53 . . . . . 29 B7
King St Mews BT12. . . . 188 C3
Kings Ave BT37 . . . . . . 133 F7
Kingsberry Pk BT6. . . . . 152 A7
Kingsbog❶ BT36 . . . . . 111 D3
Kings Brae BT5 . . . . . . 146 C3
King's Bridge BT7 . . . . . 151 D8
Kingsbury Gdns BT52 . . 174 F4
Kingschase BT7 . . . . . . 168 D4
Kingscourt Ave ❻ BT6 . 145 B3
Kingscourt Cres ❹ BT6 . 145 B3
Kings Cres BT37 . . . . . 133 F7
King's Cres BT5 . . . . . . 146 B3
Kings Ct
 Belfast BT10 . . . . . . 150 E6
 Newtownabbey BT37. . 133 F7
Kingsdale Pk BT5 . . . . . 146 C3
Kingsden Pk BT5 . . . . . 146 A3
Kings Dr BT37 . . . . 133 F7
King's Dr BT5. . . . . 146 B3
Kingsfort Cres BT48. . . . 177 B2
Kingsfort Lodge BT67 . . 166 A1
Kingsfort Rd BT48 . . . . 177 A2
Kingsgate St ❸ BT52. . . 174 D3
Kings Gdns BT37 . . . . . 133 F6
King's La BT49 . . . . 38 D7
Kingsland Cres BT38 . . 125 C6

Kingsland Dr
 Belfast BT5 . . . . 146 D3
 Carrickfergus BT38 . . . 125 C6
Kingsland Pk
 Belfast BT5 . . . . 146 D3
 Carrickfergus BT38 . . . 125 C6
Kingsley Ct BT4. . . . . . . 145 F5
Kings Link BT5 . . . . 146 D3
Kings Manor BT5 . . . . . 146 B3
Kingsmere Ave BT14 . . . 137 A2
Kingsmere Gdns BT47. . 179 D5
Kingsmoss Rd BT36 . . . 111 D3
Kings Parade BT37 . . . . 133 F7
King's Pk BT5 . . . . 146 B3
Kings Pk BT37 . . . . 133 F7
King's Rd
 Belfast BT5 . . . . 145 F4
 Coleraine BT51 . . . . . 174 A4
 ❷❼ Whitehead BT38 . 100 D1
 Whitehead BT38 . . . . 127 A8
Kings Sq Sh Ctr BT5 . . . 146 C3
King St
 Belfast BT12 . . . . . . 189 A3
 Londonderry BT47 . . . 179 A5
 Magherafelt BT45 . . . 183 D6
Kings Terr BT37 . . . . . . 133 F7
King's Vale ❹ BT5 . . . . 146 A4
Kingsway
 Carrickfergus BT38 . . . 125 C2
 Dunmurry BT17 . . . . . 160 E8
Kings Way BT37 . . . . . . 133 F7
Kingsway Ave BT5 . . . . 146 C3
Kingsway Cl BT5 . . . . . 146 C3
Kingsway Dr BT5 . . . . . 146 C3
Kingsway Gdns BT5. . . . 146 C3
Kingsway Pk BT5 . . . . . 146 C3
Kingsway Sh Ctr BT17. . 150 B2
Kingswood Pk BT5 . . . . 146 D3
Kingswood St BT5 . . . . 145 B4
King William III Cres ❷❹
 BT46 . . . . 74 D1
Kinhilt St ❸ BT42 . . . . . 181 C4
Kinkeel❶ BT54 . . . . 3 A4
Kinnaird Cl ❸ BT14 . . . . 144 C8
Kinnaird Pl ❸ BT14 . . . . 144 C8
Kinnaird St ❻ BT15 . . . . 144 C8
Kinnaird Terr ❼ BT14 . . . 144 C8
Kinnard Pk BT51. . . . . . . 58 A8
Kinnegalliagh❶ BT42 . . . 96 C8
Kinnegar Ave BT18 . . . . 139 C7
Kinnegar Cl BT18 . . . . . 139 C7
Kinnegar Ct BT18 . . . . . 139 C6
Kinnegar Dr BT18 . . . . . 139 C6
Kinnegar Rd
 Belfast BT10 . . . . . . 150 D4
 Holywood BT18 . . . . . 139 C7
Kinnego Pk BT48 . . . . . 176 B1
Kinnyglass❶ BT51 . . . . . 25 E2
Kinnyglass Rd BT51 . . . . 41 D8
Kinora Terr BT56 . . . . . 172 B6
Kinramer North❶ BT54 . . 2 C6
Kinramer South❶ BT54 . . 2 C6
Kinross Ave BT5 . . . . . 146 E3
Kinrush❶ BT80 . . . . . . 115 B1
Kinrush Rd BT80 . . . . . 115 B1
Kinsale Pk BT47 . . . . . . 179 D7
Kintullagh Cl BT43 . . . . 181 C5
Kintullagh Ct BT43 . . . . 181 C6
Kintullagh Pk BT43. . . . 181 C5
Kinturk❶ BT80 . . . . 115 C4
Kinturk Rd BT80 . . . . . . 115 C4
Kintyre❶ BT41 . . . . 186 E7
Kintyre Pk BT42. . . . . . . 181 F3
Kintyre Rd BT40 . . . . . . 182 A4
Kinune❶ BT54 . . . . 20 B1
Kirbys La BT41. . . . . . . 186 E1
Kirk Ave BT45 . . . . 183 D5
Kirkdale BT36 . . . . 132 E6
Kirkfield❶ BT53 . . . . 28 C6
Kirk Gdns BT54 . . . . 62 B7
Kirkhills❶ BT53. . . . . . . 28 B6
Kirkinriola❶ BT43 . . . . . 78 F8
Kirkinriola Prim Sch BT43 78 F7
Kirkistown❶ BT52 . . . . . 15 A2
Kirkistown Ave BT8 . . . . 151 C2
Kirkland Sq BT38 . . . . . 124 F1
Kirkliston Dr BT5 . . . . . 145 E4
Kirkliston Gdns BT5 . . . 145 E4
Kirkliston Pk BT5 . . . . . 145 E4
Kirklowe Dr BT10 . . . . . 150 A5
Kirkmoyle View BT51 . . 175 B6
Kirkpatrick Way BT40 . . 182 D7
Kirk Pk BT53 . . . . 175 E5
Kirk Rd BT53 . . . . 175 E5
Kirk St BT13 . . . . 143 F6
Kirkview Cl BT53 . . . . . 175 D5
Kirkwood Manor BT42 . . 181 D1
Kirkwood's Pk BT52 . . . 160 A5
Kirkwoods Rd BT28 . . . 160 B5
Kirley❶ BT46 . . . . 73 D1
Kirley Rd BT46. . . . . 73 D1
Kitchener Dr BT12 . . . . 188 A1
Kitchener St BT12. . . . . 188 A1
Kittybane❶ BT47 . . . . . . 51 A6
Kittybane Rd BT47 . . . . . 51 A6
Klondyke St BT13 . . . . . 144 B3
Knightsbridge
 Lisburn BT28 . . . . . . 159 C5
 Londonderry BT47 . . . 179 D4
Knightsbridge Manor
 BT9 . . . . 151 D6
Knightsbridge Mews
 BT9 . . . . 151 C6
Knightsbridge Pk BT9 . . 151 C6
Knightswood❶ BT39 . . . 110 C2
Knock❶ BT5 . . . . 146 A4

Kil–Kno 211

Knockacully❶ BT44 . . . . 32 E8
Knockadoo❶ BT80 . . . . 103 E1
Knockadoo Rd
 Cookstown BT80 . . . . 113 A8
 Magherafelt BT45 . . . 103 D2
Knockaduff❶ BT51 . . . . . 26 D1
Knockaduff Rd BT51 . . . . 42 E8
Knockagh Hts BT38 . . . 124 D2
Knockagh Rd
 Carrickfergus BT38 . . . 123 E1
 Lisburn BT28 . . . . . . 159 F1
 Newtownabbey BT36. . 128 E4
Knockahollet❶ BT44. . . . 45 C7
Knockahollet Prim Sch
 BT44 . . . . 45 C8
Knockahollet Rd BT44 . . 45 A7
Knockaleery Rd BT80 . . 112 A1
Knockalla Pk BT48 . . . . 176 D5
Knockan❶ BT47 . . . . 71 A7
Knockanavery❶ BT53 . . . 28 F4
Knockan Baan BT49. . . . 180 E5
Knockanboy❶ BT53 . . . . 28 A8
Knockancor Dr BT56 . . . 172 D5
Knockaneffrin❶ BT44. . . 49 B2
Knockane Way BT36 . . . 133 E6
Knockan Rd BT43 . . . . . . 79 B8
Knockanroe Rd BT71 . . . 113 E1
Knockans❶
 Ballycastle BT54 . . . . . . 2 F6
 Ballymoney BT53 . . . . 18 C3
 Ballymoney BT53 . . . . 44 A4
Knockans North❶ BT44 . . 32 C2
Knockans South❶ BT44 . 32 C3
Knockans The BT43 . . . . 79 C7
Knockantern❶ BT52 . . . . 26 D7
Knockantern Gr ❷ BT52. 26 C7
KNOCKANULLY BT43 . . . 63 B7
Knockanully Rd BT43. . . 63 A7
Knockavallan❶ BT53 . . . 16 D2
Knockavinnan❶ BT53 . . . 30 A4
Knockboy❶ BT43 . . . . . . 79 B8
Knockboy Rd BT43 . . . . . 62 F1
Knockbrack❶
 Ballycastle BT54 . . . . . . 9 E4
 Londonderry BT47 . . . . 52 A3
Knockbracken Cres BT8 163 D5
Knockbracken Ct BT52 . . 26 C7
Knockbracken Dr
 Carryduff BT8 . . . . . . 163 D6
 ❻ Coleraine BT52. . . . 26 C7
Knockbracken Healthcare Pk
 BT8. . . . . 163 A8
Knockbracken Manor
 BT8. . . . . 152 C2
Knockbracken Mental Health
 Services BT8 . . . . 163 B8
Knockbracken Pk
 Belfast BT6 . . . . 152 A6
 ❾ Coleraine BT52. . . . 26 C7
Knockbracken Rd BT8. . 163 C8
Knockbracken Rd S BT8 163 D2
Knockbrack Rd BT47 . . . 51 F1
Knockbreckan❶ BT8 . . . 163 D8
Knockbreda Dr BT6 . . . 152 A6
Knockbreda Gdns BT6. . 152 A6
Knockbreda High Sch
 BT6 . . . . 152 B6
Knockbreda Pk BT6 . . . 152 A6
Knockbreda Prim Sch
 BT6 . . . . 152 A6
Knockbreda Rd BT6. . . . 152 A7
Knockburn Ave BT28 . . . 159 C2
Knockburn Cl BT28 . . . . 159 C2
Knockburn Cres BT28 . . 159 C2
Knockburn Dr BT28 . . . . 159 C2
Knockburn Gdns BT28. . 159 C2
Knockburn Gr BT28 . . . . 159 C2
Knockburn Pk
 Belfast BT5 . . . . 146 C4
 Lisburn BT28 . . . . . . 159 C2
Knockcairn❶ BT29. . . . . 121 F7
Knockcairn Lodge BT29 140 C7
Knockcairn Rd BT29 . . . 140 A7
Knockcastle Pk BT5. . . . 146 A3
KNOCKCLOGHRIM BT45 . . 90 F6
Knockdarragh Pk
 Belfast BT4 . . . . 146 B7
 Lisburn BT28 . . . . . . 159 C2
Knockdene Gate ❶ BT5 . 146 B4
Knockdene Pk BT5 . . . . 146 B4
Knockdene Pk N BT5 . . . 146 B4
Knockdene Pk S BT5 . . . 146 B4
Knockdhu Pk
 Belfast BT11 . . . . . . 150 A8
 Larne BT40 . . . . 182 A5
Knock Eden Ave BT53 . . 175 D6
Knockeden Cl BT53 . . . . 175 E3
Knock Eden Cl BT53 . . . 175 D6
Knock Eden Cres BT6 . . 152 A6
Knock Eden Ct BT53 . . . 175 D6
Knock Eden Dr BT6 . . . . 152 A7
Knock Eden Gr BT6 . . . . 152 A8
Knock Eden Parade BT6. 152 A8
Knock Eden Pk BT6. . . . 152 A8
Knockeen Cres BT42 . . . 79 A3
Knockeen Rd BT42 . . . . . 79 A3
Knockenagh Ave BT36. . 133 E6
Knockenagh Wlk BT36 . 133 E6
Knockeny❶ BT44 . . . . . . 32 D4
Knockertotan❶ BT52 . . . . 4 E1
Knockfergus Pk BT38 . . 129 E3
Knock Gn BT5 . . . . 146 A2
Knock Golf Club BT16. . 146 F5

Knock Gr **4** BT5.....146 A2
Knockgullen BT47....55 A2
Knockhill Pk
  Ballymoney BT53.....175 C6
  Belfast BT5.....146 A4
Knocklade BT38.....125 A1
Knockland Pk BT5.....146 A4
Knocklands Ct **5** BT53.....175 C5
Knocklayde BT53.....175 D4
Knocklayde Cres BT40.....182 B4
Knocklayde Pk BT54.....174 A5
Knocklayde View **2** BT54.. 8 D3
Knockleigh Dr BT38.....129 E2
Knockleigh Wlk BT38.....129 E2
Knock Link **6** BT5.....146 A2
Knocklofty Ct **11** BT4.....146 A5
Knocklofty Pk BT4.....146 B5
Knockloughrim Prim Sch
  .....90 F6
Knocklynn Gr BT52.....26 C7
Knocklynn Grange **7**
  BT52.....26 C7
Knocklynn Manor **14**
  BT52.....26 C7
Knocklynn Pk **20** BT52.....26 C7
Knocklynn Rd BT52.....26 C7
Knockmacolusky**⊕** BT44.....21 B4
Knockmarloch Pk BT4 ..146 C7
Knockmore**⊕** BT28.....159 D1
Knockmore Bsns Ctr
  BT28.....169 C8
Knockmore Cres **4** BT51.. 25 E5
Knockmore Hill Ind Pk
  BT28.....159 B1
Knockmore Ind Est BT28 169 B8
Knockmore Pk
  Carrickfergus BT38.....130 B6
  Lisburn BT28.....159 C1
Knockmore Prim Sch **2**
  BT28.....169 D8
Knockmore Rd
  Ballymoney BT53.....17 B3
  Lisburn BT28.....169 C8
Knockmore Sq BT28 ....169 E8
Knockmount Gdns **2**
  BT5.....146 A2
Knockmount Pk BT5.....146 A2
Knockmoyle BT80.....185 E3
Knockmoyle Dr BT41....187 A3
Knockmult BT51.....24 F6
KNOCKNACARRY BT44.....21 A1
Knocknacarry**⊕** BT44.....32 E8
Knocknacarry Rd
  Ballymena BT44.....32 D8
  Cushendun BT44.....21 A1
Knocknacrow**⊕** BT54.....20 D2
Knocknadona**⊕** BT28 ..158 F6
Knocknadruddion**⊕** BT51.. 25 D5
Knocknagarvan**⊕** BT54....7 B4
Knocknagin**⊕** BT45.....90 B1
Knocknagin Rd BT45.....90 B1
Knocknagoney**⊕** BT18 ..139 C2
Knocknagoney Ave BT4.139 B1
Knocknagoney Dale BT4 139 A1
Knocknagoney Dr BT4 ..139 B1
Knocknagoney Gdns
  BT4.....139 B2
Knocknagoney Gn **3**
  .....139 B1
Knocknagoney Gr **2**
  BT4.....139 B1
Knocknagoney Pk BT4 ..139 A2
Knocknagoney Prim Sch
  BT4.....139 A1
Knocknagoney Rd BT4 ..139 A2
Knocknagoney Way **1**
  BT4.....139 B1
Knocknahinch**⊕** BT53.....29 D8
Knocknahushog**⊕** BT44.....45 C5
Knocknakeeragh**⊕** BT52.. 15 B1
Knocknakielt**⊕** BT46.....90 C8
Knocknakielt Rd BT46.....90 C8
Knocknarea**⊕** BT28.....158 E1
Knocknarea Rd BT28.....158 D2
Knock Nature Wlk BT5 .146 B3
Knocknogher**⊕** BT51.....24 F8
Knocknougher Rd BT51.. 24 C8
Knockoneill**⊕** BT47.....57 C1
Knockoneill Rd BT46.....57 D1
Knockramer**⊕** BT43.....63 F5
Knock Rd
  Ballymoney BT53.....175 D7
  Belfast BT5.....146 A2
  Castlereagh BT5.....145 F1
Knockreagh Gdns **4**
  BT37.....133 E5
Knocksallagh Pk BT38..129 D3
Knocksandel Dr BT52 ..174 C1
Knocksoghey**⊕** BT54.....7 D7
Knocktarna Grange **13**
  BT52.....26 C7
Knocktarna Manor BT52.. 26 C7
Knocktern Gdns BT4 ....146 B5
Knockvale Gr BT5.....146 A3
Knockvale Pk BT5.....146 A3
Knockview Ave BT36.....128 C2
Knockview Cres BT36 ..128 C2
Knockview Dr BT36.....128 C2
Knockview Gdns BT36...128 C2
Knockview Manor BT36.. 128 C2
Knockview Pk BT36.....128 C1
Knockview Rd BT36.....128 C1
Knock Way **5** BT5.....146 A2
Knockwellan BT47.....179 B2
Knockwood Cres BT5 ..145 F3

Knockwood Dr **3** BT5..146 A2
Knockwood Pk BT5.....145 F2
Knonknacarry Ave BT44..21 A2
Knowehead BT44.....46 A2
Knoweheadgrove **3** BT43 79 C7
Knowehead Rd
  Ballyclare BT39.....111 C2
  Ballymena BT43.....79 C8
Knowe The **5** BT42.....78 C4
Knoxhill Ave BT47.....178 C1
Knox Pk BT55.....173 E5
Knutsford Dr BT14.....137 A2
Kurin BT51.....58 B7
Kurin La BT51.....58 A7
Kurin Rd BT51.....58 B7
Kylebeg Ave BT51.....26 B7
Kylemore Bend **5** BT37 .133 E5
Kylemore Gdns BT40 ...182 A6
Kylemore Pk
  Belfast BT14.....137 A4
  2 Londonderry BT48 ...176 C1
  Londonderry BT48.....178 C8
Kylemore Rd BT51.....174 B2
Kyle's Brae BT51.....174 B2
Kyle St BT4.....145 D6
Labby**⊕** BT45.....88 D1

L

Laburnam Rd BT49.....38 B4
Laburnum Ct **2** BT5.....145 D5
Laburnum La **11** BT4 ....145 C5
Laburnum Pk BT17.....149 D3
Laburnum Pl BT52.....174 D5
Laburnum Row **2** BT17 .149 D2
Laburnum St **12** BT5.....145 C5
Laburnum Wlk **3** BT17 .149 D2
Lackagh BT47.....55 C3
LACKAGH BT49.....38 B3
Lackagh**⊕** BT47.....68 B7
Lackagh Pk BT47.....55 C2
Lackagh Rd BT47.....68 B6
Lacken Gdns BT36.....133 E6
Ladas Dr BT6.....145 C1
Ladas Way BT6.....145 C1
Ladas Wlk BT6.....145 C1
Ladbrook Dr BT14.....143 F8
Ladybrook Ave BT11.....150 A6
Ladybrook Cres BT11.....150 B6
Ladybrook Cross BT11 ..150 A6
Ladybrook Dr BT11.....150 B6
Ladybrook Gdns BT11 ..150 B6
Ladybrook Gr BT11.....150 B6
Ladybrook Parade BT11 .150 A6
Ladybrook Pk BT11.....150 A6
Ladye Pk BT37.....128 F1
Ladyhill BT41.....109 D8
Ladyhill La BT41.....109 C8
Ladyhill Rd BT41.....109 D8
Ladymar Gr BT12.....188 B3
Ladymar Pk BT12.....188 B3
Ladysmith La BT36.....132 E7
Ladysmith Terr BT42.....181 C3
Lady St BT12.....188 B3
Lady's Well★ BT44.....76 E3
Laganbank Rd
  Belfast BT1.....189 C3
  Lisburn BT28.....160 B1
Lagan Coll BT8.....161 D6
Lagan Lookout Visitors Ctr★
  BT1.....189 B3
Laganvale BT28.....168 E6
Laganvale Ct BT9.....151 D6
Laganvale Manor BT9 ..151 D6
Laganvale St BT9.....151 D7
Lagan Wlk BT28.....169 F7
Lagan Valley Hospl BT28..170 B8
Lagan Valley Regional Pk★
  BT28.....170 A6
Lagan Valley Regional Pk
Offices & NI RSPB HQ
  BT8.....151 D4
Laganview BT28.....170 B8
Laganview Ct BT5.....189 C3
Laganview Golf Ctr BT27 160 F6
Laganview Mews BT5 ..189 C3
Laganville Pk BT28.....169 C8
Lagan Wlk BT28.....169 F7
Lagavara**⊕** BT54.....7 C5
Lagavara Rd BT54.....7 B5
Lagge Rd BT53.....18 B2
Lagmore BT17.....149 B3
Lagmore BT28.....149 C2
Lagmore Ave BT17.....149 B3
Lagmore Dale BT17.....149 C1
Lagmore Dale Spine Rd
  BT17.....149 D1
Lagmore Downs BT17...149 D2
Lagmore Dr BT17.....149 C2
Lagmore Gdns BT28.....149 B2
Lagmore Glen BT28.....149 B2
Lagmore Gr BT17.....149 D2
Lagmore Hts BT28.....149 C1
Lagmore Mdws BT17....149 C2
Lagmore Rd BT17.....149 B4
Lagmore Rise BT28.....149 B1
Lagmore View BT17.....149 B3
Lagnagalloglagh**⊕** BT82.. 67 A1
Lagnamuck**⊕** BT51.....57 B7
Laharna Ave BT40.....182 D5
Laharna Ret Pk BT40.....182 D4
Lake Glen Ave **6** BT11 ..143 D1
Lake Glen Cl BT11.....143 D1
Lake Glen Cres **4** BT11 .143 D1
Lake Glen Dr BT11.....143 C1
Lake Glen Gn **2** BT11 ..143 D1

Lake Glen Parade **5**
  BT11.....143 D1
Lake Glen Pk **1** BT11 ..143 D1
Lakeside **8** BT39.....110 C2
Lakeside Dr BT10.....150 D2
Lake St BT67.....164 A1
Lake View BT29.....121 B8
Lakeview Ave BT36.....128 A2
Lakeview Cres BT36.....128 A2
Lakeview Gdns BT36.....128 A2
Lakeview Gr **1** BT36 ...128 A2
Lakeview Pk BT36.....128 A2
Lakeview Way BT36.....128 A2
LAMBEG (LANN BHEAG)
  BT27.....160 D5
Lambeg North**⊕** BT27....160 D6
Lambeg Prim Sch BT27..160 E5
Lambeg Rd BT27.....160 E4
Lambeg South**⊕** BT27....160 D3
Lambeg Sta BT27.....160 D5
Lambeth Way BT51.....174 B2
Lanaglug**⊕** BT80.....114 E4
Lanark Way BT13.....188 A4
Lancasterian St **3** BT38..141 A7
Lancaster St BT15.....144 D7
Lancedean Rd BT6.....152 D7
Lancefield Rd BT9.....151 A7
Landagivey**⊕** BT51.....43 A6
Landgarve Manor BT29...121 B8
Landhead BT28.....28 B2
Landhead Prim Sch BT53.. 28 B3
Landhead Rd BT53.....28 B2
Landmore**⊕** BT51.....42 F3
Landor BT47.....170 C8
Landscape Terr BT14.....144 B7
Landsdale Gdns BT53.....28 A3
Landsdale Pk BT53.....28 A3
Landsdowne Cl BT40.....182 E4
Landsdowne Cres BT40.. 182 E4
Landseer St BT9.....144 D1
Laney**⊕** BT44.....32 C7
Langarve**⊕** BT29.....121 A7
Langdale La BT40.....100 D5
Langfield**⊕** BT53.....29 C8
Langford Cl BT38.....130 D6
Langley Hall BT37.....129 D1
Langley St BT14.....144 A8
Langry Lodge BT54.....166 A2
Langtry Lodge BT39.....110 C4
LANN BHEAG (LAMBEG)
  BT27.....160 D5
Lansdale Pk BT53.....28 B3
Lansdowne Cres BT55...173 D8
Lansdowne La BT55.....173 C8
Lansdowne Pk
  Belfast BT15.....137 D5
  Lisburn BT27.....170 D8
Lansdowne Pk N BT15 ..137 D5
Lansdowne Rd
  Belfast BT15.....137 C5
  Londonderry BT47.....179 D4
Lantara BT47.....181 E1
Lanyon Pl BT1.....189 C3
Lany Rd BT67.....167 E1
Lapwing Way BT47.....179 B5
Laragh**⊕** BT46.....58 A2
Laraghaleas**⊕** BT47.....36 D5
Laragh Ct **2** BT36.....133 C1
Laragh Rd BT46.....57 F2
Laral Gdns BT36.....128 E2
Laral Pk BT36.....128 E2
Larches The **4** BT38 ...124 F1
Larchfield BT41.....187 D2
Larchfield**⊕** BT53.....28 F3
Larchfield Gdns BT51.....59 B6
Larch Gr
  Dunmurry BT17.....161 A8
  Newtownabbey BT36.....128 A2
Larch Hill BT17.....161 A8
Larch Rd
  Limavady BT49.....38 B2
  Londonderry BT47.....54 D3
Larcom Dr BT48.....177 C5
Largantea**⊕** BT49.....24 B5
Largantogher BT46.....90 B8
Largantogher **1** BT46...90 B8
Largy BT29.....116 E1
LARGY BT49.....39 B3
Largymore**⊕** BT27.....170 E6
Largymore Link
  4 Lisburn BT27.....160 D1
  Lisburn BT27.....170 D8
Largymore Prim Sch
  BT27.....160 D1
Largy Prim Sch BT49.....39 B3
Largy Rd
  Ballymena BT44.....92 F7
  Belfast BT29.....120 C8
  Carnlough BT44.....49 C3
  Limavady BT49.....39 B3
Largy Rd Cotts BT42.....93 B5
Largyreagh**⊕** BT49.....23 F1
Larkfield Ave BT10.....150 B3
Larkfield Dr BT4.....145 E7
Larkfield Gdns BT4.....145 D7
Larkfield Gr BT4.....145 E7
Larkfield Manor BT4.....145 D7
Larkfield Pk BT4.....145 E7
Larkfield Rd BT4.....145 E7
Larkhill BT48.....177 A4
Larkhill Rd BT56.....172 B2
Larkspur Rise BT11.....149 E6
Larkstone St BT12.....150 F7
Larne Golf Club BT40.....84 A4
Larne Gram Sch BT40...182 B4
Larne Harbour Sta BT40.182 F3

Larne High Sch BT40....182 D5
Larne & Inver Prim Sch
  BT40.....182 C3
LARNE (LATHARNA)
  BT40.....182 C6
Larne Leisure Ctr BT40..182 F4
Larne Rd
  Ballycarry BT38.....100 B3
  Ballyclare BT39.....111 F6
  Ballymena BT42.....181 E2
  Carrickfergus BT38.....131 C8
  Newtownabbey BT36.....111 F7
Larne Rd Link BT42.....181 E3
Larne Rd Ret Pk BT42 ..181 E3
Larne St BT42.....181 D3
Larne Town Sta BT40 ..182 E3
Larrybane Pk BT54.....7 C7
Larrycormick**⊕** BT45....104 B2
La Salle Boys Jun Sch
  BT11.....143 A1
La Salle Boys Sch BT11.. 150 B8
La Salle Gdns **1** BT12...143 F3
La Salle Mews BT12.....143 F3
La Salle Pk BT12.....143 F3
LATHARNA (LARNE)
  BT40.....182 C6
Laundry La BT36.....132 F4
Lauravale BT49.....180 D5
Laure Hill BT47.....70 A2
Laurel Ave BT51.....174 B3
Laurelbank BT17.....149 D4
Laurelbrook BT45.....183 F5
Laurel Cres BT53.....175 D4
Laurel Gr
  Coleraine BT51.....174 B1
  Lisburn BT28.....159 E4
Laurelgrove Ave BT8.....152 D2
Laurelgrove Cres **6** BT8 152 C2
Laurelgrove Ct **2** BT8...152 D2
Laurelgrove Dale **5** BT8 152 C2
Laurelgrove Manor BT8.152 D2
Laurelgrove Pk BT8.....152 D2
Laurelhill Com Coll
  BT28.....159 E3
Laurelhill Pk BT28.....159 E3
Laurelhill Rd
  Coleraine BT51.....174 B2
  Lisburn BT28.....159 E3
Laurel La BT14.....141 E8
Laurelmount Rd BT51 ..174 B1
Laurel Pk
  Ahoghill BT42.....77 E2
  Coleraine BT51.....174 B1
  Londonderry BT47.....108 A7
  10 Randalstown BT41.....108 A7
Laurel Rd BT49.....38 C3
Laurels The BT10.....150 D3
Laurelvale
  Belfast BT15.....146 A6
  Crumlin BT29.....117 A1
Laurel Way BT17.....149 F1
Laurel Wood BT8.....151 F5
Lauren Ct BT36.....132 F5
Lavens Dr BT14.....136 D2
Lavery Ave BT67.....164 A1
Lavery's Bridge Rd BT67 167 D1
Lavin Lower**⊕** BT44.....45 E7
Lavin Upper**⊕** BT44.....45 D8
Lawford St BT45.....113 E8
Lawnbrook Ave BT13.....188 A4
Lawnbrook Dr BT13.....188 A4
Lawnbrook Sq BT13.....188 A4
Lawnmount Cres BT27 ..160 D3
Lawnmount St **21** BT6...145 A4
Lawnview St BT13.....143 F7
Lawrence Hill BT48.....178 E7
Lawrence St BT7.....144 D2
Law's Ct BT1.....189 A4
Lawther Ct BT15.....137 D1
Lawyer Gdns BT12.....188 C2
Layd**⊕** BT44.....32 E6
Layde Rd BT44.....32 E6
Lead Hill BT6.....152 F8
Lead Hill Pk BT6.....152 F8
Lead Hill View **2** BT6...152 F8
Leadhill Prim Sch BT6...152 F7
Leafair Gdns BT48.....176 F5
Leafair Pk BT48.....176 F5
Leaghs**⊕** BT75.....87 C1
Lealies**⊕** BT40.....83 A2
Leaney Prim Sch BT53 .175 E3
Leansmount Rd BT67 ...164 A5
Lear**⊕** BT47.....85 D8
Learden**⊕** BT51.....25 D5
Learmount Castle★ BT47.. 70 A3
Learmount Rd BT47.....69 F3
Leat**⊕** BT82.....67 D3
Leathemstown Rd BT29 .140 C3
Lecale St BT12.....188 A1
Leck**⊕**
  Ballymoney BT53.....44 B6
  Coleraine BT51.....25 C1
  Limavady BT49.....40 B8
Leckagh**⊕** BT45.....183 D5
Leckagh Dr BT45.....183 D4
Leckey Rd
  Lisburn BT28.....156 E2
  Londonderry BT48.....178 E5
Lecky Ct BT48.....178 D3
Lecky Rd BT48.....178 D3
Lecumpher**⊕** BT45.....104 B6
Lecumpher Rd BT45.....104 B7
Ledcom Ind Est BT40....182 D3
Ledley Hall Cl **10** BT5...145 B4
Leeke**⊕**
  Bushmills BT57.....5 A2

Leeke continued
  Limavady BT49.....39 B1
  Limavady BT49.....55 B8
Leeke Rd BT57.....5 A2
Leenan Gdns BT48.....178 C5
Leeson St BT12.....188 B2
Leestone Terr **1** BT11 ..149 F6
Legacurry
  Ballymoney BT53.....29 A2
  Lisburn BT27.....171 A1
Legacurry Rd BT27.....170 C2
Legaghory**⊕** BT47.....52 B2
Legagrane**⊕** BT43.....47 C4
Legagrane Rd BT43.....47 B2
Legalaw**⊕** BT51.....25 E7
Legaloy**⊕** BT39.....97 F1
Legaloy Rd BT39.....122 C3
Legann St BT14.....136 D2
Leganoe St BT14.....136 C3
Legaterriff Rd BT28.....121 C1
Legatirriff**⊕** BT28.....121 B2
Legavallon Rd
  Limavady BT49.....56 C7
  Londonderry BT47.....55 E4
Legavannon**⊕** BT47.....53 E8
Legavannon Pot**⊕** BT49.. 56 C8
Legcloghfin**⊕** BT79.....85 F3
Legcloughfin Rd BT79...85 F5
Legg**⊕** BT44.....32 E4
Leggagh Ct **3** BT14.....136 D3
Legmail St **3** BT14.....136 D2
Legmore**⊕** BT67.....165 F3
Legnacash**⊕** BT80.....112 A2
Legnacash Rd BT80.....112 A2
Legnaduff**⊕** BT82.....50 B6
Legnagappoge**⊕** BT47...85 A5
Legnagooly**⊕** BT43.....62 F5
Legoniel
  Belfast BT14.....119 C2
  Belfast BT14.....119 D2
Leicester Ct **2** BT38 ...124 D2
Leicester Pk BT38.....124 D3
Leighinmohr Ave BT42 ..181 C3
Leighinmohr Pk BT42 ...181 C3
Leighry Rd BT49.....23 B2
LÉIM AN MHADAIDH
  (LIMAVADY) BT49.....180 A4
Leitrim⊕
  Antrim BT41.....107 E5
  Ballymoney BT53.....28 E5
  Magherafelt BT45.....91 F2
  Strabane BT82.....68 A3
Leitrim Rd
  Ballymoney BT53.....28 E5
  Magherafelt BT45.....91 E2
Leitrim St **5** BT6.....145 B3
Lelia St BT4.....145 C5
Lemberg St BT12.....188 A1
Lemnagh Beg**⊕** BT54....7 A6
Lemnagh More**⊕** BT54 ...6 F5
Lemnalary**⊕** BT44.....49 C4
Lemnalary Mountain⊕
  BT44.....48 F3
Lemnaroy**⊕** BT45.....91 A3
Lemonfield Ave BT18 ...139 E6
Lenagh**⊕** BT41.....108 D8
Lenaghan Ave BT8.....152 A3
Lenaghan Cres BT8.....152 A3
Lenaghan Ct BT8.....152 A3
Lenaghan Gdns BT8.....152 A2
Lenaghan Pk BT8.....152 A3
Lenagh Rd BT41.....108 E8
Lenamore⊕
  Limavady BT49.....11 C2
  Londonderry BT47.....56 C5
Lenamore Ave BT37.....129 B1
Lenamore Cres BT37.....129 B1
Lenamore Dr BT37.....129 B2
Lenamore Gdns
  Londonderry BT48.....176 F5
  Newtownabbey BT37.....129 B1
Lenamore Ind Est BT48.176 F5
Lenamore Link Rd BT48.176 F5
Lenamore Pk
  Lisburn BT28.....160 D1
  Londonderry BT48.....176 F5
  Newtownabbey BT37.....129 B1
Lenamore Rd BT48.....176 F7
Lennox Ave
  Carrickfergus BT38.....125 D3
  Castlereagh BT8.....152 B4
Lennox Cl BT38.....125 D3
Lennox Dr BT38.....125 D3
Lennox Mews BT38.....125 D3
Lennox Pk BT38.....125 D3
Lennoxvale BT9.....151 C8
Lenwood Hill BT28.....159 E3
Leopold Gdns BT13.....143 F7
Leopold Pk BT13.....143 F7
Leopold Pl **1** BT13.....143 F7
Lepper St BT15.....144 D8
Leroy St BT14.....136 D2
Lerris Gr BT13.....149 F5
Lesley Ret Pk BT48.....178 F5
Lesliehill BT53.....27 C3
Leslie Hill Open Farm★
  BT53.....175 A4
Lestannon Ave **3** BT38..100 D1
Lester Ave BT28.....160 B3
Lester Gdns **4** BT45 ...183 C4
Lester Pk **2** BT45.....183 C4
Lester Terr **3** BT45.....183 C4
Letteran**⊕** BT51.....103 C4
Letteran Rd BT45.....103 C2
Lettercreeve BT42.....181 D1

Letterkenny Rd BT48 . . . . 178 A2
Letterloan❶ BT55 . . . 25 C3
Letterloan Rd BT51 . . 25 D3
Letterlogher❶ BT47 . . . 70 A8
Letterlougher Rd BT47 . . 69 F7
Lettermire❶ BT47 . . . . 52 F2
Lettermuck❶ BT47 . . . 69 A6
LETTERSHENDONEY BT47. . 52 C7
Lettershendoney BT47 . . 52 C8
Lettershendoney Ave BT47 . . . . 52 C7
Leven Cl BT5 . . . 146 E2
Leven Cres BT5 . . . 146 F2
Leven Dr BT5 . . . 146 E2
Leven Pk BT5 . . . 146 E2
Leven Pl BT5 . . . 146 E2
Leveroge❶ BT8 . . . 162 D2
Leverogue Rd BT8 . . 162 E2
Lever Pk BT56 . . . 172 C5
Lever Rd BT56 . . . 172 B5
Lever St BT14 . . . 136 C4
Lewis Ave BT4 . . . 145 C5
Lewis Cl BT4 . . . 145 B3
Lewis Dr BT4 . . . 145 C5
Lewis Gdns BT4. . . 145 D5
Lewis Pk
  Ballymoney BT42. . . 181 F3
  Belfast BT4 . . . 145 C4
Leydene Ct BT28 . . . 159 F4
Leyland Ave BT54 . . 8 C3
Leyland Cres ⓲ BT54 . . 8 C3
Leyland Ct ❼ BT54 . . 8 C3
Leyland Farm BT54 . . 8 C4
Leyland Hts BT54 . . 8 C3
Leyland Mdw BT54 . . 8 C4
Leyland Pk BT54 . . 8 C3
Leyland Rd BT54 . . 8 C3
Leyland Rd Est ⓱ BT54 . . 8 C3
Leyland Rd Ind Est ❸ BT54 8 C4
Leymore❶ BT43 . . . 78 C6
Libbert East❶ BT44 . . 65 F7
Libbert West❶ BT44 . . 65 F7
Liberty Rd BT38 . . . 123 F5
Library St BT1 . . . 189 A4
Lichfield Ave BT5 . . 145 D4
Lichfield Pk BT51 . . 26 A7
Liester Pk BT39 . . . 111 C4
Liffey Ct ⓲ BT14 . . . 144 B8
Liffock❶ BT51 . . . 13 B4
Liffock Ave BT51 . . . 13 B4
Liffock Cres BT51 . . 13 B4
Liffock Cross Roads BT51 13 B3
Liffock Ct BT51 . . . 13 B4
Liffock Pk BT51 . . . 13 B4
Ligadaughtan❶ BT44 . . 21 B4
Ligg❶ BT47 . . . 36 B2
Ligoniel❶ BT14 . . . 136 C3
Ligoniel Pl BT14 . . . 136 B3
Ligoniel Prim Sch BT14 . 136 D3
Ligoniel Rd BT14 . . 136 B4
Lilac Ave
  Coleraine BT52 . . . 174 C5
  Limavady BT49 . . . 23 C2
  Strabane BT82 . . . 67 E3
Lilac Wlk BT17 . . . 160 F7
Lille Pk BT10 . . . 150 C4
Limavady Central Prim Sch
  BT49 . . . 180 C4
Limavady Coll of FE & HE
  BT49 . . . 180 B7
Limavady Gram Sch
  BT49 . . . 180 B3
Limavady High Sch BT49 180 B5
LIMAVADY (LÉIM AN
  MHADAIDH) BT49 . . . 180 A4
Limavady Rd
  Coleraine BT51 . . . 41 F1
  Garvagh BT51 . . . 57 F8
  Londonderry BT47 . . 179 B6
Lime Ct BT13 . . . 188 C4
Limegrove Sch BT49 . . 180 C4
Limehill Rd BT27 . . 170 E5
Limehill St BT14 . . . 136 C3
Limehurst Way BT27 . . 160 D2
Limekiln La
  Cookstown BT80 . . . 185 D6
  Craigavon BT67 . . . 155 C2
Lime Kiln Rd BT67 . . 167 D8
Lime Mkt St ❺ BT52 . . 174 C3
Limepark❶ BT53 . . . 29 E8
Lime Rd BT47 . . . 37 E4
Limestone Rd
  ⓭ Belfast BT15. . . 144 E8
  Limavady BT49 . . . 11 D1
Limetree Ave BT41 . . 187 C2
Lime Tree Ave BT41 . . 159 C3
Lime Tree Cl BT41 . . 187 C2
Limetree Lodge BT28 . . 159 C3
Limetree Manor BT45 . . 183 B8
Limetree Mdw BT28 . . 159 C3
Limewood Gr ❺ BT4 . . 146 A5
Limewood St BT48 . . 178 D5
Liminary❶
  Ballymena BT42. . . 79 B1
  Ballymena BT42. . . 95 A8
Liminary Rd BT42 . . 95 A7
Limnaharry❶ BT44. . . 77 C2
Lincoln Ave BT14 . . 144 C4
Lincoln Courts BT47 . . 179 B5
Lincoln Hts ⓲ BT42 . . 78 C3
Lincoln Pl BT12 . . 189 A2
Lincoln Sq BT12 . . 188 A2
Lindale Pk BT47 . . . 35 F5
Lindara Dr BT48 . . 182 A5
Linden Ave BT52 . . . 174 D5
Linden Gdns BT14. . 137 B1

Linden St BT13 . . . 188 A2
Linden Wlk BT17 . . . 161 A8
Lindenwood Pk BT48. . 176 C1
Lindsay Cl BT7 . . . 189 A1
Lindsay Ct BT7 . . . 189 A1
Lindsayville BT45 . . . 105 E2
Lindsay Way BT7 . . . 189 A1
Lindstrand Gdns BT49. . 180 E4
Linen Gn BT28 . . . 159 E5
Linen Gr BT14 . . . 136 C3
Linen Hall St W BT2. . 189 A2
Linenhall St
  Ballymoney BT53 . . . 175 C4
  Limavady BT49 . . . 180 A6
  ❷ Londonderry BT48 . . 178 F5
Linen Hall St BT2 . . . 189 A2
Linfield Ave BT12 . . . 188 C2
Linfield Dr BT12 . . . 188 C2
Linfield Ind Est BT12 . . 188 C2
Linfield Rd BT12 . . . 188 C2
Linford❶ BT40. . . 82 C7
Linford Gn BT37 . . . 133 E5
Ling❶ BT47 . . . 69 C4
Ling Rd BT47 . . . 69 C5
Link Rd
  Coleraine BT51 . . . 174 B3
  Lisburn BT28 . . . 160 A2
Links The BT55 . . . 173 E6
Linkview Pk BT9 . . . 150 A4
Linnet Pk BT28 . . . 159 E4
Linn Prim Sch BT40 . . 182 A6
Linn Rd BT40 . . . 182 A4
Linsfort Dr BT48 . . 178 B4
Linview Ct BT12 . . . 188 B2
LIOS NA GCEARRBHACH
  (LISBURN) BT27. . . 170 C6
Lir Ct BT55 . . . 8 D4
Lir Intergrated Prim Sch
  BT54 . . . 8 B3
Lisachrin❶ BT51 . . 58 C4
Lisachrin Rd BT51 . . 58 B5
Lisadell Ct BT56 . . 172 C3
Lisadell Gdns BT56 . . 172 C4
Lisaghmore Ave BT47 . . 51 F7
Lisaghmore❶ or The Trench❶
  Londonderry BT47 . . 51 C6
  Londonderry BT47 . . 179 C1
Lisaghmore Rd BT47 . . 179 A1
Lisahally Ind Est BT47. . 35 F6
Lisalbanagh❶ BT45. . 104 C5
Lisamurrikin❶ BT42 . . 79 E5
Lisanoure Castle ★ BT44 . 29 E1
Lisard Rath❶ BT47 . . 70 F7
Lisavon Dr BT4 . . . 145 D7
Lisavon Par BT4 . . . 145 D6
Lisavon St BT4. . . 145 D6
Lisbane Ave BT36 . . . 128 E2
Lisbane Dr BT37 . . . 128 E2
Lisbane Gdns BT37 . . 128 E2
Lisbellanagroagh Beg❶
  BT57 . . . 6 F6
Lisbellanagroagh More❶
  BT57 . . . 6 D5
Lisbon St BT5. . . 145 A5
Lisboy❶
  Ballymoney BT53 . . . 28 E3
  Coleraine BT51 . . . 42 A4
Lisboy La BT51 . . . 42 A4
Lisboy Rd
  Ballymena BT44. . . 45 B7
  Ballymoney BT53 . . . 29 A1
Lisbreen❶ BT43 . . 63 A5
Lisbreen Half Quarter❶
  BT43 . . . 63 A5
Lisbreen Pk BT15 . . 137 C4
Lisbunny❶ BT47 . . 68 F4
Lisbunny Rd BT47 . . 68 F4
Lisburn Ave BT9 . . . 151 A8
Lisburn Bsns Pk BT27 . 170 C8
Lisburn Central Prim Sch
  BT28 . . . 170 A8
Lisburn Ent Ctr BT28 . . 159 D1
Lisburn Golf Club BT27. . 170 D3
Lisburn Inst of FE & HE
  BT27 . . . 160 B1
Lisburn Leisure Pk BT28 170 A8
LISBURN (LIOS NA
  GCEARRBHACH) BT27. . 170 C6
Lisburn Mus & Irish Linen Ctr
  ❸ BT28 . . . 160 B1
Lisburn Rd
  Belfast BT9 . . . 188 C1
  Belfast BT29 . . . 121 D4
  Craigavon BT67 . . . 166 E4
  Lisburn BT28 . . . 168 B6
Lisburn Sq BT28 . . . 160 A1
Lisburn Sta BT28 . . . 160 B2
Liscall❶ BT51 . . . 41 D1
Liscall Rd BT51 . . . 41 C2
Liscannor Pk BT48 . . 176 C2
LISCLOON BT82. . . 68 B4
Liscloon Dr BT48. . . 177 A5
Liscloon Lower❶ BT82. . 68 B4
Liscloon Upper❶ BT82. . 68 C4
LISCOLMAN BT53. . . 16 E5
Lisconnan❶ BT53. . . 16 B1
Lisconnan Rd BT53. . . 27 F8
Liscoole BT80 . . . 185 C7
Liscoole Pk BT36 . . . 133 A6
Liscoom Rd BT42 . . 181 A3
Liscorran BT67 . . . 164 A2
Lisdarragh Pk BT14 . . 137 A5
Lisdillon Rd BT82. . . 68 A8
Lisdillon❶ BT47 . . . 51 E3
Lisdillon Rd BT47 . . . 51 E2
Lisdoonan Cl BT8 . . 163 F1
Lisdoonan Rd BT8 . . 163 F1

Lisfaddan Cres BT12 . . 188 B3
Lisfaddan Dr BT12 . . . 188 C3
Lisfaddan Pl BT12. . . 188 C3
Lisfaddan Way BT12. . . 188 C3
Lisfannon Pk ❸ BT48 . . 178 D5
Lisglass❶
  Ballyclare BT39 . . . 122 D3
  Londonderry BT47. . . 51 C4
Lisglass Rd
  Ballyclare BT39 . . . 111 F6
  Londonderry BT47. . . 51 C3
Lisgorgan Glebe❶ BT46. . 75 A6
Lisgorgan La BT46 . . . 75 B6
Lisheegan❶ BT53. . . 59 F8
Lisheegan Rd BT53. . . 59 E8
Lisheeghan La BT53. . . 59 E8
Lislaban❶ BT44 . . . 46 A4
Lislaban Rd BT44 . . . 45 F6
Lislagan Lower❶ BT53 . . 43 E8
Lislagan Rd BT53 . . . 43 E8
Lislagan Upper❶ BT53 . . 43 F8
Lislane❶ BT44 . . . 39 F3
Lislane Dr BT48. . . 178 B4
Lislane Rd BT49 . . . 39 F3
Lislaynan BT38 . . . 100 A3
Lislea❶ BT44 . . . 76 A8
Lislea Ave BT12 . . . 150 F7
Lislea Dr BT9 . . . 150 F7
Lisleen❶ BT23 . . . 153 E3
Lisleen Rd
  Belfast BT5 . . . 153 D6
  Newtownards BT23 . . 153 E3
Lisleen Rd E
  Belfast BT5 . . . 153 F4
  Newtownards BT23 . . 153 E2
Lisleen Rd S BT23. . . 153 F1
Lisles Hill Rd BT42 . . 65 A3
Lislunnan❶ BT42 . . . 95 C3
Lislunnan Rd BT42 . . 95 C3
Lismacarol❶ BT44 . . 52 A6
Lismacarrol Pk BT47 . . 51 F7
Lismacarrol Rd BT47. . . 51 F7
Lismacloskey❶ BT41. . 106 F7
Lismacloskey Rd BT41. . 106 F7
Lismain St BT6 . . . 145 B2
Lismanagh Cres BT43 . . 62 F7
Lismara Ct BT37 . . . 134 A4
Lismenary❶ BT39 . . . 97 F3
Lismenary Rd BT39. . . 97 F3
Lismoney❶ BT45 . . . 113 C4
Lismoney Rd BT45 . . 113 B4
Lismore St BT6 . . . 145 A3
Lismorrity❶ BT53. . . 17 D3
Lismoyle❶ BT46 . . 58 D2
Lismoyle Rd
  Coleraine BT51 . . . 59 A3
  Maghera BT46. . . 58 C2
  Swatragh BT46. . . 74 D8
Lismoyne Pk BT15 . . 137 B5
Lismurnaghan❶ BT42. . 77 F1
Lismurnaghan La BT42 . . 77 E1
Lismurn Pk ❻ BT42. . . 77 F2
Lismurphy❶ BT7 . . . 25 F7
Lisnabilla❶ BT67 . . . 166 E5
Lisnabilla Rd BT67 . . 166 E5
Lisnablagh Rd BT52 . . 174 F5
Lisnabraugh❶ BT53. . . 16 D2
Lisnabreeny❶ BT6 . . 152 F3
Lisnabreeny Rd BT6. . . 152 F4
Lisnabreeny Rd E BT6 . . 153 A4
Lisnacrogher❶ BT43. . . 62 C3
Lisnacrogher Rd BT43. . 62 D3
Lisnafillon❶ BT42 . . . 78 A3
Lisnafillon La BT42. . . 78 A3
Lisnafillon Rd BT42 . . . 77 F3
Lisnagalt❶ BT52. . . 15 C2
Lisnagarran❶ BT42 . . . 76 F8
Lisnagarran La BT42 . . 76 F8
Lisnagarvey Dr BT28 . . 160 A4
Lisnagarvey High Sch
  BT28 . . . 169 F8
Lisnagarvy❶ BT28 . . . 160 B2
Lisnagat❶ BT53 . . . 17 C5
Lisnagat BT53 . . . 17 A5
Lisnagaver❶ BT44 . . . 59 F6
LISNAGELVIN❶ BT47. . . 179 C4
Lisnagelvin Leisure Ctr ❺
  BT47 . . . 179 C4
Lisnagelvin Prim Sch ❻
  BT47 . . . 179 C4
Lisnagelvin Rd BT47 . . 179 C4
Lisnagelvin Ret Pk BT47. . 179 B3
Lisnagelvin Sh Ctr BT47 . 179 C4
Lisnagowan BT47 . . . 179 C7
Lisnagreggan❶ BT41. . 107 E7
Lisnagrib❶ BT49. . . 23 E4
Lisnagroat❶ BT51 . . . 59 D2
Lisnagrot Rd
  Coleraine BT51 . . . 59 C2
  Maghera BT46. . . 75 E8
Lisnagunogue Lower❶
  BT57 . . . 6 B5
Lisnagunogue Upper❶
  BT57 . . . 6 C4
Lisnahall❶ BT71. . . 113 F1
Lisnahall Rd T BT71. . . 113 F1
Lisnahawley❶ BT47. . . 177 F6
Lisnahay North❶ BT44. . 66 B4
Lisnahay South❶ BT44. . 66 B3
Lisnahilt❶ BT42 . . . 79 F3
Lisnahuncheon Rd BT44. . 60 C4
Lisnahunshin❶ BT42. . . 77 A8
Lisnahunshin Rd BT42. . 77 A8
Lisnakilly❶ BT49 . . . 39 A8

Lisnalinchy❶ BT39. . . 111 D5
Lisnalinchy Rd
  Ballyclare BT39 . . . 184 D1
  Newtownabbey BT36. . 111 D3
Lisnalinchy Rd W BT39. . 111 D4
Lisnamanny❶ BT43 . . . 62 F8
Lisnamanny Rd BT43 . . 62 F8
Lisnamorrow❶ BT45. . 105 C4
Lisnamuck❶
  Coleraine BT51 . . . 42 C7
  Maghera BT46. . . 89 B8
Lisnamuck Hill BT46 . . 89 C8
Lisnamuck Rd
  Coleraine BT51 . . . 42 B7
  Maghera BT46. . . 89 C7
Lisnamurrican Prim Sch
  BT42 . . . 79 E5
Lisnamurrican Rd BT42. . 79 E5
Lisnaragh Irish❶ BT82 . . 68 A1
Lisnaragh Rd BT82 . . 67 F2
Lisnaragh Scotch❶ BT82. 68 A2
Lisnarea Ave BT48 . . . 177 A2
Lisnarick❶ BT52. . . 15 C3
Lisnascreghan❶ BT51. . 57 A5
Lisnascreghog Rd BT51. . 57 A6
Lisnasharragh High Sch
  BT6 . . . 152 D8
Lisnasharragh Pk BT6. . 152 E8
Lisnasharragh Prim Sch
  BT6 . . . 152 D8
Lisnasoo❶ BT44 . . . 45 D1
Lisnasoo Rd BT44. . . 45 E1
Lisnastrean❶ BT27 . . . 171 A4
Lisnastrean Rd BT27 . . 171 A4
Lisnataylor❶ BT29 . . . 117 F5
Lisnataylor Rd BT29. . . 117 F5
Lisnatruck (Blaris)❶
  BT27 . . . 160 E1
Lisnatrunk (Lambeg)❶
  BT27 . . . 160 F2
Lisnavar Ct BT47. . . 179 B2
Lisnawhiggel❶ BT42. . . 94 F6
Lisneal❶
  Limavady BT49 . . . 38 A5
  Londonderry BT47. . . 179 F5
Lisneal Coll BT47 . . . 179 A3
Lisneal Coll (Drumahoe
  Campus) BT47. . . 179 E1
Lisneal Ct BT47 . . . 179 E2
Lisnevanagh❶ BT41. . . 94 F1
Lisnevenagh Rd
  Antrim BT41. . . 108 F8
  Ballymena BT42. . . 94 D6
Lisnisk❶
  Ballymena BT44. . . 29 C1
  Ballymoney BT53 . . 15 D2
Lisnode Rd BT27 . . . 171 F6
Lisnoe❶ BT27 . . . 170 C3
Lisnoe Pk BT27 . . . 170 B2
Lisnoe Rd BT27 . . . 170 B2
Lisnoe Wlk BT28 . . . 169 E8
Lisrodden❶ BT44 . . . 76 F7
Lissadell Ave BT56 . . . 172 D2
Lissadell Dr BT45 . . 183 B6
Lissadell Gdns BT56 . . 172 C4
Lissadell Gr BT56 . . . 172 C4
Lissadell Mews BT56 . . 172 C4
Lissaghmore❶ BT51 . . 43 A8
Lissan❶ BT80 . . . 112 E7
Lissan Cl
  Belfast BT6 . . . 152 B7
  Cookstown BT80 . . 185 C7
Lissan Demesne❶ BT80 . 112 E7
Lissan Dr BT80 . . . 185 C6
Lissanduff Ave BT57. . . 5 C5
Lissan Prim Sch BT80 . . 112 F7
Lissan Rd BT80 . . . 185 B7
Lisserluss❶ BT57 . . 6 A7
Lissue Cres BT28 . . 169 E8
Lissue E Ind Est BT28 . . 169 A8
Lissue Hospl BT28 . . . 158 F1
Lissue Rd BT28 . . . 169 A8
Listress❶ BT47 . . . 52 E5
Lisvarna Hts BT12 . . 188 B2
Lisvarna Pl BT12 . . . 188 B2
Liswatty Lower❶ BT52. . 15 C1
Liswatty Rd BT52 . . . 27 A8
Liswatty Upper❶ BT52. . 15 B1
Little Ballymena BT39 . 111 F6
Littlebridge Rd
  Cookstown BT80 . . . 113 F2
  Magherafelt BT45 . . 114 A3
Little Charlotte St BT7 . . 189 B1
Little Deer Park❶ BT44 . . 66 A7
Little Derry BT49. . . 40 B4
Little Diamond The BT48 178 E5
Little Donegall St BT1. . 189 A4
Little Edward St BT1. . . 189 B4
Little Flower Girls Sch
  BT15 . . . 137 D4
Little Glebe❶ BT53 . . 13 A1
Little James St BT48 . . 178 E5
Little May St BT2 . . . 189 B2
Little Patrick St BT15. . 189 A4
Little Victoria St BT2 . . 189 A2
Little Wenham BT67 . . 145 A4
Little York St
  Belfast BT15 . . . 189 A4
  ❷ Belfast BT15. . . 144 E7
Livery Lower❶ BT53 . . 28 F7
Livery Rd BT53. . . 28 F7
Livery Upper❶ BT53 . . 28 F7
Living Rivers Christian Sch
  BT42. . . 181 C3
Loan❶ BT47 . . . 77 C7
LOANENDS BT29. . . 118 C6

Loanends Prim Sch
  BT29 . . . 118 C6
Loanends Rd BT39 . . . 118 D7
Loan Rd BT42. . . 77 D7
Locan St BT12 . . . 143 E4
Locarden BT48. . . 177 E8
Lochinver Dr BT5 . . . 146 E2
Loch Lao (Lough Lea)
  BT5 . . . 145 A5
Lockhart's La BT38. . . 125 D2
Lockside BT9 . . . 151 D7
Locksley Bsns Pk BT6. . 145 E1
Locksley Dr BT10 . . . 150 D5
Locksley Gdns BT10. . . 150 D4
Locksley Grange BT10. . 150 D5
Locksley Parade BT10. . 150 D4
Locksley Pk BT10 . . . 150 D3
Locksley Pl BT10. . . 150 E4
Lockstown BT38 . . . 99 E4
Lockvale Manor BT67 . . 155 C2
Lockview Rd BT9 . . . 151 E7
Lodge❶ BT52. . . 174 E2
Lodge Manor BT52 . . 174 D2
Lodge Pk BT52 . . . 174 E2
Lodge Rd
  Coleraine BT52 . . . 174 D3
  Larne BT40 . . . 182 F3
Lodge The BT28 . . . 147 D5
Loguestown❶
  Coleraine BT52 . . . 174 F6
  Portstewart BT55 . . 173 C4
Loguestown Ct BT52 . . 174 E6
Loguestown Ind Est
  BT52 . . . 174 E6
Loguestown Pk BT52 . . 174 E7
Loguestown Rd
  Coleraine BT52 . . . 14 C5
  Portstewart BT55 . . 173 C4
Logwood Rd BT39. . . 184 F1
Lombard Ave BT28 . . 159 E3
Lombard Pk BT28 . . . 159 E3
Lombard St BT1 . . . 189 A3
Lomond❶ BT49. . . 22 F2
Lomond Ave BT4 . . . 145 D5
Lomond Hts BT80 . . 185 D3
Lomond Rd BT49. . . 22 E3
Lomond St BT4 . . . 145 D5
Londonderry❶ BT48. . . 178 E4
LONDONDERRY (DOIRE)
  BT47. . . 179 A7
Londonderry Model Prim Sch
  ❿ BT48. . . 178 E6
Londonderry (Waterside) Sta
  BT48. . . 178 F4
London Rd BT6 . . . 145 A3
London St
  Belfast BT6 . . . 145 A3
  Londonderry BT48. . . 178 C3
Lone Moor Gdns BT48. . 178 C3
Lone Moor Rd BT48. . . 178 C4
Lonemore Rd BT48. . . 178 D5
Longacre BT8 . . . 152 A5
Long Comm BT42 . . 181 A1
Long Commons BT52. . 174 D3
Longfield❶
  Ballymena BT44. . . 65 C5
  Magherafelt BT45 . . 89 F1
Longfield Beg❶ BT38. . 37 A6
Longfield Gdns BT38 . . 129 F3
Longfield Ind Est BT47 . . 36 F6
Longfield La
  Magherafelt BT45 . . 103 F8
  Newtownabbey BT38. . 129 E4
Longfield Level (Intake)❶
  BT47. . . 36 F8
Longfield More❶ BT47. . 36 F7
Longfield Rd
  Londonderry BT47. . . 36 F6
  Magherafelt BT45 . . 103 F8
Long Kesh BT27 . . . 169 E4
Long La BT53 . . . 43 F6
Longland❶ BT47. . . 52 D8
Longland Rd
  Londonderry BT47. . . 69 C5
  Strabane BT82. . . 67 E4
Longlands BT44. . . 76 C4
Longlands Ave BT36. . 133 D2
Longlands Ct BT36 . . 133 D2
Longlands Rd BT36. . . 133 D2
Longmore❶ BT43. . . 64 A5
Longmore Rd BT43. . . 63 C4
Long Rig Rd BT29 . . 117 F3
Long's Glebe❶ BT51. . 13 A2
Longshot The BT39 . . 111 B4
Longstone Prim Sch BT42 92 D3
Longstone St BT28 . . 159 F1
Longtower Prim Sch ⓳
  BT48. . . 178 E4
Longtown❶ BT44 . . . 49 D4
Long Twr Ct BT48. . . 178 E4
Long Twr St ❶ BT48 . . 178 E4
Longwood Rd BT37. . . 133 E2
Lonsdale Ct. . . 134 D8
Loonburn❶ BT39 . . . 96 C3
Loopland Cres BT6. . . 145 B2
Loopland Dr BT6. . . 145 B2
Loopland Gdns BT6 . . 145 C2
Loopland Parade BT6. . 145 C2
Loopland Rd BT6. . . 145 B2
Loran Ave BT40. . . 182 A4
Loran Parade BT40. . 182 A4
Loran Rd BT40. . . 182 A4

Loran Way BT80 . . . . 185 D3
Lord St BT5 . . . . 145 B4
Loreto Coll BT51 . . . . 174 A5
Lorne St BT9 . . . . 144 B1
Losset◑ BT54 . . . . 9 B1
Lothair Ave BT15 . . . . . . 137 C1
Lothian Ave BT5 . . . . 146 E3
Louden St Ind Est BT13 . . 188 C4
Louden St BT13 . . . . 188 C4
Loughabin
  Ballymena BT44 . . . . 45 B6
  Ballymoney BT53 . . . . . . 28 F2
Loughabin Rd BT53 . . . . . . 44 F8
Loughan◑ BT54 . . . . 20 F6
LOUGHAN BT44 . . . . 49 C7
Loughan Hill BT43 . . . . . 181 A6
Loughan Hill◑ BT52 . . . . 174 F7
Loughan Hill Est BT52 . . 174 F7
Loughan Hill Ind Est
  BT52 . . . . 174 F7
Loughanhill Pk BT52 . . . . 174 D8
Loughan Island◑ BT26 . . . 26 D5
Loughanlea La BT39 . . . . . 99 F4
Loughan Marina BT52 . . . . 26 E5
Loughanmore◑ BT41 . . . . 110 B3
Loughanmore Rd
  Antrim BT41 . . . . 187 E4
  Ballyclare BT39 . . . . . . 110 C3
Loughan Rd
  Coleraine BT52 . . . . 26 E4
  Strabane BT82 . . . . 67 F2
Loughanreagh North◑
  BT52 . . . . 26 E7
Loughanreagh South◑
  BT52 . . . . 26 D7
Loughan Sch BT43 . . . . . 181 C6
Loughareema Rd
  Ballycastle BT54 . . . . 20 D3
  Ballymena BT44 . . . . 20 D1
Loughash◑ BT82 . . . . 68 E2
Loughash Prim Sch BT82 . . 68 D2
Loughash Rd BT82 . . . . 68 C1
Lough Beg Pk BT8 . . . . . 163 C3
Loughbeg Rd BT41 . . . . . . 92 D2
Lough Brin Pk BT8 . . . . . 163 C3
Lough Caragh Pk BT8 . . 163 C3
Loughconnelly◑ BT43 . . . . 63 F3
Lough Derg Pk BT8 . . . . 163 C3
Loughdoo Rd BT40 . . . . . . 82 C6
Lough Dr BT40 . . . . 100 C3
Loughduff◑ BT40 . . . . 82 C7
Loughermore◑ BT47 . . . . . 53 F7
Loughermore Rd
  Limavady BT49 . . . . 38 B3
  Londonderry BT47 . . . . . . 54 A8
Lough Erne Pk BT8 . . . . . 163 C2
Lough Fea Rd BT80 . . . . . 112 D7
Lough Fine Pk BT8 . . . . . 163 C3
Loughgall Gdns BT37 . . . 134 A8
LOUGHGUILE BT44 . . . . . . 30 A2
Loughill◑ BT44 . . . . 45 F3
Loughill Pk BT45 . . . . 89 F5
Loughill◑ BT45 . . . . 89 F5
Loughill Rd BT44 . . . . 45 F3
Loughinsholin Pk BT45 91 C2
Lough Lea (Loch Lao)
  BT5 . . . . 145 A5
Lough Leane Pk BT8 . . . 163 C3
Loughloughan◑ BT43 . . . . 63 E2
Loughlynch◑ BT53 . . . . . . 16 F5
Loughmagarry◑ BT43 . . . . 78 D8
Loughmagarry Rd BT43 . . 78 C8
Loughmoney Pk BT37 . . . 133 F5
Lough Moss Ctr BT8 . . . 163 D2
Lough Moss Pk BT8 . . . . 163 D2
Lough Mourne Pk BT8 . . 163 D2
Loughmourne Rd BT38 . . 99 C1
Lough Rd
  Antrim BT41 . . . . 186 C4
  Ballymena BT44 . . . . 65 A1
  Carrickfergus BT38 . . . . . 99 D1
  Larne BT40 . . . . 100 C3
  Lisburn BT28 . . . . 121 C2
  Magherafelt BT45 . . . . . 105 F5
Loughrelisk◑ BT28 . . . . . 156 F5
Loughrey Ct BT51 . . . . . . 137 C2
Loughshore Ed & Resource
  Ctr BT36 . . . . 137 E2
Loughside Ind Pk BT3 . . 137 F4
Loughside Recn Ctr
  BT15 . . . . 137 E5
Lough Swilly Pk BT8 . . . 163 C3
Loughtilube◑ BT47 . . . . . . 70 A4
Loughview◑ BT67 . . . . . . 120 H4
Loughview Ave
  Carrickfergus BT38 . . . . 125 C2
  Holywood BT18 . . . . 139 D4
Loughview Bglws BT40 . . 182 E4
Loughview Bsns Pk BT3 . 138 C3
Loughview Dr
  Carrickfergus BT38 . . . . 125 E2
  Castlereagh BT6 . . . . . . 152 B6
Loughview Gn BT14 . . . . 136 E5
Loughview Hts BT14 . . . . 136 E5
Lough View Integrated Prim
  Sch BT6 . . . . 152 E7
Loughview Manor BT14 . 136 E5
Loughview Mdws BT14 . . 136 E5
Loughview Pk 4 BT51 . . . 59 C5
Loughview Rd BT29 . . . . 116 C5
Loughview St 2 BT14 . . . 136 E5
Loughview Terr
  4 Belfast BT15 . . . . 137 E4
  Newtownabbey BT38 . . . 129 D3
Loughview Village BT38 . 125 E2

Loup Prim Sch BT45 . . . . 105 A1
Loup Rd
  Antrim BT41 . . . . 92 E3
  Magherafelt BT45 . . . . . 114 A8
  Moneymore BT45 . . . . . 113 F8
Lourdes Prim Sch BT38 . 127 A8
Lovatt St BT5 . . . . 145 D4
Lovedale BT45 . . . . 105 E2
Love La BT38 . . . . 125 A2
Love's Corkey◑ BT44 . . . . 30 C1
Loves Rd BT45 . . . . 183 F5
Lower Alla◑ BT47 . . . . 69 B6
LOWER BALLINDERRY
  BT28 . . . . 155 E8
Lower Ballinderry Rd
  BT28 . . . . 155 E7
Lower Ballyboley Rd BT39 97 E3
Lower Ballycaghan◑
  BT51 . . . . 25 E1
Lower Ballyleighery◑
  BT49 . . . . 11 F1
Lower Balteagh◑ BT51 . . . 25 B5
Lower B'arton Rd BT47 . . . 69 B7
Lower Braniel Rd
  6 Castlereagh BT5 . . . . 146 A1
  Castlereagh BT5 . . . . . . 153 B8
Lower Brockagh◑ BT51 . . . 57 B6
Lower Brone◑ BT51 . . . . . 42 C4
Lower Cairncastle Rd
  BT40 . . . . 182 B4
Lower Cam◑ BT51 . . . . 41 C8
Lower Campsey◑ BT47 . . . 36 B6
Lower Clarendon St 6
  BT48 . . . . 178 E6
Lower Clonard St BT12 . . 188 A2
Lower Coole Glebe◑
  BT51 . . . . 26 E3
Lower Corndale◑ BT49 . . . 23 A2
Lower Ctres BT13 . . . . . . 188 A3
Lower Doaghs◑ BT49 . . . . 11 C7
Lower Drummans◑ BT49 . 11 C5
Lower Galliagh Rd BT48 . 176 D5
Lower Garfield St BT1 . . . 189 A4
Lower Gateside BT39 . . . 184 B8
Lower Gortagherty◑
  BT47 . . . . 36 D4
Lower Grange Rd BT80 . . 113 C1
Lower Kilburn St BT12 . . 188 A1
Lower Kildress BT80 . . . . 112 C3
Lower Kiltinny◑ BT51 . . . . 25 C4
Lower Lansdowne Rd
  BT55 . . . . 173 D8
Lower Middle Doaghs◑
  BT49 . . . . 11 D6
Lower Mill St BT43 . . . . . 181 D4
Lower Moyknock◑ BT51 . 59 F2
Lower Mullan◑ BT80 . . . 115 C5
Lower Nassau St BT48 . . 178 D7
Lower Newmills Rd
  BT52 . . . . 174 F4
Lower Paddocks 4 BT51 . 26 A7
Lower Quilley◑ BT51 . . . . 13 E2
Lower Rashee Rd BT39 . . 97 A1
Lower Rd
  Belfast BT29 . . . . 121 B3
  Londonderry BT48 . . . . 178 E6
Lower Regent St (Sráid
  Ríona Íochtir) BT13 . . . 189 A4
Lower Rockview St BT12 188 A1
Lower Rogan Manor
  BT36 . . . . 132 B7
Lower Rusky◑ BT80 . . . . 114 C4
Lower Sizehill Rd BT39 . 184 A1
Lower Slievenacloy
  BT28 . . . . 147 B8
Lower Stanfield St BT7 . . 189 B2
Lower Town◑ BT51 . . . . . . 59 C2
Lowertown Rd
  Magherafelt BT45 . . . . . 183 B8
  Strabane BT82 . . . . 67 A5
Lower Tully◑ BT47 . . . . . . 50 E4
Lower Tullyally◑ BT47 . . . 51 D6
Lower Tullykittagh◑
  BT44 . . . . 62 D8
Lower Violet St BT47 . . . 179 A4
Lower Waterloo Rd
  BT40 . . . . 182 D5
Lower Windsor Ave BT9 . 144 B1
Lower Woodlands BT38 . . 100 A3
Lowes Ind Est BT8 . . . . . 163 D2
Lowland Ave BT5 . . . . . . 146 E3
Lowland Gdns BT5 . . . . . 146 E3
Low Rd
  Larne BT40 . . . . 100 C6
  Lisburn BT27 . . . . 160 D2
Lowry Ct BT7 . . . . 151 E6
Lowry Pk BT49 . . . . 180 D3
Lowry's La BT48 . . . . 178 C8
Lowtown◑ BT40 . . . . 98 D3
Lowtown Rd
  Ballyclare BT39 . . . . . . 110 F1
  Belfast BT29 . . . . 121 F2
Low Town Rd BT28 . . . . . 121 F3
Lowtown Terr 2 BT42 . . . 77 F7
Low-Wood◑ BT15 . . . . . . 137 C6
Lowwood Gdns BT15 . . . 137 D5
Lowwood Pk BT15 . . . . . 137 E5
Lowwood Prim Sch
  BT15 . . . . 137 D5
Loy◑ BT80 . . . . 185 D5
Loy St BT80 . . . . 185 D4
Lúb Bholcáin (Vulcan Link)
  14 BT5 . . . . 145 A5
Lubitavish◑ BT44 . . . . 32 B5
Lúb Tullach Phoitínséir
  (Mountpottinger Link) 36
  BT5 . . . . 145 A5

Loup Prim Sch BT45 . . . . 105 A1
Lucerne Par BT9 . . . . 151 D7
Lucknow St 5 BT13 . . . . 143 F5
Ludlow Sq
  2 Belfast BT15 . . . . 144 D8
  4 Belfast BT15 . . . . 144 D8
Lumen Christi Coll 3
  BT48 . . . . 178 D4
Lumford Ave 6 BT38 . . . 100 D1
Luney◑ BT45 . . . . 90 D1
Luney La BT45 . . . . 90 D2
Luney Rd BT45 . . . . 104 D8
Lunnon Rd BT40 . . . . 84 D1
Lupin Ave BT82 . . . . 67 E4
Lurganagoose◑ BT45 . . . . 90 F5
Lurganagoose Rd BT45 . . 90 F4
Lurgan Rd
  Belfast BT29 . . . . 120 F4
  Craigavon BT67 . . . . . . 164 E7
  Londonderry BT47 . . . . . 36 D5
  Moira BT67 . . . . 166 A1
Lurgansemanus◑ BT67 . 165 F7
Lurgantarry◑ BT67 . . . . . 164 A1
Lurganteneil◑ BT29 . . . . 121 E3
Lurganure◑ BT28 . . . . . . 168 D6
Lurganure Rd BT28 . . . . 168 C6
Lurgan West◑ BT41 . . . . 107 F6
Lurgill◑ BT28 . . . . 120 E2
Lurigethan◑ BT44 . . . . . . 32 C2
Luxor Gdns BT5 . . . . 145 E4
Lyehill Gn BT39 . . . . 110 D1
Lylehill Rd
  Ballyclare BT39 . . . . . . 118 F5
  Templepatrick BT39 . . . 110 D1
Lylehill Rd E BT39 . . . . . 118 F8
Lylehill Rd Lower BT14 . . 119 B3
Lynda Ave BT37 . . . . 134 B8
Lynda Cres BT37 . . . . . . 134 B8
Lynda Farm
  Newtownabbey BT37 . . . 129 A1
  Newtownabbey BT37 . . . 134 A8
Lynda Gdns BT37 . . . . . . 129 A1
Lyndale Cl BT36 . . . . 132 D7
Lynda Mdws BT37 . . . . . 134 A8
Lyndhurst Ave BT13 . . . . 143 C7
Lyndhurst Cl BT13 . . . . . 143 C7
Lyndhurst Cres BT13 . . . 143 C7
Lyndhurst Ct BT13 . . . . . 143 C7
Lyndhurst Dr BT13 . . . . . 143 C7
Lyndhurst Gdns BT13 . . . 143 C7
Lyndhurst Gr BT13 . . . . . 143 C7
Lyndhurst Hts BT13 . . . . 143 C7
Lyndhurst Link BT13 . . . . 143 C7
Lyndhurst Manor BT47 . . 179 D4
Lyndhurst Mdws BT13 . . 143 C7
Lyndhurst New Rd BT13 . 143 C7
Lyndhurst Par BT13 . . . . 143 C7
Lyndhurst Path BT13 . . . 143 C7
Lyndhurst Pk BT13 . . . . . 143 C7
Lyndhurst Pl BT13 . . . . . 143 C7
Lyndhurst Rd BT47 . . . . . 179 D4
Lyndhurst Rise BT13 . . . 143 C7
Lyndhurst Row BT13 . . . 143 C7
Lyndhurst View Ave
  BT13 . . . . 143 C7
Lyndhurst View Cl BT13 . 143 C7
Lyndhurst View Rd BT13 . 143 C7
Lyndhurst Way BT13 . . . 143 C7
Lynhurst View Ave BT13 . 143 C7
Lynnwood Mews BT5 . . . 121 B5
Lynwood Pk BT18 . . . . . 139 E5
Lyric Players Theatre
  BT9 . . . . 151 D8
Lyttledale BT51 . . . . 57 F8

M

M2 Bsns Pk BT3 . . . . 137 F2
Mabel Ct BT12 . . . . 188 C1
Maboy Rd BT44 . . . . 76 E8
McAdam Gdns BT12 . . . . 188 C2
McAdam Pk BT12 . . . . . . 188 C2
Mcafee Pl BT53 . . . . 175 D5
McAllister Mews BT4 . . . 145 C6
McArthur Ave BT53 . . . . . 28 A8
McArthur Ct BT4 . . . . . . 145 A6
Mcart's Fort* BT4 . . . . . . 137 A8
MacAuley Pk 9 BT54 . . . . 8 C3
Mcauley St BT7 . . . . 189 B2
Mccamphill Pk BT44 . . . . 44 F4
Mccandless St 3 BT13 . . 144 A7
Mccarey's Loanen BT40 . 182 B6
Mccarter Pk BT47 . . . . . 179 C5
Mccartney Pk BT48 . . . . 176 F1
Mccartney Pl BT67 . . . . . 166 C1
Mccaughan Rd BT3 . . . . 138 A1
Mccavans Pl BT2 . . . . . . 189 A2
Mccleery St BT15 . . . . . . 144 D7
McClelland Rd BT44 . . . . 44 F4
Mcclintock St BT2 . . . . . 189 A2
McCloy Gdns BT47 . . . . . 179 B3
McClure St BT7 . . . . 189 A1
Mccooles Rd BT45 . . . . . . 91 A3
Mccorley Rd BT41 . . . . . 106 D7
McCrae's Brae BT38 . . . 100 D2
Mccurry Wlk BT47 . . . . . 180 E5
Mcdonald's Fort* BT41 . . 108 B4
Mcdonnell Ct BT12 . . . . . 188 B2
Mcdonnell St BT12 . . . . . 188 B2
Mcfall St 3 BT40 . . . . 83 B3
Macfinn Lower◑ BT53 . . . 26 F4
Macfinn Upper◑ BT53 . . . 26 E3
Mcgarel Cl 3 BT40 . . . . . 182 D4
Mcgarel Gdns BT40 . . . . 182 C4

Mcgarvey Ct BT47 . . . . . 179 C5
Mcgeagh Tr BT40 . . . . . . 182 A3
Mcgeagh's Well* BT80 . . 185 B7
Macgill Ct BT48 . . . . 176 A2
Mcgovern Dr BT80 . . . . . 185 C4
MACHAIRE FÍOLTA
  (MAGHERAFELT) BT45 . 183 B5
MACHAIRE MORNA
  (MAGHERAMORNE)
  BT40 . . . . 99 F8
MACHAIRE RÁTHA
  (MAGHERA) BT46 . . . . . 74 E1
Mcivor's Pl BT13 . . . . . . 188 C4
Mckeens Ave BT38 . . . . 131 B8
Mckeens Gn 2 BT38 . . . 131 B8
McKenna Rise 16 BT46 . . 74 D1
McKennas La BT45 . . . . . 91 D7
Mackenny◑ BT80 . . . . . . 112 C3
Mackenny Rd BT80 . . . . 112 B3
Mackey St BT15 . . . . 137 D1
Mckibben's Ct BT1 . . . . . 189 A4
Mckinney Ind Est BT36 . 132 A5
Mckinney Pk BT80 . . . . . 185 A6
Mckinney Prim Sch
  (Dundrod) BT67 . . . . . 140 C8
Mckinstry Rd BT17 . . . . . 160 C7
Macknagh◑ BT46 . . . . . . 74 E4
Macknagh La BT46 . . . . . 74 E5
Macknagh Rd BT46 . . . . . 74 E5
McLean & Partners
  Division◑ BT47 . . . . . . 36 E6
McLean Rd BT47 . . . . . . 36 D6
Macleary◑ BT51 . . . . 25 E5
Macleary Rd BT51 . . . . . . 25 F5
Maclevennon Rd
  Portrush BT56 . . . . 14 C5
  Portstewart BT55 . . . . . 173 E1
Mc Master Cres 1 BT45 . 91 C1
Mcmaster St BT4 . . . . . . 145 B5
Mcmullans La 2 BT6 . . . 145 A4
Mcnaul Pk BT47 . . . . 179 C5
Macneice Cl BT48 . . . . . 176 A2
McNeill Pk BT42 . . . . 95 E8
Macosquin◑ BT51 . . . . . . 25 E5
MACOSQUIN BT51 . . . . . . 25 E5
Macosquin Prim Sch
  BT51 . . . . 25 E5
Mcquillan Pk BT49 . . . . . 180 B1
Mcquillan's Grave* BT54 . 19 B1
Mcquillan St BT13 . . . . . 188 A2
Macroom Gdns BT38 . . . 125 A2
Macrory Pk BT47 . . . . . . 179 B7
McVickersland◑ BT39 . . . 96 C3
Madams Bank Rd BT47 . 179 E8
Madam's Bank Rd BT48 . 177 A4
Maddenbeny BT55 . . . . . 173 B1
Maddybenny Beg◑
  BT55 . . . . 173 B1
Maddybenny More◑
  BT52 . . . . 14 C5
Maddybenny Pk BT55 . . 173 C1
Maddydoo Upper◑ BT53 . 43 C3
Maddykeel Lower◑ BT53 . 43 B3
Maddykeel Upper◑ BT53 . 43 C4
Madigan Pk BT38 . . . . . . 125 C2
Madison Ave
  Belfast BT15 . . . . 137 B3
  Eglinton BT47 . . . . 36 E4
Madison Ave E 3 BT47 . . 145 D5
Madrid Ct (Cúirt Maidrid) 6
  BT5 . . . . 145 A5
Madrid St BT5 . . . . 145 A5
Magazine St Upper 4
  BT48 . . . . 178 E5
Magazine St BT48 . . . . . 178 E5
Magdala St BT7 . . . . 144 D2
Magee Pk BT40 . . . . 182 C7
Magees Rd
  Craigavon BT67 . . . . . . 155 F5
  Lisburn BT28 . . . . 156 B6
MAGHABERRY BT67 . . . . 167 A8
Magherry BT67 . . . . 167 A8
MAGHABERRY BT67 . . . . 167 B7
Maghaberry Manor BT67 167 B8
Maghaberry Prim Sch
  BT67 . . . . 167 A7
Maghaberry Rd BT67 . . . 166 E7
Maghadone◑ BT45 . . . . . 104 E1
Maghadone La BT45 . . . 104 E1
Maghadone Rd
  Limavady BT49 . . . . 12 D5
  Magherafelt BT45 . . . . . 114 A8
Magherabane◑ BT47 . . . . 54 C3
Magherabeg◑ BT41 . . . . . 94 C3
Magherabeg Rd BT41 . . . 94 C3
Magheraboy
  Ballycastle BT54 . . . . 7 B6
  Ballymena BT44 . . . . 46 D4
  Londonderry BT47 . . . . . 55 E1
  Portstewart BT55 . . . . . 173 D3
Magheraboy Ave BT55 . . 173 D3
Magheraboy Gdns BT55 . 173 D3
Magheraboy Hollow 4
  BT55 . . . . 173 D3
Magheraboy Lower◑
  BT53 . . . . 29 A5
Magheraboy Rd
  Ballymena BT44 . . . . 60 B7
  Coleraine BT52 . . . . 14 C5
  Portstewart BT55 . . . . . 173 D3
Magheraboy Terr (Ardán An
  Mhachaire Bhuí) BT47 . 55 E1
Magheraboy Upper◑
  BT53 . . . . 28 E1
Magherabrack Rd BT47 . 70 D4
Maghera Bsns Pk BT46 . 74 E1
Magheracanon◑ BT47 . . . 50 F5
Magheracashel◑ BT54 . . . 7 D4

Magheraclay◑ BT52 . . . . 174 A8
Magheracross◑ BT57 . . . . 5 A3
Magherafelt High Sch
  BT45 . . . . 183 C5
MAGHERAFELT (MACHAIRE
  FÍOLTA) BT45 . . . . 183 B5
Magherafelt Prim Sch
  BT45 . . . . 183 D5
Magherafelt Rd
  Castledawson BT45 . . . . 91 C1
  Magherafelt BT45 . . . . . 89 B3
  Moneymore BT45 . . . . . 113 F8
  Tobermore BT45 . . . . . . 89 F5
Magheragall◑ BT52 . . . . 158 D2
Magherageery◑ BT27 . . . 169 D5
Maghera High Sch BT46 . 90 B8
Magherahoney◑ BT53 . . . 30 C7
Magheralane◑ BT41 . . . . 94 B1
Magheralane Rd BT41 . . 108 A3
Magheralave Ct BT28 . . . 160 A5
Magheralave Grange
  BT28 . . . . 160 A5
Magheralave Pk E BT28 . 160 B3
Magheralave Pk N BT28 . 160 A3
Magheralave Pk S BT28 . 160 A3
Magheralave Rd BT28 . . 160 A3
Magheralave (Upper
  Belfast)◑ BT28 . . . . . . 160 B6
Magheralave (Upper
  Massereene)◑ BT28 . . 159 E6
Magheralis◑ BT47 . . . . . . 53 F2
Magheraliskmisk◑
  BT28 . . . . 157 C3
MAGHERA (MACHAIRE
  RÁTHA) BT46 . . . . 74 E1
MAGHERAMASON◑ BT47 . 50 E3
Magheramason Rd BT47 . 50 E3
Magheramenagh◑
  BT55 . . . . 173 D5
Magheramenagh Cres 1
  BT55 . . . . 173 D3
Magheramenagh Dr
  BT55 . . . . 173 D3
Magheramenagh Gdns
  BT55 . . . . 173 D3
Magheramenagh La
  BT55 . . . . 173 D4
Magheramenagh Pk 2
  BT55 . . . . 173 D3
Magheramesk◑ BT67 . . . 166 E6
Magheramore◑
  Ballycastle BT54 . . . . . . 18 C5
  Coleraine BT51 . . . . 57 F6
  Limavady BT49 . . . . 38 E2
  Londonderry BT47 . . . . . 37 B5
  Londonderry BT47 . . . . . 71 E5
Magheramore Rd
  Ballycastle BT54 . . . . . . 18 C6
  Coleraine BT51 . . . . 57 F6
  Londonderry BT47 . . . . . 71 D7
MAGHERAMORNE
  (MACHAIRE MORNA)
  BT40 . . . . 99 A8
Magheramorne Sta BT40 . 99 F7
Magheramully◑ BT43 . . . . 63 E2
Maghera Prim Sch 27
  BT46 . . . . 74 D1
Maghera Rd
  Maghera BT46 . . . . 90 A7
  Magherafelt BT45 . . . . . 89 F6
Magherascullion◑ BT45 . 104 A1
Magheraskeagh◑ BT49 . . 23 C2
Maghera St BT51 . . . . . . 59 C5
Magherboy Dr 3 BT55 . . 173 D3
Magherboy Wlk 5 BT55 . 173 D3
Maghereagh◑ BT41 . . . . 108 D6
Maghereagh La BT41 . . . 108 D6
Maghereagh Rd BT41 . . . 108 D6
Maghereeroy◑ BT44 . . . . 32 E7
Magheridonnel◑ BT54 . . . 9 A4
Magherintendry◑ BT57 . . 6 B2
Maghernahar◑ BT54 . . . . 7 C3
Maghery Ct BT47 . . . . . . 50 D3
Maghery Rd BT54 . . . . . . 7 C5
Maghies Pl 1 BT6 . . . . . 145 A3
Magilligan Martello Twr*
  BT49 . . . . 11 C8
Magills Ave BT49 . . . . . . 125 D1
Mahee Cl BT8 . . . . 151 C2
Main Bentra Rd BT38 . . . 126 D8
Maine Bank BT41 . . . . . 108 A8
Mainegrove BT42 . . . . . . 78 A6
Maine North◑ BT49 . . . . . 39 F2
Maine Pk BT42 . . . . 78 B3
Maine Rd BT42 . . . . 94 C6
Maine South◑ BT49 . . . . . 55 F8
Maine Valley BT43 . . . . . 61 D2
Main Rd BT40 . . . . 99 C8
Main St
  Ahoghill BT42 . . . . 77 F2
  Ballycarry BT38 . . . . . . 100 A3
  Ballycastle BT54 . . . . . . 7 C7
  Ballyclare BT39 . . . . . . 184 C5
  Ballykelly BT49 . . . . 38 C7
  Ballymena BT44 . . . . . . 32 D2
  Ballymoney BT53 . . . . . 175 C4
  Ballynure BT39 . . . . 97 F2
  Belfast BT29 . . . . 121 B5
  Bellaghy BT45 . . . . 91 F5
  Broughshane BT42 . . . . 79 D7
  Bushmills BT57 . . . . 5 E3
  Castledawson BT45 . . . . 91 C2
  Castlerock BT51 . . . . . . 13 A5
  Claudy BT47 . . . . 69 B8
  Clogh Mills BT44 . . . . . . 45 E3
  Coleraine BT51 . . . . 42 A1
  Cookstown BT80 . . . . . 114 C3
  Crumlin BT29 . . . . 117 A1

Main St continued
Cullybackey BT42 . . . . 77 F6
Cushendun BT44 . . . . 21 A1
Doagh BT39 . . . . 111 A6
Dungiven BT47 . . . . 55 C2
Eglinton BT47 . . . . 36 E5
Garvagh BT51 . . . . 58 A8
Kells BT42 . . . . 95 A6
Larne BT40 . . . . 182 D4
Limavady BT49 . . . . 180 B6
Maghera BT46 . . . . 74 D1
Magherafelt BT45 . . . . . . 104 B8
Moira BT67 . . . . 166 C2
Portglenone BT44 . . . . . . 76 D4
Portstewart BT55 . . . . . . 173 D7
Randalstown BT41 . . . . . 108 A7
Rasharkin BT44 . . . . 60 B6
Swatragh BT46 . . . . 74 D8
Tobermore BT45 . . . . 89 E5
4 Cookstown BT80 . . . . 114 C3
Majestic Dr BT12 . . . . . . 188 C1
Major St 6 BT5 . . . . 145 B5
Makeestown La BT42 . . . 94 C6
Mala Chluain Ard (Clonard Rise) **4** BT14 . . . . 188 A3
Malcolmson St BT13 . . . 188 A2
Malcolm Villas BT45 . . . 90 F6
Maldon Ct BT12 . . . . 188 A1
Maldon St BT12 . . . . 188 A1
Malfin Ct BT9 . . . . 150 E4
Malfin Dr BT10 . . . . 150 E4
Malin Cres BT56 . . . . . . 172 C6
Malin Gdns BT48 . . . . . 178 C6
Malinmore Pk BT11 . . . . 149 F6
Mallaboy Rd BT44 . . . . . 44 F3
Mallendober 0 BT57 . . . . 5 F2
Mallon Villas 1 BT45 . . . 89 A3
Mallory Pk BT47 . . . . 36 D5
Mall The BT52 . . . . 174 C4
MALLUSK BT36 . . . . 119 C8
Mallusk Dr BT36 . . . . . . 132 C5
Mallusk Ent Pk BT36 . . . 132 C5
Mallusk Gdns BT41 . . . . 186 F5
Mallusk Prim Sch BT36 . . 119 D8
Mallusk Rd BT36 . . . . . . 132 B6
Malone Ave
  Belfast BT9 . . . . 144 B1
  4 Whitehead BT38 . . . 100 D1
Malone Beeches BT9 . . . 151 A5
Malone Ct BT9 . . . . 151 A5
Malone Ct Mews BT9 . . . 151 A5
Malone (Detached Portion) **0** BT8 . . . . . . 151 D4
Malone Gdns BT17 . . . . 150 A2
Malone Golf Club BT9 . . . 161 E8
Malone Grange BT9 . . . . 151 A5
Malone Hill Pk BT9 . . . . 151 A5
Malone Hts BT9 . . . . 150 E3
Malone Integrated Coll
  BT10 . . . . 150 D6
Malone Lower 0 BT9 . . . 144 B1
Malone Manor BT9 . . . . 151 A5
Malone Mdws BT9 . . . . . 151 A4
Malone Pk
  Belfast BT9 . . . . 150 F6
  Londonderry BT47 . . . . 179 C6
Malone Pk Central BT9 . . 151 A6
Malone Pk La BT9 . . . . . 150 F6
Malone Pl BT12 . . . . 188 C1
Malone Rd BT9 . . . . 151 A3
Malone Upper 0
  Belfast BT9 . . . . 151 A5
  Belfast BT17 . . . . 150 F1
Malone Valley Pk BT9 . . . 151 A4
Malone View Av BT9 . . . . 150 E3
Malone View Cres BT9 . . 150 E2
Malone View Pk BT9 . . . . 150 E2
Malone View Rd BT9 . . . . 150 E2
Maloon 0 BT80 . . . . 185 B6
Maloon Ct BT80 . . . . 185 B6
Maloon Dr BT80 . . . . 185 B6
Maloon Hill BT80 . . . . . . 185 B6
Maloon Hts BT80 . . . . . . 185 B6
Maloon Manor BT80 . . . . 185 B6
Maloon Pk BT80 . . . . 185 B6
Maloon Pl BT80 . . . . 185 B6
Maloon Rd BT80 . . . . 185 A6
Maloon View BT80 . . . . . 185 B6
Maloon Way BT80 . . . . . . 185 B6
Malory Gdns BT28 . . . . . 159 E5
Malory Pk BT47 . . . . 36 D4
Malton Ct BT9 . . . . 150 E4
Malton Dr BT9 . . . . 150 E4
Malton Rise BT9 . . . . . . 150 F3
Malton Vale BT9 . . . . . . 150 E4
Malvern Cl BT13 . . . . . . 144 B7
Malvern Prim Sch BT13 . . 144 C7
Malvern St BT13 . . . . . . 188 B4
Malvern Terr BT47 . . . . . 179 A4
Malvern Way BT13 . . . . . 188 B4
Malwood Pk BT9 . . . . . . 150 E4
Managh Beg 0 BT47 . . . . 52 A8
Managher 0 BT51 . . . . . . 26 D1
Managher Rd BT51 . . . . . 26 C2
Managh More 0 BT47 . . . 52 A8
Manderson St BT14 . . . . 145 C5
Mandeville Ave BT27 . . . 160 C1
Mangan Ct BT48 . . . . . . 176 B2
Manister 0 BT53 . . . . 17 C4
Manister Rd BT53 . . . . . 17 C4
Manna Gr BT5 . . . . 145 D2
Manner's Town 0 . . . . . . 34 C4
Manning Way BT47 . . . . 176 C4
Mann's Rd BT23 . . . . . . 153 E5
Manola Wood 0 BT53 . . . 43 E2
Manor Ave BT45 . . . . . . 183 C3
Manor Banks BT45 . . . . 183 C3

Manor Cl
  Belfast BT14 . . . . 144 B8
  Carrickfergus BT38 . . . . 125 B2
  Magherafelt BT45 . . . . . 183 C3
Manor Ct
  2 Belfast BT14 . . . . . . 144 B8
  Kilrea BT51 . . . . 59 D5
  1 Moira BT67 . . . . 166 C2
Manor Downs BT45 . . . . 183 C3
Manor Dr 17 BT14 . . . . . 144 B8
Manor Farm BT27 . . . . . 161 C1
Manor Golf Club BT51 . . . 59 D5
Manor La BT45 . . . . 183 D3
Manor Lodge
  Belfast BT17 . . . . 150 A4
  Magherafelt BT45 . . . . . 183 C4
Manor Mews
  Belfast BT10 . . . . 150 A4
  Magherafelt BT45 . . . . . 183 C3
Manor Pk
  6 Eglinton BT47 . . . . . 36 E5
  4 Lisburn BT28 . . . . . 169 F8
  Magherafelt BT45 . . . . . 183 C3
Manor Pl BT45 . . . . 183 C3
Manor Rd BT45 . . . . 183 C3
Manor St BT14 . . . . 144 B8
Manorwood BT47 . . . . . 179 D3
Manse 1 BT52 . . . . 15 C5
Manse Ave BT55 . . . . . . 173 D7
Manse Ct 36 BT36 . . . . . 111 F1
Manse Dr
  Carryduff BT8 . . . . 163 E5
  Newtownabbey BT36 . . . 111 F1
Mansefield St BT44 . . . . 76 E5
Mansefield Gr BT48 . . . . 177 A6
Manse Gdns BT36 . . . . . 163 E5
Manse Gn 40 BT36 . . . . 111 F1
Manse Pk BT8 . . . . 163 E5
Manse Rd
  Ballymena BT44 . . . . . . 62 A6
  Belfast BT36 . . . . 152 D5
  Carrickfergus BT38 . . . . 99 E3
  Carryduff BT8 . . . . 163 E5
  Castlereagh BT8 . . . . . . 152 A3
  Crumlin BT29 . . . . 117 B2
  Newtownabbey BT36 . . . 132 E8
Manse Rise 32 BT36 . . . 111 F1
Manse Terr 37 BT36 . . . . 111 F1
Manse The BT48 . . . . . . 177 A6
Manse Way BT36 . . . . . . 128 A2
Manse Wlk 31 BT36 . . . . 111 F1
Maple Cres BT17 . . . . . . 161 A8
Maple Ct BT18 . . . . 139 D5
Maple Dr BT52 . . . . 174 D6
Maple Gdns BT38 . . . . . 124 F1
Maplehill BT41 . . . . 187 D3
Maple Rd BT48 . . . . 34 E5
Mara Gdns BT18 . . . . . . 139 D7
Maralin Ave BT28 . . . . . 169 E8
Maralin Pl 12 BT15 . . . . 144 D8
Marchioness Gn BT12 . . . 188 B2
Marchioness St BT12 . . . 188 B2
March St BT13 . . . . 143 F6
Marconi Pk 1 BT54 . . . . . 7 F3
Marcus Ward St BT2 . . . 189 A1
Margaret Ave
  Ballyclare BT39 . . . . . . 184 C6
  Ballymoney BT53 . . . . . 175 B5
Margaret Sq BT53 . . . . . 175 B5
Margaret St
  2 Londonderry BT47 . . 179 A4
  9 Londonderry BT47 . . 179 A4
Margaretta Ct BT47 . . . . 149 E5
Margaretta Pk BT17 . . . . 149 E5
Marguerite Pk BT10 . . . . 150 D5
Margymonaghan 0 BT49 . . 11 D2
Marianus Pk BT48 . . . . . 176 B1
Marina Pk BT5 . . . . 145 E2
Marine Ave BT38 . . . . . . 127 B8
Marine Ct BT37 . . . . 134 B6
Marine Highway BT38 . . . 131 B8
Marine La BT38 . . . . 127 B8
Marine Par
  Holywood BT18 . . . . 139 C5
  2 Whitehead BT38 . . . 100 D1
  Whitehead BT38 . . . . . . 127 B8
Marine Rd BT44 . . . . 49 C2
Marine St 1 BT15 . . . . . . 144 E8
Marino Pk BT18 . . . . 139 F8
Marino Sta BT18 . . . . . . 139 F8
Marino Sta Rd BT18 . . . . 139 F8
Maritime Dr BT38 . . . . . . 130 F7
Market Pl
  Carrickfergus BT38 . . . . 131 A7
  Lisburn BT28 . . . . 160 A1
Market Rd BT43 . . . . 181 D5
Market St Trade Ctr
  BT53 . . . . 175 C5
Market Sq
  Ballyclare BT39 . . . . . . 184 C5
  Lisburn BT28 . . . . 160 B1
  Toome BT41 . . . . 106 C7
Market St
  Ballycastle BT54 . . . . . . 8 C3
  Ballymoney BT53 . . . . . 175 C5
  Belfast BT2 . . . . 189 B2
  Limavady BT49 . . . . 180 B6
  Lisburn BT28 . . . . 160 B1
  Londonderry BT48 . . . . 178 F5
  Magherafelt BT45 . . . . . 183 D6
  Moneymore BT45 . . . . . 113 E8
Mark St La BT55 . . . . . . 173 D7
Mark St
  Ballymena BT44 . . . . . . 65 F8
  Portstewart BT55 . . . . . 173 D7
Markstown Cl BT43 . . . . 78 A7
Markstown Cres 1 BT43 . . 78 A6

Marlborough Ave
  6 Belfast BT9 . . . . 151 A8
  Londonderry BT48 . . . . 178 D6
Marlborough Cl BT38 . . . 125 A4
Marlborough Cres
  Carrickfergus BT38 . . . . 125 A4
  Carryduff BT8 . . . . 163 C3
Marlborough Ct 5 BT9 . . 151 A8
Marlborough Dr BT38 . . . 125 A4
Marlborough Gate 1
  BT9 . . . . 151 B7
Marlborough Gdns
  Belfast BT9 . . . . 151 B7
  Carrickfergus BT38 . . . . 125 A4
Marlborough Hts BT6 . . . 152 F7
Marlborough Pk
  8 Belfast BT9 . . . . 151 A8
  2 Belfast BT9 . . . . 151 B7
  2 Carrickfergus BT38 . . 125 A3
  Carryduff BT8 . . . . 163 C3
Marlborough Pk Central
  BT9 . . . . 151 A8
Marlborough Pk Cross Ave
  BT9 . . . . 151 B7
Marlborough Pk N BT9 . . 151 A8
Marlborough Pk S BT9 . . 151 A7
Marlborough Rd BT48 . . . 178 D6
Marlborough St
  Belfast BT1 . . . . 189 B3
  Londonderry BT48 . . . . 178 D5
Marlfield Dr BT5 . . . . . . 146 C1
Marlfield Rise BT5 . . . . . 146 C1
Marmont Cres BT4 . . . . . 146 A8
Marmont Dr BT4 . . . . . . 146 A8
Marmont Pk
  5 Belfast BT4 . . . . 139 A1
  Belfast BT4 . . . . 146 A8
Marmount Gdns BT14 . . . 136 F3
Marnabrae BT28 . . . . . . 160 B5
Marnabrae Pk BT28 . . . . 160 B5
Marquis St BT1 . . . . 189 A3
Marrian Hill BT41 . . . . . . 92 F2
Marsden Gdns BT15 . . . . 137 B2
Marshalls Rd BT41 . . . . . 145 D1
Marshallstown Mews
  BT38 . . . . 125 A4
Marshallstown Rd BT38 . . 125 B5
Martinez Ave BT5 . . . . . . 145 D4
Martin Pk BT37 . . . . 134 A3
Martin's Brae 1 BT52 . . . 174 D4
Martin St 4 BT5 . . . . . . 145 B5
Martins Terr 13 BT46 . . . 74 D1
Martinstown 0 BT43 . . . . 62 F6
MARTINSTOWN BT43 . . . 62 F6
Martinstown Rd BT43 . . . 62 F6
Martinvale Pk 25 BT46 . . 74 D1
Martinville Pk BT8 . . . . . 152 A2
Marvista BT39 . . . . 184 B4
Maryland Ind Est BT23 . . 153 C2
Marylebone Pk BT9 . . . . 151 D6
Mary St BT54 . . . . 8 C4
Maryville Ave 3 BT9 . . . . 151 A8
Maryville Ct BT7 . . . . . . 189 A1
Maryville Pk BT9 . . . . . . 151 A6
Maryville St BT7 . . . . . . 189 A1
Mashona Ct BT6 . . . . . . 145 B3
Mason Rd BT47 . . . . 50 D2
Massereene Barracks ★
  BT41 . . . . 186 B5
Massereene Com Coll
  BT41 . . . . 187 A6
Massereene Gdns BT41 . . 186 C6
Massereene Golf Club
  BT41 . . . . 186 C3
Massereene St BT41 . . . . 186 D4
Massey Ave
  Belfast BT4 . . . . 146 C7
  Limavady BT49 . . . . 180 B5
Massey Ct BT4 . . . . 146 D6
Massey Gn BT4 . . . . 146 C6
Massey Pk BT4 . . . . 146 C7
Masteragwee BT51 . . . . 13 E2
Masteragwee Rd BT51 . . 13 F2
Matapan Ave BT41 . . . . 186 C6
Matchet St BT13 . . . . . . 144 A7
Mater Infirmorum BT14 . . 144 C7
Matilda Ave BT12 . . . . . 188 C1
Matilda Dr BT12 . . . . . . 188 C1
Matilda Gdns BT12 . . . . 188 C1
Maureen Ave BT48 . . . . 178 E4
Mavis Rd BT47 . . . . 52 B4
Mawilliam Rd BT45 . . . . 114 B6
Mawilliam 0 BT45 . . . . . 114 B7
Maxwell's Pl BT12 . . . . . 188 C1
Maxwell Rd BT42 . . . . . . 95 D5
Maxwell St BT12 . . . . . . 188 C1
Maxwells Walls 0 BT42 . . 95 F5
Mayboy 0 BT51 . . . . 41 D5
Mayboy Rd BT51 . . . . . . 41 D5
Maybrook Ave 17 BT52 . . 26 C7
Maybrook Mews BT48 . . . 176 F1
Maybrook Pk
  2 Coleraine BT52 . . . . 26 C7
  Londonderry BT48 . . . . 176 E2
Maydown 0 BT47 . . . . . . 36 A5
Maydown Ctr BT47 . . . . . 35 F5
Maydown Ind Est BT47 . . 35 F5
Maydown Rd BT47 . . . . . 35 F5
Mayers La BT52 . . . . 15 A2
Mayfair Ave BT6 . . . . . . 145 C1
Mayfield Ave BT36 . . . . . 132 C4
Mayfield Ct BT36 . . . . . . 132 C4
Mayfield Dale BT36 . . . . 132 C4
Mayfield Gdns BT36 . . . . 132 C4
Mayfield High St BT36 . . 132 C4
Mayfield Hts BT36 . . . . . 132 C4

Mayfield Mansion Sq
  BT36 . . . . 132 C4
Mayfield Pk BT36 . . . . . . 132 C4
Mayfield Rd BT36 . . . . . 132 C4
Mayfields BT28 . . . . 160 B5
Mayfield Sq BT10 . . . . . 150 B5
Mayfield St 2 BT9 . . . . . 151 A8
Mayfield Village BT36 . . . 132 C4
Mayfield Wlk BT36 . . . . . 132 C4
Mayflower St BT5 . . . . . 145 C4
Mayo Ct BT13 . . . . 143 F6
Mayo Dr BT54 . . . . 8 C3
Mayoghill 0 BT51 . . . . . . 42 D2
Mayoghill Rd BT51 . . . . . 42 D2
Mayo Link BT13 . . . . 143 F6
Mayo Pk BT13 . . . . 143 F6
Mayo Pl BT13 . . . . 143 F6
Mayo St BT13 . . . . 143 F6
Maysfield Leisure Ctr
  BT7 . . . . 189 C2
May's Mdws BT7 . . . . . . 189 C2
May St
  Belfast BT1 . . . . 189 B2
  Londonderry BT47 . . . . 179 A5
Maythorn Ave BT52 . . . . 174 F4
Maze 0 BT27 . . . . 168 E4
Maze Pk BT28 . . . . 169 E8
Maze Prim Sch BT27 . . . . 168 D3
Maze Race Course BT27 . . 168 C5
Mazes 0 BT53 . . . . 17 F4
MAZETOWN BT28 . . . . . 168 D4
Meadowbank
  Ballymena BT43 . . . . . . 62 F7
  Newtownabbey BT37 . . . 129 B1
Meadowbank Ave BT48 . . 178 C6
Meadowbank Ct 1 BT37 . . 129 C2
Meadowbank Dr BT4 . . . . 183 E4
Meadowbank La BT37 . . . 129 B2
Meadowbank Pk BT37 . . . 128 F2
Meadowbank Pl BT9 . . . . 144 A1
Meadowbank (Plás Bhruach Na Cluana) **2** 37 C5
Meadowbank Rd
  Carrickfergus BT38 . . . . 130 C6
  Magherafelt BT45 . . . . . 183 D3
Meadowbank Recn Ctr
  BT45 . . . . 183 E4
Meadowbank St 1 BT9 . . 144 B1
Meadowbrook
  Ballymoney BT53 . . . . . 15 D1
  Larne BT40 . . . . 84 E1
Meadow Cl
  Ballyclare BT39 . . . . . . 184 C6
  7 Belfast BT15 . . . . . 144 D8
  Lisburn BT28 . . . . 156 E7
Meadow Ct BT57 . . . . 5 E4
Meadow Dale BT37 . . . . 129 C3
Meadow Dr
  Antrim BT41 . . . . 186 D7
  Ballyclare BT39 . . . . . . 184 C6
Meadow Gdns
  Ballyclare BT39 . . . . . . 184 C5
  Portrush BT56 . . . . 172 E5
Meadowhill
  Belfast BT17 . . . . 149 E8
  Carrickfergus BT38 . . . . 124 D3
Meadowhill Cl BT38 . . . . 124 D3
Meadowhill Grange
  BT17 . . . . 149 E8
Meadowhill View BT17 . . 149 E8
Meadowlands
  Antrim BT41 . . . . 186 C8
  1 Magherafelt BT45 . . 106 A8
  Newtownabbey BT37 . . . 129 C2
  Portrush BT56 . . . . 172 C1
Meadowlane Sh Ctr
  BT45 . . . . 183 C6
Meadow Parks 0
  Bushmills BT57 . . . . 5 D4
  Portstewart BT55 . . . . . 173 F5
Meadow Pk
  Larne BT40 . . . . 182 C3
  Portballintrae BT57 . . . . 5 C4
  Portrush BT56 . . . . 172 E5
Meadow Pl 6 BT15 . . . . 144 D8
Meadow Rd BT67 . . . . . . 167 A4
Meadow St BT43 . . . . . . 181 D5
Meadows The
  Ballymoney BT53 . . . . . 175 B3
  Broughshane BT43 . . . . 79 C7
  Craigavon BT67 . . . . . . 167 A7
  Londonderry BT48 . . . . 176 C4
  Randalstown BT41 . . . . 108 B7
  Toome BT41 . . . . 106 D7
Meadow The BT41 . . . . . 186 D7
Meadowvale
  Ballymena BT42 . . . . . . 181 F2
  Lisburn BT27 . . . . 170 A6
  1 Portstewart BT55 . . . 173 D4
Meadowvale Ave BT8 . . . 163 D2
Meadowvale Cl 3 BT8 . . . 163 D2
Meadowvale Gdns 1
  BT8 . . . . 163 D2
Meadowvale Pk
  Carryduff BT8 . . . . 163 D2
  Limavady BT49 . . . . 180 D4
Meadowvale Rd 4 BT8 . . 163 D2
Meadowview BT37 . . . . . 129 B3
Meadow View BT53 . . . . 175 D6
Meadowview Cres BT48 . . 178 C6
Meadow Villas BT45 . . . . 90 F8
Mealough 0 BT8 . . . . 163 A4

Mealough Rd BT8 . . . . . 162 C3
Meavemanougher 0 BT51 . . 41 D6
Medway St BT4 . . . . 145 B6
Meehans Terr 4 BT47 . . . 179 A5
Meenacrane 0 BT79 . . . . . 85 B1
Meenagh Hill 0 BT82 . . . . 50 C2
Meenagh Rd BT82 . . . . . . 50 C2
Meencraig 0 BT49 . . . . . . 40 E6
Meetinghouse Ave 8
  BT46 . . . . 74 D1
Meetinghouse La BT43 . . 181 D4
Meeting House La BT27 . . 160 D1
Meeting House Rd BT28 . . 157 C7
Meetinghouse St
  1 Ballymoney BT53 . . . 175 D4
  6 Larne BT40 . . . . 182 C4
Meeting St
  Magherafelt BT45 . . . . . 183 D5
  Moira BT67 . . . . 166 C2
Megalith ★ BT54 . . . . 7 E3
Megargy 0 BT45 . . . . . . 104 D6
Megargy Rd BT45 . . . . . 183 A3
Megheramesk La BT67 . . 166 E6
Melbourne St BT14 . . . . 188 C4
Melfort Dr BT5 . . . . 146 C4
Melmore Dr BT17 . . . . . 160 D8
Melmore Gdns BT48 . . . . 178 C5
Melrose Ave BT5 . . . . . . 145 D4
Melrose St BT9 . . . . 144 B1
Melrose Terr BT47 . . . . . 179 A4
Melvin St BT47 . . . . 179 B6
Menagh 0 BT51 . . . . 42 C6
Menin Rd BT41 . . . . 186 D4
Mercer Ct 1 BT27 . . . . . 160 C1
Mercer St BT27 . . . . 160 C1
Mercy Prim Sch BT14 . . . 136 E1
Meredi St BT12 . . . . 188 A1
Merion Ave BT39 . . . . . . 184 B6
Merion Pk BT39 . . . . 184 B6
Merkland Pl BT13 . . . . . 143 F6
Merok Cres BT6 . . . . . . 152 D8
Merok Dr BT6 . . . . 152 D8
Merok Gdns BT6 . . . . . . 152 D8
Merok Pk BT6 . . . . 152 D8
Merriman Ct BT48 . . . . . 176 A2
Merrion Pk BT17 . . . . . . 149 E6
Merryfield Dr BT5 . . . . . 137 B5
Merryland Cross Roads
  BT23 . . . . 153 D2
Mersey St Prim Sch BT4 . . 145 C6
Mersey St BT4 . . . . 145 C6
Merston Gdns BT36 . . . . 137 D8
Merville Gdn Village
  BT37 . . . . 133 E2
Merville Mews BT37 . . . . 134 A2
Mervue Ct 18 BT15 . . . . 144 D8
Mervue St
  3 Belfast BT15 . . . . . . 137 D1
  Belfast BT15 . . . . 144 D8
Meskan Stone ★ BT47 . . . 69 A8
Messines Pk BT41 . . . . . 186 E2
Methodist Coll BT9 . . . . 144 C2
Metropole Ave 3 BT55 . . 173 D5
Mettican Glebe 0 BT51 . . 42 A2
Mettican Rd BT51 . . . . . . 41 F1
Mews The BT28 . . . . 147 C5
Meyrick Pk BT11 . . . . . . 136 F4
Mica Dr BT12 . . . . 143 E4
Mica St BT12 . . . . 143 E4
Michael Davitt's GAC
  BT46 . . . . 58 B1
Michelin Rd BT36 . . . . . 132 C6
Middle Braniel Rd BT5 . . 153 B8
Middle Brockagh 0 BT51 . . 57 B7
Middle Division 0 BT38 . . 124 D4
Middle Doaghs Upper 0
  BT49 . . . . 11 E5
Middle Park 0 BT44 . . . . 32 E4
Middlepark Ave BT44 . . . 32 D4
Middlepark Cres BT44 . . . 32 D4
Middlepath St BT5 . . . . . 189 C3
Middle Pk Rd BT44 . . . . . 32 D3
Middle Quarter 0 BT51 . . 41 C3
Middle Rd
  Carrickfergus BT38 . . . . 124 C3
  Larne BT40 . . . . 100 C8
Middleton Pk BT40 . . . . 100 D3
Middle Town 0 BT51 . . . . 59 B2
Midland Cl 12 BT15 . . . . 144 E8
Midland Cres 11 BT15 . . 144 E8
Mid Ulster Hosp BT45 . . . 183 C7
Milburn Ave BT80 . . . . . 185 B6
Milburn Cl BT80 . . . . . . 185 C6
Milburn Pk BT80 . . . . . . 185 C6
Milebush Cl BT38 . . . . . 124 F4
Milebush Cres BT38 . . . . 124 F3
Milebush Dr BT38 . . . . . 124 F3
Milebush Pk BT38 . . . . . 124 F3
Mileriver St BT15 . . . . . 137 D1
Milestone Sh Ctr The
  BT39 . . . . 110 C1
Milesworth Plaza BT80 . . 185 D5
Milewater Cl 8 BT36 . . . . 111 F1
Milewater Dr BT36 . . . . . 111 F1
Milewater Rd BT15 . . . . 137 E1
Milewater St BT15 . . . . . 137 E1
Milewater Way 14 BT36 . . 111 F1
Milford Pl BT12 . . . . 188 B3
Milford Rise BT12 . . . . . 188 B3
Milford St BT12 . . . . 188 C3
Milfort Ave BT17 . . . . . . 150 A4
Milfort Terr BT17 . . . . . . 150 A4
Millar Ave 4 BT53 . . . . . 28 B8
Millar St BT6 . . . . 145 A2
Mill Ave BT14 . . . . 136 B4

Millbank Ave BT56......172 C6
Millbank Ct BT56......172 C6
Millbank Gdns BT53......28 E3
Millbank Rd BT39......111 A1
Millbank Rd E BT39......111 A1
MILLBAY BT40......100 A8
Millbay Rd BT40......100 A8
Mill Brae
Broughshane BT42......79 D7
Larne BT40......182 B3
Millbrook **7** BT47......36 E5
MILLBROOK BT40......83 B2
Millbrook Ave BT56......172 C4
Millbrook Ind Est BT40......83 B2
Millbrook Manor BT53......175 C2
Millbrook Pk
Drumahoe BT47......179 D2
Portrush BT56......172 C4
Millbrook Wlk BT27......160 C2
Millburn BT52......174 C6
Millburn Ct BT8......151 D2
Millburn Mews BT39......184 C4
Millburn Prim Sch BT52 174 D5
Millburn Rd BT52......174 C4
Mill Church Manor BT36...128 B2
Millcottage Dr BT53......28 E7
Millcottage La BT53......28 E7
Millcottage Way BT53......28 E7
Mill Cotts BT56......172 C3
Mill Cres BT56......89 F5
Mill Ct **3** BT51......58 A8
Milldale Cres BT47......51 E6
Millennium Forum (Theatre
& Con Centre) 9 BT48..178 F5
Millennium Way BT12...143 E4
Millers Cl BT47......69 F7
Miller St BT48......178 E4
Mill Farm BT53......17 B4
Millfield
Ballymena BT43......181 D8
Belfast BT13......188 C4
Millfields BT53......27 C2
Mill Five Acres BT53......18 A1
Millfort Cl BT56......172 C3
Mill Gdns BT56......172 C3
Mill Grange
Ballymoney BT53......175 C2
3 Newtownabbey BT36...119 C7
Millgrove Pk BT47......36 E4
Millgrove Pl BT56......172 C5
Millhaven Pk BT56......172 C5
Mill Hill La BT67......167 E4
Mill Hollow BT43......47 C2
Mill La
Carrickfergus BT38......100 C4
6 Moneymore BT45......113 E8
Mill Loughan BT52......26 D6
Millmount BT41......108 A7
Millpath BT47......36 E4
Mill Path BT47......36 E4
Mill Pk (Inishrush Park)
BT44......76 A4
Mill Pl BT40......180 B7
Mill Pond Ct **4** BT5......145 C4
Millquarter BT53......175 D1
Mill Quarter
Antrim BT41......92 E4
Coleraine BT51......41 B2
Millquarter Prim Sch
BT41......92 E4
Millrace Terr BT53......29 C8
Mill Rd
Ballyclare BT39......184 B3
Carryduff BT8......163 B6
Crumlin BT29......117 B1
Doagh BT39......110 F7
Kilrea BT51......59 C5
Larne BT40......182 B3
Limavady BT49......39 F2
Lisburn BT27......161 F5
Newtownabbey BT36......133 E1
Portrush BT56......172 C4
Mill Rd W BT8......163 A7
Millriver Mews BT39......184 C3
Millrush Dr BT56......172 D3
Millrush Dr BT56......172 D2
Millrush Mews BT56......172 D2
Millrush Pk BT56......172 D3
Millside Cres BT47......70 A3
Mill Sq BT53......15 D1
Millsquare BT56......172 C4
Mill St
Ballymena BT43......181 D4
2 Coleraine BT52......174 D4
Cushendall BT44......32 D4
Lisburn BT27......160 D3
Millstone BT56......172 C3
Millstone Ave BT56......172 C3
Millstone Ct BT56......172 C3
Millstone Gr BT56......172 C3
Millstone Mews BT56......172 C3
Millstone Pk BT56......172 C3
Mill Strand Integrated Prim
Sch BT55......173 B5
Millstream Ct BT40......182 C3
Mill Tenement BT44......49 C2
MILLTOWN BT41......106 F7
Milltown BT44......45 B3
MILLTOWN
Ballymoney BT53......175 B2
Coleraine BT51......42 E8
Maghera BT46......90 A8
MILL TOWN BT41......108 E5
Mill Town BT49......23 B7

Milltown Ave
Ballymoney BT53......175 B3
Dunmurry BT28......160 B8
Milltown Cres
Drumahoe BT47......179 D1
Dunmurry BT28......160 B8
Milltown Ct BT53......175 B2
Milltown Gdns BT28......160 A8
Milltown Hill BT8......151 C1
Milltown Pk BT28......160 B8
Millvale BT40......83 B7
Millvale Mews BT39......184 E5
Millvale Rd BT28......155 D8
Mill View BT45......91 C2
Millview Cl BT39......184 C3
Millview Ct BT14......136 D3
Millview Dr BT39......184 C4
Millview Gdns
Ballyclare BT39......184 C3
7 Garvagh BT51......58 A8
Millview Pk BT53......15 E1
Millwater Ct **1** BT42......77 F2
Millwater Lodge **3** BT42..77 F2
Milner St BT12......188 A1
Mimosa Ct **2** BT47......179 A3
Minearny BT49......22 F7
Minegallagher Glebe
BT47......37 B2
Mineral St BT15......137 E2
Ministers Wlk BT45......113 E8
Minnis North BT44......66 B6
Minnis South BT44......66 B6
Minnowburn Beeches *
BT8......151 B2
Minnowburn Dr **1** BT8..151 D2
Minnowburn Gdns **2**
BT8......151 D2
Minnowburn Mews BT8..151 B2
Minorca Dr BT38......130 E8
Minorca Pl BT38......130 F7
Minstrel Cl BT49......180 D4
Mistyburn BT42......80 F2
Mitchelin Ac BT42......79 B5
Mitchell House Sch BT4 146 A8
Mitchel Pk **5** BT47......55 D2
Mizen St BT11......149 F7
Moat Link BT42......181 E3
Moat Rd
Antrim BT41......110 A4
Ballymena BT42......181 E3
Moat St BT8......178 E3
Moboy BT44......60 C1
Mobuoy BT47......36 A3
Mobuoy Rd BT47......35 F3
Mobuoy BT45......103 A3
Mobuy La BT80......103 A2
Mobuy Rd BT80......102 F3
Model Ave BT38......130 F7
Model Ct BT53......175 C6
Model Sch Rd
2 Ballymoney BT53......175 C5
Coleraine BT51......174 B4
MOIRA BT67......166 D2
Moira Ct (Cúirt Mhaigh Rath)
5 BT5......145 A5
Moira Demesne BT67..166 B3
Moira Ind Est BT67......166 A1
Moira Mews **2** BT67......166 B2
Moira Pk **1** BT28......169 D8
Moira Prim Sch BT67..166 B2
Moira Rd
Belfast BT29......121 B3
Lisburn BT28......168 C6
Moira Sta BT67......166 D4
Molesworth Ct BT80......185 D5
Molesworth Rd BT80......185 D5
Molesworth St BT80......185 D5
Moltke St BT12......188 A1
Molyneaux Ave BT40......83 B2
Molyneaux Dr **1** BT28..159 D3
Molyneaux St **5** BT15..144 E7
Molyneaux Wlk BT28......159 D3
Monadore Rd BT47......70 B3
Monaghan BT43......62 B2
Monagh Bypass BT11......143 B2
Monagh Cres BT11......143 B2
Monagh Dr BT11......143 B3
Monagh Gr BT11......143 B2
Monagh Link BT11......143 B2
Monagh Par BT12......143 B3
Monagh Rd BT11......143 B3
Monanclogh BT53......18 C4
Monarch Par BT12......188 A1
Monarch St BT12......188 A1
Monaville Ave BT28......159 F2
Monaville Cl BT28......159 F2
Monaville Dr BT28......159 F2
Monaville Gdns BT28......159 F3
Monaville Pk BT28......159 F3
Monehanegan BT47......53 B7
Moneybrannon Rd BT51..42 C8
Moneybrannon BT51......26 A2
Moneycannon Rd
Ballymoney BT53......43 E6
Strabane BT82......68 D3

Moneycanon
Ballymoney BT53......43 F6
Strabane BT82......68 D4
Moneycarrie Lower
BT51......42 C4
Moneycarrie Rd BT51......42 B4
Moneycarrie Upper
BT51......42 B3
Moneyconey BT79......101 F8
Moneyconey Rd BT45......101 F7
Moneycrumog BT28......157 B5
MONEYDIG BT51......42 F1
Moneydig BT51......58 F8
Moneydig Pk BT51......42 E1
Moneydig Rd BT51......59 A7
Moneydig Showjumping
Ctr * BT51......42 E1
Moneydollog BT42......77 F4
Moneyduff BT44......46 C2
Moneyduff Rd BT44......62 C8
Moneyglass BT41......92 E1
MONEYGLASS BT41......92 F2
Moneygobbin BT53......27 C3
Moneygran BT51......59 E3
Moneygran Rd BT51......59 E3
Moneyguigy
Limavady BT49......40 E1
Magherafelt BT45......89 C5
Moneyhaw BT45......113 F6
Moneyhaw Rd BT45......113 F5
Moneyhoghan BT47......70 D3
Moneyleck BT44......60 B6
Moneyleck Pk BT44......60 B6
Moneyleck Rd BT44......60 A6
Moneyletra Kill BT51......58 C6
Moneymore
Maghera BT46......74 E1
Magherafelt BT45......113 F8
MONEYMORE (MUINE MÓR)
BT45......113 E8
Moneymore Prim Sch **11**
BT45......113 E8
Moneymore Rd
Cookstown BT80......185 E7
Magherafelt BT45......183 B2
Moneyneagh BT44......46 C6
Moneyneany BT45......88 A8
MONEYNEANY BT45......88 D6
Moneyneany La BT45......88 B7
Moneyneany Rd
Londonderry BT47......87 F6
Magherafelt BT45......88 A7
Moneynick BT41......107 B5
Moneynick Prim Sch
BT41......107 B6
Moneynick Rd
Antrim BT41......107 A6
Toome BT41......106 D7
Moneyrannel BT49......38 F7
Moneyrannel Rd BT49......39 A8
Moneyreagh Rd BT23......153 D2
Moneyrea St BT6......145 B3
Moneyrod BT41......107 C7
Moneyrod Rd BT41......107 C7
Moneysallin BT51......59 B2
Moneysallin Pk BT51......59 B1
Moneysallin Rd BT51......59 C1
Moneyshanere BT45......89 D5
Moneysharvan BT46......74 D6
Moneysharvan Rd BT45......74 D5
Moneystaghan-Ellis
BT44......76 B3
Moneystaghan-MacPeake
BT44......76 A3
Moneyvart BT44......32 E5
Monkstown BT36......128 F3
MONKSTOWN BT37......128 F2
Monkstown Ave BT37......133 F7
Monkstown Com Sch
BT37......128 E2
Monkstown Gdns BT37......128 F1
Monkstown Ind Est BT37 133 E8
Monkstown Rd BT37......133 E8
Monnaboy BT37......37 B2
Monnaboy Rd BT47......53 C7
Monnabuoy Rd BT47......36 F2
Monrush BT80......185 D7
Montague Ave BT42......181 C2
Montague Ct BT56......172 C2
Montague Pk BT42......181 C1
Montgomery Chase BT6..152 C8
Montgomery Cl **4** BT47..179 B5
Montgomery Commercial &
Bsns Pk BT6......145 C1
Montgomery Ct **2** BT6...152 C8
Montgomery Dr
2 Lisburn BT27......160 C1
Lisburn BT27......170 C8
Montgomery Rd BT6......152 D8
Montgomery St
Ballymena BT42......78 B2
Belfast BT1......189 B3
Montiaghs BT67......154 C5
Montreal St BT13......143 F7
Montrose Gdns **3** BT48..178 D7
Montrose St S BT5......145 B5
Montrose St **20** BT4......145 B5
Monument Rd BT38......129 C7
Monuments & Bldgs
Record * BT1......189 B4
Moon BT51......26 D1
Moorcroft Rd BT8......162 F5
Moordyke BT40......82 D1
Mooreland Cl BT43......181 D8
Mooreland Cres BT11......150 D7
Mooreland Ct **6** BT28......159 D3
Mooreland Dr
Belfast BT11......150 D7

Mooreland Dr continued
5 Lisburn BT28......159 D3
Mooreland Pk
Belfast BT11......150 C7
7 Lisburn BT28......159 D3
Moore Lodge BT53......43 D1
MOORESIDE COTTAGES
BT45......103 F8
Mooreside Villas BT45..103 F8
Moore St BT47......179 A4
Moore Wlk BT48......178 D3
MOORFIELDS BT42......95 E8
Moorfields Prim Sch
BT42......95 E8
Moorfields Rd BT42......95 E8
Moorfield St BT5......145 D4
Moorgate BT53......15 D2
Moorgate St BT5......145 D4
Moorlands BT41......93 B4
Moor Pk Ave BT11......150 A5
Moor Pk Dr BT11......150 A5
Moor Pk Gdns BT11......150 A5
Moor Pk Mews BT11......150 A5
Moor Rd BT53......29 C2
MOORTOWN BT80......115 C2
Moorville BT71......113 F1
Moran's Cross Roads
BT51......59 A1
Moreland Ave BT36......133 A4
Morgan Cl BT80......185 B6
Morgan Dr BT80......185 B6
Morgan Ind Est BT38......125 D3
Morgans Cl **1** BT45......183 C4
Morgans Hill Rd BT80......185 B6
Mormeal BT45......89 C3
Morningside
Ballymena BT42......181 A1
Lisburn BT27......170 D6
Mornington Ave BT28......159 C1
Mornington Mews BT7...151 E6
Mornington Pl
Belfast BT7......151 F6
Lisburn BT28......159 C1
Mornington View BT28...159 C1
Morpeth St BT13......188 B4
Morrison Pk BT55......173 C5
Moscow Rd BT3......138 E3
Moscow St BT13......188 B4
Mosley Pk BT41......179 D4
Mossband Rd BT80......114 D3
Mossbawn BT45......183 B7
Mossgrove Pk BT36......132 E6
Mossgrove Prim Sch
BT36......132 D6
Mosside Gdns BT53......17 B4
Mosside Mews BT17......160 D8
Mosside Rd BT17......160 D8
Moss La
Belfast BT29......121 F3
Lisburn BT28......155 B7
MOSSLEY BT36......128 A2
Mossley Prim Sch BT36..128 A2
Mossley Rd BT39......111 C4
Mossley W Sta BT36......128 A3
Moss Pk BT48......176 D4
Moss Rd
Ballyclare BT39......98 B6
Carryduff BT8......163 B1
Cookstown BT80......114 F3
Craigavon BT67......154 B5
Holywood BT18......146 E8
Lisburn BT27......160 C6
Londonderry BT48......176 E4
Magherafelt BT45......105 F5
Newtownabbey BT36......132 E6
Moss-Side BT39......110 D8
MOSS-SIDE BT53......17 B4
Moss-side BT53......17 B4
Mossvale BT51......25 D8
Mossvale Pk
Ballyclare BT39......184 B4
Coleraine BT52......174 E6
Mossvale Rd BT36......111 E2
Mossvale St BT13......143 F7
Mostragee BT45......28 E8
Mostragee Rd BT53......28 E8
Motalee BT45......90 D1
Motalee La BT45......104 D8
Motalee Rd BT45......183 A8
Motelands BT4......146 B8
Mount Aboo Pk BT10......150 D4
Mountainhill Rd BT14......136 C3
Mountainhill Wlk BT14......136 C3
Mountainvale Cres BT36 132 E5
Mountainvale Dr BT36...132 E5
Mountainvale Gdns
BT36......132 E5
Mountain Vale Pk BT28..159 F1
Mountainvale Rd BT36...132 E6
Mountain View BT47......179 A3
Mountainview Cl BT53......15 E1
Mountainview Cres BT53 15 E1
Mountainview Ct BT53......15 E1
Mountainview Dr
Ballymoney BT53......15 E1
Belfast BT14......143 E8
Mountainview Gdns
BT14......143 E8
Mountainview Hts BT53..15 D1
Mountainview Par BT14 143 E8
Mountainview Pk
1 Belfast BT14......143 E8
1 Dungiven BT47......55 D2
Mount Alverno BT12......143 B4
Mountbatten Ave BT43..181 A6
Mount Carmel BT15......137 C4
Mountcashel St BT13......143 F6

Mountcastle BT82......67 B6
Mount Charles BT7......144 D2
Mountcollyer Cl **4** BT15 137 D1
Mountcollyer Rd BT15...137 E1
Mountcollyer St BT15......137 D1
Mount Con & Bsns Ctr The
BT56......145 A4
Mountcoole Gdns BT14..137 A5
Mountcoole Pk BT14......137 A5
Mountcourt **6** BT52......26 B7
Mount Davys Rd BT42......77 F5
Mount Eagles Ave BT28..149 A2
Mount Eagles Dr BT17...149 B3
Mount Eagles Mews
BT28......149 B2
Mount Eagles Pk BT28......149 A2
Mount Eagles Rd BT17...149 B3
Mount Eagles Sq BT28...149 A2
Mounteden BT49......180 A3
Mount Eden Pk BT9......151 A5
Mount Edwards BT44......32 D3
Mountedwardshill BT44...32 D3
Mountfield Dr BT52......26 B7
Mountfield Rd BT47......69 E8
Mountforde Ct (Cúirt
Thulach Forde) **18** BT5..145 A5
Mountforde Dr (Céide
Thulach Forde) **16** BT5..145 A5
Mountforde Gdns (Garraithe
Thulach Forde) **17** BT5..145 A5
Mountforde Pk **27** BT5..145 A5
Mountforde Rd (Bóthar
Thulach Forde) **28** BT5..145 A5
Mount Gilbert Com Coll
BT13......143 D7
Mount Hamilton BT44......45 E3
MOUNT HAMILTON OR
SPERRIN BT79......86 B2
Mount Hamilton Rd BT44 45 D3
Mount Hilary BT41......93 D5
Mounthill Ave BT44......45 E3
Mounthill Ct BT44......45 E3
Mounthill Dr BT44......45 E3
Mount Hill Rath * BT41...95 A1
Mounthill Rd BT40......98 E6
Mounthill Way BT44......45 E3
Mountjoy St
Belfast BT13......188 A4
5 Londonderry BT48......178 E4
Mount Merrion Ave BT6..152 B7
Mount Merrion Cres
BT6......152 A7
Mount Merrion Dr BT6..152 B7
Mount Merrion Gdns
BT6......152 A7
Mount Merrion Pk BT6...152 A7
Mount Michael Dr BT8..152 B5
Mount Michael Gr BT8..152 B4
Mount Michael Pk BT8..152 B4
Mount Michael View
BT8......152 C5
Mount Ober Golf & Ctry Club
BT8......152 E3
Mount Oriel **1** BT8......152 A4
Mount Oriel Ct BT41......186 E5
Mountpleasant BT48......177 A3
Mount Pleasant
Ballymena BT44......76 E8
Belfast BT9......151 B8
Mount Pleasant Ave
BT37......129 A2
Mount Pleasant Dr BT37 129 A2
Mount Pleasant Gdns
BT37......129 A2
Mount Pleasant La BT37 129 A2
Mount Pleasant Pk BT37 129 A2
Mount Pleasant Rd BT37 129 A2
Mountpottinger Ctr **39**
BT5......145 A4
Mountpottinger Link (Lúb
Tullach Phoitinséir) **36**
BT5......145 A5
Mountpottinger Rd (Bóthar
Thulach Phoitinséir)
7 Belfast BT5......145 A5
7 Belfast BT5......145 A5
Mount Prospect Pk BT9 144 B2
Mount Rd BT29......117 C1
Mount Royal
Lisburn BT27......170 E8
Magherafelt BT45......183 C6
Mount St Michael's Prim Sch
12 BT41......108 E7
Mount St S **13** BT5......145 A4
Mount Sandel BT52......26 B7
Mountsandel Fort **12**
BT52......26 B7
Mountsandel Rd BT52...174 D1
Mountsandel Sh Ctr **13**
BT52......26 B7
Mount Shalgus BT41......107 F5
Mount Shalgus La BT41 107 F6
Mount St
Ballymena BT43......181 D5
15 Belfast BT6......145 A4
Coleraine BT52......174 C2
2 Londonderry BT48......178 D7
Newtownabbey BT36......137 E8
Mountstafford Rd BT44..76 C5
Mount The BT5......145 A4
Mount Vernon BT48......177 F8
Mount Vernon Dr BT15..137 D4
Mount Vernon Gdns
BT15......137 D5
Mount Vernon La BT15..137 E4
Mount Vernon Pass
BT15......137 E4

Mount Vernon Pk BT15. . 137 D4
Mount Vernon Rd BT15. . 137 E4
Mount Vernon Wlk BT15. 137 E4
Mountview Cl **1** BT45. . . 104 B1
Mountview Cres **3** BT45 104 B1
Mountview Ct
  11 Belfast BT14. . . . . 144 B8
  1 Moneymore BT45. . . . . 113 E8
Mountview Dr BT27 . . . . 160 B5
Mountview Gdns
  Coleraine BT51 . . . . 174 A2
  2 Moneymore BT45. . . . 104 B1
Mountview Hts BT37 . . . . 134 A4
Mountview Pass BT37. . . 134 A4
Mountview Pk
  Lisburn BT27 . . . . 160 C5
  4 Moneymore BT45. . . . 104 B1
Mountview Pl BT14. . . . . 144 B8
Mountview St **9** BT14. . . 144 B8
Mourefort BT7. . . . . 27 B2
Mournebeg Dr BT37. . . . 133 F5
Mournebeg Way **2** BT37 133 F4
Mourne Dr BT45 . . . . 179 B3
Mourne St **16** BT5. . . . . . 145 A5
Mourneview BT8. . . . . . . 163 D5
Mourneview Cresent
  BT28 . . . . 159 D4
Mourneview Pk **3** BT38 124 D2
Mourne View Pk BT28. . . 159 C4
Movanagher BT51. . . . . . . 59 B8
Movanagher Rd BT51. . . . 59 B8
Movenis Hill BT51. . . . . . . 58 B3
Movenis or
  Catherwoodstown **①**
  BT51 . . . . 42 C1
Movenis Rd BT51. . . . . . . 42 C2
Movie House ★ BT7 . . . . 189 A1
Movilla Gdns BT56. . . . . 172 D5
Movilla Pk BT37 . . . . 133 E5
Movilla Rd BT56. . . . . . . 172 C6
Mowhan St BT21. . . . . . . 151 A8
Moyadam **①** BT39 . . . . . . 110 D4
Moyadam Ct BT39. . . . . . 110 C4
Moyadam Pk BT39 . . . . . 110 C4
Moyagall **①** BT45. . . . . 75 C1
Moyagall Rd
  Ballymena BT44. . . . . 76 A3
  Magherafelt BT45. . . . . . . 91 A8
Moyagh **①** BT82. . . . . 67 A5
Moyagh Rd BT47. . . . . 67 A7
Moyagoney **①** BT44. . . . . 75 F7
Moyagoney Rd
  Ballymena BT44. . . . . 76 A6
  Maghera BT46. . . . . 75 F8
Moyan Rd
  Ballymena BT44. . . . . 45 C7
  Ballymoney BT53. . . . . . . 29 B3
Moyard **①** BT79 . . . . 101 D7
Moyard Cres BT12. . . . . 143 C5
Moyard Gdns BT38. . . . . 129 C2
Moyard Par BT12. . . . . . 143 C5
Moyard Pk BT12. . . . . . . 143 C5
Moyard Rd BT45. . . . . . . 101 E6
Moyarget Lower **①** BT54. . . 18 A6
Moyarget Rd
  Ballycastle BT54. . . . . 17 F6
  Ballymoney BT53. . . . . . . 16 E3
Moyarget Upper **①** BT54. . . 7 E1
Moyasset **①** BT42 . . . . 77 E4
Moyaver Lower **①** BT53. . . 29 E8
Moyaver Upper **①** BT53 . . 29 E8
Moybeg Kirley **①** BT45. . . 89 D6
Moybeg Rd BT45. . . . . . . 89 D6
Moycraig Hamilton **①**
  BT53. . . . . 17 A4
Moycraig Lower **①** BT53. . 17 A2
Moycraig MaCallister **①**
  BT53. . . . . 17 A3
Moycraig Rd
  Ballymoney BT53. . . . . . . 28 E8
  Bushmills BT57. . . . . 6 E2
Moycraig Upper **①** BT53. . 17 B5
Moydamlaght **①** BT45. . . 88 C8
Moydamlaght Rd
  Londonderry BT47. . . . . . . 72 C3
  Magherafelt BT45. . . . . . . 88 B8
Moygarriff **①** BT28. . . . . 156 B4
Moyheeland **①** BT45. . . . . 89 A4
Moykeeran **①** BT45. . . . . . 88 F4
Moykeeran Cres **6** BT45. . 89 A3
Moykeeran Dr BT45. . . . . 89 A4
Moykeeran Gdns **3** BT45. 89 A4
Moyknock **①** BT51. . . . . . . 59 E2
Moylarg **①** BT43. . . . . 61 D1
Moyle Ave BT54. . . . . 8 C4
Moyle Ct BT54. . . . . 8 D4
Moyle Ent Ctr **2** BT54. . . . 8 C4
Moyle Gdns
  Carnlough BT44. . . . . 49 C3
  Larne BT40. . . . . 182 D6
Moyle Hospl BT40. . . . . . 182 D4
Moylena Ct **3** BT41. . . . 186 E3
Moylena Gr BT41. . . . . . . 186 E3
Moylena Pk BT41. . . . . . 186 F2
Moylena Rd BT41. . . . . . 186 F3
Moylinnan Mdw BT41. . . 186 F3
Moyle Par BT40. . . . . . . 182 D6
Moyle Pk BT54. . . . . 8 C4
Moyle Prim Sch BT40 . . 182 C5
Moyle St BT54. . . . . 8 D4
Moyletra Kill **①** BT51. . . . 58 C6
Moyletra Toy **①** BT51. . . . 58 D5
Moyle View BT44 . . . . 32 E4
Moyle Wlk BT8 . . . . 151 C2
Moylinney **①** BT41. . . . . . 187 B2
Moylinny **①** BT41. . . . . . . 187 A2
Moymucklemurry **①**
  BT45 . . . . 104 C3

Moyne Pk BT5 . . . . 146 D2
Moyola Ave **2** BT45. . . . . 91 C1
Moyola Ct BT45. . . . . 91 D1
Moyola Dr BT48. . . . . . . 177 A4
Moyola Gdns **1** BT45. . . . 91 C2
Moyola Pk
  Magherafelt BT45. . . . . . . 91 C3
  Newtownabbey BT36. . . . 132 E6
Moyola Rd BT45. . . . . 91 D2
Moyola View **3** BT45. . . 106 A8
Moyola Wlk BT45 . . . . . . 177 A4
Moyra Manor **3** BT39. . . . 96 F1
Moyra Rd BT39. . . . . 110 F8
Moyrusk **①** BT67. . . . . . . 167 F7
MOYRUSK BT67. . . . . . . 168 A7
Moy Rusk Rd BT67. . . . . 168 A7
Moys **①** BT49. . . . . 38 F2
Moys Rd BT49. . . . . 38 F2
Moytown Rd BT67. . . . . . 154 D2
Muckamore BT41. . . . . . 109 D1
MUCKAMORE BT41. . . . 187 B1
Muckamore Abbey Hospl
  BT41 . . . . 109 D1
Muckamore Ind Est
  BT41 . . . . 187 C1
Muckleramer **①** BT41. . . . 93 D3
Muckleramer Rd BT41. . . 93 D2
Muckrim **①** BT41. . . . . 92 F2
MUFF BT47. . . . . 34 G9
Muff **①**
  Cookstown BT80 . . . . . . 113 B6
  Londonderry BT47. . . . . . . 36 F5
Muff Rd BT80 . . . . 113 B6
MUILEANN NA BUAISE
  (BUSHMILLS) BT57. . . . . . 5 D3
MUINE MÓR (MONEYMORE)
  BT45 . . . . 113 E8
Mulberry Cres BT37. . . . 128 F2
Mulberry Gdns BT52. . . . 174 E7
Mulberry Grange **1**
  BT37 . . . . 128 F2
Mulberry Mews **5** BT37. 128 F2
Mulberry Pk
  8 Dunmurry BT17. . . . . 149 D2
  1 Newtownabbey BT37. 128 F2
Mulderg **①** BT41. . . . . 53 C1
Mulderg Dr BT36. . . . . . 133 D1
Mulderg Rd BT45. . . . . . 105 B3
Muldonagh **①** BT47. . . . . 53 F3
Muldonagh Rd BT47. . . . . 54 B2
Mulhouse Rd BT12. . . . . 188 B2
Mulkeeragh **①**
  Limavady BT49. . . . . 38 E6
  Londonderry BT47. . . . . . . 55 D8
Mullaboy **①** BT47. . . . . . . 52 D5
Mullaboy Prim Sch BT47 52 C7
Mullagh **①**
  Limavady BT49. . . . . 180 A3
  Maghera BT46. . . . . 90 B7
Mullaghacall Cres BT56. 172 B4
Mullaghacall North **①**
  BT56. . . . . 172 C5
Mullaghacall Rd BT56. . . 172 B4
Mullaghane **①** BT44. . . . . 66 A6
Mullaghboy **①**
  Bellaghy BT45. . . . . 91 F5
  Magherafelt BT45. . . . . . 183 C6
Mullaghboy Cres
  Magherafelt BT45. . . . . . . 91 E6
Mullaghboy Glen BT45. . 183 B6
Mullaghboy Hill BT45. . . 183 A6
Mullaghboy Hts
  Larne BT40. . . . . 84 E1
  Magherafelt BT45. . . . . . 183 B6
Mullaghboy La BT45. . . . 183 B6
Mullaghboy Rd
  Ballymena BT44. . . . . 75 E2
  Larne BT40. . . . . 84 E1
Mullaghcarton **①** BT28. . 158 A2
Mullaghcarton Rd
  Craigavon BT67. . . . . 157 E2
  Lisburn BT28 . . . . 158 B2
Mullagh Cl **22** BT46 . . . . 74 D1
Mullaghconnelly **①** BT44. 65 E6
Mullagh Ct **3** BT46 . . . . 90 B8
Mullaghdoo **①**
  Larne BT40. . . . . 100 D4
  Londonderry BT47. . . . . . . 85 C5
Mullaghdubh Prim Sch
  BT40 . . . . 100 D4
Mullaghduff **①** BT53. . . . 17 E2
Mullaghduff Big **①** BT53. 17 F2
Mullaghduff Little **①** BT53 17 E2
Mullaghgaun **①** BT41. . . 107 A5
Mullaghglass **①** BT28. . . 148 D4
Mullaghglass Rd BT28. . . 148 E3
Mullaghinch **①** BT51. . . . . 42 E5
Mullaghinch Rd BT51. . . . 42 E5
Mullagh La
  23 Maghera BT46. . . . . 74 D1
  Maghera BT46. . . . . 90 B8
Mullaghmeash Pk (Páirc
  Mhullach An Mháis)
  BT47. . . . . 70 E6
Mullaghmeash Rd BT47. . 70 E7
Mullaghmore **①** BT51. . . . 42 E7
Mullaghmore
  12 Maghera BT46 . . . . 74 D1
  2 Maghera BT46. . . . . . 90 B8
Mullaghmore Glebe **①**
  BT51 . . . . 42 F8
Mullaghmore Pk BT38. . 129 D4
Mullaghmore Rd BT40. . . 99 F5
Mullaghnamoyagh **①**
  BT44 . . . . 76 A3

Mullaghnamoyagh Rd
  BT44 . . . . 76 A3
Mullagh Pk BT46. . . . . 90 C8
Mullagh Pl BT49. . . . . . . 180 B5
Mullagh Rd
  21 Maghera BT46 . . . . . 74 D1
  Maghera BT46. . . . . 90 A7
Mullaghsandall **①** BT40. . 82 B5
Mullaghsandall Rd BT40. . 82 C5
Mullaghtironey **①** BT80. . 114 B2
Mullaghwortragh **①**
  BT80 . . . . 114 F2
Mullan **①**
  Ballymoney BT53. . . . . . . 44 E8
  Coleraine BT51 . . . . 42 A7
  Coleraine BT51 . . . . 59 A8
Mullane **①** BT49. . . . . 23 E2
Mullanhead **①** BT51. . . . . 13 F2
Mullan Rd
  Ballymena BT44. . . . . 60 C8
  Ballymoney BT53. . . . . . . 43 F6
  Coleraine BT51 . . . . 59 A7
  Cookstown BT80 . . . . . . 115 B4
Mullans **①** BT53. . . . . 44 A2
Mullan Upper **①** BT80 . . 115 B4
Mullarts **①**
  Ballycastle BT54. . . . . 8 E2
  Ballymena BT44. . . . . 32 C8
Mull Ct BT44. . . . . 76 E4
Mullenan Rd BT48. . . . . . 50 C6
Mullennan **①** BT48. . . . . . 50 D5
Mullinabrone **①** BT51. . . . 42 C3
Mullinaskeagh **①** BT44 . . 32 A2
Mullindreen Rd BT42. . . . 64 D4
Mullindress **①** BT54 . . . . . 3 B6
Mullinsallagh **①** BT44. . . . 76 F4
Mullintill Rd BT47. . . . . . . 69 A1
Mull Pk BT44. . . . . 76 E4
Mull Rd BT41. . . . . 186 D8
Mulnavoo **①** BT45. . . . . . 89 A5
Mulnavoo La BT45. . . . . . 89 A5
Mulnavoo Rd BT45. . . . . . 88 F5
Mulroy Gdns BT48. . . . . 178 B5
Multyhogy **①** BT45. . . . . 145 E2
Munalahog Rd BT47. . . . . 54 D3
Munalohug **①** BT47. . . . . 54 D3
Munie **①** BT44 . . . . 65 C4
Munie North **①** BT44. . . . . 65 C5
Munie Rd BT44 . . . . 65 A3
Munie South **①** BT44. . . . 65 C3
Munreery **①** BT47. . . . . . . 54 A2
Murder Hole **①** BT49. . . . 24 D6
Murlough Rd BT54. . . . . . . 9 E4
Murob Pk BT43. . . . . 181 C7
Murrayfield Sh Ctr **2**
  BT48. . . . . 182 D4
Murray St BT1. . . . . 188 C2
Museum of Free Derry **11**
  BT48 . . . . 178 E5
Musgrave Channel Rd
  BT3 . . . . 145 B8
Musgrave Pk Bsns Ctr
  BT9. . . . . 150 D7
Musgrave Pk Ct BT9. . . . 150 E6
Musgrave Pk Hospl BT9 150 D6
Musgrave Pk Ind Est
  BT9. . . . . 150 D7
Musgrave St BT1. . . . . . . 189 B3
Music Hall La BT1. . . . . . 189 B2
Muskett Ave BT8. . . . . . . 163 C1
Muskett Cl BT8 . . . . 163 C1
Muskett Cres BT8. . . . . . 163 D2
Muskett Ct BT8 . . . . 163 C1
Muskett Dr **1** BT8. . . . . . 163 C1
Muskett Gdns BT8 . . . . . 163 C2
Muskett Glen BT8 . . . . . . 163 C2
Muskett Mews **3** BT8. . . 163 C1
Muskett Pk BT8. . . . . 163 C1
Muskett Rd BT8. . . . . 163 C1
Mussenden Cl BT51. . . . . 13 B3
Mussenden Cres BT51. . . 13 B3
Mussenden Gdns BT51. . . 13 C3
Mussenden Gr BT51. . . . . 13 B3
Mussenden Grange BT51. 13 B3
Mussenden Rd BT51. . . . . 13 A4
Mussenden Temple ★
  BT51. . . . . 12 F5
Mussenden View BT51. . . 13 C3
My Lady's Mile BT18. . . 139 D6
My Lady's Rd BT6 . . . . . 145 A3
Myroe Level (Intake) **①**
  BT49. . . . . 22 C4
Myrtledene Dr BT8. . . . . 152 B2
Myrtledene Rd BT8. . . . . 152 B2
Myrtlefield Pk BT9. . . . . . 151 A6
Myrtlefield Rd BT47. . . . 179 C5
Myrtle Pk BT53. . . . . 175 F2
Myrtle Rd BT47. . . . . 53 B6

N

Nailor's Row BT48. . . . . 178 E4
Nansen St BT12. . . . . . . 143 F3
Nappan **①** BT44. . . . . 49 C8
Nare **①** BT56. . . . . 172 E4
Nare Manor BT56. . . . . . 172 D5
Naroon Pk BT11. . . . . . . 149 F7
Narrowgauge Rd BT40. . 182 C3
Narvik Dr BT41. . . . . 186 C5
Nassau Cres BT48. . . . . . 178 D7
Naval La BT44 . . . . 76 A6
Navan Gn BT11. . . . . 150 B8
Navery Rd BT53. . . . . 28 F4

Nazareth House Prim Sch
  BT48. . . . . 178 E3
Ned **①** BT49. . . . . 38 B5
Nedd Rd BT49. . . . . 38 A5
Neillsbrook Pk BT41 . . . 108 A7
Neillsbrook Rd BT41. . . . 108 A7
Neill's Hill Pk BT5. . . . . . 145 F3
Neill's La BT38. . . . . 129 D2
Nelson Dr BT47 . . . . 179 D6
Nelson St
  Belfast BT15. . . . . 189 B4
  2 Carrickfergus BT38 . 131 A7
Nendrum Gdns
  Belfast BT5. . . . . 145 D4
  Newtownabbey BT37. . . 133 F5
Nessagh Rd BT47. . . . . . . 54 A8
Ness Gdns BT47. . . . . . . 179 B4
Netherlands Dr BT17 . . . 149 E4
Netherlands Pk BT17. . . 149 E4
Netherleigh Mews BT4 . 146 C7
Netherleigh Pk BT4 . . . . 146 C6
Nettlefield Prim Sch
  BT6. . . . . 145 A4
Nettlehill Rd BT28. . . . . 159 D4
Nettle Hill Rd BT28. . . . 159 D4
Nevis Ave BT4 . . . . 145 D5
Newal Rd BT53. . . . . 175 D5
New Barnsley Cres BT12. 143 C4
New Barnsley Dr BT12. . 143 C4
New Barnsley Gdns
  BT12 . . . . 143 C4
New Barnsley Gn BT12 . 143 C4
New Barnsley Gr BT12 . . 143 C4
New Barnsley Par BT12. . 143 C4
New Barnsley Pk BT12 . . 143 C4
New Bldgs Ind Est BT47. . 50 E4
New Bridge Dr BT12 . . . . 26 D7
Newbridge Pk **22** BT52. . 26 C7
Newbridge Rd
  Ballymoney BT53. . . . . . 175 A6
  Coleraine BT52 . . . . 174 E2
Newbridge Sean O Leary
  GAC BT41 . . . . 106 A8
New Buildings **①**
  Ballymoney BT53. . . . . . . 43 B3
  Cookstown BT80 . . . . . . 185 F5
NEW BUILDINGS BT47. . . 50 F5
New Buildings North **①**
  BT53. . . . . 27 D7
New Buildings or Maddydoo
  Lower **①** BT53. . . . . 43 B3
Newbuildings Prim Sch
  BT47. . . . . 50 F5
New Buildings South **①**
  BT53. . . . . 28 A1
Newcastle Manor **1**
  BT4 . . . . 145 B6
Newcastle St **15** BT4 . . . 145 B5
NEWFERRY BT45. . . . . . . 92 C6
Newferry Rd BT45. . . . . . 92 B7
Newforge Ctry Club BT9 151 C4
Newforge Dale BT9 . . . . 151 B5
Newforge Grange BT9 . . 151 B5
Newforge La BT9 . . . . . . 151 B5
New Hampshire St BT13. 188 C4
Newhill **①** BT53 . . . . 175 E6
Newhill Pk BT53 . . . . . . 175 D5
Newington Ave
  Belfast BT15. . . . . 137 C1
  Larne BT40. . . . . 182 D5
Newington St **1** BT15. . 137 C1
Newlands **①** BT40 . . . . . . 99 D6
Newlands Cres BT55 . . . 172 B2
Newlands Rd BT40. . . . . . 99 D6
New Line BT38. . . . . 124 C3
Newline Rd BT49. . . . . . . 55 B8
New Line Rd
  Ballyclare BT39. . . . . 98 E1
  Carrickfergus BT38. . . . . 123 E7
New Lodge Pl **①** BT15. . 144 D8
New Lodge Rd BT15. . . . 144 C8
Newlyn Terr **7** BT47. . . . 179 A4
Newmarket St **1** BT48. . 178 F5
NEWMILL BT39. . . . . 110 D6
Newmill Rd BT39. . . . . . . 110 D7
Newmills Bsns Pk BT52 . 174 F3
Newmills Rd BT52. . . . . . 174 F3
New Mkt St BT52 . . . . . . 174 C3
Newpark BT53 . . . . 175 D5
Newpark **①** BT51. . . . . . . 42 A4
Newpark BT40. . . . . 99 E7
New Park BT41 . . . . 187 C4
Newpark Ind Est BT41. . 187 C4
Newpark Ring Rd BT41. . 187 D2
New Rd
  Ballymena BT42. . . . . 93 E8
  Cookstown BT80 . . . . . . 112 A5
  Dunloy BT44. . . . . 44 F3
  Kilrea BT51 . . . . 59 C5
New Row
  4 Castledawson BT45. . 91 D2
  Coleraine BT52 . . . . 174 C3
New Row Prim Sch **7**
  BT45. . . . . 91 C2
Newry St BT6. . . . . 145 B3
New St
  Ballymoney BT53. . . . . . . 18 A1
  Lisburn BT27 . . . . 160 C2
  Londonderry BT47. . . . . 176 F2
  Randalstown BT41. . . . . 107 F6
  3 Dungiven BT47. . . . . . 55 C2
Newtownabbey Bsns Pk
  BT36. . . . . 133 C4

Newton Gdns BT36. . . . 133 E1
Newton Hts BT8 . . . . 152 C3
Newton Pk BT8 . . . . 152 B4
Newton Rd BT49 . . . . . . 180 E5
Newtown **①** BT44. . . . . . . 49 C3
NEWTOWNABBEY (BAILE NA
  MAINSTREACH) BT36. . 133 C7
Newtownabbey Comm High
  Sch BT37 . . . . 133 F2
Newtownabbey Indep
  Christian Sch BT36 . . . . 111 F1
Newtownards Rd BT5 . . 145 A5
NEWTOWNBREDA BT8. . 151 E4
Newtownbreda Dr BT8 . 151 F4
Newtownbreda Factory Est
  BT8 . . . . 151 F2
Newtownbreda High Sch
  BT8 . . . . 151 F3
Newtownbreda Prim Sch
  BT8 . . . . 152 A4
Newtownbreda Rd BT8. . 151 E2
NEWTOWN-CROMMELIN
  BT43 . . . . 47 A2
NEWTOWNHAMILTON. . . 50 B4
Newtown Limavady alias
  Rathbrady Beg **①** BT49. 180 A6
Niblock **①** BT41. . . . . . . 109 B6
Niblock Gr BT41. . . . . . . 109 A6
Niblock Oaks BT41. . . . . 109 A6
Niblock Rd BT41. . . . . . . 186 C8
Niblock Rd S BT41. . . . . 186 D8
Nicholas Pk **6** BT47 . . . . 37 C5
Nicholson Dr BT36. . . . . 132 C7
Nicholson Gdns
  Lisburn BT28 . . . . 170 B8
  Londonderry BT47. . . . . . 51 F5
Nicholson Sq BT48. . . . . 178 D6
Nicholson Terr BT48. . . . 178 D6
Ninth St BT13. . . . . 188 A4
NIXON'S CORNER BT48. . 50 E7
Norbloom Gdns **2** BT5. 145 D3
Norburgh Pk BT48 . . . . . 176 B1
Norbury St BT11. . . . . . . 143 C5
Norcross St **5** BT48. . . . 178 D7
Norfolk Ct BT11 . . . . 187 B5
Norfolk Dr BT11 . . . . 143 C2
Norfolk Gdns BT11. . . . . 143 C2
Norfolk Gr BT11 . . . . 143 C2
Norfolk Par BT11 . . . . . . 143 C2
Norfolk Rd BT11 . . . . 143 C2
Norfolk Sq BT41. . . . . . . 187 B5
Norfolk Way BT11 . . . . . 143 C2
Norglen Cres BT11. . . . . 143 C3
Norglen Ct BT11 . . . . 143 C3
Norglen Dr BT11 . . . . 143 B3
Norglen Gdns BT11 . . . . 143 C2
Norglen Gr BT11 . . . . 143 B3
Norglen Par BT11. . . . . . 143 C3
Norglen Rd BT11. . . . . . . 143 B3
North Ballinteer **①** BT51. . 25 D8
North Ballylagan BT52 . . 14 E3
North Ballyleese **①** BT56. 172 E3
North Bank BT6. . . . . . . 152 B8
North Bellemont **①** BT55. 14 C5
North Boundary St BT13. 188 C4
Northbrook Gdns BT9. . . 144 A1
Northbrook Ind Est BT52 174 F2
Northbrook St BT12. . . . 144 A1
North Circular Rd
  Belfast BT14. . . . . 137 A4
  Lisburn BT28 . . . . 160 A2
North City Bsns Ctr
  BT15. . . . . 144 D8
North Cl BT118 . . . . 139 C5
North Coast Integrated Coll
  BT55 . . . . 174 F5
Northcroft Sh Ctr BT36. . 132 C5
North Derby St BT15. . . . 137 E1
North East Division **①**
  BT38 . . . . 125 B7
North Edward St **2**
  BT48 . . . . 178 E6
North E Institue of F&H Ed
  BT38 . . . . 181 E4
North E Inst of FE BT43 . 181 E4
North E Inst of FE (Antrim
  Campus) **1** BT41 . . . . . 186 E4
North E Inst of F&H Ed
  BT45 . . . . 183 C5
North End BT54. . . . . . . 184 C5
Northern Ireland Fire
  Brigade HQ **4** BT27 . . 160 B2
Northern Ireland Hospice
  (Somerton House)
  BT15. . . . . 137 C3
Northern Rd **2** BT3. . . . 144 E8
Northfield Rise BT5 . . . . 146 A1
North Gdns BT5. . . . . . . 145 E3
North Gn BT11. . . . . 150 B8
North Hill St BT15. . . . . . 144 D7
North Howard Ct BT13 . . 188 B4
North Howard Link BT13. 188 B4
North Howard St BT13. . 188 B4
North Howard Wlk BT13. 188 A4
North King St BT13. . . . . 188 C4
Northland BT38. . . . . . . 124 F2
Northland Ave BT48. . . . 178 E7
Northland Cres BT48. . . 178 E7
Northland Cres BT13 . . . 188 A4
Northland Dr
  Londonderry BT48. . . . . 178 E7
  1 Moneymore BT45. . . 113 E8
Northland Gdns
  Cookstown BT80 . . . . . . 185 D7
  3 Moneymore BT45. . . 113 E8

Northland Ind Est BT48 . . 176 C1
Northland Par BT48 . . . . . 178 E7
Northland Rd
 Londonderry BT48 . . . . . 178 D8
 2 Moneymore BT45 . . . . . 113 E8
Northlands Pk BT10 . . . . . 150 B5
Northland St BT13 . . . . . 188 A4
Northland Terr **2** BT48 . . 178 E7
Northland Way **5** BT48 . . 178 E7
North Link BT11 . . . . 150 C8
North Mdws BT48 . . . . . . 176 B1
North Par BT7 . . . . 144 F1
North Queen St BT15 . . . 144 D8
North Rampart BT52 . . . . 174 C4
North Rd
 Ballymena BT43 . . . . 181 C4
 Ballymoney BT53 . . . . . . 175 B4
 Belfast BT5 . . . . 145 E4
 Carrickfergus BT38 . . . . 131 A8
Northside Village Ctr
 BT48 . . . . 176 F4
North Sperrin BT5 . . . . . 146 D3
North St
 Ballycastle BT54 . . . . 8 D4
 Belfast BT1 . . . . 189 A4
 Carrickfergus BT38 . . . . 131 A7
 Lisburn BT28 . . . . 156 E7
Northumberland St
 BT13 . . . . 188 B4
North View BT13 . . . . . . 133 C1
Northwest Inst of Further Ed
 & H Education BT48 . . . . 176 D2
Northwick Dr BT14 . . . . . 136 F1
North W Ind Hospl BT49 . . 38 D7
North W Inst of F&H Ed
 BT48 . . . . 178 E6
Northwood Cres **5** BT15 137 E3
Northwood Dr BT15 . . . . 137 D3
Northwood Par BT15 . . . 137 D3
Northwood Rd BT15 . . . . 137 D3
Norton Dr BT9 . . . . 151 A5
Norwell BT51 . . . . 13 A4
Norwood Ave BT4 . . . . . 145 F6
Norwood Cres BT4 . . . . . 145 F7
Norwood Ct
 Belfast BT4 . . . . 145 F7
 Coleraine BT52 . . . . 174 F3
Norwood Dr BT4 . . . . . . 145 F6
Norwood Gdns BT4 . . . . 145 F6
Norwood Gr BT4 . . . . . . 145 F6
Norwood Pk BT4 . . . . . . 146 A6
Norwood St BT2 . . . . . . 189 A2
Notting Hill BT9 . . . . 151 B7
Notting Hill Ct BT9 . . . . 151 C7
Nottinghill Manor **4**
 BT9 . . . . 151 B7
Novally**i** BT54 . . . . .8 B3
Novally Rd BT54 . . . . .8 B3
Novara Pk BT41 . . . . 186 F3
Nualamont Dr BT48 . . . . 178 D4
Nubia St BT12 . . . . 188 A1
Nun's Wlk BT18 . . . . 139 D5
Nursery Ave BT53 . . . . . 175 D6
Nursery Gr BT41 . . . . . . 187 B2
Nursery Pk BT41 . . . . . . 187 A2
Nursery Rd BT42 . . . . 93 F7
Nursery View BT42 . . . . . 93 F7
Nutgrove Rd BT45 . . . . . . 89 E1
Nutts Cnr Rd BT29 . . . . . 117 D2

O

Oakbridge Pk BT48 . . . . 176 F6
Oakburn BT41 . . . . 187 C2
Oakdale Manor BT41 . . . 187 A4
Oakdale Pk BT47 . . . . 70 E6
Oakdale St BT4 . . . . 145 C5
Oakdene Cres BT49 . . . . . 38 D7
Oakdene Dr BT4 . . . . . . 145 D6
Oakdene Par BT4 . . . . . . 145 D6
Oak Fern BT36 . . . . 132 D6
Oakfield BT41 . . . . 187 A4
Oakfield Ave BT48 . . . . . 178 D6
Oakfield Cres BT48 . . . . 178 D6
Oakfield Dr
 Carrickfergus BT38 . . . . 125 A3
 Londonderry BT48 . . . . . 178 D6
Oakfield Pk BT53 . . . . . . 175 B4
Oakfield Pl BT51 . . . . 59 C5
Oakfield Prim Sch BT38 125 A4
Oakfield Rd BT48 . . . . . . 178 D5
Oakglen BT41 . . . . 187 A4
Oak Gr
 Castledawson BT45 . . . . . 91 C1
 Greysteel BT47 . . . . 37 C5
Oakgrove BT48 . . . . 176 F7
Oakgrove Integrated Coll
 BT47 . . . . 177 E3
Oakgrove Integrated Prim
 Sch BT47 . . . . 179 B6
Oakhill BT47 . . . . 170 A4
Oakhurst Ave BT10 . . . . 150 A4
Oak La BT45 . . . . 91 C1
Oakland Ave BT4 . . . . . . 145 E5
Oakland Cres BT38 . . . . 125 A3
Oakland Dr **3** BT38 . . . 125 A3
Oakland Gdns BT38 . . . . 125 A3
Oakland Pk BT38 . . . . . . 125 A3
Oaklands BT41 . . . . 187 B4
Oaklands**i** BT80 . . . . . . 112 B2
Oaklands **5** BT42 . . . . . . 78 A6
Oaklands Ave BT36 . . . . 128 F3
Oakland's Ave BT55 . . . . 173 D5
Oaklands Cl BT36 . . . . . . 128 F3

Oaklands Ct BT36 . . . . . . 128 F3
Oaklands Dr BT36 . . . . . . 128 F2
Oaklands Mdw **6** BT36 . 128 F3
Oaklands Pk BT36 . . . . . 128 F3
Oaklands Rd BT36 . . . . . 112 B1
Oaklands Rise BT36 . . . . 128 E3
Oaklands View BT36 . . . . 128 F2
Oaklands Way **8** BT36 . 128 F2
Oakland Way **2** BT17 . . 160 F8
Oaklea Rd BT45 . . . . 105 C2
Oakleigh Pk **1** BT6 . . . . 145 A2
Oakley Ave BT18 . . . . . . 139 C5
Oakley Pk BT53 . . . . 16 E5
Oakley St BT14 . . . . 136 D2
Oakman St BT12 . . . . . . 143 F4
Oakmount Dr BT15 . . . . 137 E4
Oak Pk BT45 . . . . 88 C4
Oakridge Ave BT27 . . . . 160 B5
Oakridge Cre BT27 . . . . 160 C5
Oakridge Cres BT27 . . . . 160 B5
Oakridge Gds BT27 . . . . 160 B5
Oakridge Pk BT27 . . . . . 160 B5
Oak St BT7 . . . . 189 A1
Oaks The
 Lisburn BT28 . . . . 159 E5
 3 Newtownabbey BT37 . 133 F3
 Randalstown BT41 . . . . . 107 F7
Oak Terr BT47 . . . . 179 F2
Oaktree Dr BT41 . . . . . . 186 F6
Oakvale Ct BT17 . . . . . . 149 F3
Oakvale Gdns BT17 . . . . 149 F3
Oakvale Manor BT45 . . . 183 B4
Oakvale Pk BT52 . . . . . . 174 D7
Oak View BT39 . . . . 119 A8
Oak Way BT7 . . . . 189 A1
Oakwood BT37 . . . . 134 B5
Oakwood Ave BT8 . . . . . 163 C1
Oakwood Ct BT9 . . . . . . 151 A5
Oakwood Gr BT9 . . . . . . 151 A5
Oakwood Hts BT8 . . . . . 163 C1
Oakwood Integrated Prim
 Sch BT17 . . . . 160 D8
Oakwood Mews BT9 . . . 151 A5
Oakwood Pk BT9 . . . . . . 151 A5
Oakwood Rd BT38 . . . . . 124 E1
Oakwood Sch BT9 . . . . . 150 F4
Oasis The BT45 . . . . 183 D5
Oatlands**i** BT51 . . . . 42 B4
Oberon St BT6 . . . . 145 B2
O Cahan Pl BT47 . . . . 55 D2
O'cahanplace **1** BT47 . . 55 D2
O'cahans Castle★ BT49 . . 39 B4
O'cahan Way BT49 . . . . . 180 B3
O'casey Ct **1** BT48 . . . . 176 B3
Oceanic Ave BT15 . . . . . 137 C1
O'connor Ct **2** BT48 . . . 176 B2
O'dempsey St BT15 . . . . 137 E2
Odessa St (Sráid Odása)
 BT13 . . . . 188 A3
O Donnell Ave BT48 . . . 176 B2
O'donovan Rd BT48 . . . . 177 C5
O'donovan Rossa GAC
 BT12 . . . . 143 D2
Ogales Rd BT28 . . . . 120 E2
Oghill**i**
 Limavady BT49 . . . . 38 B6
 Londonderry BT47 . . . . . . 52 D7
Ogilvie Ct BT40 . . . . 182 A3
Ogilvie St BT6 . . . . 145 B3
Ogles Gr BT26 . . . . 169 C1
O'hara Dr BT55 . . . . 172 A3
O'hara Rd BT46 . . . . 74 D1
Ohio St BT13 . . . . 143 F8
OIRTHEAR MAÍ (ARMOY)
 BT53 . . . . 18 A1
Old Antrim Rd BT42 . . . . 181 D1
Old Ballybracken Rd
 Ballyclare BT39 . . . . 110 E8
 Ballymena BT42 . . . . 96 B4
Old Ballyclare Rd BT39 . 110 D3
Old Ballymoney Rd BT43 181 B7
Old Ballynahinch Rd
 BT27 . . . . 171 C3
Old Ballyrobin Rd BT14 . 109 D8
Old Ballyrobin Rd
 Antrim BT41 . . . . 117 E7
 Ballyclare BT39 . . . . 118 A8
Old Ballysillan Rd BT14 . 136 F4
Old Bann Rd BT45 . . . . . 106 C8
Old Belfast Rd BT40 . . . . 83 B2
Oldbridge BT47 . . . . 178 E2
Old Carrick Rd BT37 . . . 128 D3
Old Castle Ct BT55 . . . . . 173 A5
Oldcastle Rd BT38 . . . . . 100 D1
Old Castle Rd BT41 . . . . 108 B6
Old Cavehill Rd BT15 . . . 137 B5
Old Channel Rd BT3 . . . . 145 A6
Old Church**i** BT47 . . . . . 65 C5
Old Church Entry **4**
 BT43 . . . . 181 D4
Old Church La BT67 . . . . 166 B7
Old Church Rd BT36 . . . 133 E2
Old City Ct BT48 . . . . . . 178 C3
Old Cl The **6** BT43 . . . . 78 A6
Old Coach Ave BT9 . . . . 150 E2
Old Coach Gdns BT9 . . . 150 E2
Old Coach La BT9 . . . . . 150 E2
Old Coach Mews **1**
 BT39 . . . . 110 D2
Old Coach Rd
 Ballyclare BT39 . . . . 119 A8
 Belfast BT9 . . . . 150 E2
 Portrush BT56 . . . . 172 C5
Old Coagh Gill BT80 . . . 185 E6
Old Coagh Rd BT80 . . . . 185 E6
Old Coleraine Rd BT56 . 172 C2
Old Colin Rd
 Belfast BT17 . . . . 149 D5

Old Colin Rd continued
 Dunmurry BT17 . . . . 149 B4
Old Crebilly Rd BT42 . . . 181 F3
Old Crosskennan Rd
 BT41 . . . . 109 D6
Old Ct Manor BT44 . . . . . 45 E3
Old Cullybackey Rd
 BT43 . . . . 181 A6
Old Cultra La BT37 . . . . 135 B1
Old Cultra Rd BT37 . . . . 135 B1
Old Cushendun Rd BT43 . 47 A4
Old Distillery BT52 . . . . 174 D2
Olderfleet Castle★ BT40 . 182 F2
Olderfleet Prim Sch
 BT40 . . . . 182 F4
Old Ferris Bay Rd BT40 . . 84 A3
Old Forde **15** BT38 . . . . 100 D1
Old Forde Gdns **9** BT38 100 D1
Old Foreglen Rd BT47 . . . 52 D2
Old Forge**i** BT17 . . . . . . 150 C1
Old Forge BT29 . . . . 121 B6
Old Forge**i** BT17 . . . . . . 150 B1
Old Forge Manor
 Belfast BT10 . . . . 150 D2
 Larne BT40 . . . . 83 B2
Old Forge Mews BT28 . . 168 E7
Oldfort Ave BT67 . . . . . . 166 A2
Oldfort Gdns BT67 . . . . . 166 A2
Oldfort Pk BT67 . . . . 166 A2
Old Freehold**i** BT40 . . . . 82 D3
Old Frosses Rd BT44 . . . . 61 E7
Old Galgorm Dale BT42 . 181 A3
Old Galgorm Rd BT42 . . 181 A3
Old Glenarm Rd BT40 . . 182 C7
Old Gn Rd **8** BT42 . . . . . 95 A6
Old Golf Course Rd
 BT17 . . . . 150 A4
Old Grange Ave
 Ballymena BT42 . . . . 181 B2
 Carrickfergus BT38 . . . . 125 B2
Old Grange Dr BT38 . . . 125 C2
Old Grange Gn BT38 . . . 125 B2
Old Grange Way BT38 . . 125 B2
Old Holywood Rd BT4 . . 146 B8
Old Irish Highway BT37 . 133 C5
Old Kilmore Rd
 Craigavon BT67 . . . . 164 D5
 Moira BT67 . . . . 166 A1
Old Larne Rd
 Ballymena BT42 . . . . 79 A2
 Ballynure BT39 . . . . 97 F2
Old Lodge Rd BT13 . . . . 144 B7
Old Lough Rd BT41 . . . . 186 D4
Old Lurgan Rd BT67 . . . . 164 E5
Old Magheragh Rd BT41 108 C6
Old Manse Ct BT37 . . . . 134 C7
Old Manse Rd BT37 . . . . 134 B7
Old Mill BT41 . . . . 109 F1
Old Mill**i** BT40 . . . . 83 B8
Old Mill Bsns Pk BT41 . . 187 C1
Old Mill Cotts BT28 . . . . 160 B8
Old Mill Cres **4** BT36 . . 119 C8
Old Mill Ct
 Londonderry BT48 . . . . . 176 E1
 7 Moneymore BT45 . . . . 113 E8
Old Mill Dr BT36 . . . . . . 133 E1
Old Mill Grange BT56 . . 172 C3
Old Mill Hts
 Hillsborough BT26 . . . . . 169 B1
 Larne BT40 . . . . 83 B2
Oldmill Mews BT39 . . . . . 96 F1
Old Mill Mews BT47 . . . . 179 F1
Old Mill Rd BT14 . . . . . . 136 C3
Old Mill The BT26 . . . . . 169 B1
Old Milltown Rd BT8 . . . 151 C2
Old Mill Way BT14 . . . . . 136 C3
Old Model Ct BT51 . . . . 174 B4
Old Moira Rd BT28 . . . . 156 E6
Old Moria Rd BT29 . . . . 121 B4
Old Mus Arts Ctr The★
 BT12 . . . . 188 C3
Old Orch The BT67 . . . . 155 C3
Old Park**i** BT14 . . . . 119 F2
Oldpark Ave
 Ballymena BT42 . . . . 78 C4
 Belfast BT14 . . . . 137 B1
Oldpark Dr **2** BT42 . . . . 78 C4
Oldpark Manor **1** BT42 . 78 C4
Oldpark Rd
 Ballymena BT42 . . . . 78 C4
 Belfast BT14 . . . . 144 B8
Oldpark Sq **1** BT14 . . . . 137 A1
Oldpark Terr BT14 . . . . . 137 A2
Old Pk Rd BT28 . . . . 159 E7
Old Pollee Rd BT43 . . . . . 63 B3
Old Portglenone Rd BT44 . 77 B3
Old Quay Ct BT18 . . . . . 139 F8
Old Quay Rd
 Holywood BT18 . . . . 139 F8
 Newtownabbey BT37 . . . 135 B1
Old Rathbeg Rd BT41 . . 187 E8
Old Rathmore Rd BT41 . 187 E7
Old Rd BT28 . . . . 167 A8
Old Rectory Cl BT80 . . . 185 C2
Old Rectory Cres BT80 . 185 C2
Old Rectory Ct BT80 . . . 185 C1
Old Rectory Glen BT80 . 185 C2
Old Rectory Hts BT80 . . 185 C1
Old Rectory Mdws BT80 185 C2
Old Rectory Pk BT80 . . . 185 C2
Old Roguery Rd BT41 . . . 92 E1
Old Rough Rd BT14 . . . . 109 B7
Old Saintfield Rd BT8 . . 163 C7
Old Sch Ct BT29 . . . . . . 121 B6
Old Sch Field The BT47 . 179 F1

Old Sch La
 Antrim BT41 . . . . 93 B4
 Londonderry BT48 . . . . . 176 F5
Old Shore Rd E BT38 . . . 130 C5
Old Shore Rd W BT38 . . 130 B5
Old Springfarm Rd BT41 186 D6
Old Staffordstown Rd
 BT41 . . . . 107 F6
Old Steeple St BT41 . . . 109 B7
Oldstone**i** BT41 . . . . 109 C1
Old Stone Cl BT38 . . . . . 129 E1
Oldstone Hill BT41 . . . . 117 A8
Oldstone Pk BT41 . . . . . . 62 B7
Oldstone Rd BT41 . . . . . 187 B1
Old Suffolk Rd BT11 . . . 149 E7
Old Throne Rd BT36 . . . 133 C1
Old Town**i** BT57 . . . . 15 D4
Old Town Deer Park**i**
 BT45 . . . . 91 F4
Old Town Downing**i**
 BT45 . . . . 91 E5
Oldtown Rd
 Ballymena BT42 . . . . 94 F5
 Ballymoney BT53 . . . . . . 15 E4
 Magherafelt BT45 . . . . . . 91 E4
Oldtown Rd BT80 . . . . . . 185 C6
Old Tullygarley Rd BT42 . 78 C2
Old Tully Rd BT29 . . . . . 117 C5
Old Turn BT38 . . . . 125 E1
Old Tyanee Rd BT44 . . . . 76 B4
Old Warren**i** BT28 . . . . . 170 A8
Old Warren Prim Sch
 BT28 . . . . 169 F7
Old Westland Rd BT14 . . 137 B3
Oldwood BT36 . . . . 132 D7
Oldwood Rd BT41 . . . . . . 94 D2
Old Wood Rd BT41 . . . . . 94 E1
Olive St BT13 . . . . 143 F7
Olivia Ctr The BT36 . . . . 132 E5
Ollardale Pk BT39 . . . . . 184 B4
Olympia St BT12 . . . . . . 144 A2
Olympia Leisure Ctr
 BT12 . . . . 144 A1
Olympia Par BT12 . . . . . 144 A2
Olympia St BT12 . . . . . . 144 A2
Omco Est BT42 . . . . 79 B4
Omeath St BT6 . . . . 145 B3
Omerbane La BT44 . . . . . 46 C3
Omerbane Rd BT44 . . . . . 46 B3
O'naullian Cres BT48 . . . 176 B3
O'NEILL PARK BT45 . . . . 105 E4
O'neill Rd BT36 . . . . 133 E5
O'neill's Pl BT18 . . . . . . 139 D7
O'neill St BT13 . . . . 188 A3
Onslow Gdns BT6 . . . . . 145 B1
Onslow Par BT6 . . . . 152 B8
Onslow Pk BT6 . . . . 145 B1
Open Univ BT7 . . . . 144 D2
Ophir Gdns BT15 . . . . . . 137 B4
Orangefield Ave BT5 . . . 145 E3
Orangefield Cres BT6 . . 145 C1
Orangefield Dr BT5 . . . . 145 E3
Orangefield Dr S BT5 . . . 145 E3
Orangefield Gdns BT5 . . 145 E3
Orangefield Gn BT5 . . . . 145 E3
Orangefield Gr BT5 . . . . 145 E3
Orangefield High Sch
 BT5 . . . . 145 F2
Orangefield La BT5 . . . . 145 E3
Orangefield Par BT5 . . . 145 E3
Orangefield Pk BT5 . . . . 145 E3
Orangefield Prim Sch
 BT5 . . . . 145 E2
Orangefield Rd BT5 . . . . 145 E4
Orange Hall La BT28 . . . 159 D4
Oranmore Dr BT11 . . . . 149 F5
Oranmore Pk
 2 Londonderry BT48 . . 176 B1
 Londonderry BT48 . . . . . 178 B8
Oranmore St BT13 . . . . 143 F5
Orby Cl BT5 . . . . 145 E1
Orby Ct BT5 . . . . 145 D3
Orby Dr
 Ballymoney BT53 . . . . . . 16 E6
 Belfast BT5 . . . . 145 E2
Orby Gdns BT5 . . . . 145 C2
Orby Gn BT5 . . . . 145 C2
Orby Gr BT5 . . . . 145 D2
Orby Grange BT5 . . . . . . 145 C3
Orby Link BT5 . . . . 145 C3
Orby Mews BT5 . . . . 145 D3
Orby Par BT5 . . . . 145 C2
Orby Pk BT5 . . . . 145 D2
Orby Pl BT5 . . . . 145 D2
Orby St BT5 . . . . 145 E1
Orchard Bank **5** BT44 . . 76 C4
Orchard Bsns Pk BT4 . . 176 E1
Orchard Cl
 Antrim BT41 . . . . 187 C4
 Belfast BT5 . . . . 146 C3
 Lisburn BT28 . . . . 170 A7
 Portglenone BT44 . . . . . . 76 D5
Orchard Ct BT38 . . . . . . 139 B2
Orchard Dr **2** BT44 . . . . 76 D4
Orchard Gn BT41 . . . . . 107 F8
Orchard Gr **4** BT29 . . . 117 B1
Orchard Hill
 5 Crumlin BT29 . . . . . 117 B1
 Crumlin BT29 . . . . 121 B8
Orchard La BT41 . . . . . . 180 C6
Orchard Rd
 10 Crumlin BT29 . . . . . 117 B1
 Crumlin BT29 . . . . 121 B8
Orchard Rise BT8 . . . . . 152 A4
Orchard Row BT43 . . . . 178 E3
Orchard St BT48 . . . . . . 178 F5
Orchardtown**i** BT47 . . . . 36 E6

Orchard Vale BT6 . . . . . 152 E7
Orchard View **1** BT45 . . 105 A1
Orchardville **1** BT51 . . . 174 A1
Orchardville Ave BT10 . . 150 C6
Orchardville Cres BT10 . 150 C5
Orchardville Gdns BT10 . 150 C5
Orchard Way
 Antrim BT41 . . . . 187 C4
 Portglenone BT44 . . . . . . 76 D4
Oregon Gdns (Orkan
 Gairdens) BT13 . . . . . . 143 F7
O'riada Ct BT48 . . . . 176 A2
Oriel Ct BT41 . . . . 186 D5
Oriel Pk BT41 . . . . 186 F5
Oriel Rd BT41 . . . . 186 E5
Orient Gdns BT14 . . . . . 137 B1
Orkan Gairdens (oregon
 Gdns) BT13 . . . . 143 F7
Orken La BT67 . . . . 155 D5
Orkney Dr BT42 . . . . 79 A3
Orkney St
 Antrim BT41 . . . . 186 D8
 Belfast BT13 . . . . 188 A4
Orlock Cres **3** BT40 . . . . 83 B4
Orlock Sq BT10 . . . . 150 D3
Ormeau Ave BT7 . . . . . . 189 B1
Ormeau Bsns Pk BT7 . . 189 B1
Ormeau Emb BT7 . . . . . 189 C1
Ormeau Golf Club BT7 . 144 F1
Ormeau Rd BT7 . . . . 189 B1
Ormeau St BT7 . . . . 189 B1
Ormiston Cres BT4 . . . . 146 A5
Ormiston Dr BT4 . . . . . . 146 A4
Ormiston Gdns BT5 . . . . 146 A4
Ormiston Par BT4 . . . . . 146 A5
Ormiston Pk BT4 . . . . . . 146 B4
Ormonde Ave
 Belfast BT10 . . . . 150 C4
 Newtownabbey BT36 . . . 132 E8
Ormonde Gdns BT6 . . . . 145 C2
Ormonde Pk BT10 . . . . . 150 B4
Oronsay Cres BT40 . . . . . 83 B5
O'rorke's Row BT38 . . . . 124 D1
Orpen Ave BT10 . . . . . . 150 C4
Orpen Dr BT10 . . . . 150 C4
Orpen Pk
 Belfast BT10 . . . . 150 C4
 Londonderry BT47 . . . . . 179 C4
Orpen Sh Ctr BT10 . . . . 150 D4
Orpinsmill Rd BT39 . . . . . 97 A2
Orritor Cres BT80 . . . . . 185 C5
Orritor La BT80 . . . . 185 C6
ORRITOR (NA CORACHA
 BEAGA) BT80 . . . . 112 C5
Orritor Prim Sch BT80 . 112 B4
Orritor Rd BT80 . . . . 185 A6
Orritor St BT80 . . . . 185 C6
Orr Rd BT45 . . . . 105 C4
Orrs La BT27 . . . . 161 A2
Ortus Bsns Pk BT13 . . . 188 B3
Orwood Mews BT36 . . . 133 A5
Osborne Dr BT9 . . . . 151 A7
Osborne Gdns BT9 . . . . 151 A6
Osborne Pk
 Belfast BT9 . . . . 151 A6
 Coleraine BT51 . . . . 174 A3
Osborne St BT48 . . . . . . 178 C6
Osman St BT12 . . . . 188 B3
Osprey Dr BT47 . . . . 179 B2
Ossian's Grave Chambered
 Grave★ BT44 . . . . 32 A5
Osterley Pk BT36 . . . . . . 133 A6
Oswald Pk BT12 . . . . . . 188 B1
Ottawa St BT13 . . . . 143 F7
Otterbank Rd BT47 . . . . 177 F4
Otter Pk BT47 . . . . 177 F5
Oughtagh**i** BT47 . . . . 52 F4
Oughtagh Rd BT47 . . . . . 52 E4
Oughtboy**i** BT79 . . . . 85 E4
Oughtdoorish**i** BT79 . . . 85 D3
Oughtmame**i** BT79 . . . . . 86 B4
Oughtnamwella**i** BT79 . . 86 D4
Oughtymore**i** BT49 . . . . . 11 D4
Oughtymoyle**i** BT49 . . . . 23 A8
Oughtymoyle Ave BT49 . . 23 A8
Ouna or Eagle Hill**i**
 BT44 . . . . 31 C5
Our Lady of Lourdes High
 Sch BT53 . . . . 175 B3
Our Lady of Lourdes Prim
 Sch BT36 . . . . 137 C7
Our Lady of Mercy Girls Sch
 BT14 . . . . 136 E3
Our Lady Queen of Peace
 Prim Sch BT17 . . . . 149 F3
Our Lady & St Patrick's Coll
 BT5 . . . . 146 D2
Our Lady's Girls Prim Sch
 BT14 . . . . 137 A3
Outal**i** BT44 . . . . 61 D6
Outdoor Pursuits Ctr★
 BT52 . . . . 4 E1
Outhill**i** BT52 . . . . 15 C5
Oval Ct BT4 . . . . 145 C6
Ovil**i** BT47 . . . . 54 D1
Owenbeg**i** BT47 . . . . 55 B2
Owencloghy**i** BT44 . . . . . 81 C5
Owenmore Pk BT47 . . . . 177 F6
Owenreagh**i** BT45 . . . . . 102 C8
Owenreagh Dr BT37 . . . 133 F4
Owenreagh Rd BT45 . . . . 88 C1
Owensland**i** BT39 . . . . . . 96 E1
Owenstown Rd BT40 . . . 182 A1
Owenvale Mews BT13 . . 143 F5
Owenvarragh Gdns BT11 150 C7
Owenvarragh Pk BT11 . . 150 C7
Oxford Ave BT28 . . . . . . 160 B4
Oxford St BT1 . . . . 189 B3

Ozone Ave BT53 . . . . 175 D4
Ozone Leisure Ctr BT7 . . 189 C1

P

Pacific Ave BT15 . . . . 137 C1
Paddock La BT48 . . . . 177 A6
Paddocks The 3 BT51 . . 26 A7
Paddock The
  6 Ballymena BT42 . . . . . 78 C3
  Lisburn BT28 . . . . 159 C3
  Newtownabbey BT38 . . . . . 129 D4
Páirc Bhaile Andarsan
  (Andersonstown Pk) 8
  BT11 . . . . 143 D1
Páirc Mhullach An Mháis
  (Mullaghmeash Pk)
  BT47 . . . . 70 E6
Páirc Na Sceiche (Hawthorn
  Pk) 8 BT47 . . . . 37 C5
Páirc Radharc An Fheabail
  (Foyle View Pk) BT47 . . 37 A5
Paisley Rd BT38 . . . . 123 F6
Pakenham St BT7 . . . . 189 A1
Palace Gdns BT15 . . . . 137 B4
Palace Gr BT18 . . . . 139 D3
Palace Mews BT18 . . . . . . 139 C3
Palace St BT48 . . . . 178 E5
Palestine St BT7 . . . . 144 E2
Palmer Ave BT28 . . . . 160 B3
Palmer Ct 6 BT13 . . . . . . 143 F8
Palmer St BT13 . . . . 143 F7
Palmerston Pk
  Belfast BT4 . . . . 145 E7
  Londonderry BT47 . . . . . 179 C7
Palmerston Rd BT4 . . . . . . 145 E7
Pandora St BT12 . . . . 188 B1
Pansy St BT4 . . . . 145 B5
Pantridge Rd BT17 . . . . . . 149 D5
Papworth Ave BT48 . . . . . . 177 C5
Parade Rd BT43 . . . . 79 A7
Paradise Ave BT42 . . . . . . 181 D3
Paradise Pk BT39 . . . . 110 C4
Paradise Wlk BT39 . . . . . . 110 C3
Parishagh○ BT44 . . . . 65 E8
Paris St
  10 Belfast BT13 . . . . . . 144 A7
  Belfast BT13 . . . . 188 A4
Park○ BT53 . . . . 17 F1
PARK BT47 . . . . 70 A3
Park Ave
  Ballyclare BT39 . . . . 184 A4
  Belfast BT4 . . . . 145 D6
  Cookstown BT80 . . . . 185 C5
  Holywood BT18 . . . . 139 D6
  Londonderry BT48 . . . . . 178 D7
Park Cotts BT47 . . . . 69 C7
Park Dr BT18 . . . . 139 D6
Parkend St BT15 . . . . 137 D1
Parker Ave BT55 . . . . 173 D5
Parker St BT4 . . . . 145 B5
Parkfield BT29 . . . . 117 B1
Parkfield Rd BT42 . . . . 77 D2
PARKGATE BT39 . . . . 110 C4
Parkgate Ave BT4 . . . . 145 D5
Parkgate Cres 4 BT4 . . 145 C6
Parkgate Dr 4 BT4 . . . . 145 C6
Parkgate Gdns BT4 . . . . . . 145 C6
Parkgate Par BT4 . . . . 145 C6
Parkgate Prim Sch BT39 110 D5
Parkgate Rd
  Ballyclare BT39 . . . . 110 B4
  Ballymena BT42 . . . . 95 D3
Park Gn 3 BT41 . . . . 107 F7
Park Grange 3 BT4 . . . . 145 D6
Park Hall BT41 . . . . 187 A5
Parkhall Coll BT41 . . . . . . 186 E6
Parkhall Prim Sch BT41 . 186 F5
Parkhall Rd BT41 . . . . 186 F6
Park House Manor BT18 . 139 F8
Park La
  Ballymoney BT53 . . . . . . 175 B6
  Belfast BT9 . . . . 144 C1
  Magherafelt BT45 . . . . . . 183 D4
Parkland Ave BT28 . . . . . . 159 F4
Parkland Dr BT28 . . . . 159 F4
Parklands
  Antrim BT41 . . . . 186 D6
  Ballymoney BT53 . . . . . . 175 D2
  Larne BT40 . . . . 182 C7
  Londonderry BT47 . . . . . 179 D7
Parklea BT56 . . . . 172 B5
Parkley 6 BT29 . . . . 117 A1
Park Lodge BT8 . . . . 151 F3
Park Manor 2 BT36 . . . . 119 C8
Park Mews BT17 . . . . 149 F3
Parkmore BT45 . . . . 183 C4
Parkmore Ave BT45 . . . . . . 183 C4
Parkmore Cl
  Ballymena BT43 . . . . 181 B4
  Magherafelt BT45 . . . . . . 183 D4
Parkmore Cres 5 BT45 . 183 C4
Parkmore Dr
  Ballymena BT43 . . . . 181 B4
  Magherafelt BT45 . . . . . . 183 D4
  Strathfoyle BT47 . . . . 177 F5
Parkmore Gdns BT45 . . . . 183 D4
Parkmore Hts BT45 . . . . . . 183 D4
Parkmore Mews BT45 . . . . 183 D4
Parkmore or Aganlane○
  BT44 . . . . 47 F6
Parkmore Rd BT45 . . . . . . 183 D4
Parkmount Ave BT7 . . . . . . 151 F8
Parkmount
  Cookstown BT80 . . . . 185 C5
  Lisburn BT27 . . . . 160 C2

Parkmount Ave
  Ballymena BT43 . . . . 181 B6
  1 Larne BT40 . . . . 182 C5
Parkmount Cl 1 BT15 . . 137 D1
Parkmount Cres BT43 . . . . 181 B6
Parkmount Ct 5 BT36 . . 119 C8
Parkmount Dr BT43 . . . . . . 181 B6
Parkmount Gdns
  Belfast BT15 . . . . 137 E6
  4 Larne BT40 . . . . 182 C5
Parkmount La BT15 . . . . . . 137 E6
Parkmount Par BT15 . . . . . 137 D6
Parkmount Pass BT15 . . . . 137 E6
Parkmount Pl BT15 . . . . . . 137 E6
Parkmount Rd
  Ballymena BT43 . . . . 181 B6
  Belfast BT15 . . . . 137 C6
  1 Newtownabbey BT36 . . 119 C8
Parkmount St BT15 . . . . . . 137 D1
Parkmount Terr BT15 . . . . . 137 E6
Parkmount Way BT15 . . . . . 137 E6
Parknasilla Cl BT67 . . . . . . 164 F8
Parknasilla Cres BT67 . . . . 164 F8
Parknasilla Way BT67 . . . . 164 F8
Park Par BT6 . . . . 145 A3
Park Rd
  Belfast BT7 . . . . 144 F1
  Larne BT40 . . . . 98 D8
  Newtownabbey BT36 . . . . 119 C8
Parkside Dell BT43 . . . . . . 181 C6
Parkside Gdns BT15 . . . . . 137 D1
Parkside Rise BT43 . . . . . . 181 C6
Park St
  Ballyclare BT39 . . . . 184 C5
  Coleraine BT52 . . . . 174 C3
Park The
  Ballymoney BT53 . . . . . . 17 F1
  Belfast BT17 . . . . 149 F3
Parkview
  Ballyclare BT39 . . . . 184 C5
  Ballymoney BT53 . . . . . . 175 D5
Park View
  Ballymoney BT53 . . . . . . 175 D6
  3 Castledawson BT45 . . 91 D2
Parkview Cl BT53 . . . . 175 D6
Parkview Manor BT5 . . . . . 146 C2
Parkview Specl Sch
  BT28 . . . . 159 C2
Parkville Ct BT15 . . . . 137 C3
Parkway BT4 . . . . 146 B8
Park Way BT43 . . . . 181 C5
Parkwood BT27 . . . . 160 C4
Pasadena Gdns 2 BT5 . . 146 A4
Pass The BT67 . . . . 120 A1
Patrick Pl BT42 . . . . 181 D3
Patrick St BT48 . . . . 178 E6
Pats Brae 2 BT43 . . . . . . 181 D4
Pattens Fall○ BT44 . . . . . . 32 F7
Patterson Dr 3 BT38 . . . 125 C1
Patterson's Pl BT1 . . . . . . 189 A3
Paulett Ave 11 BT5 . . . . . 145 B4
Paul's La BT51 . . . . 174 A5
Paxton St BT5 . . . . 145 B4
Pearl St BT5 . . . . 145 B4
Pearse Pk GAA BT51 . . . . . 59 B3
Peel Gdns BT28 . . . . 156 E7
Pelham Rd BT47 . . . . 179 D3
Pembridge Ct BT4 . . . . 146 A6
Pembroke Ct 3 BT17 . . . 149 D6
Pembroke Loop Rd
  BT17 . . . . 149 C6
Pembroke Manor BT17 . . 149 D6
Pembroke St BT12 . . . . 188 B1
Pembrooke Ct 7 BT36 . . 132 F7
Pembrooke Mews 9
  BT36 . . . . 132 F7
Penge Gdns BT9 . . . . 151 D7
Pennethorn Ct 6 BT47 . 179 A5
Pennington Pk BT52 . . . . . 152 B2
Pennybridge Ind Est
  BT42 . . . . 181 F1
PENNYBURN BT48 . . . . . . 178 E8
Pennyburn Ct BT48 . . . . . . 178 F1
Pennyburn Ind Est BT48 . 176 F1
Pennyburn Pass BT48 . . . . 176 F1
Pennyhill BT42 . . . . 181 A2
Pennyhill Dr BT42 . . . . 181 A1
Penrose St BT7 . . . . 144 E2
Pentagon Ret Pk 4
  BT43 . . . . 181 C4
Percy Pl BT13 . . . . 188 B4
Percy St BT13 . . . . 188 B3
Pernau St BT13 . . . . 188 A4
Perry Ct BT5 . . . . 145 C4
Peter Pan Ind Est BT12 . . 143 F5
Peter's Hill BT13 . . . . 188 C4
Peters Rd BT43 . . . . 56 C6
Petrie Way BT48 . . . . 177 C5
Pharis○ BT53 . . . . 29 D2
Pharis Rd BT53 . . . . 29 D2
Phennick Dr BT10 . . . . 150 D4
Phillip St BT48 . . . . 178 F8
Picardy Ave BT6 . . . . 152 C8
Pigeontown Rd BT29 . . . . . 121 A6
Pillar Brae Rd BT43 . . . . . . 79 A8
Pilot Pl 4 BT1 . . . . 144 E7
Pilot St BT1 . . . . 144 E7
Pim's Ave BT4 . . . . 145 D6
Pim St BT15 . . . . 144 C7
Pine Crest BT18 . . . . 139 E5
Pinecroft Pk BT28 . . . . 159 F3
Pine Ct BT42 . . . . 79 D7
Pine Gr BT18 . . . . 139 D4
Pinegrove Cres BT43 . . . . . 181 B7
Pinegrove Pk BT43 . . . . . . 181 B7
Pinehill
  Lisburn BT27 . . . . 171 C6

Pinehill continued
  Ballymena BT43 . . . . 183 D4
Pinehill Ave 17 BT46 . . . 74 D1
Pinehill Rd
  Ballymoney BT53 . . . . . . 29 A1
  Lisburn BT27 . . . . 161 F4
Pineridge Rd BT43 . . . . . . 181 B7
Pine St
  Belfast BT7 . . . . 189 B1
  Londonderry BT47 . . . . . 179 A5
Pines The
  Cookstown BT80 . . . . 185 B4
  Randalstown BT41 . . . . . 107 F6
Pinetrees BT48 . . . . 176 B5
Pineview Dr BT36 . . . . 133 C2
Pineview Gdns BT36 . . . . . 133 C2
Pineview Pk BT36 . . . . 133 C2
Pineview Rd BT36 . . . . 133 C2
Pine Way BT7 . . . . 189 A1
Pinewood Ave BT38 . . . . . 124 F1
Pinewood Cres BT47 . . . . . 69 C8
Pinewood Gdns BT47 . . . . 179 F1
Pinewood Pk BT27 . . . . . . 162 A3
Piney Hill BT45 . . . . 183 D5
Piney Hills BT9 . . . . 151 B5
Piney La BT9 . . . . 151 B4
Piney Pk BT9 . . . . 151 B4
Piney Way BT9 . . . . 151 B4
Piney Wlk BT9 . . . . 151 B4
Pipe Rd BT41 . . . . 94 D3
Pirrie Pk Gdns BT6 . . . . . . 145 A1
Pirrie Rd BT4 . . . . 146 A6
Plains The BT39 . . . . 96 E1
Plantation Ave
  Carrickfergus BT38 . . . . . 125 C5
  Lisburn BT27 . . . . 170 D8
  9 Newtownabbey BT36 . . 111 F1
  Newtownabbey BT36 . . . . 128 A2
Plantation Cl BT27 . . . . . . 170 D8
Plantation Ct BT27 . . . . . . 170 E8
Plantation Dr
  Carrickfergus BT38 . . . . . 125 C6
  Lisburn BT27 . . . . 170 D8
Plantation Gr BT27 . . . . . . 170 E7
Plantation Mews BT27 . . 170 E7
Plantation Rd
  Coleraine BT51 . . . . 57 A8
  Limavady BT49 . . . . 38 C5
  Lisburn BT27 . . . . 170 E7
  Londonderry BT47 . . . . . 69 F1
Plás Bhruach Na Cluana
  (Meadowbank) 2 BT47 . 37 C5
Plás Chluain Ard (Clonard
  Pl) 2 BT13 . . . . 188 A3
Plas Merdyn BT18 . . . . 139 E6
Plateau The BT9 . . . . 151 B4
Playhouse Theatre 13
  BT48 . . . . 178 E5
Plunkett Ct (Cúirt
  Phluincéid) BT13 . . . . . 189 A4
Point Rd
  Limavady BT49 . . . . 11 C7
  Magherafelt BT45 . . . . . . 105 F4
Point St BT40 . . . . 182 C3
Poleglass○ BT17 . . . . 149 C5
Polepatrick○ BT45 . . . . . . 105 B8
Police Ct BT48 . . . . 178 E5
Polintamny○ BT53 . . . . . . 44 A7
Pollard Cl (Clós Pholaird) 2
  BT12 . . . . 143 F5
Pollard St (Sráid Pholaird)
  1 BT12 . . . . 143 F5
Pollee○ BT43 . . . . 63 B2
Pollee Rd BT43 . . . . 63 B2
Pollock Rd BT15 . . . . 144 E8
Pollysbrae Rd BT49 . . . . . . 39 A2
Pollys Brae Rd BT47 . . . . . 54 E7
Pomeroy○ BT51 . . . . 57 B8
Pomeroy Rd BT80 . . . . 185 A2
Pommern Par BT6 . . . . 145 C2
Pomona Ave BT4 . . . . 145 D5
Pond Pk Ave BT28 . . . . 159 F4
Pond Pk Cres BT28 . . . . . . 159 F4
Pond Pk Hts BT28 . . . . 159 D6
Pond Pk Prim Sch BT28 . 159 E4
Pond Pk Rd BT28 . . . . 159 C8
Pond Pk Rd E BT28 . . . . . . 159 D7
Ponsonby Ave BT15 . . . . . 137 C1
Poobles○ BT67 . . . . 165 F5
Poplar Rd
  Belfast BT29 . . . . 121 C8
  Crumlin BT29 . . . . 117 C1
  Londonderry BT47 . . . . . 179 B2
Poplars The
  3 Newtownabbey BT36 . . 119 C8
  Randalstown BT41 . . . . . 107 F6
Portallo St BT6 . . . . 145 B3
PORTBALLINTRAE (PORT
  BHAILE AN TRÁ) BT57 . . 5 B5
PORT BHAILE AN TRÁ
  (PORTBALLINTRAE) BT57 . 5 B5
PORTBRADDAN BT57 . . . . 6 E7
Portbradden Rd BT57 . . . . 6 E6
Port Davy Rd 10 BT38 . . 100 D1
Porter Rd BT10 . . . . 150 C4
Porters Bridge Rd BT28 . 121 F1
PORT GHLUAIN EOGHAIN
  (PORTGLENONE) BT44 . . 76 E5
Port Glen Manor 4 BT44 . 76 D4
Portglenone GAA BT44 . . . 76 D4
PORTGLENONE (PORT
  GHLUAIN EOGHAIN)
  BT44 . . . . 76 E5
Portglenone Prim Sch
  BT44 . . . . 76 E4
Portglenone Rd
  Ahoghill BT42 . . . . 77 E2
  Antrim BT41 . . . . 107 F8

Portland Ave BT36 . . . . . . 132 F5
Portland Rd BT40 . . . . 182 F4
Portland St BT40 . . . . 182 F4
Portlee○ BT41 . . . . 107 A2
Portlee Rd BT41 . . . . 107 A3
Portlee Wlk BT41 . . . . 186 F4
Portlock Pl BT48 . . . . 177 C5
Portmore○ BT28 . . . . 120 E1
Portmore Ave BT28 . . . . . . 156 E7
Portmore Hill BT36 . . . . . . 133 C1
Portmore Lea BT28 . . . . . . 155 D8
Portmore Rd
  Lisburn BT28 . . . . 155 D8
  Portrush BT56 . . . . 172 B6
Portmuck○ BT40 . . . . 84 D3
Portmuck Castle★ BT40 . 84 E3
Portmuck Rd BT40 . . . . 84 D2
Portna○ BT44 . . . . 59 F5
Portnamona Ct 2 BT11 . 143 B1
Portna Rd
  Ballymena BT43 . . . . 59 F5
  Coleraine BT51 . . . . 59 E4
Portneal○ BT44 . . . . 59 D6
Port Rd
  Larne BT40 . . . . 100 D3
  Strathfoyle BT47 . . . . 177 F6
PORT ROIS (PORTRUSH)
  BT56 . . . . 173 C7
Portrush○ BT56 . . . . 172 D7
Portrush Countryside Ctr★
  BT55 . . . . 173 D8
PORTRUSH (PORT ROIS)
  BT56 . . . . 173 C7
Portrush Prim Sch BT55 . 173 E6
Portrush Rd
  Ballymoney BT53 . . . . . . 175 B6
  Coleraine BT52 . . . . 174 D7
  Portrush BT56 . . . . 172 D7
Portrush Sta BT55 . . . . . . 173 D6
Portside Bsns Pk BT3 . . 138 E4
Portsmouth Gdns BT38 . . 125 C3
Portstewart Golf Club
  BT55 . . . . 172 A1
Portstewart Golf Links
  BT56 . . . . 172 C6
Portstewart Old Golf Course
  BT56 . . . . 172 C6
PORTSTEWART (PORT
  STÍOBHAIRD) BT55 . . . 172 B7
Portstewart Prim Sch
  BT56 . . . . 172 B5
Portstewart Rd
  Coleraine BT52 . . . . 174 C6
  Portstewart BT55 . . . . . . 173 C5
PORT STÍOBHAIRD
  (PORTSTEWART) BT55 . 172 B7
Portula Dr BT28 . . . . 159 E4
Portview Trade Ctr BT4 . . 145 C5
Poseyhill Rd BT39 . . . . 110 E7
Posnett Ct BT7 . . . . 189 A1
Posnett St BT7 . . . . 189 A1
Postboys Wlk BT53 . . . . . . 175 B5
Pothill La BT27 . . . . 171 E1
Pottagh○ BT51 . . . . 13 D3
Pottagh House★ BT51 . . . 13 D3
Potterswalls○ BT41 . . . . . . 109 C7
Potterswalls La BT41 . . . . . 109 C7
Pottingers Entry BT1 . . . . 189 B3
Pottinger St
  Belfast BT5 . . . . 145 B4
  Cullybackey BT42 . . . . . . 77 F6
Pound Rd BT45 . . . . 183 F6
Pound St BT40 . . . . 182 C4
Powerscourt Pl BT7 . . . . . . 189 B1
Prehen○ BT47 . . . . 50 F6
Prehen Pk BT47 . . . . 178 C1
Prehen Rd BT47 . . . . 178 C2
Premier Bsns Ctr BT2 . . 189 B2
Premier Dr BT15 . . . . 137 D3
Premier Gr BT15 . . . . 137 D3
Presbytery La BT44 . . . . . . 45 A3
Prestwich Dr BT14 . . . . . . 136 F3
Prestwick Pk BT14 . . . . . . 136 F4
Pretoria St BT9 . . . . 144 D1
Priestland East○ BT57 . . . 5 C1
Priestland Rd BT57 . . . . . . 15 D6
Priestland W BT57 . . . . 5 B1
Priestland West○ BT57 . . 5 B1
Priestown La BT45 . . . . 91 A8
Priestown Rd BT44 . . . . . . 77 B1
Priests La BT27 . . . . 169 E7
Priest's Well○ BT80 . . . . . 112 A6
Primary Sch BT14 . . . . 119 F1
Primity○ BT47 . . . . 50 F5
Primity Cres BT47 . . . . 50 F5
Primity Gdns BT47 . . . . . . 50 F5
Primity Pk BT47 . . . . 50 F5
Primity Terr BT47 . . . . 50 F5
Primrose Cl BT55 . . . . 173 E3
Primrose Cres BT55 . . . . . . 173 D3
Primrose Dr BT55 . . . . 173 E3
Primrose Gdns BT55 . . . . . 173 D4
Primrose Gdn Village
  BT28 . . . . 170 A7
Primrose Hill BT55 . . . . . . 152 B1
Primrose Pk BT55 . . . . 173 E3
Primrose St
  Belfast BT7 . . . . 151 F8
  4 Belfast BT14 . . . . 136 D2
  Londonderry BT47 . . . . . 179 A4
Prince Andrew Gdns
  BT12 . . . . 188 B1
Prince Andrew Pk BT12 . 188 B1
Prince Andrew Way
  BT38 . . . . 125 B2
Prince Arthur St 2
  BT48 . . . . 178 E5

Prince Charles Way
  BT36 . . . . 132 F8
Prince Edward Dr BT9 . . . 151 D7
Prince Edward Gdns
  BT9 . . . . 151 D7
Prince Edward Pk BT9 . . . 151 D7
Prince of Wales Ave
  Belfast BT4 . . . . 146 D5
  Whitehead BT38 . . . . 127 A8
Prince Regent Commercial
  Pk BT5 . . . . 145 E1
Prince Regent Rd BT5 . . . 145 E1
Princes Ave BT37 . . . . 133 F6
Princes Cres BT37 . . . . . . 133 F6
Princes Dr BT37 . . . . 133 F6
Princes Gdns BT40 . . . . . . 182 D4
Princes Pk BT37 . . . . 133 F6
Princes Pl BT43 . . . . 181 C4
Princess Ave BT80 . . . . . . 185 C7
Princess Dr 4 BT45 . . . . 183 D5
Princess Gdns
  Clogh Mills BT44 . . . . . . 45 E3
  Coleraine BT51 . . . . 174 A5
  3 Magherafelt BT45 . . . 183 D5
Princess Pk BT38 . . . . 127 A8
Princess St BT55 . . . . 173 C8
Princes St
  Ballymena BT43 . . . . 181 C4
  Londonderry BT48 . . . . . 178 E6
Prince's St BT1 . . . . 189 B3
Princes Terr BT45 . . . . 183 D5
Princes Terr 1 BT45 . . . . 178 E6
Princes Way BT38 . . . . 125 C1
Prince William Rd BT28 . 159 D4
Prince William Way
  BT38 . . . . 125 B1
Printshop Rd BT39 . . . . . . 118 C6
Priormore Gr BT40 . . . . . . 84 D2
Priors Lea BT18 . . . . 139 D3
Priory Cl
  Carrickfergus BT38 . . . . . 130 D6
  Lisburn BT27 . . . . 160 D5
Priory Dr BT38 . . . . 130 D6
Priory End BT18 . . . . 139 D5
Priory Gdns
  Belfast BT10 . . . . 150 D5
  Larne BT40 . . . . 182 B3
Priory Integrated Coll
  BT18 . . . . 139 D6
Priory La BT47 . . . . 55 D1
Priory Pk
  Belfast BT10 . . . . 150 D5
  Holywood BT18 . . . . 139 E7
Priory Pl BT40 . . . . 182 B3
Priory Rd BT47 . . . . 55 D2
Priory The BT39 . . . . 184 B7
Procklis○ BT41 . . . . 93 D5
Prolusk○ BT57 . . . . 7 A3
Promenade
  Castlerock BT51 . . . . 13 B5
  Portstewart BT55 . . . . . . 173 D5
Promontory Fort★
  Ballymena BT44 . . . . 49 D8
  Coleraine BT51 . . . . 13 A4
  Larne BT40 . . . . 82 E7
Prom The BT56 . . . . 172 B6
Prospect BT42 . . . . 181 B3
Prospect○ BT53 . . . . 27 C3
Prospect Ave
  Carrickfergus BT38 . . . . . 124 E2
  Portstewart BT55 . . . . . . 172 A3
Prospect Cres BT38 . . . . . 124 D1
Prospect Ct BT44 . . . . 32 E4
Prospect Downs BT38 . . . 124 E1
Prospect Downs S BT38 . 124 E1
Prospect Dr BT38 . . . . 124 E1
Prospect Gdns BT38 . . . . 124 D1
Prospect Gn BT38 . . . . . . 124 D2
Prospect Gr BT38 . . . . 124 D2
Prospect Hts BT38 . . . . . . 124 D2
Prospect Loanen 1
  BT38 . . . . 124 D2
Prospect Pk
  Belfast BT14 . . . . 144 A8
  Carrickfergus BT38 . . . . . 124 D1
  Lisburn BT28 . . . . 159 E4
  Portstewart BT55 . . . . . . 172 A3
Prospect Pl 3 BT43 . . . . 181 D4
Prospect Rd
  Carrickfergus BT38 . . . . . 124 D2
  Portrush BT56 . . . . 172 B3
Prospect St 2 BT38 . . . . 131 A8
Protestant St BT49 . . . . . . 180 A5
Pubble○ BT47 . . . . 53 E6
Pullans North○ BT52 . . . . 27 A6
Pullans Rd BT52 . . . . 27 A6
Pullans South○ BT52 . . . . 27 A6
Pump St BT48 . . . . 178 E5
PURDYSBURN BT8 . . . . . . 162 D8
Purdysburn Hill BT8 . . . . . 162 C7
Purdysburn Rd BT8 . . . . . . 151 F1
Purdy's La BT8 . . . . 152 A5
Purity St BT7 . . . . 131 B7

Q

Quadrant Pl BT12 . . . . 188 C3
Quarry Hill
  Castlereagh BT5 . . . . 153 A8
  Portrush BT56 . . . . 172 E7
Quarry Hts BT42 . . . . 77 E2
Quarry Rd
  Belfast BT4 . . . . 146 B8
  Magherafelt BT45 . . . . . . 90 B3

Quarry St BT48 178 D3
Quarry The BT43 62 F6
QUARRYTOWN BT43 62 E1
Quarrytown Rd BT43 62 E1
Quarterlands Rd
Belfast BT29 140 F7
Larne BT40 84 A3
Lisburn BT27 161 C5
Quarter Lenagh Ⓣ BT41 108 F8
Quaterlands Rd BT29 140 D8
Quay La BT38 126 E7
Quay Rd
Ballycastle BT54 8 D3
Newtownabbey BT37 133 F1
Quayside BT38 131 A7
Quayside Office Pk BT3 137 F3
Quayside Sh Ctr 7 BT48 178 E6
Quay St BT40 182 D4
Queen Elizabeth Bridge
BT1 189 B3
Queenora Ave BT56 172 B5
Queen's Arc BT1 189 A3
Queens Ave
Ballymoney BT53 175 B6
Cookstown BT80 185 C6
Magherafelt BT45 183 D5
1 Newtownabbey BT36 132 F6
Queensberry Pk BT6 152 A7
Queensbrae BT8 163 C3
Queen's Bridge BT1 189 B3
Queens Cres
Carryduff BT8 163 D3
Newtownabbey BT36 132 F6
Queens Ct BT52 174 F4
Queensdale BT8 163 C3
Queens Dr BT36 132 F7
Queensfort Ct BT8 163 D4
Queensfort Pk BT8 163 D3
Queensfort Pk S BT8 163 D3
Queensfort Rd BT8 163 D4
Queens Gdns BT36 132 F7
Queenside BT8 163 C3
Queen's Island Ⓣ BT3 145 B8
Queen's Leisure Complex
BT18 139 D7
Queen's Par BT15 144 D7
Queen's PE Ctr BT9 144 D1
Queens Pk
Ballymena BT42 77 E6
Ballymoney BT53 44 C6
Coleraine BT51 174 A5
Newtownabbey BT36 132 F6
Queens Quay BT48 178 E6
Queen's Quay
Belfast BT3 189 C4
Londonderry BT48 178 F7
Queen's Quay Link BT3 189 C3
Queens Rd BT41 187 A5
Queen's Rd BT3 145 A8
Queens Rd S BT27 160 C1
Queens Sq BT38 125 C2
Queen's Sq BT1 189 B3
Queen St
Ballymena BT42 181 D3
Ballymoney BT53 175 D4
Belfast BT1 189 A3
Carrickfergus BT38 131 A7
Coleraine BT52 174 C3
Londonderry BT48 178 E6
Magherafelt BT45 183 C4
Queen's Univ of Belfast 5
BT9 144 C1
Queensway
Carrickfergus BT38 125 C2
Carryduff BT8 163 D3
Dunmurry BT17 160 D7
Lisburn BT27 160 D4
Queens Way BT45 183 D5
Queensway Pk BT17 160 D7
Queen Victoria Gdns 1
BT15 137 D3
Queen Victoria St BT5 145 D5
Quickthorn Pl BT52 174 F4
Quiggy Ⓣ BT79 86 B1
Quilly Ⓣ BT45 104 B3
Quilly Rd
Coleraine BT51 13 D2
Magherafelt BT45 104 A4
Quinton St BT5 145 C3
Quinville BT18 139 E6
Quolie Ⓣ BT43 63 F8
Quolie La BT43 63 D5

R

Raby St BT7 151 F8
Racavan Ⓣ BT42 80 C5
Racavan Rd BT42 80 C4
Racecourse Rd
3 Londonderry BT48 176 F4
Londonderry BT48 177 B7
Race Rd BT44 77 A5
Raceview BT41 187 C1
Raceview Ave BT53 175 D3
Raceview Dr BT53 175 D3
Raceview Rd BT42 79 B6
Radharc Na Binne
(Mountainview Pk) 1
BT47 55 D2
Radnor St 26 BT6 145 A4
Raftery Cl BT48 176 A2
Raholp Pk BT37 134 A8
Railway Ct
Dungiven BT47 55 D3
Railway Ct *continued*
Newtownabbey BT37 129 B1
Railway Halt BT37 128 E2
Railway La 9 BT47 55 D2
Railway Pk BT43 47 C2
Railway Pl 3 BT52 174 D4
Railway Rd
Coleraine BT52 174 D4
Londonderry BT47 178 F4
Railway St
Antrim BT41 186 D4
Ballymena BT42 181 C2
Belfast BT12 188 C2
Dunmurry BT17 150 A2
Lisburn BT28 160 B2
Railway Terr BT53 18 A1
Railway View BT53 27 A3
Rainey Ct BT45 183 B6
Rainey Endowed Sch
BT45 183 C6
Rainey St BT45 183 C6
Rainey Way BT7 189 A1
Raleigh St BT13 144 B7
Rallagh Ⓣ BT47 71 C8
Rallagh Rd BT47 71 B5
RALOO BT40 99 A5
Raloo Ave BT40 182 B4
Raloo Rd BT40 98 F7
Ramin Pk BT47 179 F1
Ramoan Ave BT54 8 C2
Ramoan Ct 13 BT54 8 C3
Ramoan Dr BT11 150 A8
Ramoan Gdns
14 Ballycastle BT54 8 C3
Belfast BT11 150 A8
Ramoan Rd BT54 8 C3
Ramore Ave BT55 173 C8
Ramore Gdns BT48 178 B4
Ramore Gn BT40 182 A5
Ramore Pk BT10 150 E3
Ramore St BT55 173 C7
Ramper Rd BT80 102 D1
Ramsey Pk 6 BT51 25 E5
Ranaghan Ⓣ BT41 107 B6
RANAGHAN BT45 88 B6
Ranaghan La BT46 73 E2
Ranaghan Rd
Antrim BT41 107 B5
Maghera BT46 73 F3
Magherafelt BT45 88 B7
Rananagh Ⓣ BT44 32 E8
Randal Pk
Belfast BT9 151 A7
Portstewart BT55 173 F6
Randalstown Ⓣ BT41 107 F7
RANDALSTOWN (BAILE
RAGHNAILL) BT41 107 E7
Randalstown Central Prim
Sch BT41 107 F7
Randalstown Rd BT41 186 C5
Randalstown Rd Bsns Pk
BT41 186 C7
Randalstown Tir na nog GAC
BT41 108 C7
Randox Ⓣ BT29 117 C3
Randox Rd BT29 117 C3
Ranelagh St BT6 145 B2
Ranfurly Dr 8 BT4 145 E6
Rankinstown Rd BT42 94 F8
Rannyglas 3 BT47 55 D2
Rannyglass 4 BT47 55 D2
Ransevyn Ct 16 BT38 100 D1
Ransevyn Dr BT38 100 D1
Ransevyn Gdns 7 BT38 100 D1
Ransevyn Pk BT38 100 D1
Raphael Pk 12 BT42 78 C3
Raphael Rd BT38 127 A8
Raphael St BT2 189 B2
Raphael Way BT42 78 B3
Rascahan Ⓣ BT49 38 F7
Rasharkin Prim Sch BT44 60 B6
RASHARKIN (ROS EARCÁIN)
BT44 60 A6
RASHEE BT39 97 B1
Rashee Cres BT39 184 B7
Rashee Ct BT39 184 B7
Rashee Dr BT39 184 B7
Rashee Pk BT39 184 C7
Rashee Rd BT39 184 A8
Raspberry Hill Ⓣ BT47 68 B6
Ratcliffe St BT7 189 A1
Rathbeg Ⓣ BT41 187 F6
Rathbeg BT80 185 C4
Rathbeg Ave BT51 174 A6
Rathbeg Dr BT49 180 C5
Rathbeg Rd BT41 187 E7
Rathbeg Rdbt BT41 187 F6
Rathblane BT41 187 A4
Rathbone St BT2 189 B2
Rathbrady More Ⓣ BT49 180 C6
Rathbrady Rd BT49 180 B5
Rathcavan Dr BT42 181 A2
RATHCOOLE BT37 133 D4
Rathcoole Cl BT37 133 F2
Rathcoole Dr 1 BT37 133 F3
Rathcoole Prim Sch
BT37 133 D4
Rathcool St BT9 151 A8
Rathdrum Pk 1 BT37 133 F4
Rathdrum St BT9 151 A8
Ratheane Ave
8 Coleraine BT52 26 B7
Coleraine BT52 174 D1
Ratheen Ave BT80 185 C4
Rathenraw Ⓣ BT41 187 C5
Rathenraw Ind Est BT41 187 C4
Rathenraw Integrated Sch
BT41 187 B5
Rathfad Ⓣ BT49 23 C5
Rathgar St BT9 151 A8
Rathglynn BT41 187 A5
Rathkeel Ⓣ BT42 79 F4
Rathkeele Way BT48 178 B4
Rathkeel Rd BT42 79 E6
Rathkenny Ⓣ BT43 62 E4
Rathkyle BT41 187 A4
Rathlin Ave BT54 8 D4
Rathlin Ct BT54 8 D4
Rathlin Dr
Ballymena BT43 181 B7
Londonderry BT48 178 B4
Rathlin Gdns BT48 178 B4
Rathlin Hts BT38 124 D3
RATHLIN ISLAND
(REACHLAINN) BT54 2 E7
Rathlin Rd BT54 8 D4
Rathlin Rspb Seabird
Viewpoint★ BT54 2 B6
Rathlin St BT13 143 F7
Rathmena Ave BT39 184 B6
Rathmena Dr BT39 184 B6
Rathmena Gdns BT39 184 B6
Rathmena Pk BT39 184 B6
Rathmore Ⓣ BT41 187 F4
Rathmore BT80 185 C3
Rathmore Ave
Belfast BT10 150 C3
Lisburn BT28 159 E2
Rathmore Bsns Pk BT48 178 D5
Rathmore Cres BT48 178 B5
Rathmore Ct
Cookstown BT80 185 D4
Portstewart BT55 173 E6
Rathmore Depot Rd
BT41 110 A4
Rathmore Dr
Newtownabbey BT37 133 D3
Portstewart BT55 173 E4
Rathmore Ed Guidance Ctr
BT41 187 F5
Rathmore Gdns
Antrim BT41 187 B3
Belfast BT10 150 C3
Rathmore Golf Club
BT55 173 F6
Rathmore Gram Sch
BT10 150 C2
Rathmore Hts BT43 181 B7
Rathmore Pk
Belfast BT10 150 C3
Lisburn BT28 159 E2
Rathmore Rd
Antrim BT41 187 F4
Limavady BT49 180 C6
Londonderry BT48 178 B5
Rathmore Sh Ctr BT48 178 C5
Rathmore St 22 BT6 145 A4
Rathmore Trench★
BT41 187 E5
Rathmore Way BT37 133 D3
Rathmoyle Pk BT38 125 D2
Rathmoyle Pk W BT38 125 D2
Rathmullan Dr BT37 133 E4
Rathowen Pk BT48 178 B3
Rathsherry Ⓣ BT43 63 A4
Rathvarna Ave BT28 159 D3
Rathvarna Cl BT28 159 C4
Rathvarna Dr BT28 159 D4
Rathvarna Gdns BT28 159 C4
Rathvarna Pk BT28 159 D4
Rathvarna Wlk BT28 159 C4
Rath View BT38 124 C1
Ravarnet Gdns BT27 170 B2
Ravarnet Rd BT27 170 B3
Ravel Ct BT43 47 C2
Ravel Manor BT43 47 C2
Ravelston Ave BT36 128 B1
Ravelston Cres BT36 128 B1
Ravelston Gdns 4 BT36 128 B1
Ravelston Gr
6 Newtownabbey BT36 128 B1
Newtownabbey BT36 133 B8
Ravelston Link 5 BT36 128 B1
Ravelston Par 4 BT36 133 B8
Ravelston Pk BT36 128 B1
Ravelston Rd 5 BT36 133 B8
Ravelston Way BT36 128 B1
Ravenhill Ave BT6 145 A2
Ravenhill Cres BT6 145 A2
Ravenhill Ct BT6 145 A2
Ravenhill Gdns BT7 145 A2
Ravenhill Par BT6 145 B2
Ravenhill Pk BT6 152 B8
Ravenhill Pk Gdns BT6 152 A8
Ravenhill Rd BT7 151 F7
Ravenhill Reach BT6 189 C1
Ravenhill Reach Ct BT6 189 C1
Ravenhill Reach Mews
BT6 189 C2
Ravenhill St 1 BT6 145 A3
Ravenscroft Ave BT5 145 D4
Ravenscroft St BT5 145 C5
Ravensdale BT36 128 B2
Ravensdale Cres 8 BT5 145 B3
Ravensdale St BT6 145 B4
Ravensdean Ave BT47 179 E5
Ravensdene Cres BT6 145 A1
Ravensdene Mews BT6 145 A1
Ravensdene Pk BT6 145 A1
Ravensdene Pk Gdns
BT6 145 A1
Ravenswood BT41 187 C3
Ravenswood Cres BT5 146 B1
Ravenswood Pk
Castlereagh BT5 146 A1
Prehen BT47 178 C1
RAVERNET BT27 170 B3
Rawbrae Rd
Carrickfergus BT38 126 E7
Whitehead BT38 100 C1
Rawdon Pl BT67 166 C1
REACHLAINN (RATHLIN
ISLAND) BT54 2 E7
Reahill Rd BT36 128 B5
Rea's Wood Nature Reserve
BT41 186 C1
Recreation Rd BT40 182 E6
Rectory Gdns BT42 79 C7
Rectory Pk BT51 42 A1
Rectory Rd
Ballyclare BT39 111 A7
Coleraine BT52 15 B3
Larne BT40 99 C8
Magherafelt BT45 89 D3
Red Bay Ⓣ BT44 32 D3
Red Brae Rd BT38 124 F5
Red Bridge Rd BT45 113 E4
Redburn Ctry Pk★ BT18 139 E3
Redburn Prim Sch BT18 139 D4
Redburn Sq BT18 139 D7
Redcar St BT6 145 B3
Redcliffe Dr 1 BT4 145 C6
Redcliffe Par BT4 145 C6
Redcliffe St BT4 145 C6
Redford Rd BT43 78 A8
Redfort Dr BT38 125 B5
Redfort Pk BT38 125 B5
Redhall Ⓣ BT38 100 B3
Redhall Cl BT38 100 A3
Redhall Dr BT38 100 B3
Redhill Manor BT10 150 D3
Redlands Cres
Coleraine BT51 174 B6
Larne BT40 182 E3
Redlands Ind Est BT40 182 E3
Redlands Rd BT40 182 E2
Redpoll Ave BT28 159 E4
Redthorn Ct BT52 174 F5
Redwood BT37 134 B7
Redwood Pk
9 Coleraine BT51 26 A7
Drumahoe BT47 179 F1
Ree Ⓣ BT51 27 A1
Ree La BT51 42 F8
Reformed Theological Coll
BT8 152 D1
Regency Ct BT45 183 C7
Regent Ave
Ballyclare BT39 184 E5
Carrickfergus BT38 125 D3
Regent Cres BT38 125 D3
Regent Gdns BT39 184 E5
Regent Pk
Carrickfergus BT38 125 D3
Portrush BT56 172 B3
Regents Pk
Ballymena BT43 181 D6
Larne BT40 182 D6
Regent St (Sráid na Ríona)
BT13 144 C7
Reids Rd BT40 100 D3
Reid St BT6 145 B2
REIDSTOWN BT44 92 E8
Renagh Pk BT36 133 E5
Renown Ct BT41 186 D5
Renwick St BT7 188 C1
Repulse Ct BT41 186 D5
Reservoir Rd BT44 46 D8
Retreat or Cloghglass Ⓣ
BT44 48 A8
Revallagh North Ⓣ BT57 15 D6
Revallagh Rd BT57 15 D6
Revallagh South Ⓣ BT57 15 D5
Rhanbuoy Cl BT38 130 E7
Rhanbuoy Ct BT38 130 E6
Rhanbuoy Pk BT38 130 E6
Rhencullen Pk BT44 60 B6
Riada Ave BT53 175 F3
Riada Cl 2 BT4 145 B6
Ribble St BT4 145 C5
Richard Branson Activity Ctr
The★ BT54 3 B6
Richardson St BT6 145 A3
Richburn Gdns 1 BT47 179 C4
Richdale Dr BT18 139 F8
Richhill Cres BT5 146 A3
Richhill Pk BT5 146 A3
Richill Pk BT47 179 D4
Richmond Ave
Ballymoney BT53 175 E5
Belfast BT4 139 B2
Lisburn BT28 159 F3
Newtownabbey BT36 132 F7
Richmond Cl BT4 139 B2
Richmond Cres
Ballymoney BT53 175 E5
Lisburn BT28 159 F3
Londonderry BT48 178 F8
Newtownabbey BT36 132 F7
Richmond Crt BT27 160 C3
Richmond Ct
Belfast BT4 139 B2
Lisburn BT27 160 C3
Richmond Ctr Sh Centre 7
BT48 178 F5
Richmond Dr
Coleraine BT52 174 E6
Lisburn BT28 159 F3
Newtownabbey BT36 132 F7
Richmond Gdns BT36 132 F8
Richmond Gn BT4 139 B2
Richmond Gr 1 BT36 132 F7
Richmond Hts BT4 139 B2
Richmond Mews BT28 159 F2
Richmond Par BT36 132 F8
Richmond Pk
Ballymena BT43 181 D6
Ballymoney BT53 175 E4
Belfast BT10 150 D5
Carrickfergus BT38 124 F4
Lisburn BT28 159 F3
11 Newtownabbey BT36 132 F7
Richmond Pk E 2 BT36 132 F7
Richmond Rd BT36 132 F7
Richmond Sq BT15 137 C2
Richmond Way BT36 132 F7
Richview St BT12 188 B1
Rickamore Ⓣ BT39 118 C8
Rickamore Brae BT39 118 C8
Rickamore Rd BT39 118 E8
Rickamore Rd Upper
BT39 118 D8
Riddell Ed Ctr BT13 188 B4
Ridge Pk BT28 160 A8
Ridgeway Dr BT47 51 D6
Ridgeway St
Belfast BT9 151 D8
Lisburn BT28 160 A1
Riga St BT13 188 A4
Rigby Cl BT15 137 B3
Ringfad Ⓣ BT44 49 D5
Ringford Cres BT11 149 F6
Ringford Pk 2 BT11 149 F6
Ringfort Rd BT48 176 B1
Ringrash Beg Ⓣ BT51 25 D7
Ringrash More Ⓣ BT51 25 C8
Ringrash Rd BT51 25 D6
Ring Rd BT52 174 D1
RINGSEND BT51 41 C7
Ringsend Cl BT46 74 D8
Ringsend Rd BT49 39 E8
Rinmore Dr BT48 178 B5
Rinnalea Cl BT11 149 F7
Rinnalea Gdns BT11 149 F7
Rinnalea Gr BT11 149 F7
Rinnalea Way BT11 149 F7
Rinvarna Ct BT52 174 D4
Rise Gdns BT28 149 C1
Risk Ⓣ
Bushmills BT57 15 D5
Coleraine BT51 43 A3
Moira BT67 166 B3
Ritters Ct BT49 180 B3
Riverbridge BT47 179 E1
River Cl BT11 150 A6
River Ct BT17 160 E8
Riverdale
Ballymena BT42 181 A1
Larne BT40 182 C3
Randalstown BT41 108 A8
Riverdale Cl
Ballyclare BT39 184 D6
Belfast BT11 150 C7
Riverdale Gdns BT11 150 B7
Riverdale Lodge 5 BT57 5 D3
Riverdale Pk
Ballyclare BT39 184 D6
Belfast BT11 150 B6
Portglenone BT44 76 D5
Riverdale Pk Ave BT11 150 B7
Riverdale Pk Dr BT11 150 B7
Riverdale Pk E BT11 150 C7
Riverdale Pk N BT11 150 B7
Riverdale Pk S BT11 150 C6
Riverdale Pk W BT11 150 B7
Riverdale Pl BT11 150 C7
Riverdale Rd BT28 120 F2
Riverforde BT38 100 C1
Rivergate La BT27 169 F6
River Gr BT17 160 E7
River La BT44 76 B4
Riverlea BT44 62 C6
River Mdw 6 BT39 96 F1
River Mews BT17 160 E7
River Rd
Dunmurry BT27 160 E6
Magherafelt BT45 88 E2
Riversdale Cres BT52 174 C4
Riversdale Rd
Coleraine BT52 174 C4
Prehen BT47 178 C1
Riverside
Antrim BT41 186 D3
Ballynure BT39 97 F2
1 Broughshane BT42 79 C7
Cookstown BT80 113 B5
Doagh BT39 110 F6
Holywood BT18 139 E7
6 Portglenone BT44 76 D4
Riverside Commercial Ctr 5
BT27 160 C1
Riverside Cotts BT49 38 C7
Riverside Ct BT29 121 B6
Riverside Dr
Cookstown BT80 185 B2
Lisburn BT27 160 C4
Riverside Gdns 2 BT45 91 D2
Riverside Mews BT41 186 E3
Riverside N 1 BT45 91 D2
Riverside Pk BT47 179 D1
Riverside Pk E BT51 174 C1
Riverside Pk N BT51 174 C1
Riverside Pk S BT51 174 C1
Riverside Rd BT57 16 A6
Riverside Regional Ctr
BT51 174 C1
Riverside Ret Pk BT51 174 C1
Riverside Specl Sch
BT41 186 E4
Riverside Sq BT12 188 B2
Riverside Theatre★
BT52 174 B7

Riverside View BT7 151 E7
River Terr BT7 189 B1
Riverview
Ballyclare BT39 184 C4
Ballykelly BT49 38 C6
Ballymoney BT53 29 C8
Moneymore BT45 113 E8
River View
Ballymena BT42 181 F3
Londonderry BT48 177 A1
Riverview Ave BT51 174 B4
Riverview Cl BT53 175 C3
Riverview Cres BT44 21 A1
Riverview Glen BT47 36 E4
Riverview Pk
Ballymoney BT53 175 C3
Maghera BT46 74 F5
Riverview Ridge BT11 149 E7
Riverview St BT9 151 D8
Riverview Terr 3 BT47 179 A4
Riverwatch Visitor Ctr★
BT47 178 C2
River Wlk BT37 128 E1
RNLI Mus★ BT55 173 D7
Roadside BT51 41 F6
Robbery Rd BT67 168 A3
Robert St BT47 179 A3
Robina Ct BT15 137 D1
Robina St BT15 137 D1
Robinson Ave BT53 175 D5
Robinson Ctr The BT6 152 E8
Robinson Ent Pk BT48 176 D1
Robinson Meml BT53 175 E5
Robinson's Row BT38 131 A8
Rochester Ave BT6 152 C8
Rochester Ct BT52 174 E6
Rochester Dr
Belfast BT6 152 C8
Londonderry BT47 179 E5
Rochester Rd BT6 152 D7
Rochester St 6 BT6 145 A3
Rocheville BT80 185 D4
Rockbrook Rd BT45 105 C3
Rockdale St BT12 143 E3
Rock Dr BT55 172 A3
Rockfergus Ave BT38 125 A4
Rockfergus Cres BT38 125 A4
Rockfergus Mews BT38 125 A4
Rockfield BT48 177 B4
Rockfield Gdns BT53 17 B4
Rockfield Hts BT42 95 B5
Rockgrove Brae BT43 181 B6
Rockgrove Hts BT43 181 B6
Rockgrove Valley BT43 181 B6
Rock La BT67 155 C1
Rockland Ave BT56 172 D5
Rockland Crescent
BT57 15 E4
Rockland Crescnet BT44 60 B6
Rockland Dr BT56 172 D4
Rockland Gdns BT56 172 D4
Rockland Pk 1 BT51 25 E5
Rockland St BT12 188 A1
Rockmore Rd BT12 143 E3
Rockmount Gdns BT51 13 C3
Rockmount St BT12 143 E3
Rockport Pk BT47 179 B7
Rock Rd
Lisburn BT28 147 F8
Londonderry BT48 178 E7
Magherafelt BT45 114 A7
Rockstown Rd BT43 62 C3
Rock Terr BT48 178 E7
Rocktown BT45 91 B6
Rocktown La BT45 91 A6
Rocktown Rd BT45 91 B6
Rockview La
Newtownabbey BT36 133 B5
Portrush BT56 172 D5
Rockview St BT12 188 A1
Rock Villas BT45 90 F6
Rockville St BT12 143 E3
Rocky Rd BT8 152 D6
Roddens Cres 5 BT5 146 A1
Roddens Ct BT40 182 C5
Roddens Gdns BT5 145 F1
Roddens Pk BT5 145 F1
Roddens The BT40 182 B5
Roddensvale Sch BT40 182 C5
Rodeing Foot BT53 175 D4
Roden Pas BT12 188 B2
Roden Sq BT12 188 B2
Roden St BT12 188 B1
Roden Way BT12 188 B2
Rodgers Bay 130 F6
Rodgers Quay BT38 131 A7
Rodney Dr BT12 143 F2
Rodney Par BT12 143 F2
Rodney Sq BT55 173 D5
Roe Gdns BT47 179 B3
Roemill Ct BT49 180 B4
Roemill Gdns BT49 180 B4
Roemill Rd BT49 180 B3
Roemmele Haven BT49 180 D4
Roe Pk Golf Acad BT49 180 A3
Roe St BT1 189 A3
Roe Valley Country Park
BT49 180 A1
Roe Valley Ctry Pk★ BT49 39 C3
Roe Valley Hospl BT49 180 C5
Roe Valley Integrated Prim
Sch BT49 180 B3
Roe Valley Leisure Ctr
BT49 180 C4
Roeview Pk BT49 180 B4
Rogan Manor BT36 132 B7
Rogan Wood BT36 132 B7
Rogers Pk BT8 152 A4
Rogers Pl 2 BT8 152 A4
Roguery Rd BT41 106 D8
Rogully Rd BT45 114 E7
Rona Gdns BT42 79 A4
Ronald St BT40 182 C4
Ronan Ct BT45 183 D5
Ronan Dr BT45 183 E4
Ronan Sh Ctr BT45 183 E5
Ronan Valley Golf Course
BT45 183 E3
Rooghan BT42 80 A5
Roonivoolin BT54 3 A2
Roosevelt Rise BT12 188 B1
Roosevelt Sq BT12 188 B1
Roosevelt St BT12 188 B1
Rope Wlk The BT51 174 A2
Rory Dall Dr BT49 180 E4
Rory's Glen BT40 82 E1
Rosapenna Ct 14 BT14 144 B8
Rosapenna Dr BT14 137 B1
Rosapenna Par 4 BT14 137 B1
Rosapenna Sq BT11 149 E7
Rosapenna St BT14 144 B8
ROS EARCÁIN (RASHARKIN)
BT44 60 A6
Rosebank Ent Pk BT13 143 F8
Rosebank St BT13 143 F8
Rosebery Gdns BT6 145 B3
Rosebery Rd BT6 145 A3
Rosebery St BT5 145 D4
Rosebrook BT47 55 B6
Rosebrook BT47 55 C7
Rosebrook Ave BT38 125 A1
Rosebrook Gr BT38 131 A8
Rose Ct
Carrickfergus BT38 125 A1
Londonderry BT47 179 A3
Rosedermot BT44 46 A3
Rosedermot Rd
Ballymena BT44 45 F3
Clogh Mills BT44 45 F3
Rose Dr BT36 132 E6
Rose Gdns
Carrickfergus BT38 125 A1
Limavady BT49 180 E3
Rosehill Rd BT42 80 B8
Roseland Pl BT12 188 C1
Roseleigh St 5 BT14 144 B8
Roselick Beg BT55 14 C5
ROSELICK MORE BT56 172 F4
Roselick Rd
Portrush BT56 172 F4
Portstewart BT55 173 A2
Rosemary Dr BT28 170 A7
Rosemary Pk BT9 151 A4
Rosemary Pl BT52 174 D6
Rosemary Rd BT47 68 E8
Rosemary St BT1 189 A3
Rose Mdws BT28 159 D2
Rosemount BT53 28 C6
Rosemount
Clogh Mills BT44 45 E3
Lurgan BT67 164 B1
Rosemount Ave
Belfast BT5 146 E4
Londonderry BT48 178 D7
Rosemount Cres BT37 129 A2
Rosemount Ct BT37 129 A2
Rosemount Gdns
Belfast BT15 137 C2
4 Londonderry BT48 178 D7
Rosemount Pk
Castlereagh BT5 152 F7
Newtownabbey BT37 129 A2
Rosemount Prim Sch
BT48 178 C6
Rosepark BT5 146 E4
Rosepark Central BT5 146 E4
Rosepark E BT5 146 E4
Rosepark Mdws BT5 146 E4
Rosepark S BT5 146 E4
Rosepark W BT5 146 E4
Rose Pk
Limavady BT49 180 E3
Lisburn BT27 160 B5
Newtownabbey BT36 132 E6
Rosetta Ave BT7 151 F7
Rosetta Dr BT7 151 F7
Rosetta Par BT7 151 F7
Rosetta Pk BT6 152 A7
Rosetta Prim Sch BT6 152 A7
Rosetta Rd BT6 152 B7
Rosetta Rd E BT6 152 B7
Rosetta Way BT6 152 A7
Rosevale BT41 186 F4
Rosevale Ave BT27 161 D6
Rosevale Gdns BT27 161 D5
Rosevale Mdws BT28 169 C8
Rosevale Pk BT27 161 D6
Rosevale St 4 BT14 144 B8
Roseville Cres BT41 108 B7
Roseville Gdns BT27 160 C2
Roseville Pk BT27 160 C2
Roseville Wlk BT27 160 C2
Rosewood Glen BT28 159 D3
Rosewood Pk BT6 152 F8
Roseyards BT53 28 C6
Rosganna Dr BT38 125 E3
Rosgarran BT45 90 E2
Rosgarron Rd BT45 90 E2
Rosgoill Gdns BT11 149 F7
Rosgoill Pk BT11 150 A7
Roshure BT45 104 C8
Roslea BT47 50 F5
Roslyn St BT6 145 A3
Rosnashane BT53 43 E1
Rosnashane Rd BT53 43 E1
Ross BT42 95 C6
Rossair Rd BT49 180 E4
Rossan Gdns BT48 178 B5
Rossapenna BT49 180 E3
Rossbay BT47 179 B7
Rossburn Manor BT42 95 B5
Rosscoole Pk BT14 137 A5
Ross Ct BT12 188 B3
Rossdale BT47 179 C6
Rossdale Gdns 1 BT8 152 C2
Rossdale Glen 2 BT8 152 C2
Rossdale Hts 4 BT8 152 C2
Rossdale Par BT8 152 C2
Rossdale Pk 6 BT8 152 C3
Rossdale Rd 3 BT8 152 C2
Rossdowney Ave BT47 179 C4
Rossdowney Dr BT47 179 B4
Rossdowney Gdns BT47 179 B4
Rossdowney Pk BT47 179 B4
Rossdowney Rd BT47 179 D5
Rosseden Dr BT49 180 E4
Rosseden Pk BT49 180 E4
Rossendale Ave BT49 180 E3
Rosses Ave BT42 78 D2
Rosses Farm BT42 78 D2
Rosses La BT42 181 A1
Rosses Mdw BT42 181 A1
Rosses Stables BT42 78 D2
Ross Gn La BT42 95 C7
Rosskeen Pk BT48 176 A1
Ross La BT42 95 D6
Rossland Pk BT43 79 C8
Rosslea Gdns BT49 180 E3
Rosslea Way BT37 133 E4
Rosslyn Cl BT47 179 D7
Rosslyn Pk BT28 159 E1
Rossmara BT49 180 F4
Rossmore BT80 112 F7
Rossmore BT47 179 C6
Rossmore Ave BT7 151 F7
Rossmore Cres BT7 151 F7
Rossmore Dr BT7 151 F7
Rossmore Gn BT38 129 E3
Rossmore Pk
Belfast BT7 151 F7
Portstewart BT55 173 E4
Rossmore Pl
Limavady BT49 180 F4
Strathfoyle BT47 177 F5
Rossnagalliagh BT47 50 E4
Rossnagalliagh BT48 176 D4
Rossnareen Ave BT11 150 A8
Rossnareen Ct
2 Belfast BT11 150 A8
Limavady BT49 180 E3
Rossnareen Pk 3 BT11 150 A8
Rossnareen Rd 4 BT11 150 A8
Rossnavanna BT49 180 E3
Ross Pk BT42 78 F1
Ross Rd BT12 188 B3
Ross Rise BT12 188 B3
Ross's Ave BT39 184 B6
Ross St BT12 188 B3
Rosstulla Ave BT37 134 C8
Rosstulla Dr BT37 134 C8
Rosstulla Pk BT37 134 C8
Rosstulla Sch BT37 134 C8
Rossvale Gdns BT49 180 E3
Rossview Dr BT49 180 E3
Rossville St BT48 178 E5
Rosswater BT47 179 D8
Rosure Rd BT45 104 D8
Rotherwood Dr BT47 179 E5
Rotterdam Ct BT5 189 C3
Rotterdam St BT5 189 C3
Roughan Rd BT42 80 A5
Roughfort Rd
Ballyclare BT39 111 A1
Newtownabbey BT36 119 B8
Rough Hedges BT51 42 F2
Rough La BT41 109 C6
Roulson Ave BT47 179 A5
Roumania Rise BT12 188 B3
Roundhill St BT5 145 B5
Round Twr Commercial Pk
BT3 138 A4
Round Twr Integrated Schl
BT41 186 D8
Rousky BT82 67 F1
Rousky Rd BT82 67 F1
Route Ave BT53 175 C6
Rowallane Dr BT43 181 C7
Rowan Ct 5 BT36 133 A8
Rowan Ctr BT27 160 C2
Rowan Gdns BT43 181 E7
Rowanglynne BT46 74 D2
Rowan Gr 3 BT36 128 A2
Rowan Rd BT53 175 D3
Rowland Way BT12 188 C2
ROXHILL BT41 93 E1
Royal Ave
Belfast BT1 189 A4
Portrush BT56 172 B3
Royal Belfast Academical
Inst BT1 188 C3
Royal Belfast Hospl for Sick
Children BT12 188 A2
Royal Ct BT42 78 B3
Royal Lodge Ave BT8 152 A1
Royal Lodge Ct BT8 152 A2
Royal Lodge Gdns BT8 152 A1
Royal Lodge Mews BT8 152 A2
Royal Lodge Pk BT8 152 A1
Royal Lodge Rd BT8 151 F1
Royal Maternity Hospl
BT12 188 A2
Royal Mews BT17 150 A3
Royal Oaks
Castlereagh BT8 152 A1
Royal Oaks *continued*
Newtownabbey BT37 129 A1
Royal Portrush Golf BT56 4 D3
Royal Portrush Golf Club
BT55 173 F7
Royal Terr BT53 27 B2
Royal Ulster Rifles Mus★
BT1 189 B3
Royal Victoria Hospl
BT12 188 A2
Rugby Ave
Belfast BT7 144 E2
Coleraine BT52 174 E1
Rugby Ct BT7 144 D1
Rugby Par BT7 144 D1
Rugby Rd
Belfast BT7 144 D2
Larne BT40 182 F4
Rugby St BT7 144 D2
Rugby Terr 5 BT40 182 C4
Rumford St BT13 188 B4
Runkerry Gdns 1 BT40 83 B4
Runkerry Rd BT57 5 D6
Runnymede Dr BT12 144 A2
Runnymede Par BT12 144 A2
Rupert Stanley Coll
BT13 136 C1
Rural Coll The BT45 88 E5
Rural Gdns 1 BT36 132 F5
Rushall Rd BT47 51 C4
Rush Croft Ave BT47 179 C4
Rush Croft Cl BT47 179 D4
Rush Croft Dr 4 BT47 179 C4
Rush Croft Gdns BT47 179 C4
Rush Croft Pk BT47 179 C4
Rusheen Gdns BT37 133 F4
Rushey Hill BT53 43 C4
Rusheyhill Rd BT28 148 A7
Rushfield Ave BT7 151 F8
Rushfield Rd BT39 111 E4
Rushie Pk BT49 40 A2
Rushmore Cres BT28 159 C2
Rushmore Dr BT28 159 C2
Rushmore Gdns 2 BT28 159 D2
Rusholme St BT13 144 B7
Rushvale Rd BT39 122 A3
Rushy Island Rd BT43 47 A3
Ruskey BT49 39 F7
Ruskey Rd
Cookstown BT80 114 D7
Magherafelt BT45 105 A1
Ruskin Hts BT27 170 A6
Ruskin Pk BT27 170 B6
Rusky BT51 42 D8
Rusky Pk BT51 42 E8
Rusky Upper BT80 114 C4
Russell Manor BT39 184 A4
Russell Pk BT5 146 E2
Russell Pl BT2 189 B2
Russell St BT2 189 B2
Russeltown Rd BT42 78 A3
Rutherglen St BT13 143 E8
Rutland St BT7 144 E2
Ryan Pk BT5 153 A5
Ryans Ct BT27 170 B7
Rydalmere St BT12 188 A1

S

Sackville Ct BT13 188 C4
Sackville St
2 Lisburn BT27 160 B2
Londonderry BT48 178 E6
Sacred Heart Prim Sch
BT14 137 B1
Saelscoil an Lonnain
BT13 188 A3
Sagimor Gdns BT5 145 D4
Sailsbury Cres BT47 179 E5
St Agnes Dr BT11 150 B7
St Agnes Pl BT11 150 B7
St Aidans Christian Brothers
Prim Sch BT12 143 B4
St Aidan's Magilligan Prim
Sch BT49 11 F3
St Aidans Terr BT48 176 F2
St Aloysius High Sch
BT44 32 E4
St Aloysius Prim Sch
BT28 159 E1
Saint Andrews BT48 176 E7
St Andrew's Sq E BT12 188 C2
St Anne's Cath BT1 189 A4
St Anne's Cl BT10 150 B4
St Annes Cres BT36 132 E8
St Anne's Cres BT10 150 B4
St Annes Gdns BT47 37 B5
St Anne's La BT10 150 B4
St Annes Prim Sch BT48 178 D7
St Anne's Prim Sch
Ballymena BT44 46 B6
Dunmurry BT10 150 C3
St Anne's Rd BT10 150 B4
St Anthony's Prim Sch
Larne BT40 182 A5
Limavady BT49 23 C5
St Aubyn St 3 BT15 137 E3
St Bernadette's Girls Prim
Sch BT12 143 C4
St Bernard's Prim Sch
Belfast BT6 152 B6
Newtownabbey BT36 133 A5
St Bride's Prim Sch 4
BT9 144 C1
St Bride's Prim Sch BT9 151 B8
St Brides St BT38 131 A8
St Brigids Ave 1 BT48 176 F1
St Brigid's Coll 1 BT48 176 F4
St Brigids Prim Sch
Maghera BT46 74 A4
Magherafelt BT45 91 A8
St Brigid's Prim Sch
Ballymoney BT53 175 C3
Clogh Mills BT44 45 F3
St Brigid's Prim Sch 2
BT48 176 F4
St Brigid's Prim Sch BT79 85 F1
St Canice Prim Sch BT47 70 F5
St Canices Pk BT47 36 E5
St Canice's Prim Sch
BT47 55 D1
St Catherine's Prim Sch
BT12 188 A2
St Cecilia's Coll BT48 178 D4
St Ciaran's Prim Sch BT44 32 E8
St Clement's Retreat House★
BT36 137 B8
St Colman's Cres BT38 125 D2
St Colman's Prim Sch
BT27 160 C6
St Colmcille's Prim Sch
BT47 69 B8
St Colm's High Sch
Draperstown BT45 89 A3
Dunmurry BT17 149 E2
St Columba's Convent Infants
Prim Sch BT48 178 D4
St Columbas Pk BT51 41 C5
St Columba's Prim Sch
Coleraine BT51 41 D4
Kilrea BT51 59 C6
Londonderry BT47 50 F4
St Columba's Prim Sch
(Straw) BT45 88 E2
St Columbas Wlk 5 BT47 37 C5
St Columba's Wlk BT48 178 D4
St Columbkille's Stone★
BT51 58 B7
St Columb's Coll BT48 176 E3
St Columbs Ct 13 BT48 178 E4
St Columbs Leisure Ctr
BT47 179 A6
St Columb's Prim Sch
BT45 103 E8
St Columb's Rd BT47 179 A6
St Columb's Stone★
BT48 176 F2
St Columbs Wells BT48 178 E5
St Colum's Prim Sch
BT56 172 B5
St Comgall's Coll BT40 182 F5
St Comgall's Prim Sch
BT41 186 D5
Saint Cunning BT40 66 D2
St Dominic's High Sch
BT12 188 A2
St Eda's Prim Sch BT8 152 A1
St Eithne's Pk BT48 178 A8
St Eithne's Prim Sch
BT48 176 B1
St Ellen Ind Est BT8 161 F8
St Ellens BT8 161 F8
St Eoghan's Prim Sch
BT45 88 C6
Ss Patrick's & Brigid's Prim
Sch BT54 8 D4
St Eugene's Prim Sch 9
BT48 178 E6
St Eugene's RC Cath
BT48 178 D6
Saintfield Pk 3 BT27 160 D1
Saintfield Rd
Belfast BT8 163 C8
Carryduff BT8 163 C6
Castlereagh BT8 152 A3
4 Lisburn BT27 160 C1
Lisburn BT27 170 E7
St Francis de Sales Sch
BT12 143 E4
St Francis Terr BT48 176 F2
St Gabriel's Coll BT14 136 E1
St Galls GAC BT12 143 E2
St Gemma's High Sch
BT14 144 A8
St Genevieve's High Sch
BT11 150 B7
St George's Gdns BT12 188 C1
St Helen's Bsns Pk BT18 139 D6
St Ives Gdns BT9 151 C8
St James Ave BT12 143 F3
St James Mdw BT29 117 A1
St James Pk BT12 143 E3
St James' Prim Sch
BT37 134 A7
St James Rd BT27 168 B2
St James's Cres BT12 143 F2
St James's Dr BT12 143 E2
St James's Gdns BT12 143 F2
St James's Par BT12 143 E3
Saint James's Pk BT53 175 C5
St James's Pl BT12 143 E2
St James's Rd
Ballymoney BT53 175 B5
Belfast BT12 143 E2
St James St 6 BT15 144 C8
St Jeans Cotts BT80 185 B5
St John's Ave BT7 151 F7
St John's Cl BT56 172 B4
St John's Pk
Belfast BT7 151 F6
Londonderry BT48 176 E2
Moira BT67 166 C2

St Johns Pl **2** BT40 . . . . . **182** C4
St John's Pl BT51 . . . . . **174** A3
Saint Johns Pl E **3**
BT40 . . . . **182** C4
St John's Prim Sch
  Carnlough BT44 . . . . . . **49** C2
  Coleraine BT51 . . . . . . **174** B3
  Londonderry BT48 . . . . **178** C4
  Swatragh BT46 . . . . . **74** D8
St John's Prim Sch
  (Dernaflaw) BT47 . . . . . **55** A1
St John the Baptist Prim Sch
  BT11 . . . . **150** B7
St Joseph's Boys Sch
  BT48 . . . . **178** C6
St Joseph's Coll
  Belfast BT6 . . . . **152** A8
  Coleraine BT52 . . . . . . **174** D2
  BT47 . . . . **69** D3
St Josephs Prim Sch
  Belfast BT5 . . . . **145** F4
  Lisburn BT27 . . . . **160** C1
St Joseph's Prim Sch
  Antrim BT41 . . . . **187** B4
  Ballymena BT43 . . . . . **181** C8
  Belfast BT12 . . . . **188** B2
  Carryduff BT8 . . . . . . **163** C6
  Coleraine BT51 . . . . . . **57** C5
  Crumlin BT29 . . . . **121** A8
  Dunloy BT44 . . . . **44** F3
St Judes Ave BT7 . . . . . **151** F8
St Judes Cres BT7 . . . . . **151** F8
St Judes Par BT7 . . . . . . **151** F8
St Jude's Sq BT7 . . . . . . **151** F8
St Katherines Rd BT12 . . **143** F2
St Kevin's Prim Sch
  BT12 . . . . **143** E2
St Kieran's Prim Sch
  BT17 . . . . **149** C4
St Kilda Ct BT6 . . . . **189** C2
St Leonard's Cres **11**
  BT4 . . . . **145** B5
St Leonard's St **12** BT4 . . **145** B5
St Louis Convent Prim Sch
  BT43 . . . . **181** C5
St Louise's Comp Coll
  BT12 . . . . **143** F2
St Louis Gram Sch BT43 **181** C5
St Loury's Well★ BT49 . . . **40** C7
St Luke's Cl BT13 . . . . . . **188** B4
St Lukes Maintained Prim
  Sch BT17 . . . . **149** E3
St Luke's Wlk BT13 . . . . . **188** B4
St Lurachs Rd **2** BT46 . . **74** D1
St Macnissis Coll BT44 . . **49** D8
St Macnissi Prim Sch
  BT40 . . . . **182** E4
St Macnissi's Prim Sch
  BT37 . . . . **128** C2
St Macnisuis Prim Sch
  BT41 . . . . **94** F3
St Malachy's Coll BT14 . . **144** C7
St Malachy's High Sch
  BT41 . . . . **187** A6
St Malachy's Pk BT80 . . **115** D2
St Malachy's Prim Sch
  Belfast BT7 . . . . **189** B2
  Coleraine BT52 . . . . . . **174** D2
  Magherafelt BT45 . . . . **113** F3
St Mark's Prim Sch BT17 **149** E2
St Mark's Wood BT28 . . **159** D4
St Mary's Altinure Prim Sch
  BT47 . . . . **70** B3
St Mary's Coll
  Ballymena BT44 . . . . . . **76** B4
  Londonderry BT48 . . . . **178** C5
St Marys Cres **2** BT48 . . **176** F1
St Mary's Ct **4** BT13 . . **144** A7
St Marys (Faughanvale) GAC
  BT47 . . . . **37** D6
St Mary's GAC BT47 . . . . **52** E8
St Mary's Gdns BT12 . . **143** E4
St Marys Gram Sch BT43 **181** E6
St Mary's High Sch BT49 **180** B5
St Marys-on-the-hill Prim
  Sch BT36 . . . . **119** F8
St Mary's-on-the-hill Prim
  Sch BT36 . . . . **133** A7
St Mary's Prim Sch
  Ballycastle BT54 . . . . . . **3** A6
  Ballymena BT42 . . . . . **181** D4
  Belfast BT12 . . . . **188** C3
  Bellaghy BT45 . . . . **91** F5
  Castledawson BT45 . . . . **91** C1
  Coleraine BT51 . . . . . . **42** F5
  Craigavon BT67 . . . . . **154** A6
  Cushendall BT44 . . . . . **32** D4
  Portglenone BT44 . . . . . **76** E4
St Mary's Prim Sch
  (Glenview) BT46 . . . . . **74** C1
St Mary's Star of the Sea
  Prim Sch BT15 . . . . . **137** D2
St Mary's Univ Coll BT12 **143** F4
St Matthew's Ct (Cúirt
  Naoimh Maitiú) **22**
  BT5 . . . . **145** A5
St Matthew's GAC BT49 . . **40** A1
St Matthew's Prim Sch **40**
  BT5 . . . . **145** A5
St Matthew's Prim Sch
  BT49 . . . . **40** B1
St Meryl Pk BT11 . . . . . **143** C1
St Michael's Gram Sch
  BT67 . . . . **164** C1

St Michael's Prim Sch
  BT6 . . . . **145** A1
St Nicholas Prim Sch
  BT38 . . . . **130** F7
St Olcan's High Sch **11**
  BT41 . . . . **108** A7
St Olcan's Prim Sch BT53 **18** B1
St Oliver Plunkett Prim Sch
  BT11 . . . . **149** E7
St Oliver Plunkett's Prim Sch
  Strathfoyle BT47 . . . . . **177** F4
  Toome BT41 . . . . **106** C7
St Patricks Ave
  Craigavon BT67 . . . . . **164** F8
  Whitehead BT38 . . . . . **127** A8
St Patrick's Ave BT52 . . **174** D2
St Patrick's Coll
  Ballymena BT43 . . . . . **181** E7
  Belfast BT15 . . . . **189** B1
St Patrick's Coll **26** BT46 . **74** D1
St Patrick's High Sch
  Dungiven BT47 . . . . . . **55** D1
  Lisburn BT28 . . . . **159** E1
St Patrick's Pk BT53 . . . **175** D4
St Patrick's Prim Sch
  Ballymena BT42 . . . . . . **93** B6
  Coleraine BT51 . . . . **57** F8
  Craigavon BT67 . . . . . **164** F8
  Holywood BT18 . . . . . **139** D6
  Londonderry BT48 . . . . **176** E2
  Maghera BT46 . . . . **74** B1
  Moneymore BT45 . . . . **113** F8
  Portstewart BT55 . . . . . **173** E6
  Rasharkin BT44 . . . . . . **60** B6
  Strabane BT82 . . . . **67** E3
St Patrick's & St Brigid's Sch
  6 BT47 . . . . **69** C8
St Patrick's St BT45 . . . . **89** A3
St Patrick's Wlk **4** BT4 . **145** B5
St Paul's Coll BT51 . . . . . **59** D5
St Paul's Ct BT28 . . . . . **159** E1
St Pauls GAC BT11 . . . . **149** F8
St Paul's Prim Sch
  Belfast BT12 . . . . **143** E4
  Londonderry BT48 . . . . **176** E4
St Paul's St **5** BT15 . . . **144** E8
St Peter & Paul Prim Sch
  BT47 . . . . **54** B2
St Peter's Cath (RC)
  BT12 . . . . **188** B3
St Peter's Cl BT12 . . . . . **188** B3
St Peter's Ct BT12 . . . . **188** B3
St Peter's High Sch
  BT48 . . . . **178** A3
St Peter's Prim Sch
  Belfast BT12 . . . . **188** B3
  Cookstown BT80 . . . . . **115** C1
St Peter's Sq E BT12 . . . **188** B3
St Pius X High Sch BT45 **183** C5
St Quentin Ave BT36 . . . **133** A6
St Quentin Pk BT36 . . . . **132** F5
St Rose's High Sch **12**
  BT12 . . . . **143** F4
Saintsbury Ave BT27 . . . **170** A6
St Stephen's Ct BT13 . . **188** C4
St Teresa's Prim Sch
  BT67 . . . . **164** B2
St Theresa's Prim Sch
  BT11 . . . . **143** B1
St Therese of Lisieux Prim
  Sch BT15 . . . . **137** C4
St Thérèse's Prim Sch
  BT17 . . . . **149** B4
St Therese's Prim Sch
  BT48 . . . . **176** F5
St Treas Prim Sch BT45. . **105** F5
St Vincent De Paul Prim Sch
  Belfast BT14 . . . . **119** E2
  Belfast BT14 . . . . **136** C3
St Vincent St **2** BT15 . . **137** E3
Saleen Pk BT18 . . . . . . **139** D7
Salia Ave BT38 . . . . **125** A1
Salisbury Ave BT15 . . . . **137** B4
Salisbury Ct BT7 . . . . . . **189** A1
Salisbury Gdns BT15 . . . **137** B4
Salisbury La BT7 . . . . . . **189** A1
Salisbury Pl **2** BT17 . . . **150** A2
Salisbury St BT7 . . . . . . **189** A1
Sallagh✪ BT40 . . . . **82** E6
Sallagh La BT40 . . . . **82** F8
Sallagh Pk BT40 . . . . . . **182** D5
Sallagh Pk Central BT40 **182** D5
Sallagh Pk N BT40 . . . . . **182** D5
Sallagh Pk S BT40 . . . . . **182** D5
Sallowilly✪ BT47 . . . . . . **69** B4
Sallowilly Rd
  Londonderry BT47 . . . . . **69** B5
  Strabane BT82 . . . . **68** F2
Sallybush Rd BT36 . . . . **111** D3
Sally Gdn La BT17 . . . . . **149** C5
Sally Gdns BT36 . . . . . . **132** F6
Salmon Fishery★ BT57 . . . **6** C8
Salters Castle★ BT45. . . **115** C7
SALTERSTOWN BT45 . . . . **115** B7
Salterstown Rd BT45 . . . **115** B7
Salt Works✪ BT47 . . . . . **36** C7
Samuel St BT13 . . . . . . **189** A4
Sancroft St BT13 . . . . . . **144** B7
Sanda Dr BT40 . . . . **83** B5
Sandale Pk BT48 . . . . . . **176** F6
Sanda Rd BT37 . . . . **133** F1
Sandbank Pk BT48 . . . . . **176** F6
Sandbrook Gdns **2** BT4 **145** D7
Sandbrook Gr **1** BT4 . . . **145** D7
Sandbrook Pk BT4 . . . . . **145** D7
Sandel Ct **8** BT52. . . . . . **26** C7
Sandeldale **16** BT52 . . . . **26** C7

Sandelfields **13** BT52 . . . **26** C7
Sandelford Sch BT52. . . . **174** E1
Sandel Gr **10** BT52 . . . . . **26** C7
Sandel Pk BT52. . . . . . . **174** E1
Sandel Village Ctr BT52 . . **26** D7
Sandelwood Ave **5** BT52 . **26** C7
Sandes Ct **3** BT38 . . . . **124** F1
Sandford Ave
  Belfast BT5 . . . . **145** E4
  Larne BT40 . . . . **83** B3
Sandhill Dr
  Belfast BT5 . . . . **145** E3
  Portstewart BT55 . . . . . **173** D6
Sandhill Gdns BT5 . . . . . **145** F3
Sandhill Gn BT5 . . . . . . **145** F3
Sandhill Pk BT5 . . . . . . **145** F3
Sandholes Rd BT80 . . . . **185** B1
Sandhurst Dr BT9 . . . . . **151** D8
Sandhurst Gdns BT9 . . . **144** D1
Sandhurst Rd BT7. . . . . **144** E2
Sand Leford Ct BT52 . . . **174** C2
Sandmount Dr BT42. . . . . **78** B4
Sandmount Pk BT42 . . . . **78** B3
Sandmount Rd BT42 . . . . **78** B4
Sandown Dr
  Belfast BT5 . . . . **145** F4
  Londonderry BT47 . . . . **179** C5
Sandown Pk
  Ballymena BT43 . . . . . **181** D7
  1 Belfast BT5. . . . . . **146** A4
  Lisburn BT28 . . . . **159** E2
Sandown Pk S BT5 . . . . **145** F4
Sandown Pk BT5. . . . . . **145** F4
Sand Rd BT42. . . . . **78** B4
Sandringham Ave BT38. . **124** E3
Sandringham Ct BT38 . . **124** E2
Sandringham Dr BT47. . . **178** C1
Sandringham Gn BT38 . . **124** E3
Sandringham Hts BT38 . . **124** E3
Sandringham Mews BT38 **146** B4
Sandringham Pk BT38. . . **124** E3
Sandringham Pl **3** BT9 . **144** B1
Sandringham St **3** BT9 . **144** B1
Sandy Braes BT45 . . . . . **183** E6
Sandy Gr BT45 . . . . **183** E6
Sandy Hill BT27 . . . . . . **161** B6
Sandy Hill Ave BT27 . . . **161** B6
Sandy Hill Gdns BT27 . . **161** B5
Sandy Hill Gr BT27 . . . . **161** B6
Sandy Hill Pk BT27 . . . . **161** B6
Sandyholme Pk **6** BT36 **132** D6
Sandyholme Way **1**
  BT36 . . . . **132** D6
Sandyknowes Ave BT36 . **132** D6
Sandyknowes Cres BT36 **132** D6
Sandyknowes Dr **5**
  BT36 . . . . **132** D6
Sandyknowes Gdns **2**
  BT36 . . . . **132** D6
Sandyknowes Gr **4**
  BT36 . . . . **132** D6
Sandyknowes Pk **7**
  BT36 . . . . **132** D6
Sandyknowes Way **3**
  BT36 . . . . **132** D6
Sandy La BT27 . . . . **161** A5
Sandymount BT27 . . . . . **161** A6
Sandy Mount BT45 . . . . . **183** E6
Sandymount Cl BT27 . . . **161** A6
Sandymount St BT9 . . . . **151** D8
Sandy Row BT12 . . . . . . **188** C2
Sanford Ave BT40 . . . . . . **83** B2
Sans Souci Pk BT9 . . . . . **151** C8
Sarajac Cres BT14 . . . . . **137** A4
Sark St BT4 . . . . **145** B5
Savagh✪ BT44 . . . . **31** F7
Sawelabeg✪ BT79 . . . . . . **86** E2
Sawel Hill BT11 . . . . . . **150** B8
Sawel Pl
  Dungiven BT47 . . . . . . **55** D2
  Lisburn BT28 . . . . **159** F1
Sawmill Rd BT39 . . . . . . **97** B3
Sawmills✪ BT51 . . . . **43** A6'
Scally Pk BT44 . . . . **30** A2
Scalty✪ BT51 . . . . **26** E1
Scaryhill✪ BT44 . . . . **49** B5
Sch of Dentistry BT12 . . **188** A2
Schomberg Ave **2** BT4. . **146** B6
Schomberg Ct **1** BT38 . . **131** A8
Schomberg Dr BT12 . . . . **188** C1
Schomberg Lodge **3**
  BT4 . . . . **146** B6
Schomberg Pk BT4 . . . . **146** B6
School Ct
  Belfast BT4 . . . . **139** B2
  Carrickfergus BT38 . . . **125** C3
School Hill BT40 . . . . **83** B7
School La
  Castlerock BT51 . . . . . . **13** A4
  Lisburn BT28 . . . . **157** F6
  Magherafelt BT45 . . . . . **91** A8
  Newtownabbey BT38. . . **129** E4
School of Ed BT7 . . . . . **144** D2
School of Nursing &
  Midwifery BT9 . . . . . **144** C2
School Rd
  Belfast BT6 . . . . **153** C4
  Castlereagh BT8 . . . . . **152** A4
  Londonderry BT47. . . . . **37** A5
School St BT39 . . . . **184** C5
Schooner Ct BT37. . . . . . **129** E1
Science Research Pk
  BT52 . . . . **174** B8
Scoil na Fuiseoige BT17 **149** D2
Scolboa✪ BT41 . . . . **109** F8
Scolboa Mdw BT42 . . . . **109** F8
Sconce✪ BT51 . . . . **24** F7
Sconce Rd BT51 . . . . . . **24** E7

Scotch Boleran or Golds
  Town✪ BT51 . . . . **41** C5
Scotch Cah✪ BT51 . . . . . **41** F3
Scotchomerbane✪ BT44 . **46** D2
Scotch Quarter BT38 . . . **131** B8
Scotchtown✪ BT80 . . . . **185** E3
Scotchtown Carrowmuddle✪
  BT49 . . . . **22** F6
Scotchtown La BT80 . . . . **115** A5
Scotchtown Rd BT49 . . . . **23** A7
Scots Rd BT67 . . . . **164** F3
Scotstown Rd BT28 . . . . **147** E2
Scotts Rd BT45 . . . . **114** E8
Scott St BT12 . . . . **188** C1
Scottstown Rd BT42. . . . . **95** D8
Scrabo St BT3 . . . . **189** C4
Screen Rd BT51. . . . . . . **174** C1
Scribe Rd
  Ballymena BT44 . . . . . . **75** F1
  Magherafelt BT45 . . . . . **91** E8
Scriggan✪ BT47 . . . . **55** D4
Scriggan Rd BT49. . . . . . **180** D7
Scroggy Cl BT49 . . . . . . **180** C4
Scroggy Pk BT49. . . . . . **180** C6
Scroggy Rd
  Ballymoney BT53 . . . . . **43** D6
  Belfast BT29 . . . . **121** B4
  Limavady BT49 . . . . . . **180** C3
  Lisburn BT28 . . . . **121** B3
Scroil an Droichid & An
  Droichead Cultural Ctr
  BT7 . . . . **189** B1
Scullions Rd BT36 . . . . . **132** C6
Seabank Par **8** BT15. . . **137** E3
Seabourne Par BT15 . . . . **137** D3
Seacash✪ BT29 . . . . **117** A4
Seacash Dr BT41. . . . . . **186** F5
Seacash Rd BT29 . . . . . **116** F5
Seacliff Ct BT40 . . . . . . **182** D7
Seacliff Rd BT40 . . . . . . **182** C7
Seacoast Rd BT49 . . . . . . **39** A8
Seacon Beg✪ BT53 . . . . . **27** C5
Seacon High✪ BT53 . . . . **27** B5
Seacon Lower✪ BT53 . . . **27** B5
Seacon More✪ BT53 . . . . **27** B6
Seacon North✪ BT53 . . . **27** A5
Seacon Pk BT53 . . . . . . **27** B5
Seacon Rd BT53 . . . . . . **175** A6
SEACOURT BT40 . . . . . . **182** C8
Seacourt Rd
  Larne BT40 . . . . **182** C7
  Limavady BT49 . . . . . . **23** A7
Seafield Pk BT56. . . . . . **172** B3
Seafield Pk S BT56. . . . . **172** B4
Seaforde Ct (Cúirt Suí Forde)
  20 BT5. . . . . **145** A5
Seaforde Gdns (Garraithe Suí
  Forde) **19** BT5. . . . . **145** A5
Seaforde St (Sráid Suí
  Forde) **21** BT5. . . . . **145** A5
Seaforth Ave BT56 . . . . . **172** C3
Seagoe Gdns BT37 . . . . **134** A8
Seagrove Par **7** BT15 . . **137** E3
Seagrove Pl BT15 . . . . . **137** D3
Seahaven Ct BT56 . . . . . **172** B3
Seahaven Dr BT56 . . . . . **172** C4
Seahaven Pk BT56 . . . . . **172** C4
Seahill Rd BT40 . . . . . . **182** D7
Seaholm Par BT15 . . . . . **137** D3
Sealands Par BT15 . . . . . **137** D3
Seal Rd BT3 . . . . **138** B3
Sealstown Rd BT36 . . . . **119** B7
Seamount **1** BT15 . . . . **137** E3
Seamount Par BT15 . . . . **137** D3
Seapark BT51. . . . . **13** B4
Seapark Ave BT18 . . . . . **139** E8
Seapark Ct BT18 . . . . . . **139** E8
Seapark Dr BT15 . . . . . . **137** D3
Seapark Gr BT18 . . . . . . **139** E8
Seapark La BT18 . . . . . . **139** F8
Seapark Mews BT18 . . . . **139** E8
Seapark Terr BT18 . . . . . **139** E8
Seapatrick Rd BT47 . . . . **36** E5
Seapoint BT38 . . . . **130** E6
Seaport Ave BT57 . . . . . . **5** C5
Sea Rd
  Castlerock BT51 . . . . . . **13** B5
  Coleraine BT51 . . . . . . **13** B3
Seascape Par **2** BT15 . . **137** D3
Seaview Cl **2** BT15 . . . . **137** D1
Seaview Dr
  Belfast BT15 . . . . **137** D3
  Portrush BT56 . . . . . . **172** B4
Seaview Dr N BT56. . . . . **172** B4
Seaview Gdns **6** BT15 . . **137** E3
Seaview La BT15 . . . . . . **132** F6
Seaview Prim Sch
  Ballymena BT44 . . . . . . **65** F8
  Belfast BT15 . . . . **137** D3
Seaview St **1** BT15 . . . . **137** E1
Seaview Terr BT18 . . . . . **139** E7
Sedgemoor **20** BT51. . . . **26** A7
Seefinn Rd BT46 . . . . . . **73** F3
Sefton Dr BT4 . . . . **145** E6
Sefton Pk BT4 . . . . **145** E6
Selby Cl BT38. . . . . **125** D3
Selby Ct
  Belfast BT12 . . . . **188** B2
  Carrickfergus BT38 . . . **125** D3
Selby Rd BT38 . . . . **125** D3
Selby Wlk BT12 . . . . . . **188** B2
Semicock✪ BT53 . . . . . . **175** C6
Semicock Ave BT53 . . . . **175** C6
Semicock Pk BT53 . . . . . **175** C6
Semicock Rd BT53 . . . . . **175** B6
Seneirl✪ BT57. . . . . **15** F5

Seneirl Rd BT57. . . . . **16** A5
Sentry **2** BT51. . . . . . . **111** F1
Sentry Hill BT43 . . . . . . **181** B7
Sentry Hill Sports Hall
  BT43 . . . . **181** C7
Sentry La BT36 . . . . **132** B7
Sepon Pk BT28 . . . . **160** A2
Sequoia Hts BT37 . . . . . **134** B7
Serpentine Gdns **2**
  BT36 . . . . **137** D8
Serpentine Par **1** BT36 . **137** D8
Serpentine Rd BT36. . . . **137** D8
Sersons Rd BT45. . . . . . . **90** F1
Servia St BT12 . . . . **188** B2
Seskin Ave BT39 . . . . . . **122** D8
Seskin Pk BT39 . . . . **122** D8
Seskin Rd BT39 . . . . **123** A7
Sesnagh✪ BT49 . . . . **39** A5
Sesnagh Ave BT49 . . . . . **39** A6
Sessia✪ BT80 . . . . **114** C3
Sevastapol St (Sráid
  Seibheástopol) **1**
  BT13 . . . . **188** A3
Seven Mile Straight
  Antrim BT41. . . . . **187** B1
  Belfast BT29 . . . . **118** D5
Sevenoaks BT47 . . . . . . **179** D4
Seventree Rd BT47. . . . . **179** C4
Seven Twrs Leisure Ctr
  BT42 . . . . **181** E3
Severn St BT4 . . . . **145** C4
Seygorry✪ BT51 . . . . **42** A5
Seymour Dr BT53 . . . . . **175** C3
Seymour Gdns BT47. . . . **179** D6
Seymour Hill Ind Est
  BT17 . . . . **150** A4
Seymour Hill Mews
  BT17 . . . . **150** A4
Seymour Hill Prim Sch
  BT17 . . . . **160** F8
Seymour La BT1 . . . . . . **189** B3
Seymour Pk BT27 . . . . . **170** D8
Seymour Row BT1 . . . . . **189** B3
Seymour St
  Ballymoney BT53 . . . . . **175** C4
  Belfast BT1 . . . . **189** B3
  Lisburn BT27 . . . . **160** C2
Shaftesbury Ave BT7. . . . **189** B1
Shaftesbury Cross **2**
  BT38 . . . . **124** F1
Shaftesbury Dr BT38 . . . **131** A8
Shaftesbury Pl **1** BT38. . **124** F1
Shaftesbury Recn Ctr
  BT7 . . . . **189** A1
Shaftesbury Sq BT2 . . . . **189** A1
Shaftesbury Sq Hospl
  BT2 . . . . **189** A1
Shalom BT5 . . . . **152** F8
Shamrock Ct **7** BT6 . . . **145** A4
Shamrock Pl **8** BT6. . . . **145** A4
Shamrock St **5** BT6. . . . **145** A4
Shanaghy Rd BT53 . . . . . **43** D3
Shanaghy Upper✪ BT53. . **43** D3
Shancoole Pk BT14 . . . . **137** A5
Shandarragh Pk BT15 . . **137** B4
Shandon BT28 . . . . **159** F4
Shandon Hts BT5 . . . . . **153** B8
Shandon Pk
  Ballymena BT42 . . . . . **181** B3
  Ballymoney BT53 . . . . **175** F2
  Belfast BT5 . . . . **146** B2
  3 Castledawson BT45 . . **91** C2
  Londonderry BT48 . . . . **176** E2
Shandon Pk Golf Club
  BT5 . . . . **146** A1
Shane Ct
  Ballymena BT43 . . . . . **181** E6
  Broughshane BT43 . . . . **79** C7
Shaneen Pk BT14 . . . . . **137** A5
Shane Hts BT38 . . . . . . **124** C3
Shane Manor BT43. . . . . . **79** B7
Shanemullagh✪ BT45. . . . **91** C2
Shaneoguestown✪
  BT41 . . . . **109** E1
Shanes✪
  Ballymoney BT53 . . . . . **30** A7
  Ballymoney BT53 . . . . . **30** A7
Shane's Castle★ BT41. . . **108** C4
Shane's Castle La BT41. . **108** C5
Shane's Castle Park✪
  BT41 . . . . **108** B6
Shanescastle Pk BT41. . . **108** C5
Shane's Castle Pk★
  BT41 . . . . **186** A6
Shanescourt **2** BT41. . . **108** A7
Shaneshill Rd
  Ballymena BT42 . . . . . . **97** D8
  Larne BT40 . . . . **98** A7
Shanes Pk BT44 . . . . **21** A1
Shanes St BT41 . . . . . . **108** A7
Shanes Terr **1** BT41 . . . **108** A7
Shangarry Pk BT14. . . . . **137** A5
Shaninish✪ BT44 . . . . . . **32** A7
Shankbridge Rd BT42 . . . **94** C3
Shankhill Graveyard **3**
  BT13 . . . . **143** F2
Shankill Ctr BT13 . . . . . **188** B4
Shankill Leisure Ctr
  BT13 . . . . **188** B4
Shankill Par BT13 . . . . . **188** C4
Shankill Rd BT13. . . . . . **188** B4
Shankill Terr **6** BT13 . . **188** C4
Shanks Pk **1** BT40. . . . . **83** B2
Shanlea Dr BT40 . . . . . . **182** A6
Shanlieve BT42 . . . . **181** D1
Shanlieve Pk BT14 . . . . . **137** A5
Shanlieve Rd BT11 . . . . **150** C8
Shanlongford✪ BT51 . . . . **41** B6

Shanlongford Rd BT51 ... 41 B6
Shanmullagh Pk **2** BT45.. 88 E2
Shannagh Ave BT38.... 129 E2
Shannon Ct BT14 ...... 144 B7
Shannon Gdns BT40.... 182 C3
Shannon St BT14 ...... 144 B8
Shanoguestown Rd E
BT41 .... 109 F1
Shanoguestown Rd W
BT41 .... 109 F1
Shanowen BT42 .... 181 E1
Shanreagh **①** BT49 ...... 39 A7
Shanreagh Pk
Limavady BT49 ...... 180 C5
Londonderry BT48..... 176 B1
SHANTALLOW BT48 ..... 176 F4
Shantallow Ave BT48.... 176 F3
Shanvey **①** BT49....... 23 C5
Sharman Cl BT9 .... 151 D6
Sharman Dr BT9 .... 151 D6
Sharman Gdns BT9 .... 151 D6
Sharman Pk BT9 .... 151 D6
Sharman Rd BT9....... 151 D7
Sharman Way BT9 ..... 151 D6
Sharonmore Ave BT36.. 133 B8
Sharonmore Gdns **①**
BT36 .... 133 B8
Sharonmore Par **2**
BT36 .... 133 B8
Sharonmore Pk **3** BT36. 133 B8
Sharvogues **①** BT41 ..... 94 C4
Shaw Ct BT48.......... 176 B4
Shawfield La BT38 ..... 126 F8
Shaw's Ave BT11....... 150 A7
Shaws Bridge BT9 ..... 151 A2
Shaws Cl BT11 .... 149 F8
Shaw's Ct **2** BT11 ...... 150 A7
Shaw's Hill BT42....... 96 B4
Shaw's Pk **①** BT11 .... 150 A7
Shaw's Pl BT11 .... 150 A7
Shaw's Rd BT11........ 149 F8
Shaw St BT4........... 145 E6
Shearwater Way BT47... 179 B5
Sheascanview BT47..... 54 C2
Sheddings Rd BT53 .... 27 C3
Sheelin Pk BT48 .... 176 B3
Sheepwalk Rd BT28 .... 147 C2
Shelahs Rd BT82....... 68 B5
Shelbourne Rd BT6 .... 145 B1
Shellbridge Pk BT52.... 174 D6
Shellfield **①** BT53 .... 16 A2
Shelling Ct BT27....... 170 A3
Shellinghill La **②** BT42... 77 F7
Shellinghill Rd
Ballymena BT43....... 61 D1
Cullybackey BT42 ..... 77 F7
Shelling Pk BT27....... 170 B3
Shelling Ridge BT27 ... 170 A3
Shell Rd BT47.......... 36 B5
Shelton North **①** BT53.. 30 D5
Shelton Rd BT44....... 30 B2
Shelton South **①** BT53.. 30 D4
Shepherds Glen **①** BT47. 179 B4
Shepherd's Gr **①** BT47. 179 B4
Sheraton Pk **3** BT48... 176 C1
Sherbourne Hts BT45... 183 C1
Sherbourne Pk **7** BT45. 183 C3
Sherbourne Pl **6** BT45.. 183 C4
Sherbrook Cl BT13...... 188 C4
Sherbrook Terr **5** BT13. 188 C4
Sheridan Ct **10** BT15.... 144 D8
Sheridan Pk BT28...... 159 E5
Sheridan St BT15 ...... 144 D8
Sheriff's Land **①** BT40... 83 A2
Sheriffs Rd BT48....... 178 A8
Sheriff's View BT48 .... 178 B7
Sheringhurst Ct BT15... 137 E5
Sheringhurst Pk BT15... 137 E5
Sherriff's Mountain **①**
BT48 .... 34 E2
Sherry La BT47 .... 70 E6
Sherwood Ave BT36.... 132 D8
Sherwood Pk **①** BT47.. 179 D5
Sherwood Pks BT36.... 132 D8
Sheskin Cres BT47..... 179 B4
Sheskin Pk **7** BT47.... 37 C5
Sheskin Rd BT47....... 37 B4
Sheskin Way BT6 ...... 152 B8
Shetland Gdns BT42.... 79 A3
Shetland Pk BT42...... 79 A4
Shetland St BT41....... 186 D8
Shiels Ct BT53 .... 175 C4
Shiels St BT12......... 143 F4
Shillanavogy **①** BT42... 81 A5
Shillinavogy Rd BT42... 96 F8
Shimna Cl BT6......... 152 B8
Shingle Cove BT44 .... 49 C2
Shinny Rd BT51........ 41 C8
Shipbuoy St BT15 ..... 144 E7
Shipquay Pl **3** BT48... 178 F5
Shipquay St BT48...... 178 F5
Ship St
Belfast BT15 .... 144 E8
Larne BT40 .... 182 F2
Shona Gn BT42........ 181 F3
Shore Ave
Limavady BT49 ...... 22 C4
Newtownabbey BT37... 134 D8
Shore Cres BT15....... 137 E6
Shorelands BT38....... 129 F2
Shorelands Gdns BT38.. 129 F2
Shore Rd
Antrim BT41.......... 106 D4
Ballymena BT44....... 32 D4
Belfast BT15 .... 137 E2
Holywood BT18....... 139 D7

Shore Rd *continued*
Larne BT40 .... 100 A6
Lisburn BT28 .... 120 D4
Londonderry BT47..... 37 E6
Magherafelt BT45..... 115 B7
Newtownabbey BT15... 137 E7
Short St BT1.......... 144 E7
Short Strand BT5 ..... 189 C3
Shrewsbury Dr BT9 ... 151 A5
Shrewsbury Gdns BT9.. 150 F5
Shrewsbury Pk BT9.... 151 A5
Shuttle Hill BT51...... 174 B3
Sibs Stone ★ BT28.... 148 C7
Sicily Pk
Belfast BT10 .... 150 E4
4 Dunmurry BT17..... 150 A2
3 Londonderry BT47... 179 C4
Sidings Office Pk The
BT28 .... 160 A2
Sillerburn Pairk
(Silverstream Pk) BT14.. 136 E3
Silver Birch Courts BT13. 188 B4
Silverbirch Cres BT47... 179 C5
Silverbrook Pk BT47.... 50 F5
Silverspring BT54...... 8 D4
Silversprings **①** BT53.. 175 C5
Silverstream Ave BT14.. 136 D3
Silverstream Banks
BT38 .... 129 E1
Silverstream Cres BT14.. 136 E3
Silverstream Dr BT14.. 136 E3
Silverstream Gdns BT14.. 136 E3
Silverstream Par BT14.. 136 E3
Silverstream Pk (Sillerburn
Pairk) BT14............ 136 E3
Silverstream Rd
2 Belfast BT14....... 136 D3
Newtownabbey BT37... 129 D1
Silverstream Terr BT14.. 136 D3
Silverthorn Ave BT52.. 174 F4
Silvio St BT13......... 144 A7
Simpsons Brae BT47... 179 A4
Sinclair Rd BT3........ 138 A1
Sinclair St BT5......... 145 F4
Sinton Ct BT80........ 185 B5
Sintonville Ave **4** BT5.. 145 D5
Siskin Dr BT28........ 159 E4
Sistrakeel **①** BT49...... 38 B4
Sistrakeel Prim Sch BT49. 38 B3
Sistrakeel Rd BT49..... 38 B4
Sixmile Leisure Ctr
BT39 .... 184 D5
Sixmile Manor BT39... 184 D5
Sixtowns Rd BT45..... 101 D5
Skeagh **①** BT40........ 82 A6
Skegoneill **①** BT15..... 137 D3
Skegoneill Ave BT15... 137 D2
Skegoneill Dr BT15.... 137 D2
Skegoneill St BT15..... 137 E2
Skelton Cl BT38....... 131 A8
Skelton Ct BT38....... 131 A8
Skeoge Ind Pk BT48... 176 E6
Skerdan Rd BT44...... 76 F7
Skerrybeg Ave **2** BT55.. 173 E5
Skerry Ct BT43........ 181 E5
Skerry East **①** BT43.... 47 A4
Skerrymore Pl BT55.... 173 E5
Skerry Rd E BT43...... 46 F1
Skerry Rd W BT43..... 46 F3
Skerry West **①** BT43.... 46 F3
Skerrywhirry **①** BT42... 82 A1
Skeskburn Ave BT54.... 8 E4
Skeskburn Recn Ctr BT54. 8 E3
Skeyhoogan **①** BT47.... 54 E6
Skilganaban **①** BT39.... 97 E1
Skipper St BT1........ 189 B4
Skipton St BT5........ 145 C5
Skye Pk BT42......... 79 A4
Skyline Dr BT27....... 160 C4
Slaght **①** BT42........ 94 C8
Slaghtaverty **①** BT51... 57 E5
Slaghtaverty Rd BT51... 57 D6
Slaghtfreeden **①** BT79.. 102 B3
Slaght La BT14........ 60 F6
Slaghtmanus **①** BT47... 53 B6
Slaghtneill **①** BT46.... 74 A6
Slaght Rd
Ballymena BT42....... 94 C7
Cookstown BT80 ...... 102 B2
Slaghtybogy **①** BT46... 90 E8
SLANE BT44........... 64 D4
Slane Rd BT44......... 64 F5
Slatady **①** BT5......... 153 A5
Slaughterford Rd BT38.. 100 C1
Slaughtmanus Rd BT47.. 52 D5
Slaughtneill Rd BT46.... 74 A6
Sleans **①** BT41........ 21 B1
Slemish Coll BT42..... 181 E2
Slemish Dr
Ballymena BT43....... 181 E5
Larne BT40 .... 182 D6
Slemish Hts BT38..... 124 D2
Slemish Pl BT51....... 174 B3
Slemish View BT45..... 183 D5
Slemish Way
Belfast BT11 .... 150 C8
Lisburn BT28 .... 159 E1
Sliabh Mor BT11...... 143 D1
Slievard Hts BT38..... 124 D3
Slieveban Dr BT11..... 150 B7
Slievebane **①** BT44..... 66 A5
Slieve Banna BT51..... 174 A5
Slieveboy Pk BT47..... 69 F4
Slievebuoy Rd BT47.... 69 D3
Slievecoole Pk BT14.... 137 A5
Slievedarragh Pk BT14.. 137 A5

Slievegallion Dr BT11... 150 B8
Slieve Gallion Dr **9** BT45.. 89 A3
Slieve Gallion Pk **3** BT45.. 89 A3
Slievegoland Rd BT36... 137 C8
SLIEVEMORE BT48...... 176 C4
Slievemore Pk BT48.... 176 D3
Slievemoyne Pk BT15... 137 C5
Slievenacloy **①** BT28... 148 C7
Slievenagh **①** BT44..... 76 F3
Slievenaghy BT53...... 44 A1
Slievenaghy Rd BT53... 44 A1
Slievenagravery **①** BT17.. 141 E1
Slievenanee BT43...... 47 C3
Slievetoye Pk BT14..... 137 A5
Slievetrue Rd BT36..... 128 F7
Slimag BT52........... 15 A6
Sloan's Ave BT8 ...... 163 D3
Sloan St BT27......... 160 C1
Sloefield Dr BT38...... 130 C6
Sloefield St BT38...... 130 D6
Sluggada **①** BT47...... 85 F6
Smallquarter **①** BT53... 44 F8
Smeaton Pk BT67..... 166 A2
Smiley St BT40........ 182 D4
Smithfield Pl BT43..... 181 C4
Smithfield Sq N BT1.... 189 A4
Smithfield St BT28..... 160 B1
Smith St BT45......... 113 E8
Smulgedon **①** BT51.... 56 D8
Smyth Cres BT44...... 76 E5
Snugville St BT13...... 188 A4
Society Ct **4** BT52..... 174 C3
Society St BT48....... 178 E5
Solar **①** BT44......... 66 C5
Soldierstown Cres BT67.. 155 C2
Soldierstown Rd BT67... 165 F7
Solway St **3** BT4...... 145 B6
Somerdale Ave BT14... 136 E1
Somerdale Grange **14**
BT51 .... 26 A7
Somerdale Pk **2** BT14.. 136 E1
Somersby Ave BT51.... 26 A7
Somerset **①** BT51...... 26 A7
Somerset Cres **10** BT51.. 26 A7
Somerset Ct
Antrim BT41.......... 187 C5
11 Coleraine BT51....... 26 A7
Somerset Dr BT51 .... 174 B3
Somerset Gdns BT41... 187 B5
Somerset Par BT41..... 187 C5
Somerset Pk
Antrim BT41.......... 187 C5
Coleraine BT51....... 26 A7
Somerset Rd BT51..... 174 B1
Somerset Ridge **6** BT51.. 25 F7
Somerset St BT7...... 151 F8
Somerton Cl BT15..... 137 C4
Somerton Ct BT15..... 137 C3
Somerton Dr **3** BT15... 137 C4
Somerton Gdns BT15... 137 C3
Somerton Grange
Belfast BT15 .... 137 C5
1 Coleraine BT51....... 26 A7
Somerton Lodge **13** BT51.. 26 A7
Somerton Mews BT15.. 137 D3
Somerton Pk BT15..... 137 D4
Somerton Rd BT15..... 137 C4
Somervale Grange BT51.. 26 A7
Somme Dr BT6........ 152 C7
Sorella St BT12........ 188 A2
Sorrel Ave BT37...... 128 F3
Sorrell Dr - Sorrell Ave
BT37 .... 128 F3
Sorrell Pk - Sorrell Ave
BT36 .... 128 F3
Soudan St BT12....... 188 A1
Sourhill Rd BT42...... 181 A2
Sourhill Rd BT42...... 181 A1
South Ballintoy **①** BT54.. 25 D7
South Ballylagan BT52.. 14 F5
South Ballyleese **①** BT56.. 172 F2
South Bank BT6 ...... 152 B8
South Bellemont BT52.. 14 C5
South Cl BT18 .... 139 D5
South Cres BT8 ...... 151 D2
Southend Pk BT48 .... 178 D3
Southland BT5........ 146 A1
Southlink BT40 .... 182 A5
South Link BT11 ...... 150 C8
SOUTH MULLAGHACALL
BT56 .... 172 D3
Southport Ct **10** BT14.. 144 B8
South Sperrin BT5 .... 146 D3
South Terrydoo Walker **①**
BT49 .... 40 B6
SOUTHTOWN BT48..... 66 C3
Southview St **7** BT7... 144 E1
Southway BT48 .... 178 B3
Southwell St BT15..... 144 D7
Spallan Rd BT49...... 38 D8
Spamount St BT15..... 144 C8
Spawell Gdns **13** BT52.. 26 C7
Spawell Rd BT80...... 102 D3
Spectrum Ctr ★ BT13.. 188 A4
Speerstown Rd BT42... 95 F6
Spence Cres **3** BT42... 78 A6
Spencer Rd BT47...... 179 A4
Spencer St BT18...... 139 D6
Sperrin Ct BT80....... 185 D6
Sperrin Dr
Belfast BT5 .... 146 E3
Sperrin Her Ctr ★ BT79.. 86 A2
Sperrin Hts BT44...... 76 E5

Sperrin Integrated Coll
BT45................. 183 E7
Sperrin Mews
Cookstown BT80 ...... 185 E5
Magherafelt BT45..... 183 D5
Sperrin Pk
Belfast BT5 .... 146 E3
Londonderry BT47..... 179 D7
Sperrin Rd
Limavady BT49 ...... 180 B4
Londonderry BT47..... 86 D8
Omagh BT79 .... 86 D4
Sperrin View
Cookstown BT80 ...... 185 A6
Magherafelt BT45..... 183 D5
Portglenone BT44..... 76 D5
Sperrin Wlk BT5....... 146 E3
Spier's Pl BT13........ 188 B4
Spinnershill La BT14.... 136 C3
Spinner Sq BT12 ...... 188 A3
Spires Integrated Prim Sch
BT45................. 183 B3
Spires Sh Mall BT1..... 189 A2
Spires The
Cookstown BT80 ...... 185 D4
Holywood BT18....... 139 F5
Spiresway BT41 ...... 92 F2
Spittle Hill **①** BT52..... 174 E6
Spoutfields BT51...... 174 B4
Springbank Cl **4** BT17.. 149 D6
Springbank Ind Est BT17. 149 C6
Springbank Rd BT51.... 12 F4
Springburn Pk BT27.... 170 A6
Springburn Rd BT47... 179 C4
Springdale Gdns BT13.. 143 E5
Spring Farm **①** BT41.. 186 E8
Springfarm Ind Est BT41. 186 C7
Springfarm Mews BT41.. 186 D6
Springfarm Rd BT41... 186 D7
Springfield **①** BT53..... 28 C5
Springfield Ave (Ascaill
Chluanaí) BT12....... 143 F5
Springfield Cl BT13..... 143 C5
Springfield Cres (Corrán
Chluanaí) **8** BT12.... 143 F5
Springfield Ct **①** BT12.. 143 F5
Springfield Dr (Céide
Chluanaí) BT56 ..... 172 D3
Springfield Hts BT12... 143 D5
Springfield Mdws BT12.. 143 D5
Springfield Par BT13... 143 D5
Springfield Pk
Belfast BT13 .... 143 C5
Bellaghy BT45 .... 91 F5
Springfield Prim Sch
BT13 .... 143 E6
Springfield Rd
Belfast BT12 .... 143 B3
Coleraine BT51....... 58 E4
Londonderry BT48..... 177 C7
Belfast BT13 .... 143 C4
Belfast BT12 .... 188 A3
Springgrowth Bsns Pk
BT48................. 176 D2
Springham Pk BT48.... 176 D1
Springham St BT48.... 178 E7
Springhill BT44........ 65 F7
Spring Hill **①** BT48..... 34 E2
Springhill Ave BT12.... 143 D4
Springhill Cl BT12..... 143 D4
Springhill Cres BT12.... 143 D4
Springhill Dr BT12..... 143 D4
Springhill House ★ BT45.. 113 F7
Springhill Hts BT12.... 143 D4
Springhill Mews BT28.. 159 D5
Springhill Prim Sch
BT13 .... 143 C6
Springhill Rd
Londonderry BT48..... 178 A5
Magherafelt BT45..... 114 B5
Moneymore BT45..... 113 F7
Springhill Rise BT12... 143 D4
Springmadden Ct BT12.. 143 D4
Springmartin BT13..... 143 D6
Springmartin Rd BT13.. 143 D5
Spring Mdws
Coleraine BT51....... 174 B1
Craigavon BT67...... 166 F8
Spring Mount **①** BT44.. 61 F7
Springmount Rd BT44.. 61 F6
Spring Pl **18** BT6....... 145 A4
Spring Rd BT80....... 114 F6
Spring St **18** BT6...... 145 A4
SPRING TOWN BT48.... 176 D1
Springtown Bsns Pk
BT48................. 176 C2
Springtown Cl BT48.... 176 A1
Springtown Ind Est BT48.. 176 C2
Springtown Pk BT48... 176 C1
Springtown Rd BT48... 176 A1
Springtown Sh Ctr BT48.. 176 C2
Springvale BT45....... 113 C7
Springvale Bsns Pk
BT12................. 143 E5
Springvale Dr BT14.... 136 D3
Springvale Gdns BT14.. 136 D2
Springvale Hts BT39... 97 A1
Springvale La BT51.... 13 B4
Springvale Par BT14... 136 D3
Springvale Pk
Belfast BT14 .... 136 D3
Londonderry BT48..... 176 C4
Springvale Rd BT39... 97 A2
Springview St BT12.... 188 A2

Springview Wlk BT13... 188 A3
Springwell Crescent **①**
BT51 .... 25 A4
Springwell Rd BT39.... 111 C3
Springwell St BT43..... 181 D5
Sprucefield BT41....... 187 D2
Sprucefield Cl BT27.... 169 F5
Sprucefield Ct BT27.... 170 A4
Sprucefield Dr
Coleraine BT52....... 174 E7
18 Maghera BT46....... 74 D1
Sprucefield Ret Pk BT27. 169 E5
Sprucefield Sh Ctr BT27. 169 F5
Spruce Hill BT17....... 149 C8
Spruce Mdws BT48.... 177 D8
Spruce Pk BT43....... 181 E7
Spruce St BT27........ 160 D2
Squires Hill Cres BT14.. 136 D3
Squires Hill Pk BT14.... 136 D3
Squires Hill Rd BT14.... 136 D4
Sráid An Chaisleáin BT1.. 189 A3
Sráid Árann (Arran St) **2**
BT5 .... 145 A5
Sráid Bholcáin (Vulcan St)
10 Belfast BT5 .... 145 A5
Belfast BT13 .... 188 C2
Sráid Chill Dara (Kildare St)
4 BT13 .... 188 C4
Sráid Chúbar (Cupar St
Upper) **4** BT13 ..... 143 F5
Sráid Earnáin (Arnon St) **3**
BT13 .... 188 C4
Sráid Elswick (Elswick St) **3**
BT12 .... 143 F5
Sráid Harper (Harper St) **24**
BT5 .... 145 A5
Sráid Loch Altáin (Alton St)
1 BT13 .... 188 C4
Sráid Na Bhalla (Wall St)
BT13 .... 188 C4
Sráid na gceimiceán
(Chemical St) **15** BT5.. 145 A5
Sráid na Ríona (regent St)
BT13 .... 144 C7
Sráid Odása (odessa St)
BT13 .... 188 A3
Sráid Pháirc na Feá
(Beechfield St) **34** BT5.. 145 A5
Sráid Pholaird (Pollard St)
1 BT13 .... 143 F5
Sráid Ríona Iochtir (Lower
Regent St) BT13 ..... 189 A4
Sráid Seibheástopol
(Sevastapol St) **1**
BT13 .... 188 A3
Sráid Suí Forde (Seaforde
St) **21** BT5.......... 145 A5
Sráid Thír Eoghain (Tyrone
St) **2** BT13......... 188 C4
Stable La
Castlerock BT51 ..... 13 B4
Coleraine BT52....... 174 C4
Londonderry BT48..... 178 E5
Staffa Dr BT42........ 79 A3
Stafford Rd BT36..... 132 B6
Staffordstown **①** BT47.. 107 C3
Staffordstown Rd BT41.. 106 C3
Stanalane BT57....... 5 D3
Stanfield Pl **①** BT7..... 189 B2
Stanfield Row BT7..... 189 B2
Stanhope Dr BT13..... 188 C4
Stanhope St BT15..... 144 D7
Stanley Ct BT12....... 188 C3
Stanley St BT12....... 188 C2
Stanley's Wlk BT48.... 178 D4
Stanne's Mews BT36... 132 E8
Starbog Rd
Ballymena BT44....... 81 E7
Larne BT40 .... 82 D3
Star Bsns Pk BT45..... 105 C2
Starfield BT41......... 108 A8
Star of the Sea Prim Sch
BT14................. 144 C8
STARTHFOYLE BT47.... 35 F5
Station Ave **①** BT47... 55 C2
Station Mews BT4..... 145 E7
Station Pk BT41....... 106 D7
Station Rd
Antrim BT41.......... 186 E4
Ballycastle BT54...... 8 D3
Ballymena BT44....... 61 D6
Ballymoney BT53..... 28 B8
Belfast BT4 .... 145 E7
Belfast BT29 .... 116 F3
Carrickfergus BT38.... 125 F3
5 Castledawson BT45... 91 C2
Coleraine BT51....... 42 A1
Craigavon BT67...... 166 D5
Cullybackey BT42 .... 78 A6
Doagh BT39 .... 111 A6
Dungiven BT47....... 55 C2
2 Garvagh BT51....... 58 A8
Kells BT42 .... 95 A6
Larne BT40 .... 182 D3
Limavady BT49 ...... 38 B8
Lisburn BT27 .... 160 D5
Londonderry BT47..... 36 D6
Maghera BT46....... 74 D1
1 Magherafelt BT45.... 90 E1
Magherafelt BT45..... 183 D8
Moira BT67........... 166 C3
Moneymore BT45..... 113 C8
Newtownabbey BT37... 133 F6
Portrush BT56........ 172 E4
6 Randalstown BT41... 108 A7

Station Rd Ind Est BT45 . 183 E7
Station St Flyover BT3 . 189 C4
Station Sq Ret Pk BT80. 185 D5
Station St
  Ballycastle BT54 ...... 8 D3
  Belfast BT3 .... 189 C3
Station View
  Ballymena BT44......... 61 D5
  Dunmurry BT17...... 150 A2
Steadings The BT27... 161 C6
Steam Mill La BT1 ... 189 B4
Steedstown Rd BT28 ... 147 D7
Steelstown Prim Sch
  BT48............... 177 A4
Steelstown Rd BT41 ... 177 A4
Steens Row 5 BT5.... 145 C4
Steeple 5 BT41....... 186 E6
Steeple Gdns BT41.... 186 F6
Steeple Gn BT41...... 186 F6
Steeple Ind Est BT41.... 186 F5
Steeple Rd
  Antrim BT41........ 186 E5
  Ballymena BT42...... 95 B3
Steepleview BT41...... 186 F5
Stephen's Ct 4 BT48... 176 B2
Stephen St BT1 .... 189 A4
Stevenson Pk BT47...... 51 D6
Stewart Ave BT80...... 185 D3
Stewart's Pl BT18...... 139 D7
Stewart St BT7 .... 189 C2
Stewart's Terr BT48.... 178 D6
Stewartstown Ave BT11. 149 F7
Stewartstown Dr BT40.. 98 D8
Stewartstown Gdns
  BT11............... 149 F7
Stewartstown Pk BT11 . 149 F7
Stewartstown Rd
  Belfast BT11....... 149 F6
  Dunmurry BT17...... 149 D4
Stiles 5 BT41........ 187 B4
Stiles Farm BT41...... 187 B4
Stiles Way BT41...... 186 F6
Stirling Ave BT6 ...... 152 D8
Stirling Gdns BT6..... 152 C8
Stirling Rd BT6 ...... 152 C8
Stirling St BT41...... 186 E8
Sturach's Gdns 2 BT46.. 74 B1
Sturach's Terr 1 BT46.. 74 B1
Stock Car & Short Circuit
  Racing BT51........ 43 A6
Stockdam Glen BT28... 159 F4
Stockdam Rd BT28.... 159 F5
Stockman's Ave BT11.. 150 D7
Stockman's Cres 3
  BT11............... 150 D8
Stockman's Ct (Cúirt Mhic
  Giolla Stoic) 1 BT11.. 150 D8
Stockman's Dr BT11... 150 D8
Stockman's Gdns 2
  BT11............... 150 D8
Stockman's La BT9.... 150 D7
Stockman's Pk BT11... 150 D7
Stockman's Way BT9... 150 D7
Stoke Rd BT36........ 132 B5
Stonard St BT45...... 113 E8
Stonebridge Ct BT28... 147 D5
Stoneburn Pl BT47...... 51 D6
Stone Park BT51....... 25 B5
Stone Row BT52...... 174 C3
Stone Row Upper BT52.. 174 C3
Stoneyfalls BT82...... 67 E3
Stoneyfalls Pk BT82.... 67 E3
Stoneyford Rd BT28.... 147 D5
Stoney La BT42....... 79 D7
Stoney Path BT47..... 50 F6
Stoney Pk BT46....... 74 D8
Stoney Rd BT16....... 146 F6
Stoney Wood BT47..... 178 B1
STONYFORD BT28..... 147 D6
Stonyford St BT5..... 145 C5
Stonyhill BT44........ 49 C1
Stony Hill BT44....... 49 C1
STONY QUARTER BT42.. 80 E7
Stormont Castle* BT4.. 146 E6
Stormont Cres 16 BT5.. 145 B4
Stormont House* BT4.. 146 E6
Stormont La 13 BT5... 145 B4
Stormont Pk BT4...... 146 C5
Stormont Rd BT3...... 138 A1
Stormont St BT5...... 145 B4
Stormount Ct BT5..... 146 D4
Strabane Old Rd BT47.. 178 F3
Stracam Cnr BT6..... 152 C7
Stradowen Dr BT47.... 177 F6
Stradreagh 1 BT49.... 23 F5
Stradreagh Beg BT47.. 178 F4
Stradreagh Hospl BT47.. 177 E3
Stradreagh More 1
  BT47.............. 177 F2
Straham View 5 BT53.. 28 B8
Strahull 1 BT79...... 86 C1
STRAID
  Antrim BT41........ 93 F7
  Ballyclare BT39...... 122 C8
Straid 1 BT42....... 93 F8
STRAID BT57......... 6 F3
Straid 1 BT47....... 70 B5
Straidballymorris 1
  BT39.............. 110 A1
Straidbilly 5 BT53.... 16 E6
Straidbilly Prim Sch BT53 16 E6
Straidhavern 1 BT29... 117 F4
Straidhavern Prim Sch
  BT29.............. 117 F3
Straidhavern Rd BT29.. 117 F3

Straidkilly 1 BT44...... 49 D1
Straidkilly Rd BT44..... 65 E8
Straid (Main Portion) 1
  BT44............... 32 D8
Straidnahanna 1 BT39.. 122 C2
Straid Prim Sch BT39... 122 D8
Straid Rd
  Ballycastle BT54 ..... 7 B3
  Ballyclare BT39...... 122 C8
  Ballymena BT42...... 94 A8
  Bushmills BT57 ...... 5 E3
  Londonderry BT47..... 70 B5
Straid View BT47...... 70 A7
Straid Wlk BT38...... 125 A3
Straight The BT6...... 152 B7
Stranabrosny 1 BT82... 67 B5
Stranagalwilly 1 BT47.. 85 A7
Stranagard 1 BT45.... 90 A1
Strand Ave
  Holywood BT18....... 139 E7
  Portrush BT56....... 4 E3
Strandburn Cres 2 BT4. 145 E6
Strandburn Ct 1 BT4.. 145 D6
Strandburn Dr 1 BT4.. 145 E6
Strandburn Gdns 2 BT4 145 D6
Strandburn Par BT4... 145 E7
Strandburn Pk BT4.... 145 E6
Strandburn St BT4.... 145 D7
Strand Cl (Clós na Trá) 9
  BT5................ 145 A5
Strand Cotts BT54..... 8 E3
Strand Cres BT55..... 172 A3
Strand Mews
  Holywood BT18....... 139 D7
  11 Belfast BT5....... 145 A5
Strand Pk BT44...... 45 E3
Strand Prim Sch 5 BT4. 145 D7
Strand Rd
  Ballyclare BT39....... 110 E5
  Coleraine BT51...... 174 C2
  Londonderry BT48..... 178 E6
  Portstewart BT55..... 172 A2
Strand Studios BT4.... 145 D6
STRANDTOWN BT4..... 145 E6
Strandtown Prim Sch
  BT4............... 145 E5
Strandview Ave BT56... 172 B3
Strandview Cotts BT51. 13 A5
Strandview Dr BT56.... 172 B3
Strandview Gdns BT54.. 8 D4
Strandview Pk BT44... 21 B1
Strandview Rd BT54... 8 D4
Strandview St BT9..... 151 D8
Strangford Ave BT9.... 150 F5
Strangford Pk BT48.... 176 B1
STRANMILLIS BT9..... 151 C7
Stranmillis Ct BT9.... 151 D8
Stranmillis Emb BT9... 144 C1
Stranmillis Embank BT9 151 D8
Stranmillis Gdns BT9... 151 C8
Stranmillis Mews BT9... 151 C8
Stranmillis Rd BT9.... 144 D1
Stranmillis Prim Sch
  BT9............... 151 D6
Stranmillis Rd BT9.... 151 C7
Stranmillis St BT9.... 151 C8
Stranmillis Univ Coll Campus
  BT9............... 151 C7
STRANOCUM BT53..... 28 E7
Stranocum BT53...... 28 F6
Stratford Gdns BT14... 136 F1
Strathall 1 BT47..... 52 B4
Strathallen Pk BT10... 150 D2
Strathard Cl BT51.... 174 B2
Strathearn La BT4.... 146 A6
Strathearn Mews 10 BT4 145 E6
Strathearn Pk BT4.... 146 A7
Strathearn Prep Sch
  BT4.............. 146 A6
Stratheden St BT15.... 144 C8
Strathern Ct BT18.... 139 C5
STRATHFOYLE BT47.... 177 F5
Strathfoyle Prim Sch
  BT47.............. 35 F5
Strathmore Pk BT15... 137 C5
Strathmore Pk N BT15. 137 B6
Strathmore Pk S BT15. 137 B5
Strathroy Pk BT14.... 136 F1
Strathyre Pk BT17.... 150 D2
Straw 1
  Londonderry BT47..... 55 C7
  Magherafelt BT45..... 88 F2
Strawbridge Pk BT57... 5 D4
Strawmore 1 BT45.... 88 E4
Strawmore La BT45.... 88 D3
Strawmore Rd BT45.... 88 E3
Straw Mountain 1 BT45. 103 A7
Strawpark 1 BT39..... 110 D7
Straw Rd BT47....... 55 C6
STREEVE BT49........ 180 D8
Strifehill Rd BT80..... 185 C1
Stroan 1 BT53....... 18 E4
Stroan Lower 1 BT53... 28 A7
Stroan Rd BT53...... 28 B7
Stroanshesk Pk BT54... 8 D4
Stroan Upper 1 BT53.. 28 B7
Stroma Dr BT42...... 79 A4
Stroud St BT12....... 188 C1
Strule Gdns 3 BT47.... 179 B4
Stuart Pk BT53....... 175 E3
Stuarts Gdns BT56.... 172 B5
Stylux Ind Est BT40.... 182 D5
Suffock Cl BT11...... 149 D7
Suffock Hts BT11..... 149 D7
Suffock Rise BT11.... 149 D7
Suffock Way BT11.... 149 D7
Suffolk 1 BT17...... 149 E6

Suffolk Ave BT11...... 150 A6
Suffolk Cl BT41...... 187 C5
Suffolk Cres BT11..... 150 A6
Suffolk Ct BT11...... 149 D7
Suffolk Dr BT11...... 149 F6
Suffolk Par BT11..... 150 A6
Suffolk Prim Sch BT11. 149 F5
Suffolk Rd BT11...... 149 E7
Suffolk Sq BT41...... 187 C5
Suffolk St BT43...... 181 E5
Sugarfield St BT13.... 188 A4
Suilnamona Ct 1 BT11.. 143 B1
Sulatober Cl BT38.... 125 A4
Sulatober Sq BT38.... 125 A4
Sullatober Row BT38... 125 A4
Sullenboy 5 BT80.... 185 B4
Sullenboy Pk BT80... 185 C4
Sullivan Ct BT18...... 139 D7
Sullivan Pl BT18...... 139 D7
Sullivan St BT18...... 139 D6
Sullivan Upper Sch
  BT18.............. 139 D6
Summerfield Mews
  BT43.............. 181 E5
Summerfield Rd BT43.. 181 E5
Summer Hill BT47..... 178 C1
Summerhill Ct
  16 Belfast BT14...... 144 B8
  Larne BT40........ 182 C2
Summerhill Dr BT17... 149 E2
Summerhill Gdns BT17. 149 E1
Summerhill Gr BT48.. 176 F3
Summerhill Grange 1
  BT17.............. 149 E2
Summerhill Par BT5... 146 D4
Summerhill Pk
  Belfast BT5........ 146 D4
  3 Londonderry BT47... 149 E2
Summerhill Rd BT17... 149 E2
Summerhill Rd BT17... 149 E2
Summer Mdws Manor
  BT47.............. 179 F5
Summer Mdws Mews
  BT47.............. 179 F5
Summer Mdws Pk BT47. 179 F6
Summer Mdws View
  BT47.............. 179 F6
Summer St BT14..... 144 B8
Sunbury Ave BT5.... 145 D4
Sunderland Rd BT6... 152 C8
Sunningdale Dr
  Belfast BT14....... 137 A4
  Prehen BT47....... 178 B1
Sunningdale Gdns BT14. 136 F4
Sunningdale Gr BT14... 136 F4
Sunningdale Pk
  Ballymena BT43..... 181 A5
  Belfast BT14....... 137 A4
Sunningdale Pk N BT14. 137 A4
Sunninghill Dr BT14.. 137 A4
Sunninghill Gdns BT14. 136 F4
Sunninghill Pk BT14... 136 F4
Sunnyhill Pk BT17.... 149 F2
Sunnylands Ave BT38.. 130 F8
Sunnylands Com Ctr
  BT38.............. 124 F1
Sunnylands Dr BT38... 130 F8
Sunnylands Gr BT38... 125 A1
Sunnylands Pass BT38. 131 A8
Sunnylands Prim Sch
  BT38.............. 124 F1
Sunnymede Pk BT17... 149 F2
Sunnyside Cres BT7... 151 E8
Sunnyside Dr
  Belfast BT7........ 151 E8
  Maghera BT46...... 74 D2
  Rasharkin BT44..... 60 A6
Sunnyside Pk
  Ballymena BT42..... 78 E2
  4 Belfast BT7....... 151 E8
  Maghera BT46...... 74 C2
Sunnyside Rd BT80... 114 D1
Sunnyside St BT7.... 151 E8
Sunnyvale Ave BT55... 173 F5
Sunset Pk BT56..... 172 C5
Sunset Ridge BT56... 172 C5
Sunvale Pk BT47..... 37 B5
Sunview Pk BT43..... 47 A2
Sunwich St 4 BT6.... 145 A3
Surrey St BT9....... 144 A1
Susan St BT5....... 145 A5
Sussex Ct BT41...... 187 B5
Sussex Pl BT2....... 189 B2
Sussex Sq BT41..... 187 B5
Sutton Gdns BT47.... 179 D5
Sutton Gr BT47..... 179 D5
Swanston Ave BT36... 132 D6
Swanston Cres BT36... 132 E6
Swanston Dr BT36.... 132 E6
Swanston Gdns BT36.. 132 E6
Swanston Pk BT36.... 132 E6
Swanston Rd BT36.... 132 D6
Swanston Rd N 8 BT36. 132 D6
Swatragh 1 BT46.... 58 B1
SWATRAGH (AN
  SUAITREACH) BT46... 74 D8
Swatragh Bsns Pk BT46. 58 B1
Sweathouse* BT49.... 24 B3
Sweat House* BT46... 74 A3
Sweep Rd BT80...... 185 D2
Sweetwall Rd BT41.... 110 A3
Swift Ct 2 BT48..... 176 B3
Swift Pl BT48...... 145 A4
Swifts Quay BT38.... 130 F6
Swift St 12 BT6...... 145 A4
Swilly Dr BT56...... 172 D6

Swilly Gdns BT48...... 178 B5
Swilly Pk BT56...... 172 D6
Swilly Rd BT56...... 172 C6
Swine Craes The* BT42. 80 D7
Sycamore Cl BT37.... 129 A1
Sycamore Dr
  20 Maghera BT46.... 74 D1
  Newtownabbey BT37... 129 A1
Sycamore Gdns BT47.. 179 F1
Sycamore Gr 12 BT4... 145 E6
Sycamore Hts BT47... 70 A2
Sycamore Pk BT37.... 129 B1
Sycamore Rd BT29.... 141 A5
SYDENHAM BT4...... 145 F8
Sydenham Airlink BT3. 145 E8
Sydenham Ave BT4.... 145 F6
Sydenham Bsns Pk BT3. 138 F5
Sydenham By-pass BT3. 145 E8
Sydenham Cres BT4... 145 E6
Sydenham Dr 3 BT4... 145 E6
Sydenham Flyover BT3. 145 A5
Sydenham Gdns BT4... 145 E6
Sydenham Intake 1 BT3. 138 F3
Sydenham Pk BT4.... 145 E6
Sydenham Prim Sch 6
  BT4.............. 145 D7
Sydenham Rd BT3.... 145 A6
Sydney St W BT13.... 144 A7
Sylvan St 5 BT14.... 137 B1
Symons St BT12..... 188 B1
Synge Ct 11 BT48.... 176 B2
Taboe Glebe 1 BT82.. 67 E8

T

Taboe Rd BT82...... 67 E6
Tagharina 1 BT47.... 50 E3
Tagharina Rd BT47.... 50 E3
Taghey 1 BT53...... 27 B3
Taghnabrick 1 BT27... 170 C4
Talbot Pk BT48...... 177 A2
Talbot St BT1....... 189 A4
Tamar Bsns Ctr BT4... 145 C5
Tamar Commercial Ctr
  BT4.............. 145 B6
Tamar Commerical Ctr
  BT4.............. 145 C5
Tamar Ct BT4....... 145 C5
Tamar St BT4....... 145 C6
Tamery Pass BT5.... 145 B4
Tamlagh Rd BT80.... 185 D8
Tamlaght
  Antrim BT41....... 93 F5
  Ballymena BT44..... 48 E8
  Ballymena BT44..... 60 B3
  Coleraine BT51..... 43 B1
  Cookstown BT80.... 112 B4
  Limavady BT49..... 38 F6
  Magherafelt BT45... 114 B3
Tamlaghtduff 1 BT45.. 91 E7
Tamlaghtduff Pk BT45. 91 F6
Tamlaghtduff Rd BT45. 91 E7
Tamlaghtmore 1 BT80. 113 B6
Tamlaghtmore Rd BT80. 113 B6
TAMLAGHT O'CRILLY
  BT46.............. 75 C7
Tamlaght (part of Glebe) 1
  BT49.............. 23 B8
Tamlaght Rd
  Ballyclare BT39..... 110 F2
  Ballymena BT44..... 59 F4
  Coleraine BT51..... 59 A1
  Maghera BT46...... 75 C7
  Magherafelt BT45... 114 B3
Tamlough Pk BT47.... 38 D7
Tamlough Rd BT41.... 93 F4
Tamnabrack La BT44.. 65 C3
Tamnabrady 1 BT82... 50 B1
Tamnabrady Rd BT82.. 50 B1
Tamnabrock 1 BT53... 43 C1
Tamnaclare 1 BT82... 50 B2
Tamnadeese 1 BT45... 91 C2
Tamnadeese Pk 2 BT45. 91 C2
Tamnadeese Rd BT45.. 91 C2
Tamnaderry 1 BT41... 107 B3
Tamnadoey 1 BT45... 104 C1
Tamnagh 1 BT47.... 85 F7
Tamnaghmore 1 BT41. 107 A8
Tamnaghmore Rd BT41. 106 F8
Tamnagh Rd
  Londonderry BT47.... 86 A8
  Omagh BT79....... 85 F3
Tamnaherin 1 BT47... 52 F8
Tamnaherin Rd BT47.. 52 C7
Tamnakeery 1 BT82... 50 C1
Tamnamoney 1 BT51.. 26 A6
Tamney Cres BT47.... 74 D1
Tamneymartin Rd BT46. 90 D8
Tamneymore BT47.... 178 F2
Tamneyreagh Pk BT47. 36 E1
Tamniaran 1 BT45.... 91 D2
Tamnyagan 1 BT47... 70 F4
Tamnyaskey 1 BT45.. 89 E4
Tamnyhagan 1 BT80.. 112 D7
Tamnymartin 1 BT46.. 74 E1
Tamnymore 1
  Coleraine BT51..... 41 E1
  Coleraine BT51..... 41 E2
  Londonderry BT47.... 52 C4
Tamnymullan 1 BT46.. 74 D2
Tamnymullan La BT46.. 74 D3
Tamnyrankin 1 BT46.. 58 A2
Tamnyrankin Rd BT46.. 57 F2
Tamnyreagh 1 BT47... 52 D8
Tamnyvane 1 BT67... 165 A6
Tamworth Cres BT47.. 179 D4

Tamybuck 1 BT42..... 64 D2
Tanderagee 1 BT56.... 4 F3
Tandragee Fort* BT47.. 70 F6
Tannaghmore 1 BT41.. 107 D8
Tannaghmore North 1
  BT67.............. 164 A1
Tannaghmore Rd BT41. 107 E8
Tanners Ct BT67..... 166 C2
Tansy La BT28...... 121 E1
Tansy Rd BT28...... 147 A1
Tara Pk BT48....... 177 A4
Tarawood BT37...... 135 B1
Tarawood Mews BT8... 151 E5
Tardee Pl BT28...... 159 F1
Tardee 1 BT42...... 95 F3
Tardee Gr BT43..... 181 E4
Tardee Hts BT38.... 124 D2
Tardee Rd BT42..... 95 E2
Targarville La BT46... 74 E5
Tarnreagh Pk 1 BT4.. 178 C8
Tarragon Pk BT41.... 186 E3
Tarry La BT67...... 164 B2
Tartnakilly 1 BT49... 38 C3
Tartnakilly Rd BT49... 38 A4
Tate's Ave BT12..... 144 A2
Tate's Fort* BT53.... 43 C4
Tates La BT43...... 47 A1
Tatnagilta 1 BT80.... 112 E6
Taughey Rd BT53.... 27 B3
Taughmonagh 1 BT9.. 150 E5
Taughmonagh Prim Sch
  BT9.............. 150 F4
Taunton Ave BT15.... 137 D5
Tavanaghan La BT44.. 32 C5
Tavanagh St BT12.... 188 A1
Tavnaghan 1 BT44... 32 C5
Tavnaharry 1 BT44... 32 B3
Tavnaghboy 1 BT54.. 19 A5
Tavnaghdrissagh 1 BT44. 32 B6
Tavnaghmore 1 BT41. 94 E3
Tavnaghmore Rd BT41. 94 E4
Tavnaghoney 1 BT44. 32 A6
Tavnaghowen 1 BT44. 32 C5
Tawnybrack 1 BT42.. 95 A7
Taylor Pk BT49..... 180 C4
Taylors Ave BT38.... 131 B4
Taylors Fort* BT29... 121 E6
Taylor Sq BT28..... 169 F8
Taylors Row BT52.... 174 D3
Taylorstown BT41.... 93 A3
Taylorstown Hill BT41.. 93 B3
Taylorstown Rd BT41.. 93 A3
TEAMPALL PHÁDRAIG
  (TEMPLEPATRICK)
  BT39.............. 110 C2
Tedburn Pk BT114.... 136 D2
Teeavan 1 BT47.... 72 A5
Teeavan Rd BT47.... 71 F8
Teeling Ave BT17.... 149 B3
Teeling Gr BT17.... 149 B3
Teeling View BT17.... 149 B3
Teenagh Rd BT47.... 69 F5
Teenaght 1 BT47.... 69 F6
Teeshan 1 BT43.... 78 C7
Teeshan Rd BT43.... 78 B7
Tehorny 1 BT44.... 60 B3
Telfair St BT1....... 189 B3
Temain 1 BT49..... 40 D3
Temain Rd BT49.... 40 D3
Templar Ave BT27... 170 C8
Templastragh 1 BT57.. 6 E4
Templeard BT48..... 177 E8
Templecormac 1 BT28. 121 C7
Temple Ct
  Londonderry BT48.... 176 B4
  2 Templepatrick BT39. 110 D2
Temple-effin 1 BT38.. 100 C2
Templefinn Pk BT37... 134 A4
Templegrove BT48.... 176 C3
Templemore Ave BT4.. 145 C6
Templemore Pk BT48.. 178 D7
Templemore Pl 8 BT5.. 145 B4
Templemore St BT5... 145 B5
Templemoyle 2 BT42.. 95 A5
Templemoyle 1
  Limavady BT49..... 39 B1
  Londonderry BT47.... 36 D3
  Londonderry BT47.... 71 C3
Templepatrick 1 BT39. 110 C2
Templepatrick Prim Sch
  BT39.............. 110 C1
Templepatrick Rd BT39. 184 D4
TEMPLEPATRICK (TEAMPALL
  PHÁDRAIG) BT39.... 110 C2
Temple Pk
  Coleraine BT51..... 13 A4
  Londonderry BT48.... 176 D5
Temple Rd
  Coleraine BT51..... 57 B7
  Lisburn BT28...... 121 A4
  Londonderry BT47.... 56 E6
  Strathfoyle BT47.... 35 F5
Temple Rise BT39.... 110 D2
Temple St 9 BT5.... 145 B4
Templeton Pk 2 BT39. 110 C2
Templetown 1 BT47... 35 F4
Templetown Mews BT47. 35 F5
Templetown Pk BT47.. 35 F5
Templewell 7 BT39... 110 C2
Tenaghs 1 BT54.... 19 C1
Tennent St BT13..... 188 A4
Teraghafeeva or Lissue 1
  BT28.............. 169 A8
Termonbacca 1 BT48.. 50 E8
Termoncanice Prim Sch
  BT49.............. 180 A5

Termon St 5 BT47......179 A5
Ternamuck BT51......56 E8
Tern Cres BT38......125 A3
Tern St BT4......145 B6
Terrace Row BT52......174 C2
Terressan BT80......113 C2
Terrydoo Clyde BT49....40 B5
Terrydoo Rd BT49......39 F4
Terrydreen BT47......70 C5
Terrydreen Rd BT47......70 C6
Terrydremont North
BT49......39 D4
Terrydremont South
BT49......39 D3
Terrydrum BT49......39 A4
Terrygowan BT41......93 D4
Terrywhinny La BT80......112 A2
Terrywinny BT80......112 A1
Tervillin BT54......9 E4
Teutonic Gdns BT12......188 C1
Thackery Pl BT49......180 B7
Thalia St BT12......188 B1
Thames Ct BT12......143 F3
Thames St 11 BT12......143 F4
Thanksgiving Sq BT1......189 B3
THE BATTERY BT80......115 D2
The Creagh (Etre & Otre)
BT41......106 B8
Thecrescent BT53......27 B2
The Cross BT47......52 A5
THE DRONES BT53......29 D5
The Gort alias Eglish
BT80......115 B3
The Hollow BT47......55 C1
The Holly Bush BT48...35 E8
The Holme BT44......45 F3
The Isle Hill BT44......59 F1
The Isles BT44......45 A5
The Leap BT44......59 E5
The Leven BT47......52 D6
The Loop BT44......45 B8
THE LOUP BT45......105 A1
The Oaks BT47......52 B4
Theodore St BT12......188 A2
The Park BT44......30 C2
The Pass BT51......25 A7
The Pillars BT44......46 A2
The Plains BT53......43 D3
The Quarter BT51......42 D1
THE SIX TOWNS BT45......102 B7
The Wood BT51......42 E3
THE WOODS BT45......105 D4
Thiepval Ave BT6......152 C8
Thiepval Ct BT49......180 A5
Third St BT13......188 A3
Thirlmere Gdns BT15...137 B4
Thistle Ct BT5......145 A5
Thistlemount Pk BT28...159 D4
Thistlewood Cres BT41...187 B3
Thistlewood Pk BT48...176 C1
Thomas St
Ballymena BT43......181 D5
Belfast BT15......144 D7
Carrickfergus BT38......131 A8
Thompson Cres BT51....58 A8
Thompson Gdns 15 BT46...74 D1
Thompson House Hospl
BT28......160 A3
Thompson Prim Sch The
BT39......111 C4
Thompson's Grange BT8 163 C2
Thompson's Point BT38...130 C5
Thompson Wharf Rd
BT3......138 B1
Thorburn Rd BT36......137 C8
Thornberry Ave BT14...136 B3
Thornberry Mews BT14...136 B3
Thornberry Rd BT14....136 B3
Thornbrook
Ballymena BT42......77 E3
Lisburn BT27......170 F2
Thornbrook Croft BT42...77 E3
Thornbrook Rd BT67......167 B3
Thorndale
Limavady BT49......180 D3
Londonderry BT48......177 A6
Thorndale Ave BT15....144 C8
Thorndale Cl BT41......187 C2
Thorndale Pk BT8......163 C2
Thorndale Rd BT29......141 C8
Thorndale Rd S BT8......163 C2
Thorndale Sq BT38......124 F2
Thorndene Pk BT38......124 F4
Thorndyke St 10 BT5...145 B5
Thornfield Ct BT38......124 F2
Thornfield Sch BT37....134 C8
Thornhill Ave
Lisburn BT28......159 F5
Magherafelt BT45......183 B3
Thornhill Coll BT48......177 D6
Thornhill Cres
Belfast BT5......146 C4
Dunmurry BT17......149 D2
Lisburn BT28......159 F5
Thornhill Ct
2 Dunmurry BT17......149 E2
Magherafelt BT45......183 B3
Thornhill Dr
Ballyclare BT39......184 A5
Belfast BT5......146 C4
Magherafelt BT45......183 B3
Thornhill Gdns
Ballyclare BT39......184 A5
3 Belfast BT9......151 B7
Lisburn BT28......159 F4
Thornhill Gr BT5......146 C4
Thornhill Malone BT9...151 B7

Thornhill Par
Ballyclare BT39......184 A5
Belfast BT5......146 C4
Thornhill Pk
Belfast BT5......146 C4
Lisburn BT28......159 F5
Londonderry BT48......177 E7
Magherafelt BT45......183 B3
Thornhill Rd
Antrim BT41......109 A8
Dunmurry BT17......149 F2
Thornhill Roadt BT17...149 F1
Thornlea Ave BT43......181 A5
Thornlea Dr BT52......174 E7
Thornlea Gdns BT47......179 A2
Thornleigh BT39......110 E2
Thornleigh Ave BT41...107 F6
Thornleigh Cl BT28......159 F2
Thornleigh Dr BT28......159 F2
Thornleigh Pk
Ballymoney BT53......43 F8
Lisburn BT28......159 E2
Randalstown BT41......107 F6
Thorn Way BT41......187 C2
Thralcot Link BT38......125 C6
Three Mile Wr Conservation
Pk★ BT37......128 D2
Three Taghmores BT51...24 F2
Throne Ctr The BT36...133 C2
Throne Terr BT36......133 C4
Thyme Pk BT41......186 E3
Ticloy BT44......64 E5
Tierney Gdns BT12......188 C1
Tievebulliagh BT44......31 F3
Tiger Ct BT41......186 D5
Tildarg BT39......96 D5
Tildarg Ave BT11......149 F5
Tildarg Prim Sch BT39...96 F4
Tildarg Rd
Ballyclare BT39......96 D4
Ballymena BT42......95 F4
Tildarg Rd S BT39......96 F4
Tildarg St BT6......145 B2
Tillies Brae BT48......178 E4
Tillysburn Dr 4 BT4...139 A1
Tillysburn Gr BT4......146 A8
Tillysburn Pk
3 Belfast BT4......139 A1
Belfast BT4......146 A8
Timacon Way BT46......75 A8
Timaconway Rd
Coleraine BT51......58 E1
Maghera BT46......75 A8
Timbey Pk BT7......151 E8
Timoyle BT44......31 F2
Timpan BT44......31 F7
Tinamara BT38......129 D4
Tindall Cotts 9 BT39...110 C2
Tintagh BT45......103 D4
Tirbracken 2 BT48......52 B8
Tirbracken Rd BT47......51 F7
Tirconnelly BT82......68 B4
Tircorran BT49......23 D4
Tircreven BT49......12 A1
Tircreven Rd BT49......23 D4
Tiree St BT41......186 D8
Tireighter BT47......70 A2
Tireighter Cotts BT47...70 A1
Tireighter Rd BT47......70 A1
Tirgan BT45......103 F4
Tirgan Rd BT45......103 F3
Tirgarvil BT46......74 F5
Tirgarvil Rd BT46......75 A4
Tirglassan BT47......70 B7
Tirglassan Rd BT47......70 B7
Tirgoland BT47......55 F3
Tirgracey BT41......109 B1
Tirgracey Rd BT41......117 A8
Tirhugh BT46......74 C8
Tireighter Rd BT47......69 F1
Tirkane BT46......73 F5
Tirkane Ct 9 BT46......74 D1
Tirkane Rd BT46......73 F5
Tirkeeran BT51......57 F7
Tirkeeran Rd BT51......57 F7
Tirkeerin Pk BT47......35 F4
Tirkeeveny BT47......50 F1
Tirkilly BT44......32 B6
Tirmacoy BT49......38 A6
Tirmacoy Rd BT49......37 F5
Tirmacshane BT80......112 A5
Tirmaquin BT49......40 A7
Tirnageeragh BT46......75 B4
Tirnanog BT80......115 C2
Tir-na-n'og Prim Sch
BT39......184 B5
Tirnony BT46......74 C3
Tirnony Rd BT46......74 C3
Tirowen Dr BT28......169 D8
Tirowen Way BT28......159 D1
Tirruadh Ct 5 BT45......89 A3
Tirruadh Dr BT45......89 A3
Tirruadh Hts 2 BT45...89 A4
Tirruadh Mews 7 BT45...89 A3
Tirruadh Rd 1 BT45......89 A4
Tirruadh Sq 11 BT45...89 A3
Tiscallen BT67......164 E7
Tiscallen Rd BT67......164 C7
Titania St BT6......145 B2
Titterington Gdns BT27...162 A2
Tivoli Gdns BT15......137 B4
Tivoli Pk BT48......176 C1
Tobar-glen BT36......133 B4
Tobar Pk 4 BT42......78 A6
Toberagnee BT39......118 E8
Toberbilly
Ballycastle BT54......18 D6

Toberbilly continued
Ballymoney BT53......29 A3
Tobercooran Ave BT36...133 A5
Tober Ct BT42......77 F7
Toberdoney 6 BT53......16 E3
Toberdoney★ BT44......45 F3
Toberdoney Cross Roads
BT53......16 E3
Toberdoney Rd 2 BT53...28 B8
Toberdornan BT52......15 B6
Toberdowney BT39......97 F2
Toberdowney Ave BT39...97 F2
Toberdowney Dr BT39...97 F2
Toberdowney Gdns BT39...97 F2
Toberdowney Manor
BT39......97 F2
Toberdowney Pk BT39...97 F2
Toberdowney Valley BT39 97 F2
Tobergel La BT40......83 C6
Tobergill Gdns BT41......186 F5
Tobergill Rd BT39......110 A6
Tobergill St
9 Belfast BT13......144 A7
Belfast BT13......188 A4
Tobergill Wlk BT41......186 F6
Toberhead BT45......90 F3
Toberhead Rd BT45......91 A3
Toberkeagh BT57......6 F2
Toberkeagh Rd BT57......6 E2
Toberlane BT80......112 D4
Toberlane Rd BT80......112 D4
Tobermore BT45......89 F6
TOBERMORE (AN YOBAR
MÓR) BT45......89 E5
Tobermore Bsns Ctr 4
BT45......89 F5
Tobermore Prim Sch
BT45......89 F5
Tobermore Rd
Draperstown BT45......89 A4
Maghera BT46......90 A8
Magherafelt BT45......183 B8
Tobernagola BT53......29 C2
Tobernaveen BT41......95 C1
Tober Rd
Ballymena BT44......45 D8
Ballymoney BT53......29 C2
Toberslane BT82......50 A6
Toberwine BT44......48 B5
Toberwine St 1 BT44...65 F8
Tobin Pk BT80......115 C1
Tokio Gdns BT15......145 A8
Tollnamona Ct 3 BT11...143 B1
Tomb St BT1......189 B4
Tonagh BT28......159 F2
Tonagh Ave BT28......159 F1
Tonagh Dr BT28......159 F1
Tonagh Hts BT45......88 F3
Tonagh Mews BT28......159 F1
Tonagh Pk BT28......159 F1
Tonagh Prim Sch BT28...159 F1
Tonaght BT45......88 F2
Tonaght Rd BT45......102 F8
Tonduff BT57......6 A7
Tonduff Mountain BT57...6 A8
Tonedluff BT47......52 C1
Tongue Loanen BT38...125 F5
Toome BT41......106 D7
TOOME (DROICHEAD
THUAMA) BT41......106 C7
Toome Rd BT42......181 D1
Top of the Hill 6 BT47...179 A3
Topp Lower BT53......28 D4
Topp Rd BT53......28 D5
Topp Upper BT53......28 E4
Torard BT44......30 B2
Torcorr BT44......21 A6
Toreagh Prim Sch BT40...98 F6
Torglass BT54......9 F4
Tornabodagh BT54......9 A4
Tornagrough BT17......141 E4
Tornamoney BT44......21 A4
Tornaroan BT54......9 A4
Tornaroy BT17......142 A4
Tornaroy Rd BT17......141 E4
Toronto St BT7......145 A3
Torrens Ave
Belfast BT14......137 A1
Londonderry BT47......179 B6
Torrens Cres BT14......137 A1
Torrens Ct
2 Belfast BT14......137 A1
Belfast BT14......137 A1
Torrens Dr BT14......137 A1
Torrens Gdns BT14......137 A1
Torrens Pk BT53......43 F8
Torrens Rd BT14......137 A1
Torr Gdns BT40......83 B4
Torr Rd
Ballycastle BT54......9 E3
Ballymena BT44......21 B5
Torr Way BT10......150 D4
Torwood BT67......166 B2
Tosh Ave BT47......179 C6
Tower Rd
Ballymena BT44......49 D8
Larne BT40......182 F4
Tower St BT4......145 B5
Tower Way BT41......186 F4
Town Brae BT44......65 F7
Town & Ctry Sh Ctr BT8...15 F6
Townend BT57......15 F6
Townhall St BT53......175 C4
Townhead Rd BT44......76 D6
Town La BT40......100 D4

Townland Rd BT29......116 D4
Town Parks
Ballycastle BT54......8 D4
Ballymena BT44......65 F8
Ballymoney BT53......175 D4
Belfast BT13......144 C7
TOWN PARKS BT13......188 C4
Town Parks 6 BT40......182 C4
Townparks N BT21......186 E5
Town Parks of Magherafelt
BT45......183 C6
Townsend Ent Pk BT13...188 C4
Townsend St BT13......188 C4
Townsley St 2 BT4......145 C5
Towns Parks BT41......186 D5
Tracy's Way BT47......55 D1
Trafalgar St 3 BT15...144 E7
Traherne Gdns BT27...170 A6
Trailcock Rd BT38......125 E3
Trainfield St 5 BT15...144 D8
Tralee BT80......114 C5
Tralee Rd BT80......114 B5
Tramway Dr BT57......5 D4
Tramways Sh Ctr 4
BT36......132 F5
Tranarossan Ave BT48...176 B1
Trassey Cl BT6......152 B8
Travers Pl 6 BT53......28 B8
Trea Gdns BT45......106 D7
Treetops La BT36......133 E7
Trenchard BT11......149 F5
Trench Ave BT11......150 B6
Trench Ct 9 BT42......95 A5
Trenchill Ave BT39......97 B2
Trenchill Rd BT39......97 B2
Trench La BT36......119 C7
Trench Pk BT11......150 B6
Trench Rd
Hillsborough BT26......168 E1
Londonderry BT47......179 A2
Newtownabbey BT36......132 A7
Trench Rd Prim Sch
BT47......179 A2
Trench Rd Sh Ctr BT47...179 A2
Tresna Pk BT41......107 F8
Trevor St BT18......139 D6
Trienaltenagh BT51......58 E6
Trigo Par BT6......145 D2
Trillick Ct 7 BT5......145 B4
Trillick St 4 BT5......145 B4
Trinity Ave BT55......172 B2
Trinity Dr BT53......175 D5
Trinity Terr BT28......160 A1
Tromery Ct BT29......121 B8
Tromery Dr
3 Crumlin BT29......117 B1
Crumlin BT29......121 B8
Tromery Pk BT29......121 B8
Tromra Ct BT44......32 C7
Tromra Rd BT44......32 C7
Trooperhill 5 BT15......25 B4
Trinity Ave
Belfast BT6......152 D7
Newtownabbey BT37......134 B8
Tudor Ct BT6......152 D7
Tudor Dale BT4......145 F7
Tudor Dr
Belfast BT6......152 D7
Carrickfergus BT38......125 C5
Tudor Gdns BT38......125 D5
Tudor Gr
Belfast BT13......144 B7
Newtownabbey BT37......134 B8
Tudor Grange BT28......159 E4
Tudor Link BT38......125 C5
Tudor Oaks
3 Ballymoney BT53......175 C5
Holywood BT18......139 E7
Tudor Pk
Carrickfergus BT38......125 C5
Holywood BT18......139 E7
Newtownabbey BT36......119 C7
Tudor Pl BT13......144 B7
Tudor Rd BT38......125 C5
Tudor Vale BT42......77 F2
Tuftarney BT43......47 B3
Tuftarney Rd BT43......47 B2
Tullagh BT80......185 B4
Tullaghans BT44......44 C4
Tullaghans Rd BT43......43 F3
Tullaghans Top BT44...44 D3
Tullaghbane BT44......46 A3
Tullaghbeg BT41......107 A4
Tullaghboy Rd BT80......113 B5
Tullagh Brow BT42......78 D1
Tullagh Dr BT80......185 B5
Tullaghgarley
Ballymena BT42......78 D1
Ballymena BT43......61 F2

Tullaghgore BT53......27 D6
Tullagh Hts BT42......78 D1
Tullaghmurry East
BT56......172 B4
Tullaghmurry West
BT56......172 A3
Tullaghore BT53......18 E3
Tullagh Pk BT11......150 A8
Tullagh Rd BT80......185 A5
Tullagh Vale BT42......78 D1
Tullagh View BT80......185 A4
Tullanee BT47......36 F4
Tullanee Rd BT47......36 F4
Tullans 2 BT52......26 D8
Tullans Pk BT52......26 D8
Tullaville BT80......185 B4
Tulleevin Dr BT36......133 E6
Tulleevin Wlk BT36......133 E6
Tullintrain BT47......69 D5
Tulloghgore Rd BT53......27 C6
Tullog La BT42......80 C5
Tully
Ballymena BT42......79 D1
Ballymena BT44......32 C4
Ballymena BT44......65 D7
Belfast BT29......117 D5
Limavady BT49......38 E7
Londonderry BT47......36 C5
Tullyally Rd
Drumahoe BT47......179 D1
Londonderry BT47......51 C5
Tullyard
Lisburn BT27......171 E7
Strabane BT82......67 D4
Tullyardan BT48......35 F8
Tullyard Rd BT27......171 E6
Tullyard Way (Heichbrae
Airt) BT6......152 E8
Tullyarmon BT49......23 D2
Tullyarton BT52......174 E5
Tullyballydonell BT28...156 A6
Tullybane BT53......17 D1
Tullybeg Ave BT51......174 A5
Tullyboy BT45......113 C5
Tullybrick BT45......102 A6
Tullybrick Rd BT45......102 C5
Tullybrisland BT47......37 B6
Tullycall BT80......112 D5
Tullycall Rd BT80......112 D4
Tullycapple BT53......27 C8
Tullycarnet Prim Sch
BT5......146 F3
Tullycreenaght BT41...108 F7
Tully Cres BT44......32 C4
Tullydagan BT67......164 D3
Tullydagan Rd BT67......164 C3
Tullygare BT80......185 F6
Tullygarley Rd BT42......181 A1
Tullyglass Pk BT42......78 C3
Tullygowan BT42......78 B1
Tullygrawley Rd BT43...78 B8
Tullyheran BT46......74 B2
Tullyheran Rd BT46......74 B1
Tullyhoe BT49......38 E7
Tullykeeran Mountain
BT46......73 D5
Tullykittagh Rd BT44...46 D2
Tullykittagh Rd N BT44...46 A4
Tullykittagh Rd S BT44...62 D7
Tullykittagh Upper
BT44......46 E1
Tullylinkisay BT45......105 B7
Tullyloob BT67......165 B3
Tullymain BT49......38 A6
Tullymore BT43......79 D8
Tullymore Dr BT11......150 A8
Tullymore Gdns BT11...150 A7
Tullymore Pk BT42......181 C3
Tullymore Rd
Ballymena BT43......79 D8
Drumahoe BT47......51 D6
Tullymore Wlk 5 BT11...150 A8
Tullynacross BT27......160 F4
Tullynacross Rd BT27...160 F4
Tullynagee BT45......103 F3
Tullynagee Rd BT45......103 D5
Tullynahinnion BT47......77 A6
Tullynahinnion Rd BT44...77 A6
Tullynamullan BT41......94 C5
Tullynamullan Rd BT42...94 D5
Tullynewbane BT29......121 E6
Tullynewbank BT29......121 E5
Tullynewbank Rd BT29...121 E5
Tullynew★ BT44......62 B4
Tully North BT44......30 B2
Tullynure BT80......112 E8
Tullynure Rd BT80......112 E8
Tullyraw BT80......113 E1
Tully Rd
Ballykelly BT49......38 D7
Ballymena BT42......95 B8
Belfast BT29......117 D5
Limavady BT49......38 E6
Tullyreagh BT44......61 F5
Tullyreagh Rd BT44......61 F5
Tullyroan BT45......45 F4
Tullyroan BT45......89 E3
Tullyronnelly BT67......164 E3
Tullyrusk BT29......140 E3
Tullyrusk Fort★ BT29...140 B4
Tullyrusk Rd BT29......140 B4
Tully South BT44......30 A1
Tully Upper BT44......30 B1
Tullyvar Pk BT28......159 E5
Tullyveagh BT80......113 D1

Tullyveagh Rd BT80 . . . . . . 113 D1
Tullyverry❶ BT47 . . . . 37 D6
Tullyweery❶ BT71 . . . . . . 113 E1
Tullywest Rd BT29 . . . . . 117 D4
Tullywiggan Rd BT80 . . 185 D1
Tulymore Dale BT42 . . . . . . 79 D7
Tummock Rd BT53 . . . . 28 D2
Tunnel Brae BT51 . . . . 13 A5
Tuppenny Mdws BT42 . . . . 78 B2
Tuppenny Rd BT42 . . . . 78 B2
Turasmore Pk BT48 . . . . . 178 B8
Tureagh❶
  Ballymoney BT53 . . . . 18 E1
  Larne BT40 . . . . 98 F5
Tureagh Pk BT40 . . . . . . 182 B4
Tureagh Rd BT40 . . . . 99 A4
Turfahun❶ BT57 . . . . 6 A3
Turf Lodge❶ BT11 . . . . . 143 C3
Turin St BT12 . . . . 188 B2
Turmeel❶ BT47 . . . . 71 F8
Turmeel Rd BT47 . . . . 71 F8
Turnaface❶ BT5 . . . . . . 113 C8
Turnaface Rd BT45 . . . . 113 C8
Turnagrove❶ BT53 . . . . . . 29 C3
Turnakibbock❶ BT52 . . . 26 F7
Turnarobert❶ BT53 . . . . . 18 B2
Turnarobert Pk BT53 . . . . 18 A2
Turnavedog❶ BT44 . . . . . . 30 A3
Turnberry Mews BT56 . . 172 C1
Turnerstown La BT51 . . . . 59 A1
Turraloskin❶ BT54 . . . . 8 A1
Turraloskin Pk BT54 . . . . . 7 F2
Turrasaglin Well★ BT47 . . 69 F3
Turrygoogan❶ BT53 . . . . . 29 B3
Tutor Ct BT48 . . . . 178 D7
Twaddell Ave BT13 . . . . . 143 E8
Twenty Acres❶
  Ballycastle BT54 . . . . 9 D3
  Coleraine BT51 . . . . 42 A1
Tweskard Lodge BT4 . . . 146 C7
Tweskard Pk BT4 . . . . . . 146 C7
Twinbrook❶ BT17 . . . . . 149 D2
Twinbrook Rd BT17 . . . . 149 D3
Twinburn Cres BT37 . . . . 128 E2
Twinburn Dr BT37 . . . . . 128 E2
Twinburn Gdns BT37 . . . 128 E2
Twinburn Hill BT37 . . . . 128 D2
Twinburn Pk BT37 . . . . . 128 E2
Twinburn Rd BT37 . . . . . 128 E2
Twinburn Way BT37 . . . . 128 D2
Twin Spires Ctr BT13 . . . 188 B3
Twiselside BT18 . . . . 139 E7
Twr Mus The ⓬ BT48 . . 178 E5
Tyanee❶ BT44 . . . . 76 B6
Tygore❶ BT47 . . . . 36 F3
Tyler Ave BT49 . . . . 180 C7
Tyler Pk BT49 . . . . 180 C6
Tyler Rd BT49 . . . . 180 C6
Tynan Dr BT37 . . . . 129 A1
Tyndale Cres BT14 . . . . . 136 E4
Tyndale Dr BT14 . . . . . . 136 E4
Tyndale Gdns BT14 . . . . 136 E4
Tyndale Gn BT14 . . . . . . 136 E4
Tyndale Gr BT14 . . . . . . 136 E4
Tynedale Cres BT28 . . . . 159 E5
Tynedale Pk BT28 . . . . . 159 E5
Tyne St BT13 . . . . 188 B4
Tynure BT80 . . . . 112 F7
Tyrconnell St BT48 . . . . 178 D5
Tyrone St (Sráid Thír
  Eoghain) ❷ BT13 . . . . . 188 C4

U

Ulidia Integrated Coll
  BT38 . . . . 125 B3
Ulster Ave BT17 . . . . . . 150 A2
Ulster Coll of Music BT9 144 B1
Ulsterdale St BT5 . . . . . 145 D4
Ulster Mus★ BT9 . . . . . 144 D1
Ulster Science & Tech Pk
  BT48 . . . . 176 C2
Ulster Sports Club BT1 . 189 B4
Ulster St BT1 . . . . 189 B4
Ulsterville Ave
  Belfast BT9 . . . . 144 B2
  ❷ Londonderry BT47 . . 179 B5
Ulsterville Dr BT9 . . . . . 144 B2
Ulsterville Gdns BT9 . . . 144 B2
Ulsterville Pl BT9 . . . . . 144 B2
Umbra❶ BT49 . . . . 12 C4
Umgall Rd BT39 . . . . . . 118 F5
Umrycam❶ BT47 . . . . 70 E5
Umrycam Rd BT47 . . . . . 70 C4
Umry Gdns BT41 . . . . . . 186 B6
Unagh❶ BT80 . . . . 112 D5
Unagh Rd BT80 . . . . 112 E5
Union Bridge BT27 . . . . 160 C1
Uniondale St BT5 . . . . . 145 D4
Union Hall Pl BT48 . . . . 178 F5
Union Pl BT80 . . . . 185 D5
Union Rd BT45 . . . . 183 D6
Union St
  ❸ Ballymoney BT53 . . . 175 D4
  Belfast BT1 . . . . 189 A4
  Coleraine BT52 . . . . . . 174 C4
  Cookstown BT80 . . . . . 185 D5
Unity St BT38 . . . . 131 A8
University Ave BT7 . . . . 144 D2
University Ct BT52 . . . . 174 C8
University Gdns BT52 . . 174 C8
University of Ulster at
  Jordanstown BT38 . . . 129 D1
University of Ulster (Belfast
  Campus) BT1 . . . . 189 A4
University of Ulster
  (Coleraine Campus)
  BT52 . . . . 174 B8
University of Ulster Magee
  Campus BT48 . . . . 178 E7
University of Ulster (School
  of Hotel; Leisure &
  Tourism) BT55 . . . . . . 173 F5
University of Ulster Science
  Pk BT48 . . . . 178 F7
University Pk BT52 . . . . 174 C8
University Rd BT9 . . . . . 144 C2
University Sq BT7 . . . . . 144 D2
University St BT7 . . . . . 144 D2
University Sta BT52 . . . 174 C8
University Terr ❶ BT9 . . 144 C2
Unshanagh❶ BT44 . . . . . 32 B8
Unshinagh❶ BT44 . . . . . . 44 A5
Unshinagh Mountain❶
  BT44 . . . . 64 F8
Unshinagh North❶ BT44 65 B8
Unshinagh South❶ BT44 65 A8
Upper Arthur St BT1 . . . 189 A3
UPPER BALLINDERRY
  BT28 . . . . 156 F7
Upper Ballyboley Prim Sch
  BT39 . . . . 97 F5
Upper Ballyboley Rd BT39 97 E5
Upper Ballynahinch
  BT27 . . . . 171 A1
Upper Balteagh❶ BT51 . . 24 F4
Upper Bennett St ❼
  BT48 . . . . 178 E4
Upper Braniel Rd BT5 . . 153 C7
Upper Cairncastle Rd
  BT40 . . . . 182 B6
Upper Cam❶ BT54 . . . . . 25 B1
Upper Canning St BT15 . 144 D8
Upper Carneal Rd BT40 . . 99 C3
Upper Castle Pk BT15 . . 137 B5
Upper Cavehill Rd BT15 . 137 A5
Upper Charleville St
  BT13 . . . . 144 A7
Upper Church La BT1 . . . 189 B3
Upper Coole Glebe❶
  BT51 . . . . 26 E3
Upper Cres BT7 . . . . 144 D2
Upper Cross St ❶ BT40 . 182 C4
Upper Ctyd BT7 . . . . 151 E7
Upper Drummans❶ BT49 . 11 E4
Upper Dunmurry La
  BT17 . . . . 149 E5
Upper Frank St ❶ BT5 . . 145 B4
Upper Galliagh Rd BT48 . 176 B5
Upper Galwally Rd ❸
  BT8 . . . . 152 A6
Upper Gateside❶ BT39 . 184 D8
Upper Glenariff Mountain
  East❶ BT44 . . . . 48 D5
Upper Glenariff Mountain
  West❶ BT44 . . . . 48 C4
Upper Gn BT17 . . . . 149 F3
Upper Heathmount BT56 172 B5
Upper High Rd BT56 . . . 172 B6
Upper Hightown Rd
  Belfast BT14 . . . . 136 E7
  Newtownabbey BT36 . . 132 C3
Upper Hollybrook Hts
  BT36 . . . . 132 D3
Upper Kildress Rd BT80 . 112 B2
Upper Killea Rd BT48 . . . 50 C8
Upper Killyglen Rd BT40 . 82 E4
Upper Kiltinny❶ BT51 . . . 25 A3
Upper Knockbreda Rd
  BT6 . . . . 152 B6
Upperland❶ BT46 . . . . . . 74 F6
UPPERLANDS BT46 . . . . 74 E5
Upperlands Rd BT46 . . . . 74 E8
Upper La Rd BT47 . . . . . . 37 B3
Upper Liester Pk BT39 . . 111 C4
Upper Main St BT40 . . . 182 C4
Upper Malone Cl BT9 . . . 150 E3
Upper Malone Cres BT9 . 150 E3
Upper Malone Gdns BT9 150 E3
Upper Malone Rd BT17 . . 161 D7
Upper Malvern Cres BT8 ❽
  BT8 . . . . 152 C3
Upper Malvern Dr ❼
  BT8 . . . . 152 C3
Upper Malvern Pk BT8 . . 152 C3
Upper Malvern Rd BT8 . . 152 C2
Upper Mdw St BT15 . . . 144 C8
Upper Mealough Rd BT8 163 A5
Upper Meehan St BT13 . . 144 B7
Upper Moyknock❶ BT51 . 59 D2
Upper Nassau St BT48 . . 178 D7
Upper Newtownards Rd
  BT5 . . . . 145 B4
Upper Prince's St BT43 . . 181 B5
Upper Queen St BT1 . . . 189 A3
Upper Quilley❶ BT51 . . . 13 E1
Upper Riga St BT13 . . . . 188 A4
Upper Springfield Rd
  Belfast BT17 . . . . 141 F3
  Lisburn BT28 . . . . 141 E2
Upper Stanfield St BT7 . . 189 B2
Upper Sta Rd BT39 . . . . 184 B7
Upper Suffolk Rd BT11 . 149 D7
Upper Timaconway❶
  BT46 . . . . 75 A8
Uppertown❶ BT44 . . . . . 45 B3
Uppertown Dr BT36 . . . 128 A2

Uppertown Rd BT40 . . . . 99 A6
Upper Townsend Terr
  BT13 . . . . 188 C4
Upper Tullans❶ BT52 . . . 14 F1
Upper Tully Rd BT47 . . . . 50 E2
Upper Tullyvally❶ BT47 . 51 D6
Upper Violet St BT47 . . . 179 A4
Upper Waterloo Rd
  BT40 . . . . 182 E5
Upton Ave BT10 . . . . . . 150 C4
Upton Cotts BT11 . . . . . 143 C2
Upton Ct
  Belfast BT11 . . . . 143 C2
  ❻ Templepatrick BT39 . 110 C2
Upton Pk BT10 . . . . 150 C4
Urbal❶
  Ballymena BT44 . . . . 45 B3
  Ballymoney BT53 . . . . . . 16 E1
  Cookstown BT80 . . . . . 114 C2
Urbal La BT80 . . . . 114 D2
Urbal Rd
  Ballymoney BT53 . . . . . . 16 F2
  Cookstown BT80 . . . . . 114 C3
  ❹ Cookstown BT80 . . . 114 C3
Urbalreagh❶ BT56 . . . . . . 4 F2
Urbalshinney Rd BT46 . . 74 A3
Utility St BT12 . . . . 188 C1
Utility Wlk BT12 . . . . . . 188 C1

V

Vaddegan Ave BT36 . . . . 133 A3
Vaddegan Dr BT36 . . . . . 133 A3
Vaddegan Gdns BT36 . . . 133 A3
Vaddegan Pk BT36 . . . . . 133 A3
Vaddegan Rd BT36 . . . . . 133 A3
Vale Pk BT55 . . . . 173 D4
Vale Rd
  Londonderry BT47 . . . . . 37 C3
  Portstewart BT55 . . . . . 173 D4
Valiant Ct BT41 . . . . 186 E5
Valley Bsns Ctr BT37 . . . 133 C4
Valley Leisure Ctr The
  BT36 . . . . 133 D3
Valley Rd BT42 . . . . 94 D6
Valley Ret Ctr BT37 . . . . 133 C3
Valleyside BT12 . . . . . . 143 E6
Vancouver Dr BT15 . . . . 137 C2
Vandyck Cres BT36 . . . . 137 D8
Vandyck Dr BT36 . . . . . . 137 D8
Vara Dr BT13 . . . . 143 F6
Varren Gdns BT55 . . . . . 173 B5
Vauxhall Pk BT9 . . . . . . 151 D6
Velsheda Ct BT14 . . . . . 136 E1
Velsheda Pk BT14 . . . . . 136 F1
Venal Way ❶ BT14 . . . . . 136 E1
Vennel Streeet ❸ BT44 . . 65 F8
Ventry La BT2 . . . . 189 A1
Ventry St BT2 . . . . 189 A1
Verbal Arts Ctr ⓮ BT48 . 178 E5
Vere Foster Prim Sch
  BT12 . . . . 143 C5
Vere Foster Wlk BT12 . . 143 C5
Verner Ct BT7 . . . . 189 B2
Verner St BT7 . . . . 189 A1
Vernon St BT7 . . . . 189 A1
Veryan Gdns BT36 . . . . 137 D8
Vicarage Gdns BT41 . . . 186 E5
Vicinage Pk BT14 . . . . . 144 C8
Victoria Ave
  Belfast BT4 . . . . 145 E7
  Whitehead BT38 . . . . . 127 A8
Victoria Cl BT39 . . . . . . 184 C3
Victoria Coll (Cranmore
  Campus) BT9 . . . . 151 B7
Victoria Coll (Richmond
  Lodge Campus) BT9 . . 151 B8
Victoria Cres
  Carrickfergus BT38 . . . 125 C3
  Lisburn BT27 . . . . 160 C2
Victoria Ct
  Ballyclare BT39 . . . . . . 184 B7
  Belfast BT4 . . . . 145 E7
  Carrickfergus BT38 . . . 125 C3
Victoria Dr BT4 . . . . 145 E7
Victoria Gate BT47 . . . . 178 E2
Victoria Gdns
  Ballyclare BT39 . . . . . . 184 B7
  Belfast BT15 . . . . 137 B4
  Carrickfergus BT38 . . . 125 C2
  ❶ Dunmurry BT17 . . . 150 A2
Victoria La BT37 . . . . . . 128 E1
Victoria Manor BT39 . . . 184 C7
Victoria Par BT15 . . . . . 144 D7
Victoria Park❶ BT3 . . . . 145 D7
Victoria Pk BT43 . . . . . . 181 D7
Victoria Pl ❻ BT48 . . . . 178 E4
Victoria Prim Sch BT38 . 125 C1
Victoria Rd
  Ballyclare BT39 . . . . . . 184 B7
  Belfast BT4 . . . . 145 E7
  Carrickfergus BT38 . . . 125 B3
  Holywood BT18 . . . . . . 139 E7
  Larne BT40 . . . . 182 D4
  Londonderry BT47 . . . . . 50 E4
  Prehen BT47 . . . . 178 D2
  Strabane BT82 . . . . 50 B1
Victoria Rd Link BT47 . . 178 F4
Victoria Rise BT38 . . . . 125 C3
Victoria Sq BT1 . . . . . . 189 B3
Victoria St
  Ballymoney BT53 . . . . . 175 C4
  Belfast BT1 . . . . 189 B3
  ❸ Carrickfergus BT38 . 131 A8
  Portstewart BT55 . . . . 173 D6
Victoria Terr BT56 . . . . 172 B6
Victor Pl BT6 . . . . 145 A4

Victory St BT27 . . . . . . 160 D2
Vidor Ct BT4 . . . . 145 E7
Vidor Gdns BT4 . . . . . . 145 E7
Viewfort Pk BT17 . . . . . 150 D2
Village Ct
  Castlereagh BT8 . . . . . 151 F4
  ❻ Newtownabbey BT36 . 133 A8
Village Gn
  Doagh BT39 . . . . 111 A6
  Moira BT67 . . . . 166 B2
Village Gn The BT6 . . . . 145 C1
Village Hill Mews BT39 . 122 D8
Village La BT48 . . . . . . 176 F4
Village Mews ❶ BT67 . . 166 B2
Village The
  Londonderry BT48 . . . . 178 C6
  Templepatrick BT39 . . . 110 C2
Vines The BT10 . . . . 150 D3
Violet St BT12 . . . . 188 A2
Vionville Cl BT5 . . . . . . 146 F2
Vionville Ct BT5 . . . . . . 146 F3
Vionville Gn BT5 . . . . . . 146 E3
Vionville Gdns BT5 . . . . 146 E3
Vionville Hts BT5 . . . . . 146 F3
Vionville Pk BT5 . . . . . . 146 F3
Vionville Pl BT5 . . . . . . 146 F3
Vionville Rise BT5 . . . . . 146 F3
Vionville View BT5 . . . . 146 F3
Vionville Way BT5 . . . . . 146 F2
Virginia Ct BT47 . . . . . . 179 A3
Virginia St BT7 . . . . 189 A1
Virginia Way BT7 . . . . . 189 A1
Vistula St BT13 . . . . 144 A7
Voltaire Gdns
  ❹ Newtownabbey BT36 . 133 D1
  Newtownabbey BT36 . . 137 D8
Vow❶ BT53 . . . . 43 C2
Vow Rd BT53 . . . . 59 D7
Vulcan Ct (Cúirt Bholcáin) ⓬
  BT5 . . . . 145 A5
Vulcan Gdns (Gairdíní
  Bholcáin) ⓭ BT5 . . . . . 145 A5
Vulcan Link (Lúb Bholcáin)
  ⓮ BT5 . . . . 145 A5
Vulcan St (Sráid Bholcáin)
  ⓾ Belfast BT5 . . . . . . 145 A5
  Belfast BT12 . . . . 188 C2

W

Wakehurst Ind Est BT42 . 181 D2
Wakehurst Pk BT42 . . . . 181 D2
Wakehurst Rd BT42 . . . . 181 D2
Wakeside Link BT47 . . . 179 A5
Walker Ct ❼ BT6 . . . . . 145 B3
Walkers Farm BT26 . . . . 169 B1
Walkmill❶ BT39 . . . . 96 F2
Walk Mill❶ BT57 . . . . 5 D2
Wallace Ave BT27 . . . . . 160 B2
Wallace Ct BT28 . . . . . . 159 B2
Wallace High Sch BT28 . . 160 A3
Wallace Hts BT47 . . . . . . 50 D3
Wallace Pk BT44 . . . . . . 60 B6
Wallace Studios ❸ BT27 160 B2
Wallasey Pk BT14 . . . . . 136 F3
Walled Gdn The ❼ BT51 . 26 A7
Wall St
  Newtownabbey BT37 . . 134 B6
  Belfast BT13 . . . . 188 C4
Walmer St BT7 . . . . 151 E8
Walnut Ave BT40 . . . . . . 83 B4
Walnut Ct BT7 . . . . 189 B1
Walnut Dr ⓾ BT40 . . . . . 83 B4
Walnut Gdns ❷ BT40 . . . 83 B4
Walnut Gr ❸ BT40 . . . . . 83 B4
Walnut Hill BT27 . . . . . . 168 E1
Walnut Mews BT7 . . . . . 189 B1
Walnut Pk ❾ BT40 . . . . . 83 B4
Walnut Rd ❼ BT40 . . . . . 83 B4
Walnut St BT7 . . . . 189 B1
Walworth❶ BT49 . . . . . . 38 A7
Walworth Pk BT49 . . . . . 38 C7
Walworth Rd BT49 . . . . . 38 C7
Wandsworth Cres ⓬
  BT4 . . . . 146 A5
Wandsworth Ct ❸ BT4 . 146 A5
Wandsworth Dr BT4 . . . 146 A6
Wandsworth Gdns BT4 . 146 A5
Wandsworth Glen BT51 . 59 B3
Wandsworth Par BT4 . . 146 A5
Wandsworth Pl BT4 . . . 146 A5
Wandsworth Rd BT4 . . . 146 B5
Wansbeck St BT9 . . . . . 151 D7
Wapping La BT48 . . . . . 178 E4
Warbleshinny❶ BT47 . . . 51 B5
Ward Ave BT28 . . . . 169 F8
Warden St BT43 . . . . . . 181 E5
Wardlow Cres BT42 . . . . 79 B2
Wardlow Rd BT42 . . . . . . 79 B2
Ward Rd BT47 . . . . 36 D2
Wardsborough Rd ❶
  BT28 . . . . 160 B1
Waringfield Ave BT67 . . 166 A1
Waringfield Dr BT67 . . . 166 A1
Waringfield Pk BT67 . . . 166 B1
Waringmore BT67 . . . . . 166 A1
Waring St
  Ballymena BT42 . . . . . 181 D3
  Belfast BT1 . . . . 189 A3
Warke Pl BT51 . . . . 13 B5
Warnocks La BT52 . . . . . 26 D7
Warren❶ BT44 . . . . 32 E2
Warren Ct BT28 . . . . . . 169 F7
Warren Cres BT56 . . . . . 172 C5
Warren Gdns BT28 . . . . 169 F7

Warren Gr
  Castlereagh BT5 . . . . . 146 B1
  Lisburn BT28 . . . . 169 F7
Warren Mourn BT28 . . . 169 F8
Warren Pk BT28 . . . . . . 169 F7
Warren Pk Ave BT28 . . . 170 A8
Warren Pk Dr BT28 . . . . 169 F8
Warren Pk Gdns BT28 . . 170 A8
Warren Rd BT82 . . . . 67 F7
Warren The
  Antrim BT41 . . . . 187 A3
  Ballymoney BT53 . . . . 175 C6
Washington Dr BT52 . . . 174 D6
Watch Hill Rd BT39 . . . . 98 E2
Water Bank BT47 . . . . . 179 C7
Waterfall Rd
  Ballymena BT44 . . . . . . 49 A3
  Larne BT40 . . . . 98 F4
Waterfoot Pk BT47 . . . . 179 C6
Waterfoot Rd BT45 . . . . 105 E6
Waterford Dr BT52 . . . . 174 C2
Waterford Gdns BT13 . . 188 A3
Waterford St BT13 . . . . 188 A3
Waterfront Hall★ BT1 . . 189 B3
Waterloo Gdns
  Belfast BT15 . . . . 137 C6
  Larne BT40 . . . . 182 D6
Waterloo Pk BT15 . . . . . 137 C6
Waterloo Pk N BT15 . . . 137 C6
Waterloo Pk S BT15 . . . 137 C6
Waterloo Pl ❶ BT48 . . . 178 E5
Waterloo Rd BT27 . . . . . 170 C4
Waterloo St BT48 . . . . . 178 E5
Watermouth Cres BT12 . 143 E5
Waterside❶ BT51 . . . . . 174 A4
Waterside
  Coleraine BT51 . . . . . . 174 A3
  Lisburn BT28 . . . . 170 B8
WATERSIDE BT47 . . . . . 179 B4
Waterside Hospl BT47 . . 177 E1
Water St BT48 . . . . 178 F5
Waterstone Pk BT47 . . . 179 B1
Waterville St BT13 . . . . 188 A3
Watt St BT6 . . . . 145 A2
Watt's Town❶ BT52 . . . 174 F1
Wattstown Bsns Pk BT52 . 26 C6
Wattstown Cres BT52 . . . 26 C6
Wauchope Ct BT12 . . . . 188 B1
Waveney Ave
  Ballymena BT42 . . . . . 181 C4
  Belfast BT15 . . . . 137 D6
Waveney Brow BT43 . . . 181 D7
Waveney Dr BT15 . . . . . 137 D6
Waveney Gr BT15 . . . . . 137 D6
Waveney Hospl BT43 . . . 181 D6
Waveney Hts BT15 . . . . 137 E6
Waveney Mews
  Ballymena BT42 . . . . . 181 C4
  Londonderry BT47 . . . . 179 C4
Waveney Pk
  Belfast BT15 . . . . 137 D5
  Londonderry BT47 . . . . 179 C4
Waveney Rd BT42 . . . . . 181 C4
Waverley Ave
  Lisburn BT28 . . . . 170 A3
  Newtownabbey BT36 . . 133 A8
Waverley Cres ❶ BT36 . 128 A1
Waverley Dr BT36 . . . . . 128 A1
Waverley Gr BT36 . . . . . 128 A1
Waverley Pk ❹ BT36 . . . 133 A8
Waverley Rd BT36 . . . . . 128 A1
Wayland St BT5 . . . . . . 145 C3
Wayside Cl ❽ BT5 . . . . 146 A1
Wayside Gn BT43 . . . . . 181 D5
Weatherly Way BT49 . . . 180 E4
Weavers Ct Bsns Pk
  BT12 . . . . 188 C1
Weavershill La BT14 . . . 136 C3
Weavershill Wlk BT14 . . 136 C3
Weavers Mdw BT29 . . . 121 B8
Weddell Bridge Rd BT45 . 88 F4
Wedderburn Ave BT10 . . 150 C3
Wedderburn Gdns BT10 . 150 C3
Weirside BT41 . . . . 108 A4
Welland St BT4 . . . . 145 C5
Wellbourne Cres BT80 . . 114 C3
Wellbourne Gr ❶ BT42 . . 95 E8
Wellbrook Rd BT80 . . . . 112 A4
Wellesley Ave BT9 . . . . 144 C3
Wellington Ave BT40 . . . 182 E6
Wellington Gn BT40 . . . 182 E6
Wellington Par BT40 . . . 182 E6
Wellington Parks BT67 . . 167 A8
Wellington Pk BT9 . . . . 144 C1
Wellington Pk Ave BT9 . . 144 C1
Wellington Pk Terr BT9 . 144 C1
Wellington Pl BT1 . . . . . 189 A3
Wellington St
  Ballymena BT43 . . . . . 181 D4
  Belfast BT1 . . . . 189 A2
Well Pl ⓰ BT6 . . . . 145 A4
Wellwood Ave ❹ BT4 . . 145 D7
Wellwood Cl ❸ BT4 . . . 145 D7
Wellwood St ❷ BT12 . . 188 C1
Welsh St BT7 . . . . 189 B2
Wesleyan Mews BT45 . . 183 C6
Wesley Ave BT40 . . . . . 182 B6
Wesley Ct
  Belfast BT7 . . . . 189 A1
  Carrickfergus 130 F6
Wesleydale BT39 . . . . . 111 C4
Wesleydale Ct BT39 . . . 111 C4
Wesley St
  Belfast BT7 . . . . 189 A1
  Lisburn BT27 . . . . 160 C2
  ❶ Londonderry BT48 . . 178 D7
West Ave BT56 . . . . 172 B4

West Ballycarry South❶
BT38 . . . . .100 A2
West Ballymaclevennon❶
BT55 . . . . .173 D1
Westbank Bsns Pk BT3. .138 C4
West Bank Cl BT3 . . . . . . .138 C4
West Bank Dr BT3 . . . . . .138 C4
West Bank Rd BT3 . . . . . .138 C4
West Bank Way BT3 . . . . .138 C5
Westbourne Ave BT43 . . . .181 B6
Westbourne Cres BT51 . . . .174 B2
Westbourne St ❶ BT5. . . .145 B5
Westbrook Ct BT52 . . . . . .174 C4
Westbury Cl BT80 . . . . . . .185 B3
Westbury Cres BT80 . . . . .185 B3
Westbury Dr BT80. . . . . . .185 B3
Westbury Gdns BT80 . . . . .185 B3
Westbury Way BT80 . . . . .185 B3
West Circular Cres BT13 143 E6
West Circular Rd BT13 . . .143 D6
Westcott St BT5 . . . . .145 C4
West Cres BT37. . . . . .133 D3
West Crossreagh❶
BT52 . . . . .172 B1
West Ct BT28 . . . . .159 F2
West Division❶ BT38. . . . .129 D8
West Dr BT56 . . . . .172 B4
West End Pk BT48 . . . . . .178 D5
Westfield Pk BT53 . . . . . .27 B5
Westgate BT53 . . . . .175 C3
West Glebe❶ BT45 . . . . . .91 F6
West Gn BT18 . . . . .139 C5
West Lake BT47 . . . . .177 E4
Westland Ave
Ballymoney BT53 . . . . . . .175 B6
Londonderry BT48 . . . . . . .178 D5
Westland Cres
Cookstown BT80 . . . . .185 B5
❶ Greysteel BT47 . . . . .37 C5
Westland Ct BT80 . . . . . .185 C3
Westland Dr
Belfast BT14 . . . . .137 B3
Cookstown BT80 . . . . .185 B5
Magherafelt BT45 . . . . . . .183 C5
Westland Gdns
Belfast BT14 . . . . .137 B2
Magherafelt BT45 . . . . . . .183 C5
Westland Pk BT80 . . . . . .185 B5
Westland Rd
Belfast BT14 . . . . .137 B3
Cookstown BT80 . . . . .185 B5
Magherafelt BT45 . . . . . . .183 C5
Westland Rd S BT48 . . . . .185 B4
Westland St BT48 . . . . . . .178 D5
Westland Terr BT48 . . . . .178 D5
Westland Way BT14 . . . . .137 B3
Westlink BT12 . . . . .188 A1
West Link
Holywood BT18 . . . . .139 C5
Larne BT40 . . . . .182 A6
Westlink Ent Ctr BT12. . . .188 B2
Westminster Ave ❶ BT4 145 D5
Westminster Ave N ❺
BT4 . . . . .145 D5
Westminster Pk BT56 . . . .172 B2
Westminster St BT17. . . . .144 E2
Westmount Ave BT14 . . . .130 F7
Weston Bsns Pk BT38 . . . .124 D2
Westoncroft BT53. . . . . . .175 B4
Westoncroft Pk BT53. . . . .175 B3
Weston Dr BT9 . . . . .150 E6
West Park❶ BT57 . . . . . . .5 A1
West Pk
Lisburn BT28 . . . . .159 E2
Portrush BT56 . . . . .172 B4
West Quarter of Ballyleese❶
BT56 . . . . .172 E1
West Rd BT41 . . . . .76 E5
Westrock Cl BT12 . . . . . . .143 E4
Westrock Cres BT12 . . . . .143 D4
Westrock Ct BT12. . . . . . .143 D4
Westrock Dr BT12. . . . . . .143 D4
Westrock Gdns BT12 . . . . .143 D4
Westrock Gn BT12 . . . . . .143 D4
Westrock Gr BT12 . . . . . .143 E4
Westrock Par BT12. . . . . .143 D4
Westrock Pk BT12 . . . . . .143 D4
Westrock Pl BT12 . . . . . . .143 D4
Westrock Sq BT12 . . . . . .143 E4
Westrock Way BT12 . . . . .143 E4
West St
Ballycarry BT38 . . . . .100 A2
Carrickfergus BT38 . . . . . .131 A7
West Strand Rd BT55. . . . .173 C5
West Torr❶ BT54 . . . . . . .10 A3
Westway BT48 . . . . .178 C6
Westway Cres (Wastairt
Bowe) BT13 . . . . .143 C7
Westway Dr BT13 . . . . . . .143 D7
Westway Gdns BT13 . . . . .143 C8
Westway Gr BT13 . . . . . . .143 C7
Westway Hill BT13 . . . . . .143 C7
Westway Par BT13 . . . . . .143 C7
Westway Pl BT13 . . . . . . .143 C7
Westwood Sh Ctr BT11. .150 D8
Weyburn Rd BT40 . . . . . . .83 A8
Whappstown❶ BT42 . . . . .96 B6
Whappstown Rd BT42 . . . .95 F6
Wheatfield ❶ BT47 . . . . . .36 E5
Wheatfield Ave BT51 . . . .174 A1
Wheatfield Cres
Belfast BT14 . . . . .136 D2
Coleraine BT51 . . . . .174 A1
Wheatfield Dr
Belfast BT14 . . . . .136 E2
Coleraine BT51 . . . . .174 A1
Wheatfield Gdns
Belfast BT14 . . . . .136 E1

Wheatfield Gdns continued
Coleraine BT51 . . . . .174 A1
Wheatfield Hts BT40 . . . .83 B8
Wheatfield Pk BT51 . . . . .174 A1
Wheatfield Prim Sch
BT14 . . . . .136 E2
Wheatsheaf Rd BT51 . . . .14 B2
Wheelers Rd BT17 . . . . . .141 F4
Whelan's Pk BT41 . . . . . .108 B7
Whinburn Cl BT41 . . . . . .187 B3
Whincroft Rd
❷ Castlereagh BT5 . . . . . .145 F1
❷ Castlereagh BT5 . . . . . .146 A1
Whincroft Way BT5 . . . . .146 A1
Whinfield BT40 . . . . .182 C7
Whinfield La BT38 . . . . . .130 A4
Whinfield Wlk BT38 . . . . .124 E1
Whinknowe Rd BT39 . . . .110 E8
Whinney Hill BT28 . . . . . .158 C8
Whinney Hts BT38 . . . . . .152 A3
Whinnyhill Dr BT8 . . . . . .151 C1
Whin Park BT41. . . . . . . .109 C6
Whin Pk BT17 . . . . .149 D2
Whin Rd BT40 . . . . .83 B8
Whinsmoor Ave BT42 . . . .79 C6
Whinsmoor Pk BT42 . . . . .79 C6
Whins The
Larne BT40 . . . . .182 B4
Portstewart BT55 . . . . . . .173 C5
Whispering Pines
Castlereagh BT6 . . . . .152 C6
Limavady BT49 . . . . .180 E4
Whistlebare❶ BT47 . . . . . .55 B6
WHITEABBEY BT37. . . . . .134 B7
White Abbey❶ BT37 . . . . .134 A6
Whiteabbey Halt BT37. . . .134 A6
Whiteabbey Hospl BT37. .133 F5
Whiteabbey Prim Sch
BT37. . . . . .134 B7
White City❶ BT36. . . . . . .133 D1
Whitecliff Cres BT12 . . . .143 D3
Whitecliff Par BT12. . . . . .143 C4
Whitefalls❶ BT51 . . . . . . .58 C8
Whitefalls Rd BT51. . . . . .58 C8
White Gables Raloo BT40 98 F5
White Glen BT17 . . . . . . .149 B3
Whitehall Ave BT54 . . . . .8 C3
Whitehall Cl ❶ BT54. . . . .8 C3
Whitehall Cres ❶ BT54. . . .8 C3
Whitehall Ct ❶ BT54. . . . .8 C3
Whitehall Dr ❶ BT54. . . . .8 C3
Whitehall Gdns
❻ Ballycastle BT54 . . . . . .8 C3
Belfast BT7 . . . . .151 F8
Whitehall Hts ❷ BT54. . . .8 C3
Whitehall Mews BT7 . . . . .151 F8
Whitehall Par BT7 . . . . . .151 F8
Whitehall Pk ❺ BT54. . . . .8 C3
Whitehall Pl ❸ BT54. . . . .8 C3
Whitehall Rd BT67 . . . . . .164 D7
WHITEHAVEN (AN CIONN
BÁN) BT38. . . . . .100 C1
Whitehaven Mews BT56 . .172 B3
WHITEHEAD (AN CIONN
BÁN) BT38. . . . . .100 C1
Whitehead Golf Club
BT38 . . . . .100 D2
Whitehead Prim Sch
BT40. . . . . .100 E1
WHITEHILL BT41 . . . . . . .108 C7
Whitehill❶ BT47 . . . . .36 D3
Whitehill Lodge BT28 . . . .159 E2
Whitehill Mews BT28 . . . .159 E2
Whitehill Pk BT49 . . . . . .180 D2
Whitehill Rd
Antrim BT41 . . . . .108 C7
Ballymena BT44. . . . . . . .49 B2
Londonderry BT48 . . . . . . .36 D3
Whitehouse❶ BT82 . . . . . .50 B4
White House❶
Ballymena BT44. . . . . . . .20 F2
Newtownabbey BT37. . . . .133 F3
Whitehouse Ct BT37 . . . . .134 A3
Whitehouse Gdns BT37. . .134 A2
White House or
Ballymagrorty❶ BT48 . .34 C3
Whitehouse Pk
Londonderry BT48 . . . . . . .176 B4
Newtownabbey BT37. . . . .134 A2
Whitehouse Prim Sch
BT37. . . . . .133 F3
Whitehouse Rd BT48 . . . .176 A3
White La BT28 . . . . .157 D3
White Mountain Rd
BT28 . . . . .159 B7
White Park❶
Ballycastle BT54 . . . . .7 A7
Ballyclare BT39 . . . . .184 F8
Whitepark Dr ❹ BT54. . . .8 C3
White Pk Rd
Ballycastle BT54 . . . . .7 D7
Bushmills BT57 . . . . .5 E4
White Rise BT40 . . . . .182 B5
Wilshere Dr BT44 . . . . . . .146 A7
Whiterock Bsns Pk BT12 143 B5
Whiterock Cl (Clós na
Carraige Báine) BT12. .143 C3
Whiterock Cres BT12. . . . .143 D3
Whiterock Dr BT12. . . . . .143 D3
Whiterock Gdns BT12 . . . .143 D3
Whiterock Gr BT12. . . . . .143 C3
Whiterock Leisure Ctr
BT12. . . . . .143 C3
Whiterock Par BT12. . . . . .143 E3
Whiterock Rd BT12 . . . . . .143 C3
Whiterock Rd Upper
BT12 . . . . .143 B5
WHITESIDES CORNER
BT41 . . . . .93 E5
Whitesides Cotts BT42 . . .78 C1

Whitesides Fort★ BT29. .121 A7
Whitesides Rd
Antrim BT41. . . . . .93 D4
Ballymena BT42. . . . . . . .94 A7
Whitethorn BT38. . . . . . . .129 C4
Whitethorn Dr BT47. . . . . .51 D6
Whitewater Ct ❶ BT45. . . .88 E2
Whitewell Cres BT36 . . . . .137 D8
Whitewell Dr BT36 . . . . . .137 D8
Whitewell Mews BT36. . . .133 C3
Whitewell Par BT36 . . . . .137 E8
Whitewell Rd BT36 . . . . . .137 E8
Whitla Cres BT28 . . . . . . .160 B4
Whitla Rd BT28 . . . . .160 B4
Whitlas Brae BT40 . . . . . .182 C3
Whitla St ❻ BT15 . . . . . . .144 E8
Whittaker St BT48 . . . . . .178 F5
Whowhatwherewhenwhy★
BT3 . . . . .189 C4
Whyns Cres BT56 . . . . . . .172 C5
Wigton St BT13 . . . . .188 B4
Wildeen BT27 . . . . .160 C4
Wildflower Way BT12 . . . .150 F8
Wilgar Cl BT4. . . . . .145 E5
Wilgar St BT4. . . . . .145 E5
Willan Dr BT55 . . . . .173 E4
Willcroft Mdws BT39 . . . .111 C3
Willesden Pk BT9 . . . . . . .151 D6
William Alexander Pk
BT10 . . . . .150 B4
William Ct BT45. . . . . . . .91 F5
William St S BT11 . . . . . .189 A3
William St Swimming Baths
BT48 . . . . .178 E5
Williamson Park❶ BT53. .27 C5
William St
Ballymena BT43. . . . . . . .181 D5
Belfast BT1 . . . . .189 A4
Bellaghy BT45 . . . . .91 F5
Cookstown BT80 . . . . .185 D5
Limavady BT49 . . . . .180 A5
❸ Londonderry BT48 . . . . .178 E6
Willisfield Ave BT10. . . . .150 D3
Willisfield Gdns BT10 . . . .150 D3
Willisfield Pk BT10. . . . . .150 D3
Willowbank Cres BT8 . . . .152 C6
Willowbank Dr BT6 . . . . . .152 B6
Willowbank Gdns BT15. . .137 B2
Willowbank Pk BT6 . . . . . .152 B7
Willowbank Rd BT40 . . . . .83 B2
Willow Brook BT42. . . . . .95 A5
Willowbrook La BT52 . . . .174 C8
Willow Brook Pk BT52. . . .174 C5
Willow Cres BT40 . . . . . . .182 A4
Willow Ct ❸ BT17. . . . . . .160 F8
Willowdale BT41 . . . . . . .187 C3
Willowdale Pk BT53 . . . . .43 C8
Willow Dr BT52 . . . . .174 C8
Willowfield BT41. . . . . . . .107 F8
Willowfield Ave
❸ Belfast BT6 . . . . .145 B3
Coleraine BT52 . . . . .174 D8
Willowfield Cres ❷ BT6. .145 B3
Willowfield Dr BT6. . . . . .145 A3
Willowfield Gdns
Belfast BT6 . . . . .145 B3
❶ Coleraine BT52. . . . . . .174 D8
Willowfield Par BT6. . . . . .145 A3
Willowfield Pk
Coleraine BT52 . . . . .174 C8
Drumahoe BT47. . . . . . . .179 F1
Willowfield St BT6 . . . . . .145 B3
Willow Gdns BT17 . . . . . .161 A8
Willowholme Cres BT6. . . .145 B2
Willowholme Dr BT6 . . . . .145 B1
Willowholme Par ❹ BT6 145 B2
Willowholme St BT6 . . . . .145 B2
Willow Hts ❶❶ BT36 . . . . .133 A8
Willow Lodge BT28 . . . . . .167 A8
Willow Mews ❸ BT52 . . . .174 D8
Willow Pk
Carrickfergus BT38 . . . . . .130 F8
❸ Newtownabbey BT37 . .133 F4
Willow St BT12 . . . . .188 C2
Willows The
Ballyclare BT39 . . . . .111 C4
❶❸ Ballymena BT42. . . . . .78 C3
Castlereagh BT6 . . . . .152 C6
Magherafelt BT45 . . . . . . .183 B4
Willowvale Ave BT11. . . . .150 A6
Willowvale Gdns BT11. . . .150 A6
Willowvale Gr BT40 . . . . .100 D3
Willowvale Mews BT11. . .150 A6
Willowvale Pk BT40 . . . . .100 D3
Wilmar Rd
Dunmurry BT27 . . . . .160 C7
Lisburn BT27 . . . . .160 C7
Wilmohr Pk BT42 . . . . . . .77 F2
Wilmont Pk BT17 . . . . . . .150 D1
Wilmuir Cres BT40 . . . . . .182 B5
Wilson Ave BT42 . . . . . . .181 E2
Wilson Bsns Pk BT36. . . . .119 C7
Wilson Cres BT42 . . . . . . .181 E2
Wilson Ct BT1 . . . . .189 B3
Wilson St
Belfast BT13 . . . . .188 C4
Lisburn BT27 . . . . .160 C2
Wilton St BT13. . . . . .188 A4
Wimslow Manor ❶❷ BT51. .26 A7
Winchester Ave BT8. . . . . .163 D1
Winchester Cres BT8. . . . .163 D1
Winchester Dr BT8. . . . . . .163 D1
Winchester Gdns BT8. . . . .163 D1
Winchester Gr ❷ BT8. . . . .163 D2

Winchester Pk
Carryduff BT8 . . . . .163 D1
Londonderry BT47 . . . . . . .179 E6
Winchester Rd BT8 . . . . . .163 D1
Windermere Ave
Carrickfergus BT38 . . . . . .125 C2
❷ Castlereagh BT8 . . . . . .152 C3
Windermere Cl ❸ BT8 . . .152 C3
Windermere Cres BT8. . . . .152 C3
Windermere Dr BT8. . . . . .152 C3
Windermere Gdns BT15 . .137 B4
Windermere Gn ❶ BT8 . . .152 C3
Windermere Pk BT8 . . . . . .152 C3
Windermere Rd
Carrickfergus BT38 . . . . . .125 C2
Castlereagh BT8 . . . . .152 C3
Lisburn BT28 . . . . .159 D2
Windermere Village ❹
BT8 . . . . .152 C3
Windmill Ave BT38. . . . . .130 F7
Windmill Pk BT38. . . . . . .130 F7
Windmill Terr ❶ BT48 . . .178 D4
Windmill View BT48. . . . . .50 C6
Windridge Dr BT47. . . . . .179 A2
Windrush Ave BT8 . . . . . .152 C4
Windrush Pk BT8 . . . . . . .152 C4
Windslow Cl BT38. . . . . . .124 E3
Windslow Cres BT38 . . . . .124 E3
Windslow Ct BT38 . . . . . .124 E3
Windslow Dr BT38 . . . . . .124 D3
Windslow Gdns BT38 . . . .124 E3
Windslow Gn BT38 . . . . . .124 E3
Windslow Gr BT38 . . . . . .124 E3
Windslow Hts BT38 . . . . .124 E3
Windslow Mews BT38 . . . .124 E3
Windslow Pk BT38 . . . . . .124 E3
Windslow Rise BT38 . . . . .124 E3
Windsor Ave
Belfast BT9 . . . . .151 C8
Coleraine BT52 . . . . .174 D4
Holywood BT18 . . . . .139 E6
Limavady BT49 . . . . .180 C6
❷ Lisburn BT28 . . . . .169 F8
Whitehead BT38 . . . . .127 A8
Windsor Ave N BT9 . . . . .144 C1
Windsor Bsns Pk BT12 . . .151 B8
Windsor Cl BT9 . . . . .151 B8
Windsor Cres
Cookstown BT80 . . . . .185 B5
❷❷ Whitehead BT38. . . . .100 D1
Windsor Dr BT9 . . . . .151 B8
Windsor Gr BT9 . . . . .151 B8
Windsor Gr S BT38 . . . . . .175 F2
Windsor Hts BT40 . . . . . .182 C7
Windsor Manor ❹ BT9 . . .144 B1
Windsor Mews
Belfast BT9 . . . . .151 B8
❶❼ Whitehead BT38. . . . . .100 D1
Windsor Pk BT9 . . . . .151 B8
Windsor Pl
Cookstown BT80 . . . . .114 C3
❶ Portstewart BT55. . . . . .173 E5
Windsor Rd BT9 . . . . .144 A1
Windsor Terr ❷ BT80 . . . .114 C3
Windsor Villas ❶ BT80. . .114 C3
Windsor Wlk BT43 . . . . . .181 D7
Windy Hall❶ BT52 . . . . . .26 D7
Windyhall Pk BT52. . . . . .26 D8
Windyhill❶ BT82 . . . . . . .67 A3
Windyhill Rd
Coleraine BT51 . . . . .14 A1
Limavady BT49 . . . . .180 C8
Strabane BT82. . . . . .67 A3
Winecellar Entry BT1 . . . .189 A3
Winetavern St BT1 . . . . . .189 A4
Wingrove Gdns BT5 . . . . .145 D4
Winston Dr BT56. . . . . . . .172 B3
Winston Gdns BT5 . . . . . .146 A4
Winston Way BT51 . . . . . .174 B3
Witham St BT4 . . . . .145 C5
Wm Pinkerton Meml Prim
Sch ❼ BT53. . . . . .28 B8
Wolfend Dr BT14. . . . . . . .136 C3
Wolfend Rd BT14 . . . . . . .136 C3
Wolff Cl ❸❷ BT4 . . . . . . .145 A5
Wolff Rd BT3 . . . . .138 C1
Wolfhill Ave S BT14 . . . . .136 B3
Wolfhill Dr BT14 . . . . . . .136 B4
Wolfhill Gdns BT14. . . . . .136 B4
Wolfhill Gr BT14 . . . . . . .136 B4
Wolfhill Rd BT13 . . . . . . .136 A2
Wolseley St BT7 . . . . .189 A1
Woodbank La BT18 . . . . . .139 F7
Woodbourne Cres BT17. . .149 E6
Woodbourne Ct BT11 . . . .149 E6
Woodbreda Ave BT8 . . . . .152 A3
Woodbreda Cres ❷ BT8. .152 A3
Woodbreda Dr ❶ BT8 . . . .152 A3
Woodbreda Gdns ❶
BT8 . . . . .152 A3
Woodbreda Pk BT8 . . . . . .152 A3
Woodbrook BT48 . . . . . . .176 C5
Woodbrook W BT48. . . . . .176 C4
Woodburn❶ BT52 . . . . . . .14 D4
Woodburn Ave
❷ Carrickfergus BT38 . . . .124 E1
Carrickfergus BT38 . . . . . .130 E8
Woodburn Cres BT52 . . . .174 D7
Woodburn Dr BT15. . . . . .137 B4
Woodburn Pk BT47 . . . . . .179 C4
Woodburn Prim Sch
BT38 . . . . .124 C2
Woodburn Rd BT38 . . . . . .130 E8
Woodcot Ave BT5. . . . . . .145 D4
Woodcroft Ave ❸ BT42. . .78 C4
Woodcroft Brae ❼ BT42 . .78 C4
Woodcroft Chase ❺ BT42 78 C4
Woodcroft Hill ❷ BT42 . . .78 C3

Wes–Woo 227

Woodcroft Hollow ❹
BT42 . . . . .78 C3
Woodcroft Hts
❽ Ballymena BT42. . . . . . .78 C4
Castlereagh BT5 . . . . .153 A8
Woodcroft La ❼ BT42. . . .78 C3
Woodcroft Rise
❶ Ballymena BT42. . . . . . .78 C4
Castlereagh BT5 . . . . .153 A8
Wood End BT18. . . . . .139 D5
Woodend Pk BT51 . . . . . .13 C3
Woodfield BT37. . . . . .129 B2
Woodfield Dr BT37. . . . . .129 B2
Woodfield Glen BT37. . . . .129 B2
Woodfield Gr BT37. . . . . .129 B2
Woodford Ave
Drumahoe BT47. . . . . . . .179 F1
Newtownabbey BT36. . . . .128 C2
Woodford Cres BT36 . . . . .128 B2
Woodford Dr BT36 . . . . . .128 B2
Woodford Gdns BT36 . . . .128 C2
Woodford Gn BT8. . . . . . .152 B2
Woodford Gr BT36 . . . . . .128 B2
Woodford Manor BT36 . . .128 C2
Woodford Par BT36 . . . . . .128 B2
Woodford Pk
❺ Coleraine BT51. . . . . . .26 A7
Newtownabbey BT36. . . . .128 B2
Woodford Pk E BT36 . . . . .128 B1
Woodford Rd BT36 . . . . . .128 C2
Woodglen Cres BT80 . . . . .185 B7
Wood Gn BT37 . . . . .134 C7
Woodgrange BT18 . . . . . .139 F7
Wood Grange BT37 . . . . . .134 C3
Woodgreen
Antrim BT41. . . . . .187 C2
Newtownabbey BT38. . . . .129 D5
Woodgreen Ave BT42 . . . .94 E5
Woodgreen Pk BT42 . . . . .94 E6
Woodgreen Rd BT42 . . . . .94 E5
Woodgrove BT43 . . . . . . .78 C5
Woodhall BT67 . . . . .166 B2
Woodland Ave
Ballymena BT42. . . . . . . .181 A3
❷ Belfast BT14. . . . . .137 C1
Carrickfergus BT38 . . . . . .124 C1
Lisburn BT27 . . . . .160 C6
Woodland Ct BT37 . . . . . .134 A4
Woodland Cres BT37. . . . .134 A3
Woodland Ct
❶ Bushmills BT57 . . . . . . .5 E4
Lisburn BT28 . . . . .159 C3
Woodland Dr
Cookstown BT80 . . . . .185 E5
Lisburn BT27 . . . . .160 C6
Newtownabbey BT37. . . . .134 A4
Prehen BT47 . . . . .178 C1
Woodlanddrive BT47. . . . .55 A2
Woodland Gdns BT27 . . . .160 C6
Woodland Gr BT41 . . . . . .186 D2
Woodland Grange BT10 . .150 B5
Woodland Hts BT45 . . . . .88 F3
Woodland Mews BT28. . . .159 C3
Woodland Pk
Ballymena BT42. . . . . . . .80 B6
Coleraine BT52 . . . . .174 D1
❻ Kilrea BT51 . . . . .59 C5
Lisburn BT27 . . . . .160 C6
Woodland Pk N BT27. . . . .160 C6
Woodland Pl BT37 . . . . . .134 A4
Woodland Rd BT45. . . . . .88 F3
Woodland Rise BT39 . . . . .184 D5
Woodlands
Ballycarry BT38 . . . . .100 A3
❹ Broughshane BT43. . . . .79 C3
Holywood BT18 . . . . .139 F7
Woodlands Cl BT28 . . . . . .159 C3
Woodlands Dr BT45 . . . . . .183 B7
Woodlands Gr BT45 . . . . . .183 B7
Woodland Terr BT37. . . . .134 A4
Woodlawn
Antrim BT41. . . . . .187 C3
Carrickfergus BT38 . . . . . .124 C1
Woodlawn Ct BT38. . . . . .130 E8
Woodlawn Prim Sch
BT38. . . . . .124 F1
Woodlee BT48 . . . . .35 E7
Woodlee St BT5 . . . . .145 C4
Wood Rd BT45. . . . . .89 E4
Woodside BT28. . . . . .170 A7
Woodside Dr BT17 . . . . . .149 D3
Woodside Hts BT47 . . . . .178 E2
Woodside Ind Est (East)
BT42. . . . . .79 B5
Woodside Ind Est (West)
BT42. . . . . .79 A5
Woodside Pk
Dunmurry BT17 . . . . .149 D3
Lisburn BT28 . . . . .170 A7
New Buildings BT47 . . . . . .50 F5
Woodside Rd
Ballymena BT42. . . . . . . .79 B5
Londonderry BT47 . . . . . . .178 E1
Woodside View BT17 . . . .149 C2
Woodside Wlk BT17. . . . . .149 C3
Woods Prim Sch BT45. . . .105 D3
Woods The BT40 . . . . . . .182 C6
Woodstock Link BT5 . . . . .145 A4
Woodstock Pl ❶❶ BT6 . . . .145 A3
Woodstock Rd BT6. . . . . . .145 B3
Woodtown❶
Coleraine BT51 . . . . .58 D6
Limavady BT47 . . . . .58 D7
Woodtown La BT51 . . . . . .58 D6
Woodtown Rd BT43 . . . . . .181 A7

Woodvale BT28 . . . . **159** D5
Woodvale Ave BT13 . . . . . **143** F6
Woodvale Cres 🏠 BT45 . **113** E8
Woodvale Dr BT14 . . . . . . **143** F8
Woodvale Gdns BT13. . . . **143** E8
Woodvale Par BT13 . . . . . **143** E8
Woodvale Pass BT13 . . . . **143** F6
Woodvale Pk BT57 . . . . **5** E3
Woodvale Rd
  Belfast BT13 . . . . **143** F8
  Eglinton BT47 . . . . **36** E4
  Magherafelt BT45 . . . . **105** A3
  Portrush BT56 . . . . **172** C2
Woodvale St BT13 . . . . . **143** F7
Woodview ❶ BT49. . . . . . . **39** F4
Woodview Cres BT28. . . . **170** A7
Woodview Dr
  Castlereagh BT5 . . . . **146** C1

Woodview Dr *continued*
  Lisburn BT28 . . . . **170** A7
Woodview Pk BT53 . . . . . **175** B6
Woodview Pl BT5 . . . . **146** C1
Woodview Terr BT5. . . . . **146** C1
Workhouse Mus ✶ BT47 . **179** B5
Workman Ave BT13 . . . . . **143** E6
Workman Rd BT3 . . . . **138** C1
Work W Enterprise Ctr
  BT11 . . . . **149** E8
Wye St BT4 . . . . **145** B5
Wynard Pk BT5 . . . . **146** B3
Wyncairn Ave BT40 . . . . . **182** B5
Wyncairn Dr BT40. . . . . . . **182** B5
Wyncairn Gdns BT40 . . . **182** B5
Wyncairn Par BT40. . . . . . **182** B6
Wyncairn Pk BT40 . . . . . . **182** B5
Wyncairn Rd BT40 . . . . . . **182** B5
Wyncairn Rd E BT40. . . . . **182** C6
Wynchurch Ave BT6. . . . . **152** B6
Wynchurch Gdns BT6 . . . **152** B6

Wynchurch Pk BT6. . . . . . **152** B6
Wynchurch Rd BT6 . . . . . **152** B6
Wynchurch Terr BT6 . . . . **152** A6
Wynchurch Wlk BT6 . . . . **152** B6
Wyncroft Cres BT28 . . . . . **159** F2
Wyncroft Gdns BT28 . . . . **159** F2
Wyndham St BT14 . . . . . . **137** A1
Wyndway Ct BT38. . . . . . . **130** E7
Wynfield Ct BT5 . . . . **145** E4
Wynford Pk BT27 . . . . **170** C8
Wynford St BT5. . . . . **145** D4
Wynfort Lodge BT67 . . . . **166** A2
Wynnland Ave BT36. . . . . **132** F8
Wynnland Cres ❸ BT36 . **132** F8
Wynnland Dr BT36 . . . . . . **132** F8
Wynnland Gdns BT36. . . . **132** F8
Wynnland Pk BT36. . . . . . **132** F8
Wynnland Rd
  ⓴ Newtownabbey BT36. . **111** F1
  Newtownabbey BT36. . . . . **132** F8
Wynthrop Gr BT37 . . . . . . **134** A4

Y

Yarrow St BT14 . . . . **144** A8
Y Bridge Rd BT28 . . . . **147** B7
Yeats Ct ❾ BT48. . . . . **176** B2
Yew St BT13 . . . . **143** F7
Yewtree Hill Rd BT67. . . . **167** C7
Yew Tree Wlk BT17 . . . . . **149** F1
York Ave
  Portrush BT56 . . . . **172** C6
  Whitehead BT38 . . . . **127** A8
York Cres BT15 . . . . **137** E3
York Dr BT15 . . . . **137** E3
York Link BT15 . . . . **144** E7
York Par BT15 . . . . **137** E3

York Pk
  Belfast BT15 . . . . **137** E3
  Portrush BT56 . . . . **172** C5
York Rd BT15 . . . . **137** E2
York St
  Belfast BT1 . . . . **189** A4
  ❷ Londonderry BT47 . . . **179** A5
Young St BT27 . . . . **160** C1
Ypres Pk BT37 . . . . **134** A6
Yukon St BT4 . . . . **145** C5

Z

Zenda Pk BT17. . . . . **161** B6

Name and Address	Telephone	Page	Grid reference

Addresses

Name and Address	Telephone	Page	Grid reference

Name and Address	Telephone	Page	Grid reference